Operations Management

Strategic context and managerial analysis

TERRY HILL
University of Oxford

palgrave

First published 2000 by
PALGRAVE
Houndmills, Basingstoke, Hampshire RG21 6XS and
175 Fifth Avenue, New York, N.Y. 10010
Companies and representatives throughout the world

PALGRAVE is the new global academic imprint of
St. Martin's Press LLC Scholarly and Reference Division and
Palgrave Publishers Ltd (formerly Macmillan Press Ltd).

ISBN 0–333–77592–9

This book is printed on paper suitable for recycling and made from fully managed and sustained forest sources.

A catalogue record for this book is available from the British Library.

Editing and origination by
Aardvark Editorial, Mendham, Suffolk

10 9 8 7 6 5 4 3 2
09 08 07 06 05 04 03 02 01

Printed and bound in Great Britain by
Antony Rowe Ltd, Chippenham, Wiltshire

Operations Management
Strategic context and managerial analysis

Other publications by Terry Hill:

Small Business: Production/Operations Management (Macmillan, 1987)

Manufacturing Strategy: the Strategic Management of the Manufacturing Function Second Edition (Macmillan, 1993)

The Essence of Operations Management (Prentice Hall, 1993)

The Strategy Quest (AMD Publishing, 1998: Albedo, Dousland, Devon, UK, PL20 6NE)

Manufacturing Strategy: Text and Cases Second Edition (Macmillan, 2000)

Manufacturing Strategy: Text and Cases Third Edition (Irwin/McGraw Hill, 2000)

Contents

part four

IMPROVING OPERATIONS 469

part five
MANAGING PEOPLE 525

part six
CASE STUDIES 551

Preface to the First Edition

The area of operations management (OM) is often misunderstood by both students of business and managers within firms. This misunderstanding is generated partly by the way the subject is presented and taught, and partly by the way the function is perceived and explained by operations managers to their fellow executives.

However, part of the problem also lies in the changing field of study. Originally, the conceptual orientation and emphasis within OM was towards the management of the area. Later, specialist developments introduced techniques that made useful, sometimes fundamental, contributions to help manage operations. From this developed a strong, often overriding, impetus to teach and develop OM as a body of techniques involving detailed analysis and tactical considerations, but often not discriminating between the usefulness or relevance of one approach or technique to another. Furthermore, this emphasis towards the quantitative perspective as a way to resolve and present OM issues also increasingly included explanations and mathematical derivations of the formulae and solutions proposed.

The outcomes were significant. In the academic world OM became uninteresting and apparently lacked business relevance. Demand fell and growth in faculty resources, research and teaching did not match the general expansion experienced in business education at the undergraduate, postgraduate and post-experience levels. Within the manufacturing and service sectors of the economy the role became devalued. Consequently, the critical perspectives of this large and substantial function were not clearly recognized and were often inadequately presented. Typical results were unbalanced corporate argument, inappropriate allocation of key management resources to operations and a failure to attract the necessary management talent into the area by matching task, responsibilities and contribution with appropriate status, influence and reward.

From the increasingly competitive nature of markets in the last 15 to 20 years of the old millennium has re-emerged the key role of operations in bringing about growth and profitability of organizations. Fast and on-time delivery, providing products and services right first time and the need to cut costs were increasingly important factors in most markets. How well operations was managed to bring these about became a key corporate issue. As a function responsible for 60–70 per cent of costs, assets and people (while also typically contributing much to the way organizations compete), the emphasis swung in terms of what was key in operations from a bias towards techniques to one that stressed and highlighted the effective management of this large business function. This book is designed to contribute to this focus and perspective. It is orientated towards a managerial perspective of operations and is set within the context of its significant contribution to the overall success of an organization.

PEDAGOGICAL FEATURES

Operations Management: Strategic Context and Managerial Analysis includes a number of features that help the learning process:

Diagram providing an overview of the book opposite the first page of each chapter. This diagram overviews the whole book by positioning each chapter throughout the operations role of transforming inputs, such as materials and information, into the service and product outputs a company sells. The particular chapter you are reading will be identified as well as the chapters that have been covered so far. This will help you position the chapter you are reading and also provide an overview of the topics already addressed.

Chapter overviews at the start of each chapter provide an outline of the topics to be covered and so help guide the reader through the material that follows.

Case examples are appropriately provided to help illustrate the concepts, issues and developments introduced in each chapter. Most include questions to help further their usefulness by asking the reader to consider relevant issues and reflect on a case example's message.

Exhibits are provided throughout all chapters. These present some of the concepts, issues, perspectives and approaches that are introduced within a chapter, in the form of graphs and tables, to further illustrate the points involved.

Cartoons provide additional emphasis. The picture and format is not only intended to bring a smile but also to reinforce the point in question.

Concepts and practice characterize the field of management and the applied approach within the book emphasizes the link between concepts and approach and the reality of putting these ideas into practice.

Chapter summary and discussion questions are included at the end of each chapter. The former provides a short recapitulation on the key issues addressed in a chapter, while the discussion questions are intended to help test a reader's understanding of core concepts and to facilitate classroom and group discussion.

Further reading lists are given as suitable references for additional reading to give pointers to help extend a reader's understanding of the key concepts contained in a chapter.

Case studies at the end of the book narrative cover the range of topics within the book. These are intended to form the basis of class discussion as part of the approach to learning using the case method.

Data disc is included with all copies of the book. This contains the exhibits for all cases at the end of the book that include data. The form in which it is provided will facilitate students and managers to analyse the numbers as a key part of analysing these case studies.

Index at the end of the book is included to help the reader search out relevant information and make this book a valuable resource for both studying and managing the field of operations.

Website. Lecturers' resource material is available at http://www.macmillan-business.co.uk.

THE PLAN OF THE BOOK

The book is divided into six major parts. These reflect the different, broader perspectives within the OM field and are explained below.

Part One: Operations management – day-to-day and strategic roles

The two chapters within this part directly relate to the title. Chapter 1 introduces the operations management task and highlights the key issues involved, while Chapter 2 explains how to develop a functional strategy in operations and sets this within the corporate strategy of a business.

Part Two: Product, service and process development

With the scene set, the next area to be addressed concerns developing products, services and processes. As operations transforms inputs into outputs the fundamental nature of product/service development and the delivery system involved are examined in detail.

Part Three: Managing and controlling the operations system

The core of the book, certainly in terms of the number of chapters (it totals 7 of the 15 chapters in the book itself) is in this section. A glance at the chapter list shows the heavyweight substance of these areas – capacity management, technology developments, the day-to-day control and scheduling of operations, management and control of inventory, managing the supply chain, the need for process reliability and maintaining the delivery system. These represent the central tasks of managing the internal functions in operations besides the supply-chain management issues that result from the make-or-buy decisions that companies take.

Part Four: Improving operations

Operations management's role does not end at managing the dimensions and issues involved. It also includes the essential task of improving the operations function and the two chapters in this section introduce this key part of an operations manager's role.

Part Five: Managing people

The key dimension of people management is highlighted throughout the book. This section brings these several items together and underpins them with the concepts that relate to this key task.

Part Six: Case studies

This section includes over 20 case studies that cover the topics presented in the book. As explained in the pedagogical comments above, they are intended to form the basis of class discussion as part of the approach to learning using the case method.

By providing a conceptual view of the issues of the OM task and discriminating between the useful and less useful by the coverage given to topics, it is hoped to serve the needs of those who are or who intend to take on the OM role and those whose roles will relate to this function in a range of businesses. The book, therefore, is designed to provide for its readers in the following ways:

1. As part of a course of study, with explanations and further application through class discussion and the use of appropriate case studies.

2. For managers who can apply the knowledge, concepts and ideas to their own situation to increase their understanding of how to improve their contribution to the overall business performance.

To all those who use this book, I trust you will find it helpful. It is vital that operations takes its full part in the running of companies and that the concepts and issues involved form part of a more complete understanding of business.
    Good luck!

TERRY HILL

Acknowledgements

The author and publishers wish to thank the following for permission to use copyright material:

The Ambassador Hotel, Kuala Lumpar for Exhibit 3.10.

Lloyds TSB Bank for Exhibit 3.11.

Courtyard by Marriott for Exhibit 3.12.

Forte Hotels for Exhibit 3.13.

Holiday Inns International for Exhibit 3.14.

Upper Crust for Exhibit 3.15.

Land Rover for Exhibits 4.7 and 7.6.

Steigenberger Hotel for Exhibit 5.19.

Gartner Group for Exhibit 5.20.

Roger Beale, whose cartoons well illustrate many dimensions in the book, for Exhibits 5.21, 7.11, 8.23, 11.14, 11.15, 11.19 and 15.7.

Vollman, TE, Berry, WL and Whybark, DC for the original diagram and insights on which Exhibits 6.6 and 8.2 are based.

Schofield, N for Exhibit 7.1.

Open University (UK) for Exhibits 7.3, 7.4 and 7.8.

Ford Motor Company for Exhibit 7.5.

Scott Adams for the use of his cartoons as Exhibit 9.22.

Oliver Wight for the parody that concludes Chapter 10.

Disney Enterprises Inc. for the use of the case study 'What they teach you at Disney U'.

Professor Bill Berry (Ohio State University) for his help on several aspects.

Every effort has been made to trace all the copyright holders but if any have been inadvertently overlooked the publishers will be pleased to make the necessary arrangements at the first opportunity.

## part one

Operations Management:

Day-to-day and Strategic Roles

CHAPTER ONE

The content and planning of this book: an overview of what is involved, what has been addressed so far and what is covered in this chapter

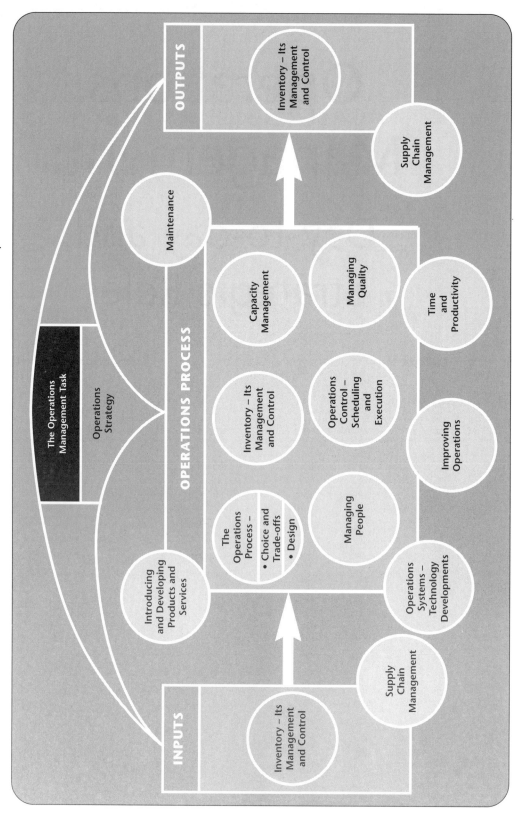

The Operations Management Task

Chapter overview

The diagram opposite highlights the position of this chapter within the whole of the book. As you would anticipate, it is shown as having an overarching dimension to depict the all-embracing nature of this topic. In particular, the aspects covered here relate to the role of operations management within organizations and reviews the following:

- **The nature of organizations** – with the growth of businesses, groups of tasks are completed by a number of departments or functions – one of these is operations

- **The operations manager's task** – transforming inputs into saleable outputs is at the core of operations management. What this involves is discussed and illustrated

- **Operations management in a developing economy** – the varying nature of the operations task in the primary, secondary and tertiary sectors is discussed and the mix between these within nations is examined

- **The purchase** – a mix of manufactured items and services – purchases contain a mix of products and services. How these differ and the operations management response are examined

- **Size of the operations task** – that operations typically comprises 60–70 per cent of people, assets and costs is discussed

- **The role of the operations manager** – the variety and nature of the tasks that comprise operations are outlined

- **Manufacturing versus services** – the similarities and differences between these two sectors are reviewed and examples given to illustrate the issues involved.

INTRODUCTION

The contribution and value-adding role of operations management is at the heart of most organizations. Whether it is a pair of jeans, midday snack, live concert, haircut, personal computer or hospital check-up, operations is central to its provision. To successfully manage operations within a business concerns two distinct but interrelated sets of activities:

- the day-to-day, 'making it happen' role and
- supporting the needs of markets, the strategic role.

The breadth of these tasks and range of management skills involved make the area a demanding and, at the same time, fascinating role. It links strategy to action, requires co-ordination across functions and involves managing the largest part of an organization. To accomplish this, operations manages most of the assets, costs and resources necessary to produce the goods and services sold to consumers or other organizations. On the strategy dimension, the operations' role is especially fulfilling as it supports many of the attributes that help sell the products and services involved; for example, being on time, to specification, fast and low priced.

The operations role is best described as exciting, rich in issues, full of problems, central to the process of a business and about managing through and with people. The day-to-day role is full of interest and variety while its strategic contribution is central to maintaining and growing market share.

ORIGINS OF THE NAME 'OPERATIONS MANAGEMENT'

The term 'production management' was predominantly used in the past with the early emergence of the manufacturing sector. Indeed, in many companies this title is still appropriately in use. However, the enlargement of the role to include responsibility for other tasks in the supply chain, such as purchasing and despatch led to a change in title to that of 'operations management'. Furthermore, the growth of the service sector in industrially developed countries has reinforced the change to using the term 'operations management' as a more appropriate, general title. The title of this book, therefore, reflects both this shift and the dual emphasis of the operations task in the manufacturing and service sectors.

THE NATURE OF ORGANIZATIONS

To provide a product or service requires certain tasks to be completed. Essentially, they include design, buying materials and/or services from others, creating the products and services to meet the needs of customers (for example by adding to them in some way, changing the shape of materials, assembling parts, giving advice, processing information or requests, arranging services or selling a product to customers), selling them and accounting for the cash or credit transactions involved. When an organization is small, several of these tasks are typically completed by one person. As a business grows, sets of tasks are separated off into departments or functions and managed by different people. While the tasks remain the same (albeit typically larger in size and complexity) the organizational structure to manage and provide them has altered.

Certain sets of tasks and responsibilities are classed as line or executive functions (for example, operations and sales) while others are referred to as staff or support functions (for example, accounting and human resources). As the function responsible for providing the products and services that are sold to customers, operations plays a key role in any organization, no matter what its size.

THE OPERATIONS MANAGER'S TASK

The operations function is that part of an organization responsible for producing the goods or providing the services that a company sells in its markets. Some organizations produce physical items such as furniture, building materials and stationery, while others provide services such as medical care, banking facilities, processing information and requests and retail sales.

The operations task, however, is common to all the diverse range of goods and service activities that make up a national economy. It concerns the transformation process that involves taking inputs and converting them into outputs together with the various support functions closely associated with this basic task. Exhibit 1.1 provides a simplified overview of what is involved. The level of complexity within the operations function will depend upon several factors, including:

■ The size of an organization and associated product/service volumes
■ The nature of the products and services provided
■ The technology levels embodied in both the products/services involved and processes used within the operations function
■ The extent to which the products and services are made in-house.

Exhibit 1.2 illustrates these differences by providing more details of the inputs, operations process and outputs involved in a range of businesses, while the following section places the operations manager within the context of an organization.

Exhibit 1.1   *Overview of the operations process – transforming inputs into outputs*

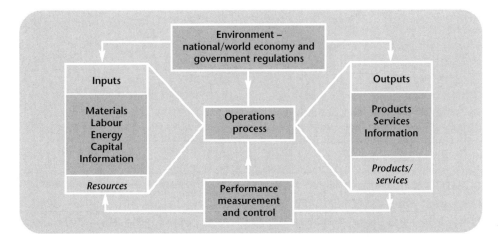

Exhibit 1.2   *An overview of different organizations in the manufacturing and service sectors outlining the inputs, operations process and outputs involved*

Sector/organization		Inputs	Operations process	Outputs
Manufacturing	Bakery	Buildings Equipment Food ingredients Packaging Energy People	Mixing Baking Packaging Equipment maintenance Distribution	Range of packed bakery items delivered to warehouses and retail outlets that are fresh and in line with consumer shopping patterns
	Garments	Range of threads Accessories (for example, buttons and ribbons) Buildings Equipment Energy People	Cloth-making Cutting Garment making Packaging Equipment maintenance Warehousing Distribution	Range of garments Distribution to warehouses and retail outlets to meet seasonal demand patterns
	Packaging	Buildings Equipment Paper and film Inks Energy People	Cylinder and plate preparation Equipment maintenance Printing Slitting Packing Distribution	Packaging to meet customer specifications Distribution to customers' manufacturing plants in line with agreed schedules
Services	Air passenger transport	Airports Booking systems Aircraft Aircrews Ground staff Fuel Food	Passenger reservations Flight schedules Check-in Aircraft and equipment maintenance Aircraft cleaning and provisioning Meals and crew scheduling Boarding procedures In-flight procedures Baggage claim	Customers booked on appropriate flights in terms of timing and convenience Customers progressed through the pre-boarding phase of the service delivery system Customers transported safely and on time to chosen destinations
	Computing centre	Buildings Computing equipment Stationery Toner Energy People	Updating records Printing Enveloping Distribution	Information to internal and/or external customers using agreed distribution alternatives and in line with agreed schedules
	Restaurant	Buildings Equipment – kitchen and table Food Energy People	Table setting Order taking Food preparation and cooking Table waiting Drinks provision Dishwashing General cleaning	Food, wine and other drinks provided in line with customers' selection and preferred timings. Aim is to lead to satisfied customers who will return to dine again

Notes

1. In manufacturing, products are processed.
2. In services, customers (or their requests/enquiries) and/or information are processed.
3. As you will see later, customers may provide capacity as part of the 'inputs' – for example, in fast-food restaurants.

THE OPERATIONS MANAGER WITHIN THE ORGANIZATION

As explained earlier, the operations manager is usually responsible for a whole range of functions within an organization. These functions will differ depending upon whether it is a manufacturing or service business, and the nature of the items provided. Exhibits 1 and 2 in the case study 'Too short, the day' at the end of the book show the position of the operations manager within a theatre and the functions reporting to him. Likewise, Exhibit 1.3 shows a typical organizational set-up for an operations manager within a large manufacturing company.

These two examples are further complemented by Exhibit 1.4. This provides examples of typical line and support tasks in operations as well as support functions to operations in three diverse businesses.

OPERATIONS MANAGEMENT IN A DEVELOPING ECONOMY

National economies comprise a mix of the primary (for example, agriculture), secondary (for example, manufacturing) and tertiary (for example, services) sectors. As economies develop, the balance between these different sectors changes, as clearly illustrated in Exhibit 1.5. Looking at some of the differences under the three headings, it is possible to see that they reflect the general activities associated with the

Exhibit 1.3 *Operations management functions in a large manufacturing company*

Chief Executive Officer					
V-P Human Resources	**V-P Marketing**	**V-P Operations**	**V-P Research and Development**		**V-P Finance**
Maintenance	Process engineering	Production planning and control	Manufacturing	Despatch	Purchasing
Plant	Tool room	Scheduling	Other production processes	Finished goods inventory	Supplier evaluation
Buildings	Industrial engineering	Materials control and call-offs	Assembly	Ware-housing	Contract negotiations
Repair shop	Continuous improvement		Component inventory		

Notes

1. The descriptions 'director' and 'vice-president (V-P)' are used in organizations to denote similar roles.
2. Quality assurance (see later in Chapter 9) here reports to the V-P Research and Development.
3. Inspection is undertaken by the operator responsible for completing the task.
4. Many of the activities within industrial engineering (for example, continuous improvement – see Chapter 14) are undertaken with the staff who have the prime responsibility for completing the task. Here the industrial engineering staff train and advise throughout.

Exhibit 1.4 *Operation jobs and typical support functions in three different organizations*

| Type of business | Some typical jobs in operations | | Typical support functions to operations that report elsewhere in an organization |
	Line tasks	Specialist or support functions	
Hospital	Hospital director Medical staff: – Doctors – Ward sisters – Nurses	Reception Maintenance Cleaning Porters	Micro-biology Pathology Pharmacy Physiotherapy
Print company	V-P operations Print manager Finishing manager Supervisors Team leaders Operators	Ink manager Warehousing Plate production Purchasing Production scheduling	Design Salaries Accounts Quality assurance
Transport company	V-P operations Depot manager Drivers	Vehicle maintenance Scheduling Purchasing	Building and equipment maintenance Pay office Accounting

Exhibit 1.5 *Per cent of GDP by sector group for selected countries, 1980 and 1996*

| Country | Per cent of gross domestic product by sector | | | | | |
| | 1980 | | | 1996 | | |
	Primary	Secondary	Tertiary	Primary	Secondary	Tertiary
Australia	12	28	60	8	22	70
Belgium	3	39	58	2	34	64
Canada	12	33	55	8	30	62
France	6	40	54	4	33	63
Germany	4	47	49	2	41	57
Italy	7	40	53	3	31	66
Japan	5	41	54	2	40	58
Norway	24	28	48	21	22	57
Singapore	2	36	62	1	36	64
South Africa	31	29	40	15	33	52
Spain	8	40	52	4	30	66
Sweden	5	41	54	3	36	61
UK	7	38	55	4	33	63
USA	8	29	63	4	24	72

These sectors include the following activities:
Primary   – agriculture, mining and quarrying.
Secondary – manufacturing and construction.
Tertiary   – utilities, wholesale/retail trade, transport, services and others. ('Others' are unclassified activities that constitute in all instances a relatively high percentage of the total GDP. This category is included in 'tertiary' since the activities are neither 'primary' nor 'secondary'.)

Source: UN Bulletin of Statistics.

individual countries involved. For example, the relatively high percentage of gross domestic product (GDP) created by the primary sector in both Norway and South Africa reflects respectively the North Sea oil and gas exploration and mining activities within these countries. Similarly, the high percentage of GDP created by the secondary sector of Japan has been maintained over the period, signalling its role as a major manufacturing nation.

However, looking at the overall mix change from 1980 to the mid-1990s shows a similar pattern. The service sector continues to grow in itself and as a percentage of each country's GDP.

The operations management role, no matter what sector, is similar in terms of task and significance. Growing foodstuffs, extracting minerals, making products or providing services are parts of the basic task of any business and central to its continued success. Therefore, whether or not you are or intend to be in operations it is essential that you understand the concepts and approaches that are involved, the interfaces this function has within a business and its key role in helping to grow sales and to meet an organization's short- and long-term financial goals.

Finally, although it is useful to separate activities into primary, secondary and tertiary sectors in order to help identify, understand and discuss the whole, in reality they form part of a total economy. The mutual interdependence between the sectors is acknowledged and addressed within developed countries at both the national and corporate levels. Arguments suggesting that developed nations can rely on the tertiary sector as a way of sustaining standards of living or as a means of improving below-average trade performance are without foundation. Each sector is not only an integral part of the same whole but performance in one sector will often have an impact on another. For example, a large part of many service sales comprises a product provided by activities in the primary and/or secondary sectors (for example, foodstuffs and equipment). Equally, the economic success of countries such as Japan and Germany and the rapid emergence of countries like South Korea highlight the critical nature of a sound secondary base. On reflection, it is also not surprising that in the 1990s, several of the largest (assets) banks in the world were Japanese.

To sustain or improve corporate prosperity it is essential to achieve the level of effectiveness required to compete successfully in chosen markets. To do this, it is necessary for those activities responsible for the provision of goods or services to be well managed. These tasks are, therefore, critical to the success of an organization. Operations managers oversee these tasks. They control the inputs and processes that together produce the goods or provide the services that a business sells. But, as with other functional executives, operations managers have a strategic, as well as operational, dimension to their responsibilities. They have to develop a functional strategy as part of the corporate debate that identifies and agrees the strategic direction that an organization needs to follow.

It is, therefore, the development and control in both these main-thrust activities that constitute the role of the operations manager and are the ones which this book addresses.

THE PURCHASE – A MIX OF MANUFACTURED ITEMS AND SERVICES

Goods are tangible items purchased by individuals or organizations for subsequent use. Services are intangible items that are consumed at the time of provision, with a

Exhibit 1.6   *Different product/service mixes provided in a range of purchases*

The purchase	Mix	
	100% goods	100% services
Vending machines		
Low-cost consumable goods		
Make-to-order, high-cost goods		
Meal in a fast-food restaurant		
High quality restaurant meal		
Regular maintenance		
Breakdown maintenance		
Computer bureau		
Management consultancy		
Health farm		

customer taking away or retaining the benefits of that service. However, in many situations, what is provided or produced by an organization can be a mixture of both goods and services. In some instances there will be a heavy accent on product, and in others, the reverse. Exhibit 1.6 shows a range of items sold and the mix between the product and service content provided. The purchase mix represented here is intuitively derived, and others may consider the balance to differ from that shown. It is important, therefore, when considering Exhibit 1.6, to bear in mind that its purpose is to draw attention to the produce/service mix that constitutes a business. Hence, the question to be answered is 'Are we a manufacturing organization with an auxiliary service, or a service organization with a facilitating good?'[1]

Thus, products and services are packages of explicit and implicit benefits made or provided by a supporting set of processes often using services and/or goods respectively as part of the package provision. For example, compare a cup of coffee provided by a vending machine and the same item provided in the lounge of a good hotel. The former service offers convenient, twenty-four-hour, fast delivery of a product. The product specification is largely influenced by the nature of the service delivery system and hence the product range offered is limited both in terms of width and specification: coffee is provided in a number of combinations (for example, regular or decaffeinated, with or without milk and sugar) and in a disposable cup. On the other hand, coffee provided in the lounge of a good hotel comprises significantly different service factors – choice, presentation, comfort and normally a slower, 'more leisurely' service at a higher price. In the former coffee provision, the ratio of goods to service in the total package mix would be considerably higher than in the latter.

In order to compete, some organizations will change this mix to provide a more attractive package. For instance, look at Case examples 1 and 2.

SIZE OF THE OPERATIONS TASK

Operations management is concerned with the management of physical resources for the production or provision of an item or a service. To accomplish this, the available

Case example

1

To compete in the fast-food market Burger King and Hardees both introduced a product offering that allows customers to select from a range of ingredients and so make a burger of 'their choice'. These moves and other developments in the fast-food sector saw more diverse offerings being introduced and competition growing faster than demand. The impact on McDonald's has been significant. Average annual per-store operating profits in the USA dropped from around $140 000 to less than $80 000 by 1996/97.

At the root of all this is the menu. Indeed consumers ranked McDonald's food 87th out of 91 chains in early 1999. Until recently, McDonald's last launched a successful new product in 1983 – Chicken McNuggets. Recognition that changes needed to be made came in 1998 when Jack M. Greenberg was appointed CEO. Since then he has cut 23 per cent of the headquarters' staff and given franchisees and corporate field managers more say in when to discount and what foods to test. One result has been some success with new products including a bagel breakfast sandwich and the McFlurry sundae. These were the big reasons why average annual per-store operating profits in the USA rose to about $125 000 in 1998 and overall company revenues rose 9 per cent to $12.4bn. Greenberg's contribution was to bring a real sense of urgency and get rid of corporate arrogance. In parallel to new products introductions, McDonald's has launched successful promotions such as Teenie Beanie Babies and miniature Furley dolls. But, as Alan D. Feldman (President of Mcdonald's US) said, 'We've just got to improve our menu.'

To this end, McDonald's started a $500m upgrade in almost all its US kitchens to support its 'made for you' initiative. Instead of keeping food in warming bins, the system uses computers to project customer volumes and a process that keeps lettuce cool and burgers hot while making customized orders as simple as they are at rivals Burger King and Hardees. In the past it had been a real imposition to make a customized order often resulting in 'long' waits and cold meals. Greenberg has moved the company away from major product changes such as pizzas, the Arch Deluxe and the confusing Campaign 55 discounts and focused on getting things right. One thing they are trying to do, though, is to improve McDonald's appeal to adults (the breakfast bagel sandwich is one such move and will be in most restaurants by 2000) while allowing local decision-making on when to launch discounts. As one competitor reflected, the recent 29 cent and 39 cent burgers have been a great success.

Case example questions

1.1 How is McDonald's coping with the competitive threats in the fast-food sector in the USA?

1.2 What developments in operations will need to result to meet such changes?

Case example

2

British Airways' introduction of arrivals lounge facilities at its UK terminals in the London airports extends the operations process. Now business customers can shower, change and breakfast before the start of another working day. In this way the service delivery package has been differentiated and made more attractive. At the same time the operations process was enlarged to include more of the post-flight phase of the service delivery system.

Case example questions

2.1 Do such changes bring a different operations task?

2.2 What needs to be understood and allowed for in the structure and procedures within operations to handle this change?

facilities need to be managed to meet current market requirements within the cost constraints laid down and, in the longer term, it will also be involved in the design or extension of facilities insofar as they affect the operating system. In addition, this task is made more complicated by the presence of two factors:

■ The dynamic nature of today requires the effective management of these resources in times of economic uncertainty and social change

■ The size of the task compounds the problems associated with managing operations, as this function is unique in terms of its overall size, as now explained below.

1. *People.* The operations task concerns the management of a large number of people. Most employees are usually involved in the main-thrust activities of a business (that is, those making products or providing services). A high percentage of the support staff will also come under an operations manager's control as illustrated earlier in Exhibits 1.3 and 1.4. The result is that the total number in this function usually accounts for 60–70 per cent of all those employed by an organization.

2. *Assets.* Operations is responsible for the effective use of some of 60–70 per cent of an organization's total assets. On the fixed assets side, it is usually accountable for land and buildings together with plant and equipment, and these make up a large percentage of the total fixed asset investment list. On the current assets side, it is responsible for the inventory holding, which, as shown in Chapter 10, is a high percentage of the current assets investment. Since these together constitute a large part of the total investment made, the operations function takes on the responsibility for effectively managing the most significant proportion of an organization's use of funds.

3. *Costs.* Lastly, the operations function accounts for the major proportion of an organization's expenditure. As the majority of the direct costs, such as labour and materials, are incurred in this area, together with much of the overhead costs involved, then it is by far the largest budget area within a business.

These features mean that the efficient management of the operations process is critical to both an organization's short- and long-term success. The efficient use and control of the assets and costs involved are core to the cost structure and budgets of a business. Similarly, as markets are changing quickly, understanding the business capability of operations is a key facet of delivering a successful corporate strategy. However, translating these tasks into the right combination of plant, equipment, people, procedures and processes to meet the needs of customers and markets is a difficult and time-consuming job. These areas of activity are not only large in themselves but they are all closely interrelated parts of the whole task. Furthermore, decisions made in this area are difficult to change because of their complicated nature and the high investment cost usually associated with past actions and future proposals.

THE ROLE OF THE OPERATIONS MANAGER

As explained above, the operations management task is large. Furthermore, this wide range of internal dimensions needs to be managed within the context of a company's markets and other external variables. While the book principally covers the relevant operational tasks, it attempts to set these within a strategic context.

The former are addressed within the various chapters of the book. The latter (the external variables) relate to changes in markets, competition, financial resources and economic trends. The task thus consists of controlling a sizable part of an organization in terms of the effective management of the delivery system in line with customers' needs and corporate targets and within a context of changing markets.

These features of the operations task, their size and their importance, together create a situation that is difficult to manage. It is concerned with detail yet must address corporate issues of significant size and importance. To understand more of what is involved, some key aspects of the job are now outlined.

1. Managing a cost centre

As explained in the previous section, operations accounts for a large part of the asset investment and typically has the largest budget within an organization. One consequence is that operations managers are responsible for a large cost centre. If operations budgets and output levels are met, then the cost structure of a business will be sustained.

2. Managing the short and long term

It is necessary that operations is managed efficiently in the short term. The task of producing goods or providing services is a short-term function. A day's lost output will never be recovered without additional costs being incurred. Customers who go elsewhere are lost business, sometimes for ever. That is the nature of the operations' short-term task. It is thus essential that the day-to-day activities are well controlled and co-ordinated, and meet budgeted outputs. To meet monthly targets requires that each day's target is met. Other departments, such as sales, work on a different time basis with no one expecting the period sales target to be met pro rata each day. As a consequence, substantial pressure is, and has to be, exerted to meet the short-term operations requirement.

In fact, operations management 'is problem orientated, indeed in this sense its practicability is overwhelming'.[2] 'Pressure is also a distinctive feature'[3] of the job due to the tasks involved, the time constraints imposed and the dependency upon a whole range of activities, some of which are outside the direct control of the operations function either in terms of the organization's reporting system or in that they are externally sourced.

The time pressures on operations managers often result in their having to make as good a decision as possible in any given situation. To think of a better decision at a later date is usually of little value. It would be too late and the consequences of the delay would normally outweigh the gains involved. It is essential, therefore, that operations managers use their experience to good effect as there is little opportunity for discussion with colleagues.

But it is equally important that the longer-term requirements do not take a secondary role. In a function controlling such a large portion of revenue expenditure, the longer-term developments of the operations function need to be given the necessary time and attention. For here, small percentage improvements invariably lead to large actual savings.

3. Manager of technology

The operations manager is a manager of technology, both product and process. However, the degree of technology will differ from industry to industry and from one organization to the next. And, in many situations the level of technology involved is quite low. In most instances, however, the task is the same. The operations manager needs not so much to understand the technology itself as the level of technology involved and, more importantly, the business trade-offs that can be delivered by the technology in use or being proposed. In this way, operations uses technology to make products or provide services for a company's markets, with technical expertise provided by support staff.

4. Co-ordinating the whole

Like managers of other departments, the operations manager breaks down the total task into subsystems as a way to control the whole. This is essential in order to cope. However, the manager's role is to control these subsystems while trying to control the total system. As the operations task is large, the subsystems will usually be both numerous and interrelated.

In addition, many support and specialist functions will form part of the organizational structure, with much of their activity being concerned with the main thrust of the organization, as illustrated earlier in Exhibit 1.4. Therefore, it is equally important for operations managers to be involved with and contribute to the specialist's tasks and activities as far as they relate to their own area of responsibility. They need to set the agenda for these support activities and to be proactive in establishing directives and agreeing the tasks and specification for the work on hand.

5. Managing the work and money flow

Operations is responsible for both the work flow and money flow. The role of controlling the work flow has been discussed before; it forms an essential part of the job. However, this task is linked to part of the money flow within an organization as illustrated in Exhibit 1.7, which shows current assets and the relationship to work and money flows. Components materials (money out) will, in work-flow terms, become work-in-progress with labour and any additional material inputs (money out), and similarly will eventually become finished goods or services (more money out). Until it is a finished good or service it is not possible to sell the item to create a debtor (except for cash sales). Eventually a payment is made against the invoice (money in) by the customer.

In some businesses (for example, retail outlets) the transactions are cash or credit card sales only. Also, in make-to-order situations, stage payments are often negotiated and, therefore, parts of the above loop are circumvented. But the principle still holds (see the note with Exhibit 1.7). Thus the money flow is tied to the work flow with collection and payment falling within the accounting function, working on normal commercial rules.

Exhibit 1.7   *Work and money flows*

Money flow		Current assets		Work and materials flow	Activity description
Out	**In**				
✓		Inventory	Raw materials and components	Materials/components	The necessary materials/components are bought from outside
✓			Work-in-progress (WIP)	Labour and other materials/components added	The necessary tasks to produce the product or provide the service are completed
✓			Finished goods	More labour and materials/components added	Product/service now complete and is or can be sold
	✓	Cash sales		Finished goods/services are sold	Cash sales
		Debtors		Finished goods/services are sold	Credit sales
	✓	Cash			Payment made for credit sales

Note

1. In some cases, payments are made when certain stages have been completed (for example stage payments may be made in the building/construction industry) or at the end of a time period (for example management consultations usually invoice on a weekly basis)

It is for this reason that the 'end of the month rush' takes place in some organizations. Here, the pressure on money flow to get goods or services completed and submit an invoice before the end of the month (thus accelerating payment (money in)) will override the efficiency needs within the process. Thus, improved cash flow becomes a trade-off with the increased costs that will result from the decrease in efficiency inherent in the 'end of the month rush' activity.

6. Using the common denominator of time

The operations function has to be controlled on both a time and money basis. Time constitutes the common denominator for the control of the process, and money the common denominator for corporate reporting systems. It is essential that managers in these functions understand both bases in order to contribute to their design and development, to be able to understand more fully the essential nature of the reporting systems, and to explain the results to others.

7. Tangible outputs

One distinguishing feature of the operations management (OM) task is that it is characterized by tangible outputs. Unlike many other functions, each stage in the operations process (see Exhibit 1.1) can be measured. While this offers intrinsic satisfaction to the incumbents, it may also tend to reinforce other characteristics. For example, as a consequence of this feature many organizations evaluate OM performance by a series of well-specified and objective measures; this, in turn, often reinforces the incumbents' concern for the short-term aspects of the task (those which are more tangible in nature and, therefore, more specific in application) and the organization's failure to incorporate OM perspectives when determining corporate strategy (an issue addressed at some length in the next chapter).

8. Linking the thinking and doing ends of a business

The operations function forms the interface between the thinking end and the doing end of a business. It provides the essential link between the corporate view and the operational task. On the strategy dimension it links direction to action. Without action, strategic discussion and debate has little value. Translating strategy into action is fundamental and operations has a key role in getting this done. In the same way, operations links corporate philosophies and values with the views of work held by those who complete the task. Linking the top and bottom of businesses helps forge coherence and co-operation essential for successful enterprises.

9. Managing complexity

The dimension that best embodies the tasks outlined here is that of being a manager of complexity. The size and diversity of the tasks involved and the implications of decisions in terms of investment, costs and people are enormous. The challenge in the OM job comes not from the nature of the individual tasks and decisions for which the operations manager is responsible – in themselves they are often quite simple – but from the number of these that have to be completed or made at the same time and the complex interrelationships that exist. As the main-thrust activities constitute the core of an organization, then the work of specialists will be largely related to the activities of this function. They will be involved not only with improving this function *per se* but also with developing the interrelated activities of this and other departments. To illustrate, take the example of the Post Office (Case example 3).

MANUFACTURING VERSUS SERVICES

The statistics in Exhibit 1.5 show the relative size and importance of the manufacturing and service sectors within the economies of selected industrial nations. This pattern is similar in most developed countries and underscores the emphasis given to these two sectors within this book.

As a consequence, the similarities and distinctions that characterize the operations management task in the manufacturing and service environment, and which have been highlighted in this chapter, will feature throughout. However, in essence operations management in a manufacturing and service business is the same – it entails managing the operations process that transforms inputs into outputs in an efficient way and in line with the needs of agreed markets. These core activities and the characteristics of the operations management role described in the last section are central to the task in both sectors. But, while there are many similarities there are also features distinctive to the one as opposed to the other. Some of the key differences are reviewed below. But, although these differences are real, they are also a matter of

Case example

3

The Post Office is one of the UK's largest companies with annual sales revenues of more than £7bn and 194 000 employees. It comprises the letters business (Royal Mail), Parcel Force, the UK's leading carrier business, the retailing network, Post Office Counters Ltd, and SSL, a market leader in customer management and telebusiness services. Since the mid-1970s the Post Office has operated profitably and without taxpayers' subsidy (a rare achievement among the world's postal authorities) and contributed over £2.4bn to UK government funds in the last twenty years. Pre-tax profits in the last three years were:

Year	Pre-tax profits (£m)
1998/99	608
1997/98	664
1996/97	577

Royal Mail – the letter business

Delivering mail quickly and keeping costs down have been at the heart of the Royal Mail. To handle increasing volumes (77 million letters, cards and packages everyday) the company in 1998/99 invested £200m in a high-tech sorting process (an Integrated Mail Processor) that now enables 90 per cent of all mail to be handled automatically. This helps increase the Royal Mail's next-day delivery targets for first-class mail (see below) and handle volumes at peak times such as Christmas (in the Christmas 1998 period the Royal Mail handled a record 2.5bn letters).

Year	% next-day delivery – first-class mail
1988	74.5
1996	92.3
1998	92.3

To do this the Royal Mail employs 169 000 people (and a further 30 000 temporaries in the Christmas period) and has a transport fleet of 29 000 vehicles. It maintains and collects from 112 000 post boxes and delivers to 26m addresses.

In partnership with Microsoft Network, it has launched Relay One™, a world-wide service that has effectively put a postbox on each customer's computer. Using Relay One, text and pictures sent by the Internet from anywhere in the world are received at the Royal Mail's electronic services centre in London where they are printed, put into distinctive envelopes and despatched by first-class mail the same day.

Case example questions

3.1 Relate the sections on 'Size of the operations task' and 'The role of the operations manager' to the Royal Mail example.

3.2 What features in this illustration best reflect the operations management task?

degree. Not only are purchase packages typically a mix of products and services, as explained earlier, but also the nature of the offering directly affects the characteristics involved. This section provides an introduction to these differences that will be more fully explained in later chapters. These will highlight relevant perspectives with some including a section summarizing any pertinent issues in the service sector. The reason for this is not just to highlight differences but to emphasize the need to distinguish between and yet recognize the considerable overlap that exists in terms of the management of the operations function within organizations.

Operations concerns the task of processing products, information or services. As highlighted before, the purchase will often be a mix of these but the examples in Exhibit 1.8 are intended to illustrate the principal orientation.

Exhibit 1.8　　*Examples of product, information and service processing*

Processing task	Examples
Products	Chemicals, furniture, motor vehicles, personal computers, food and pharmaceuticals
Information	Tax accountants, lawyers, computing centres and insurance
Customers	Beauty salons, hospitals, health farms, physiotherapists and restaurants

OVERVIEW OF THE DIFFERENCES BETWEEN PRODUCT, INFORMATION AND CUSTOMER PROCESSING

Producers of goods, information and services need to recognize the key differences that affect their business; this factor is a feature of the subject area and one that needs to be recognized and borne in mind in order to help understand the management task within operations. Exhibit 1.9 summarises some of those that will be reviewed throughout the book and are now briefly explained.

- *Nature of the product/service* – the characteristics of product, information and customer processing vary in several ways. For example, services are consumed by the customer at the point of provision which results in an inability to store capacity in the form of inventory and the perishable nature of capacity that results. This contrasts sharply with the option of making products to inventory as a way of handling the capacity demand imbalances as they occur. Information-based businesses, on the other hand, are typically able to schedule the processing task until the most suitable time for completion, thus enabling demand to be spread in line with available capacity or cumulate volumes to help lower processing costs. Even so, the length of time over which scheduling alterations can be made within information processing will normally be limited in scale compared to the manufacturer of products. Whereas with products, inventory can be made, if required, ahead and independent of demand profiles, information processing will invariably be an integral part of a customer's own overall service or procedure. The result is that the

Exhibit 1.9　　*Some aspects of product, information and customer processing*

Aspect	Processing of		
	Product	Information	Customer
Nature of the product/service	Tangible Durable Highly specified	————→ ————→ ————→	Intangible Perishable Server discretion
Organizational arrangements	Back office	————→	Front office
Level of customer involvement in the operations process	Low	————→	High
Competitive environment	Traded	————→	Sheltered

processing task can only commence on receipt of relevant data and needs to be completed to fit in with a customer's own requirements.

Similarly, the presence of customers in the system also brings the aspect of server interpretation into the delivery of a service – referred to as 'service discretion'. In turn, this makes it more difficult to control quality conformance in terms of establishing service levels and measuring performance against these. In the provision of goods, the issues of quality control and measuring performance against specification is more easily managed given the separation of the making and purchasing events and the control over what and how a product is made.

■ *Organizational arrangements and level of customer involvement in the operations process* – at the product end, the operations process is largely, or more often than not, totally separated from the customer, whereas in the service sector customers are involved in the provision. Where possible the service delivery system is split between the front office and back office. In the former the system interfaces with customers and, for example, handles requests or provides the given service. However, systems and procedures are so designed to undertake certain tasks in the back office and, in that way, delay processing until a more convenient time and cumulate activities in order to gain economies of scale and justify investments as part of the way to reduce costs. Being separated from the customers in the back office also allows procedures and tasks to be undertaken without making essential responses to customers' immediate requirements.

■ *Competitive environment* – the tangible nature of products has enabled work and supporting technologies to be easily transferred, in product form, from the place of manufacture to markets throughout the world. In this way, products have always been referred to as being 'traded'. Many services on the other hand, are classed as being 'sheltered'. This is intended to highlight the fact that the extent of competition is restricted by the geographical boundaries of such markets – the 'you-do-not-go-to-Hong-Kong-for-a-Chinese-takeaway' syndrome.

CONCLUSION

Few operations managers would consider their role to be other than demanding, challenging, absorbing and satisfying. They would also tell of its frustrations and complexity: this is bound to be so where a function is required a handle a large number of variables and to achieve many, diverse and complicated short- and longer-term objectives.

To manage such a task effectively requires a range of executive qualities as indicated in the section outlining the OM role. To this list need to be added hard work, intellect and experience. The OM task is, among other things, about hard, physical work. To complete the day-to-day tasks requires much physical effort. However, to perceive the whole and instigate through others appropriate initiatives and developments also requires both intellect and experience. The former to be able to appreciate the issues and perspectives involved and the latter to help alert potential problem areas.

High levels of complexity involving key roles in both the efficient management of most of an organization's assets and costs, and market support in terms of the many different needs of customers are the hallmarks of tasks the resolution of which is intellectually demanding. Unless operations managers are able to understand the whole,

Exhibit 1.10 *The levels of learning*

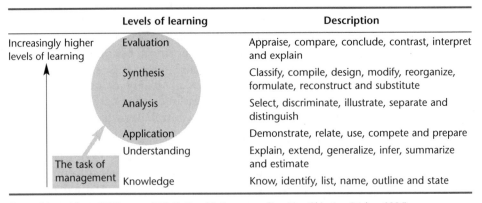

	Levels of learning	Description
Increasingly higher levels of learning	Evaluation	Appraise, compare, conclude, contrast, interpret and explain
	Synthesis	Classify, compile, design, modify, reorganize, formulate, reconstruct and substitute
	Analysis	Select, discriminate, illustrate, separate and distinguish
	Application	Demonstrate, relate, use, compete and prepare
	Understanding	Explain, extend, generalize, infer, summarize and estimate
The task of management	Knowledge	Know, identify, list, name, outline and state

Source: Adapted from: BS Bloom and DR Krathwohl, *Taxonomy of Learning Objectives* (Makay, 1956).

take it apart, fix the parts required and put it back together, then they will not be able to efficiently and effectively manage the tasks involved. Exhibit 1.10 is included here to underline this point. As you will see, management concerns the high levels of learning, application through to evaluation. The operations task is classic of these demands, a fact gaining increasing recognition not least because of the success of industrial nations and the emphasis placed by the more successful upon the management of the operations function. By the early 1980s it was becoming clear that Japanese success was not based upon greater investment in processes but in management, particularly operations. Similarly, the successful growth of international retailers such as Wal-Mart and Ikea has been built on world-class operations capability. Some believe that the managers needed to convert operations into 'a competitive resource may have to be the best rounded and most intellectually able of all corporate managers'.[4] The competences identified included: 'a knowledge of technology... as well as every business function... a thinking style that includes the ability to conceptualize as well as analyse complex trade-offs... [and] managers who are architects of change not house-keepers'.[5]

Recognition of these operations management qualities is a prerequisite for both the manufacturing and service sectors. Those nations that have been unsuccessful in carrying out the operations tasks in manufacturing industries have stood by and watched this sector diminish dramatically in the period of a few years. Next on the list are parts of the service sector. Passenger airlines, banks and other parts of the financial sector have already experienced the full weight of global competition. This will not abate in these sectors and is already surfacing elsewhere. The sound management of operations both in terms of its internal and external roles has a key contribution to make in the success of companies, sectors and hence nations.

The rest of this book reviews the essential tasks involved and some of the important perspectives that need to be understood by an operations manager. The book attempts both to present the concepts underlying this function and to show which approaches are the most useful to adopt in order to analyse and evaluate each major part of the whole OM task. The emphasis, therefore, is not on covering all existing techniques or mathematical approaches and explanations. As shown in Exhibit 1.10, the higher levels of learning are those concerned with application, analysis, synthesis and evaluation. Knowledge and understanding are the easier, lower levels of learning; the most difficult task is to do the job effectively. This requires the application of relevant knowledge, the analysis of the results of that application, the building back together of the results into an improved form (synthesis) and the evaluation of this in terms of what has to be done. Effective managers are those who are able to do this as a way of continuously developing their own set of responsibilities. Thus, as well as describing the relevant concepts, approaches, tools and techniques within OM, the book also emphasizes the managerial dimension of the task. The book concerns operations management and the text, chapter questions and case studies provide the opportunity to introduce materials to meet the requirements of all the six learning levels.

SUMMARY

The operations process transforms inputs into outputs that the organization then sells in its chosen markets. Exhibit 1.1 overviews this core task while Exhibit 1.2 provides examples from both the manufacturing and service sectors.

As operations accounts for 60–70 per cent of the costs, assets and people within a typical organization then its sheer size makes it a difficult management task. In addition, to undertake these activities operations comprises a wide range of functions and support roles, examples of which are given as Exhibits 1.3 and 1.4 together with Exhibits 1 and 2 in the case study 'Too short the day' at the end of this book.

Most companies deliver a mix of both product and services as illustrated in Exhibit 1.6 and where an organization chooses to be on this product/service mix continuum will influence its competitive position and the operations task involved. The fast-food and passenger airline examples illustrate this. While most offerings are a combination of products and services there are important distinctions in managing operations in the manufacturing and service sectors. These are outlined and overviewed in Exhibit 1.9.

The intention of this chapter is to set the scene for the rest of the book. The next chapter in operations strategy completes this overview and together they provide the appropriate context for the issues that follow.

Discussion questions

1. Select two service and two manufacturing businesses of your own choice. From an operations perspective what are the similarities and differences that exist?

2. What is operations management? What are the key elements of the operations task? Illustrate your answer with examples.

Discussion questions (cont'd)

3. Based on Exhibits 1.1 and 1.2, select one manufacturing and one service business other than those used in Exhibit 1.2 itself. Then, complete a similar analysis to that given in Exhibit 1.2.

4. Look through McDonald's website (www.mcdonalds.com) and list the dimensions that concern operations. How many outlets are there throughout the world and how do you think the company ensures effective control over the operations task in order to maintain its desired standards within the service delivery system?

5. Select two other functions within a service or manufacturing business. For each, identify three links to operations and explain the key dimensions of the activities involved and how they would assist operations to complete its tasks and responsibilities.

6. Analyse the operations function in the university or college department in which you are registered or in the company in which you work in terms of:

 - the key operations responsibilities
 - the size of the operations task
 - the operations function in the context of the rest of the university/college department or organization
 - four factors that illustrate the complexity of the operations task. Give reasons for your choice.

7. Make a list of the top ten companies in the *Financial Times* or *Fortune 500* from 1965, 1985, 1995 and the current day. Compare these to the current list. Identify the fundamental differences and give reasons for these changes.

8. Identify an operations system in your own life. What are the inputs, operations process activities and outputs involved?

9. Consider the following processes that you frequently encounter

 - enrolling on a course
 - taking lunch
 - buying a ticket for a concert

 Identify the inputs, operations process and outputs involved.

Notes and references

1. Sasser, WE *et al.*, *Management of Service Operations* (Boston: Allyn & Bacon, 1978), p. 10.
2. Lawrence, PA *Operations Management: Research and Priorities*, Report to the Social Services Research Council (April 1983), p. 2.
3. Ibid., p. 14.
4. Meyer, R 'Wanted: a new breed of manufacturing manager', in *Manufacturing Issues 1987* (New York: Booz Allen, 1987), pp. 26–9.
5. Ibid., p. 28.

Further reading

Albrecht, K and Bradford, LJ *The Service Advantage*, Dow Jones Irwin, Homewood, IL (1990).

Armistaed, CG (ed.) *The Future of Service Management*, Kogan Page, London (1994).

Caltanach, RE, Holdreith, JM, Reinke, DP and Sibik, LK *The Handbook of Environmentally Conscious Manufacturing*, Irwin Professional Publishing, Chicago (1995).

Collier, DA *Service Management: Operating Decisions*, Prentice-Hall, Englewood Cliffs, NJ (1987).

Etienne-Hamilton, EC *Managing World Class Service Business*, South Western College Publishing, Cincinnati (1998).

Flaherty, MT *Global Operations Management*, McGraw-Hill, New York (1996).

Heskett, JL *Managing in the Service Economy*, Harvard Business School Press, Boston, MA (1986).

Loog BV, Van Dierdonck, R and Gemmel, P *Services Management: An Integrated Approach*, Financial Times*/Pitman Publishing, London (1998).

Melnyk, SA and Denzler, DR *Operations Management: a Value-driven Approach*, McGraw-Hill/Irwin, Chicago (1995).

Ould, MA *Business Processes*, John Wiley & Sons, New York (1995).

Schmenner, RW *Service Operations Management*, Prentice-Hall, Englewood Cliffs, NJ (1995).

Schneider, B and Bowen DE *Winning the Service Game*, Harvard Business School Press, Boston (1995).

Schonberger, R *Building a Chain of Customers*, Hutchinson Business Books, New York (1990).

Shafer, SM and Meredith, JR *Operations Management*, John Wiley & Sons, New York (1998).

Slack, N, Chambers, S, Harland, C, Harrison, A and Johnson, R *Operations Management* (2nd edn), Pitman Publishing, London (1997).

CHAPTER TWO

The content and planning of this book: an overview of what is involved, what has been addressed so far and what is covered in this chapter

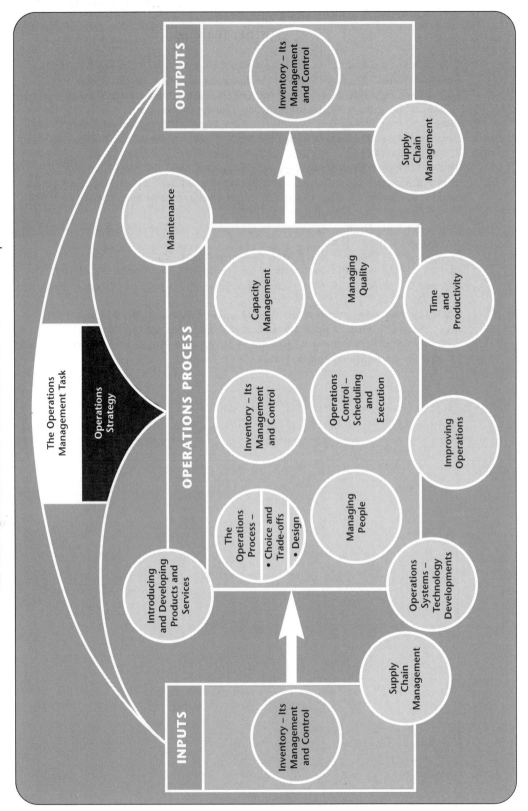

Operations Strategy

Chapter overview

Faced with the pressures of increasing competition, businesses have an even greater need to co-ordinate the activities of their principal functions within a coherent strategy. The reality is that companies typically do not do this. When developing their corporate strategies they fail to embrace all the functional contributions and insights essential to understanding, resolving and agreeing strategic direction. One common and glaring omission in this process is the views and involvement of the operations function.

To explain this phenomenon and to introduce the key concepts and ideas that underpin operations strategy this chapter addresses the following:

- **Executive roles** – a review of the operational and strategic dimensions of an executive's task
- **Levels of strategy** – introduces the different levels of strategy from corporate through firm/business unit to functional together with a review of business units strategy and formulation
- **Reactive role of operations in strategy development** – provides an in-depth explanation of why operations continues to play a reactive role in strategy development
- **Recognizing difference within strategy formulation** – as today's markets are increasingly different then understanding difference is a central feature of strategy development
- **Linking marketing and operations** – this section introduces the need for and approach to linking markets and operations and how this is achieved through markets
- **Developing and implementing an operations strategy** – an approach to developing an operations strategy is explained and how this is implemented is outlined in detail.

Finally, the diagram opposite shows the position of this topic within the book and illustrates its over-arching nature within the operations management field.

EXECUTIVE ROLES – OPERATIONAL AND STRATEGIC DIMENSIONS

As businesses grow, activities are separated out into clusters of similar tasks. These are then managed as functions. The sense in this is simply one to do with providing a structure to handle the growing complexity that comes with larger organizations.

Within each of these functions, executives have two sets of tasks:

■ *Operational* – to manage and control the range of activities that fall within their area of responsibility as well as the crossovers between functions
■ *Strategic* – to develop a functional strategy in line with the needs of agreed markets.

The core, day-to-day tasks that make up the operational role within operations management are embraced by the contents of this book. A glance at the chart at the front of this chapter will give you an overview of what is involved. In simple terms it concerns managing and controlling those tasks necessary to make products or provide services and to deliver them to customers. However, there is an equally essential role that concerns developing an operations strategy to support the needs of agreed markets. Though parts of the same executive task they are different in orientation. For operations management:

■ *The operational role* is to manage and control the various, wide-ranging tasks involved in making products and providing services and to do this efficiently.

■ *The strategic role* is to contribute to the debate about and agreement on the markets in which to compete in terms of retaining customers, growing market share and entering new markets. Operations then needs to develop and invest in the processes and infrastructure to provide those competitive dimensions for which it is responsible – for example, price and delivery speed. In this way, operational capabilities are guided by strategic requirements (the needs of agreed current and future markets) and so help provide competitive advantage.

Thus, while operational tasks are built on internal efficiency, strategic tasks need to be orientated to external effectiveness. Or, put another way, whereas the operational role is to do things right, the strategic role is to do the right things.

LEVELS OF STRATEGY

For most businesses, strategy needs to be developed at three levels:

■ *Corporate* – concerns decisions by the business as a whole in terms of the industrial and/or service sectors in which it wishes to compete.

■ *Firm/Business unit* – within each chosen industrial and/or service sector an organization will usually have, depending on the terminology used, one or more firms, companies or business units. These will typically serve different segments within a sector although there may be some overlap. Such overlaps could be for reasons of history, convenience, preference, to reflect customer wishes or failure to reach agreement within the overall business.

Each of the firms/business units will need to develop a strategy in terms of its markets. Agreement on the current and future markets in which to compete is an essential strategic task and one in which all relevant functions must be involved. It is in these debates that functional differences need to be recognized and where resolution of strategic direction is taken. In that way, decisions on the markets in which to compete (the core task of strategy) is taken appropriately at the level of the business and not at the level of functions.

■ *Functional* – functional strategies prioritize developments and investments in line with the needs of agreed current and future markets. Examples of those criteria that relate to different functions are provided in Exhibit 2.1. The strategic task for a function is to improve its level of support for relevant performance criteria. These can either be the sole responsibility of a function (for example, meeting the delivery speed requirements of customers is solely an operations management responsibility) or the joint responsibility of two or more functions (for example, reducing product/service development lead times is the joint responsibility of the design marketing/engineering and operations functions).

BUSINESS UNIT STRATEGY

This chapter concerns developing an operations strategy. But, before addressing this dimension let us first look at how a business unit strategy should be developed compared to how it typically is.

As discussed earlier, organizations use functions in order to facilitate the management task involved. However, businesses are not a number of different parts or functions, but are wholes. An essential task, therefore, is to rebuild the parts back into wholes. And, nowhere is this more critical than at the strategic level within a firm.

Discussion and agreement about current and future markets have already been highlighted as a core task in strategy development. This step requires functions to discuss their views on markets and to address and resolve differences in terms of what is best for the business overall. Similarly, the outcome of this debate would be a major input into developing a strategy at the firm/business unit level, with the desired process being in line with that outlined in Exhibit 2.2. Functions would debate current and future markets, and highlight constraints and opportunities as part of their input into developing a strategy for the firm. Similarly, opportunities and strategic initiatives would be signalled at the business unit level and form part of the essential debate and strategic outcome.

Exhibit 2.1   *Examples of criteria for which different functions have sole responsibility*

Function	Examples of criteria for which it is solely responsible
Design	Product/service design[1]
Engineering	Delivery system development
Marketing	Brand name and customer relations
Operations	Delivery reliability and quality conformance

Note

1. In a service company the design function is typically part of marketing's strategic responsibility.

Exhibit 2.2   The requirement for developing a firm or business unit strategy

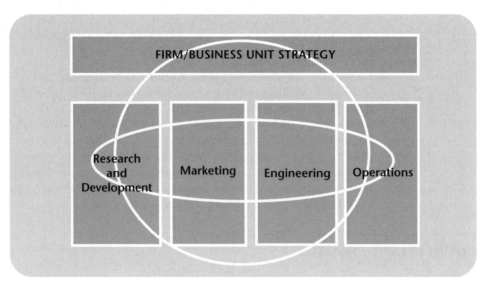

Reality is far from this. 'In many firms, business unit strategy is developed as a series of independent statements. Lacking essential integration, the result is a compilation of distinct, functional strategies which sit side by side, layer on layer in the same corporate binder. Integration is not provided if, in fact, it was ever intended.'[1] The outcome, rather than being similar to that represented by Exhibit 2.2, is more like that shown in Exhibit 2.3.

Exhibit 2.3   The reality of how a firm or business unit strategy is developed

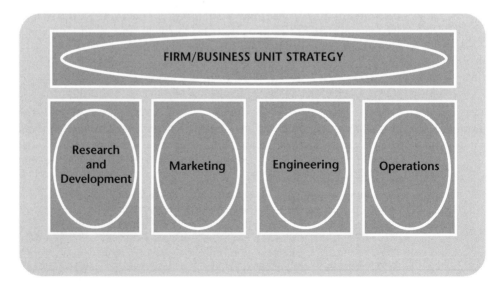

REASONS FOR CURRENT APPROACHES TO DEVELOPING STRATEGY

If the reality of strategy development is so divorced from the essential integrated nature of the task, the question which at once comes to mind is, why? There are several reasons.

1. Statements on strategy developments stop at the interface

Statements put forward by academics, consultants and other strategy specialists on how companies should go about developing a strategy allude to integration but in reality ignore this essential step. They stop at the interface. For example, a review of major textbooks and articles on both corporate strategy and marketing strategy would show that they fail to embrace the dimension of operations. Whether it would inhibit the approaches and arguments put forward, make it too complex to describe and explain or signal an implicit belief that delivering strategy is not an integral part of its development, the reality is that the essential interfacing central to Exhibit 2.2 is never aspired to, let alone delivered in most (if not all) approaches to corporate and marketing strategy development.

2. History of functional dominance

Approaches to developing corporate strategy have a history of being dominated by single functions. In many manufacturing companies, for example, the operations function dominated the corporate strategy process until about the mid-1960s. In a world where, up to that time, there was an undercapacity in relation to demand, selling what you could make was typically the dominant thrust of strategy. As the capacity/demand imbalance redressed itself, selling into markets became more difficult and heralded the birth of marketing's key role in the success of companies. This strategic role has, in many companies, been strengthened with the continued growth in competition, especially where markets are increasingly characterized by over-capacity as emerging nations develop or companies enter existing markets in which they currently do not compete. As with operations before, marketing has acquired the mantle of providing strategic direction not only in its own eyes but typically in the eyes of others and the firm as a whole. The outcome is that marketing's view much of the time goes undiscussed and unchallenged.

3. Markets versus marketing

Coupled with the last point is the fact that many firms fail to make the critical distinction between markets and marketing. Whereas markets comprise the business itself, marketing is a function. Thus, while marketing will play a necessary role in the debate and agreement about markets, it is critical that its views of market needs are countered, challenged and enlarged. For, while its insights are essential to the understanding of markets they are limited in the perspective they offer on two counts:

- The reality of delivering the needs of markets is only fully understood by those functions charged with undertaking those tasks. While marketing has the responsibility for meeting several of these criteria, there are many that are in the domain of others. In fact in some, if not several, instances, marketing's strategic role is limited in that other functions are responsible for supporting most, if not all, the needs of a company's chosen markets.

■ The timescales and investment implications involved in maintaining or improving support for those performance criteria that relate to market success can only be gauged and assessed by the function involved.

Not recognizing these essential differences and not incorporating all relevant perspectives within the strategy debate will only lead to inadequate and superficial outcomes.

4. The proactive role of marketing in strategy development

One consequence of the last two points is that marketing expects to, is expected to and does take a proactive role in strategy development. While this is the desired stance to be adopted by all relevant functions, many organizations in acknowledging and supporting marketing's proactive role fail to recognize the need to incorporate other perspectives essential to the discussion and agreement on markets and corporate strategy. The proactive stance adopted by marketing is seen as an implicit (if not explicit) statement that markets and marketing are one and the same and that marketing has a singular role in these essential strategy decisions that are central to the business as a whole.

5. The reactive role of operations in strategy development

The fact that the operations function has an exacting and critical corporate role to play is never in dispute. Couple this with the high cost and fixed nature (changes take a long time to bring about) of its investments, then it is paramount for a company to understand the business trade-offs involved in operations decisions. As operations is a principal player in providing those criteria that maintain and improve market share and in successfully entering new markets then not knowing how operations will ensure the provision of that support is risk-taking of the highest order especially given the highly competitive and fast changing nature of today's markets on the one hand and the fixed and high cost dimensions involved in developments and investments on the other.

REASONS FOR OPERATIONS' REACTIVE ROLE IN STRATEGY DEVELOPMENT

Given this scenario, why is it that operations executives adopt their current reactive role and why does the situation not appear to improve? There are several reasons, including those listed below.

1. Operations managers' view of themselves

A major contribution to this current position is that operations managers also see themselves holding a reactive corporate brief. They believe their role concerns a requirement to react as well as possible to all that is asked of the operations or service delivery system. They see their role as the exercise of skill and experience in effectively coping with the exacting and varying demands placed on the system and then to reconcile the trade-offs as best they can.

But rarely do they explain or provide data to illustrate these trade-offs as part of the corporate strategy debate and so allow these decisions to be made at the level of the business rather than the level of the operations function.

2. The company's view of the operations manager's role

The operations' view of its own role is reinforced by the company's view of its strategic contribution. Though top executives are actively (and appropriately) engaged in discussions with marketing about decisions on markets and customers, the same level of time investment is typically not given to understanding key operations decisions and their impact on market support. A lack of recognition is hereby reflected in the typically low level of involvement that results.

3. Too late in the corporate debate

Very often operations executives are not involved in corporate policy discussions until the decisions have started to take shape. The result is that they have less opportunity to contribute to decisions on strategy alternatives and, consequently, always appear to be complaining about the unrealistic demands made of them and the problems that invariably ensue.

4. Lack of language

One the whole, operations managers do not have a history of explaining their function clearly and effectively to others within the organization. This is particularly the case in terms of the strategy issues that need to be considered and the operations consequences that will arise from the corporate decisions under discussion. Reasons for this failure, however, cannot wholly be placed at the operations manager's door. The knowledge base, concepts and language so essential to providing explanations and insights have not been developed in the same way. Surrogates for strategy in the form of panaceas have more often than not taken the place of strategic inputs, and the support given to these approaches by academics and consultants have reinforced this stance. The regular heralding of just-in-time (JIT) and total quality management (TQM)-type initiatives (explained more fully in Chapters 8 and 10 respectively) have been seen, in part at least, as operations' strategic contribution. In a similar way, calls to become flexible, for instance, point to an apparent state in operations that offers a capability to do most (if not all) things. Purposefully general, these overtures are without essential definition and direction and, more importantly, purport to offer the rest of the business an ability to support any strategic alternative equally well and with no trade-offs to be made. Furthermore, when the superficiality of this state is exposed the pundits for such strategic alternatives merely switch the phrase (to become versatile and then agile are two more recent proposals), arguing that the subtle differences in definition remedy the serious misgivings inherent in the discarded phrase. The cycle then restarts.

For many businesses, corporate strategy comprises the independent inputs of different functions. However, this invariably leads to functional conflicts that, without a way of being resolved, will result in inappropriate corporate decisions being taken. Where this concerns process and/or infrastructure investments it involves two important characteristics. These investments are large in size and fixed in nature.

Consequently, they typically take a long time to determine and install, and even longer to change. Thus, it is essential that companies understand the relevance of proposed investments in terms of their current and future markets.

THE NEED TO RECOGNIZE DIFFERENCE AT THE LEVEL OF STRATEGY FORMULATION

Any executive being asked 'Are all your businesses the same?' or 'Are all parts of one business the same?' would answer 'no' to both questions. Strategy formulation must acknowledge that reality. To describe a company's strategy as being the same ignores the essential difference that characterizes today's markets.

In the same way, as markets are different then the strategic response by functions needs to recognize and reflect those differences. None more so than in operations, which involves large investments based on change times that are too long to allow errors of judgement – the large and fixed syndrome alluded to earlier.

Developing a functional strategy involves deciding on development and investment priorities that are, in turn, determined by those market needs for which the function is solely or jointly responsible. The book addresses two sets of different but related issues:

1. How does operations management contribute to the corporate strategy debate in such a way that

   ■ its perspectives are understood
   ■ the needs of the different markets in which a company competes are agreed
   ■ the investments to develop and the performance criteria to measure those operations capabilities necessary to support the needs of current and future markets are clearly identified?

2. To illustrate the different approaches at the operational level within operations so that appropriate consideration can be given to alternatives both in terms of market support (doing the right things) and internal efficiency (doing things right).

This chapter outlines the approach to developing an operations strategy.[2] The rest of the book details the alternative approaches that may be used at the operational level. Which ones are best for a company will depend upon the nature of the business itself, factors such as size and product/service complexity and the requirements of the markets in which a firm competes. It is necessary, therefore, to review the options detailed in each of the following chapters, both in terms of themselves and also within the context of the strategic trade-offs that have to be made.

Finally, most parts of a business have an impact on one another. Operations investments are both substantial (about 60 to 70 per cent of the corporate total) and embody a set of fixed trade-offs that will not change unless deliberately changed. The competitive dimensions that operations can support will be reflected in the trade-offs embodied in its investments. What operations can do well and less well needs to be clearly recognized as it will impair its level of support in different markets and will signal the desired changes in trade-offs which future investments must provide.

Similarly, marketing has an impact upon operations. Its decisions make demands upon both processes and infrastructure provision. Incremental change, so often the way in which a company's markets move, usually results in a gradual and increasing mismatch between the demands on the operations function and its ability to respond. While operations managers intuitively recognize the consequences of these changes, they typically do not have, as highlighted earlier, the concepts and language to argue their case and to alert the company to such issues of strategic importance. The result is frustration and an ever-widening gap between the marketing and operations functions even though they are both essential contributors to the business, its strategy formulation and overall success.

This chapter addresses the need to close the gap by providing approaches to strategy building that bring together marketing and operations, facilitate open discussion about the business, and enable sensible resolution of functional differences at the corporate level.

LINKING MARKETING AND OPERATIONS

The importance of linking marketing and operations is as paramount as it is logical. They are, after all, two sides of the same coin. Together, they constitute the basic task in any business – the sale and delivery of products and services. On the surface it would seem simple to unite their efforts to meet the needs and expectations of customers. The reality is often far removed from what should be the desired goal of those involved.

Many current strategy approaches reinforce corporate misunderstanding and promote interfunctional differences and rivalry. Functional dominance in corporate strategy development is a typical source of such problems. The result is that key functions tend 'to treat one another as competitors for resources rather than coming together to serve the external customers'.[3] This is well illustrated by Exhibit 2.4 that lists the different, often opposing, views held by operations and marketing on a range of issues. There is an urgent need to close the gap, to increase corporate awareness of the differences and difficulties involved in the status quo and to facilitate discussion based on an improved understanding of functional perspectives, business options and overall consequences. The way forward is to resolve interfunctional differences not at the level of the function as so often it is now, but at the level of the business. These genuine conflicts need to be addressed and resolved in terms of what is best for the business as a whole. In that way the tensions, concerns and rivalries that typically characterize the marketing/operations relationship can be set to one side. The focus can then shift from competing functional views about what is best overall, to each function doing its part to implement the chosen strategy.

The question is how? First, however, let us consider examples that illustrate how the link has been established and the successful outcomes that result.

Exhibit 2.4   *Operations and marketing perspectives on some key issues*

Issues		Perspectives and goals	
		Operations	Marketing
Products/ services	Range	Restricting range enhances volumes, helps reduce cost and simplifies control	Customers typically seek variety. Restricting range reduces segment coverage
	Standardization vs Customization	Lack of change reduces uncertainty and room for error. Limiting server discretion maintains cost and throughput profiles	Customization often important particularly in mature markets. Server discretion personalizes service often at little cost – enhances customer retention
Costs and profit		Measured on meeting cost budgets. Resist orders that increase costs. Has no control over pricing	Sales revenue is the key performance measure. Profit implications are not part of the decision or evaluation. Higher costs are not part of its budget considerations
Productivity improvements		Reduce unit costs	May cause a decline in quality conformance provision
Facilities location		Considerations concern costs and the convenience for suppliers and staff	Customers may find it unattractive, undesirable and, for a service business, inaccessible
Managing capacity		High utilization of capacity has an effect on costs and assets. Pressure to manage capacity and thereby keep investment as low as possible	Product/service may be unavailable when needed. Quality compromised in high demand periods
Job design		Orientated to minimizing errors and waste. Simplify tasks and use technology where possible	Employees orientated to operations task and not customer need. Restricts ability to meet changing requirements as they occur
Queues		Optimize use of available capacity by planning for average throughput	Increases lead times. Customers facing long lead times or queues may go elsewhere

Case examples   1

The advent of the warehouse model for distributing food and dry goods provides a good example of companies competing on a price leadership strategy.

■ Sam's, the US-based chain of outlets and Aldi, the German-based food chain,

provide examples of how this has been successful because they supported the price leadership strategy with a clear integration of marketing and operations that co-operated rather than competed in providing this strategic deliverable. The basis of these retail offerings is a no-fuss concept. It is designed to be simple yet make it easy to shop. Wide gangways, bare floors, bright but inexpensive (basic strip lights but in abundance) lighting, basic (often the manufacturer's original packaging) displays comprising warehouse-style racking and sturdy wire mesh cages and limited support staff keep costs down. Of the product range on offer, Aldi keeps a limited, (typically about 25 per cent of the range offered by traditional supermarket competitors) mainly own label range of goods. Sam's, on the other hand, matches its own market requirements for a one-stop shopping experience, that constitutes the customer expectation in the free-spending, low-price, no-hassle US consumer market.

■ IKEA, the Swedish firm that specializes in complete furnishings for the home from floor coverings and curtains to tables, chairs, bookcases and bedroom suites, provides a further example. In essence, IKEA is a chain of self-service warehouses that are currently visited by over 126 million people with revenues of about $16bn. Operations is clearly linked to the price leadership strategy of the business and delivers a no-fuss, broad and easy to-take-away or to-be-delivered range of products. The provision of play areas and restaurant facilities as part of the service delivery system reflects and encourages the concept of the family-based shopping expedition that characterizes these outlets.

2

In the mid-1960s Luciano Benetton and his sister Giuliana started designing and making brightly coloured clothes. With leading edge designs, the company grew sales and profits year on year. An integral part of this success story has been the company's operations development to support the whole supply chain as the following examples illustrate.

■ In fashion markets, forecasting which styles and colours would sell best is difficult. An integrated information system to provide feedback on current actual sales at each retail outlet coupled with a manufacturing process that makes woollen garments and then dyes them in line with actual sales led to major gains. Inventory and consequently the size of retail outlets was cut and the products that are selling well are the ones that manufacturing makes. Fast feedback, short manufacturing lead times and quick deliveries better meet market needs while cutting inventory and asset investments.

■ The mid-1990s saw the opening of the state-of-the-art manufacturing plants in Castrette, north of Venice. The latest developments are part of a $350m investment to make tailored apparel, skirts, jeans and

cotton garments. These plants have been integrated with the woollen plant built in 1986 and the automated warehouse handles all the storage, invoicing, pick-up and shipment of garment boxes to the 7000 points of sale around the world. The aim of the latest investments was to reduce staff in the existing cutting and packing operations as a way of matching unit costs from alternative suppliers in the Asia Pacific and other low-cost areas of the world, while maintaining its local subcontractors' base comprising 200 companies and their 30 000 employees. While many competitors now outsource from countries such as Indonesia and Turkey, Benetton has continued to develop its local supply base while achieving its essential cost reductions through combined investments in operations. In this way it is able to reflect the short lead time requirement of its markets with its in-house and outsourcing policies. High investment in the front and back end of garment making with local subcontractors providing a short response service – a high-tech sandwich encasing a more labour-intensive tailoring filling providing low costs and fast response advantages in a competitive, fashion-led market.

Case examples (cont'd)

3

American Express is able to charge a price premium for its card both to its customers and the businesses that accept it for payment by differentiating itself from other credit cards. Support for this differentiation strategy has, in part, been provided by operations – replacing lost cheques anywhere in the world, immediate use where cards have been lost, mislaid or stolen (with 24-hour replacement to follow) and year-end summaries of card use.

4

Restructuring within the healthcare industry grew apace in the 1990s with worldwide annual mergers and acquisitions into four figures and over $60bn. Delivering the potential is proving harder to bring about. Those that have are looking to changes in delivering care and the operations support involved. Quantum Health Resources, an Indianapolis-based firm specializing in the treatment of haemophiliacs has reduced by over 20 per cent the typical annual patient bill of $100 000 by assigning 'personal care managers'. In this way drugs are managed, hospitalization due to lack of personal care is cut and drug regimes are under constant review, improving fit and eliminating waste. Paradigm is a California-based company specializing in caring for people with catastrophic injuries such as brain damage and serious burns. Annual patient care costs can run as high as $2m but this has been cut by half through specializing support for patients, treating more people at home and assignng support teams to sets of patients thereby improving operational support and lower costs.

The growing need to control and reduce the operational costs of delivering healthcare has led, in the USA, to a spurt of vertical integration by insurance companies moving into the management of hospitals and health clinics. In that way, they recognize that the essential need to link sales and operations can be made so enabling business to grow, deliver a better service and become more profitable.

Case examples questions

Review the examples given in this section and consider the following questions:

1. Identify the key way in which operations supports each company's markets.

2. Now compare each review with one another and table the similarities and differences involved.

UNDERSTANDING AGREED MARKETS – THE REALITY

Let us start by restating the important distinction made earlier in the chapter. Markets and marketing are not the same thing. Whereas markets constitute the business itself, marketing is a function. As there will typically be several markets within a business then the relevant criteria to keep and grow existing market share and to enter new markets will differ from market to market as well as from each other. The strategic role of functions (including marketing and operations) is to support those criteria for which they are solely or jointly responsible. In that way, the company becomes market (as opposed to marketing) driven.

The cornerstone in all of this is understanding markets. Markets are the essence of a business, the very reason for its existence. Consequently, you can never know too much about them. Identifying differences, supporting these insights with clear explanations and descriptions and verifying them with supporting data would, therefore, be reasonable to expect. The reality is, however, that the necessary clarity is usually not provided. The examples given earlier are the exception rather than the rule. Instead, current approaches to corporate strategy development typically fail to provide sufficiently adequate insights on which to build functional strategies. Current approaches to market reviews usually embody a number of characteristics that contribute to the general nature of the outcomes and provide statements that lack essential meaning. The result is descriptions of markets that imply a similarity that does not exist. For example:

■ Markets are usually only looked at and described from a marketing point of view. Segment descriptions are typically based on factors such as geographical regions (for example Europe and North America) and sectors in which customers operate (for example food and financial services) or product/service clusters. While this has a sound rationale from a sales/marketing viewpoint in terms, for instance, of arranging promotional and sales activities and the orientation of technical literature and support, the assumption is carried forward (as it is implied) that such segments are each coherent in terms of the way a company needs to compete. A pause for reflection will lead to a recognition that this is both an unreal and inaccurate inference to draw. Although from the viewpoint of marketing, Europe/North America or financial services, for example, are coherent segments, from an operations point of view there will be different sets of demands from groups of customers within these marketing segments and hence these will constitute different markets.

■ Views of markets are positioned at too high a level in the strategy process. As markets are increasingly different rather than increasingly similar, the only way to uncover this essential difference is to dig deep. Current approaches fail to do this and result in statements about markets that are broad-brush in nature and superficial in terms of the insights they provide.

■ The inadequacy of the outputs that result from the approaches above is further compounded by a use of general phrases to provide market descriptions. Words and phrases such as 'customer service' and 'delivery' are examples of this. Each can be defined in more than one way and, once there is more than one meaning, misunderstanding and a failure to clarify will follow. The result is that general descriptions are used to explain markets that in themselves embody more than one segment. One dimension compounds the other with the result that generalities mask critical and essential insights and necessary clarity is replaced by unhelpful ambiguity.

The result is that the key, first step of clarifying and agreeing markets, the basis on which to link corporate direction and relevant functional support, is not provided. As a consequence, the failure to co-ordinate strategic direction continues, interfunctional rivalries are reinforced and the approaches used to develop corporate strategy do not deliver the very essence of what is required or intended.

Given the increasingly dynamic, competitive and fast-changing nature of markets it is of paramount importance that companies improve the way they develop corporate strategy and particularly the need to forge the link between marketing and operations. In summary, what typically happens now is that:

■ Market descriptions are limited to the views of marketing. While these views give essential insights from a marketing perspective, they fail to yield the key differences and provide essential insights into markets from the view of other functions and particularly that of operations.

■ The words and phrases used to describe markets are not sufficiently precise to provide the clarity needed to yield the necessary insights.

■ The procedures followed are not sufficiently exacting to expose and challenge these critical deficiencies, and inadequate outcomes result.

The question is then, how does a company improve its approach to strategy development?

LINKING OPERATIONS AND MARKETING THROUGH MARKETS

The framework given in Exhibit 2.5 is intended to help explain what currently happens as well as what needs to take place so that the link between corporate marketing decisions and operations can be made. A glance at Exhibit 2.5 shows that the framework has five columns. Each represents a step as follows:

1. Define corporate objectives.
2. Determine marketing strategies to meet these objectives.
3. Assess how different products/services win orders against competitors.
4. Establish the most appropriate mode to manufacture these sets of products or provide these sets of services – process choice.
5. Provide the infrastructure needed to support the operations process.

Most companies draw up a set of objectives and then, as the next step, turn to marketing and ask for a strategy to meet these. As corporate bedfellows, this initial step makes sense. Discussion and reconciliation between the corporate requirement and marketing's response take place. The problem is that the strategy discussion stops at this point, the debate ends – a fact which the space between columns 2 and 3 of Exhibit 2.5 is intended to illustrate. The assumption is that operations (as well as other functions) can meet the outcomes of these discussions. However, not only is this simplistic in essence but foolhardy in application, a point highlighted throughout much of this chapter.

The task facing operations then is how to get into this strategy debate at the right time and the right level. Only then will it be able to put forward its views and perspectives before decisions in reality have been or are being closed down. The way forward is to get the business to address its markets by answering the simple but key question – how do you qualify and win orders in the marketplace? In this way the centre of the strategic discussion turns, as it should do, around markets. Once markets have been discussed and agreed, operations can then develop its strategic response as depicted in columns 4 and 5.

Exhibit 2.5   *Framework for reflecting operations strategy issues in corporate decisions*

1 Corporate objectives	2 Marketing strategy	3 How do you qualify and win orders in the market place?	Operations strategy	
			4 Process choice	5 Infrastructure
Growth Survival Profit Return on investment Other financial measures	Product/service markets and segments Range Mix Volumes Standardization versus customization Level of innovation Leader versus follower alternatives	Price Quality conformance Delivery: speed reliability Demand increases Colour range Product/service range Design leadership Technical support supplied Brand awareness New products and services – time to market	Choice of various processes Trade-offs embodied in the process choice Process positioning Capacity: size timing location Role of inventory in the process configuration	Function support Operations planning and control systems Quality assurance and control Systems engineering Clerical procedures Payment systems Work structuring Organizational structure

Notes
1. Although the steps to be followed are given as finite points in a stated procedure, in reality the process will involve statement and restatement, for several of these aspects will impinge on each other.
2. Step 3 concerns identifying both the relevant order-winners and qualifiers.

UNDERSTANDING AGREED MARKETS – THE APPROACH TO FOLLOW

Clarity of markets is essential. Difference not similarity characterizes today, a fact that leads to one outcome. Companies are in multiple markets and the outcomes of the discussions on markets should provide a clear understanding of and identify the differences that exist.

The steps to secure these insights are as follows:

1. *Avoid general words and phrases* – as markets are the core, the very essence of a business, using general words and phrases needs to be rigorously avoided. Each dimension should be expressed on its own and a single definition needs to be associated with each word or phrase used. In this way, each dimension put forward as being relevant can be discussed separately and then either deleted or retained on the list.

2. *Order-winners and qualifiers* – a further step to improve clarity is to separate relevant criteria into order-winners and qualifiers. Qualifiers get a product/service into a marketplace or on to a customer's shortlist, and keep it there. They do not in themselves win orders. Conversely, failure to provide qualifiers at appropriate levels will lead to a loss of orders. Thus, in such situations competitors do not win orders from a rival, rather the rival loses orders to its competitors. However,

having gained entry to a market is only the first step. The problem then is to know how to win orders against competitors who have also qualified to be in the same market. With qualifiers, you need to match customers' requirements (as do competitors) whereas with order-winners you need to provide them at a level better than competitors. Finally, when applying this concept there are some key points to remember:

- Qualifiers are not less important than order-winners, they are different. Both are essential. With qualifiers, a company needs to qualify and requalify at all times to stay on a customer's shortlist. If you are not on the list you cannot compete.
- Order-winners and qualifiers are time- and market-specific – they will be different market to market and will change over time within a market.
- The relevance and importance of order-winners and qualifiers will typically be different to retain market share, grow share in existing markets and enter new markets.
- Not all criteria will be either a qualifier or an order-winner. Some criteria do not relate to some markets.

3. *Weighting qualifiers and order-winners* – to improve clarity still further, it is essential to weight qualifiers and order-winners in the following way:

- *Qualifiers* – it is adequate and appropriate to limit the classification of qualifiers into two categories. Qualifiers (denoted by a Q) and order-losing sensitive qualifiers (denoted by a QQ). The latter is intended to alert a company to the fact that failure to provide criteria which are considered to be 'order-losing sensitive' will lead to a rapid loss of business.

- *Order-winners* – the appropriate step here is to allocate 100 points across all the order-winners within a market. This forces the different levels of importance to be exposed and in that way provides an essential step in distilling out importance. It is essential, therefore, to avoid procedures where stars (for example) are allocated as a way of indicating importance as this approach avoids confronting and resolving the key step of determining the relative importance of one criteria with another. As the alternative procedure allows all criteria to be given any level of importance then the need to discriminate is bypassed.

DEVELOPING AN OPERATIONS STRATEGY

As highlighted earlier, markets are the common denominator of functional strategies. With markets analysed in depth and agreement reached on the current and future directions to follow, the strategic task in operations is to develop the relevant capabilities to support relevant order-winners and qualifiers. As columns 4 and 5 show, this concerns investments in the processes to make products or deliver services and the infrastructure to help provide and sustain these activities. Some of the types of issues and decision areas involved are listed under the appropriate column in Exhibit 2.5. A glance at these will show that the investments involved have the inherent characteristics of being both large (in terms of cost) and fixed (in terms of the length of time to install and change). The need for the business as a whole to appreciate which investments have been or are being made and the trade-offs involved is imperative.

An operations strategy thus concerns making decisions about relevant investments, in terms of what trade-offs best support the agreed markets of today and tomorrow. In Exhibit 2.5 the arrow going from right to left is intended to illustrate this fact – markets set the strategic agenda for operations, as they do for all functions.

This debate thus clarifies what operations needs to be best at, specifies the time period involved, signals any anticipated changes, identifies qualifiers that have the potential to become order-winning and signals those qualifiers that are order-losing sensitive. Exhibit 2.5 illustrates the framework involved and the linkage formed by asking the question, 'How do you qualify and win orders in the marketplace?'

How the framework operates

The objectives of using the framework in Exhibit 2.5 is to produce an operations strategy for a business (columns 4 and 5). As these columns show, the range of requirements in terms of market support will affect both process and infrastructure decisions. The first step then is a review of existing and future markets in terms of how a company qualifies and wins orders. In all instances the market reviews will be based on evaluating current products/services and/or customers as the basis for gaining essential insights. The reviews will need to be based on current and future market expectations for the simple reason that operations must consider investments to support a product or service through its whole life cycle and the fact that markets change.

To reach columns 4 and 5 though, the first three steps need to be taken. With some understanding of what is to be achieved, it is useful now to consider each step in turn, explaining how the necessary interrelations between these parts come together as a whole to form a corporate strategy for a business.

Step 1: Corporate objectives

Inputs into corporate strategy need to be linked to the objectives of a business. The essential nature of this tie-up is twofold. It provides the basis for establishing clear strategic direction for the business, and demonstrates the level of strategic awareness essential to achieve corporate success. Second, it defines the boundaries and marks the parameters against which the various inputs can be measured and thus provides the hallmarks of a coherent corporate plan.

For each company, the objectives will be different in nature and emphasis, reflecting the nature of the economy, markets, opportunity and preferences of those involved. Typical measures concern profit in relation to sales and investment, together with targets for growth in absolute terms, or with regard to market share. Additionally, businesses may wish to include employee policies and environmental issues as part of their overall sets of objectives.

Step 2: Marketing strategy

Linked closely to the provision of the agreed corporate objectives, a marketing strategy needs to be developed and will typically include the following components:

1. Market planning and control units need to be established. Their task is to bring together a number of products/services or customers that have closely related

market targets and that often share a common marketing programme. This will help to identify a number of manageable units with similar marketing characteristics.

2. The second stage involves a situational analysis of current and future product/service markets that includes:

   ■ determining current and future volumes;
   ■ defining end-user characteristics;
   ■ assessing patterns of buying behaviour;
   ■ examining industry practices and trends;
   ■ identifying key competitors and reviewing the business's relative position.

3. The final stage concerns identifying the target markets and agreeing objectives for each. This will include both a broad review of how to achieve these and the short-term action plans necessary to secure the more global objectives involved.

In addition, a company should agree on the level of service support necessary in each market and assess the investments and resources needed to provide these throughout a business.

The outcome of this will be a declaration to the business of the product/service or customer-based markets and segments that the strategy proposes and the identification of the range, mix and volumes involved. Other issues pertinent to a business will include the degree of standardization/customerization involved within each product/service range, the level of innovation and product/service development proposed, whether the business should be a leader or follower in each of its markets, and the extent and timing of these strategic initiatives.

Step 3: How do you qualify and win orders in the marketplace?

This concerns the need to understand markets in-depth, an essential step emphasized throughout the chapter. The order-winners and qualifiers will differ market to market and over time, and column 3 in Exhibit 2.5 identifies some of those that may apply to a market. Although presented here as a list it does not mean that they should be used in that form and against which all markets should be checked. They are given here, as with the details in each column, as illustrations. The key is not to assume but to clarify and check. As markets are different so will be the order-winners and qualifiers. Finally, you will notice from the illustrations of order-winners and qualifiers in column 3 that some relate solely to operations (for example, delivery speed and quality conformance), some are a joint provision between operations and another function (for example, new products/services – time to market would be provided by research and development/marketing, engineering and operations) and some are solely the concern of another function (for example, brand awareness would be a strategic task of marketing) – see also Exhibit 2.1. As emphasized before, markets are the common agenda for all functional strategies. Determining and then supporting those criteria for which a function is solely or jointly responsible constitutes a function's strategic role.

Thus for operations, relevant order-winners and qualifiers may include price, quality conformance, delivery speed and delivery reliability. Which ones are qualifiers and how important the order-winners are is an integral part of setting the agenda. Operations' strategic task would then be to orientate its developments and investments in line with supporting these requirements – steps 4 and 5 of the framework.

Step 4: Process choice

Operations can choose from a number of alternative processes to make the products or services involved. The key to this choice is volume and the order-winners and qualifiers which relate to the market under review. Therefore, each choice needs to reflect the set of trade-offs involved for the various products or services. The issues embodied in these trade-offs are extensive and important. Chapter 3 has been devoted to the aspect of process choice, where implications embodied in this fundamental decision will be dealt with in detail.

Step 5: Operations infrastructure

Infrastructure comprises the non-process features within operations and includes the procedures, systems, controls, reward systems, work-structuring alternatives and organizational issues involved in managing and controlling this function.

IMPLEMENTING AN OPERATIONS STRATEGY

The reality of implementing a functional strategy is to translate the order-winners and qualifiers for which it is solely or jointly responsible into relevant actions. The rest of this book addresses the key areas in operations and the detailed approaches to both managing the wide range of tasks that comprise the operations function and the approaches to improving operations whether in terms of doing things right (the efficiency dimension integral to any management role) and doing the right things (the strategic role concerning support for those criteria in a market for which operations is solely or jointly responsible). Thus, support for markets is a mechanism for identifying those areas that need to be prioritized in terms of investments and developments.

As you will see from Exhibit 2.6, the translation from order-winners and qualifiers into actions is a straightforward step. Implementation, on the other hand, is typically far from easy. Management is an applied not a knowledge-based field as illustrated in Exhibit 1.10. That is, knowing which approach to follow for the best results and then making the developments happen is the underlying management capability. What to do and how best to do it are addressed throughout the different topics covered by this book. The place to start in terms of operations strategy is linking the strategic tasks (that is, the relevant order-winners and qualifiers) to courses of action. Exhibit 2.6 gives an overview of what needs to be completed.

Market or marketing led?

As highlighted earlier, companies do not always keep in sharp focus the critical difference between being market led and being marketing led. To substitute the business (market) perspective with a functional (marketing) perspective will invariably lead to distorted strategies and eventually to corporate disadvantage. Unfortunately, in many businesses, marketing is increasingly becoming characterized by the perceived role of creating ideas. Where this is manifest, it is invariably indicative of functional self-indulgence. Generating ideas becomes an end in itself, with the rigour of testing business fit left to others. This trend not only trivializes the important functional perspective of marketing, but detracts from its fundamental strategic contribution.

Exhibit 2.6   *An overview of some of the areas within operations that need to be reviewed in line with some typical order-winners and qualifiers for which operations has the sole or joint responsibility to provide*

Relevant order-winners and qualifiers	Typical areas for review and improvement
Price	Reducing costs in all areas particularly regarding materials and overheads which typically make up some 70–90 per cent of total costs
Quality conformance	Making products or providing services to specification. Building quality into the process and delivery system rather than checking conformance after the event. Also, improvements here impact costs
Delivery reliability	Assessing on-time delivery performance by product/service and customer. Reviewing current approaches to meeting orders – involves discussions on the extent to which products and services can be or are made to order and the role of activities and investments such as scheduling and inventory in meeting these requirements
Delivery speed	Reviewing the elements of the operations process with the purpose of reducing the lead time in the various steps comprising the production process or service delivery system
Product/service range	Review the process capability and skill base in relation to current and future product/service range requirements. Identify and supplement capabilities in line with proposed needs
Demand spikes	Assess current capacity provision in terms of the ability to rapidly increase in line with known or anticipated demand levels. Approaches include short-term capacity and inventory-holding alternatives
New products/services – time to market	Identify the elements of lead time within the new product/service development process for which operations is responsible. Assess the work involved and opportunity to reduce the task content, current start times in relation to the overall procedures and opportunities to complete part or all of the task in parallel (rather than in sequence) with other elements of the process
Meeting specific customer needs	Assess current approaches to identify how standard products and services can be modified in line with specific customer requirements and the impact on costs, lead times, quality conformance and the overall schedule

Many companies fail to appreciate the fact that the most critical orders are the ones to which a company says 'no'. For it is this decision that marks the boundaries of the business and declares those segments that fall outside its scope.

The approach illustrated in Exhibit 2.5 facilitates these debates. Asking marketing questions of the market requiring operations answers takes the strategic discussion away from functional perspectives and places it within a business context. This process helps, therefore, to reorientate the business towards corporate issues, so facilitating the resolution of interfunctional differences at the business level. It thus sets the scene and prepares the ground for essential corporate strategy resolution.

OPERATIONS STRATEGY – AN ILLUSTRATION

With an understanding of the approach to and outcomes of operations strategy developments, it is opportune to provide a short illustration of what is involved.

Exhibit 2.7 is the outcome of a company's full and extensive debate about its markets. The firm is a contract hire car company. Although it supplies cars to individual customers, the majority of its business is supplying fleets of cars to the public and private sectors.

The review provided in Exhibit 2.7 covers the three segments that make up the majority of the company's sales. There are other smaller segments but these have been omitted. The review has been further simplified by not including the forward look required to highlight any anticipated changes in the relevance of the order-winners and qualifiers and corresponding weightings.

Exhibit 2.7 *The order-winners and qualifiers in the three principal markets of a large contract hire car company*

Criteria	Market segment		
	Public sector	Private sector	
		Large fleet user	Small fleet user
Price	60	40	Q
Quality conformance	40	40	50
Financial stability of supplier	QQ	Q	–
ISO 9000 registered	Q	Q	–
Proximity of vehicle supplier	Q	–	–
Existing customer list	–	Q	–
Simplicity of documents and procedures	–	–	Q
One-stop-shop provision	–	–	20
Service specification	–	20	30

Notes

1. Quality conformance concerns fulfilling the service specification within a contract. For new customers, access to existing customer's experience to verify the level of conformance quality achievement would be provided by the company.
2. Service specification – for large fleet users this includes the ability to meet a customer's specific needs as well as the range of added value products (for example, fuel card provision) on offer.
3. Order winners have a weighting, the total of which is 100.
4. Q = a qualifier and QQ = an order-losing sensitive qualifier.

Some key points illustrated by this review and how it translates into an operations strategy is now provided.

1. *Markets* – the review illustrates, from an operations strategy point of view, the multi-segmented nature of a company's markets. That the three segments highlighted are different is eminently clear.

2. *Functional strategies* – the criteria listed in Exhibit 2.7 are the sole or joint responsi-bilities of several functions. When developing each functional strategy, these responsibilities would, in turn, need to be reflected in the priority given by relevant functions to the developments and investments necessary to maintain or improve performance on each criterion.

Exhibit 2.8 highlights those criteria that operations have to support. The remainder would form the strategic task of other functions. For example, service specifications would be a marketing task. Hence, marketing would need to review the current service specifications on offer and propose ways (if needs be) to improve the overall specific-ation as well as the range of services provided and the extent to which the specific needs of large and small fleet users are being met and how any proposed changes would improve that provision. In turn, these marketing proposals would form part of a corporate strategy debate that would include an operations review of any proposals and highlighting any investments and developments (together with timescales) that would need to be made to meet any proposed changes.

Exhibit 2.8 lists the criteria for which operations is partly or solely responsible and identifies some of the initiatives that operations may undertake to maintain or improve its provision of these – in other words, the operations strategy.

Exhibit 2.8 *A review of the criteria listed in Exhibit 2.7 for which operations has sole or part responsibility and typical actions that operations would undertake to maintain or improve its provision of current performance*

Criteria	Some operations initiatives (that is, strategy) that may result
Price	Develop supplier relations and negotiate contracts for products (for example cars) and services (for example maintenance programmes and insurance) to reduce costs while meeting specifications. Streamline internal processes and procedures to reduce costs
Quality conformance	Meeting the agreed service specification and improving its provision
ISO 9000 registration	Continue to meet the ISO provisions and requirements
Simplicity of documents and procedures	Continuously simplify documents and procedures to make them increasingly user-friendly
One-stop-shop provision	Develop the internal capability within operations to provide all aspects of the service offering

CONCLUSION

To maintain profitable growth over time requires sound direction and relevant functions providing support for the needs of agreed markets. Operations is being recognized as a major, often dominant, player in determining and securing competitive advantage. Take Wal-Mart, for example. Its considerable and continued success in the highly competitive world of discounters is in marked contrast to its major rival, Kmart, and well illustrates this point.

The year 1962 saw the birth of two retailers in the highly competitive retail market in the USA. Both were discount stores that looked alike, sold the same products, sought the same customers and bore similar names – Kmart and Wal-Mart. By the mid-1980s, Kmart was the better positioned with twice the stores, twice the sales revenue and greater visibility through its advertising and large urban presence. In 1987, Joseph Antonini was brought in to head up Kmart and was heralded as having 'get up and go', good existing locations close to highly populated areas and a sound plan for growth and profit improvement. Sam Walton, co-founder of Wal-Mart and its CEO until his death in 1992, commented in his autobiography that in the mid-1980s so much about Kmart's stores was superior that at times it looked difficult to compete.

In the years to the late 1980s, Wal-Mart had principally located outside small towns and was taking share from ageing Moms and Pops outlets. Kmart, on the other hand, had competed against other large discount retailers in competitive and expensive urban locations. When Wal-Mart decided to enter this arena, it did so on the back of its strategy to develop operations including extensive investments in sophisticated computer systems to help track and replenish its merchandise quickly and efficiently. To prepare for the encounter Mr Antonini's strategic focus was on his own strengths: marketing and merchandising. He invested heavily in nationwide television campaigns featuring glamorous television stars as presenters. Kmart's renewed emphasis on advertising and brand served to widen the gap between the two approaches. Kmart continued to be widely known through television, general advertising and its prime store locations. On the other hand, Sam Walton continued to concentrate investments and developments in operations. He invested tens of millions of dollars in a company-wide computer system linking cash registers to head office so enabling him to quickly restock goods as they were sold off the shelves. This, together with investments in trucks and distribution centres, not only increased control but also led to significant cost reduction.

On the one hand, Kmart relied heavily on a marketing-based strategy to improve its corporate image, reinforce the Kmart brand name and cultivate brand loyalty. Wal-Mart's strategy, on the other hand, was orientated to operations as its source of advantage – cost reduction to support effectively a wide product range and an operations inventory, allocation and distribution system that kept the shelves filled with the right products. Before Wal-Mart's 'invasion' of Kmart's urban-based territories, Kmart launched a five-year stores refurbishment and development initiative with a budget of $3.5bn – all part of a strategy to smarten the company's outward appearance. Although relatively few people had seen a Wal-Mart advert let alone a store, the least visible parts of its operations-based strategy were beginning to tell. Wal-Mart's sophisticated scanner, distribution and inventory systems meant that shelves had the right stock, a price discount strategy that could be supported by low-cost operations and internal store procedures such as accurate price labelling meant that delays and customer concerns over the accuracy of the store systems and procedures were rare.

Meanwhile, Kmart was filled with distribution horror stories. An internal company report highlighted major loopholes in its service delivery system – empty shelves, employees without the skills and training to plan and control inventory and an in-place replenishment system that lacked the capability to ensure that the price on the shelf was the same as that stored in the cash registers, a problem which led to an out-of-court settlement of some $1m relating to 72 instances of overcharging. Exhibits 2.9 and 2.10 show the results of the two strategies with probably the most telling statistic being that whereas Kmart's share of the total discount sales market in the period from 1982 to the mid-1990s fell from 34.5 to 22.7 per cent, Wal-Mart's grew from 20.1 to 41.6 in the same period.

Exhibit 2.9　　Sales revenue: comparisons between Kmart and Wal-Mart

| Year | Sales revenue ($bn) | | | |
| | Kmart | | Wal-Mart | |
	$bn	Index	$bn	Index
1985	22.0	100	6.4	100
1986	23.8	108	8.5	133
1987	25.6	116	11.9	186
1988	27.3	124	16.0	250
1989	29.5	134	20.6	322
1990	32.1	146	25.8	403
1991	34.6	157	32.6	509
1992	37.7	171	43.9	686
1993	36.7	167	55.5	867
1994	34.0	155	67.3	1052
1995	32.5	148	82.5	1289
1996	34.4	156	93.6	1463
1997	32.2	146	104.9	1639

Exhibit 2.10　　Earnings before tax: comparisons between Kmart and Wal-Mart

| Year | Earnings before tax | | | |
| | Kmart | | Wal-Mart | |
	$m	Index	$m	Index
1985	757	100	502	100
1986	1028	136	603	120
1987	1171	155	847	169
1988	1244	164	1069	213
1989	515	68	1326	264
1990	1146	151	1708	340
1991	1301	172	2043	407
1992	1426	188	2554	509
1993	(306)	(40)	3166	631
1994	102	13	3791	755
1995	(313)	(41)	4262	849
1996	330	44	4346	866
1997	418	55	4850	966

Case example 5

'Make no mistake', concludes Richard Tomkins,[4] 'Wal-Mart Stores is bent on world domination. Its sales already exceeded the combined revenues of McDonald's, Coca-Cola and Walt Disney. At its present rate of growth, it will soon overtake General Motors to become the world's largest company by sales revenue and, in the process, change the face of global retailing. Sam Walton, Wal-Mart's founder, never claimed to be an original thinker but [he] used to say: 'People think we got big by putting big stores in small towns. Really we got big by replacing inventory with information.' By this he meant the retailing technology that Wal-Mart pioneered.' The company was first to share point of sale information with its suppliers thereby reducing inventory and cost.

In the early 1990s it began its international expansion and by the new millennium was already the biggest retailer in Canada and Mexico and had entered Brazil, Argentina, China, South Korea, Germany and the UK. By putting the customer as #1 (for example, the company's 'Ten Foot Attitude' requires all employees coming within 10 feet of customers to look them in the eye, greet them and ask them if they need help), it has transformed the shopping experience for most customers. Now Wal-Mart is coming to Europe – first in Germany then in 1999 the £6.7bn takeover of Asda, the UK's third largest supermarket company at that time. The result, Peggy Hollinger claims,[5] is that European retailers' conversation centres on Wal-Mart. 'Fear of a European invasion by the world's largest retailer, that has already acquired a foothold in Germany, is having an effect. Retailers are trying to bolster themselves by changing operating methods, and many predict a wave of mergers within Europe.' As Cees van der Hoven, Chairman of Ahold, the Dutch-based food retailer reflects, the consolidation in the USA in the late 1990s was dramatic. South America has also fallen and the last market is Europe. When Wal-Mart entered Canada in 1993 it cut prices on everyday products. Today it is Canada's biggest retailer and highly profitable. The same approach is anticipated in Europe. And the low-cost strategy is based on highly efficient operations and distribution

systems. Germany is the first market under threat. It is large with retail sales of some £250bn but also one of the region's most inefficient. There is a high level of private ownership, overcapacity and a slow response to technology investment. For example, only 10–20 per cent of sales are automatically reordered in Germany against 70–100 per cent in the UK. The opportunities for Wal-Mart are obvious with its efficient logistics and supply chain skills underpinning lower costs but providing adequate profits. 'Europe's leading retailers insist that they are not intimidated by Wal-Mart,' explains Hollinger. She quotes Hans-Joachim Körber, CEO of Germany's large retailer Metro, who argues that Wal-Mart's success is not guaranteed because of its size. 'They are used to the politics of the American market', he says. 'You can get a licence and roll out a concept relatively quickly,' he explains. In contrast, Europe has widely different regulations and approaches to business and 28 languages, sets of eating habits and cultures, he points out.

Indeed, Wal-Mart has not always succeeded abroad. It failed in Thailand, one of the most attractive consumer markets in the Southeast Asia region because, according to former Wal-Mart executives, it refused to adapt to a different way of doing business. But those who know Wal-Mart best warn against complacency. It has declared publicly its intentions, and its sheer size (it has sales three times that of Europe's biggest retailer and a market value twice that of Carrefour, Metro, Ahold, Tesco and Kingfisher combined) and its world-class operations and distributions capability give it the wherewithal to make its ambition a reality. Indeed early warnings of this were sounded in January 2000 when Wal-Mart announced its UK plans:

■ 12 new store openings in the year 2000:
 – 4 new stores
 – 6 re-sites
 – 2 expansions of existing stores into supercentres

■ 'to plough an extra £30 million into savings (that is, price reductions) on 200 food products.'[6]

Case example questions

1. What is the key to Wal-Mart's success to date?
2. Highlight operations' strategic role in this success story.
3. What might operations have to do differently for Wal-Mart to succeed in Europe?

Companies should continuously seek to line up their functional strategies to the needs of markets. One of the major players in delivering strategy is operations. The critical nature of its role reflects the increasing importance of those order-winners and qualifiers for which it is jointly or solely responsible. As in the illustrations given throughout the chapter, getting it right in operations results in sizeable and sustainable advantage. Although not the only strategic player, in most organizations its role will be important while in many it will be central to the continued success of the business.

SUMMARY

As companies grow, clusters of activities are separated out and managed as functions. Typical of these are accounting and finance, sales and marketing, human resources, operations, and research and development. The reason for this is to facilitate the management of the increasing corporate complexity that follows growth.

Functions have a dual role to provide – the day-to-day management of the areas for which they are responsible and developing strategies to support agreed markets. The latter role is the subject of this chapter, the former is addressed in the rest of the book.

Functional strategies are one of the three levels at which strategy needs to be formulated. As with other functions, operations strategy concerns investments and developments to support the order-winners and qualifiers for which it has sole or joint responsibility. In this way it needs to be proactive in forging these discussions as they typically are expensive and involve long lead times. The reality, however, is that operations tends to wait for product, service and market-related discussions to be made and then respond to those requirements after the event. This reactive style is typical of many operations executives due in part to their own and others' perceptions of what operations' strategic role should comprise. One further, fundamental reason concerns the lack of concepts and language to help explain and deliver operations perspectives within the corporate strategy debate.

As marketing and operations fulfil the basic activity within an organization (that is, the provision and sale of products and services), then linking these together within strategy formulation is a core task. The way to achieve this is through identifying and agreeing in which markets a company wishes to compete and to grow, and then establishing the current and future order-winners and qualifiers that relate to these. Exhibit 2.5 summarizes this link while Exhibit 2.6 provides examples of how relevant order-winners and qualifiers translate into aspects of operations that need to be reviewed, developed and improved.

SUMMARY (cont'd)

Throughout, examples of how organizations have successfully developed operations strategies that support its chosen markets are provided to help explain this task. The illustrations embodied the question asking how, while the end-of-the-chapter questions cover issues raised throughout this section. Have a go at answering some of these as a way of checking your understanding.

Discussion questions

1. Identify the order-winners and qualifiers for the following enterprises:

   ■ an ambulance service
   ■ a medium size passenger car
   ■ a pharmaceutical company
   ■ a furniture removal company

   In all cases use the guidelines provided in the three steps in the section 'Understanding agreed markets – the approach to follow'.

2. What would constitute the operations strategy for the four businesses reviewed in Question 1 above.

3. Why would delivery reliability typically be designated an order-losing sensitive qualifier ('QQ') for a carton company supplying packaging to a food company?

4. In the early 1970s when the Japanese entered the European colour television market it took market share in part on the basis of providing higher levels of conformance quality. Explain how the improvement of this factor worked in terms of gaining sales.

   In the period of the early 1970s was quality conformance an order-winner or qualifier in the European colour television market? What is this criterion in today's market – an order-winner or qualifier? Explain your reasoning.

5. Why should all functions within a company, including operations, participate in business-level strategic planning?

6. Why are operations-related considerations becoming more important in formulating business strategy? Describe one example from both the manufacturing and service sectors (other than those given in this chapter) that illustrate how they have gained competitive advantage from operations.

7. Search the internet to find a European company with operations in China. What is the stated rationale for this decision? Are there any other factors involved, do you think?

Notes and references

1. Terry Hill, *The Strategy Quest*, AMD Publishing (1998) p. vii. Copies from the publisher whose address is 'Albedo', Dousland, Devon PL20 6NE.
2. These approaches and the issues involved are dealt with in greater depth in the following books by Terry Hill: *Manufacturing Strategy: The Strategic Management of the Manufacturing Function* (Macmillan, 1993); *Manufacturing Strategy: Text and Cases* (3rd edn) (Irwin/McGraw-Hill, Burr Ridge, Illinois, 2000); *Manufacturing Strategy: Text and Cases* (2nd edn) (Macmillan, 2000) and *The Strategy Quest*, op. cit.
3. Schneider, B and Bowen, DE *Winning the Service Game* (Harvard Business School Press, Boston, MA, 1995), p. 200.
4. Tomkins, R 'The formula to beat', *Financial Times*, 5 May 1999, p. 25.
5. Hollinger, P 'Who's afraid of Wal-Mart?', *Financial Times*, 5 May 1999, p. 25.
6. *Financial Times*, 10 January 2000.

Further reading

Baden-Fuller, C and Pitt M *Strategic Innovation*, Routledge, London (1996).

Fine, CH *Clockspeed*, Perseus Books, Reading, MA (1998).

Fitzsimmons, JA and Fitzsimmons, MJ *Service Management for Competitive Advantage*, McGraw-Hill, New York (1994).

Ford, H *Today and Tomorrow*, Productivity Press Inc., Cambridge, MA (1926).

Gibson, R (ed.) *Rethinking the Future*, Nicholas Brealey Publishing, London (1997).

Lovelock, CH and Yip, GS 'Developing global strategies for service business', *California Management Review*, **38**(2): 64–86.

Normann, R *Service Management: Strategy and Leadership in Service Business* (2nd edn), John Wiley & Sons, Chichester (1991).

Ortega, B 'In Sam We Trust: The Untold Story of Sam Walton and How Wal-Mart is Devouring America', *Times Business*, Random House, New York (1998).

Porter, ME 'What is strategy?', *Harvard Business Review*, November–December 1996: 61–78.

Schonberger, RJ *World Class Manufacturing: The Next Decade*, The Free Press, New York (1996).

## part two

Product, Service and Process Development

CHAPTER THREE

The content and planning of this book: an overview of what is involved, what has been addressed so far and what is covered in this chapter

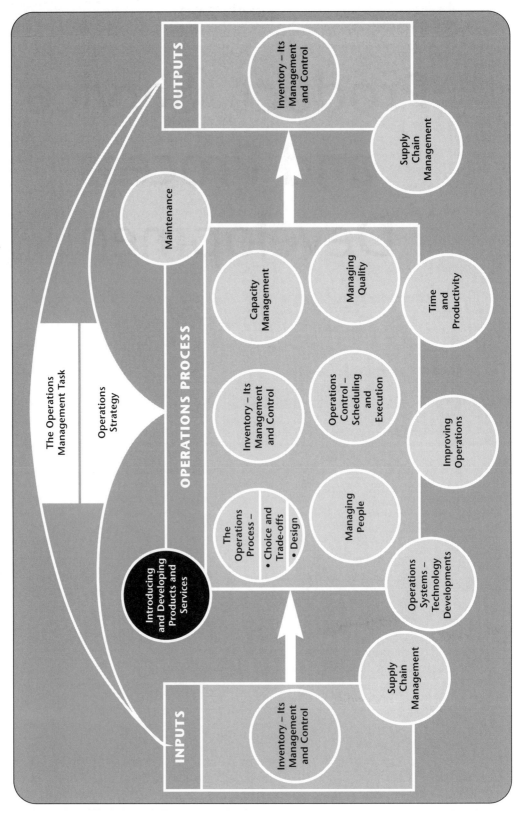

Introducing and Developing Products and Services

Chapter overview

Growth and success are based to a large extent on an organization's ability to introduce new and develop existing products and services. While a natural market may exist for some essential needs (for example, food and clothing) for many, a market has to be created. In either case, most organizations have changed from, in the past, an *ad hoc* approach to the planning of new products and services to one that is an organized activity involving a procedural cycle from generating ideas through to market launch. Here we examine the procedures involved and some of the important issues to be considered for both new and existing products and services.

This chapter covers the following sections:

- The introduction and development of products and services are the lifeblood of any organization. This part of the chapter looks at the research and development process from the phase of generating ideas through to final design.

- The key issues and considerations in product/service design including life cycles, portfolio analyses and design contributions to help support different product/service market segments. It involves the input of technology, techniques and approaches related to design including standardization, modular design, Taguchi methods, value engineering, value analysis, simultaneous engineering and variety reduction.

INTRODUCING AND DEVELOPING PRODUCTS AND SERVICES

Introducing new and developing existing products and services are the lifeblood of organizations. However, the task involves more than initiating new ideas, although that is where it typically all begins. The procedure is one of checking ideas and alternatives and verifying that what is proposed can be done within the context of the market, the organization's own targets and expectations and the impact on other parts of a business, including operations – see the overview at the beginning of the chapter and the position of this chapter and its interface with the operations process. It concerns generating ideas, setting financial hurdles and providing detailed specifications prior to the marketing and provision of the products or services in question. Some of the issues are now overviewed as a way of outlining what is involved. The sections that follow then look at the various aspects in more detail and address some of the key points to be considered throughout this core task.

Ideas come from internal or external sources depending upon an organization's allocation of resources (for example, research spend), its approach to stimulating and processing contributions and its attitude towards the degree of risk it is prepared to take; for example, whether to be a pioneer or follower in its chosen markets.

A product/service idea will raise problems of definition and clarification that call for research and that need to be answered before the specification can be finalised. The development activity will usually highlight other problems which, in turn, require further investigation. As development work concludes, final design is undertaken and, as with the development phase, this may also lead to more problems requiring more solutions. Throughout this procedure, trade-offs will have to be made between the product/service specification, existing process capabilities, operations investments and market requirements. Like much of management, the difficulty comes in handling the complexity of the task that results from the interrelated nature of the issues inherent in the parts of the process. What these involve are now looked at in more detail.

THE RESEARCH AND DEVELOPMENT PROCESS

The objective of research and development (R&D) activity is to bring about technological change and innovation within both the products and services to be sold and the process by which these will be produced. The total cycle of events to achieve this embraces programmes classified as being at the strategic and tactical levels.

Strategic programmes

These comprise activities concerned with both fundamental and applied research. Although convenient to highlight this split when defining what is involved, in reality the distinction is often blurred:

■ Fundamental research is not specifically concerned with the practical applications of its results. Its purpose is to study the basic relationships between cause and effect with the aim of increasing knowledge, making discoveries and establishing new applications that may eventually be used on a commercial basis.

■ Applied research, on the other hand, is concerned principally with practical applications and solutions to practical problems. Its function concerns classifying and interpreting basic knowledge from fundamental research activities to facilitate problem solving. The return on this research investment is quicker and more assured than for fundamental research. Since applied research is directed towards solving particular problems in the later stages of product/service planning (for example, advanced development work), the uncertainty is less and the practical usefulness of the results is inherent in the activity. However, an organization may well subcontract some or all of this task until its own research demands can justify employing its own staff.

The level of commitment to strategic programmes is an important corporate decision. The degree of commitment will vary. Organizations may decide to adopt either an offensive or a defensive design strategy while others fall in between making a moderate R&D commitment by, for instance, contracting out research or licensing other organizations' product/service designs.[1]

The offensive strategy brings with it a relatively large research spending commitment with the objective of being a leader in product/service innovation within a given market. The defensive strategy usually limits the amount of research spending to a minimum and will be largely directed towards the development of existing knowledge to enhance product/service roles in a market or in response to customer requirements.

Between these two strategies lie moderate forms of research commitment. For example, research contracts are used by governments and other organizations to buy specific research investigations and research institutes, universities and independent research laboratories are available to take on this work. A second approach is to manufacture under licence or provide a service under a franchise. Here, marketable products and products manufactured successfully elsewhere are produced under licence agreements. Franchising services (for example fast-food restaurants) is similar to licensing except that invariably the products, methods of working and environment are highly specified and supplies are from a prescribed source. In that way, a tighter control on product/service specifications and their provision is maintained.

Tactical programmes

Following these strategic activities come the tactical steps to develop a product or service. Although excellent and innovative products/services are conceived and designed by a whole range of businesses, a feature frequently experienced by many organizations is that the requirements of subsequent steps in the procedure are not adequately taken into account at the design stage. The result leads to higher than necessary costs. A good way to illustrate this is provided by the Ford Motor Company's 'effectiveness lever' that illustrates the impact upon effectiveness that can be achieved at each of the principal stages in the procedure from design through to operations (Exhibit 3.1).

Tactical programmes cover all stages throughout the development of a product or service including its launch. They are concerned with the functional aspects of design and address basic questions covering:

- What will it do?
- How will it do it?
- How will it be made or provided?
- The maintenance and repair requirement.
- Physical distribution.

Exhibit 3.1   *The Ford Motor Company 'effectiveness lever'²*

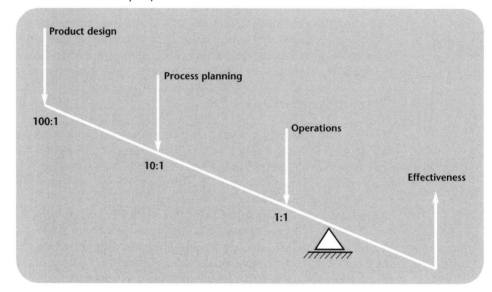

The link between market need, technology, development, design and the operations process is essential to the profitable production of a product or provision of a service and it is essential that all steps are addressed.

The approach to development involves defining a product or service by a procedure of checking successive designs until the required specifications are met as economically as possible. This usually involves testing several designs to evaluate their feasibility in terms of functionality and cost. The sections that now follow look at these steps in detail.

THE PRODUCT/SERVICE DEVELOPMENT PROCESS

The first step in developing a new or modifying an existing product or service is generating ideas. But a good idea does not necessarily indicate a successful outcome. A significant amount of development work is required before a product can be produced or service provided and made available to customers. These steps are described as the product/service development process and are outlined in Exhibit 3.2. However, before discussing these in some detail it is important to make two observations.

Reiteration – the development process consists of a series of steps. Although shown as being sequential in Exhibit 3.2, they actually involve much reiteration throughout. Questions are often posed at each stage and these take the proposal back one or more steps in order to clarify and resolve the fresh issues raised, as shown in Exhibit 3.2.

Sequential – again the process outline shows the steps as being sequential whereas in fact parts of several stages will be completed in parallel one with another. This allows for a reduction in development lead times and so enables the earlier introduction of final designs to be made.

Exhibit 3.2   *The design and development of products and services*

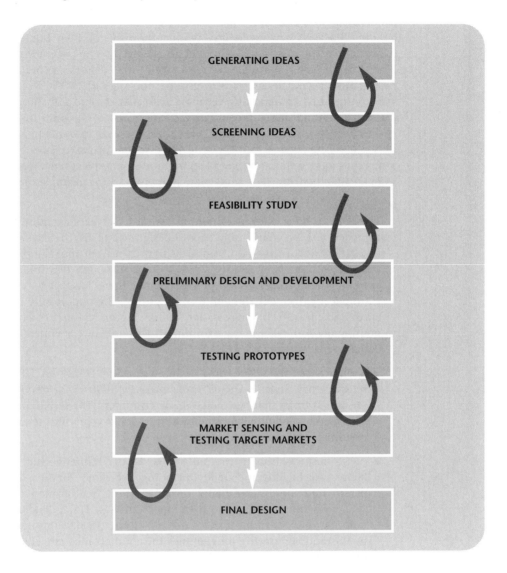

1. Generating ideas

Ideas for new products and services can arise from a variety of sources within and outside a firm. Internal sources include employees, research and development, market research, the salesforce and reverse engineering. The need to generate ideas is a key step in this process especially as the ratio between ideas and successful product and service introductions is often as low as less than 1 or 2 per cent. Companies stimulate ideas in several ways. Suggestion schemes or including the generation of ideas as part of employee evaluations has long been an effective way of getting ideas on the table. Somewhat at the other extreme is the pharmaceutical industry. Pharmaceuticals, where new product introductions are a key factor for success, has seen 'a quantum leap in the mechanics of drug research [and one that] promises to revolutionize pharmaceuticals the way PCs reinvented the computer industry'.[3] Glaxo has started to use 'combinatorial chemistry' which creates tens of thousands of new molecules – the building blocks of new medicines – within the space of a few hours, compared with conventional chemistry that results in an average of some 40 new molecules a year. Linked to this is a robotized screening station that evaluates a compound's effectiveness against specific disease-causing genes at the rate of 50 000 a week. As only one in 4000 synthesized compounds ever make it to market, and only 30 per cent of these earn back their full development costs, creating new compounds in a cost- and time-effective way is essential. Molecule selection is the essence of the pharmaceutical business and effectively generating ideas is the essential first step. Equally important, and sometimes more important than ideas from internal sources, are those ideas generated from outside the firm. Such sources are numerous as the examples below illustrate.

■ *Customers*

There has been a marked change in the last 30 years regarding the source and approach to new product and service design. Gone are the days when the role of researchers was to come up with ideas that then went into the products and services that customers were encouraged to buy. Although this still happens (see for example the section on technology below) there has been a recognition that customer involvement through focused groups, the opportunity to express preferences and ideas, technology design interfacing on products such as vehicles and housing are some of the ways to bring this source of consumer-led ideas into the design arena. For example:

■ having closed their doors on a Saturday since the late 1960s, UK banks reopened selected high street branches from the early 1990s, as a response to providing services at times that best suited many customers. The service provision has now increased to a point where an almost full service is on offer at a time when many customers are best able to use it

■ of US business trips in the mid-1990s, 15 per cent involved children. Several factors are fuelling the trend (including two-career families and more single-parent households) and many working parents see business trips as a way of squeezing in precious time with their families. Hotels and airlines are now tailoring services to meet these needs – licensed babysitter booking, children's menus and sightseeing programmes for children illustrate the service development responses in some hotels.

■ *Legislation*

Government legislation invariably leads to a need to adapt and change. Very often it requires new products and services to meet new requirements. For example:

■ The European Commission's targets for waste management (see Exhibit 3.3) will impact packaging design and stimulate the development of services to meet these future requirements.

■ Citizens' Charters introduced by many governments will increasingly have an impact on service design within several industries.

■ Legislation concerning issues such as noise and pollution has required product design changes to meet the new requirements. The increasing use of active noise cancellation in turboprop aircraft to reduce noise levels, the pressure on emission

Exhibit 3.3   *European Commission waste management*
                  targets for packaging

Activity	% total/year	
	1990	2000
Prevention	0	10
Incineration	20	20
Recycling	20	60
Landfill	60	10

levels in vehicles and the research work on battery-driven vehicles all illustrate
the impact of legislation on design.

■ *Environment*

Concerns and pressures from the 'green lobby' are forcing change often independent of government action. For example:

■ in the early 1990s, over 400 German companies set up the Duales System
  Deutschland (DSD) to establish the infrastructure needed to recover and reuse
  packaging waste. At an estimated set-up cost of £3.5bn and annual running costs
  of £0.7bn DSD is in response to growing consumer awareness of waste. The recycling targets set are given in Exhibit 3.4 and will undoubtedly influence European standards in the future. The impact on packaging and waste collection
  services will be widespread

■ the sales growth in rechargeable battery (a nickel–cadmium battery can be
  recharged 1000 times) reflects concerns not just about price but also the
  environment.

■ *Technology*

Technology shifts have a far-reaching effect on products and service design. In
some instances, the changes revolutionize design and in others, provide a plethora
of new offerings. Dupont's invention of nylon and the impact of plastics, semiconductors, integrated circuits and computing on new product and service opportunities have been significant. Just look around you to see the ranges of new
products spawned from these new technologies. Enhancing products and services
by incorporating new technologies is also widespread. For example, Federal Express

Exhibit 3.4   *Duales System Deutschland recycling targets*

Material type	Recycling targets (%) from	
	1 January 1993	1 July 1995
Glass	42	72
Tinplate	26	72
Aluminium	18	72
Board	18	64
Paper	18	64
Plastics	9	64

interlinks stages in the service system by using computers to monitor and track deliveries throughout its whole delivery system. On receipt of a customer call a Federal Express operator enters details on to a computer. This information is then radioed to a courier and displayed on a hand-held computer terminal. After pick-up, a package is logged into the company's central computer in Memphis. With the use of industrial bar codes, packages can be tracked in the system and customers can access these details at any time on request.

■ *Strategic positioning*
A key decision in product/service design concerns the strategic position taken by a company and the effect this has on ideas generation. While a market leader strategy involves high research and development spend and a need to pursue ideas generation, a follow-the-leader strategy puts little emphasis on research but high investment on development to provide the rapid technical response to market leader changes that go with this strategy. Other alternatives include an applications orientation strategy that emphasizes product/service modifications to serve particular customers' needs thereby creating specialized segments, and finally a strategy that keeps designs fixed and emphasizes efficiency and cost control as the support for price as the order-winner.

Each of these gives a different emphasis on the requirement and importance of ideas generation while also needing to be considered in the context of existing and future competitors.

2. Screening ideas

The purpose of screening ideas is to eliminate those that do not appear to have high potential and so avoid the costs incurred at subsequent stages. Using a group of people, proposals would be supported by graphics, models and an outline specification and judged against a set of criteria such as necessity to the firm's survival, role in filling out an existing product/service line, degree of overlap with existing products and services, utilization of existing processes and capabilities, reflection of the firm's interests and expertise and the impact on overall, estimated sales and profits.

To provide greater insight, organizations often score each dimension of each idea on a 0–10 scale and the apply weights to each of these dimensions. The resulting aggregate score helps in deciding which ideas to progress and which to terminate.

3. Feasibility study

Initial screening was designed to stop ideas that were not thought suitable for further consideration. The next step is to complete a more detailed check on the ideas still being considered. This part of the process will look at a whole series of dimensions that relate to a product/service idea and its intended markets, for example:

Product/service development

■ development lead time
■ previous experience
■ anticipated length of life cycle
■ uniqueness of design

Market(s)

■ related order-winners and qualifiers
■ selling price
■ sales volumes over time
■ fit with corporate strategy
■ level of existing and future competition
■ stable/seasonal demand patterns
■ advertising required
■ technical demands on support staff

Operations

■ degree of match with existing capabilities
■ quality conformance requirements
■ ability to support relevant order-winners and qualifiers
■ capacity needs
■ process investment

Financial

■ capital outlays
■ return on investment
■ cash flows

Whereas the scoring model adopted in the initial screening stage provided a rough, quantitative measurement, the purpose of the analysis at this stage in the design process is to determine more specific qualitative measures on all important dimensions. This is necessary in order to help to decide whether or not to commit further resources to the development of an idea. From this stage forward costs tend to increase significantly.

4. Preliminary design and development

This stage of the process involves developing the best design for a new idea. Here the broad outline of the new product or service will need to be specified in much greater detail. Many trade-offs will have to be made concerning features, costs and producibility. Reconciling these, often conflicting, demands is a difficult task and one that needs to be resolved at this stage.

The advent of computer-aided design (CAD) has made a significant contribution to facilitating these decisions and is dealt with in more detail in a later section addressing the impact of technology on design.

5. Testing prototypes

The physical embodiment of the functional and aesthetic requirements of a product or service is the prototype. This step in the process serves many ends. In addition to illustrating the aesthetic dimension, it serves to check the functionality of the idea, its robustness and the operations implications of it provision. In this way it tests the physical properties or use under actual operating conditions. Part of this involves questions about the need for specific capabilities, material requirements, use of standard components, process steps, layouts, packaging and despatch implications. Typically there will be several, if not many, prototypes. It is a way of checking reality beforehand and enables savings in both time and costs to be secured.

6. Market sensing and testing target markets

The last section was orientated towards testing the functionality of an idea and undertaking the continuous and critical task of checking prototypes in terms of their provision. At the same time the checking of markets continues. That the idea works and can be reproduced is one side of the coin. The other is whether customers will buy it. As with prototype testing, this step continues to be an ongoing task.

For example, in services a prototype may be the introduction of a new or revised service in one or more test sites where the concept can be evaluated and modified as necessary. Once a new service and its delivery system has been tried and proved to be successful it can be introduced into other outlets.

In the same way, product prototype testing is a way of verifying the technical and sales performance of the new idea. Test marketing in a selected geographical area is a similar approach to that outlined for services in the last section. Throughout, screening and testing is a continuous activity aimed at checking and rechecking in order to reduce uncertainty before large capital investments are committed.

7. Final design

Prototype testing often identifies necessary changes to the initial design. During the final design phase these will be incorporated. At this stage, specifications will be completed and the essential tasks of marketing plans, material supply, operations tasks and associated investments will be initiated. The detail involved forms part of the chapters which follow.

DESIGN – THE REALITY

As mentioned earlier, the design process is characterized by reiteration and a non-sequential nature. Steps into the unknown embody uncertainty and the rigours of the process are intended to flush out questions essential to arriving at a viable design. Two further issues that are also part of the reality of the design process are now highlighted.

The decision

The final decision as to whether or not to go ahead rests with top management. The levels of investment, corporate profile and reputation, and the strategic direction of the firm are invariably central to the decision. Rejection stems from a combination of experience, judgement and placing a decision in the context of other investment opportunities. Approval commits a firm's efforts and resources one way and to a course of action the success of which may not be measurable for months, even years later and yet may harm a company's success or even jeopardize its very survival.

Product/service design and process design

The design of a product or service and the design of the process or delivery system to provide it are interlinked. In the case of services, the 'product' is often the service system itself. However, the separation of these two aspects has been deliberate. Providing detail on both is essential, but making these as a single set of statements can often be confusing. Separating these adds clarity without significant disadvantages. In the discussions on process design (Chapter 5), links to product and service design will be recognized throughout.

PRODUCT/SERVICE DESIGN – ISSUES AND CONSIDERATIONS

The last section dealt with the product/service design process and explained the steps involved. These next few sections concern:

1. Overview issues in the product/service design process.
2. Design support for different market segments.
3. Developing a service specification.
4. The impact of technology on design.
5. Techniques and approaches related to design.

Throughout there will emphasis on the service sector. It reflects the intangible nature of the service provision and highlights some of the many issues to be considered.

1. Overview issues in the product/service design process

All organizations have a range of products or services at a given time. To be competitive, it is necessary to have a set that is complementary, relates to the organization's strategic decisions associated with issues such as growth and market share, and takes account of tactical considerations such as completeness of range, process capability and distribution costs. Furthermore, the mix is always undergoing change. New products or services are necessary for survival and growth. However, there are three important factors to be considered:

■ The development and introduction of new products and services are both risky and costly.
■ Products and services tend to follow a life cycle.
■ Some products and services are or have the potential to be more successful than others – product/service portfolio analysis.

The issues around the first point have been addressed earlier. Here we now look at product/service life cycles, product/service portfolios and the needs of different 'segments' and their relationship to the design process.

Product/service life cycles

The extent and rate of new product/service introductions can make a significant impact on a business. However, of equal concern in these decisions is the life cycle pattern anticipated or experienced once the product/service has been introduced.

Marketplace pressures require that designs never remain static and continuous endeavours are made to increase the fit with customer needs while scrutinizing the relationships between cost, quality and value. Despite the attention given by most organizations, many products and services enter the market and are then quickly phased out due to a lack of sales.

The process of introduction, initial growth, maturity and eventual decline in sales is referred to as the product/service life cycle (see Exhibit 3.5). It outlines the phases through which a product or service may go as it moves into and out of the market. New products and services are required to replace those already in the cycle no matter how extended the timescale may be.

Introduction

The sales pattern of many products and services initially shows a slow rate of growth. Market awareness is low and acceptance has not yet been achieved. The concept is often new, and initial teething troubles are usually experienced. This makes for low sales with slow growth,

Growth

The market has now been conditioned to the product or service. With acceptance comes a rapid growth in sales resulting from promotion, increased dependability, past sales and often a lower selling price.

Maturity

At this stage, the rate of sales increases begins to slow. This is due to the competitors who have entered the market partly due to increased demand as a product/service is now well known and established within its market segment.

Exhibit 3.5   *The generalized product/service life cycle*

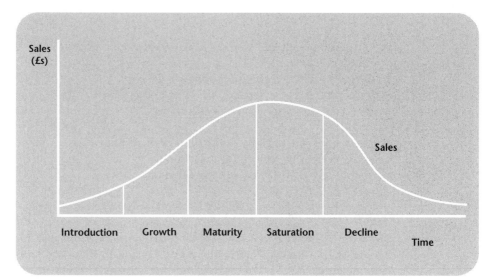

Saturation

In this stage, almost all those who want the product or service have now bought it. Market demand is restricted to replacement demand plus a small quantity of new sales. Product and service promotion is often used more extensively here not to publicize the item but to differentiate it from its competitors.

In service firms, this phenomenon is often not as marked. Restaurant chains still keep selling but often the sales levels plateau for reasons of overcapacity or those stated earlier. Also, some decline may take place as alternatives enter and prosper. For example, Kentucky Fried Chicken sales have declined in the last decade even though overall sales in the fast-food sector have grown. This is due to the success of fast-food alternatives.

Decline

In this phase, sales continue to fall off, and invariably at a rapid rate. The introduction of competing products and services, either as improvements or as substitutes, accelerate the decline to the point where it becomes obsolete. For example, the slide rule had been in the mature/saturation stage for a long time before it was replaced by the hand-held electronic calculator. Similarly, public transport services have in many country areas been replaced by private car ownership.

Reporting current and forecast sales of products and services in terms of the stage in their life cycle provides an insight into the spread of sales by phase, future patterns and the levels of new products and services that need to be targeted in the future. Also, different strategies are more relevant to one cycle stage than another. For example, an applications-orientated strategy is appropriate in the mature stage by offering modifications to existing products or services to serve particular market segments, whereas the emphasis on reducing costs and keeping designs fixed is most appropriate in the saturation phase of a typical cycle.

Product/service portfolio analysis

Portfolio analysis provides another way of helping companies look forward and decide on the allocation of resources. As shown in Exhibit 3.6, products and services can be separated into four classes, with the market share held by an organization being measured horizontally and the growth rate within the market measured vertically.

Products and services are then placed throughout or across two or more of the four segments to illustrate their relative positions against these two dimensions. The resulting 'portfolio' of products and services serves as part of the basis by which an organization can determine the appropriate allocation or concentration of corporate resources and particularly research and development funding. The interesting symbols used to describe these quadrants are explained below.

An organization that has analysed its products and services in this way is then able to look at its current or proposed mix in terms of cash and profits. This will help it to ensure continuity of a suitable product or service mix by determining a series of corporate issues. These include which markets to aim for and the degree of support required, particularly with regard to decisions on research and operations investment.

Exhibit 3.6   *Product/service portfolio analysis*

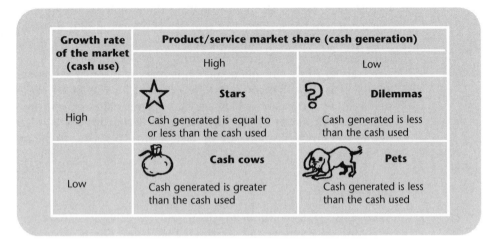

Dilemmas

A situation where products or services have a small percentage of a high growth market. In order to maintain or improve its position, an organization will have to allocate more cash than the products or services generate. Although the environment is favourable, current performance is questionable, thus requiring close examination and often remedial action. Consequently, it will be uncertain as to whether a product or service in the future will become a star or a pet.

Stars

Products and services with a high market share (typically a market leader) in a high growth market but often in a position where the cash generated is, at best, equal to (and often less than) the cash needed. Stars will eventually become cash cows if they hold their market share; they will become pets if they do not.

Cash cows

Products and services with a high percentage of a market, even though the market growth is low, and they are in the latter half of their life cycle. These are the principal generators of funds. The cash cow can be 'milked' to generate more cash than can be profitably reinvested. However, they can in no way be forgotten: they have to be managed efficiently, new developments within that product or service range have to be made and customers have to be carefully tended, with the emphasis on cash-flow rather than building market share.

Pets

Also known as cash traps, cash dogs and cash coffins, pets describe products and services where individual market share is low, market growth is low, and they are cash absorbers, with little or no hope of changing the situation. For many organizations the majority of their products and services fall into this category. They may

Exhibit 3.7   *Product/service portfolio with continuous axes and the plots for product/services A to E*

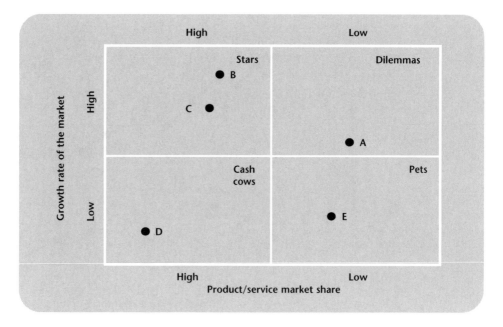

show an accounting profit but the profit must be reinvested to maintain market share. They leave no cash surplus for investment elsewhere and often absorb cash surpluses created by other products and services. As a rule, they should be deleted from the range.

The product or service portfolio analysis is essentially static but is a useful selection technique to help organizations both to understand more fully their current position and to reposition their product/service portfolio in the future. Its primary functions are to aid resource allocation and cash management by pinpointing those products and services with greatest potential and to maintain a balance within the current mix. The product/service life cycle is a dynamic model with associated market-related strategies built in. Thus, the combination of the portfolio matrix and life cycle models helps to determine or indicate tactical strategies concerning investments and harvesting in terms of cash usage. Exhibits 3.7 and 3.8 provide a simplified example to illustrate this development. In Exhibit 3.7, five products/services (A to E) are placed appropriately on the portfolio matrix, using the two dimensions as continuous scales. Showing the relevant life cycle for each product as in Exhibit 3.8 provides necessary insights into making appropriate current and future investments, together with related product/service and operations strategies.

2. Design support for different market segments

Firms invariably compete in more than one market segment. Identifying the segments within markets, therefore, is the first step in recognizing and addressing difference in terms of product/service development, marketing and the operations tasks involved. Examples of how firms have developed products and services to meet these different sets of needs are provided below.

Exhibit 3.8   *Portfolio/life cycle matrix*

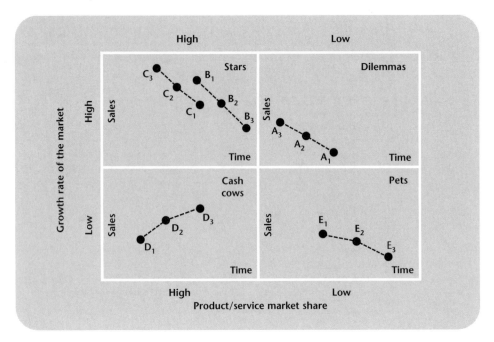

■ The concept of segmentation was originated by Alfred P. Sloan of General Motors (GM). He developed automobiles for different segments and thereby was able to compete in more parts of this growing market. Today manufacturers of consumer goods invariably offer a range of products to meet the needs and price brackets of various customers, for similar reasons to GM.

■ This separation is similarly reflected in the service sector. See Case examples 3.1 and 3.2.

Case example

1

Handels Bank NW of Zurich provides a different service offering for the following market segments:

Institutional investors
Portfolio management clients
Large investors
Standard investors
Medium investors
Small investors

These segments reflect the needs of its investors, the appropriate investment tools to be used, and the differential costs the bank applies in providing its different services. In this way, the bank more clearly identifies the type and level of service to be provided and the operations support required in that provision.

In the same way, UK banks have been segmenting their market and developing services to meet the needs of 'high earners'.[4] Tailoring products and allocating more management time are high on the agenda and linked to different segments. Natwest, for example, divides its customers by age, family status and income, and address each segment differently.

Hotels continue to emphasize segments within their offering and to support these with appropriate service developments. In the 1970s it was in-room mini-bars. Health clubs were all the rage in the 1990s. Now executive floors have emerged in the top business hotels both within North America and Europe. Billed as hotel within a hotel, the premium floors have their own check-in and check-out facilities, an executive lounge and sometimes a dedicated, express-elevator service. For five-star hotels, executive floors are a way of differentiating themselves at a time of intense competition in downtown and airport sites. For example, the Hilton Hotel in the Boulevard des Waterloo, Brussels offers for a $60 supplement, an executive floor room which includes the complimentary breakfast (normally $27), free drinks in the lounge until 2200 hours, butler service, and a library of compact discs and videos for guests to play in their room and a mobile phone loaned free and for which they can obtain their individual phone number three days in advance.[5]

Finally, with the growing number of guests who are women travelling alone on business, hotels are providing services to reflect this. The Meridien Hotel, Piccadilly, London offer a female Executive Traveller package including female room service attendants and increased awareness of security at all stages in the hotel process. The Thistle Hotel chain includes special features in its rooms allocated to women and some of its hotels offer only-women wings. A recent survey showed that 35 per cent of all business travellers are women, with the number expected to rise to 50 per cent by the year 2000.[6]

Separating services by type highlights the different development tasks and orientation required. One split concerns those services based principally on equipment and those principally on people. Within these two broad divisions, subdivisions concerning skill requirements can be identified, as illustrated in Exhibit 3.9.

Exhibit 3.9   *Types of service showing the range of operations requirements within the service delivery system*

Predominant base	Level of automation and labour skills	Examples
Equipment	Automated	Cash dispensing Photocopying Vending machines Car wash
	Monitored by unskilled/semi-skilled people	Photocopying Dry-cleaning Gardening Tree surgery Taxis
	Operated by skilled people	Airlines Computer time-sharing Word processing
People	Unskilled	Cleaning services Security guards
	Skilled	Catering Vehicle maintenance Appliance repairs
	Professional	Lawyers Management consultants Accountants

Strategies to reduce cost

Companies in various service systems have pursued strategies to reduce costs in several ways, including the following:

1. *Seeking out low-cost customers.* Some customers cost less to serve than others, without any deterioration in the perceived level of service provided. Non-smokers are eligible for lower life insurance rates and accident-free customers for lower insurance premiums. Similarly, targeting higher age groups links lower premiums to lower-risk categories. Shouldice's Hernia Hospital near Toronto carefully screens patients and only accepts those in good physical condition with forms of hernia in which it specializes. This contributes to rapid recovery rates and early discharge, which are reflected in the hospital's prices and costs.

2. *Standardizing products and services.* The growth in direct line services from insurance to mortgage lending and banking is based on standardizing products to allow the fast handling of requests and enquiries. The impact on overhead costs is reflected in the competitive prices on offer.

3. *'Do-it-yourself' customerization.* Numerous examples exist in the service sector to illustrate this phenomenon – telephone subscriber dialling, self-service salad bar provision in restaurants, automatic teller machines, hot drink and mini-bar facilities in hotel bedrooms all illustrate the provision of an acceptable level (and often preferred type) of service while reducing areas of potential customer complaints and, at the same time, taking out costs.

Strategies to enhance services

Companies basing their approach on product and service differentiation employ several strategies to bring this about, including the following:

1. *Making the intangible tangible.* One way to bring the intangible facets of a service to the attention of a customer is to make them tangible. In this way, parts of a service package that would often go unnoticed are now a visible part of the provision. For example:

   ■ Maid service in a hotel bedroom to include collars placed on toilets with words similar to 'sanitized for your personal use', end-folding toilet roll paper, folding down the bed in the evening with a personalized note and guest room checklist duly completed (see Exhibit 3.10).

   ■ Fast attentive service is signalled by prominent positioning of the '3-minute warning' notice in some high street branches of Lloyds TSB Bank (see Exhibit 3.11). Supported by the prompt opening of additional tellers when queues start to form, this draws customers' attention to this dimension of service provision.

   ■ Some hotels are increasingly making in-room hot drink provision a feature, as illustrated by Exhibit 3.12. Moreover, most hotels provide the highest quality amenities such as French-milled and smooth facial soaps, shampoo, conditioner, bath foam, hand lotion and shower caps; aftershave for male travellers with make-up remover and styling preparations for their female counterparts. And all in keeping with the hotel's standards of service provided elsewhere (see Exhibit 3.13).

Exhibit 3.10 *A typical note left for guests to see and which helps to bring to their attention an otherwise less tangible part of the hotel's service*

■ In a similar vein, hotels now display notices in the en-suite bathrooms informing guests that, should they have forgotten any essential toiletry item then just telephone reception for complimentary provision (see Exhibit 3.14).

■ Prompt service is also made tangible in one of several ways – many hotels guarantee an in-room breakfast that will be delivered within ten minutes of the

Exhibit 3.11 *Setting standards and bringing them to the attention of customers*

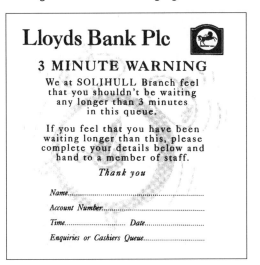

Note

In 1999, Lloyds Bank's name switched to Lloyds TSB.

Exhibit 3.12   *In-room hot drink service – advising the guest of the wider product range available*

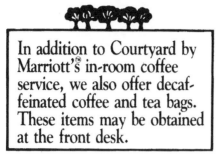

In addition to Courtyard by
Marriott's® in-room coffee
service, we also offer decaffeinated coffee and tea bags.
These items may be obtained
at the front desk.

Exhibit 3.13   *Some of the complimentary toiletry items provided by Forte*

requested period or it will be provided free of charge. Domino Pizza's promise to deliver an order to your home within 30 minutes (normal times) or 40 minutes (peak demand times) or it will be replaced or money refunded. In practice, this means that if a delivery is late customers would be asked to pay for the pizza(s) but not (say) the soft drink(s) or dessert(s). Furthermore, if a delivery is considered very late (20 plus minutes) the whole order is offered free of charge. Domino Pizza's replace or refund policy also applies to its quality guarantee.

■ In maintenance work, cleaning up after completion provides a 'reverse' example of this same perspective. Similarly, a car-wash given free with a routine service or

Exhibit 3.14   *Complimentary provision notice where guests may have forgotten an essential toiletry item*

paper covers left inside the vehicle demonstrate to the customer the level of care taken by the company.

■ Guarantees on quality are now standard for most products where reimbursement of price and postage is prompt and is encouraged by companies where a customer has any concerns whatsoever. With food, the time of preparation also signals freshness as demonstrated in Exhibit 3.15.

Exhibit 3.15   *The time stamp is the symbol of freshness*

2. *Customizing a standard product/service.* Hotel telephone receptionists addressing a guest by name, Burger King's strategy (as mentioned in a previous chapter) to increase the level of customization in its food service provision to help differentiate it from McDonald's strategy of a low price, standard menu. The issue of mass customization is discussed in a later section.

3. *Influencing quality expectations.* The definition of what constitutes good service varies by customer and transaction, 'but it is influenced as much by customer expectation as by a customer's experience of the services actually delivered'.[7] Approaches that influence expectations include identifying customer expectations and aligning these with service delivery systems capabilities or vice versa.

3. Developing a service specification

In addition to the points raised earlier in the chapter, there are other important perspectives pertinent to developing a specification that need to be recognized by an organization. For example, the following characteristics have an important bearing on their provision and both concern service definition:

1. By their very nature, services are less tangible than products. Thus while the physical dimensions of a product require specification, services lack these characteristics and hence are intrinsically less defined. It is necessary, therefore, for an organization to ensure that the task of determining the service specification is undertaken.

2. In manufacturing the products and customers are invariably decoupled in the system, for example through inventory or the wholesale/retail stages in the total process. In services, however, the provider and customer are invariably linked at the point of provision. The result is that the opportunity to interpret what is meant by 'service' is also at the point of provision. It is necessary, therefore, for organizations to determine the level of discretion to be allowed in the service delivery system concerning the interpretation of what each service should comprise.

Within the context of the characteristics described above, organizations need to address the elements of service specification in order to determine the operations issues involved within the delivery system. To help in this task, the following perspectives should be taken into account:

1. It is important to determine the product/service mix (see Exhibit 1.6) that best reflects the nature of the services provided. This will reflect the market segment(s) in which an organization wishes to compete, influenced at least in part by competitive pressure. For example, most McDonald's outlets now offer a breakfast menu in line with competing businesses. The result is an increased product range, some of which is only available before mid-morning. In addition, the overall range offered is becoming more extensive, in part reflecting the competitive pressure in the different fast-food markets.

2. Within this context, a service can be expressed as a combination of the following:[8]

    (a) a service within which there is a facilitating good;
    (b) a good that also involves a facilitating service;

(c) the explicit services provided;

(d) the implicit services provided;

(e) the supporting structural facilities.

(a) *A service within which there is a facilitating good.* A look back at Exhibit 1.6 is a reminder that most of what is purchased is a combination of goods and services. Where the mix is predominantly service, then the goods element of the package is known to be facilitating in nature.

(b) A good that also involves a facilitating service. Many purchases of goods contain an element of service. The extent of the service content within the total package will vary, for example purchasing a television set as compared with tailored kitchen units requiring installation; or a meal provided by a high-class restaurant as compared with a fast-food outlet.

(c) *The explicit services provided.* When services are purchased, customers perceive that they are receiving one or more explicit services. For example, a bank provides the explicit service of money transactions; a hotel provides food and accommodation; and a hairdresser, the styling of hair. Customers may choose from a range of quality levels concerning the provision of a service and this will typically influence their selection of the providing organization.

(d) *The implicit services provided.* In many markets the implicit services may well be as, if not more, important a factor in customer selection as the explicit service that is at the core of the purchase. For example, security and privacy within a banking system; level of attention, promptness and recognition of a regular customer by hotel staff; magazine and hot/soft drink provision and levels of cleanliness within a hairdressing salon.

(e) *The supporting structural facilities.* This aspect concerns a recognition of the need to determine support facilities that reflect the nature and customers' perceptions of the services provided. The quality of buildings, furniture, fittings and equipment, appropriate decor, level of maintenance and general upkeep are typical examples.

Establishing the level of contact with a customer

'A few manufacturing firms use the customer for do-it-yourself assembly, but basically the customer buying a product is decoupled from the factory. Service managers must decide exactly what the customer should experience and how the customer will or will not participate in the creation of the service. The degree of self-service desired in a service delivery system affects many factors including capacity provision, service levels, training requirements for company employees, and cost control.'[9]

Companies need to determine the extent of customer participation. Increases will lead to the gains mentioned while reductions decrease the level of contact and the opportunities to personalize service and encourage customer loyalty. The trade-offs need to be understood and the operations implications for supporting the service delivery system need full assessment. For example: while banks in the UK are increasingly standardizing procedures in bank loan applications, in Japan the procedure has already progressed to the use of a score sheet. Answers to several questions are graded

Exhibit 3.16 *Factors for success embracing products and services brought about by do-it-yourself approaches in selected service sectors*

Factors for success	Selected service sectors					
	Supermarkets	Fast-food outlets	Telephone services	Petrol stations	On-line shopping	Financial services
Faster service	✓	✓	✓	✓	✓	✓
Lower price	✓	✓	✓	✓	✓	✓
Improved product quality	✓	✓				
Increased product variety	✓				✓	
More convenient	✓				✓	✓
More control within the delivery system	✓		✓	✓	✓	✓

and if the customer's score is above a certain level, the loan application is handled quickly. The impact upon operations provision is significant.

The concept of do-it-yourself approaches was addressed earlier in this section. It also relates directly to the issue here. Examples of service industries increasingly using this approach include:

■ **Supermarkets** control over 80 per cent of the gross retail market and sell principally on a self-service basis.

■ **Fast-food outlets** form a growing part of overall restaurant provision.

■ **Telephone services** are principally based on subscriber dialling with most telephone calls now being made by customers.

■ **Petrol stations** use self-service as the basis for providing fuel, screen washing, and oil, water and tyre pressure checks.

■ **On-line shopping** is a rapidly growing sector of the retail industry. It requires a customer to complete the selection, application and payment parts of the procedure, with the business providing a fast delivery service once the transaction is fed into the service system.

■ **Financial services** provide an increasingly wide range of products through self-service delivery systems from automatic teller (or cash) machines (ATMs), general banking, insurance, mortgages and personal loans.

The reasons for the growth in these sectors vary. Exhibit 3.16 summarizes some factors that relate to their success.

The scheduling of customers' labour is less critical since they help themselves at the time as well as undertaking any pre- and post-service activities. However, for this to be successful companies must assess the total operations requirement of the service delivery system and carefully complement the customer inputs by well-trained staff and reliable equipment.

Case example

3

There are over 20 million private motorists in the UK and ownership continues to grow. As a result, motor insurance is big business with an £8bn annual premium spend. Launched in 1985, Direct Line was the first insurance company to use the telephone as its primary medium for sales and other transactions. Cutting out the middleman and commissions enabled it to speed up the applications process and reduce premiums. Today Direct Line is the UK's largest private motor insurer with over 2 million policy holders. Direct Line has also successfully expanded its product range and the Direct Line Group (a wholly owned subsidiary of the Royal Bank of Scotland) now offers the following:

■ *Direct Line Insurance Plc* – motor, rescue, home, travel and pet insurance

■ *Direct Line Financial Services Ltd* – mortgages, savings, personal loans and credit cards

■ *Direct Line Life Holdings Ltd* – personal pensions, life insurance and ISAs.

In 1995 Direct Line opened its first industrial scale car repair centre and now operates four throughout the UK that contribute to the quality and efficiency of the service within its overall claims business.

A strong feature of the early years was Direct Line's speed of growth. By Year 3 it was profitable even though it offered premiums that were typically 20 per cent lower than competitors. The concept of the telephone as its primary tool enabled Direct Line to deal directly with the public and to use the advantages afforded by its technological efficiency and underwriting precision to cut costs. Less than a decade after its entry, Direct Line became the UK's largest private motor insurer.

Direct Line's entry set new service standards for the insurance industry. It offers extended hours with lines open from 8am to 8pm on weekdays and 9am to 5pm on Saturdays. It enables customers to register and complete their claims by telephone and provides 24-hour emergency help lines. The idea brings greater simplicity, improves the level of customer support through the process and results in better value for money.

In 1993, when the company's flagship products were both the fastest growing in their respective markets, Direct Line extended its range adopting the same tactics of low prices, straightforward products and telephone-based service delivery systems. As the company transacts the vast majority of its business by telephone, operations is at the core of the Direct Line service proposition. To ensure standards are maintained, the company provides extensive customer care training and re-engineers processes to cut out complicated forms and jargon. One of its first revolutionary moves was to eliminate cover notes (that were traditionally sent to customers as confirmation of insurance cover but were not the official documents) by laser printing and mailing policies, insurance certificates and other documents the same day.

Innovative technology helps Direct Line keep down costs. For example, most products are paid for by credit card or direct debit allowing payments to be processed electronically and so reducing staff and overheads. Similarly, automated call handling systems ensure that the 15 million calls received each year are quickly and effortlessly rerouted between Direct Line's different call centres to minimize customer waiting time.

Today, Direct Line continues to improve its operations so as to offer additional customer benefits and better customer support. These range from the use of daily interest calculations for mortgages to a 'pet bereavement' helpline for pet insurance customers. Staff development is also a key activity with initiatives such as cross-training sales and claims staff so that the same people can handle both sets of tasks. The result is that work interest increases while customers are served more quickly.

Case example questions

3.1 Why is Direct Line so successful and how has operations supported the business growth?

3.2 How do (if at all) the products offered by Direct Line differ from its competitors?

3.3 Analyse Direct Line in terms of the 'factors for success' introduced in Exhibit 3.16.

As service industries develop, the considerations of customer-based capacity provision need to be revised. One example concerns the differential pricing arrangements in petrol stations in the USA. The price per gallon of fuel varies depending upon whether it is a self-service or full service provision.

Level of server discretion

The server–customer interface allows for discretion. It is important, therefore, for organizations to establish the appropriate level of discretion to be exercised within each service category (that is, the extent to which it is desired or appropriate that a server is allowed to interpret what should constitute the service specification actually provided). Earlier issues concerning service standardization, levels of customer contact and automation will have an impact upon server discretion levels; firms need to recognize these factors as ways of reducing or increasing customization and use them to develop a service delivery system that supports the level of customization desired. In so doing, organizations can improve their control of quality conformance within the service delivery system with given levels of customer contact and staff skills.

Off-line versus on-line

Some services are inherently on-line and do not allow the server to be separated from the customer (for example, hairdressing and passenger transport). However, other service businesses do allow for a measure of server/customer decoupling. Where this is so, on-line services can be done off-line if desired.

Furthermore, once parts of a service are off-line they can also be transferred from the front office to the back office. This not only allows them to be completed using different methods and at different times (thus enabling for instance, low-cost opportunities to be exploited by cumulating desmand and thereby increasing volumes prior to processing) but it also allows firms to improve customer perceptions of the service itself.

The Royal Bank (Canada), for instance, believes that customers' perceptions are a critical factor in service provision. The bank considers that when queues form, customers' attitudes to waiting are affected by both the server's attitude when they are eventually attended to, and the fact that when waiting, customers judge service by the level of attendance shown in the front office. Thus, if bank staff are doing jobs other than attending to customers, and the queues are long, customers' attitudes to the bank's overall regard for service quality are affected. Thus, the bank's aim is to transfer as much paperwork to head office or to the back office as possible.

Customer interface: front office or back office

Related to the last section is the need for a company to determine where the customer interface will take place - the front office or back office. The reasons for separating the service delivery system in this way is to orientate activities to one part or the other. Front office activities interface with customers and the need to meet their needs and expectations is at the forefront of the provision. The intention of the back office arrangement is to exclude customer interface thereby allowing staff to complete tasks as best suits the system. However, there are times when interfacing the back office and customers brings significant benefits.

Case example 4

An electrical repair shop recently changed the customer interface point in the delivery system. Whereas previously the customer explained the repair needs to those in the front office, the customer now takes the repair to the back office and discusses the problem with the person who will complete the repair. Everyone gains. The repair person can now ensure that all pertinent questions are covered and the customer is able to discuss the repair both before and after the service is completed. This, of course, has long been the arrangement in many good quality dressmakers and tailors.

Using limited capabilities

Businesses offering a wide range of services may well find that by carefully analysing tasks in terms of skill requirements and checking these against servers' actual skills they can realign service needs to server provision to ensure that the capacity of skilled servers is maximized. Some companies employ this approach to gain the maximum leverage of scarce resources (that is, skilled and experienced staff of whom there are typically fewer available). For example, the auditing divisions of large accounting firms employ large numbers of junior or associate staff on relatively low salaries which increases the level of sales and profit per partner. With little opportunity for advancement, the levels of staff turnover are high and so junior and associate staff are continually being replaced by new entrants so helping to maintain the sales and profit levels per partner.

4. The impact of technology on design

Technology and its role in design and operations in general is significant and widespread. Chapter 7 addresses technology applications in detail. This section is intended to signal these developments and illustrate their role both in the delivery system as well as the product/service design process itself.

The impact of rapid increases in technology that have characterized the last fifty years needs to be carefully assessed and provided for by all organizations. Product/service and process technology advances have become more stepped in nature and more frequent in occurrence. Increasingly, therefore, it is essential that organizations address these opportunities not only in terms of developing their current business base but also in assessing the impact on all corporate functions. This latter requirement is particularly important in terms of the operations function due to the relatively high asset/cost profile that is involved, and the changes in capacity and capability that will ensue. One example of this level of technology change is provided by banking:

■ *1960s* Cashless payment transactions became technologically feasible. This led to a rapid increase in customers' use of banks initiated by the direct payment of salaries and wages by employer organizations into employees' bank accounts.

■ *1980s* Known technology led to increased automation in banking with cash dispensers, multi-functional terminals, point-of-sale systems and video tape systems.

■ *1990s* The 1990s witnessed an increase in self-service activity and the resulting substantial reduction in the functions performed by bank branches. The consequence on the role of advisory *vis-à-vis* transaction services within banks, and the changing staff requirements have been significant. One development that has followed is home banking supported by video text comparisons, resulting in a greater emphasis on the advice and consultation role of banking staff within branches and less emphasis on basic data provision.

With these developments on hand, banks have been identifying those services that lend themselves to automation and those that will be provided (at least in part) by the qualified experts at a bank branch. In addition, 'given new technologies such as digital bankwide networks of terminals, many administrative activities could be handled by clerical workstations located outside a branch. Staff workstations could be set up in their own homes or in separate local or communal working places. The consequences include a drastic reduction in requirements for and use of office premises.[10] The ramifications throughout banking, especially in terms of the operations function, will, in the future, be even more significant than seen so far.

As the last section illustrated, the impact of information technology (IT) on products and services has been and will continue to be dramatic. Voice recognition (both for comprehension of vocal commands and for speech-to-text dictation) is not far away.[11] Already voice-over technology capability permits two people to discuss the data being exchanged on their personal computers, while executives can agree changes to a document while sharing the program on screen.

The impact on transmission, business travel and other services of these developments will be revolutionary, in the same way that computer-aided design (CAD) has dramatically altered the process of designing in a whole range of industries. As explained earlier, the design process is iterative in nature. Ideas, options and solutions all need to be checked, evaluated and rechecked. CAD developments have facilitated this process. A CAD system stores, retrieves, manipulates and displays graphical information with great speed and accuracy. It is based on a minicomputer with three-dimensional graphical displays. With CAD, a common engineering database is developed which is a collection of all the information about related products. Thus, once generated, the information is neither lost nor recreated. In addition, the geometric and non-geometric information stored in the engineering database is then used as the basis for manufacturing at a later stage. This then forms part of computer-aided manufacturing (CAM) systems of which more will be said in Chapter 7.

A typical CAD system consists of a central processing unit with a large storage facility and a minicomputer plus system software. Linked to this control unit will be a number of design terminals. Through these, the designer interacts with the engineering database to develop a detailed product design while monitoring the work on the display terminal. The designer creates, modifies and refines each design without putting pen to paper. Thus the design terminal provides a simple yet powerful interaction between the designer and the computer. The designer instructs the system using an electronic pen or keyboard. Initially, any completed drawings, other stored information relevant to the design task and the standard design symbols to be used are retrieved. This on-line library, therefore, eliminates both filing and information retrieval procedures. Then, by using either an electronic pen and drawing tablet or a keyboard, the designer communicates draughting instructions to the system. Graphic displays give designers an imaginary drawing board of some 20 000 square inches, any portion of which can be viewed through the display in three dimensions with zooming and rotation facilities available to view the design from any angle and allowing for interaction on any basis. In this way, operators can create and modify a design while watching it emerge on the display unit with the system automatically informing them of procedural or design rule errors. Also built into a system is the capability for assisting the designer in outline drawings, creating the third dimension at any desired angle, generating views from any side, rotating the part, changing the scale, producing a mirror image and adding the appropriate text all with a sufficient degree of precision to meet the highest engineering standards.

Once the preliminary design is created, the information is stored allowing existing designs to be readily retrieved. At any time, a hard copy of the design can be made in paper form for use outside the CAD system. When the preliminary design has been agreed, various analyses can be applied to test its viability. After making any necessary modifications, the design is ready for the manufacturing stage. Although the costs of creating preliminary three-dimensional geometrical designs are similar to those using conventional methods, the savings when revising and modifying them are substantial. For instance, a designer is able to interrogate the database to help make decisions on designs, while further large savings are made on filing, information retrieval and all the error prone, time-consuming, handwritten activities necessary with conventional methods.

CAD is now being used in all parts of the world including emerging nations and is increasingly being used in software and service applications. As shown in Exhibit 3.17 the period 1990–95 saw a compound growth in CAD/CAM sales of 12 per cent.

Exhibit 3.17   *Worldwide CAD/CAM markets*

Applications	Year ($bn)						Compound Growth (%)
	1990	1991	1992	1993	1994	1995	
Hardware	7.96	8.50	9.63	10.45	11.41	12.39	9
Software	4.07	4.72	5.44	6.35	7.33	8.49	16
Services	2.33	2.57	2.88	3.23	3.62	4.08	12
All	14.36	15.79	17.98	20.03	22.36	24.96	12

5. Techniques and approaches related to design

This final section outlines some of the techniques and approaches used to help improve the design process in the overall context of a business.

Standardization

At the two extremes of the product/service continuum the offerings range from specials where each item is unique to offerings where there is little if any choice – the Ford Model T any colour as long as it is black syndrome. For the most part, today's markets lie between these extremes. The concept of standardization helps provide a range of options while enhancing the volumes of parts from which end products and services are built. The concept can be applied to components, materials and process choice to great effect.

Components

Standardized components and subassemblies can be used to make finished items that are different in appearance and performance. This approach can be formalized into providing modular designs such that a variety of final products use only a few basic components. This approach results in economies due to component inventory reduction, longer production runs, increased opportunity to automate, purchasing advantages and improved delivery on-time and speed performance.

Materials

In a similar way to components, standardization can be applied to both direct and indirect materials. In this case, both the variety of material sizes and types can be simplified through close examination. It is important, however, to seek a balance between the cost gains due to reduced inventory, easier control and bulk purchasing, and the overspecification and lower utilization of material that will increase the materials bill.

Processes

The standardization of equipment, assuming that there is no requirement to increase flexibility, will lead to a reduction in spare parts inventory and will simplify the maintenance requirement. Where it is feasible in terms of capability to choose equipment of the same type and size, then such standardization will also lead to increased flexibility (for example, tool changes in manufacturing or compatible computer hardware and software in operations).

However, to make standardization work effectively requires the formulation of a corporate policy together with the establishment of agreed criteria that will be applied to all the products produced or services provided.

Modular design

The use of modules as standard building blocks in designing and providing products and services is an extension of the concept of interchangeable parts. Using common sets of parts enhances volumes, lowers costs and reduces inventory levels.

Case examples

5

■ Oil and gas production platforms, historically custom-designed and built to a bespoke specification, are moving towards standard designs built on a modular basis as part of a cost-cutting orientation to ensure the future profitability of big oil companies.[12]

6

■ Toyota launched its smaller, recreational vehicle Rav 4 at around half the price of most vehicles in this segment in part by using existing components and subassemblies from other cars – the engine and steering wheel from Celica, a sports car, and door mirrors from Corina, a four-door sedan.[13]

7

■ Offering modular services in support of products enabled Sonnoco's Industrial Products Division to customize its packaging of support services 'to meet more precisely the requirements of its spectrum of customers'. The concept of offering only essential services as part of the sales package and then offering modular services at set prices is enabling companies such as Sonnoco Products Company, Baxter Healthcare International, Asea Brown Boveri (ABB) and AZKO to tailor packages to customer needs and keep prices lower.

Mass customization

Although the topic of mass customization is more fully covered in Chapter 4, it is opportune to introduce the concept at this time.

The increasingly competitive nature of today's markets has increased the need to provide customers' requirements without prohibitive price and lead time implications. While process investment is at the core of this provision, the decision to customize products as the way to run a business will mean substantial changes throughout an organization. Ever since General Motors (GM), by offering choice and alternatives, took over the world leadership mantle from Ford and its 'no choice' strategy in the 1920s, the car industry has offered a wide choice on many dimensions. The result is that the potential number of different car configurations (engine types and size × colours × options) for most models runs into six figures and they are all assembled on the same process. This development is now spreading to other markets.

The proliferation of faster, smarter and more affordable computers, software and telecommunications allows more choice or customization on a mass (that is, high volume) scale. Aspects of modular designs and interchangeable parts offer choice to the customer and with the necessary process investment required in place and an organization geared to meet these offerings, the ability to customize a standard product is a viable activity. Whereas mass customization is not in itself new (the GM strategy was launched in the late 1920s) its application to a wider range of product offerings is, and the phrase 'mass customization' is intended to herald this growing phenomenon.

Taguchi methods

An approach to design developed by Japan's Genichi Taguchi has received considerable attention.[14] His principle is simple. Instead of constantly directing effort to control a process so as to assure consistent quality conformance, it is better to design the product or service to achieve desired levels of quality conformance despite the variations that will occur in the production process or service delivery system. Based on his work in manufacturing, Taguchi's approach is based on the use of statistically designed experiments to optimize design and operations costs. This approach requires a product or service to perform to specification in extreme conditions. For example:

■ above-average demand – ability of manufacturing to provide capacity uplifts
■ absenteeism – staffing plans to provide short-term cover
■ dietary needs – range of options to provide alternative menus
■ weather shifts – alternative activities to meet changeable weather patterns
■ unexpected demand – plans to meet early arrivals
■ working conditions – developing products to withstand harsh climates or extreme patterns of use.

The effects of this approach on design procedures and objectives continue to be most noticeable. In part it forces the process/delivery system and product/service design to come together and agree the parameters to meet a range of conditions and to build these into the specification.

Quality function deployment and the house of quality

There are two dimensions that affect the success of the design effort – the extent to which a product or service design meets customers' needs and how well an organization can produce or deliver the design. Quality function deployment (QFD) is a way to evaluate how well the product or service design and the operations process meet or exceed the needs of customers. Using competitors' offerings as an additional part of the assessment helps organizations to identify both where they need to improve and also the product and service features and activities that are non-value adding.

QFD had its origins in Bridgestone Tire Corporation and Mitsubishi's Kone (Japan) shipyards in the late 1960s. Professor Yoji Akao (Tamagawa University) and Shigeru Mizuno gave QFD its name in the late 1970s and popularized the concept of formalizing customer inputs into product and service design procedures. The complete QFD approach involves a sequential set of matrices (see Exhibit 3.18) through which the links between customer needs and the technical, component/material and operations requirements are identified and maintained.

The most commonly used phase of QFD is the stage 1 matrix, often called the house of quality. Exhibit 3.19 illustrates the general steps involved and will be used to show how the approach is applied, in this instance to a fast-food restaurant.

■ *Step 1:* **Customers' needs and wants** – this concerns establishing what customers need and want and the characteristics and attributes of the products and services involved. Furthermore, the relative importance of these must then be established as shown in Exhibit 3.19.

■ *Step 2:* **Establish the customers' view of competition** – this step concerns establishing how well this facility is satisfying customers' needs compared with compet-

Exhibit 3.18   *How quality function deployment links customer needs and wants to operations requirements*

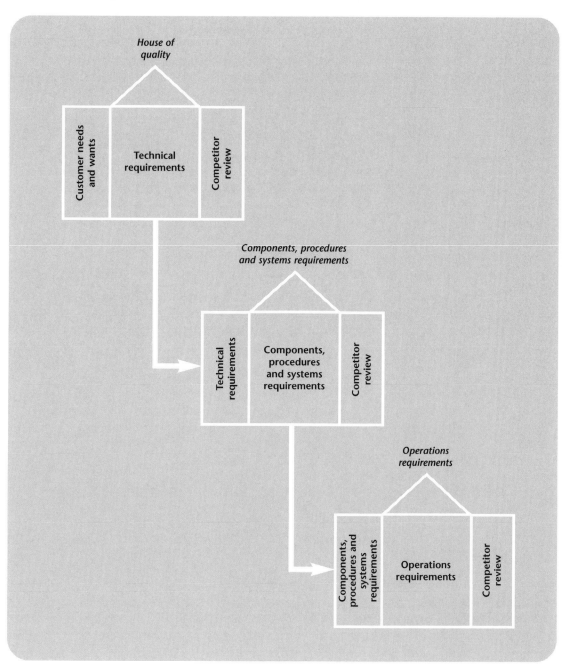

Exhibit 3.19 *An illustration of using quality function deployment–matrix I the 'house of quality'*

Customers' needs and wants		Weights %	Increase grill area	Increase server staff at peak times	Increase server stations	Increase kitchen staff at peak times	Decrease average time food is stored	Decrease maximum time food is stored	Decrease process steps – main meal	Best 1	2	3	4	Worst 5
Decor and layout		5									OP B	AC		
Menu variety	Child	5	+			+					OP C	AB		
	Adult	10	+			+				C		B	OP A	
Service speed		30	+	+	+	+	–	–	+	C		OP A	B	
Food	Tastes good	15	+	+	+	+	+	+	+		OP C	AB		
	Served warm	10	+	+	+	+	+	+	+	C	A	B	OP	
	Ingredients	5									OP C	B	A	
Low price		20	–	–		–	–	–			OP	AB		C
Technical evaluation of competitors			m²	#	#	#	mins	mins	#	Comments				
Own performance (OP)			2.5	5	5	7	6	9	8					
Competitors	A		2.4	5	5	7	6	8	6					
	B		2.7	5	5	8	6	7	6					
	C		3.0	6	7	8	4	7	5					
Target technical specifications			2.9	6	7	8	4	7	5					

itors' outlets. In Exhibit 3.19, three competing restaurants are compared, with OP (own performance) representing this outlet and A, B and C representing the competitors' facilities. Where 1 is the worst and 5 the best category comparisons are made and areas that potentially need improving are revealed.

- ■ *Step 3:* **Identify the technical requirements** – here, the technical requirements necessary to provide customers' wants and needs are identified. For example, fast service may be, in part, achieved by making food ahead of time or by reducing the process lead time involved. Measuring the factors that affect these and other dimensions would then be completed as an input into a later stage, Step 5.

- ■ *Step 4:* **Looking for links between customer needs and technical requirements** – this step looks for links between the technical requirements and their effect on the different customers' needs and wants. These are recorded in the body of the house of quality with an a + or a – sign indicating the extent to which it would potentially improve or harm relevant product or services attributes. For example, let us consider the technical requirement 'Decrease average time food is stored' listed in Exhibit 3.19. While decreasing the average storage time of food is potentially harmful (hence the – sign) to service speed (that is, the chance of being out of stock increases and, therefore, customers would be required to wait), it is also recognized as potentially helping the attributes 'food tastes good' and 'food served warm' (hence the + sign). Obviously, if we changed this technical requirement from 'decrease' to 'increase average time food is started' the + and – signs would be reversed.

- ■ *Step 5:* **Complete technical comparisons** – this stage concerns checking the extent of your technical provision with that of your competitors. The actual figures involved or using a scale of 1 to 5 helps in drawing comparisons and making subsequent assessments. In Exhibit 3.19, actual figures are used throughout.

- ■ *Step 6:* **Evaluating the trade-offs for different design features** – the final step is to record in the 'roof' section of the house of quality information relating to the trade-offs of different design features. The conclusions reached are recorded at the top of the 'house', again using + or – signs. The purpose of this step is to highlight the effect of changing the extent of one requirement on the other technical dimensions in the process.

In the example provided as Exhibit 3.19 you will see a plus sign recorded between the first and fourth technical requirements. This highlights the need for both these requirements to meet an increased menu variety and improved delivery speed. However, you will also see a minus sign between the first and fifth and again between the first and the sixth technical requirements. Whereas increasing the grill area will help improve service speed, decreasing storage times will have the reverse effect.

Value engineering and value analysis

The price of materials, components and services is the concern of the purchasing function. To a large extent, it will be influenced by world markets, competition and usage volumes. However, the other important factor determining an organization's material costs is how well it utilizes these materials. The significance of a reduction in these costs is substantial. In 1996, the cost of purchases made by all UK manufacturing industries totalled £226 909m. A small percentage reduction, therefore, would reveal a considerable amount overall. However, it is the incidence of labour costs which concerns most UK companies and where most organizations put their resources in an attempt to reduce costs. However, the *Census of Production* revealed that in 1996, the purchases of all UK manufacturing industries was 6.9 times higher than the cost of

Exhibit 3.20 *Ratio of purchases to costs of wages and salaries for selected industries and for all manufacturing industries*

| Industry | Ratio of purchases to wages and salaries | | | | | |
| | 1996 | | 1986 | | 1970 | |
	Operatives	All	Operatives	All	Operatives	All
Food, drink, tobacco	9.6	6.5	9.6	6.8	7.6	5.5
Chemical	10.2	4.0	9.6	4.5	6.6	3.5
Office equipment and computers	21.3	7.6	16.3	4.2	n.a.	n.a.
Motor vehicles	10.9	7.0	5.2	3.4	4.3	3.1
Textiles	3.6	2.4	3.3	2.4	3.5	2.6
Footwear	2.3	1.7	1.9	1.5	2.1	1.7
Furniture	3.4	2.2	3.6	2.5	2.1	1.7
Rubber products	4.0	2.4	3.2	2.0	2.8	1.9
Sports goods	6.2	2.9	4.1	2.4	2.9	1.9
Plastics products[3]	4.2	2.7	3.8	2.5	2.9	2.0
All manufacturing industries	6.9	3.5	5.0	3.0	3.9	2.6

Notes
1. Industry categories were revised in 1986.
2. Purchases include materials for use in production, and packing and fuel: these include the cost of raw materials, components, semi-manufactured goods and workshop materials, replacement parts and consumable tools not charged to capital account, packaging materials of all types, stationery and printed matter, fuel, electricity and water materials.
3. In 1970 and 1986 this category was titled 'Processing of plastics'.
4. n.a. = not available.

Source: HMSO Business Statistics Office, PA 1002 *Business Monitor Report on the Census of Production*. Summary tables for relevant years.

operatives (at £36 130m), 8.1 times higher than the cost of other wage and salary categories (at £28 043m) and three and a half times higher than all wages and salaries. For the period 1970–96, this also applies to a cross-section of industries (see Exhibit 3.20), and, as the figures illustrate, the ratios show a consistent, marked and upward trend of these patterns. For the UK to be competitive, it is essential that not only should productivity gains be sought in labour terms, but also that effective, material cost management is introduced and maintained on a corporate basis.

An important, but often underused, technique to help provide this systematic approach to reducing the cost of a product or service but without impairing its function is *value analysis*. It concerns the methodical examination of each product, component or service with the purpose of minimizing its cost without reducing its functional value.[15] Although value analysis was applied initially to existing manufactured products, it is now applied with equal success to the service sector and the overhead costs within all types of organization. The term *value engineering* is often used synonymously with value analysis but, strictly speaking, it refers to the use of this technique in the initial stages of product/service design.

Value analysis, like other methods of continuous improvement aims to reduce costs. However, its orientation is different. Continuous improvement methods (discussed in detail in Chapter 14) tend to accept the product/service as determined and concentrate on the way it is made or provided. Thus, the principle aim is to reduce aspects such as labour costs, rejects, other wastage and lead times. Value analysis, however, considers the functions that the components, products or services are intended to perform. It then reviews the present design in order to provide these functions at a lower material and staff cost, without reducing the value. However, as illustrated in Exhibit 3.20, the potential gains by reducing material costs average five times the value of equivalent reductions in direct labour costs.

The need for value analysis to be introduced and maintained throughout an organization is an essential part of any strategy for systematically reducing costs. As Lawrence Mills, who developed these concepts in the immediate post-war period, said: 'On average, one fourth of manufacturing cost is unnecessary. The extra cost continues because of patterns and habits of thought, because of personal limitations, because of difficulties in promptly disseminating ideas and because today's thinking is based on yesterday's knowledge.'[16]

Value can be classified under two headings:[17]

■ *Use value.* The properties and qualities that accomplish the function of the product or service.
■ *Esteem value.* The properties, features or attractiveness that cause people to want to own it.

Value, therefore, consists of a combination of use and esteem properties related to the cost of providing them.

The analysis of value

In attempting to analyse value, three aspects of operations are reviewed:

1. Design of the product or service.
2. Purchase of materials or services.
3. Process methods.

Design

Too often design decisions are made without due consideration of the effects on product or service costs. The reasons include the following:

■ Designers are often preoccupied with the initial task of designing to meet the functional requirements involved.
■ Traditional designs are often concerned with reliability and quality and do not ask value-for-money questions.
■ Designers often adopt a safety-first policy and thereby overspecify compared with what is required.
■ Too often there is a lack of current information available to designers. Therefore, they design too much from yesterday's principles and information sources.
■ The functional specialisms that exist help to create barriers between design, purchasing, operations and sales.
■ In the case of services, too often the specification is not clearly determined, as explained in an earlier section.

Purchasing

In many organizations too little attention is given to the need to obtain materials and services that meet design requirements at lowest cost. This is because:

■ Purchasing in most organizations is still seen largely as a paper-processing task. For this reason, the executive staff attracted to this critical role tend to be of insufficient quality to provide the essential cost and value-orientated approach.

■ It is too easy to: (a) rely on previous or known suppliers, or allow other functions to specify the source for items; (b) avoid investigation and questioning as an integral part of the purchasing procedure, and (c) be reactive in this role.

■ As in other areas, purchasing also suffers from the barriers created by functional specialisms.

Operations

Many firms are increasingly looking to improve all aspects of their organization. This has long been so in the operations function. But in the past, reviews of working procedures have been limited in the following ways:

■ The investigation has been based on an operation or department rather than the service or product through all its stages including design.
■ Study has usually concentrated on the process, the way the work is completed. In so doing, it has failed to ask essential questions regarding design and materials.

Value analysis procedure

Value analysis comprises two parts: (1) those responsible for completing the analysis, and (2) the procedure to be followed.

The make-up of those responsible for completing the analysis work is quite wide-ranging. The classic structure is to have a group comprising a full-time specialist (the value analyst) and representatives from design, purchasing, costing and operations. However, other forms have proved equally successful and, in the case of many Japanese companies, includes the groups constituted under quality circles. In each instance prerequisites to the successful application of value analysis are that those concerned are trained in the procedures involved, and that corporate goodwill is demonstrated at all points throughout, including time to complete the tasks, access to cost and other data, and liaison with outside suppliers. The steps involved are:

1. Select the item or service.
2. Gather information about it.
3. Analyse its function and its value for money.
4. Generate alternative ways to provide the same function through speculation and brainstorming.[18]
5. Assess the worth of these ideas.
6. Decide what is to be done.
7. Implement the decisions.
8. Evaluate the results.

The items selected are usually known to be of high cost and the use of the 80/20 rule will help in the procedure.[19] However, it is important not to select a product/service that is nearing the end of its life cycle. Value analysis is not a prop to help non-viable products/services become viable. It can, however, form a legitimate part of extending the life cycle of existing products or services.

When introducing value analysis, it is important that the procedure in no way brings with it an air of recrimination. It is essential that those concerned contribute to the procedure in an objective way without implying criticism of any department's or person's previous work. The following series of questions will help when applying value analysis to each item or part of the product or service:

■ Does it contribute to the esteem or use value of the product/service? If so, how?
■ What is its cost? Does the cost appear to be in proportion to its function?
■ Are all the feature essential? Which ones are questionable?
■ If it is necessary, what else could provide the same function:
  (a) Standard part?
  (b) Alternative part?
■ Is the way in which the product/service is currently made or provided in line with current volumes? Often volumes change, but the process does not.
■ Has anyone asked the supplier if an alternative is available to provide the same function?
■ Have alternative supplies been sought recently in terms of current volumes and prices?

Value analysis consists of taking each part of a product or service and looking in detail at its function. Every feature, tolerance, hole, degree of finish, piece of material, part of the service is vetted to ensure that none of these is adding to the total cost without providing a useful function.

The application of value analysis principles to products can be readily visualized. However, these principles are increasingly, and appropriately, being applied within service industries. One example is provided in a review of the Paul Revere Life Insurance Company's application of value analysis as part of achieving their corporate strategic objective of improved quality.[20] As part of this drive, management groups formed value analysis workshops to address the question, 'Are we doing the right thing?'[21] resulting in recommendations to improve basic work functions and processes. The responsibility for implementing these organizational and work process changes was delegated to those running the individual sections, with department managers themselves eventually taking part in the value analysis workshops. Having identified the more important departments and the functions within a department, standard value analysis procedures were applied. Annual savings in the first part year were $6m.

The sources of savings from value analysis come principally from materials. They include:

■ Eliminate parts (for example, components, transaction and steps in a service system) without reducing the functional qualities involved.
■ Combine the functions of two or more components or services by redesign.
■ Reduce tolerances that are unnecessarily tight and make for higher operations costs.
■ Extend the concept of standardization.
■ In conjunction with many of these savings, it will be possible to simplify the process task and consequently reduce labour costs.

Simultaneous engineering

The speed with which products and services can be designed and introduced into a market directly affects sales revenues and profit. Simultaneous engineering is an

Exhibit 3.21 *Reducing product/service development lead times by partly undertaking tasks in parallel with one another and by reducing the length of each stage*

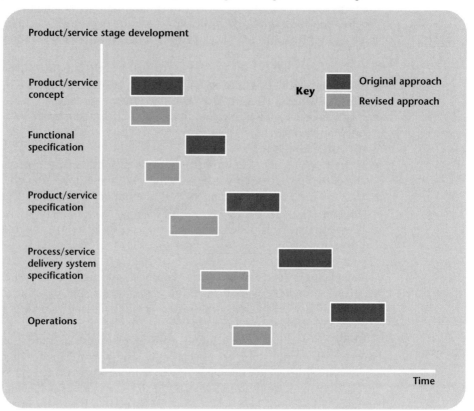

organizationally based approach to reducing design lead times. It involves all relevant functions within a business (for example, design, marketing, engineering and operations) as well as suppliers. The purpose of the approach is to undertake tasks, in part or in total, in a parallel rather than sequential way. Receiving early inputs from various functions also reduces time-consuming redesigns and consequent delays. Teamwork encourages co-ownership of design and a greater commitment to making a product/service succeed. Jobs are enriched and creativity is stimulated. Because everyone is communicating with everyone else throughout the design process, product/service quality increases, product/service lead times are dramatically shortened and product/service costs are cut.

What happens in principle is shown in Exhibit 3.21.

To achieve reductions similar to those outlined in this exhibit, companies are using a number of approaches to help speed up the process of designing and introducing products and services. These new methods (some of which have been mentioned earlier) include:

■ **Contracting out activities** – using external resources for one or more of the stages increases capacity and reduces delays. The areas of activity include R&D, engineering and prototyping.

- **Increased use of suppliers** – as explained later in Chapter 11 on 'Supply Chain Management', suppliers are increasingly being asked to take on several of the design and product or service introduction phases as part of the supplier package. The infusion of outside capacity within the design process is one advantage that results.

- **Teamwork** – forming product, service and process teams not only increases ideas but also speeds up the process and eliminates problems.

- **Combining or eliminating stages** – combining or eliminating stages by re-examining the need to undertake all or part of the existing procedure not only rigorously tests current practices but also reduces lead times throughout.

- **Overlapping stages** – as illustrated in Exhibit 3.22, by identifying opportunities to begin the next phase before the current stage is complete moves the overall procedure away from a sequential to a parallel activities format. Delays are reduced and the overall lead times improved dramatically.

- **Incremental vs breakthrough innovations** – breakthrough innovations in the past have often been the desired goal of designers. Breakthroughs are harder to come up with, typically have longer lead times in all phases of the design process and result in a higher failure rate. Switching the emphasis to incremental improvements and introducing clusters of these at the same time still leads to significant product and service improvements but reduces the lead times to bring them about.

- **Using standard parts and modular designs** – an earlier section introduced the principles and benefits using standard parts and components and modular approaches to designs. A further advantage is also gained as improvements in 'common' parts can be introduced into relevant existing designs with corresponding and substantial reductions in lead times.

- **Using new technologies** – employing new technologies such as computer-aided design (CAD) and computer-aided engineering (CAE) reduces lead times within the overall process as well as eliminating stages. For example, CAE takes CAD designs and subjects them to stress, loads and vibrations to assess their strength and reliability, thus eliminating later elements of the design and prototype phases.

Variety reduction

The approaches and techniques listed so far have addressed issues around the design itself. This last review, however, questions whether or not retaining all the products and services currently on offer is best for the business as a whole.

In the product/service range provided, some items will generate more sales, or more profit, or contribute more to the fixed costs of the organization than others. Moreover, the costs incurred and efforts involved in providing and selling these lower contributors are disproportionately higher than for other products/services. Consequently, looking closely at the contribution that they make should become part of the tactical approach in order to move towards a reduction in uneconomical variety and to an increased control of variety in the future. A more quantitative appraisal of the range of products and service on offer by a firm is that of variety reduction.

The approach is to list all the products or services into Pareto order of highest total value of sales at the top, and lowest at the bottom. This often reveals that about 20 per

Exhibit 3.22   *Product analysis by annual sales revenue*

Product reference number	Sales revenue (£000)	Percentage of total sales	Total variable costs (£000)	Total contribution (£000)	Percentage of total contribution
054-19	2480	19.5	2128	352	12.7
303-07	2134	16.8	1684	650	23.4
691-30	1720	13.5	1372	348	12.5
016-10	1440	11.3	1028	412	14.8
418-50	980	7.7	676	304	10.9
402-50	620	4.9	580	40	1.4
155-29	428	3.8	390	92	3.4
900-01	360	2.8	240	120	4.3
308-31	308	2.4	220	88	3.2
341-17	280	2.2	212	68	2.4
540-80	260	2.0	200	60	2.2
701-91	232	1.8	160	72	2.6
650-27	220	1.7	202	18	0.6
712-22	192	1.5	140	52	1.9
137-29	180	1.4	152	28	1.0
003-54	172	1.4	168	4	0.1
541-21	140	1.1	122	18	0.6
543-61	136	1.1	112	24	0.9
305-04	96	0.8	86	10	0.4
097-54	88	0.7	86	2	0.1
323-34	72	0.6	68	4	0.1
542-93	68	0.5	62	6	0.2
386-07	44	0.3	36	8	0.3
440-18	20	0.2	19	1	–
	12724	100.0	7463	2781	100.0

Notes

1. Contribution = selling price less variable costs.
2. Further analysis could be complemented by grouping like products together and showing the product group totals for columns 'percentage of total sales' to 'percentage of total contribution' inclusive.
3. The 80/20 relationship implied in the rule is only an indication of the size of the actual figures involved. Thus in the example here, 25 per cent of the products accounts for 74 per cent of sales, illustrating clearly the concept of a relatively small number of products accounting for a high percentage of the sales revenue.

cent of items accounts for about 80 per cent of the total sales revenue. This is known as the 80/20 rule (also note its use in Chapter 10). In the example given as Exhibit 3.22, the top 6 of the 24 products account for about 74 per cent of total sales (see note 3 to the exhibit) whereas the bottom 15 products account for only 17 per cent. In addition, these top 6 account for some 76 per cent of the total contribution, whereas the bottom 15 (or 62 per cent) contribute only £375 000, about 13 per cent.

The next step is to check the relative performances over the last three or four years of the items with a low percentage of the sales revenue in order to determine if the individual trend is 'upward–level–downward'. Further checks are then made on the level and downward trend items to see if their contribution can be improved by reducing variable costs and/or increasing the selling price. If this action does not bring about the required changes in terms of percentage contribution to selling price, then phasing out of the range should be considered.

Case example 8

Few products have resisted moves to standardize as much as the humble door lock. In Europe alone, several hundred thousand types are sold – a product range diversity that reflects the doors and buildings that have evolved in different countries over several centuries.

Today demand for security is growing and prospects are good. Assa Abloy (the Swedish lock maker with worldwide sales of £12.5bn) is now #1 worldwide with 6 per cent of total sales. This growth was party generic and partly by takeover, as Assa in the 1990s spent £400m on 20 lock companies worldwide. Its current sales profile is 50 per cent in Europe, 35 per cent in the USA, 10 per cent in the Pacific Rim and the remaining 5 per cent in the rest of the world. Despite this international breadth, products sold in more than one country account for only 25 per cent of sales.

Where possible Assa tries to capitalize on the potential high volumes involved – for instance, all exit bars for its fire and emergency doors are made in one plant in France. But this is more the exception than the rule. The outcome is over 40 manufacturing plants around the world, each mainly supplying its domestic market.

Case example questions

8.1 Why are some product ranges less open to variety reduction opportunities than others?

8.2 Choose a product that provides good opportunities to standardize and reduce variety. Compare and contrast this with locks.

The advantages of variety reduction are many, including:

- Longer operations runs with less down time through changeovers.
- Potential savings in plant/equipment requirements.
- Reduced inventory with the advantages in capital, control, space and costs.
- More concentrated activity in development and design, sales effort and after-sales service.
- Easier operations planning and control.
- Appropriate reallocation of capacity (particularly scarce resources) to the overall benefit of a business.

The disadvantages of this approach concern the reduction in product or service range in terms of the number of individual items produced or provided, the reduced range available and the danger of cutting out products/services which serve as loss leaders. Thus it is variety reduction's net corporate effect which needs to be considered and on which decisions should be based.

CONCLUSION

All organizations have a range of products or services at a given time. To be competitive, it is necessary to have a set that is complementary, relates to the organization's strategic decisions associated with issues such as growth and market share, and takes account of tactical considerations such as completeness of range, process capability and distribution costs. Furthermore, the mix is always undergoing change as organizations are continuously faced with the need to introduce new products and services in a never-ending requirement to keep a mix that meets the needs of their customers. However, developing and introducing new items is typically expensive, risky and involves a long time horizon. But, it also concerns the very lifeblood of business as new products and services are necessary for survival and growth.

Attitudes and norms concerning the level of innovation and the introduction of new products and services are affected by both internal and external forces. Decisions to invest in R&D or to seek to exploit developments in technology will vary from industry to industry and from company to company, and often markedly so. In product-based companies, the tradition to invest in R&D and actively to seek to introduce new products has noticeably increased over the last few decades. This varies from superficial modifications (for example, in markets such as customer durables, there is a traditional 'facelift' to existing models/products on a regular basis) to major product service changes.

A review of service industries also highlights the changes over the last decade in what is on offer. Protected for a long time by geographical distance, commercial legacies and legal constraints, many service industries remained conservative and insensitive to the needs of their customers. They competed in what are known as sheltered markets. However, the impact of deregulation, advances in data processing and increased global competition in many areas of the service industry have moved many sectors from being in sheltered into what is known as being in traded markets. For instance, deregulation and advances in data processing have made an enormous impact upon the travel industry and led directly to changes in corresponding service delivery systems. In the same way the limited competition that UK banks enjoyed from the very beginning changed with the alterations to trading rules for building societies, the opening up of financial markets, investments in data processing and the entry of non-finance organizations (for example, supermarket chains, other retailers and a wide range of other businesses) into credit sales, personal loans and banking has dramatically altered the basis and form of competition in the finance sector. A similar dramatic change in the insurance sector was highlighted earlier in the chapter.

One of the toughest business lessons that top managers need to draw from the history of progress is that most technologies, products and services will be replaced and most efforts to replace them will fail. This is somewhat a game of Russian roulette in which companies need to participate if they wish to grow and prosper. The stakes, however, will vary with the nature of the product and service and the level of change involved. But, it is easy to be misled. Changes to existing, well-established markets of a non-dramatic nature can result in major shifts in success as Case examples 3.9, 3.10 and 3.11 illustrate.

After the cost-cutting, rationalization and restructuring of the 1980s and 1990s, the corporate agenda has recognized the key role of innovation in the quest for growth. In part, this stems from a recognition that improved efficiency is no substitute for growth. Some organizations are experiencing anxious times as they are having difficulty in moving back towards an innovative culture. Many are stressing innovation as a corporate goal while others (for example, BP Chemicals, 3M, Elf Aquitaine, Siemens and British Airways) are introducing innovation schemes as a way to stimulate further these essential activities. But, the area of innovation is as difficult to

Case examples

9

Changing existing specifications do not have to be sizeable to make a significant impact. For example, increasing the freshness of food provision has enabled supermarkets not only to match local high street outlets but outperform them. Bread technologies are enabling doughs to be held for several days without deterioration. This enables in-store, supermarket bakeries to produce bread several times each day and thereby increase product freshness. In addition, part-baked breads to be oven finished at home have opened up a new dimension to fresh bread provision.

10

Traditional markets are as vulnerable to the impact of design changes as any other. For example, alternatives to pneumatic tyres for off-road vehicles in order to reduce punctures and the costs involved have been long needed. Traditional solutions of solid and foam-filled wheels have the drawbacks of lack of comfort for the driver and wear on vehicle suspension due to increased rigidity. In the early 1990s Altrack, an Australian tyre company, introduced a puncture-free wheel for construction equipment where punctures are up to 10 times more likely than on other vehicles. The new tyre design comprises a number of hollow-moulded, rubber segments that bolt on to a special wheel rim. A damaged rubber section takes only 15 minutes to replace with the vehicle (and its load) still in place.

11

The importance of design in the success of companies is a critical part of the business mix. During the most difficult competitive times in the car industry, Honda's drive towards a combination of cost-cutting and innovative products resulted in spectacular sales increases in the mid-1990s after losing market share and performing less well than the industry as a whole in the previous five years. See Exhibit 3.23.[24]

Exhibit 3.23 *Honda passenger car sales compared to the whole car industry*

Year	Honda and car industry sales (annual % increase)	
	Industry	Honda
1990	7.4	2.4
1991	(3.2)	(2.1)
1992	(7.4)	(10.4)
1993	(7.3)	(7.4)
1994	1.1	(9.3)
1995	5.3	13.3
1996	3.3	20.8
1997	3.1	18.4
1998	(0.6)	12.1

Notes

1. Figures in brackets indicate decreases in sales.
2. Figures for 1998 are the first nine months.

Source: ING Barings and *Financial Times*.

embrace as it is essential for continued success. Some pointers to these issues and ways forward include the following:

- Encouraging to be more creative only addresses part of the problem. Much of the difficulty lies in establishing a clear link between innovation and corporate success.

- One common mistake is to believe that innovation can compensate for competitive disadvantages elsewhere.

- It is a misconception to think that innovation is a technical issue. Akio Morita (the founder of Sony) dismissed descriptions of the Walkman as an innovation marvel. 'Frankly', he observed, 'it did not contain any breakthrough technology. Its success was built on product planning and marketing'.

- Need to move from a preoccupation with R&D to the totality of innovation in terms of scope (the Sony Walkman syndrome) and organizational style. Innovation is potentially in everyone and everywhere.

- Using customers is essential. One-third of the toy company Hasbro's annual sales come from new products. To ensure this trend continues, it goes to great lengths to keep its designers in touch with children. To this end it has built a crèche (known as the 'fun lab') for 25 children next to its R&D department.

- The task is to generate good products and services on a continuous basis. A culture of innovation is essential for this to happen. Ways of engendering the need to spend time on creating ideas has to become part of the corporate culture. 3M allows designers to spend up to 15 per cent of their time on any research project they wish. The Post-it note pad had bottom-up origins. Other organizations need to break down the status quo dimension that traditionally goes with innovation. They need to create a culture that encourages and develops innovation in order to bring everyone and their ideas on board.

Discussion questions

1. The section 'Developing a service specification' explained that a service can be expressed as a combination of five dimensions (that is, 'a service within which there is a facilitating good' and so on). Analyse the following businesses in line with these five dimensions:

   - a supermarket
   - a high street post-office
   - an up-market restaurant

2. Exhibit 3.16 overviewed the factors involved in six do-it-yourself (DIY) approaches within a service delivery system. Complete a similar analysis (to include additional factors for success if relevant) for the following:

   - an automatic teller machine (ATM) or cash machine
   - self-service restaurant in a motorway service station
   - telephone banking

Discussion questions (cont'd)

3. Select a product and a service that are at different points of their life cycles. Explain their progress to date, where they are now and what you expect will happen in the future.

4. In what types of organization might new ideas have:
   - a low mortality rate (that is, they last for a long time)
   - a high mortality rate (that is, they last for a short time)?

5. Since markets for services typically have lower entry barriers than product markets why do overseas companies not start with services when they first begin to compete in foreign markets?

6. A major UK shoe company launched a new range of tennis shoes. There were two styles, one for men and one for women. Within each of these two styles there were six colour combinations and the shoe sizes ranged from size 7 to 14 for men and 4 to 9 for women. How many shoes would a store have to stock to have one pair of each shoe within both ranges?

7. Explain the back office and front office arrangements in a library and supermarket.

8. Give two examples (with supporting details) for each of a service and manufacturing firm of the impact of technology in product and service design.

9. Give one example of the use of standardization and modular design for both a product and service of your choice.

10. Apply the value analysis principles to a product or service and see if you could identify opportunities for cost reduction without reducing the value.

Notes and references

1. This explanation of the design strategies was put forward by Schonberger, RJ in *Operations Management*, Plane, Texas: Business Publications (1981).
2. The graphical representation of the relationship between the functions in the design-production procedure and their impact on effectiveness is a product of the Ford Motor Company.
3. For example see Moore, SD 'Glaxo accelerates pursuit of new medicines: Glaxo lab initiates a high-speed chase in the drugs industry', *Wall Street Journal*, Europe, 6 Dec. (1996), pp. 1 and 5.
4. 'For richer, not poorer: UK banks are trying to increase revenues by devoting more time to selling services to high earners', John Gappes, *Financial Times*, 24 May (1993), p. 15.
5. Also see 'Rooms where class matters', Skapinker, M, *Financial Times*, 21 March (1994), p. 10.
6. Churchill, D 'Hotels target women', *The Times*, 2 Jan. (1997), p. 28.
7. Heskett, JL *Managing the Service Economy*, Boston: Harvard Business School Press (1984), p. 59.
8. These concepts were first introduced by Sasser, WE *et al.* in *Management of Service Operations: Text, Cases and Readings*, Boston: Allyn & Bacon (1978), pp. 10–11.

9. Collier, DA *Service Management: Operating Decisions*, Englewood Cliffs, NJ: Prentice-Hall (1987), p. 43.

10. Meier-Preschany, M 'Perspectives on banking in the 1990s', in *International Banking: Management and Strategies*, Zenoff, DB (ed.), Euromoney Publications (1985), p. 72.

11. Booth, SA 'Super-charged desktop PCs', *World Traveller*, April (1996), p. 25.

12. Corzine, R 'Uniformity on the high seas', *Financial Times*, 3 Dec. (1993), p. 12.

13. Terazano, E 'Toyota's drive for the 20-something's', *Financial Times*, 18 Aug. (1994), p. 10.

14. References include Noori, H 'The Taguchi methods: achieving design and output quality', *Academy of Management Executive*, Nov. (1989), pp. 322–6, and Taguchi, G and Clausing, D 'Robust quality', *Harvard Business Review*, Jan.–Feb. (1990), pp. 65–75.

15. Value analysis is defined in BS 3138 as: 'a systematic interdisciplinary examination of factors affecting the cost of a product or service, in order to devise means of achieving the specified purpose most economically at the required standard of quality and reliability'.

16. Miles, LD *Techniques of Value Analysis and Engineering*, Maidenhead: McGraw-Hill (1961).

17. In Chapter 4 of *The Four Kinds of Economic Value*, Harvard Business Press (1926), Walsh CM describes four kinds of value: 'Use-value is a thing's power to serve our ends. Esteem-value is its power to make us desire to possess it. Cost-value is its power to impose upon us effort to acquire it. Exchange-value is its power to procure other things in its place'.

18. It is important with brainstorming techniques to use someone with experience and to select carefully the group involved. The selection should avoid the potential problems of seniority and be designed to give a wide range of disciplines within the group. This stage is essential to the successful application of this technique and needs to be used with care.

19. The 80/20 rule concerns the phenomenon that, for example, 80 per cent of costs will be incurred by 20 per cent of the items. Chapter 10 provides another example of its application.

20. *The Paul Revere Life Insurance Company*, Case Study no. 42, Houston: American Productivity Center, February (1984).

21. Ibid., p. 1.

22. Nakamoto, M 'Drive for the home market: Honda's recent success is the result of cost-cutting and innovative products for Japan', *Financial Times*, 15 Nov. (1996), p. 17.

Further reading

Baxter M *Product Design*, Chapman & Hall (1995).

Chase RB 'The service factory: a future vision', *International Journal of Service Industry Management*, Vol. 2 No. 3 (1991), pp. 60–70.

Christensen CM *The Innovators' Dilemma*, Harvard Business School Press, Boston (1997).

Cohen L *Quality Function Deployment*, Addison-Wesley Longman, Wokingham (1995).

Heskett JL, Sasser WE and Hart CWL *Service Breakthrough: Changing the Rules of the Game*, The Free Press, New York (1990).

Pine JB II *Mass Customisation: The New Frontier in Business Competition*, Harvard Business School Press, Boston (1993).

Quelch JA and Kenny D 'Extend profits, not product lines', *Harvard Business Review*, Sept.–Oct. (1994), pp. 153–60.

Ramaswammy R *Design and Management of Service Processes*, Addison-Wesley Longman, Reading, MA (1996).

Stuart FI and Tax SS 'Planning for service quality: an integrative approach', *International Journal of Service Industry Management*, Vol. 7 No. 4 (1996).

Zeithaml VA, Parasuraman A and Berry LL *Delivering Quality Service: Balancing Customer Perceptions and Expectations*, The Free Press, New York (1990).

CHAPTER FOUR

The content and planning of this book: an overview of what is involved, what has been addressed so far and what is covered in this chapter

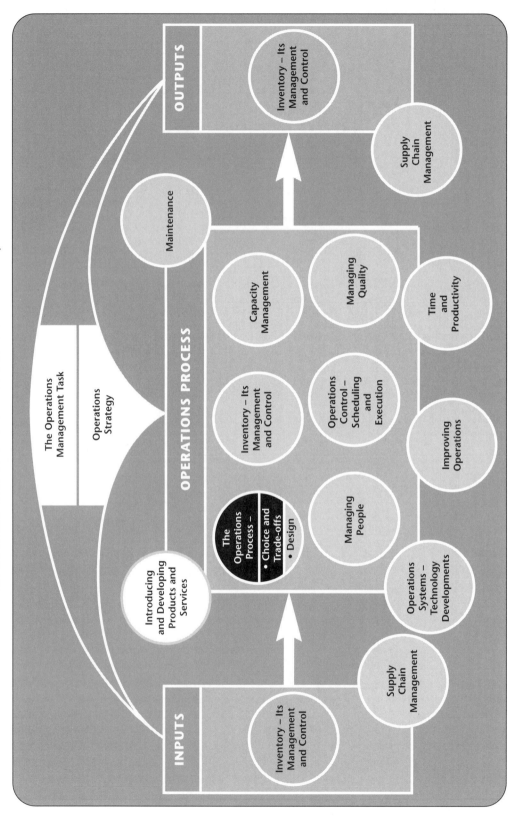

The Operations Process – Choice and Trade-offs

Chapter overview

There are many wide-ranging issues and tasks involved in managing the operations function. One key area concerns the choice of operations process made by organizations and the consequences of this decision. The explanation of this is covered in two different chapters. This chapter presents a conceptual view of process choice. It provides the reader with a sound base on which to understand better the processes themselves while highlighting the trade-offs and issues regarding products/services, operations, investments, costs and infrastructure choices that have to be made. These insights will then form part of the decision on how best to design processes, the subject of Chapter 5. In summary, this chapter comprises the following sections:

- **Types of process** – an in-depth explanation of the different processes used to make products or provide services.

- **The implications of process choice** – when choosing a process, a business also chooses a set of trade-offs. This section discusses these in detail around the major topics of products/services and markets, operations, investment and cost, and infrastructure.

- **Product/service profiling** – the trade-offs inherent when choosing a process to make products or provide services have major implications for how well operations can support the needs of markets. This section introduces an approach that allows organizations to test how well operations strategy supports markets and the effect of changes in operations and marketing strategies on future levels of alignment.

TYPES OF PROCESS

One part of the operations management task concerns the transformation process that takes inputs and converts them into outputs (see Exhibit 4.1). This section considers the different methods available to an organization by which it is able to produce goods or provide services for customers – the dimension of process choice.

As examples given later in the chapter illustrate, the methods of conversion to produce goods or provide services will often be an interrelated set of processes feeding into one another as part of the total transformation. Each of these will have its own method of conversion, selected to meet the particular requirements of that stage of the total process.

The complexity of a product or service will directly impact the number of stages or steps to complete it. In many service organizations the provision of a service is completed as a single step (for example, borrowing books from a library or paying in a cheque at a local bank), while the number of steps to manufacture the Rolls-Royce Trent 800 and 900 engines for the Boeing 777 and A330 respectively run into hundreds. How to handle the operations process requirement will, therefore, reflect this complexity factor. Furthermore, this process requirement has two dimensions as shown in Exhibit 4.1:

- **The technical dimension** concerning what has to happen technically to a product or service to meet the specification. For example, bread is baked and plastic trim for a car interior is moulded. To complete these tasks requires appropriate technology, in this instance ovens and injection moulding machines.

- **The business dimension** concerning how operations decides to make a product or provide a service and will reflect the volumes involved and the market needs (order-winners and qualifiers) to be supported.

To illustrate how these differ let us take the examples of baking bread and manufacturing a car. A village baker will choose different oven arrangements and auxiliary equipment than a large bakery company that bakes and delivers bread throughout a city and its suburbs. Similarly, to manufacture a Formula 1 or Indy car will be very different from that to assemble a mid-size family saloon or hatchback car. In both instances the product to be made (namely, bread and cars) is the same in a technical sense but the market requirements are totally different in a market sense. Hence, the process chosen will reflect these business-based differences. It is this latter dimension that constitutes the operations management task and which this chapter addresses.

Exhibit 4.1   *One part of the operations function – the transformation process*

Transformation process

Methods of conversion
- alternative choices of process
- typically use two or more types of process to provide the
  - technical capability
  - market support re factors such as volumes and speed of response

Specialist functions
- provide support to operations management in terms of control and feedback on the process and other activities
- help to improve the process

This and the following chapter are concerned with the operations management task of using technology to meet the needs of markets. To complete this the operations executive requires and will call on the support of technical specialists such as process engineers and IT specialists. In this way the operations managers of call centres would not resolve the technical dimensions of the systems their staff use but would look to specialists to fix technical problems and undertake technical developments as necessary.

The role of operations management is to use the necessary process technology together with other inputs such as staff capabilities to meet the needs of markets and the cost profiles and profit targets of the business. The essential technical role of operations management concerns, therefore, the choice and development of the process used to make products and provide services that best meet the needs of customers and markets – the concept of process choice. Working with technical experts is a key task of operations management. Each is responsible for providing different but essential inputs – the technical and business perspectives of the products and service offerings.

The need to help other functions in an organization to understand these alternative choices and their implications for the business is an integral part of an operations manager's role. Each process will have trade-offs (things it can do well and less well) and these need to be understood by a business and form part of these key investment decisions.

There are several perspectives to be taken into account in understanding the alternative choices of process that can be made. These will be addressed throughout the chapter, but first let us recap on the technology dimension of product and service provision and then explain in detail the alternative processes that operations can choose to meet the needs of markets. A company needs to select the processes by which it will make the products or provide the services it sells. In part this concerns the technical dimensions of the items involved, for example:

■ Packaging would need to be produced on printing machines and then cut to size using slitting machines.

■ Plastic containers would need to be produced by loading the appropriate tooling (designed to give the shape and detail involved) on to a machine and then injecting material under pressure to fill the cavity within the mould – a process known as injection moulding.

■ A restaurant would need to prepare food in line with the menus on offer and in line with customers' requirements. It would, therefore, need the equipment to undertake the food preparation involved.

■ A computer services bureau would need the hardware to enable it to process the information requirements of customers.

However, while this dimension of a process is a fundamental part of the investment decision, the issues we will address here (as explained earlier) concern not the technology involved but the way operations chooses to make a product or provide a service. These choices can be made from five classic types together with a number of hybrid processes. The next sections explain what these classic processes are and what they look like, while Chapter 5 will discuss the hybrid processes that have been developed as part of process design decisions.

Project

Organizations selling large-scale, complex products or services that cannot be physically moved once completed or need to be undertaken at or within a client's organization will normally provide them using a project process. Product examples include civil engineering contracts to build roads and bridges, and aerospace programmes. Service examples include management consultancy assignments involving corporate policy issues and organizational development, and a large banquet supplied to a customer's own premises. It concerns the provision of a unique product or service, the inputs for which need to be co-ordinated in line with a customer's requirements. The resource inputs will normally be taken to the point where the product is to be built or service provided.

If you reflect on the examples provided above then, in your mind's eye, you will probably be able to envisage what the process looks like. All the activities, including support functions, will normally be controlled in the form of a total system for the duration of the project and under the direction of the co-ordinating team, Similarly, resources will be allocated for the duration of the project and these, like the supporting functions, will be reallocated once their part of the task is complete or at the end of the project.

The operations manager's problem, then, is one of co-ordinating a large number of interrelated activities and resources in such a way as to achieve the customer's requirements while minimizing costs through the process.

This choice of making a product or providing a service is forced upon an organization by the simple fact that the product has to be made or the service provided on site. As you can envisage, this is not an efficient way of working as resources need to be moved to and from the assignment as it progresses. This incurs cost and militates against achieving efficiencies. Hence, companies try to produce off-site as much as possible of the product or service. This allows a more efficient process to be used with the parts then being transported to the site. For example, concrete sections and timber framing for buildings and much of the food preparation for a banquet will be made off-site and then assembled or arranged on-site as required. Overall, the improved process efficiency of making off-site outweighs the additional transportation costs of getting parts to the site. Exhibit 4.2 summarizes the main points.

Jobbing

Once products or services are transferable then companies look to another process to make or provide them. The jobbing process is designed to meet the one-off (that is,

Exhibit 4.2   *Project process – key characteristics*

Product/service

Made or provided on site as it is too large or difficult to move after completion. Examples include management consultancy assignments, large banquets on a customer's premises and building roads and bridges

Process

Resources to make or provide the service are allocated for the duration of the project and then reallocated once their part of the task is complete or at the end of the assignment unique) requirements of customers. The product or service involved is of an individual (one-off) nature and tends to be of a smaller size (and, therefore, transportable) than in the case of those provided by a project process. Product examples include a purpose-built piece of equipment, hand-made, built-in furniture to meet specified customer requirements, a customer-designed and specified control unit, and hand-made shoes or clothing. Service examples include a tailor-made management development programme, the design and installation of a computer system, a banquet at a restaurant's own premises and the decision concerning the application for a large industrial loan.

Although some elements of these products and services may be provided on-site, usually they are completed in-house and then transported to the customer. The producer then often installs and commissions the product or service before it is accepted by the customer. Jobbing, however, requires that the providing organization interprets the design and specification of the job, applying high-level skills in the conversion process. Normally, one or a small group of skilled people will be responsible for completing all or most of the product or service. It is a one-off provision which means that the product or service usually will not again be required in identical form or, if it is, the demand will tend to be either irregular or with long periods between one sale and the next. Exhibit 4.3 summarizes the main points.

Batch

Most organizations provide products and service that are deemed standard (that is, they have been provided before) rather than special. The repeat and higher volume nature associated with standard products and services signals a need to consider a different process designed to take advantage of these characteristics. A batch process is one alternative.

As the product or service has been provided before or will be provided again in the future then the opportunity to invest in the process in order to simplify and reduce costs makes sense. The level of investment that can be justified will relate to the repeat nature and total volumes involved. This investment can range from recording and establishing the best way to complete a job through to substantial investment in equipment to help make the provision of the task more efficient. For example, a bank uses printed forms, agreed procedures and an interview to handle an application for a personal loan but automatic teller machines (ATMs) to handle cash withdrawal requirements, and call centres to handle mortgage applications and personal loans of a moderate nature. The standard and high volume nature of the latter three examples

Exhibit 4.3   *Jobbing process – key characteristics*

Product/service

Special (that is, will not be repeated) products/services
Examples include the design and installation of a computer system, processing the application of a large industrial loan and hand-made shoes and clothing

Process

One or a small group of skilled people do everything including interpreting the product/service specification, clarifying issues with the customer and ensuring that what is delivered meets the specification justifies the greater level of investment and a delivery system based on predetermined procedures and sets of rules to determine whether or not to go ahead with a mortgage or loan request.

When using a batch process, the first step is to break the job into a number of stages. How many stages will depend, in part, on the complexity of the product or service involved. The provision of a product or service may be completed by a single-step batch process where the requirement is simple. For products or services that are more complex, they will be provided by a multi-step batch process as shown in Exhibits 4.4 and 4.5. Whereas in jobbing the whole task is completed by one or a small group of people, in a batch process each operation making up the whole product/service is completed separately, by different people/equipment and normally in a different part of the process. The purpose of splitting the task into smaller operations is a form of investment in itself, and is one way to help undertake the task more efficiently and to introduce the potential for specialization.

The following examples are provided to help explain how a batch process works:

■ **Making a product** – the product would first be split into an appropriate number of operations and the decision taken on how best to complete each of these. The order quantity to be produced (which may reflect the size of a customer's order, production rules concerning the quantity to be produced at any time or forecast sales projections) would then go to the process in which the first operation is to be completed. The appropriate process is then set up to undertake the first operation and the whole order quantity is then completed. In this way, each process is only set up once per order quantity. This reduces the amount of lost capacity due to setups/changeovers which, in turn, reduces costs. With operation 1 now completed, the whole order quantity then moves on to the next process on which operation 2 will be completed. Typically, the order quantity would wait for this process to become available as often there are other products being or waiting to be completed. When available, this process is then set up to complete operation 2 of the given product and the whole order quantity is processed. Meanwhile, the process needed to complete operation 1 is available to be reset to process a given operation on another product. Thus, a product goes from process to process until all the operations necessary to complete the job have been undertaken.

■ **Delivering a service** – a customer would enter a service delivery system such as a hospital. The patient (that is, the customer) would initially go to reception and the staff there would process the person in terms such as recording relevant details. The patient would then go to the next stage in the process (for example, to see a specialist consultant) and, having waited, would then go through that stage of the treatment. As with the product example, the patient would then go through the next stages in the same way until the total service was completed.

With information processing, the procedure is broken down into a number of stages the total of which completes the whole process. Then, as in the 'making a product' example above, the documents go from stage to stage with each step typically involving waiting time, a single set-up and the processing of all the documents at the one time. This waiting between stages allows processes to work independently of one another (known as decoupling) and hence more efficiently while the processing of all the documents (the equivalent of order size in the product example) at one stage reduces the number of set-ups involved.

So, a batch process is a preferred way of handling larger volume, repeat business. For example, whereas if using a jobbing process the healthcare specialist would record a patient's details, undertake the consultation, complete the X-ray, check to confirm the nature of the broken limb, apply the plaster and make the next appointment, these various tasks in a batch process environment are performed by different staff who specialize in the different areas. Thus, healthcare specialists restrict their involvement to their area of specialism, with other tasks being completed in a more cost-effective way in terms of staff skill and with each step of the process developing specialized and more effective procedures and approaches to completing the tasks involved. By processing products or customers operation by operation, the capacity at each stage in the process is used and reused to meet the different requirements of different orders or customers needs.

The service sector concerns both processing information and customers. Examples of the former include a computer bureau that processes the work of several clients on the same hardware. In addition to the hospital service delivery system described earlier, other examples of customer processing include restaurants, hairdressing and health farms. To help visualize still further how this works, Exhibits 4.4 and 4.5 provide an outline of batch processes in both the service and manufacturing sectors, with Exhibit 4.6 summarizing the key characteristics.

Exhibit 4.4   *A dental surgery – an example of a multi-step batch process*

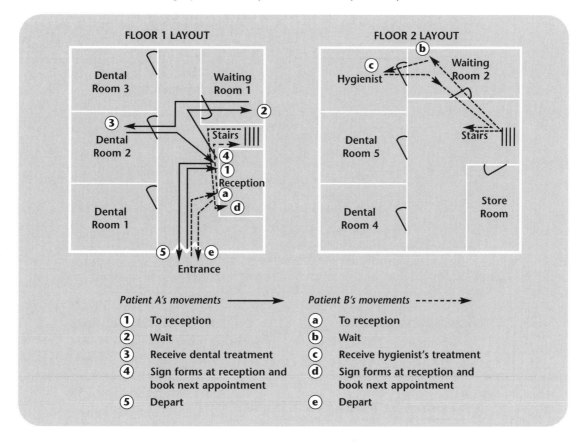

Patients attending a dental surgery would typically report at reception and be asked to take a seat in the waiting room from where they would be collected by the appropriate dental nurse. After treatment, some patients may then attend the hygienist and go through the waiting and treatment sequence once again. Finally, patients would report at reception, settle their accounts and book the next check-up. Within the service delivery system a customer (in this instance a patient) moves from stage to stage to receive the appropriate part of the total service and will typically wait between

Exhibit 4.5　　*A printing company – an example of a multi-step batch process*

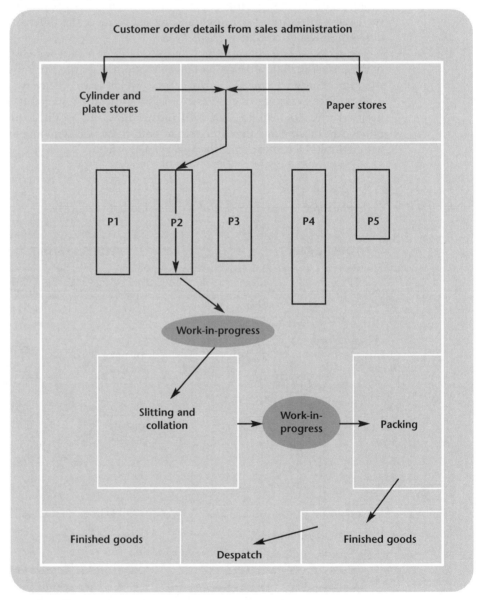

Notes

1.　The 'P' in P1 to P5 is an abbreviation for printing machine.
2.　——▶　Movement of a typical order.

one process and the next. This waiting is a form of work-in-progress inventory that decouples parts of the system from one another. The service delivery system thereby works on the principle of customers waiting for the process which then allows parts of a process to work independently and hence more efficiently.

As explained earlier, where a batch process is used to make a product it will typically be of a repeat nature. The example provided in Exhibit 4.5 is a repeat order for an existing flexible packaging product (for example, a toffee bar wrapper). In this instance, a roll of film is loaded on the front of the print machine. The choice of machine reflects the quantity required and the number of colours on the packaging product. These colours are transferred onto the film at each station on the printing machine by means of a flexographic mat. Between each application of colour the ink is dried. When the product quantity is completed the toffee bar wrapper or other product is taken off the machine again in roll form.

With an understanding of how the process technology works, let us now look at how a product would be printed using these batch processes. The flexographic mats, paper and inks would be made available in line with a customer's delivery date. At the scheduled time, the paper, mats and ink would be loaded onto the printing machine as an integral part of the set-up. Typically, the wrapper design would be printed (for reasons of lower cost) two or more times across the width of the film. The order quantity would be produced and the roll(s) of printed film would then go into work-in-progress inventory waiting to be loaded onto the slitting process. This will cut the rolls so that there will be one design per smaller role in line with the customer's own packing requirements. Following slitting, the product would again go into work-in-progress inventory awaiting packing, then in and out of inventory before being despatched. The role of inventory here is again to decouple the various processes. It is the same as in the dental surgery example and is a distinctive element of a batch process. This and other characteristics of batch processes have been summarized in Exhibit 4.6.

Line

With further increases in volume requirements, investment is made to provide a process that is dedicated to the needs of a given range of products/services. While often the range of products/services is narrow, this is not always so. For example, the number of different vehicles that an assembly line can handle will often be tens even hundreds of thousands. When the number of engine types is multiplied by the

Exhibit 4.6   *Batch processes – key characteristics*

Product/services

Standard, repeat products and services, the volume demand for which justifies the process investment. Examples include beauty parlours, banking, hospitals, injection moulding and printing.

Process

Having broken down the products/services into different operations, the order quantity to be processed (which may be, and in services often is, an order quantity of one) is taken to the process where the first operation is to be undertaken. The process is made ready/set up and whole order quantity is completed. The part-made product or part-processed customer or information typically goes into work-in-progress inventory awaiting the next process that will complete the second operation. When available the process is made ready, the whole order quantity is processed and so on or until the whole product/service is completed.

Exhibit 4.7   *Different stages on the Land Rover vehicle assembly line*

number of colours and the outcome is then multiplied by the typically wide range of options the result is a very large number of potentially different vehicles.

As with batch the product or service is split into a number of steps and the process is arranged to complete these sequentially. As the processes follow each other they are set out in a line, hence the name. The repetitive process, therefore, is one in which the product(s) or service(s) are processed, with each product or service passing through the same sequence of operations. The result is that operation 1 is completed on the first product or service which then goes immediately to operation 2. Meanwhile, operation 1 is being completed on the next product or service, and so on, The line has also been designed to cope with any item within a given range and, therefore, the essential characteristic of line (compared with batch) is that to produce another product or provide another service, the process does not have to be stopped and reset. Product examples include domestic appliances and motor vehicles. Exhibit 4.7 shows part of the vehicle assembly plant at Land Rover, Solihull, UK. Service examples are not as widespread as applications for manufactured items. However, they include certain preparatory operations in fast-food restaurants such as McDonald's. A further example (see Exhibit 4.8) is provided by Dr Svyatoslav Fyoderov's Institute of Eye Microsurgery which uses this process in the treatment of myopia.[1]

Using laser technology and assembly line methods, surgeons at the institute cure myopia using the classic principles of a line process. The institute is also a world leader in advanced eye surgery. Finally, Exhibit 4.9 provides a summary of the key characteristics of line processes.

Continuous processing

With continuous processing, one or several basic materials are processed through successive stages and refined into one or more products (for example, petrochemicals). Because the costs of stopping and starting-up are very high (often prohibitive) the process will have been designed to run all day and every day with minimum shutdowns (hence, continuous processing). The materials are transferred automatically from one part of the process to the next with the labour tasks being predominantly ones of system monitoring. This type of process is not used in the provision of a service. Exhibit 4.10 gives an example of continuous processing – ExxonMobil's ethylene cracking plant in Fife, Scotland. To close down and restart the plant would take several days due to the complex process and safety requirements involved. Finally, Exhibit 4.11 provides a summary of the key characteristics.

Exhibit 4.8   *Dr Svyatoslav's eye microsurgery unit*

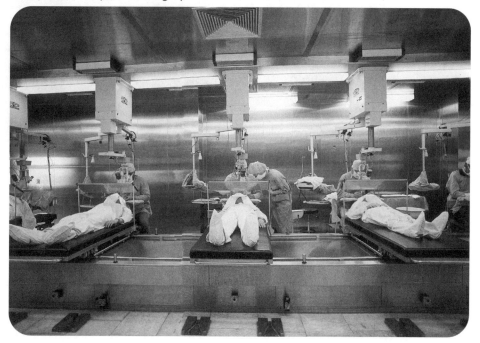

Exhibit 4.9   *Line processes – key characteristics*

Products/services

Standard, repeat, high volume products/services.
Examples include motor vehicles, domestic appliances and the preparatory operations in fast-food restaurants. Not often found in manufacturing and rarely so in services as the required volumes to justify the investment are not typical of today's markets.

Process

Products/services are separated into different operations. These are met by a series of sequential processes through which all items in a selected range pass. To the process all the products or services are the same and, therefore, the line does not have to be stopped and reset to accommodate a change in requirement. However, the line can only cope with the predetermined range for which the process has been designed.

Exhibit 4.10   *ExxonMobil's ethylene cracking plant – Fife, Scotland*

Exhibit 4.11   *Continuous processing – key characteristics*

Products/services

Standard, very high volume products.
Examples include oil refining and some petrochemicals.

Process

Materials are processed through successive stages with automatic transfer of the product from stage to stage. The costs of stopping and restarting are typically so high that the process is not stopped, hence the name – continuous processsing.

Case example 1

Meindorf GmbH is part of a large German cable company that manufactures compounds (the material used to cover the copper or aluminum conduit) to meet inter-group and external demand. It has four process units that heat and mix the various fillers and oils that make up a range of standard product specifications. Order sizes from customers range from 1 to 40 tonnes. To meet a customer order typically requires several mixings.

■ **Process Unit 1** produces natural and coloured elastomers

■ **Process Unit 2** manufactures the whole range of thermoplastics

■ **Process Unit 3** makes black elastomers

■ **Process Unit 4** produces small order quantities of thermoplastics and experimental compounds for the research and development department. This unit is not fully utilized.

On leaving these process units, the compounds move onto the next stage that involves shaping, cutting and packaging.

The mixing stage lasts between 8 and 14 minutes and the number of mixes required to meet a customer order are completed one after the other. At the end of a run the process units are changed to make the next product. The length of colour and compound changeovers take between 40 minutes and 2 hours. The most difficult colour changes involve moving from a dark to a lighter colour. In order to minimize changeovers, similar colours and similar compounds are run together wherever possible and in line with customer schedules. Typically, changeovers for Process Unit 2 account for 20 per cent of available time while changeovers for Process Units 1 and 3 account for up to 10 per cent of available time.

Delivery reliability is an order-losing sensitive qualifier for most customers and trends towards smaller customer orders is giving concern to operations in terms of meeting schedules.

Case example questions

1.1 Which process type (project, jobbing, batch, line or continuous processing) is used to heat and mix compounds in this plant?

1.2 Give reasons for the different changeover levels (10, 20 and 10 per cent respectively of available time) for Process Units 1, 2 and 3.

1.3 Why are reducing order quantities of concern to operations?

As mentioned earlier, companies often use different processes to meet the technical specification of a product or service. To illustrate, let us look at the following examples:

1. **Project** – building 60 houses which comprise four different designs would use, for example, the following combination of processes:

   ■ **project** to meet the overall requirements of bringing resources to and from the site with one person having the overall management responsibility to undertake this task in line with the effective use of resources and cost budgets involved.

   ■ **batch** processes would typically be used to meet several phases of the work. For example, once the footings had been completed on a number of houses then the concreting of the ground floor areas for all houses that had reached this stage would be completed consecutively using ready-mixed concrete in line with the

Exhibit 4.12   *The different tasks typically undertaken by jobbing, batch and line processes*

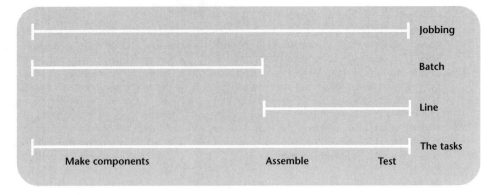

schedule. In this way, one phase would be completed on a house and then this same phase would be completed on the next house and so on until this task was completed for a number of houses.

■ **jobbing** process would typically be used on several aspects of the work. Here, skilled staff such as bricklayers and joiners, would receive drawings, interpret these and be fully responsible for fulfilling the specification(s) detailed on a drawing and for checking the results.

2. **Jobbing, batch and line** – the link between these three choices is well illustrated by Exhibit 4.12. As shown, in jobbing a skilled person makes the parts and components or completes the necessary analyses and reviews, assembles them or puts together the parts of a service and test or checks the final outcome. In manufacturing when products become standard, batch processes make the parts, components and subassemblies that feed lines with these processes undertaking the task of assembly and final test. In services, batch processes serve a customer or process information. More usually, a service will be completed at the end of one or more batch processes. The components of a service rarely go onto a line process to be completed – exceptions (as highlighted earlier) include some of the back office tasks in fast-food restaurants.

3. **Continuous processing** – as with project, continuous processing is specific to a small range of industries. The example of a chemical plant given in Exhibit 4.10 clearly shows how the processes are interconnected. Limited to products that can flow through pipes, continuous processing, as the name implies, comprises processes through which products flow from stage to stage without leaving the process (that is, continuously) until completed.

THE IMPLICATIONS OF PROCESS CHOICE

Once the choice of process has been decided or has evolved over time, the consequences will be significant. As the operations task accounts for a large proportion of the investment, expenditure and workforce, the implications for the business of the chosen process will be correspondingly important. The most significant aspects are outlined in a later section discussed under the headings products/services and markets, operations, investment and cost and organizational infrastructure. Many generalized statements are made in this section to help both explain the implications of these choices and examine the consequences that normally follow. Note that the analyses contained in these exhibits are intended as general statements relating the usual requirement of one type of process to the other four.

Thus, process choices show trends within each of these characteristics that will generally appertain to one type of process relative to the others. In a batch process there will tend, however, to be significant differences within this one process. This is because this type of process is often the transition between the lower and higher volume processes and also between the make-to-order and make-to-stock sales patterns. Furthermore, Exhibit 4.13 is presented in such a way as to illustrate the fact that the transition of processes from one to another does not occur. Organizations do not, for instance choose project and then later replace it with jobbing; similarly, companies rarely move from jobbing to batch then line. Exhibit 4.13 illustrates this while also showing that marginal transitions do take place between jobbing and low volume batch, low volume batch and higher volume batch and high volume batch and line.

Finally, you will notice that batch is depicted as an elongated shape in Exhibit 4.13 and typically the dimensions in Exhibits 4.14 to 4.17 describe batch by using an arrow. This highlights the fact that batch covers a very wide range of volumes and market characteristics, a factor explained more fully later in the chapter.

Exhibit 4.13   *Potential transitions between the different choices of process*

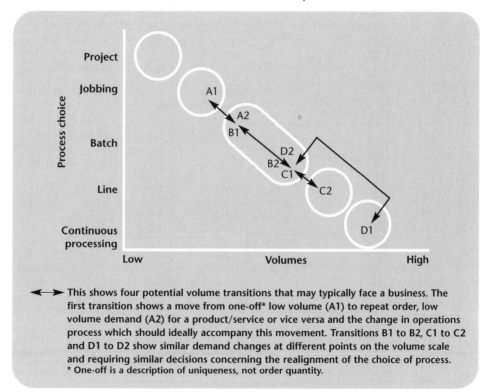

◄———► This shows four potential volume transitions that may typically face a business. The first transition shows a move from one-off* low volume (A1) to repeat order, low volume demand (A2) for a product/service or vice versa and the change in operations process which should ideally accompany this movement. Transitions B1 to B2, C1 to C2 and D1 to D2 show similar demand changes at different points on the volume scale and requiring similar decisions concerning the realignment of the choice of process.
* One-off is a description of uniqueness, not order quantity.

Source: Terry Hill, *Manufacturing Strategy: Text and Cases,* 2nd edition (Basingstoke: Macmillan, 2000).

Product, service and market implications

Project/jobbing processes tend, by definition, to be chosen to provide one-off products and services, that are made-to-order and compete predominantly on aspects such as delivery speed and unique skills rather than price (see Exhibit 4.14).

As a provider of one-off, non-standard items the organization will offer a diverse range of products and services in order to meet differing customer requirements. For this reason, the company sells a set of capabilities rather than a product or service *per se*.

In line and continuous processing, the opposite end of the spectrum prevails. Products and services are highly standardized, made-to-stock with innovation being orientated towards the process rather than the product. Products and services in these markets tend to compete primarily on price although companies will often try to

Exhibit 4.14   *Product, service and market implications of process choice*

Product/service and market implications		Typical characteristics of process choice				
		Project	Jobbing	Batch	Line	Continuous processing
Product or service	type	Special	Special ⟶		Standard	Standard
	range	High diversity	Wide ⟶		Narrow	Narrow
Customer order size (quantity)		Small	Small ⟶		Large	Very large
Degree of product/service change required in the process		High	High ⟶		Low	Nil
Make-to-	order[1]	Yes	Yes ⟶		No	No
	stock[1]	No	No ⟶		Yes	Yes
Orientation of innovation-process or product/service		Product/ service	Product/ service ⟶		Process	Process
What does the organization sell?		Capability	Capability ⟶		Standard products/ services	Standard products/ services
How does the organization win orders?	typical order winners	Capability, delivery speed	Unique capability, delivery speed ⟶		Price	Price
	typical qualifiers	Delivery reliability, price	Delivery reliability, price ⟶		Delivery reliability, quality conformance	Delivery reliability, quality conformance

Notes

1. Products and services are either specials (that is, have not been made or provided before), standards or some combination of the two. However, whereas organizations have by definition to make specials to customer delivery and specification requirements, they may choose to make standards either to stock (that is, finished goods inventory ahead of demand), only to customers' orders or in line with customers' schedules (that is, only when an order or schedule has been placed).
2. A customized product or service can be either a standard (for example, packaging that bears a customer's name and logo) or a special.

differentiate by, for instance, brand name hence moving away from price as an order-winner. (Note, when price is an order-winner it follows that profit margins will be low).

Little accommodation will be provided in the process to meet product or service change. In fact, the level of change to be handled by the process will be determined before the investment is made, with the latter being designed to make the specified range. For example, motor vehicles will typically offer the customer a whole range of options from which to choose and the process and support systems are subsequently designed to cope with any combination of options as standard procedure. Thus, the process is not required to stop in order to handle various option combinations, for to the line all motor vehicles with these different option packages are the same and can be accommodated without stopping the process. However, any customer requiring an option other than from the approved list will need to arrange this as a retro-fit (that is, post-delivery) task. In the same way some car assembly plants have been designed to build two or more models on the same process. For example, Toyota plants build Lexus and Camry cars on the same line. The principle is simple – the more you invest the more variety a process can handle. But, if you wish to make something different as well then you will need to invest some more.

Batch processes occupy the middle ground. With increases in volume, an organization will start to move from low volume to high volume markets. When this happens, competition in the relevant market segments becomes more price sensitive. This, in turn, leads to a reduction in the degree of change that can be accommodated and a move away from small-order markets. Also, it is in a batch process that the transition from make-to-order to make-to-stock is usually accommodated.

Operations implications

In project and jobbing situations, the product or service provided is one-off (that is, unique). Thus, the operations task will be variable (and often in jobbing, unknown)

Case example 2

At Toshiba's computer factory in Ome, 50 km from downtown Tokyo, a computer-based system networks the office, engineering and factory operations, providing just-in-time information as well as just-in-time parts. Ome workers assemble nine different word processors on the same line while on an adjacent one, 20 varieties of laptop computers are assembled. Usually they make 20 of one product and then change. Workers on the line have been trained to make each model and they are further supported by a computer display at every work station that shows a drawing and provides detailed instructions. When the model changes, so does the display. Product life cycles of some models are measured in months so the process developments for small order quantities help to guard against being unable to support sales peaks and overproducing when sales fall off.

Case example questions

2.1 What type of process does Toshiba use to manufacture its word processors and laptop computers?

2.2 What key operations developments have enabled the company to match process capability to its market needs?

and the operations process will need to be flexible, with many set-ups, using universal equipment and skilled labour. The effective utilization of the skilled labour will, therefore, be the dominant operations task, with relatively low equipment utilization being inherent in this choice of process (see Exhibit 4.15).

With line and continuous processing, the important perspectives change. The choice is made to provide high volume, standard products and services that usually compete on price. The operations' tasks will, therefore, be well defined using dedicated processes and equipment on a large scale. Process times will tend to be short and plant utilization the dominant task. Capacity changes in both line and continuous processing will be of a stepped nature – for example in line additional shifts or an additional process while in continuous processing only the latter is available as an option. (While in line, continuous and high volume batch processes companies will seek to refine the equipment to secure incremental throughput gains, eventually there will be no alternative than to undertake a major uplift in capacity as explained here. It is this aspect of changes in capacity that is highlighted here.)

Batch process is again the transitional, middle ground between low and high volume activities. It may, therefore, tend towards either jobbing or line and contain a mixture of their characteristics. Hence, capacity changes in high volume batch will also be stepped, requiring an additional shift or a new process.

The control of operations in terms of activities, quality conformance and capacity will also show marked differences depending upon the choice of process. In project and jobbing, because the operations tasks are variable and the process times are long, capacity will also be variable due to the uncertainty of how long the tasks will take. The internal span of process (that is, the extent of the operations process provided within each site) will be wide. This is necessary because the organization needs to have in-house as much of the capability requirement as possible. By doing this it can provide the necessary flexibility, cope more easily with product or service uncertainty, and retain a higher degree of control over the delivery schedule. Also, the large work content of the products and services provided will add to the complexity of both task and control. Quality conformance will be the responsibility of the operator plus supplementary spot checks. Lastly, productivity is more difficult to ascertain due to the problem of measuring the inputs that go into the manufacturing of a product or provision of a service.

The measurement and scheduling of operations in both line and continuous processing are much easier. The task is shorter and well defined with quality control designed into the process. Capacity is well defined due to the standard nature of the process and the product or service and hence, easier to control. The internal span of process within a line or continuous processing arrangement will tend to be narrow in terms of the work content of the finished product. However, previous parts of the process will often be provided within the same organization although not necessarily on the same site. For example, high volume car manufacturers often have separate plants for body pressings, castings and engine assembly, with the final assembly completed in yet another plant.

Again, batch processes are the transition between project/jobbing and line/continuous processing. The increase in volume is catered for by a batch process. The range of volumes that this process will be able to provide on a competitive basis will depend upon the degree of specialization within its process. But whatever the situation, the range will be very wide. As a consequence, the level of control complexity will vary, depending upon the span of the process involved and the degree of technology embodied in the product or service and in the process.

Exhibit 4.15   *Operations implications of process choice*

Operations implications		Typical characteristics of process choice				
		Project	Jobbing	Batch	Line	Continuous processing
Nature of the process technology		Universal	Universal	General purpose	Dedicated	Dedicated
Process flexibility		Flexible	Flexible	→	Inflexible	Inflexible
Ability of the process to cope with	product/service changes	High	High	→	Low	Nil
	new developments	High	High	→	Low	None
Volumes		Low	Low	→	High	High
Set-ups/ make readies	number	Many	Many	→	Few	Very few
	expense	Variable	Inexpensive	→	Expensive	Very expensive
Dominant utilization		Predominantly labour	Labour	→	Process	Process
Knowledge of the	operations task	Variable	Known but often not well-defined	→	Known	Well defined
	material requirement	Known at the tendering stage	Some uncertainty	→	Known	Well defined
Materials handing provision		Variable	Low	→	High	High
Internal span of process		Wide	Wide	→	Narrow	Narrow
Operations scheduling	key feature	Order status	Order status	→	Flow of materials	Flow of materials
	basis	System	Person	→	System	System
	ease of task	Complex	Complex	Very complex	Easy	Straightforward
Control of quality conformance		External spot checks	Monitored by the operator	→	Off-line inspection	Designed into the process
Process times		Very long	Long	→	Short	Short
Capacity	basis for calculation	Labour	Labour	→	Process	Process
	scale	Small	Small	→	Large	Very large
	definition	Variable	Variable	→	Established	Established
	nature of changes	Incremental	Incremental	→	Stepped	New facility
	control	Difficult	Difficult	→	Easy	Easy
Productivity control		Difficult	Difficult	→	Easy	Easy
Bottlenecks	number	Few	Few	Key process(es)	None	None
	position and nature	Random and movable	Random and movable	Fixed in the the short and medium term	Not relevant	Not relevant
Impact of breakdowns		Variable	Little	→	High	Enormous

Investment and cost implications

The typical primary and secondary investment consequences of each process choice will vary. In a project process, the capital (or primary) investment can be low (for example, the provision of a one-off service such as consultancy or medical specialist), through to high (for example, civil engineering projects). However, within the other four types of process, the relationship between capital investment and process choice will be more uniform (see Exhibit 4.16).

In jobbing, the capital investment will be quite low because of the universal nature of the process technology and the high level of labour skills required to meet the one-off product/service requirements. With larger volumes, investment in the process will be made in order to reduce costs, with the process technology also deskilling the manual tasks involved. An important secondary investment, however, is made in the form of inventory. Each type of process will require different levels of investment at each of the different stages. In the lower volume areas of project and jobbing, component and finished goods inventory will be low compared to line and continuous processing, where utilization of plant and make-to-stock are typical priorities. Work-in-progress (WIP) inventory, will, however, be the inverse of this. Because of the long duration and process methods used in project and jobbing, WIP will be high. In order to keep this as low as possible companies invariably agree to sell on part of the WIP at regular intervals. In civil engineering this would take the form of stage payments. In

Exhibit 4.16   *Investment and cost implications of process choice*

Investment and cost implications		Typical characteristics of process choice				
		Project	Jobbing	Batch	Line	Continuous processing
Amount of capital investment		Variable	Low	→	High	High
Economies of scale		Few	None	→	Many	Many
Level of inventory	components and raw material	As required	As required	→	Planned with buffer inventory	Planned with buffer inventory
	work-in-progress	High	High	Very high	Low	Low
	finished goods	Low	Low	→	High	High
Percentage of total costs	direct labour	High	High	→	Low	Low
	direct materials	Variable	Low	→	High	High
	overheads	Low	Low	→	High	High
Opportunity to decrease costs		Low	Low	→	High	High
Basis of cost control		Each contract	Each job	→	Throughput	Throughput

management consultancy, this would take the form of weekly invoicing. The higher volumes associated with batch processes will usually result in even higher WIP necessary to provide the important decoupling function.[2] With line and continuous processing, since each product or service is added to throughout the process, WIP is minimal, comprising whatever happens to be in the system at any one time. Lastly finished goods inventory reflects the make-to-order and make-to-stock positions; low in the former, high in the latter.

Organizational implications

In project and jobbing processes, the nature of the task is for unique, variable products and services with a need for flexible operations. Sales orders will be low, often by tender and with few formal customer ties. Similarly, supplier relationships will tend to be informal with few long-term agreements. (Note that in the case of some project organizations such as civil engineering, these relationships will often be more established and longer term). Thus, the organization more suited to these requirements is one of decentralized control with a more entrepreneurial style based on the process involved. As a consequence, the predominant managerial input is technological knowledge (see Exhibit 4.17). Here, operations managers would be expected to advise in areas of process technology and their academic and professional background would, therefore, be in an appropriate technology. The need for specialists to provide supporting advice will tend to be correspondingly small. On the labour side, the skill level required will be high, requiring flexibility to meet a wide range of tasks and to interpret customers' requirements. The technology involved in the job will also be at quite a high level and this, together with a wide range of tasks and long cycle of work, will provide the opportunity for an interesting and inherently satisfying job.

With line and continuous processing these characteristics will tend to be reversed. The highly standardized, cost-dominated tasks will be more suited to centralized control and a bureaucratic style. Thus, the process will be designed towards systems developed in line with this concept. The operations infrastructure, however, will change between line and continuous processing.

The operations management skills more suited to a line process will reflect the business orientation associated with the high volumes, levels of investment, control requirements and number of people involved. As far as the operations management role is concerned, in a line process the technology of both the product/service and process is known and well established. Furthermore, any support for either of these technical dimensions will be provided by specialist support services. Thus the investment that has gone into the process will have decreased the technical but increased the business and managerial tasks involved in managing operations. Hence, labour skill requirements will be low as will the opportunity for a work environment conductive to a meaningful set of tasks. Low skill, large plants and large volumes will tend to give rise to uninteresting jobs in the technological sense, and a lack of opportunity to have other parts of work (for example, planning) built in as a meaningful part of the task.

But with continuous processing these characteristics change. The operations management task assumes a higher technical dimension, process control is provided by technically trained staff (there are no operators in the classic sense of the word) with a high level of specialist support given the technical nature associated with this type of process.

Exhibit 4.17 *Organizational infrastructure implications of process choice*

Organizational infrastructure implications		Typical characteristics of process choice				
		Project	Jobbing	Batch	Line	Continuous processing
Customers	nature of sales	One-off tenders	One-off tenders	→	Defined prices with discounts	Well established
	degree of co-ordination	Small	Small	→	Highly organized	Highly organized often with forward integration
Suppliers	relationships	Variable	Informal	→	Formal	Long-term contracts
	degree of co-ordination	Variable	Small	→	Highly organized	Highly organized
Type of organizational	control	Decentralized	Decentralized	→	Centralized	Centralized
	style	Entrepreneurial	Entrepreneurial	→	Bureaucratic	Bureaucratic
Basis of corporate control		Individual contract	Individual job	→	Systems-based	Systems-based
Operations infrastructure	dominant operations management perspective	Technology	Technology	→	Business	Technology
	level of skill required	High	High	→	Low	High
	nature of labour skills	Technical	Technical	→	Manual	Technical
	work environment re inherent motivation	High	High	→	Low	Medium
	level of specialist support	Low	Low	→	High	High

Again, the transition comes with batch processes. The lower the volume requirement within the batch process the more akin the infrastructure requirements will be those of jobbing. The higher the volume, the more akin to line.

PRODUCT/SERVICE PROFILING[3]

Organizations need to have a clear understanding of the different implications for their business as alternative processes are chosen. The earlier sections in this chapter provided these insights.

However, when companies invest in processes they often fail to incorporate into that decision the business trade-offs involved. Similarly, as markets change or as companies enter new markets with different competitive needs, they again typically fail to check whether the changing or different needs of their markets can be supported by the operations investments already in place. But as highlighted earlier, investments in operations are characterized by their large size and fixed nature, that is, to make changes in operations typically takes a long time and a lot of money. Thus, if market needs and operations' capabilities (that is, operations strategy) are not matched a company can be seriously disadvantaged.

Now place these considerations in the context of today's competitive environment. Markets are changing faster and are increasingly different rather than increasingly similar. For operations to align its capabilities to the needs of a company's markets today and tomorrow it needs a way of assessing current alignment and of being alerted to future changes that may weaken this essential support. Similarly in its market-driving role it needs to agree with a business ahead of time, those order-winners and qualifiers it must improve to maintain or grow share in current markets or to enable it to successfully enter new markets.

As explained earlier in the chapter, on the one hand investments enable operations to meet the technical dimensions of the products and services to be provided while on the other they enable operations to meet the business dimensions (that is, the order-winners and qualifiers for which operations is solely or jointly responsible – for example, delivery speed, delivery on time and price) that make up the other part of the market requirement. The last section detailed the business trade-offs (what processes can/cannot do well) involved. This section explains how organizations can check alignment – that is how well market needs are matched by what operations is set up to provide.

The concept for undertaking this check is called product/service profiling. It offers an organization the opportunity to test the current or anticipated degree of fit between the characteristics of its market(s) and the characteristics of its existing or proposed process and infrastructure investments. The principal purpose of this assessment is to provide a method to evaluate and, where necessary, improve the degree of fit between the way in which a company qualifies and wins orders in its markets and operations' ability to support these criteria.

The ideal is to achieve this fit. In many instances though, companies will be unable or unwilling to provide the desired degree of fit due to the level of investment, executive energy or timescales involved to make the necessary changes. Sound strategy concerns improving the level of consciousness an organization brings to bear on its corporate decisions. In such circumstances product/service profiling will increase corporate awareness and allow a conscious choice between alternatives.

Inconsistency between the market and an organization's process and infrastructure capability in terms of supporting the business specification of its product and services, can be induced by changes in either market needs or process investments, or a combination of the two. Potential mismatches emanate from the fact that while investments within operations are both large and fixed, markets are affected by competition that brings about change and the fact that corporate marketing decisions can sometimes be relatively transient. While the latter allows for change and repositioning, operations decisions bind a business for years ahead. Thus, linkage between these two parts of an organization is not just a felt need but an essential requirement.

Procedure

The procedure to be followed in product/service profiling is as follows:

1. Select aspects of Exhibits 4.14 to 4.17 that are relevant to the situation under review. The key here is to keep the number of chosen dimensions small and so keep the insights sharp. Remember, this approach is a mechanism for communicating strategic issues to other parts of a business. Keeping to the point highlights the message and avoids digressing.

2. Next, put down the characteristics associated with each chosen dimension in the same way as they are displayed in Exhibits 4.14 to 4.17. Exhibit 4.18 is an example of the outcome of product/service profiling and a glance at this will show you how to proceed.

3. Now profile the product(s) or service(s) by positioning them on each of the characteristics selected. Where the circle is drawn indicates the position. The example in Exhibit 4.18 profiles two plants to illustrate why one was successful and the other was not. As the note at the foot of the exhibit shows, different circles represent the two different plants. As explained in more detail later, profiling the product and market characteristics served by both plants and also profiling the operations and investment characteristics involved checks alignment. Thus, these profiles show, on the one hand, the needs and characteristics of the market under review, while on the other, they show the capability of operations to provide these. In this way it tests the fit (current or future) between markets and operations.

4. The resulting profiles illustrate the degree of consistency between the characteristics of the market and the business specification of the process and chosen features of investment, cost and infrastructure. The higher the level of consistency, the straighter the profile will be. Inconsistencies will be shown by the dog-leg shape of a profile.

Product/service profiling, therefore, is a way of illustrating the level of fit that exists between a company's markets and operations' capabilities either in terms of the current or future requirements. The lack of alignment can be caused by a strategy that moves the company in part or in total to new markets and new requirements or an operations strategy that is not in line with the needs of current and/or future markets.

The story behind Exhibit 4.18

Faced with a decline in markets and profits, the company illustrated here undertook a major internal review of its two manufacturing plants. To provide orientation to its business it decided to manufacture different products at each of its two sites. This decision resulted in an orientation in each plant in terms of products and associated volumes. Two or three years later the number of product types handled by Plant B was eight times as many as Plant A and, as one would expect, product volume and order

Exhibit 4.18   *A profile analysis for two plants of a company illustrating the mismatch between one plant and its market induced by applying the same operations strategy to both plants*

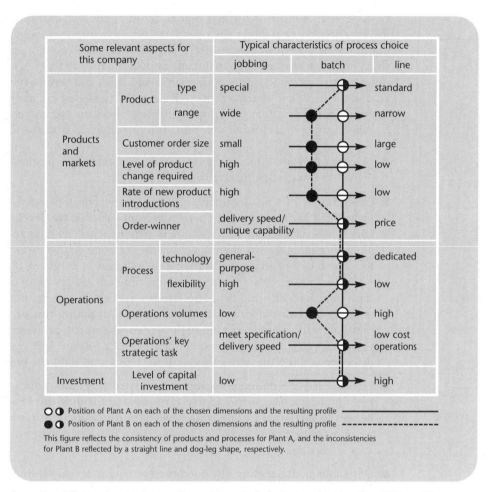

Source: Terry Hill, *Manufacturing Strategy: Text and Cases,* 2nd edn (Basingstoke: Macmillan, 2000), p. 152.

size differences resulted from this decision. While in Plant A, average volumes for individual products rose by 60 per cent, in Plant B they decreased by 40 per cent. To further help redress the overall decline in profits, the company also embarked on major operations investments at each plant, involving identical process investments and infrastructure changes. Exhibit 4.18 illustrates how these changes fitted Plant A's markets while they led to a significant mismatch for Plant B.

The procedure followed to complete Exhibit 4.18 is the one given in the previous section. Again, the first step was to choose the characteristics of markets, operations, investment/cost and infrastructure features pertinent to this business. The dimensions selected for these two plants are detailed in Exhibit 4.18. Next, the characteristics that reflect the change between jobbing, batch and line were described. On the one hand, the product range associated with jobbing is wide, and becomes increasingly narrow as it moves through to line. On the other, customer order size is small in jobbing and becomes increasingly large as it moves through to line, and so on. These dimensions represent the classic characteristics of the trade-offs embodied in process choice and as illustrated in Exhibits 4.14 to 4.17. Plant A's profile showed a straight line relationship between the markets and the process and infrastructure provision. That is, the needs and characteristics of Plant A's markets were matched by the characteristics of its operations investments and capabilities (its operations strategy). However, when the profile was drawn for Plant B it can be seen that a dog-leg occurred because the process and infra-structure investments made in that plant, although similar to those made in Plant A, did not relate to the characteristics of this particular market and hence a mismatch occurred. That is, the needs and characteristics of Plant B's markets were not matched by the char-acteristics of its operations investments and capabilities (its operations strategy).

When using product/service profiling it is important to note the following:

■ As companies are often in more than one market then profiles will need to be drawn on a market-by-market basis.

■ Other causes of non-alignment other than the one illustrated by Exhibit 4.18 include the fact that market changes are not matched by developments in oper-ations necessary to support these new requirements. As changes in markets are often incremental then the impact of the aggregate change over time goes unde-tected and lack of alignment is the result. Whereas in Exhibit 4.18 the comparison made was between two plants in the same timeframe, a review of one business over time compares one time period to another. As explained here, market changes are typically incremental and many go undetected. If during this period the strategic position of operations continues unaltered alignment problems result. As you would expect, these reviews should form part of a forward look by organizations to detect potential mismatches that leads to steps to put right the potential problem.

■ Product/service profiling is an important way of illustrating current or future align-ment problems. The picture format is the key to providing this insight and needs to be kept focused on the underlying issues within a business. As recommended in the way how to best draw a profile, keeping the number of dimensions small and rele-vant is essential.

■ One fundamental reason why alignment problems develop is that companies typi-cally wish to invest in processes just once. Propositions that companies link process investment to stages in the life cycle of products and services[4] are not borne out in reality.[5] Although theoretically attractive, this proposition is not followed on the simple basis of associated investment costs. To invest and reinvest as volume grows would involve high costs. Although companies typically use different processes at the research and development phase, once a product or service enters operations to be provided commercially, investment decisions are made on the basis of forecast volumes with the aim of minimizing associated costs. That is, they intend and plan to invest the once unless, of course, sales grow to the point where extra capacity is needed. Any transitions, therefore will tend to be restricted as explained in Exhibit 4.13.

CONCLUSION

Markets are different and they change over time. The main issue in this chapter concerns understanding markets in terms of volumes and requirements and understanding processes in terms of what, in relation to market support, they can do well and less well. Thus, as markets are different so will be the nature of operations' support. The reality in most businesses is that this essential link between operations and market need is not adequately provided. One source of this problem comes from the structure of organizations themselves.

When most organizations start to grow, the initial functional division that usually takes place separates operations from other functions. With further growth, procedures and systems are developed, and support and specialist functions are introduced to link the marketing/finance dimension with the operations dimension. Exhibit 4.19 illustrates this development.

The task facing operations is to ensure, through its joint ownership of the links between products/services and processes, between customers and producers, and between quality and attitudes that it makes its essential contribution towards the improvement of these within an organization. In many instances, operations managers have shed this major responsibility to the detriment of the operations function, their own managerial role and the business as a whole. Given the important strategic role to be provided by operations and the essential task within this of supporting agreed markets then understanding and explaining to the rest of a business the trade-offs being faced is a prerequisite in the strategy debate and its outcomes.

With organizations typically being developed on the basis of functions and specialists, the key links between products/services and processes and between customers and producers have been separated in their essential task of providing and selling products and services to customers.

Exhibit 4.19 *Binominal model of an organization*

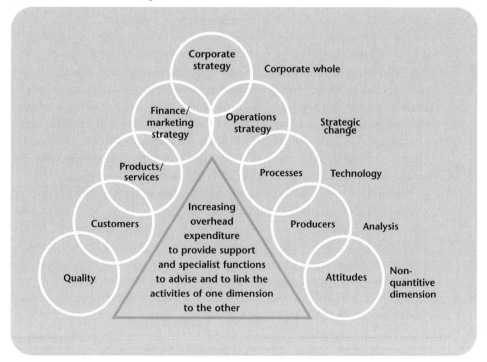

Source: Developed from NK Powell, 'Steps towards a definition of operations management', *Management Education and Development*, Vol. 9, No. 3 (1979), pp. 162–7.

The task of any business is to provide products and services and sell them in chosen markets. But, using functions and specialisms as the basic building blocks of organizations has separated the provision from the sale. The key links between products/services and processes and between customers and producers have been severed. As highlighted in Chapter 2, operations (as with other functions) needs to proactively close this gap. Providing the necessary insights to do this is a key role of all functions. Explaining the trade-offs embodied in choosing processes is one of operations' essential contributions. Only then will this allow a business as a whole to understand what is involved and to incorporate this in its strategic decisions.

SUMMARY

A key role in operations is to determine how best to make the products or provide the services an organization sells to its customers. Involved in this decision is the technical dimension and the business dimension of the products and services to be provided.

Meeting the technical characteristics leads to certain, often given, choices. To make bread commercially requires ovens of a given size. A computer-based IT system necessitates a computer with an adequate memory and capabilities. To make plastic mouldings needs injection moulding machines. And so on. While this is a key issue, alternative process technologies normally form part of the role of the engineering, IT specialist or other technical function. Operations' role is to use these technologies to make products and provide services in line with the needs of chosen markets.

Within this process provision lies operations' key role. It has to choose within the technology domain about the type(s) of process to best meet the demands of customers. This chapter (remembering that process design follows next) lays down the foundation blocks of process choice. What the differences are and, more importantly, the trade-offs associated with each alternative are explained in some detail. When you prepare one of the case studies at the back of the book or analyse operations in a real-life setting this is one of the first questions you should resolve. In doing so it will give you important insights into operations in terms of the trade-offs and the characteristics that you would expect within operations given the process choice that has been made.

The final section reminds you of the strategic dimension that forms a principal feature of this book. Product/service profiling is a most useful approach to checking alignment between what operations can do and the needs of a company's markets. This approach provides ways to check current alignment, the source of any alignment problems and to look forward to assess any changes that need to be made so that operations continues to be able to provide those order-winners and qualifiers for which it is responsible.

With these concepts in hand, the time is now ready to move on to the next associated topic – process design.

Discussion questions

1. Envisage going to the emergency unit of your local hospital with a suspected broken wrist. List the key steps in the delivery system in which you would be involved. What process is used at each?

2. Check the Internet to review one of the major petrochemical companies. Analyse one of its oil refineries and explain:
   - how it handles the product range that is processed in the plant
   - how often the plant is shut down and why.

3. What are the essential differences between:
   - project and jobbing
   - jobbing and batch
   - batch and line
   - line and continuous processing?

4. When assembling a car there will be five tyres (four plus a spare) to each vehicle. Why is it then that tyre-making would use a batch process while a car is typically asssembled using a line process?

5. Choose a service company that uses at least two of the processes detailed in this chapter. The illustrations may refer to more than one service delivery system. Explain why a company would have made such choices.

6. Select an example to illustrate the different tasks typically completed by jobbing, batch and line processes as shown in Exhibit 4.12.

7. Select a business/organization (other than the examples given in this chapter) to illustrate the five types of process – see below.

Process type	Business/organization	
	manufacturing	service
Project		✓
Jobbing		✓
Batch		✓
Line	✓	
Continuous processing	✓	

For each example, briefly explain how the process works.

8. Give an example where you consider that an operations delivery system is not aligned to an organization's market(s). Explain key aspects that illustrate this. What steps would you take to improve the level of fit between market needs and operations' capabilities?

9. For the example given in Exhibit 4.18:
   - What, for you, were the key reasons for the underperformance of Plant B?
   - What steps could you take to improve the existing level of fit?
   - Choose the one most appropriate action to follow to bring about improvement.

Notes and references

1. M Smoland and D Cohen, *A Day in the Life of the Soviet Union*, (Collins, London, 1987), pp. 66–7.

2. One function that work-in-progress (WIP) inventory provides is to help separate dependent parts of the process or delivery system by decoupling one operation from the next. It does this by providing inventory into which one operation can feed partly completed work and from which the next operation can draw its work. The extent of this inventory will depend upon the degree of certainty in the planning and control of operations. Where call-offs are firm and changes in demand are low, WIP inventory requirements will be substantially reduced. These issues are more fully covered in Chapter 10.

3. The concept of product/service profiting is more fully explained in Terry Hill's books *Manufacturing Strategy: Text and Cases*, 3rd edn (Burr Ridge: Irwin/McGraw-Hill, 2000), Chapter 6 and *Manufacturing Strategy: Text and Cases*, 2nd edn (Basingstoke: Macmillan, 2000), Chapter 6.

4. The proposition of linking process life cycles and product/service life cycle was most noticeably argued by Hayes and Wheelwright in their article, 'Link manufacturing process and product life cycles', *Harvard Business Review*, Jan./Feb. (1979), pp. 133–40.

5. A comparison between how useful these insights are in evaluating the source of alignment problems between markets and operations strategy compared with those of product/service profiling was reported in an article by the author, R Menda and DH Dilts entitled 'Using product profiling to illustrate manufacturing–marketing misalignment', *Interfaces*, Vol. 28, No. 4, July–August (1998), pp. 47–63.

CHAPTER FIVE

The content and planning of this book: an overview of what is involved, what has been addressed so far and what is covered in this chapter

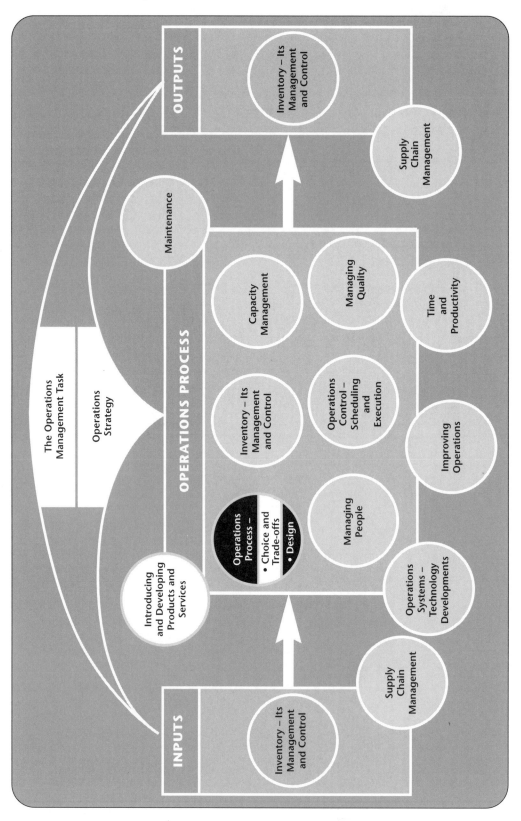

Process Design

Chapter overview

The last chapter described the basic processes that companies use to make products and deliver services. This chapter looks at how processes are designed to reflect the product or service provided, the issues involved in process design and the features incorporated in process layouts. In particular, it covers the following topics:

- **Delivering, products and services** – this is an introductory section to the chapter and highlights issues, such as the nature, category and complexity of the products and services to be provided, and the impact on process design.

- **Classic delivery systems and corresponding layouts** provides an in-depth review of process design and layouts with examples to illustrate the features involved.

- **Choosing processes** introduces the reality of companies selecting two or more processes to meet their varying requirements.

- **Hybrid processes** explains how companies develop processes that are, in fact, a mix between two of the classic systems discussed in the last chapter. These include cells, linked batch, Nagare production systems and transfer lines.

- **Service delivery systems** is a section that details the development of service delivery systems and emphasizes the impact on future sales and profits of retaining customers and the need to incorporate these issues when designing processes.

- **Other dimensions and formats** – this section introduces developments in process design that reflect the particular requirements of a business. The aspects covered include flexing processes to meet changing levels of demand, the concept of flexible offices or 'hot seating' and the impact of information technology including e-commerce.

Exhibit 5.1   *The nature of the product or service to be processed*

Nature of the product or service		Examples
Products		Power tools, domestic appliances, carpets and gardening equipment
Service	customers products information	Hairdressing, passenger airlines and healthcare Retail grocery, laundry and automated banking services Mortgage application, insurance claim and tax advice

DELIVERING PRODUCTS AND SERVICES

The products and services that companies provide and sell are different and these differences will impact the design of the process used to deliver them. It is important, therefore, to clarify at this early stage the differences that impact process design and then to reflect these dimensions in the rest of the chapter as alternatives and approaches to process design are reviewed.

The nature of the products or services

The products and services to be processed by the operations system are different not just in themselves (fast-food and high-quality restaurants provide a different product and service mix as illustrated in Exhibit 1.6) but by the nature of what is involved. Exhibit 5.1 highlights these differences and you will see from this that what is involved will impact the design of the process to deliver it. The key dimensions illustrated by these examples are:

■ the complexity of (that is, the number of steps to complete) the product or service to be provided
■ what is processed in the delivery system – customers, products or information.

Understanding, therefore, how products and services differ is an important prerequisite when designing the delivery systems to be used. Additional ways of categorizing products and services will help explain this still further and these are provided in the next section. However, before we leave this first point regarding the nature of the products and services to be delivered it is important to recognize that many organizations sell products and services that are not provided in a single process. For example, a dealership sells a new car. In the total sale is the manufacture of the car, the selling process, new car delivery and handover, warranty repair claims and servicing. All are handled by different processes that need to be designed to meet both the needs of customers and the internal requirements of the organization. The outcome is that organizations typically design and develop a number of delivery systems to provide the process needs of the products and services they sell.

Categories of products and services

The volume differences in products and services were explained and highlighted in the last chapter. Other key dimensions that further classify products and services are provided in Exhibit 5.2

A glance at this exhibit begins the important step of recognizing that products and services fall into different categories that reflect their differences and these need to be taken into account when designing the delivery process.

Complexity of the product or service

The complexity of products and services varies. Many customer-based services are relatively simple in terms of the operations process involved and can be delivered as a single step transaction; for example, the front office process in a retail bank and a take-away food restaurant. Other services need multi-step process provision. For example, whereas a 'dry cut' in a hairdressing salon is a single transaction, a shampoo and styling product would require two or more processes depending upon what was involved.

Exhibit 5.2   *Product and service categories*

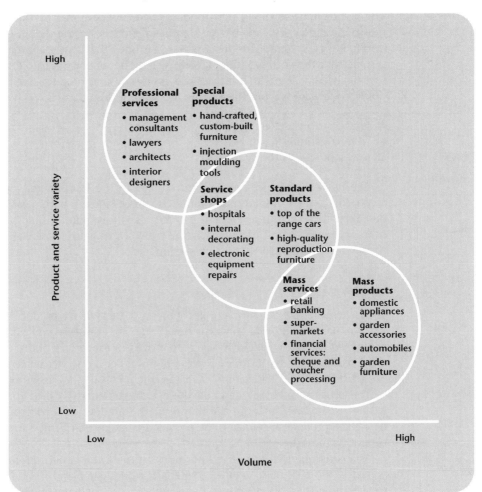

Similarly, both the back office and front office provision for dinner at the Ritz in London would involve many more stages than having dinner in a fast-food restaurant.

Volumes

How volume was critical to the issue of process choice was central to the discussion in the last chapter. This section serves only to remind you of this key factor.

Customer interface

Some service processes in particular interface with customers during the delivery system. Where the level of customer interface is high, opportunities for involving customers in the product or service provision are also high. Equally, high customer interface requires a process that is able to accommodate varying levels of demand while keeping queues to acceptable lengths.

CLASSIC DELIVERY SYSTEMS AND CORRESPONDING LAYOUTS

The last section explained that products and services differ and introduced the fact that these differences will have a significant impact on the design of the corresponding delivery system. This section now outlines the classic approaches to delivery systems and the corresponding layouts used. The sections that follow then highlight several specific factors that impact process design and product/service provision. The points to take away from this section are to understand:

■ how a process delivers a product or service
■ what constitutes a process
■ how a process is configured.

The five classic processes were introduced in the last chapter – project, jobbing, batch, line and continuous processing. The process design within each of these is now described to take into account the three take-away points listed above. These are, however, other hybrid processes that mix two or more of these classic processes and these will be explained in the next section.

Project

The last chapter defined how a project process is used when a product has to be made or a service has to be provided on a customer's site. The reason, as you will recall, is that the completed product would be too large to move (for example, a bridge or office block), it is not feasible to move it (for example, a highway) or the service needs to be undertaken on a customer's site (for example, a management consultancy assignment).

The process layout to describe these arrangements is called fixed position (see Exhibit 5.3) which refers to the nature of the product or service provision. That is, where the product or service to be provided is fixed (that is, in a fixed position) as it cannot be moved.

As a consequence of the fixed position nature of this provision, the process design concerns the task of scheduling materials, skilled staff and resources to a site and rescheduling these to other jobs on completion of their phase of the work or at the

Exhibit 5.3   *Types of layout used by different processes*

Process type	Type of layout
Project	Fixed position layout
Jobbing Batch	Process or functional layout
Line Continuous processing	Product or service layout

end of the job. The consequence is that the capabilities and resources to complete a product or service are brought to and arranged on-site, are managed on-site and then dismantled or redistributed during and at the end of a task. What constitutes the delivery system, therefore, is the process of bringing resources and skilled people to complete a product or service at a site other than where a firm has its own facilities.

Setting up and dismantling these resources makes the project process inefficient and costly. Consequently, companies make or undertake as much of the product or service away from the site using other existing processes within their own organizations.

Furthermore, and as with most delivery systems, companies will typically use a combination of processes when delivering these products and services. Whereas fixed position layouts are the overriding processes used in circumstances similar to those described in this section, on-site a company will use other processes to complete the task. For example, company auditors undertake the audit task on-site using a project process. But, to check and evaluate a company's procedures is a well-documented, highly proceduralized batch process, as will be explained in a later section. Similarly, a construction company building 50 houses would complete certain phases (for example, the footings, plastering and electrical wiring) for several of these dwellings at the same time. This again is a batch process and is chosen to lower costs by allocating skilled people and bringing in bulk materials (for example, concrete for the footings) to complete the same phase of several houses at the same time or one after another hence increasing the volume of these tasks and thus providing an opportunity to reduce the costs involved.

Jobbing

Where special products and services can be completed and undertaken within a company's own facilities the delivery process changes to jobbing. As Exhibit 5.3 shows, the type of layout now changes to be one based on processes or functions. What this means is that similar processes or functions are positioned or located in the same geographical area. The reasons for this delivery system layout are gains such as similar skills being grouped together and the utilization of processes, skilled staff and equipment is improved as assessing the availability of this total resource is made easier as it is grouped in the same area.

As these products and services are unique and will not typically be repeated, the skilled person or team decides the best process to follow and then accesses the relevant process or resource group as appropriate. Thus, the person undertaking the job will determine and then follow the best sequence of steps to complete the product or service. Hence, although the process design is often based on a skilled person's past

Exhibit 5.4   *Process layout for jobbing: a machine toolmaker*

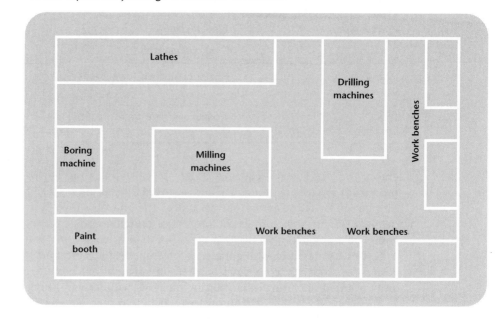

experience of similar tasks, the detailed elements of the process design will be unique to the job on hand. In the service sector, the analysis phase of (say) a management consultancy assignment would be completed using PC facilities. Here, a consultant may stay in the same location but would access or compile the relevant data and complete the appropriate analyses to meet the varying outcomes of each phase of the assignment. In addition, when discussions with executives and staff are necessary, a consultant would typically meet with them in their own office, area or location. Similarly, analysis of procedures, systems and facilities would typically be completed in the various functions or areas involved. Thus in jobbing, skilled staff take a job or task to the appropriate process, complete the work, move to the next process to complete the next step and so on until the job is completed. A further illustration of a company using jobbing and a process layout is given in Exhibit 5.4. This is a tool making company that builds unique tools and dies for customers. Having reviewed and discussed the details of a customer's drawing, a skilled toolmaker completes the whole task of machining and building the tool to the design specification required. To do this a toolmaker completes the machining requirements by taking the part-finished die from work bench to machine and from machine to machine to undertake the appropriate step until it is completed. Here, just as with the management consultancy example given earlier, both product and the skilled person move from process to process until the work is completed.

Batch

As explained in the last chapter, when products and services are completed more than once, the higher volumes and repeat nature of these requirements are more appropriately provided by a batch process. As with jobbing, what is processed (that is, products, customers or information) will impact the process design, but will be based on a process or functional layout (see Exhibit 5.3).

Examples of process layouts include:

- **Hospital** – the functions in a hospital (for example, operating theatres, pharmacy, consulting rooms, reception area, x-ray facilities, wards and laboratories) are laid out functionally. That is, the facilities and staff that constitute pharmacy services will be put together in one department, all operating theatres will similarly be located in the same area and so on.

- **Printing company** – the activities in a printing company that comprise design, plate preparation, ink laboratory and stores, printing and post-printing tasks such as cutting and creasing, slitting, collation and packing will be brought together each in their own area such that all designers and relevant equipment are in the same department, and similarly with plate preparation and so on, as shown in the illustration provided in the last chapter as Exhibit 4.5.

- **Supermarket** – the layout in a supermarket is based on similar merchandise (for example bakery items, soft drinks, wines, cheese, cooked meats, fresh vegetables and cereals) being located on shelves in the same aisles and similar activities (for example, checkouts) positioned in the same area. Where merchandise and activities are positioned will also reflect the levels of demand, traffic flows, nature of the purchase and similar factors. But the reason for locating merchandise and activities in the same area is twofold:

  – for customers it is easier to shop
  – for supermarket staff it is easier to replenish the shelves.

Now let us look at how a batch process works. First, facilities are laid out with like kinds (functions, processes or merchandise) grouped together. This enables utilization to be improved, keeps skills groups together, and reduces investment (due to higher utilization and by minimizing unnecessary process, equipment and space duplication) and operating costs. Second, the total product or service is often provided by two or more stages. For example, you go to a hospital with a suspected broken arm. To be processed you will go through the series of steps shown in Exhibit 5.5. So the way batch processes are designed is that a function or process layout brings with it economy of scale gains. However, for the products, customers or information to be processed, what is required to complete the task is broken down into a number of steps and each step is provided by a different process. This is achieved by the product, customer or information going to each function or process group in the appropriate order where the required task is then completed. In some service delivery systems, for example a fast-food restaurant, the total requirement is provided as a single step. But, the principle is the same as in a multi-step provision. Going back to the example above, if you had a suspected broken arm you would typically be processed by a hospital in the following way and with potential delays (queues) between steps as shown in Exhibit 5.5:

1. To hospital and provide details at reception.
2. Go to orthopaedic consultant and wait for your turn.
3. Consultant assesses that you have a broken right arm and now you are asked to go for an X-ray to provide the consultant with confirmation and details of the break. You queue and then an X-ray is taken of your arm in line with the consultant's written requirements.

Exhibit 5.5 *An overview of the process in a hospital for a patient with a suspected broken arm*

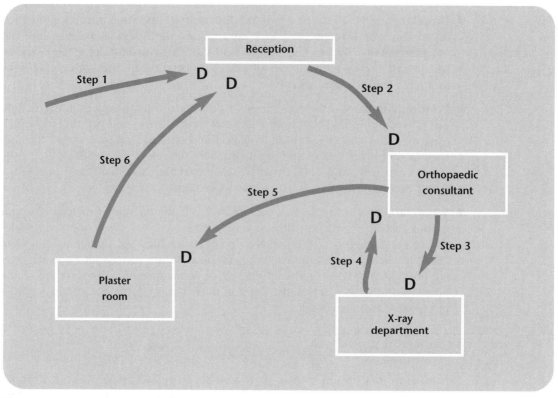

Notes

1. Explanation of steps 1 to 6 is given in the accompanying narrative.
2. D indicates a delay (in this instance, a queue).
3. Layout is not to scale.
4. The hospital layout would comprise corridors, rooms and waiting areas, and patients (that is, the customers being processed) would move, as shown above, from department to department using corridors, stairs and lifts.

4. Return to the consultant with the X-ray plates and wait. Plates are reviewed by the consultant who provides instructions to the plaster room on how the arm is to be bound and supported.
5. To plaster room to provide the necessary support. You wait and then your arm is treated.
6. Back to reception to arrange your next appointment.

As you will see from this, the customer (in this instance the patient) moves from function to function in order to be processed. This movement from one step to the next is an underlying characteristic of a batch process design. Furthermore, products, customers and information will typically wait for a process to become available. The result is that products, customers and information will queue before each stage in a process. Keeping work-in-progress as low as possible and queue lengths as short as possible (part-made products, part-processed information and part-processed customers in queues are all forms of work-in-progress) needs to be embraced by the process design itself. Minimizing inventory investment and shortening operations lead times are key issues for most businesses. Finally, before each step in the process is completed there will be a step-up or make-ready task. In the hospital example described here, reception will make ready the system and call up a patient's history if the person has undergone treatment before. Similarly, the consultant will review any patient notes, the X-ray unit will read the consultant's requirements and so on through each step of the process. The length of time a set-up takes will vary from process to process and within each step of a process. This can range from less than a minute to several hours when a complex piece of equipment is involved. Thus, before the next step in a customer, product or information requirement can be completed the process has to be made ready (or set up) before the work can be started. And this stop-and-start feature is a characteristic of a batch process.

Similarly, in the example of a supermarket, customers move from aisle to aisle selecting the food items they wish to purchase. However, when customers wish to purchase products that are not self-served within the store (for example bakery items, cheeses, meats and fish) they typically need to queue before being served. Queues also form at the checkout points especially at busy times. To ease these queuing problems many supermarkets have a ticket system to avoid uncertainty about which customer is next in the bakery or cheese queue. At the checkout assistants help to load the customers' purchases to speed up the service while certain checkout positions are designated to process customers with (say) 10 or less items.

You will see from these examples that companies often refine their basic process by designing alternatives that better meet the needs of customers. Additional examples of modifications to process designs are provided in later sections.

In manufacturing, the process layout and the way in which a product is completed follow the same format as the last examples. Similar processses are grouped together in the same geographical area (see Exhibit 5.6). Products are broken down into a number of steps and the order quantity for a product would all be processed at step 1, then move to the next stage in the process to complete step 2 and so on until all the order quantity is completed. Typically between one step and the next there will be a delay (see Exhibit 5.6) until the machine or equipment becomes available. This queuing creates work-in-progress inventory just as in the earlier examples. So, looking at Exhibit 5.6, a product that required moulding, sonic welding, hot roll stamping and final assembly would go through the necessary series of steps with periods of waiting between one step and the next as shown in this example.

Finally with functional layouts the position of processes may reflect the flow of the products or services through the different steps or stages. This would only be the case where the products or services involved all follow (at least in part) the same sequence. Hence of the examples provided so far:

- Exhibit 4.5, a printing company. You will see when you glance back at this that the functional layout reflects the sequence involved. That is, all products will start with cylinders/plates and paper stores, through printing then possibly to slitting and collation (if required), to packing and on to finished goods.

- Exhibit 5.6 is similar to Exhibit 4.5.

- Exhibit 5.4 on the other hand, does not reflect product/service flow as here products will have very different routings to one another and may, in fact, go back to earlier processes at some stage. This lack of similarity in process sequence is also well illustrated in the hospital example overview in Exhibit 5.5. As you can envisage, the sequence of steps for one patient will differ greatly from that for another patient.

Exhibit 5.6   *Process layout for batch manufacturing*

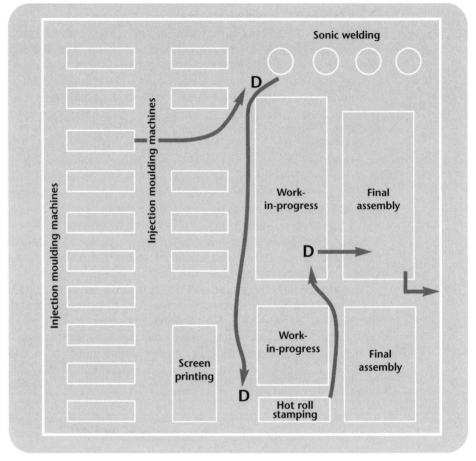

Notes

1. D indicates a delay: a product here is waiting its turn to be processed.
2. ➤ indicates product movement from injection moulding to sonic welding to hot roll stamping to work-in-progress to final assembly.

Line

A glance back at Exhibit 5.3 shows that with a line process the delivery system design changes to a product or service layout. If you recall, in the last chapter, when volumes of a product or service increase such that a set of processes can be dedicated to their provision then a layout specifically designed to make these products or provide these services can be justified. Hence, the term 'product or service layout' means that the processes are arranged as the sequential series of steps to undertake all the tasks necessary to complete the products or services in question. Whereas in jobbing and batch, the process or function layout is designed to be used and reused by a range of products and services because the volume requirements of a product or service are insufficient to justify dedicating processes to their singular use.

When volumes justify dedicating processes or functions to a given range of products or services, the process can be designed to meet the specific needs of these and the layout can reflect the order in which the steps to complete them need to be taken.

Examples include:

- **Car assembly** – the steps to assemble a car form the basis for the process design of a car assembly line with each vehicle passing along the same track where it is systematically built in line with the colour, type, engine size and other options from which customers can select. Because the steps necessary to build a car are the blueprint for the assembly line design each vehicle can pass immediately from one step to the next and the order in which these steps are completed reflects what is involved.

- **Fast-food restaurant** – burger preparation in the back stage of a fast-food restaurant is often designed as a line process. The preparation is separated into a number of steps and each burger is completed by going through each step at a time.

- **Self-service restaurant** – customers entering a self-service restaurant will walk through the service line and select the food they wish to purchase and pay the bill at the end.

As the product, customer or information service is completed step after step and does not leave the process, there is little work-in-progress inventory or queuing in this system relative to the volumes involved. You will however, often have experienced a queue at the end of the self-service restaurant system where the capacity at the checkout till is insufficient to meet the demand at certain times. Where this happens, ways to adjust capacity at the manned points on the service line need to be designed into the process in order to minimize waiting.

Continuous processing

As the last chapter explained, continuous processing is only suitable for certain products (for example, fluids and gases) and is not used to process services. The volume requirements are very high and the process is designed to run all day and every day. In many ways continuous processing is similar to line in that the fluid or gas being refined or treated moves from step to step until complete and without leaving the process. The process design reflects the sequence of steps necessary to complete a product (hence, it uses a product layout) and the volumes justify the high investment in the equipment and controls involved.

CHOOSING PROCESSES

As shown earlier in Exhibit 4.13 the project and continuous processing choices are at the two extremes of the process continuum. In most instances, the choice of either project or continuous processing goes hand in hand with the product or service to be provided. The process will, therefore, be largely predetermined, and progression from project to jobbing or from line to continuous processing is rare, normally impractical and often irrelevant. Project and continuous processing are, in most, if not all, situations, isolated from the other three process choices as shown in Exhibit 5.7. However, with jobbing, batch and line processes there is some transition from one to another but this is quite limited as was shown in Exhibit 4.13.

Companies choose processes based on volumes and markets. So, as companies support different markets and the volumes at stages in an operations process will differ then companies choose processes to reflect these differences. Thus, two or more of these process types are invariably found in the same company providing different products and services with their own distinct characteristics and reflecting the different volume levels involved. For example, vehicle components such as plastic panels will be made using a batch process but vehicle assembly would use a line process. The reason is that although the quantity is the same (one plastic panel per vehicle) the work content to make a panel is much smaller than the work content to assemble a vehicle. Hence the volume (quantity × work content) of the latter is higher than the former. Consequently, the former is completed on a batch process while the latter is completed on a line process. Regarding the batch process, what would typically happen is that the machine making panels would be scheduled and set up to complete (say) the equivalent of two weeks of vehicle assemblies. Once the schedule quantity was completed the machine would be reset to make another component and so on. Hence matching process to requirement is a basic task in process design – see Exhibit 5.3. Similarly, in a management consultancy firm, a combination of project and jobbing processes would typically be used to meet the specific requirements of a customer or client. Here, some parts of the assignment would be appropriately completed on a client's site while other tasks would be more appropriately completed in a consultancy company's own facilities. The same consultancy firm may also have developed specific solutions to address different segments of its overall business and part of this may include developing prescribed approaches and procedures to client situations and problems and in which its own consultants are trained, will follow and will implement. Such offerings would be provided using a low volume batch process. Let me explain – an assignment to deliver a consulting firm's solution to address and resolve the problems of a client will follow a prescribed approach in terms of the steps

Exhibit 5.7   *Process choices*

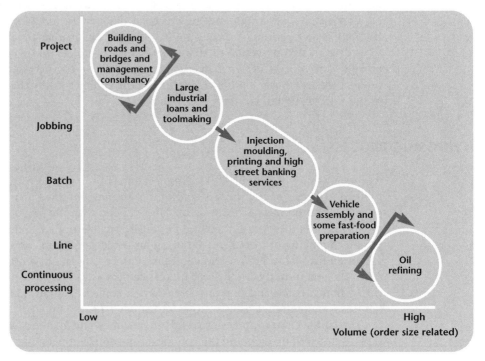

to be taken and analyses to be completed. The work will follow a given sequence and comprise a set of analyses and reviews that form an integral part of a prescribed approach. Thus, as in all batch processes, the job would be broken down into a number of steps, the work to be undertaken at each step would be listed and each step would then be completed often by a different member of the consultancy team until the job is completed.

The point that project and continuous processing go hand in hand with the product/service and industry has already been made. Furthermore, most markets today are neither characterized by the low volume, special (jobbing) nor the high volume, standard (line) ends of the product/service continuum. Consequently, most companies are competing in markets that are best supported by batch processes. Hence as shown in Exhibits 4.13 and 5.7, the elongated shape depicting batch reflects the wide spread of volumes with which batch processes can and are required to cope. It also illustrates the rationale behind drawing an arrow to represent the characteristic of batch for most dimensions listed in Exhibits 4.14 to 4.17. This shows batch as a transition between jobbing and line with low volume batch typically sharing the same characteristics as jobbing, and high volume typically sharing the same characteristics as line.

HYBRID PROCESSES

Given the increasing difference in markets, companies have responded by developing processes to reflect these changing demands. Line processes are often developed to produce a relatively wide range of products or services with a marked increase in investments typically associated with these decisions. Similarly, numerically controlled (NC) machines or machining centres provide programmable systems that can better handle the repeat, low volume demand of certain markets.[1]

In addition to investing directly in the process itself, companies often choose to rearrange or use existing processes in a different way. Some of the more common examples of these process redesigns are now explained. Both are termed hybrid processes as they are developed to provide a different set of trade-offs than was delivered by the process arrangements from which they originate.

Cells

Exhibits 4.14 to 4.17 illustrated how the trade-offs on a whole range of dimensions changed depending on the process chosen. Companies may seek to alter some of these trade-offs by rearranging processes. One such example is changing from a batch process to cells.

As explained earlier, batch processes are based on grouping similar processes or functions together in the same geographical area – for example, operating theatres in hospitals, libraries in a university, restaurant facilities in a large office complex and printing machines in a packaging company. Also see the earlier examples provided as Exhibits 4.4, 4.5, 5.5 and 5.6.

As a company choosing batch processes would be providing standard products or services, then the only practical alternative to a batch process is line. The reason why companies choose batch rather than line is based on volumes. Where products and services do not have sufficient volumes to justify the investment involved in dedicating processes, then batch is used. These processes are designed to allow products and services to share processes and thus make more sense of the utilization/investment equation. However, batch processes embody trade-offs some of which companies look to change. In particular, these include the complex scheduling and operations control problems, the long process lead times and high amounts of work-in-progress inventory that result (see Exhibits 4.15 and 4.16). Cells are a form of hybrid process that although still batch in origin (the process will still have to be stopped and reset to handle a product or service change) are in fact, a mix of batch and line that offers changes on some key variables. First let us discuss what cells are and then review the key trade-off changes that result.

| Exhibit 5.8 | *In batch, similar processes are grouped together* |

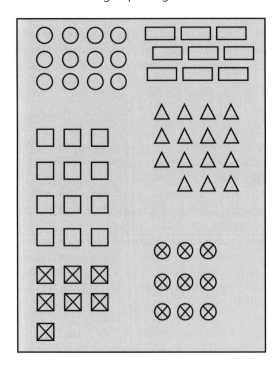

Exhibit 5.8 gives an example of a batch process and the functional layout (similar processes are grouped together in the same geographical area) that is part of these arrangements. As explained earlier, products and services are completed using a batch process because the associated volumes are insufficient to justify dedicating processes to their provision. Thus, one group of products and services share processes with other products and services, the hallmark of batch. Now the rationale underpinning cells is that grouping products or services together and treating them as being the same leads to an increase in volume (the volumes of all the products or services under consideration are added together and the aggregate is viewed as a whole) and hence allows processes to be allocated to this group for their sole use. What happens, therefore, in cells is that the necessary processes, both in terms of capability and capacity (that is, they can provide the product or service both in terms of its technical and demand dimensions), are allocated to the sole use of these product or service groups where the 'dedication' is justified by the enhanced level of volume that results – see Exhibit 5.9.

Compared to batch, this rearrangement brings with it changes in certain, key dimensions, for example:

■ process lead times become shorter
■ work-in-progress inventories reduce
■ operations scheduling and control is made easier.

The question is why? Well, it is bound up with the allocation of processes which moves this hybrid process towards line (although still on the batch process dimension) as shown in Exhibit 5.10. The production process or service delivery system will be laid out within a smaller physical area and handling a reduced range of products or services. This, in turn, simplifies the scheduling task and enables lead times and work-in-progress inventory to be reduced as waiting time between processes is more easily managed.

Exhibit 5.9 *Cellular layout: required processes are physically located in a cell as compared to the functional layout associated with batch processes as shown in Exhibit 5.8. Where products or services follow a similar sequence of steps, the process layout within the cell would reflect this, as explained earlier*

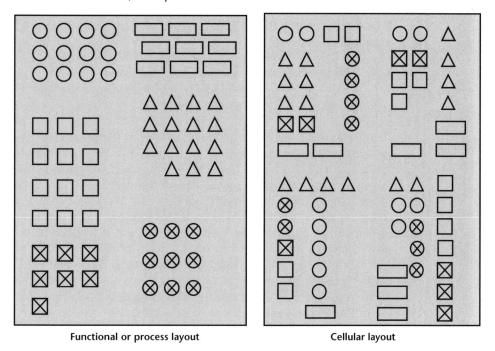

| Functional or process layout | Cellular layout |

Exhibit 5.10 *The position of cells and linked batch relative to batch and line processes*

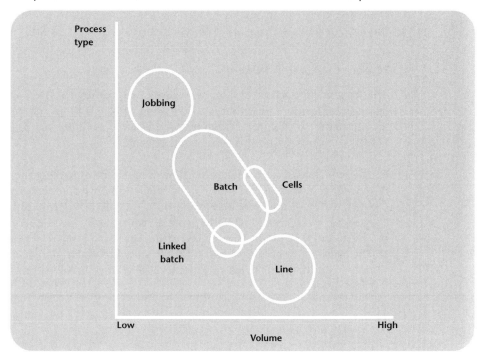

Just as these 'gains' come from moving the hybrid towards line, cells, compared to batch, also incur certain disadvantages which again are associated with their repositioning on the process continuum. Compared to batch, cells are:

- less flexible
- result in lower utilization of equipment that may require additional process capacity investment[2]

Both these are characteristic of line rather than batch.

Linked batch

Companies investing in line processes often find that, over time, the demand for the products or services may decline. With spare capacity resulting from this change in demand, companies typically seek to reuse the available process capacity by providing other products or services. The outcome of this decision is that, whereas originally the process would not have to be stopped and reset to accommodate a product or service change, it typically would now as the added products and services fall outside the original process arrangement. The result is that the process, although it still looks like a line (with processes set out sequentially) is, in fact, a batch hybrid known as linked batch (see Exhibit 5.10). The key change resulting from this move from line to a hybrid batch process is the impact of set-up or changeover times now incurred to provide different products or services. As the stages in a linked batch process are coupled (as it was originally configured as a line process) then a changeover will involve resetting all the parts of the total process before the process can again begin to make or provide products or services. Thus, although in batch all parts of the process to make or provide a product or service would have to be reset before each operation can be completed all the set-ups do not have to be done at the same time. The total set-up time, therefore, will invariably be lower as some processes would be working on other products or services while other part(s) of the total process are still to be changed.

Nagare Production System

The Nagare Production System was developed within the Disc Brake Division of Sumitomo Electric. The layout is a derivation of cells and, in the same way, provides an alternative to the process layout used in batch, as illustrated in Exhibit 5.11. The key differences between this system and cells are:

- The sequence of steps reflects the flow of materials in making the product.
- Operators move the part from step to step and hence complete a whole product.
- Operators typically produce to a just-in-time (JIT) system using a *Kanban*-type arrangement (this and JIT systems are explained fully in Chapter 8).
- The quantity of products produced at any one time is relatively small.
- The Nagare Production System is ideally suited to making products that are similar to one another. This helps keep the level of change involved low and hence set-up times are reduced.

Exhibit 5.11   *Changing from process layout to Nagare cell*

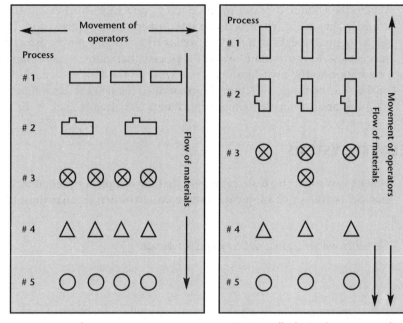

Layout by process group

Nagare cell – layout by process order

A large US telecommunications company organised its call centre on a functional basis. Using three tiers of support groups, customers' correspondence, requests and queries were initially handled at the Tier 1 level. Any issues that could not be resolved here would be passed to a Tier 2 technician. Delays on transfer between Tier 1 and Tier 2 staff frequently occurred and where a Tier 2 technician could not resolve an issue it would be passed back to the Tier 1 originator. This passing back and forth often happened two or more times. The result was that an issue requiring half an hour to resolve would take up to two days before a reply was given to a customer.

The company decided to reconfigure its call centres. Each centre retained four functional areas – inbound (payment collections), outbound (sales), technical support and research agents – and three tiers of support. However, cells were formed to handle specified groups of customers with two of the three support tiers now contained within each cell. Hand-off between Tier 1 and Tier 2 staff now occurs within a cell and this means that over 90 per cent of customer queries are resolved within a single team leader's span of control. The cell team leader is ultimately responsible for ensuring that every customer query is followed through to a satisfactory conclusion.

Case example questions

1.1   How did the original call centre structure result in delays?

1.2   How did the call-based redesign reduce delays?

1.3   What could be the different ways of routing calls into the cells?

1.4   What other advantages or opportunities would a cell-based structure offer this company?

Transfer lines

Where the volume demand for products is very high, further investment is justified. Transfer lines are a hybrid between line and continuous processing. The high demand leads to investments designed to reduce the manual inputs associated with a line process and to move more towards a process that automatically transfers a part from one station to the next, positions it, completes the task and checks the conformance quality. Furthermore, deviations from specified tolerance levels will be registered within a process and automatic tooling adjustments will often be part of the procedure.

SERVICE DELIVERY SYSTEMS

Having explained the basic principles that govern process design let us now look at a number of issues that supplement these insights when organizations take on board the

Exhibit 5.12   Elements within service delivery system design

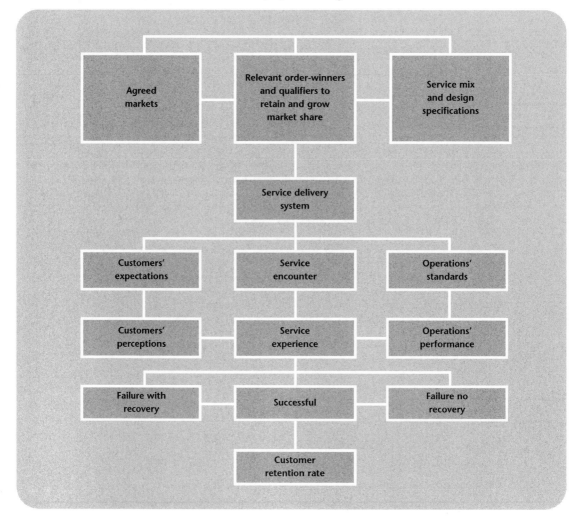

reality of designing processes to meet the needs of their markets. The first of these is a closer look at service delivery system design. Exhibit 5.12 provides a way of analysing and developing a service delivery system. You will see that as with Exhibit 2.5, the market provides the external context in which the system needs to be developed while also reflecting the internal requirements of the organization such as staffing levels and controls. While the central column represents the reality of the service encounter and the service experience itself, these need to be adjusted and developed in line with customers' expectations and perceptions while the operations' standards designed to meet the service specification need to reflect service requirements, with actual performance being measured to ensure that what is provided in the service experience meets customers' needs.

Case example 2

When push comes to shove, more than 50 per cent of airline passengers (according to an informal survey of frequent business travellers by USA Today in late 1999) cite elbow room (having an empty seat next to them is the ideal) as their first choice when it comes to extra space. In 1999, the percentage of seats filled on US internal flights rose 6 points to 72 per cent. Economy seats are about 17 in or 42 cm wide, the same as they have been for years. Making aisles dangerously narrow or putting fewer seats in rows and sacrificing revenue are difficult calls to make.

But, more elbow room is starting to influence airline choice. Denver-based Frontier Airlines cited the extra 7 in (17 cm) wider interior as 'a big selling point' in ordering twenty Airbus 318s and 319s over the new-generation Boeing 737s. Also, Continental Airlines specifically designed the coach-class seating in its new Boeing 777s in a way that increased the chances that passengers would have an empty seat next to them. As the table below shows, seat layouts in today's passenger jets have taken these issues on board.

Seat arrangements	Airplane	Percentage of seats filled before a passenger must sit next to another
3–2	■ Boeing MD80, 88, 90 ■ DC9 and Fokker F100	51
3–3	■ Boeing 727, 737, 757 ■ Airbus A-319, A-320	54
2–5–2	■ DC10 ■ Boeing MD11 ■ Lockheed L-1011	34
3–3–3	■ Boeing 777	54
3–4–3	■ Boeing 747	52

Source: Boeing.

As most airlines report, one of the biggest drivers for satisfaction is whether the seat next to a person is empty. When the seats filled crosses the 60 per cent line, customer satisfaction plummets, while at a 70 per cent load factor only 25 per cent of passengers view a flight as being satisfactory.

Case example questions

2.1 Why is elbow room on passenger airlines an increasingly important factor in the new millennium?

2.2 Why is legroom often easier to provide than elbow room in a passenger jet design?

2.3 Link this case example to Exhibit 5.12 and highlight the key dimensions it illustrates.

The level of customer retention not only has a significant impact on future sales but is also a major factor on profit margins. As shown in Exhibits 5.13 to 5.17, recognizing the size of the complaints problem, the effect of handling problems within the service delivery system, how problems are best handled in terms of response time and process, the impact on retention rates by operations' performance and the increasing profitability of customers over time are key factors to incorporate into service delivery system design.

As Exhibit 5.13 shows, the percentage of customers experiencing problems varies by sector, and the levels are high with five of the sectors close to or above the 50 per cent mark. While these are high in themselves the impact on return rates shows that potentially these sectors could lose repeat business by between 15 and 41 per cent (see Exhibit 5.14).

Exhibit 5.13 *Percentage of customers experiencing problems and the impact on retention rates*

Sector	Percentage total of customers experiencing problems	Retention rates (per cent total) for customers having	
		no problem	problem
Consumer goods	22	83	54
Appliance repairs	44	73	40
Car rentals	47	92	75
Branch banking	49	86	76
Hi-tec (business customers)	60	91	81
Air travel	69	91	77

Exhibit 5.14 *Possible overall retention rate (per cent) by sector*

Sector	Customers experiencing no problems			Customers experiencing problems			Possible overall retention rate (%)
	total (%)	retention level rate (%)	actual	total (%)	retention level rate (%)	actual	
Consumer goods	78	83	65	22	54	12	77
Appliance repairs	56	73	41	44	40	18	59
Car rentals	53	92	49	47	75	35	84
Branch banking	51	86	44	49	76	37	81
Hi-tec (business customers)	40	91	36	60	81	49	85
Air travel	31	91	28	69	77	53	81

The satisfaction levels of those customers with a problem are further influenced by the length of delay by a company in handling the complaint as well as by the way the organization deals with the problem. As you would imagine (see Exhibits 5.15 and 5.16) the length of the response time to handle a complaint and the number of people within an organization that become involved in handling a complaint directly impact the satisfaction levels of customers.

The penultimate line of Exhibit 5.12 introduces an important dimension in customer satisfaction levels, that of recovering from a service failure. Avis, the worldwide car rental company, found that the repurchase intention levels of customers alters dramatically depending how well the process design accommodates complaints – see Exhibit 5.17. As these illustrations show, the impact on future sales of how well the process meets customers' needs and expectations and the extent to which the process is designed to deal with customer complaints speedily and effectively is dramatic. The consequence of this is further enhanced when the increase in customer profit levels over time is recognised. As customers are retained, processing costs and problems decline with the result that annual levels of profit increase. In the credit card sector the increase over a five-year period is 180 per cent whereas for auto-servicing it is over 350 per cent.

Exhibit 5.15   *Percentage of customers satisfied related to response time to handle a complaint*

Response time	
# of days	% Customers satisfied
1–7	52
8–21	42
22–28	38
29+	23

Exhibit 5.16   *Percentage of customers satisfied related to the number of contacts required to handle a complaint*

Contacts to handle complaints	
#	% Customers satisfied
1	58
2	37
3	32
4	29
5+	11

Exhibit 5.17   *Customers' repurchase intention levels – Avis*

Category		Repurchase intention level (%)
No problem		92
Problem but did not complain		87
Complained and were	satisfied	92
	mollified	70
	dissatisfied	44

OTHER DIMENSIONS AND FORMATS

The previous sections have addressed the concepts and issues that relate to the general approach to process design. This section highlights other dimensions and formats that, while relating to more specific delivery systems, provide additional approaches and insights to meeting the needs of particular markets and organizational requirements.

Flexing processes to reflect demand levels

In many companies, sales demand can vary significantly. To meet these changes in activity levels companies, where possible, incorporate these factors in their process design. For example:

■ Car assembly plants are often able to increase the number of positions on an assembly line thus decreasing the work content per station and thereby allowing operations to increase the speed of the process and raise output levels.

■ Bank and post-office branches create several more teller positions than are normally required so enabling them to 'flex' capacity in line with queue lengths.

■ Some fast-food restaurants have developed a design process that can be altered to meet the requirements of peak and non-peak sales periods as shown in Exhibit 5.18.

Exhibit 5.18   *Process design permitting adaptations (and even gradual progression) between the two formats for peak and non-peak demand periods*

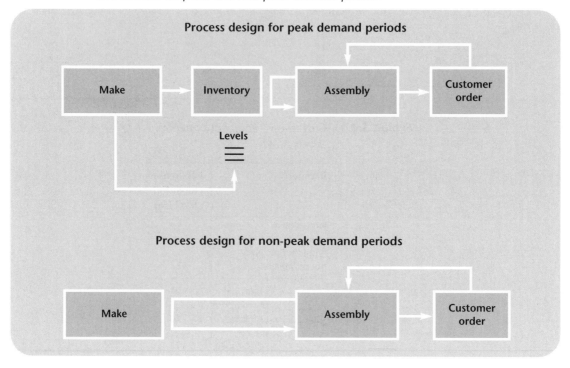

Flexible offices

For jobs such as consultants, service engineers and sales staff, the need for dedicated desks occupying expensive floor space is often unnecessary. Companies are now providing a number of desks that can be used by staff on an as-needed basis. The combination of variable space to work and somewhere to hang a coat provides the alternative descriptions of the virtual office, 'hot offices' and 'hot desks'.

Other systems use mobile desk base units that can be put out of the way when the owner is out. Similarly, computer screens that descend from the ceiling on demand are examples of other dimensions of the concept of flexible offices. Add to these changes the growing trend towards flexible working, working from home and the increasing use of part-time staff and the need for a more flexible office to accommodate fewer permanent staff is a growing phenomenon of the new millennium. Arriving at the office, picking up their personalized mobile phone from the recharging rack and then finding a place to work is the way that many staff will be accommodated in the future.

Protecting the environment

Increasingly organizations are incorporating environmentally friendly dimensions into their processes and systems. The recycling of materials and waste has been high on the agenda for some decades, and systems for separating paper, cans and glass have long been in place in the workplace. This awareness is also being extended to other delivery systems as the example provided as Exhibit 5.19 illustrates.

Information technology

Information technology developments have not only reduced costs and lead times within systems and procedures but have also enabled companies to redesign many of these processes, as the examples that follow illustrate:

■ *Automatic banking:* high street banks are continuing to cut costs by automating more of their services. Automatic teller machines (ATMs) are now the principal way to get cash from your bank account. Increasingly automated branches are adding video disc displays selling insurance, providing details of loans and screens offering share quotations. In parts of Europe and the USA fully automatic

Exhibit 5.19 *Let the guest decide: accommodating environmental issues in the delivery system design*

> Please decide: Hand-Towels thrown into the bath or shower means: Please exchange. Hand-Towels replaced on the towel-rail means: I'll use it again – for the sake of our environment.
>
> **STEIGENBERGER**
> H · O · T · E · L · S

branches are replacing existing arrangements. These offer all the usual customer services but no tellers.

maing phone

■ *Teleworking:* since the early 1980s, companies have been experimenting with teleworking, the practice of using computers and telephone links to work away from the office. Home offices are part of this growing trend while companies are making increasingly heavy use of telecommuting, a policy that allows employees to work in the office one or two days a week and spend the rest of the time with clients and working from home. Jack Nilles, the 'father of teleworking', coined the phrases 'teleworking' and 'telecommuting' in 1973 while leading a research project at the University of Southern California into the impact of IT at work.[3]

Telework brings benefits including productivity increases of 20 per cent or more, reduced office space requirements and lower staff turnover levels.[4] In addition, benefits to a nation's economy are significant. Traffic congestion cost the UK economy more than $90bn in lost productivity in 1996 while London commuters waste more than 10 hours per week going to work. In the USA, clean air legislation is obliging large firms to reduce their commuter workforce. AT&T, for instance, already had a telecommuting workforce of 35,000 in the late 1990s. While in the late 1970s there were very few teleworkers, by the late 1990s this had grown to 20 million worldwide and it is predicted to reach 200 million by 2016.

Case example 3

First Direct, Midland Bank's telephone banking business, was the first to challenge the traditional bank-based provision that characterized the banking industry in the last century. Based on call centre provision, First Direct presents itself as a gateway through which customers pass to access their money, obtain advice and control their financial affairs. Conventional banks, staff are told, are a brick wall in comparison, resolute, restrictive, secure but unresponsive. A basic tenet is to offer customers an equal relationship with their bank manager. To inculcate this into their behaviour and values staff are themselves treated with equality in the workplace. First, recruitment is based on behavioural rather than banking skills – only 5 per cent of staff have worked previously in banks. Second, the 24-hour banking service is run on flexible shift patterns where staff choose their own patterns (anything from 16 to 32 hours) while recognizing the peaks and troughs in demand. Staff also decided themselves how they should dress for work and opted for a smart dress code to better reflect the way they needed to carry out their jobs. Crèche facilities at the Leeds (UK) centre have always been available allowing staff to mix family and work commitments. Basic pay relates to an employee's skills which are heavily weighted towards the behavioural (communicating, handling stress, influencing, assessing information, judgement and decision-making) end of the skill continuum. Staff are also required to match certain standards covering call duration, availability and signed on times.

Case example questions

3.1 Why are call centres attracting customers away from conventional bank branch provision of services?

3.2 What aspects of First Direct have helped make its call centre a success?

■ *Call centres:* whether the vendor is a personal computer manufacturer providing a help desk for users, a gas or electric distribution company answering queries or a financial services company handling account, policy or general enquiries or handling mortgage and personal loan applications, a call centre has become the preferred solution. Call centres cut staff costs compared to multi-site arrangements both in terms of the number of staff required and the opportunity to locate centres in lower wage rate areas. With call centres, customers are offered free or low-rate calls to encourage their use, while international centres allow customers to call a local number while the system then transfers them to an overseas agent who speaks their own language.

In addition, some companies transfer calls from one region to another (for example, mainland Europe to the UK or Ireland and then to the eastern seaboard of the USA and so on) as a way of efficiently handling the times during the 24-hour period when the number of calls are low. For example, bookings and enquiries for Radisson Hotels in Europe and the Middle East are handled by the group's call centre in Dublin from 7am to 7pm. The operation handles more than 1000 calls daily with 22 incoming telephone lines (all free phones) operated by 25 staff speaking 11 different languages. From 7pm the service switches to operations in the USA.

The advances in computer telephony integration has enabled call centres to replace traditional service departments by linking the telephone to a computer that routes calls to the most appropriate agent, prompts the agent with caller data (known as 'screen popping') and leads the agent through a script to produce answers to thousands of different questions.

Case example 4

Thomas Cook has been providing travel services for almost 160 years and operates the world's largest network with over 100 000 retail locations worldwide including some 35 000 bureaux de change and affiliated services. Now owned by West Deutsche Landesbank, it serves 20 million customers each year in an operation worth £1bn.

In late 1998, Thomas Cook added Global Services to provide value-added travel emergency assistance services. This entails providing detailed assistance at the end of a telephone line with the use of computer telephony integration that identifies a caller's number and places that call in the queue for a call centre agent with appropriate skills. Further developments link a caller in Shanghai (say) with a map showing the location of the caller and the closest medical services displayed so the agent can talk the caller through. Details of all incidents are also stored allowing an agent to pull up a full history of customer's problems on future occasions. The main site in Peterborough (UK) can handle queries in 60 languages. The £20m investment is attracting a new group of corporate customers and is now being offered to third parties such as airlines and government agencies.

Case example questions

4.1 Why would corporate customers be attracted to this service?

4.2 How is a call centre uniquely appropriate for providing these services?

Exhibit 5.20 *Internet user population forecasts*

Region	Year (millions)				
	1996	1997	1998	1999	2000
Europe	8	14	19	24	29
Japan–Asia Pacific	3	5	12	21	30
North America	32	43	49	58	76
Other	1	1	4	7	9
Total	44	63	84	110	144

Source: Gartner Group 1997 Conference Presentation.

In addition, automated or 'predictive' dialling (that connects agents to customers just as the incoming call rings out) is being increasingly installed to cut the time to answer and also reduce the number of times a customer rings off. Favoured locations for call centres in Europe are Ireland and Scotland due in part by wage rates in a service where labour accounts for 45 per cent of total costs. For example, American Airlines relocated its European reservation centre to Dublin in the late 1990s where it estimated that staff costs were half those in Switzerland. In fact, it was estimated in the late 1990s that Ireland alone now accounts for 30 per cent of all pan-European call centres in the European Union. The problem, however, that Dublin, Edinburgh and Glasgow and their immediate hinterlands now face is how to keep staff. The concern is not so much one of losing staff to competitors but to other job opportunities.

E-commerce

Dealing with customers and suppliers through e-commerce has profound implications for the way companies operate and, as more users gain access to the Internet (see Exhibit 5.20), the need for organizations to embrace relevant technologies into the design of their processes is critical.

What the Internet offers is the capability to personalize the service to customers. It has the ability to tailor itself to every one its 100 million users.[6] Furthermore, the Internet crosses borders, which means that pressure on prices is going to increase almost overnight. For example, European companies will find it tough competing with US competitors in many retail markets. For instance, books in the UK and CDs in Europe and Japan are both about 30 per cent more expensive than in the US.

The benefits on the retail end of the spectrum have also been increasingly embraced by company inter-trading. But e-commerce is not just shopping by another name. It encompasses companies' relationships with their suppliers as well as their customers. Corporate intranets will be linked in order to provide a safe, secure, manageable, business-to-business environment, and e-commerce will be an integrated part of customer/supplier partnership and these issues are discussed in more detail as part of Chapter 11 on supply chain management.

CONCLUSION

Process design embraces the need to deliver the technical dimension of products and services, to meet the needs of chosen markets and reflect the internal requirements of

Case example

5

■ Jeri Capozzi only shops for plants at the on-line nursery Garden Escape Inc. The reason is not just that the World Wide Web site offers unusual plants, but also because Garden Escape created a personal store just for her. Greeted by name on her personal page each time she visits, Capozzi can make notes on a private on-line notepad, tinker with garden plans using the site's interactive design program, and get answers from the Garden Doctor. So far, Jeri has spent $600 in less than 12 months and has no plans to shop elsewhere. With service that personal, she says, 'I probably will never leave it'.[7]

■ Pekka Nurmisanta wanted to buy several hard-to-find books on marketing. Rather than search the bookshops of Brussels where he lives, he hit the Internet. Several mouse clicks landed him at Amazon.com.Inc., the online bookstore in Seattle. He ordered three titles, paid by credit card and the books arrived two weeks later.[8]

Case example question

5.1 What are the advantages of shopping on the Internet? Do you see any problems?

organizations such as capacity, utilization, inventory levels, queue lengths, the interface with customers and IT developments.

Although the way a company chooses to meet the technical specification of its products and services will impact the design of the process, operations managers must also ensure that the design decisions reflect market needs and the internal requirements of the organization for which it is responsible. At the same time, operations needs to be alert to incorporating IT and other development opportunities in order to help keep the business competitive and make it better at meeting customers' requirements.

Within the design process, operations managers have the key task of interfacing with technical specialists whose predominate perspective is typically that of technology rather than markets. As the operations' task is to use and manage technology to supply products and services, putting forward the business dimensions of these developments falls clearly and appropriately within the remit of operations. The danger is that technology is left with the experts and is not recognized as needing to be driven and embraced by business requirements – behind the humour in Exhibit 5.21 is a critical but often unrecognized truism.

At the core of this chapter has been the need for businesses to recognize the key differences that exist between products and services and this difference needs to be incorporated in the design of the process that provides them. At one extreme in services, customers are processed by the system and they are present throughout – healthcare, restaurants, hotels and passenger transport are classic of these. At the other end of the continuum, the process does not involve customer contact. In manufacturing, products are made and transported to customers while similarly in some service businesses such as mail order, distribution and repairs the process handles 'customer surrogates' in the form of information or customer's goods. Identifying where on the continuum a company is positioned (and it may be in more than one position as typically companies offer different products and services) is a key step in the process design and redevelopment.

Exhibit 5.21   *Technology is a business as well as a technical issue*

As markets evolve, however, many companies are deliberately expanding their positions in the product/service mix dimension in order to increase sales revenue and move into more profitable areas. Exhibit 5.22 provides examples of recent acquisitions by companies that increases the mix.

As the service element becomes increasingly significant for some companies or the source of change comes from IT developments, companies need to reassess what is involved and the process design to best meet these new and changing requirements. Yet another facet of change, developing and refining processes to better meet the needs of markets while also delivering the internal requirements of organizations, is a task that is central to the operations function's corporate contribution.

Exhibit 5.22   *Manufacturing companies move increasingly into the service dimension of their business to both sales and profits[9]*

Company	Prime business	Recent developments or acquisitions
Boeing (USA)	Aircraft maker	In 1999, set up a division to service aircraft
Ford Motor Company (USA)	Automobile maker	In 1999, purchased Kwik-Fit, a UK chain of tyres and exhaust fitters for £1bn
Körber (Germany)	Engineering	In 1999, purchased service companies totalling £169m
Svedala (Sweden)	Rock-crushing equipment maker	In 1998, 40 per cent of its £1.1bn sales and 80 per cent of its profits came from its after-sales services
Jungheinrich (Germany)	Lift truck maker	Virtually all its profits come from its after-sales maintenance contracts
ABB (Sweden)	Heavy equipment manufacturer	The service part of its business has grown from less than 10 to about 25 per cent of its $32bn sales

SUMMARY

This chapter and Chapter 4 are two halves of the same dimension. While the latter outlined the processes and delivery system alternatives from which companies can choose and explained how they differ and the business trade-offs that result, this chapter focuses on process design.

The initial part of the chapter re-emphasized points from earlier. One key issue in process design is that the complexity of a product or service will have a direct impact on the delivery system. This gives rise to

single-step *vis-à-vis* multi-step processes

In single-step processes, the product or service is completed in a single operation – for example a meal in a fast-food restaurant. Many products and services comprise, however, a multi-step process where the product, customer or information goes through more than one step to be completed.

The earlier part of the chapter, however, linked the five classic processes (project, jobbing, batch, line and continuous processing) to their different layouts as shown in Exhibit 5.3. Throughout this section, illustrations and diagrams help to explain the process design entailed and the key differences between alternatives.

There follows a section on hybrid processes that demonstrate why and how companies choose alternative delivery systems to those classic processes outlined earlier in the chapter. These comprised cells, linked batch, Nagare Production System and transfer lines.

The chapter then addresses some key points on service delivery system design, with an overview (Exhibit 5.12) as well as other particular examples.

The final section introduces the key area of e-commerce and links this to a more extensive coverage provided in Chapter 11 on supply chain management.

Discussion questions

1. Select a single-step and a multi-step process example from both a manufacturing and service organization. Explain how they work.

2. How are process choice and process design two halves of the same operations dimension? Illustrate your points with examples.

Discussion questions (cont'd)

3. Provide an outline layout for:
   - a supermarket
   - a high street post office.

   Describe what process layout is involved and explain how the process design works.

4. Why is work-in-progress an integral part of a batch process design?

5. For a service company of your choice explain:
   - the process design
   - how the company could reduce the work-in-progress queue within the system.

6. For a manufacturing company of your choice explain:
   - the process design
   - how the company could reduce the work-in-progress inventory.

7. Review the data provided in Exhibits 5.13 to 5.17. Why do the results seem to make sense?

Notes and references

1. NC refers to the operation of machine tools from numerical data stored on magnetic tape, computer storage or direct information. The development of machining centres results from the concepts of NC. In a machining centre, a range of operations is provided using a carousel with up to 150 tools or more (that is, embodied in the centre) from which the program will select as required, with some taking place simultaneously as required. Consequently, a machining centre is not only able to cope with a wide range of product requirements, it can also be scheduled to complete single products in any desired sequence.

2. If you compare the functional or process layout to the cellular layout in Exhibit 5.9 you will notice that additions to some process types have been made. This is because when similar processes or capabilities are brought together and managed as a single group utilization and reutilization will be facilitated, and this is what happens in process layouts. Process design in cells, on the other hand, moves away from the principle that underpins batch processes of grouping all similar processes together and one outcome is that process utilization levels fall. At one extreme, if a company has a single process or capability and moves from a process-based arrangement to (say) two cell-based arrangements that both require this capability then a company would have to buy another process or unit of capability to have a source of capacity in each cell. In other circumstances, the high utilization levels that go hand in hand with batch typically fall with cellular designs for similar reasons.

3. J Nilles's books include *Managing Telework*, (New York: John Wiley, 1998).

4. Nairn, G 'The future of work', *Financial Times Information Technology Review*, 8 Jan., 1997, p. X.

5. Brown, JM 'Call centres: keeping staff is a problem', *Financial Times Survey*, 21 May 1998, p. V.

6. *Business Week* Special Report, 'Now it's your Web', 5 Oct. 1998, pp. 68–76.

7. Adapted from *Business Week*, Oct. 1998, p. 68.

8. Adapted from Woodruff, D 'E-shop till you drop', *Business Week*, 9 Feb. 1998, p. 14.

9. These and other examples are highlighted in P Marsh's article, 'At your service', *Financial Times*, 12 May 1999, p. 24.

## part three

Managing and Controlling the Operations System

CHAPTER SIX

The content and planning of this book: an overview of what is involved, what has been addressed so far and what is covered in this chapter

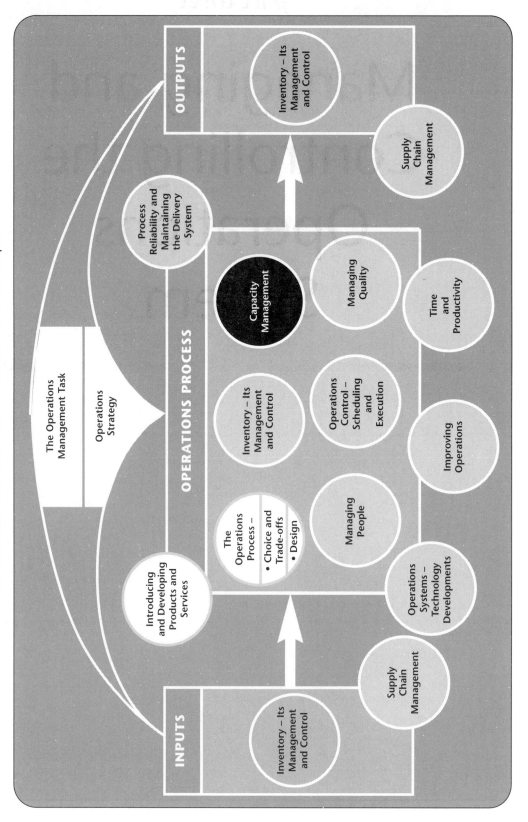

Capacity Management

Chapter overview

The overview diagram of the book (opposite) shows the central position of capacity management within the operations process. This chapter addresses this key topic and contains the following sections. You will see from these that it is intended to provide an understanding of how capacity is measured and what the statements of capacity look like before addressing the planning and management of capacity and the systems for doing this. The order of the principal sections is as follows:

- **Capacity** – measurement, definitions and expressions of output are discussed. In order to further help your understanding, examples from both the manufacturing and service sector are provided.

- **Defining capacity** – factors affecting the definition of capacity including make vs buy, product/service range, process design and the choice of process made to complete the task.

- **Determining how much capacity** – when determining capacity, both demand- and capacity-related issues need to be addressed.

- **Resource planning** – typically looking some two to five years ahead, this embraces general issues around aspects such as global capacity through to factors influencing the choice of region or country.

- **Location** – where to position new or to extend existing facilities is a key decision facing organizations.

- **Rough-cut planning** – typically concerns the one to two-year time frame and details the options available to achieve the plan.

Finally, this chapter addresses the important operations perspectives of capacity investment decisions that need to be considered by a business. By taking this orientation it is recognized that other aspects (outside the scope of this book) need to form part of these decisions. Notable among these is investment appraisal that covers the various ways in which the necessary financial assessment of a particular investment can be made.[1]

INTRODUCTION

When organizations develop their short- and long-term business objectives, one important consideration concerns the provision of appropriate capacity to meet current and future sales levels. In turn, these capacity decisions will need to relate both to process capability and volumes. (Note: the process choice issues that reflect order size and the nature of a company's markets were covered in Chapter 3.) The capability provision will vary depending on the nature and range of product and service designs. Similarly, a consideration of actual and forecast sales will underpin the size of the capacity requirements to be provided. However, the uncertainty of forecasts and the certainty of reality will continue to create situations of false starts, underutilization of capacity or an inability to cope with actual demand. Furthermore, capacity considerations in service industries and the perishable nature of service capacity create their own set of difficulties.

The costs incurred by investing forward when increased sales do not materialize and the lost sales involved in not being able to meet demand support both argument and counter-argument for alternative business strategies. The residues of past strategies have made their mark on all aspects of the operations function. Even successful strategies place substantial strain on organizations as they attempt to change direction. To be successful requires responses both at the strategic and tactical levels, and this calls for a high level of co-ordination to fit the parts together.

The initial steps in capacity investment will always command corporate attention. New markets, new customer contracts, new products and new services are high profile by nature while decisions concerning additional staff and new plant, equipment, buildings and site locations are characterized by investments of large size. As such, these prime tasks are approached with thoroughness and care due to the vetting and control exercised in corporate appraisal systems and the level of executive self-interest in making sound decisions that normally accompany such proposals.

However, it is equally essential that an analysis of the other important functions and tasks involved when capacity is changed are also linked into this rigorous approach, especially as the self-generated interest factor mentioned above will often not be as apparent.[2] But, too often organizations fail to appreciate the full impact of uplifts in capacity upon all parts of a business. This may be due to a failure to understand, overoptimism or 'turning a blind eye' as part of a desire to minimize the total investment involved so as to improve the financial attractiveness of the proposal under review. No matter what, the outcome is often an underprovision of much of what is required to make the initiative work successfully (for example, too little training, insufficient lead time before going live or too few support staff). In addition, when companies later, through necessity, rectify these omissions this underprovision will often prove to be more costly and time-consuming than it would have been had it formed an integral part of the original investment package. Moreover, these characteristics are found not only in growth scenarios but also in times of downsizing. Cutting staff without assessing the tasks that no longer need doing or failing to re-engineer current practices is typical in these situations.

CAPACITY – MEASUREMENT

There are two common denominators used in businesses to express, calculate and measure activities – time and money. In most parts of a business, money is the dimension used to express and evaluate activity – for example sales revenue and profit. In operations, the common denominator is time. Statements and measures of performance, for example regarding capacity and output, are calculated by using time as the base. So, all products and services will need to be measured in terms of the time taken to complete them. Checks can then be made, for instance, to assess how much capacity is needed and how well it has been used. The second aspect to be clarified concerns whether a firm should use staff or plant/equipment as the basis of these capacity statements particularly where both are used in providing the products and services to be sold. The base will differ depending upon the process chosen, as discussed in Chapter 4 (see especially Exhibit 4.14). The sections that follow explain the aspects around measuring capacity but, before addressing the principles involved, it will be useful to discuss capacity statements and measurements in general.

General issues

Statements and measurements of capacity will often differ within and between the various parts of an organization to reflect the issues and dimensions involved. Taking a hospital as an example, let us clarify what this means.

- **Overall size** – a hospital will typically use the number of beds it has as one indicator of overall size. This provides a useful statement about an important dimension of its capacity.

- **Emergency unit** – capacity in the emergency unit of the same hospital would relate to the expected levels of demand at different times through each day of a week. This would then be translated into the number and mix of staff (the ratio of doctors, nurses and support staff) required at different times of a week, month and year.

- **Consultant clinics** – based on the average length of appointments, a clinic would be arranged on a number of days each week or each month. Appointments would then be made in line with the scheduled capacity. The number of clinics would reflect known and future demand levels and this would be adjusted to reflect changes in demand over time.

In this way, expressions of capacity will differ, with each emphasizing the dimension that underlines the aspect of capacity being described. However, you will notice from the three examples above that the last two use a time base. Assessing how many emergency staff and how many clinics are required will use time as the means of calculating appropriate numbers.

Capacity – unit of measurements

The question posed earlier was whether the measurement of capacity should be based on staff or plant/equipment. The approach to be used will reflect the process involved, as follows:

- **Project and jobbing** – in these businesses, skilled staff provide the product or service, with plant and equipment helping them to complete the task. Here, staff hours would be the measure of capacity available and used.

- **Line and continuous processing** – with these processes, the plant/equipment makes the product and people support the plant/equipment in this task. Although the speed of a line process can, within certain limits, be adjusted to reflect demand and these adjustments will also require changes to staffing levels, the statement of capacity in these businesses will typically be based on the quantity the process is able to produce per hour.

■ **Batch** – high volume batch is more like line and so plant/equipment hours are typically the basis used for statements on capacity. Conversely, businesses more towards the low volume end of batch will use labour as the basis of capacity calculations. This is because in these situations people rather than plant will be the factor governing output.

So, the measure of capacity will reflect which input (people or plant) into the process is the one that is key in the provision of the products and services involved. Examples have been provided later to help you understand these differences.

Capacity – definitions

There are several definitions that surround the provision and use of capacity. Recognizing and recording these is a necessary first step to avoid confusion and to allow the expressions of 'how much' and 'how well' to be made with both understanding and insight.

■ **Planned (or available) capacity** – although theoretically operations could run or be open 24 hours each day throughout a year, in reality this is not normally required nor does it typically make sense. An exception to this are those companies using continuous processing where the costs involved of stopping and starting a process are so high that the process is run continuously (see Chapter 4). Planned (or available) capacity, therefore, is a statement of the intended, or planned, number of hours to be made available in a given period.

■ **Utilization** – this measures the actual number of hours staff worked, a plant was used or a department or firm was open compared with the planned hours.

■ **Efficiency** – this compares actual output to the level of output expected given the number of hours worked.

You will already detect from these definitions that there are some important nuances that need to be clarified. The next section also concerns definitions. After this, a simple example will be provided to illustrate these points and to highlight differences.

Capacity – expressions of output

The earlier section on units of measurement pointed to time as the common denominator used in operations. How much operations capacity is necessary will be assessed in relation to the size and type of expected demand and these dimensions are then translated into time as the way of comparing like with like. For example, a postal service concerns delivering letters. However, the time taken, for example, to deliver letters in the centre of a town, would be considerably shorter than to deliver them in rural districts. Using the number of letters posted would not reflect demand or capacity. The time taken would need to reflect the number delivered and the distances and other difficulties involved.

In some organizations, however, while time is the underlying means of assessment, discussions do not typically use time as the means of expression or the form of calculation for either output or performance. Where the products and services are similar (for example, vehicles produced in a car plant or meals served in a fast-food restaurant) or it is more meaningful to analyse a business in terms of the products and services involved, then units would be more appropriately used as the statement of capacity. For example, the capacity of an oil refinery would be expressed as the number of gallons or litres processed per day, the capacity of a car plant by the number of vehicles assembled per day, the capacity of a restaurant by the number of meals served at given times in a day and the capacity of a hairdresser by the number of appointments handled in a day. In turn these would form the basis for statements on capacity and calculations made on utilization and efficiency.

Capacity and output – examples

The examples that follow are provided to help you understand the issues raised earlier in the chapter. They are based on real examples although they have been simplified to help get across the key points.

Example 1 – Conform

Conform is a small manufacturing business. It has five machines. One is often fully used but the other four machines always have spare capacity. Conform's business is subcontract work for a number of customers whose work is typically completed on two or more of the machines. The manufacturing process is simple, with all products being completed as a single operation on one machine. Following machining, the products are packed before being designated to customers against schedules or in line with orders. Conform employs three operators who complete the necessary set-ups on machines and undertake all the machining operations. In addition there is one full-time and one part-time packer. The former is also responsible for despatch.

Planned operator capacity – from Monday to Friday the three machine operators each work daily a single shift of seven and a half hours:

$$\begin{aligned} \text{Planned capacity} \ &= \ \text{Normal working hours} \\ &= \ 3 \text{ operators} \times 7.5 \text{ hours} \times 5 \text{ days} \\ &= \ 112.5 \text{ hours} \end{aligned}$$

Operator utilization – week 1

In week 1, the company arranged on each of four days for one hour of overtime for each of two of the operators. The utilization of operators in this week is shown below. As you will see, it compares total hours against planned capacity. In this way, it signals to the company that the number of hours required is higher than planned and allows the company to monitor capacity and adjust accordingly.

$$\begin{aligned} \text{Operator utilization} \ &= \ \frac{\text{Actual hours worked}}{\text{Planned hours}} \times 100 \\ &= \ \frac{120.5}{112.5} \times 100 \\ &= \ 107 \text{ per cent} \end{aligned}$$

Exhibit 6.1   *The different levels of machine utilization at Conform*

	Week	
Machine	**1**	**2**
1	41.5 hours worked 37.5 hours available = 111 per cent	37.5 hours worked 37.5 hours available = 100 per cent
2	9.0 hours worked 37.5 hours available = 24 per cent	8.0 hours worked 37.5 hours available = 21 per cent
3	22.0 hours worked 37.5 hours available = 59 per cent	20.0 hours worked 37.5 hours available = 53 per cent
4	35.0 hours worked 37.5 hours available = 93 per cent	31.0 hours worked 37.5 hours available = 83 per cent
5	13.0 hours worked 37.5 hours available = 35 per cent	13.0 hours worked 37.5 hours available = 35 per cent
Total hours worked on the five machines	120.5	109.5

Notes

1. The above calculations use the number of hours available (that is, the hours when the firm was open and the machines were available to be used) as the denominator. However, you will also see that the company would not plan to run machines 2 to 5 all the time. Demand for products on these machines did not require all the available hours and so current manning levels reflected this. Thus, the figures calculated are intended to show the additional capacity available on machines 2 to 5 under the present working arrangements. The utilization figures also show that more people would need to be employed should demand increase. Similarly, the week 1 utilization of machine 1 is shown as 111 per cent. The rationale for showing this as an 'overutilization' position is the reverse of that for showing the 'underutilization' of machines 2 to 5. In week 1 the planned available time was 37.5 hours. But with overtime, machine 1 actually worked 41.5 hours. If over a period of time the utilization of machine 1 increased then the 'overutilization' figures would signal the need to consider buying a new machine, modifying, if possible, one of the machines 2 to 5 to do the same type of work as machine 1 or working an additional shift on that machine.
2. The hours worked includes productive time (when products were being machined) and non-productive time (when machines were being reset). The reason why both categories of work are taken into account when calculating utilization is that in neither instance would a machine be available to make another product. Set-up time is recognized as being an essential part of making a product and referred to as non-saleable productive hours as opposed to saleable productive hours when a machine is making products.
3. A glance at the above utilization figures shows the spare capacity available on machines 2 to 5 and highlights the lack of meaning which an average utilization figure for weeks 1 and 2 (in this instance 64 and 58 per cent respectively for all five machines and 53 and 46 per cent respectively for machines 2 to 5) would provide. An average would only have value where two or more of the machines could undertake the same type of work. Thus, if machines 3 and 5 were the same then averaging the utilization of these would be the relevant way of assessing availability. Signalling that in weeks 1 and 2 machines 3 and 5 had an average utilization of 47 and 44 per cent respectively provides a clearer statement of available capacity within current working arrangements than recording one as being 59 and 53 and the other 35 per cent utilized.
4. Here, the phrase 'hours available' is the same as 'planned capacity'.
5. Using operator and machine utilization figures gives a more complete picture of Conform's position.

Operator utilization – week 2

In week 2 no overtime was worked. In addition, there was a period of three hours without machining work for one operator. This operator (as was normal in these circumstances) was reassigned to packing. Utilization, therefore, was

$$\text{Machine operator utilization} = \frac{\text{Actual hours worked}}{\text{Planned hours of work}} = \frac{109.5}{112.5} = 97 \text{ per cent}$$

Machine utilization – Weeks 1 and 2

The company has five machines on which the three operators make a range of products. The hours worked on each machine vary. The calculations on machine utilization highlight these differences, as shown in Exhibit 6.1.

Efficiency – operators

Whereas utilization compares the number of hours worked with the number available or planned, efficiency (also known as effective performance) measures the amount of work produced in the hours worked and compares this figure with the amount expected (known as the standard). In a business where the products are the same (for example, an automotive company), then the calculation would be the number of cars produced in a day compared with the number expected. Where a company makes or provides several different products or services, comparisons are made by converting the latter into the hours of work they should have taken to complete and then comparing the total hours produced (that is, the number of units produced × the time per unit it should have taken to complete) with the total hours worked.

In our last example, the three operators on machining each worked 7.5 hours on day 1 of the week with two operators also each working one hour of overtime. If during this day they made the products listed in Exhibit 6.2, then their overall efficiency would be calculated as shown at the foot of the table (Normally, this calculation would be made for a whole week. Taking a single day keeps the example short yet still illustrates the principles and calculations involved.)

Exhibit 6.2   *Calculating efficiency for machine operators at Conform*

Product reference	# standard minutes to machine/complete	# produced products	minutes
1612	10.0	14	140
4725	5.5	8	44
3408	25.0	3	75
0184	18.5	6	111
1229	36.0	4	144
4120	4.5	10	45
3678	12.0	30	360
2185	27.5	6	165
2766	3.0	25	75
Set-ups	15.0	9	135
		Total – minutes	1294
		– hours	21.6

$$\text{Efficiency} = \frac{\text{\# hours of work produced}}{\text{\# hours worked}} = \frac{21.6}{24.5} = 88 \text{ per cent}$$

Notes

1. As two operators on day 1 of the week each worked one overtime hour then this made a total hours worked of 3 × 7.5 + 2.0 = 24.5 hours.
2. Set-ups or changeovers took 15 minutes. Work produced, therefore, included 1159 saleable productive and 135 non-saleable productive minutes as explained in Note 2, Exhibit 6.1. The issues around this are dealt with in more detail in Chapter 13.
3. Standard minutes (column 2 above) are explained more fully in Chapter 13 as are the issues and expectations around levels of efficiency.

Example 2 – John Michael

John Michael is a hairdresser in the centre of town. It has seven hairdressing chairs that are used at different times during a week in line with expected demand, as shown in Exhibit 6.3.

The working pattern illustrated reflects the mix of full-time (chairs 1 to 4) and part-time staff (chairs 5 to 7), while opening hours reflect expected demand levels each day.

Utilization – facilities

As the facilities are the same, calculating overall utilization is a more appropriate statement than calculating the utilization of each chair. However, as service provision needs to match demand levels during each day, then planned capacity will be at different levels to reflect this. For John Michael, whereas on Monday to Thursday the salon opened for 8 hours, on Friday and Saturday the planned capacity (that is, salon opening) was 10 hours. During a week the daily utilization calculations need to reflect this, as shown in Exhibit 6.4.

Utilization – hairdressers

The statement in *Utilization – facilities* (above) concerns the utilization of the seven chairs available. Similar calculations assessing the utilization of each hairdresser during each day would also be appropriate. In John Michael's case, the schedule for a

Exhibit 6.3   *Salon opening and hairdressing hours on each day of the week*

Day	# opening hours	# hours available/chair							Total hours
		1	2	3	4	5	6	7	
Mon	8	–	8	8	8	–	–	–	24
Tue	8	8	8	8	–	4	–	–	28
Wed	8	8	–	8	8	–	4	4	32
Thu	8	8	8	–	8	4	4	–	32
Fri	10	10	10	10	10	8	8	8	64
Sat	10	10	10	10	10	10	10	10	70

Exhibit 6.4   *Daily utilization levels at John Michael's salon*

Day	Utilization (%)
Mon	43
Tue	50
Wed	57
Thu	57
Fri	91
Sat	100

Note

Utilization on Monday $= \dfrac{\text{Hours used}}{\text{Hours available}} = \dfrac{24}{56} = 43$ per cent

Hours available = 7 chairs x 8 hours (the opening hours of the salon)

hairdresser was based on 15-minute booking slots with longer jobs being allocated more than one 15-minute slot. A simple check on the number of slots not filled during each day gave the owner an adequate statement on the utilization of each hairdresser.

Efficiency – hairdressers

The efficiency of the seven hairdressers may be calculated in two ways. The first would be based on standard times for each type of service – alternatives such as trim, restyling, shampoo and wash, highlighting and other forms of hair colouring would take different lengths of time. Calculations of efficiency would be similar to those completed in Exhibit 6.2.

A second method is available where businesses are not complicated and the services provided are similar to one another or will tend to average out over a given period. This uses a simpler, 'broad-brush' calculation such as the revenue generated by each hairdresser per hour worked. With prices reflecting, in part, the time involved and with each hairdresser undertaking a similar mix of work, then a 'revenue per hour worked' calculation would give a rule of thumb assessment of efficiency. It would be easy to calculate and yet provide a check on the efficiency required. In fact, the owner of the John Michael salon used this measure as follows, with net hours equalling attendance hours less non-booked time by clients:

$$\frac{\text{Revenue generated}}{\text{Net hours worked}} = \text{Revenue per hour worked}$$

FACTORS AFFECTING THE DEFINITION OF CAPACITY

So far we have looked at capacity decisions and definitions without introducing factors that affect their definition. This section now introduces some of the factors that need to be taken into account when defining capacity.

1. Make or buy decision[3]

Theoretically, every item, process or service currently purchased from an outside supplier is a candidate for in-house provision, and vice versa. In reality, however, the choice is not so extensive, as often buying from an outside supplier is the only option. Nevertheless when alternatives are available the decision to make or buy needs to be taken with due care. For the issues are not just about the level of capacity required – this fundamental decision needs to be considered at both the strategic and tactical levels. These issues include the following:

■ **Longer-term competitiveness needing operations support** – some organizations in the pursuit of short-term financial improvements decide to subcontract tasks traditionally completed within their own operations function. In some instances it makes sense, but there are issues to be checked before making such a change. For example, a decision to subcontract may be taken as a matter of expediency. Facing a difficult problem requiring managerial time and expertise to put right can often be the stimulus for subcontracting without undertaking essential checks on the long term impact. Similarly, some companies have painted themselves into the 'hollow corporation syndrome'[4] with the long-term consequences of an eroded operations base (both process and infrastructure) from which it will normally be more difficult to initiate change.[5]

■ **Delaying investment decisions by initially subcontracting** – process investment to meet the needs of new markets brings with it added uncertainty. One way of reducing the uncertainty is initially to subcontract operations until market demand is more clearly defined. A company making household products, for example, used subcontract capability in the early stages of the life cycle of a new product range until it was able to ascertain the volumes involved. When the picture became clearer and volumes more certain it could then choose from the following alternatives – allocate the new range to a part of its own manufacturing facility in keeping with forecast volumes, leave it with the existing supplier or switch the contract to another supplier, again based on volume fit. In this way it was able to reduce the investment risk and increase the fit between processes and requirements.

■ **Handling technology uplifts** – stepped changes in technology often result in an organization having to buy in that technology. Although initially there may not be an alternative, it is essential for organizations to consider future make or buy positions once the technologies are more available and internal provision becomes a option. Too often organizations do not reconsider these fundamental decisions when circumstances have changed.

■ **Tactical issues** – there are several tactical issues to be considered including:
  – internal technical/skill capability to meet product and service specifications
  – the position of each item in the process and its effect on lead times
  – the degree of dependence that a final product or service has on a subcontract item, process or service
  – availability of suppliers to meet the volumes and specifications involved
  – comparative costings need to incorporate checks that the internal data in making these decisions reflect true costs, the real impact on internal overhead cost structures with volume changes and likely future actions by suppliers
  – decisions to make in-house result in increased aggregate volumes and consequently contribute to overhead recovery and facilitate the balancing of demand and capacity over time
  – the protection of product, process and service ideas
  – avoiding subjective decisions concerning beliefs about internal capabilities and cost structure costings that have not been checked.

2. Product/service – range and specification

The role of operations is to provide the products and services a company sells. Determining the range, degree of change and extent of available options is, therefore, fundamental to establishing the capabilities and capacity required. Similarly, agreeing the specification of products and services within the range will involve like outcomes. The issues and details concerning product and service design have already been covered in Chapter 3.

3. Process design

Although the subject of the last chapter, aspects of process design have a major impact on the provision of capacity within the operations process. Some key issues are now discussed:

■ **Use of customers** – as mentioned earlier, because of the inherent producer/
consumer interaction within a service delivery system, the customer becomes a
potential source of capacity. The extent of that provision within different service
delivery systems is an important decision in terms of the overall source of capacity
provision, and this unique opportunity needs to form part of the process design.
The benefits of this involvement include:

– it cuts costs

– it helps to provide capacity at points in the delivery system where all or part of
the service is consumed. For example, in a self-service restaurant, the job of the
waiter is provided partly by the customer. In turn, this requires decisions on key
aspects such as the movement and flow of customers and the roles of both server
and customer in the system design

– some customers prefer to be able to make their own choices. For example, self-
service food shopping and salad bar provision in a restaurant are often preferred
by customers because of the increased control or choice being exercised by them.

Customers have proved willing to take part in the service delivery system if it can be
shown to be profitable, it is supportive of their needs, convenient or it enhances the
sociable nature of the total process. Examples include self-service facilities of all kinds,
direct telephone dialling, purchases by television, on-line shopping, investment
brokerage services, other financial services (including cash machines) and travel
arrangements.[6] The impact upon the provision and type of capacity is considerable.

Similarly, manufacturing companies need to recognize that what they sell invariably involves a service element (see Exhibit 1.6), and then determine a customer's
potential role within this element. For example, a small company offering specialized material finishing capabilities experienced difficulties in keeping pace with the
growth in demand. It recognized that one loss of capacity resulted from its earlier
decision to collect and deliver the items from/to customers. Not only was this time-
consuming in itself but it invariably involved delays at customers' premises. A
policy change requiring customers to deliver and collect enabled the company to
improve its delivery turnround, with this being a major aspect of the total service
and one that, for most customers, was an order-winner.

■ **The perishable nature of services** – service capacity is perishable. It cannot be put
into inventory for use or sale in a future time period. A major task thus concerns
adjusting capacity provision or influencing levels of demand in order to improve the
trade-offs involved in the effective use of capacity while meeting the varying levels of
customer demand. The alternative ways available are discussed later in the chapter.

■ **Back office versus front office** – within a service business, a distinction needs to
be made between the two basic parts of the process – the back office and front
office. A fundamental distinction between these two parts of the system concerns
customer interface. In the front office customers are present (for example, in person
or on the telephone) and the service system has to manage customers in the
delivery of the service. In the back office, customers are not present in the system
and the pressure to respond immediately is not there. Consequently, capacity
requirements, the opportunity to spread demand and the potential to use technology will differ from one part to another.

Back office – because activities in the back office are decoupled from the
customer, tasks can be delayed until cumulated volumes are sufficiently large to

secure the advantages of size or their completion better fits the overall schedule. This not only increases the opportunity to manage demand fluctuations more efficiently but cumulated volumes (often from more than one location) also justify investment in technology. Being able to cumulate volumes facilitates the use of the latter which not only improves productivity but also impacts capacity requirements.

Front office – this part of a process involves interfacing with customers and providing services to meet their requirements. Service provision and consumption are simultaneous. Capacity provision needs to meet demand not only in terms of the range of services provided but also to reflect the differing levels of demand during the day, week or longer time periods. When demand is greater than capacity customers either wait or go elsewhere. Getting the balance right between capacity levels and queue lengths is an important decision affecting a business and ways of handling these trade-offs are discussed later in this chapter.

■ **Ensuring adequate capacity at each stage of a system** – where products or services require a single operation to complete them then the task of determining the necessary capacity is relatively easy. Often however, to make a product or provide a service involves several steps and also differing amounts (due to the mix of volumes and longer time requirements to complete one operation compared to another) of time at each step. This makes determining how much capacity is required a more difficult task, as there are more stages and hence it is more complex. The importance of getting it right makes a significant impact on costs and customer support which, in turn, affects overall sales revenue and profit.

4. Choice of process and equipment

The need for operations managers to understand the technology of the process and equipment used in providing products and services varies, as shown earlier in Exhibit 4.17. However, understanding the business implications is essential no matter what

---

Case examples

1

A restaurant experiencing a high demand increased capacity in two ways. It added more tables in the existing dining areas and increased the speed of service in an attempt to improve throughput. Both provisions made a direct impact on the customers' experience. Although the quality of the food and wine remained the same, customers' perception of the service specification on offer changed. Bookings fell, and sales and profit declined.

2

Dell computers believe its place in the top five PC manufacturers, with sales in excess of £2bn, is in a large part, due to customer loyalty. More than 80 per cent of its custom is repeat business. Key to sustaining this is the company's strong field support for its customers when they use its PCs. Direct selling to customers instead of through dealers not only meant lower prices but also removed those personnel who traditionally supported a computer installation. To meet these needs Dell provides European sales and customer support through a telephone operation located close to Dublin. Highly trained, multi-lingual staff offer 24-hour, seven-day support for Dell users across Europe. Providing a hotline with continuous support is key for customers with computer problems and is considered to be an essential part of Dell's success.

market or process is involved. Several of these implications directly impact capacity and provision including:

- **Break-even analysis** – the throughput speed of equipment will have a direct bearing on the amount of capacity required. The two dimensions involved when choosing which equipment to use are set-up time (the length of time to prepare the equipment to process a product or service) and throughput speed (the time taken to actually process a product or service).

  The relationship between set-up time and process time helps us choose between options by using the break-even concept:

$$\text{Break-even} = \frac{\text{Additional setting-up time for a process}}{\text{Reduction in process time per unit or product/service}}$$

- **Flexibility** – the different dimensions of flexibility need to be recognized and reflected in capacity calculations. These include the ability to:

  - produce part or all of the current/anticipated range of products and services
  - respond to increases in demand on a timescale that cannot be met by the purchase of additional process capacity – the seasonal demand factor
  - meet delivery promises leading to a high level of both delivery speed and delivery reliability
  - cope with customer specification changes during the process.

- **Product/service definition** – the technical capability of the process can often have an impact on the definition of a product/service. For example, direct access within the travel industry by computers allows for part of the booking-in procedure to be completed ahead of time (for example, seat reservation) and affords the opportunity to pre-list customer options for parts of the service such as alternative menus and preferred seat allocations.

- **Skills and mix** – the introduction of technology into facets of the operations process will lead to changes in skill requirements and staff mix. This alters the capacity requirements and so needs to be part of the decision process.

ISSUES IN DETERMINING CAPACITY NEEDS

Plant/equipment capacity, once created, is usually an irreversible investment decision. Labour and staff capacity once created is an expensive decision to change. Growth and its associated decisions present a difficult and challenging task. Not only are all these dimensions difficult in themselves but they also involve the interrelated aspects of market position and competitors' decisions on the size and timing of their capacity changes.

The process is complex. Organizations are faced with several difficult decisions, such as:

- Anticipating the end of growth
- Avoiding overcapacity
- Choosing to plan ahead of growth or to plan to follow growth
- What action to take in a situation of overcapacity – divest or diversify?

Similar dilemmas are involved in downsizing. The timing and extent concern not only questions of cost but also the impact on sales and market share. And, in the same way as capacity investment, once made they are usually too difficult to reverse.

But this has to be managed and is an essential part of the operations role. Before considering these tasks, this section highlights some of the important issues involved.

1. Demand-related issues

An organization focuses its planning efforts towards meeting the requirements of its customers. To do this it needs to manage demand. This involves identifying the nature and size of demand and determining how it is best going to meet it. One characteristic of demand that further complicates this provision and makes managing it more difficult is that it is never the same twice over. Some of these variations are, however, more predictable than others, as explained below.

Predictable variations

Although demand levels will vary, very often there are characteristics of sales from which patterns can be identified and that enable fluctuations to become more predictable. For example:

■ **Seasonality** – the seasonal nature of many products and services is well recognised. Defined as variation that repeats itself at fixed intervals, seasonal patterns are caused by many factors including the weather (for example patterns in holidays and sales of air conditioners and ice cream) and time of the year (for example patterns in the demand for holiday bookings, air travel, types of clothing, gardening equipment, fireworks, training courses and tax processing).

■ **Peaks** – whereas seasonality of demand occurs over a yearly interval, predictable variations in demand also occur at shorter intervals. To distinguish the two, the latter patterns are normally known as peaks. As with seasonality of demand, these are caused by recurring factors that can be identified. For example, working hours affect traffic volumes; the day of the week will affect demand for example, the emergency unit in a hospital will be busier than usual late on a Saturday night; time of the day will affect the level of demand for sandwiches; and a firm's policies such as billing patterns and the push to meet sales targets will be reflected in the activity levels during a month.

Unpredictable variations

Other demand characteristics are less predictable but still need to be managed. For example, to protect against 'no shows', airlines overbook on flights. This policy is also adopted by hotel operators, particularly those in locations where the uncertainty of showing up or the frequency of late cancellations brings uncertainty in the pattern of demand and the resulting loss of revenue from having turned business away.

2. Capacity-related issues

As with demand, there are issues in the provision of capacity that increase the difficulty of this management task. Again, some of these are more predictable than others as explained below.

Predictable aspects of capacity

The demands placed on capacity will vary to reflect the mix of products and services and the sales levels involved. For this reason there are bottlenecks in the process where capacity is less than the demand placed on it. However, bottlenecks are medium- to long-term phenomena and so are predictable in terms of their position and extent. Knowing where they are is essential as this enables a business to manage capacity within this constraint, while directing attention and resources to increasing capacity in these parts of a process.

Unpredictable aspects of capacity

As with demand, some aspects of capacity are less predictable and these introduce problems of a more *ad hoc* nature:

■ **Absenteeism** – people stay away from work for a number of reasons. Estimates in the mid-1990s placed the direct and indirect costs for UK businesses as high as £16bn and absence rates on average were running at about 3.5 per cent.[7] In 1994, the average number of days' absence through sickness for the manufacturing and service sectors is given in Exhibit 6.5 with a high of 12.1 average days in government agencies.[8]

The short-term impact of this adds difficulty to the effective management of capacity. Ways of attempting to cope with this have centred on recognizing absenteeism as a management problem and attempting to reduce it to manageable levels. In the mid-1990s, Lewisham Borough Council in the Greater London area was affected by absentee levels averaging 17 days a year for each employee. Better monitoring helped bring this down to less than 11 days per year in just 24 months. Others argue that unpaid sick leave encourages employees to believe that no one loses when they are away. Paying for sickness, including the penalty of taking away this benefit for abuse of the system, is part of why Nissan believes it has achieved absence levels of less than 2 per cent at its plant in Washington in the north-east of England.

■ **Short-term demand changes** – short-term demand variations can often result in a temporary shortage of capacity with the difficulties this presents in managing demand, a point highlighted in a previous section.

Exhibit 6.5 *Average number of days sickness absence by sector in the UK during 1994*[9]

Full-time staff category	Sector		
	Manufacturing	Service	All
Manual	9.0	11.0	9.7
Non-manual	5.1	7.6	6.1
Total	7.3	8.4	7.8

Case example

PRET A MANGER

Lunch-time food for workers in major towns and cities is big business, but being able to find fresh and tasty sandwiches and other snacks was never easy, until the advent of Prêt à Manger.

The founders of the chain of sandwich shops recognized an unfilled need to provide high specification and freshly made food in a market where demand for good food was growing. Initially, targeting central London, Prêt à Manger (meaning ready to eat) has now been successfully launched in other major cities, for example Birmingham.

Prêt sandwiches and cakes are all made to a high specification and genuinely are ready to eat, ready wrapped and freshly made. Made at each location many lunchtime favourites do not appear on the outlet shelves until an hour or so before time. The fresh ingredients are kept properly chilled until they are ready to be used as sandwich fillings. Coffee is made from the finest Arabica beans that are freshly ground in line with each customer's request.

If a day's sandwiches do not sell they get loaded on to one of the Prêt trucks and are distributed to the homeless free of charge – last year this totalled over 14 000 left-over sandwiches.

Case example question

3.1 How do you think Prêt à Manger copes with the predictable and unpredictable aspects of demand and capacity when determining staffing levels at its outlets?

PLANNING AND MANAGING CAPACITY

The purpose of the first section of this chapter has been to introduce key definitions, provide an overall review of capacity and illustrate the purpose and outcomes of the task of its provision. The rest of the chapter concerns planning and managing capacity. It will address the longer-range tasks of resource planning and rough-cut planning with short-term operations control and scheduling being discussed in Chapter 8.

Capacity management is an essential responsibility of the operations function. The objective is to match the level of capacity to the level of demand both in terms of quantity (how much) and capability (the skill mix to meet the product/service specification). Simple though it sounds, meeting this basic requirement concerns issues of:

■ **uncertainty** – forecasting demand is inherently uncertain
■ **timescales** – the task concerns long-term capacity planning through to day-to-day scheduling
■ **alternatives** – choosing from the different ways of providing capacity to meet demand
■ **execution** – fulfilling the plan.

The optimum approach to planning and managing capacity is to separate the task into its major elements and to position these in terms of the time phases in which they need to occur. Exhibit 6.6 is a simplified schematic of these tasks showing their position in each phase of the planning and control system.[10] The level of planning

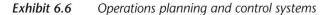

Exhibit 6.6   *Operations planning and control systems*

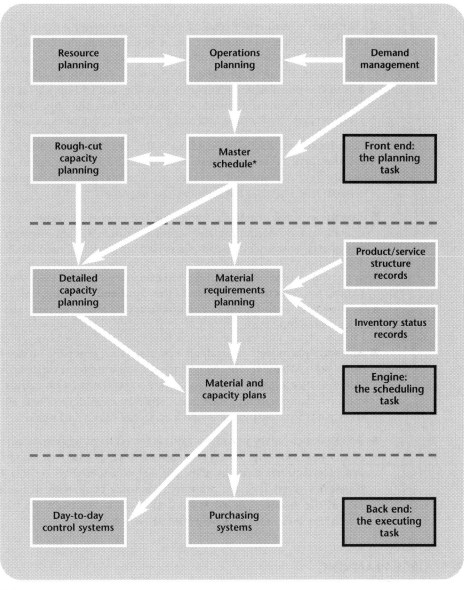

Note

* Referred to in manufacturing planning and control systems as the 'master production schedule' or MPS.

Source: Adapted from Vollman *et al., Manufacturing Planning and Control Systems,* 4th edn, Irwin/McGraw Hill (1997), p. 69.

and control detail involved will reflect the complexity of the products and services provided. As you will no doubt appreciate, managing a sandwich bar will be less complex that managing a large hotel, as would a small assembly shop compared with a large pharmaceutical plant making chemical formulations and a wide range of pack sizes and alternatives. In essence though the tasks are the same, as explained below:

- **Planning** – front-end planning provides key communication links between top management and operations. It helps form the basis for translating strategic objectives into operations plans and resources and is essential in determining what can be achieved, the investments and decisions to be made and the timescales involved. It is in this phase where companies look forward and decide on the 'game plan' for the future. How far forward will depend upon the investments and timescales involved and these will be discussed in detail in the next section.

- **Scheduling** – the scheduling phase is the 'engine' of the system. It involves determining capacity several weeks, months and sometimes up to one year ahead. It details how demand will be met from available facilities and ensures that the capacity and material requirements are in place.

- **Execution** – the 'back end' phase of the system concerns executing day-to-day operations by determining and monitoring material and capacity requirements to ensure that customer demand is met and resources are used efficiently.

Both the dimensions of scheduling and execution are fully discussed in Chapter 8.

Exhibit 6.6 depicts several facets of the 'front-end planning task'. All are considered to be long term with regard to the timescales involved. In turn, these can be further split on a time base into:

- **Resource planning** – a strategic business issue generally involves looking five or more years ahead. It aims to provide for the long-term capacity requirements and resource allocations to meet the future organizational objectives by planning for capacity changes in line with major shifts in existing products and services and to meet plans for new products, services, technologies and markets.

- **Rough-cut capacity planning (also referred to as aggregate planning)** – used to plan for periods one to two years ahead. It details how demand will be met from available facilities that, in principle, are considered to be at a fixed level. (The timescales given here are arbitrary. For some businesses (for example oil exploration) the resource planning horizon could be greater than five years while for others, the long-term horizon could be two or less.)

RESOURCE PLANNING

Anticipating future demand in terms of its size (associated volumes) and nature (the product/service mix) is an essential strategic decision. It needs to address three critical dimensions:

- **amount** – how much is required
- **timing** – when the capacity is needed
- **location** – where the capacity should be located.

What makes long-term capacity decisions difficult are the timescales involved and the fact that the above are not stand-alone questions. All three impinge on one another. For example, determining size is not just a question of total requirement but will need to address issues concerning units of capacity, their location and when they need to be available. Consequently, these elements of long-term operations planning need to be considered as an integrated whole and, in so doing, need to take into account many issues. Before addressing these let us outline the steps involved in resource planning. As Exhibit 6.6 shows, resource planning is the initiating step in capacity planning. It is the most highly aggregated and has the longest capacity planning horizon. It typically involves taking the two to five-year time frame and converting monthly and annual data from the operations plan into statements of aggregate resources such as total labour or staff hours, floor space and machine/equipment hours. This level of planning potentially involves new capital investments such as buildings, warehousing and equipment that often have lead times of months or years.

As Exhibit 6.6 indicates, the operations planning task takes demand and resource planning information that gives details of what is required and what is available and then highlights possible constraints in terms of lead times and levels of investment. These issues are large in size, complex in nature and concern the types of critical capacity issues listed earlier around amount, timing and location. These and other aspects that also need to be taken into account, and that in turn add to the complexity of these discussions, are now discussed.

1. General issues

Competition

As markets become more global and as countries increasingly build up their own national capability to make products and deliver services then recognizing and incorporating these trends into long-term plans become more essential. In a world where demand is not growing as quickly as supply, overcapacity results. The impact in traditional industries such as steel, shipbuilding and automobiles is well reported. But, the same is happening in newer industries and also in segments of the service sector. Since the late 1980s there has been overcapacity in the semiconductor industry. The passenger airline industry is in a similar position. In the mid-1990s, 92 per cent of airline passengers in the USA bought their tickets at a discount, paying on average just 35 per cent of the full fare.[11] Although in part due to the response to deregulation since the late 1970s, these characteristics largely reflect the overcapacity in the industry. Similar patterns have been emerging in Europe since the early 1990s. Setting future capacity levels, therefore, needs to recognize the potential actions of competitors and possible new entrants and the result these will have on overall capacity within a given market.

Developing countries

The need for developing countries to increase the size of their wealth-creating sectors is fundamental to their own longer-term national prosperity. The resulting demand by governments to build local facilities increasingly affects the factors of location, size and timing in the capacity decisions of internationally based companies.

Technology

Changes in product/service, process and other technologies not only impact directly on levels of demand and capacity but also offer the opportunity to reposition capacity.

The development of information technology is allowing companies to reposition the workplace of individual people (for example home versus office) and also to provide a fuller support service. For example, the support unit answering a customer query can be located anywhere in the world to reflect issues of cost and time of the day. Lower-cost countries in Europe (for example Eire) are increasingly being used as support unit locations. Similarly, as offices close for the day in Europe, calls are initially transferred to the east coast of the USA and then progressively westwards to be handled by staff working during their normal hours.

Similarly, being able to send data via satellite has enabled information-based service companies to relocate relevant processing capacity to anywhere in the world. News-papers are often composed in one location but printed in two or more locations close to their respective markets. The gains are not only the reduction in transport costs but also the speed of transfer that enables printing to be delayed until the very last moment. Similarly, companies involved in data processing are beaming the tasks to lower-cost centres in countries such as India and South Africa without incurring the long lead times that previously would have made such decisions infeasible.

A final example is healthcare. In most developed countries the post-Second World War period saw a growth in hospitals that reflected the impact of the baby boom and people's expectations about health provision. Government-owned facilities were the largest healthcare provider and subsidies continued to be found to support existing capacity. Since the mid-1980s, dramatic improvements in medical technology and procedures have made hospital visits less necessary and the length of in-hospital stays shorter. The result has been a lower demand for hospital beds and an overall reduction of hospital facilities has followed.

2. Amount of capacity

Deciding on the amount of capacity needs to incorporate forecasts of demand, make versus buy decisions and how much capacity a company intends to hold in relation to anticipated demand. The factors involved in these complex decisions are now discussed:

Forecasting demand for products and services

One prerequisite for capacity planning is a statement of demand. Organizations need to forecast demand in order to anticipate future capacity requirements as well as the other resources in a business (for example buildings and facilities). But demand fore-casting is difficult. No matter which method is used, it will not (by definition) be accu-rate. But despite this inaccuracy, it is essential to forecast demand, for the alternative is to have no forecast at all. Next, it is necessary to recognize the capacity planning horizon of different businesses. These will differ depending upon lead times. Where capacity is in the form of labour and staff (for example in a business using a jobbing process and in most service businesses), the relevant time horizon will normally be shorter than where investment in plant and equipment is involved. Manufacturing examples illustrating the dimension of long lead times come readily to mind – for instance, new vehicle assembly and petrochemical plants. Also, service industries with a similar dependency on equipment will experience long lead times – for example, most elements of the transport industry.

Thus forecasting demand for products/services is critical in planning capacity. Without the international scheduled passenger projections illustrated in Exhibit 6.7, for instance, plans for aircraft production and purchase would probably not be anywhere near the actual requirement for this decade.

There are many books explaining the options for demand forecasting. It is not intended to cover these here, but for those who wish to study them a list of suitable material is given at the end of this chapter.[12]

While demand forecasts are often completed elsewhere in a business, it is necessary for those involved in capacity planning to understand the forecasting procedures used, the assumptions made and the implications for the operations function. To help appreciate these issues, some of the features involved are now described. To help in this explanation, what follows is a short review of the dimensions to be taken into account when planning capacity within the air travel industry as a way of illustrating the general issues and perspectives that may be involved. It is not, of course, intended to be comprehensive, merely illustrative.

The level of growth depicted in Exhibit 6.7 is significant. Couple this with aircraft replacement requirements in terms of investment costs, lead times and known aircraft developments (for example Boeing and European Airbus products) then the time frames are uncertain yet crucial. Put this within a framework of airline profitability trends on international scheduled services as given in Exhibit 6.8 and you will see that the need not only to plan capacity but also to be accurate in terms of amount and timing is critical to a company's overall financial success.

Within this scenario there are also current trends to be assessed in terms of the impact of deregulation on increased competition, customers who will become more

Exhibit 6.7   *Air traffic growth – total international scheduled passengers (1970–2010)*

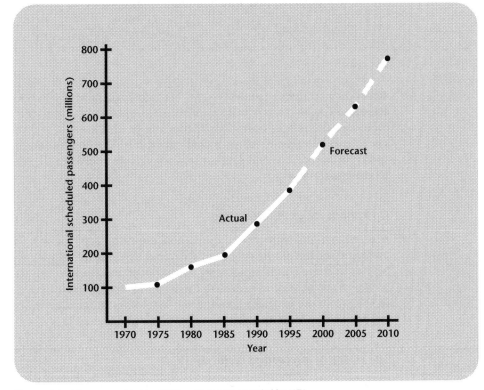

Sources: Actual figures provided by ICAO and forecasts provided by IATA.

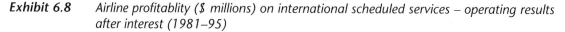

Exhibit 6.8 *Airline profitablity ($ millions) on international scheduled services – operating results after interest (1981–95)*

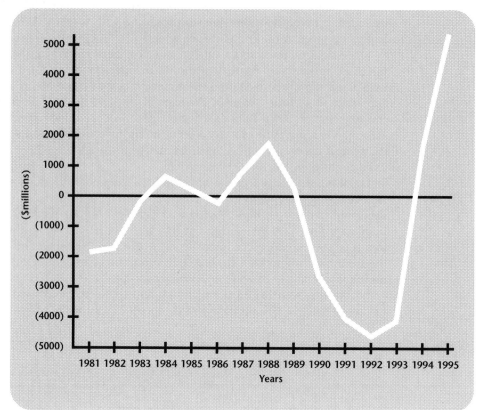

Source: IATA.

demanding (through familiarity and being offered greater choice) and the need to achieve adequate returns on investment. The impact upon capacity forecasts and provision, and the role of operations within the process are and will remain significant. The long-term capacity issues, including airports (size and location), aircraft (number and type), operations and support services, are significant in themselves and in their fundamental nature.

Operations issues in forecasting

A key operations issue in forecasting concerns accuracy. The more general the statement and the longer the time period covered by the forecast, the more accurate it will be. But, at some point, projections have to be translated into the actual products and services to be made and provided. Establishing assumptions, forcing clarification and moving from the general to the specific in terms of mix, volumes and other key operational differences is an essential operations management task.

The choice of forecasting method

The inherent difficulties of forecasting have led to many forecasting models being developed in the past 50 years. And, as would be expected, different models are based on different sets of assumptions. Understanding these assumptions, particularly those that may have an impact on operations, is an essential first step. Key factors to clarify so as to better understand forecast outcomes and to signal aspects that need to be revisited at appropriate times within the long-term planning process include the following:

■ The accuracy level of predictions sought and achieved and the trade-offs involved.

■ The extent to which a model assumes that past behavioural patterns and relationships will continue in the future. A continuous check on presumed levels of stability between the past and future has to be embodied in the forecasting procedure in order to evaluate this feature of a model.

■ Establishing the appropriate forecasting horizon that reflects the capacity lead time currently experienced.

■ The need to establish a match between the selected forecasting model and the data patterns that are present in a particular business. The most common patterns are described as being constant, trend, seasonal and cyclical. A business needs to ascertain its own data patterns to ensure that the model chosen reflects them appropriately.

3. Make versus buy

The question of determining the make versus buy policy has already been signalled as a key step in the process of determining capacity. The issues and dimensions involved have been highlighted elsewhere (Chapter 11) and this section serves solely to restate its fundamental role in these decisions.

4. Size of operations units

How large to build an operations unit is bound up with many issues and is made for a variety of reasons. The principal factors include:

■ **Scale** – there are conflicting views concerning scale – the size of operations units. The economies of scale argument is based on the premise that large units yield lower costs as fixed costs are spread over more products or services. In some sectors (for example petrochemical plants) there is a minimum size below which it is difficult to justify the necessary process investment. Scale economies are truly present in these situations. Whereas some companies follow the economies of scale principle, others limit the size of units in order to avoid what they consider to be the disadvantages of large scale, including remoteness, poor motivational climate for staff, increased complexity and the difficulties of managing a larger organization. For these reasons, some businesses put an upper limit on size after which a new unit would be built.

An example of where large scale does not appear to be working is provided by the Tandy Corporation's Incredible Universe Super Store chain in the USA. These glitzy emporiums, the size of two (American) football fields, seem to have gone too far. The average location offers 85 000 products in an area of 185 000 square feet. The outcome is that to break even it needs to generate an estimated $70m sales per year and this seems to be proving difficult to achieve and has resulted in losses of over $60m in the five years to 1996 and a forecast loss in 1997 of over $10m.[13]

■ **Catchment area** – in some industries and particularly in the service sector, units are built to serve a certain catchment area. Demand outside this area will be met by building another facility. Examples include retail chains, banks and restaurants.

■ **Distribution costs** – products have different distribution cost-to-item-value ratios. Those companies where distribution costs are high in relation to the product value will tend to build more plants than where the ratio is low.

■ **Innovation levels** – many companies wish to encourage innovation and tend to operate smaller units in order to avoid the bureaucracy and centralized control that usually militate against innovative behaviour.

5. Timing of capacity

As levels of demand change over time, when to increase or decrease capacity is a key business issue for both long-term (five or more years ahead) and medium-term (up to two years ahead) planning horizons. This section deals with the former; the medium-term responses to this and other relevant aspects of capacity will be discussed later in the section entitled 'Rough-cut planning'.

Businesses need to choose the amount of capacity to be provided in relation to demand forecasts. Based on assumptions of average demand an organization can choose to provide adequate capacity to meet peaks, to meet average demand patterns or to maximize its utilization of capacity. Which one to choose will need to reflect the requirements of, and chosen responses in, the different markets in which it competes.

The essential question though on timing is whether to lead or follow anticipated demand. How the alternatives work in practice are described as follows:

■ **Proactive strategy** – concerns building capacity in advance of forecast levels of demand. In this way an organization maintains a positive capacity cushion by aiming always to have capacity in excess of demand. Depending upon the nature of demand increases (incremental through to stepped as explained in Exhibit 4.14), a company seeks to keep a positive capacity cushion while limiting the size of the excesses at any time.

Certain industries always adopt a proactive strategy regarding capacity provision by planning to ensure that customers' demands can always be met. Utility companies such as gas and electricity aim for this level of provision. Hospital emergency units have similar objectives. In the case of the former, long-term decisions on capacity are essential given the timescales involved. Examples where a sector's failure to plan sufficiently far ahead in order to ensure that demand levels are met include water utilities in several Western countries. Increasing demand, changing weather patterns and the long timescales in provision have led to a growing shortage of water at certain times of each year.

■ **Reactive strategy** – concerns building capacity to follow demand. This results in a negative capacity cushion where there is insufficient capacity to meet demand. As the gap grows, investments in additional capacity are made with companies seeking to manage the gap in line with their strategy decisions on capacity and demand. Many of the medium-term ways of coping with this will be dealt with later in the section on 'Rough-cut planning'.

For many companies, the preferred approach is to allow demand to grow and then invest in capacity in line with known demand. The reason is to reduce risk.

Follower strategies are less risky and many companies prefer to manage the problems of excess demand rather than to create a position of building excess capacity and the exposure that such strategies embody.

■ **Combination strategy** – as the phrase suggests, this strategy is a mixed approach. Initially, capacity is allowed to move into a negative cushion position. Then capacity investments are made that match, or more often exceed, current demand levels and so create a positive capacity cushion. Demand continues to grow and the cycle is repeated.

■ **Strategic positioning** – the decision when to build capacity may be driven by considerations of strategic positioning. Developments within the European Union (EU), for example, triggered decisions by many international companies to build manufacturing facilities or take over existing businesses in order to meet the EU criteria on imported goods. The growth in Japanese investments in Europe provides an example of this.

Similarly, the decision to 'be in on the ground floor' has led to organizations entering countries and regions with high growth economies. For example, the investment bank Morgan Stanley (and Morgan Stanley is not alone – Merill Lynch, Goldman Sachs and J P Morgan are all investing heavily) made growth in Asia its top priority in the 1990s. The number of its employees in this region outside Japan soared from 90 to 540 between 1990 and 1995, with staff costs alone of $200m.

What drives the timing of these capacity decisions is primarily gaining position and helping to influence and shape developments rather than short-term profit – in the same period Morgan Stanley's return on equity fell from a 24 per cent high in 1993 to less than 9 per cent a year later. While 1995 saw a recovery to about 15 per cent this was still lower than for the late 1980s. Going first is always perceived as being risky unless it clearly pays off. The title of *Business Week*'s 1996 review of these decisions says it all in the title 'Global gamble: Morgan Stanley is charging into the Third World. Will it get burned?'[14]

6. Location

Where to position new or develop existing facilities is a key decision facing organizations. For companies involved in worldwide markets, the positioning of facilities concerns regional and country-level decisions as well as the more local concerns of where to locate within a given region. This section addresses the location issues at the regional/country level, while the more detailed decision of choosing the actual location is discussed later.

General issues

Although the choice of where best to locate should, as with other management decisions, be set against objective criteria, the constraints of reality often limit available options. Two classic examples of this concern the historical origins of existing sites and the growing political pressure from governments throughout the world.

■ **The origins of existing locations** – many organizations are where they are due to decisions made in the past and where the cost of changing to a more suitable location cannot be justified. Reasons that may have led to choosing locations are often no longer valid at a later time. Being close to a founder's residence or near to the source of materials or customers for the original prime business are typical of the historical decisions that have underpinned past choices of where best to locate at that time. As organizations grow and the investment to meet that expansion also grows then the cost to relocate compared with extending an existing site can often become prohibitive.

■ **Politically based constraints** – as highlighted earlier, countries wish to develop their own industrial and service sectors in order to create the wealth essential for national prosperity. One step being increasingly taken by governments is to require multinational companies (MNCs) to build facilities within their own country so as to reduce imports and create value-adding activities. Joint ventures are an increasingly common way of meeting these requirements. Such arrangements dictate the location and often size of facilities as MNCs seek to increase global presence.

These pressures do not only relate to developing nations. Marked balance of payment deficits are also resulting in governments putting pressure on foreign competitors to locate facilities locally. For example, this is one of the reasons why Japanese car makers have located plants in the USA and are continuing to increase the capacity of these over time.

Whereas the last section highlighted potential constraints, other developments and changes have brought fresh options to the list of alternative locations:

■ **Technology developments are changing the levels of freedom on where to locate** – technology is not specific to a location, and in that way, is redefining the role of geography in businesses. While physical proximity to aspects such as the marketplace or raw material source will invariably remain an important factor, the age of high technology and electronic communications means that it may no longer be essential. The speed and opportunities that these technologies are providing have already changed the pattern of locations in several industries – see the examples given earlier in this chapter.

■ **New countries are opening up** – areas of the world that for decades have been closed to investments due to factors such as political dogma or social/economic instability have now opened up. Notable examples of these in the 1990s were China and Eastern Europe. Factors such as nearness to new markets, low labour costs and the opportunity for companies to take over existing, often not well-managed, facilities have driven recent location decisions.

The final set of general issues have economic origins. Although, in part, these could be listed under the next section detailing specific issues, the examples given here are considered to be more general in nature:

■ **Market access–local presence in large consumer markets** – there is no more clearcut example of how large markets are attractive locations for businesses than the recent and continuing investments in North America and Europe. The reason primarily concerns market access. The USA is a very large market in its own right. The North America Free Trade Agreement (NAFTA) has swelled the consumer base by over 40 per cent to 360 million consumers. Becoming direct participants in this highly competitive and highly innovative market is one of the reasons that led Honda and Toyota to build plants and establish joint venture agreements in the

1980s and continue to expand these facilities through the 1990s. This was also part of the rationale for BMW and Mercedes-Benz building their first manufacturing plants outside Germany and locating them in South Carolina and Alabama respectively. Similar patterns are also present in Europe where the total market continues to grow as EU membership increases. One outcome reflecting the growing importance of this combined market is the level of foreign direct investment within Europe. Since the mid-1990s this has been more than 40 per cent of the world total.

■ **Currency value fluctuations** – as the relative values of currencies change, the impact on costs may force a company to rethink the location of its manufacturing plants particularly those serving local markets. The most marked example of this is Japan. In order to enable it to remain competitive, particularly in export markets, a whole range of Japanese companies have moved the location of their manufacturing plants to the regions in which they export. The motor industry examples above were also influenced by this factor. Other examples include electronics and consumer products companies.

Specific issues

Choosing the region or country in which to locate is also influenced by a range of decisions concerning cost and practicality. Typical examples of these are now discussed:

■ **Workforce availability** – in a 1996 survey of the factors cited by senior executives as important location determinants, over 70 per cent chose workforce availability as the most important single issue. Concerns about the skill levels and flexibility of the workforce are at the forefront of choice given the long-term dimensions inherent in location decisions.

■ **Cost structures** remain a critical issue in location decisions and concern the several dimensions that make up total costs:

   – **labour costs** – locating in lower labour cost areas of the world such as Mexico, Eastern Europe and parts of the Asia Pacific region is often fundamental in the decision process. Very often these decisions concern less skilled staff but the developments in IT and communications discussed earlier have extended this location alternative to higher skilled people

   – **energy costs** – where energy costs of processing are high, companies may often choose to locate near to a less expensive source of power such as hydroelectricity

   – **transportation costs** – concern the aspects of both raw materials and the distribution of finished goods. The costs involved not only include the actual costs of haulage but also excise duties and tariffs that may vary depending on the country of origin

   – **hospitable business climate** – the long-term nature of location decisions places the business climate high on the agenda. The combination of an environment of free trade, free thought and the opportunity to create wealth are key factors in attracting investors. For this reason, Europe and North America attract a high percentage of global foreign investment

   – **quality of life for employees** – factors concerning schools, accommodation and social infrastructure have an impact on the quality of life for employees, particularly expatriates. As concerns about and recognition of the family dimension of executives' lives have grown, this factor has become increasingly important

– **support services** – the availability of appropriate services within the context of general business support is an increasingly important factor in location decisions. For example, the growing base of technology and the particular role of IT are placing greater emphasis on the requirement for local support to meet the short lead-time needs of companies. Similarly, well-developed transportation and other aspects of infrastructure are high on the list of requirements for companies when they choose where to locate at the country and regional level

– **availability of suitable land** – an important constraint on relocation activity in certain areas of the world is the availability of suitable land. In densely populated regions such as Europe, the failure of some governments to identify and account for this factor has curtailed opportunities and hence attracted less relocation investments. While Eire, France and the Netherlands, for example, can supply land to suit most requirements, Denmark, Greece and Italy are seen to be short of suitable relocation sites and consequently are not considered attractive areas

– **barriers and licences** – individual countries and trading blocs may impose restrictions in the form of quotas or increased tariff levels for different importers. To overcome or circumvent such restrictions often leads MNCs in particular to choose locations that reduce or even eliminate such disadvantages.

7. Support guarantees

Developments in IT and appropriate applications in processing data have increased the level of dependence on processing technology to the point where support guarantees in terms of back-up IT provision are a part of both internal and external customer requirements. Data processing and printing centres, for example, are faced with the need to be able to supply guarantees of client support in circumstances where loss of capacity due, for example, to fire would otherwise lead to having no production capability. To avoid providing additional, off-site capacity for this purpose with its attendant high investment and low return outcomes, companies agree reciprocal deals with other companies (often competitors) having similar facilities. By 'spread agreements' involving as many as three or four other companies, major catastrophes can be overcome while keeping underutilized investment to a minimum.

ROUGH-CUT CAPACITY PLANNING

Rough-cut capacity planning (also referred to as aggregate planning) for periods of between one and two years[15] ahead is used within the overall framework of the long-term plan. It consists of establishing feasible medium-term plans to meet agreed output levels in situations where capacity is considered to be relatively fixed. As the name 'rough-cut' implies, this step in the planning process is designed to look ahead and resolve, in broad terms, the approach to follow to best provide sufficient capacity to meet forecast levels of demand and reflect the needs of customers. It examines the effects of the proposed master schedule (see Exhibit 6.6) on key areas of capacity (for example skilled staff categories, departments and equipment), to assess any capacity changes that would need to be made, how feasible those would be to accomplish and the stages that need to be taken to meet the timescales involved. It also incorporates decisions about ways of managing demand and capacity in order to help in this essential task. It does this by adjusting demand and capacity variables within the control of the organization in order to help fine-tune the capacity plan. Alternative approaches are discussed in some detail later in this chapter.

As shown in Exhibit 6.6, the master schedule (referred to in manufacturing planning and control systems language as the master production schedule or MPS) takes statements of demand (both forecast sales and known orders) and translates them into operations requirements. The rough-cut capacity plan takes these requirements and checks them against the capacity available from existing known resources. This activity sets the overall planned level of output from period to period.

Although small adjustments to sales patterns can be accommodated from one sales period to another, it is necessary to develop rough-cut capacity plans in order to cope with an overloading or underloading of facilities in the longer term. In this way, an orderly and systematic adjustment of capacity can be made to meet any significant changes in aggregate demand and sales mix while facilitating the achievement of delivery commitments to customers and internal operating efficiency targets.

As sales orders are received, detailed schedules of the products and services to be provided are developed and the plans adjusted upwards or downwards to accommodate the actual as against forecast sales position. It is at this stage that the short-term operations control activities of scheduling and execution (see Exhibit 6.6) take over. Thus, rough-cut planning helps to control medium-term changes while allowing the short-term, fine-tuning of the system to remain within manageable proportions.

Steps in rough-cut capacity planning

Earlier in the chapter an explanation of the steps involved in resource planning and rough-cut capacity planning was provided. This section gives a more detailed explanation of what is involved, with the final section providing details of some of the ways in which the plan is achieved.

1. **Develop the master schedule**. Sales forecasts and known orders for each product or service within each time period are translated into statements of what operations needs to provide. Initial forecasts will be adjusted by the known trends in actual sales, hereby hardening the information on future requirements.

2. **Make-or-buy decision**. The make-or-buy decisions based on both the strategic and tactical perspectives will be under review. Changes in these decisions must be measured in capacity terms, initially through the rough-cut capacity plans, and where major shifts occur, against resource plans.

3. **Select common measures of aggregate demand**. The next step is to aggregate demand for all products and services into statements of common or like capacity groups. For single product/service organizations this is often not difficult. For the brewer it could be gallons of beer; the doctor, patient visits; a coal mine, tonnes of coal. For multi-product or service organizations great care has to be used in arriving at appropriate measures.

4. **Develop rough-cut capacity plans**. Rough-cut capacity plans need to be developed to achieve agreed corporate goals. Primary objectives include meeting demand at lowest cost and supporting other relevant order-winners and qualifiers. It is also

essential to agree secondary objectives such as providing continuity of employment as they form part of the basis on which these decisions may have to be made.

5. **Select the planning horizon**. For each business, it is necessary to select an appropriate planning horizon for the rough-cut capacity plan. While this will cover several time periods, the plans will typically be considered on a month-by-month basis due to the interrelated nature of the operations decisions that need to be made from one month to the next. Decisions made in one time period will often limit the decisions that can be made in the next. In addition, many operations decisions are, in effect, part of a composite set of decisions that need to form a consistent whole. Decisions that ignore future consequences will often prove costly.

6. **Achieving the rough-cut capacity plan**. This step involves choosing between a range of options to best achieve the plan. These concern taking steps to adjust demand patterns and ways of providing appropriate capacity. The next section discusses these in detail.

7. **Select the rough-cut capacity plan**. The final step is to select the most suitable rough-cut capacity plan to meet the corporate objectives determined earlier in the procedure.

Achieving the rough-cut capacity plan

The pattern of demand for products and services will vary over time and within a given period. Capacity to meet these variations will need to be provided as part of the rough-cut plan in order to reflect the timescales involved and the implications of the available options for a business. As explained in step 6 of the rough-cut capacity planning procedure, the alternative ways to achieve the plan are now discussed in some detail.

However, before outlining the alternatives it will be helpful to discuss the inherent nature of the problem that underlies this task – that is, the nature of demand and capacity are markedly different. The rate and product/service mix uncertainties of demand are in stark contrast to the relatively fixed nature of capacity. It is, therefore, not possible to make products or provide services in one time period that exactly match the pattern of demand in the same period without using some combination of inventory, order backlog/queues or underused capacity. Often, companies choose a combination of options that may, in turn, be different in different time periods.

Before reviewing these options in detail let us explain how the basic options work. Firstly, there are two prime ways of adjusting the imbalance that occurs between demand and capacity. One is to allow the length of the order backlog/forward load to increase or decrease as demand fluctuates. The other is to allow the level of inventory to similarly adjust to the changing patterns of demand.

These alternatives are depicted in Exhibits 6.9 and 6.10 respectively with 6.11 illustrating a combination of the two approaches.

The second basic issue concerns which capacity plan a business decides to adopt. The alternative approaches are:

- level capacity
- chase demand
- mixed plan

and these are now described.

Exhibit 6.9   *Order backlog/forward load as a mechanism for handling demand/capacity differences*

Demand/capacity differences held
in order backlog/forward load

Companies working on a make-to-order basis will use the length of their order backlogs/forward loads as a mechanism for coping with variable demand patterns. If demand continues to grow and hence the order backlog/forward load increases then raising capacity will need to be considered in terms of lengthening lead times and customer requirements.

Companies using this approach will normally be handling special and low volume, standard products and services. However, some high volume businesses (for example Western car companies) also manage demand/capacity in this way.

Exhibit 6.10   *Finished goods and work-in-progress inventory as a mechanism for handling demand/capacity differences*

Demand/capacity differences met
by work-in-progress inventory

Demand/capacity differences met
by finished goods inventory

Companies working on a make-to-stock or assemble-to-order basis will use finished goods or work-in-progress inventory levels respectively as a mechanism for coping with variable demand patterns.

Companies using this approach will be those handling higher volume products and services where future demand is more predictable and products are made in anticipation of customer sales. In service companies, decisions to make ahead of demand will invariably concern the product content of the sale, for example publishers printing books and restaurants part-preparing menu items.

Exhibit 6.11   *The use of both order backlog/forward load and finished goods inventory for handling demand/capacity differences*

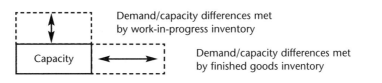

Demand/capacity
differences held,
in part, in order
backlog/forward load

Demand/capacity
differences met,
in part, by finished
goods inventory

Companies making standard products can also use a mixed approach to handle demand/capacity differences. In the illustration above, the company allows order backlog to grow to the equivalent of four weeks of sales (position 1). At this point a production order equivalent to 12 weeks of sales is initiated. During the process lead time, two further weeks of order backlog/forward load accumulate (position 2). When the order quantity is completed in production, the six weeks of backlog orders are met and the balance creates finished goods inventory to meet future sales (position 3).

Companies using this approach will be typically those making low/medium volume standard products.

Level capacity plans

In a level capacity plan, operations capacity is set at the same level throughout the planning period, irrespective of the pattern of forecast demand. In this way, companies uncouple capacity and demand rates. In make-to-stock situations, this allows throughout levels to be smoothed by transferring capacity available in low demand periods to higher demand periods in the form of work-in-progress and finished goods inventory. This smoothing is used by companies to create stability in their capacity requirements with several attendant benefits, especially regarding people's continuity of employment. Exhibit 6.12 provides an illustration of this for a 12-month rough-cut planning period. This principle was earlier illustrated in Exhibit 6.10, with Exhibit 6.9 offering an alternative approach to reducing inventory levels by using order backlog/forward load as part of the overall mechanism for handling the capacity/demand differences experienced by companies.

In make-to-order situations, the level of order back-log/forward load is the adjusting mechanism to enable capacity levels to remain level (see Exhibit 6.9).

Chase demand capacity plans

The opposite of a level capacity plan is one designed to adjust capacity in line with anticipated changes in levels of demand. Known as a chase demand capacity plan, this involves changing capacity levels from one period to another by adjusting some combination of staff numbers, working hours and available equipment. As you can imagine, this approach is more difficult to manage than a level capacity plan due to the increased complexity of the task. Changing variables, ensuring availability, training and retaining staff and the potential impact on quality conformance, are some of the dimensions involved.

Whereas manufacturing companies making standard products can take advantage of a level or mixed plan (see the next section below), service organizations and busi-

Exhibit 6.12   *A level capacity plan and its effect on capacity and inventory for the rough-cut planning period*

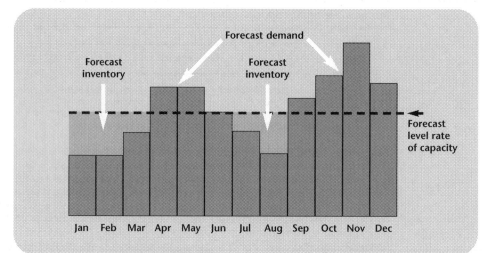

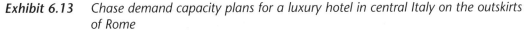

Exhibit 6.13   *Chase demand capacity plans for a luxury hotel in central Italy on the outskirts of Rome*

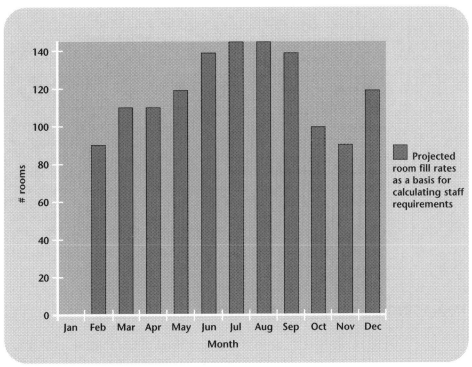

Note

The hotel has a total of 153 rooms.

nesses making special products usually cannot. Because most services cannot be stored and special products, by definition, cannot be made ahead of demand then either chase demand (see Exhibit 6.13) or order backlog (see Exhibit 6.9) are the only viable option open to these organizations.

The decisions, however, not only concern by how much to increase capacity but also need to embrace issues around timing and the extent to which a business is prepared to carry excess capacity as an alternative to the costs and concerns of repeatedly changing capacity and the potential inability to meet required customer lead times due to lengthening order backlog/forward load positions.

Mixed capacity plan

The third option to handle capacity/demand differences is to choose a mixed capacity plan. Here, some inventory is accumulated to make effective use of existing capacity and some capacity changes are made to reflect changes in demand. For example, Exhibit 6.14 shows an increase in capacity during September to December. This has been based upon the introduction of a temporary evening shift (18.30–22.00hrs) to help reduce inventory holdings throughout the 12-month period.

Exhibit 6.14   *A mixed plan involving level capacity (for eight months of the year), inventory and an increase in capacity from September to December inclusive*

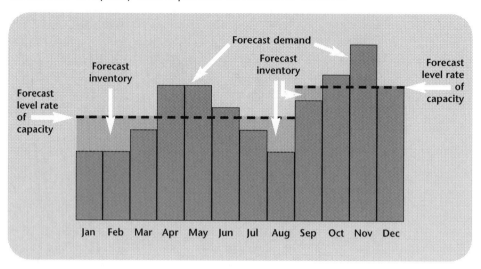

MANAGING DEMAND AND CAPACITY

So far we have discussed the concept and role of rough-cut capacity planning and the alternative approaches from which a business may choose. This section discusses the options for adjusting levels of demand and capacity within the overall plan. These will be within the control of the organization and are designed to help fine-tune the capacity plans so as to better meet the objectives of the business as well as the needs of the market.

1. Managing demand

Demand is inherently variable at all times and at all points on relevant timescales. That is the nature of market demand and the task that operations needs to manage and discharge.

Within its overall chosen approach, however, operations can select from alternatives to manage demand in order to better meet the needs of the business and its customers. These alternatives fall within a number of categories that are now discussed.

Changing the pattern of demand

One way of adjusting demand and capacity differences is to change the pattern of demand. Examples include:

■ **Altering price levels** to differentiate, for example, between peak and off-peak periods. In this way, some customers are persuaded to choose periods where demand levels are normally lower in exchange for paying less. Lower, off-peak prices also attract customers who may not otherwise have purchased the service or product as well as those who switch from one alternative to another. For example, off-season holidays, matinee cinema and theatre prices, night-time and weekend telephone rates, factory discounts for early- or late-season purchases, off-peak rail travel for otherwise road users and early-evening menu discounts at restaurants. The purpose of these pricing schemes is to help level demand through different time periods.

■ **Advertising** can be used to stimulate demand. Often working hand in hand with price changes, the purpose is to stimulate demand in periods of otherwise low demand. As with pricing, the purpose is to change the pattern of demand and/or create new sales that otherwise would not have been made. Examples include extending the season for beach and ski resort holidays respectively, increasing demand in the summer months for meat products by preparing food for weekend barbecues and stimulating demand throughout the year for products that have traditionally been purchased at festive or seasonal times – for example turkey sales other than to celebrate Thanksgiving and Christmas.

■ **Complementary products and services** can be developed with counter-cyclic, seasonal trends. In this way demand for the complementary products and services will be in the periods of lower sales for the current products and services. Examples include the use of hotels in the winter for conferences, coach tour operators providing school bus services, fast-food restaurants offering breakfast menus and garden tractor and mower companies developing a range of blowing equipment to handle autumn leaves and winter snow.

Product/service design

Companies use a combination of materials, labour and process capacity to make products or provide services. In order to alter the shape and size of demand, companies are looking to redesign their product and service range in order to reduce the labour and process content not only to lower direct costs but also to flatten high demand periods and with it the capacity to meet these peak periods. Buying in more work in the form of materials and subassemblies reduces demand on internal capacity, while getting the customer to provide more capacity within the system will have similar outcomes. For example, customers undertaking more of the front end (for example completing essential information or self-assessment tasks) or back end (for example self-assembly of knock-down products) of the service.

Scheduling

A third way is to develop elements of the scheduling procedure aimed specifically at modifying demand patterns. They include the following:

■ **Reservations and appointments** are an effective way of helping to manage demand. In essence they are a mechanism to pre-sell capacity within a service delivery system. When preferred slots are already taken, demand can be deflected into other available time slots within the system or to alternative systems within the same company. Many service delivery systems use this mechanism including hospitals, dental and other health practices, passenger airlines, hairdressing and beauty salons, hotels and restaurants.

- **Fixed service schedules** are often used by companies to enhance the effective use of capacity by forcing customers to adapt their requirements to the capacity schedule available. All forms of public transport use the fixed service schedules as the basis for managing capacity.

- **Advertising**, as described earlier, is a way to help change the pattern of demand. In addition it is used to change forecast demand into known orders by inducing (often through offering some kind of discount or complementary benefit) customers to make confirmed bookings at an early date. Besides possibly increasing overall sales in the period, the other significant advantage is that it converts forecast sales into known orders which facilitates the scheduling task by reducing the inherent level of demand uncertainty.

- **Educating customers** to work within the scheduling system parameters also helps companies to alter the incoming shape of demand so that the inherent fit with capacity provision is enhanced.

Managing uncertainty

Demand is uncertain, even where companies have developed ways of moving some requirements from 'forecasts' to 'known' orders. One classic example of the problem is the latent uncertainty within reservation systems. In some service systems pre-payment is coupled to pre-booking which obviates the problem of lost sales. In other systems penalties are imposed that relate to the number of days a cancellation notice is given and the service has been reserved (for example in dental practices and pre-booked holidays). Some companies use these mechanisms as well as alternatives. On fares, passenger airlines offer a 'no change' deal through to a totally flexible ticket depending upon the level of price discounting offered. Those passengers buying a non-discounted ticket have complete freedom to change. One result of offering this degree of flexibility is the number of 'no-shows' that airlines experience. To protect capacity from this phenomenon flights are typically overbooked to reflect past experience with the aftermath being managed where and when there are too few seats for the passengers waiting to take a flight.

2. Managing capacity

The other principal area where companies can manage the demand/capacity difference is to consider different ways to manage capacity. These include the following.

Short-term capacity adjustments

These can be made in two ways – overtime and using temporary labour. Though the use of overtime is being reduced in many more developed economies, the use of temporary labour is increasing. The EU's aim is to limit the number of hours worked in any week to a maximum of 48. In some countries (for example, Germany and Japan) overtime levels are nominal. In others the tradition of substantial overtime still remains – for example in the UK overtime accounts for more than 10 per cent of hours worked. In the EU the UK currently tops the hours worked list with an average of 43.4 compared with Belgium at the bottom of the list with an average 38.2 hours.

Temporary staff have long been used in many businesses as the preferred way of handling marked changes in demand for which overtime working is not a sustainable option. Traditionally, employment agencies principally provided staff to cover sickness, holidays and known seasonal peaks. By the mid to late 1980s as companies restructured to cope with the new business climate and slimmed down in an effort to reduce overall costs they were left with a core of permanent staff that represented insufficient capacity to cope with demand at peak times. Temporary and contract staff have increasingly been used to provide the necessary capacity on a need-to-have basis and are proving to be an ideal way of providing capacity to meet predictable and random demand patterns that can be of a weekly, monthly or seasonal nature. In 1995, it was estimated that in the UK there were 700 000 temporary and contract staff employed through agencies at any one time.

Flexible capacity

The last section dealt with ways of adjusting planned capacity levels. This section considers ways of being able to change capacity within the limits of the plan or to alter the provision to reflect the needs of both a business and its customers.

- **Flexible staff** provide the option of moving capacity to reflect changes in demand, both those that are anticipated and those that arise unexpectedly. Training to increase each person's range of skills is fundamental to this option. Switching staff to meet the varying requirements in line with forecast sales and known orders has been an integral part of manufacturing businesses for many years. As product options increase then being able to switch staff to reflect sales trends and the need to meet the short-term needs of customers are a by-product of the changes typical of most markets. In service delivery systems this option is widely used. In fast-food restaurants, for example, staff switch from serving to cleaning tasks during periods of low demand.

- **Different capacity levels within given time periods** needs to reflect the anticipated pattern of demand. Part-time staff, temporary staff, shift patterns and staggered working hours including break times are some of the more common ways of changing capacity in line with demand.

Changing the form and nature of capacity

To meet the increasingly dynamic nature of markets and the varying patterns and fluctuations in demand that follow, companies have been changing the form and nature of capacity. Some of the more commonly used approaches are now discussed:

- **Annualized hours** entails calculating working time on an annual rather than weekly or monthly basis with employees contracted to work, for example, 1748 hours per year rather than 38 hours per week. (This example comprises 52 weeks less 6 weeks of holidays x 38 hours per week.) The system gives companies more flexibility when scheduling work, allowing for longer standard hours at some periods and shorter hours at others. Overtime is not ruled out in these arrangements, but being able to match capacity to seasonal patterns of demand leads to marked reductions in overtime. Companies also point in these situations to lower levels of absenteeism. The use of annualized hours began to grow in Europe from

Case example

4

One of BMW's key tasks when it took over the Rover car plant in the UK was to increase productivity and bring levels of output per worker up to those of its factories in southern Germany. BMW estimated the gap in 1999 at some 30 per cent and explained in discussions with Rover management and workers that the options were to close the gap or face significant job cuts. The changes sought concerned working practices that during the last decade had transformed BMW's shopfloor into one of the world's most productive.

One of the most important changes that BMW was looking for was the introduction of flexible working. In its own plants, BMW had dispensed with the standard eight-hour day and five-days-a-week shifts. Instead BMW employees work varied shift patterns (including a regular requirement to work on Saturday at no extra pay) that, on average, add up to four days a week. The shift patterns are very varied (about 250 models) to meet different sets of needs. For instance, at one factory in rural Bavaria there is one model for a handful of workers who are also farmers and need to get home early to tend their livestock.

The result is that BMW's expensive plants run longer and are not idle at the weekend thereby cutting the actual costs per car by one-quarter compared to traditional work patterns. With machines costing as much as $250m each, the savings are big.

Another element of flexible time BMW is looking to introduce is the time accounting module. This allows the company to increase or decrease hours (up to a maximum at any time of 200 hours) in line with demand and with workers later taking time off or working longer, again at no extra cost.

Case example questions

4.1 Explain how these arrangements helped BMW become more competitive.

4.2 Give an example of when a company would use the two elements of flexible working described here – flexible working and the time accounting model.

the late 1970s, particularly in France and Germany. In the UK, recent estimates show that well over 10 per cent of all employees now work on this basis. Companies adopting this approach include BP Chemicals (Grangemouth), British Airways, Findus Foods (Newcastle), Bristol and West Building Society, television companies such as ITN, Yorkshire and HTV, Fisons Pharmaceuticals, Tesco Distribution, Matsushita Electric, Scottish Power, Manchester Airport and a number of national health trusts.

■ **Substituting capacity** by increasing the application of technology or use of customers in providing the product or service not only decreases costs but also helps flatten demand peaks in terms of capacity provision.

■ **Subcontracting** similarly allows companies to spread the task of handling capacity/demand differences by requiring suppliers to manage part of the capacity implications resulting from changes in demand.

■ **Sharing capacity** is a concept designed to spread the cost of expensive equipment or highly skilled labour resources that would normally be underutilized. For example, hospitals may agree to share expensive medical equipment with doctors having admitting privileges within the agreement. Similarly, smaller passenger and freight airlines reach agreement on sharing a range of facilities with other airlines from terminals to baggage handling equipment and ground personnel.

Additional examples include the discussions between Mazda and Ford to consider the joint use of car-assembly capacity in Japan. 'Such a move would give Ford additional auto-production capacity in Asia while making use of Mazda's idle capacity resulting from the sluggish auto demand in Japan'.[16]

Case example

5

A JOB TO SUIT THE BUSINESS AND YOUR LIFESTYLE

Staff at Lloyds TSB (one of the major UK banks) are encouraged to work flexibly. Under the Work Options initiative staff no longer have to explain to their managers why they want to change their working hours: their case will be decided purely on whether it makes sense for the business. One outcome is that about 17 000 employees of Lloyds TSB work flexible or reduced hours. From now on, the bank is adapting practices used successfully in the USA and the rest of Europe to allow staff to work differently. Under this new system employees choose from a menu of options: job sharing, reduced hours, a compressed working week (for example, four longer days), variable starting and finishing times and working off-site for one to three days a week. Staff can also propose alternative arrangements.

Applicants need to explain how they will fulfil their duties, how colleagues and customers will be affected, how the bank could benefit and how they propose to detect and handle any problems.

The approach was triggered after the merger of Lloyds and TSB in the mid-1990s, and an environment characterized by increasing competition (for example from supermarkets), the trend to 24-hour banking for which staff had to provide extended cover and the growing need to recruit and retain staff in a more competitive labour market. The new system aims to make flexible working a mainstream business practice, not an entitlement or a benefit. Past arrangements were recognized as being too dependent on individual relationships between employee and manager. The aim is to move these arrangements from the category of 'a favour' and to give everyone more control over when work was done, with the emphasis switching to output rather than the time spent at work. Employees need to think through how this will work for them and how they and their respective managers will review how well the process is working.

Part of the launch involved briefing managers on the new perspectives of work as well as the taboos of flexible working – for example, that teleworking is impractical for managers. Time working at home gives thinking and planning more time often unavailable in the workplace. While each arrangement has to be supported by a business case, a change in attitude to work and work practices and the emphasis on the outputs and work contributions made will bring benefits to employees and the business alike.

Case example questions

5.1 How will flexible working help Lloyds TSB run its business better?

5.2 What benefits do you see for employees?

5.3 Make a business case for working a condensed week of four longer days.

CONCLUSION

Managing operations capacity is complicated. The complexity factor comes from its size, getting all facets of capacity to work well in themselves and together and managing in an environment where demand is increasingly dynamic and less predictable.

For example, the data in Exhibit 6.15 provide an illustration of the size and inter-related nature of capacity. This is what it takes Delta to feed one day's passengers from Atlanta airport. To assess the dimensions of internal and subcontract capacity and the co-ordination involved in this one aspect of running a passenger airline is a sizeable task in itself and well illustrates the forward-looking as well as the day-to-day nature of capacity management.

But all of this is in an environment characterized by high levels of risk. As markets open up, capacity and location decisions, for instance, will have an impact on future market position and opportunity. For example, several major car companies have built assembly plants to help position themselves early in relation to the potential market opportunities in China. All have found it tough, as Exhibit 6.16 shows. The same story is true for pharmaceutical companies where concerns include new moves by the Chinese government to protect the local drug industry, fresh restrictions on foreigners' ability to sell drugs and serious problems experienced by foreign investors concerning the protection of intellectual property as patents are broken and substitute products are made locally.[19] While some companies, such as Xian-Janssen and Smith Kline Beecham, have earned good profits, others are below target. With 1996 prescription and over-the-counter sales exceeding $5bn, companies believe they cannot afford not to be present and are thus planning not only to stay, but to expand. Companies such as Bristol Myers Squibb, Glaxo Wellcome, Novo Nordisk, Pfizer and Pharmacia Upjohn see 'such huge sales beckoning [that they] are still betting China is worth the headache'.[20]

Exhibit 6.15   *What it takes Delta to feed its passengers from Atlanta airport on one day[17]*

Aspects		Quantity
#	passengers	36 800
	flights	274
	trucks	60
	assembly lines	16
Kilograms	chicken	1 130
	pasta	535
	broccoli	23
	spinach	100
	tomatoes	140
	lettuce	1 120
	butter	235
	coffee	420
#	dinner rolls	18 500
	apples	5 800
Litres	olive oil	86
	wine	6 320

Exhibit 6.16   *Position in 1997 for four car plants in China[18]*

Company	1997 Position
Peugeot	Halted production at its Guangdong plant, where demand has fallen far short of capacity
Citroën	Producing at a fraction of capacity at its $1.4bn Wuhan plant
Volkswagen	New 150 000 unit plant in Changchun lost an estimated $100m
Mercedes	Its $1bn plant to make mini vans in Guangzhou is bogged down in negotiation. Many analysts think it unviable

For any business, whether to increase or decrease capacity is typically a major decision. It comprises not only the level of permanency involved but also the issue of timing. A loss in market share always goes to a competitor. The competitor who adds capacity first does not necessarily make a profit. But the competitor that trails on the growth/capacity path will find great difficulty in regaining its future market share position, whether or not it decides to increase capacity at a later date. On the other hand, adding capacity that subsequently is underused is bound up with unnecessary costs and high exposure. There are few areas of decision-making where the outcomes are under such an intense spotlight. Buying capacity that does not get used or having insufficient capacity to meet demand will always be reviewed with a level of incredulity by those outside a company due to the fundamental nature of capacity provision in transacting business.

Within this scenario, therefore, one critical strategic dimension of capacity acquisition concerns whether to lead or follow demand. Most organizations opt for the latter, principally because it is less risky. The reason that companies select the 'follow' course of action is that the decision is easier to make rather than it being for reasons of strategy. Companies facing uncertainty often cope by not endeavouring to increase their understanding of the sets of issues involved. As a consequence, they choose options that enable them to postpone the resolution of these dimensions. One result is that strategic decisions have to be resolved at the tactical level. It is here where the yes/no choice has to be taken. With regard to capacity it will typically lead to inefficiencies and higher costs on the one hand and an inability to support key order-winners and qualifiers such as delivery reliability and delivery speed, on the other. The examples given earlier concerning China reflect the size and nature of the dilemma. Furthermore, the dimensions underpinning these decisions are becoming more difficult to embrace as the timescales become shorter and the risks get bigger. As this chapter has highlighted, the issues impacting demand and capacity have an increasing measure of these characteristics. The dynamic nature of today's markets is matched by the developments in technology, the concept of work, the issue of where work needs to be undertaken, changes in organizational structures and repositioning in terms of the make/buy mix and their impact on capacity. The outcome serves only to reinforce the key decisions involved in the choice and management of capacity.

SUMMARY

Managing the provision of capacity is central to the basic business task of providing products and services in line with customer demand. As all the assets and all the people contribute to operations capacity then its central role is further emphasized by the dimension of size.

A key step in managing capacity is determining how it is most appropriately measured. Choice of definition reflects the issues and dimensions involved not only business to business but within a business itself.

The desired position in capacity is neither to have too much nor too little. But, corporate decisions concerning make versus buy, product/service range, process design and the perishable nature of capacity (particularly in the service sector) are among the several variables that impact this issue. Within an environment where definitions of capacity are impacted by uncertainty, operations needs to plan and manage capacity by identifying those parts of capacity that can be predicted, on the one hand, while influencing demand profiles on the other.

This chapter addresses the longer-term horizons of capacity provision, particularly resource planning (often five or more years ahead) and rough-cut planning that manages the medium-term (typically one or two years ahead), with Chapter 8 introducing the short-term scheduling and control dimensions. The sections on resource and rough-cut planning also provide illustrations of alternative approaches that may be used. In resource planning, the aspects of amount, timing and location are central to the section. In rough-cut planning, the steps used to provide a plan are detailed together with alternative approaches to achieving the plan – level capacity, chase demand or a mixed plan.

The final section in the chapter introduces alternative ways of managing demand (including changing demand patterns, and scheduling) and managing capacity (for example short-term adjustments, forms of flexible capacity and changing its basic form).

Discussion questions

1. How do the capacity considerations in a hospital, wine bar and a company making lawn mowers differ?

2. Discuss the major differences between a call centre and a soft drinks company producing own-label products for major retailers with respect to:
   - capacity provision
   - facilities location

3. Should an organization always attempt to match its capacity to its forecast and known demand patterns? Give two examples to illustrate your views.

Discussion questions (cont'd)

4. Discuss the advantages and disadvantages of the following approaches for meeting demand:
   - the build-up and depletion of finished goods inventory
   - subcontract work
   - using part-time workers

5. Which approaches to capacity management would you favour using in an Italian ski-resort hotel? Explain your choice.

6. A fully integrated oil company would be involved in the following major steps in the business process:
   - searching for new oil fields
   - drilling for oil
   - building a new or extending an existing oil refinery
   - managing an oil refinery
   - delivering different fuel grades to petrol stations
   - managing the sale of non-fuel goods at a petrol station

   What are the likely capacity planning time horizons for each of the above activities? Then, fit them into the long-, medium- and short-term time frames introduced in this chapter.

7. Under what circumstances would it be best for a business to adopt a lead and when best a follow capacity provision policy? Give two examples for each alternative to illustrate your arguments.

8. What are your views on the business ethics of companies, such as hotels and airlines, that overbook their fixed capacity facilities knowing that sometimes they will have to turn away customers with a 'guaranteed reservation'? How do you think companies handle these times when more customers show than available capacity can accommodate?

9. Which approaches (order backlog/forward load or work-in-progress/finished goods inventory or a mix of the two) would the following organizations use to help handle the rough-cut capacity plan issues discussed in the chapter:
   - an architect's office?
   - a high quality, reproduction furniture manufacturer?
   - a management consultancy company?

Notes and references

1. Books that cover the subject of investment appraisal include Brealy, R and Myers, SS *Principles of Corporate Finance*, 6th edn (New York: McGraw-Hill, 1999); Luenberger, DG *Investment Science* (Oxford: Oxford University Press, 1997) and Dixit, A and Pyndyck, RS *Investment under Uncertainty* (Princeton, NJ: Princeton University Press, 1994).

2. In their article 'Coupling strategy to operating plans', *Harvard Business Review*, May/June (1977), Hobbs, JM and Heany DF, discuss problems concerning the gap between strategic

plans and those prepared at the operating or functional level, and offer some practical steps to help improve this situation.

3. This issue is also discussed in Chapter 11 on Supply Chain Management.

4. See, for example, 'The hollow corporation', Special Report, *Business Week*, 3 March 1986.

5. These strategic aspects of the issue are dealt with in some detail in Terry Hill, *Manufacturing Strategy: Text and Cases*, 2nd edn, (Basingstoke: Macmillan, 2000), Ch. 9.

6. However, if involvement in all or part of the delivery system does not meet expectations, then customers fail to participate in or do not complete their perceived involvement. For example, supermarket shopping trolleys (an integral part of the self-service provision) are often left abandoned after use because of the long distances involved in returning them to their designated areas. The resulting inconvenience and added costs have stimulated most large supermarket chains to introduce a deposit system, thus penalizing unco-operative shoppers.

7. Wesson, S and Humphreys A, *Managing Absence: 1995 Survey Results* (Boston, MA: CBI/Centre File Publication, 1996).

8. Ibid., p. 12.

9. Ibid., p. 10.

10. The overview provided in Exhibit 6.6 will again be used as Exhibit 8.2. The decision to show the same illustration twice is to help provide continuity between the related topics in this chapter and those concerning scheduling and execution addressed in Chapter 8 on operations scheduling.

11. Smith, TK 'Why air travel doesn't work', *Fortune*, 3 April 1995, pp. 26–36.

12. Books and articles that cover the subject of forecasting include: Fisher ML, Hammond, JH, Obermeyer, WR *et al.* 'Making supply meet demand in an uncertain world', *Harvard Business Review*, **72** (May–June 1994), pp. 83–93; Georgoff, DM and Murdick, RG 'Managers' guide to forecasting', *Harvard Business Review*, **64** (Jan–Feb 1986), pp. 110–20; Makridakis, S, Wheelwright, SC and McGeeve, VE *Forecasting: Methods and Applications* (New York: John Wiley, (1998); Sager, L and Cortese, A 'IBM: why good news isn't good enough', *Business Week*, 23 Jan, 1995, pp. 22–33; Willis, RE *A Guide to Forecasting for Planners and Managers* (Englewood Cliffs, NJ: Prentice-Hall, 1987) and Wilson, JH and Keating, B *Business Forecasting*, 3rd edn, (Homewood, Il: McGraw-Hill, 1998).

13. Anderson Forest, S 'Incredible universe: lost in space', *Business Week*, 4 March 1996, p. 36.

14. Spiro, LN *et al.* 'Global gamble: Morgan Stanley is charging into the Third World. Will it get burned?', *Business Week*, 12 Feb. 1996, pp. 35–40.

15. As already highlighted. although the timescales for resource and rough-cut planning are classically referred to as two to five years and one to two years ahead respectively, for many organizations the need to plan so far ahead is not required as the lead times involved are not of that duration. While large, long-time scaled facilities are characteristic of some sectors (for example, oil refining and car plants) for many organizations one to two years may well be the furthest they need to look ahead without limiting options and opportunities.

16. 'Mazda and Ford consider joint use of car-assembly capacity in Japan', *The Wall Street Journal Europe*, 18 Jan. 1995, p. 7.

17. Diamond, J 'Mile high menus', *Traveler*, June (1994), p. 146.

18. Roberts, D 'Where's that pot of gold?', *Business Week*, 3 Feb. 1997, p. 24.

19. Ibid., p. 25.

20. Ibid., p. 26.

Further reading

Blackstone, JH *Capacity Management*, South-Western, Cincinatti (1989).

Fisher, ML, Hammond, JH, Obermeyer, WR and Raman, A 'Making supply meet demand in an uncertain world', *Harvard Business Review*, **72** (May–June 1994), pp. 83–93.

Fitzsimmons, JA and Fitzsimmons, MJ *Service Management for Competitive Advantage*, McGraw-Hill, New York (1994).

Harmon, RL *Reinventing the Factory II: Managing the World Class Factory*, The Free Press, New York (1992).

Heskett, JL *Managing in the Service Economy*, Harvard Business School Press, Boston, MA (1986).

Parasuraman, A, Berry, LL and Zeithami, VA 'Understanding customer expectations of service', *Sloan Management Review*, **32**(2) (Spring 1991), pp. 39–48.

Senge, P *The Fifth Discipline, The Art and Practice of the Learning Organization*, Doubleday, New York (1990).

Vollman, TE, Berry, WL and Whybark, DC *Manufacturing Planning and Control Systems*, 4th edn, Irwin, Homewood, Il (1997).

CHAPTER SEVEN

The content and planning of this book: an overview of what is involved, what has been addressed so far and what is covered in this chapter

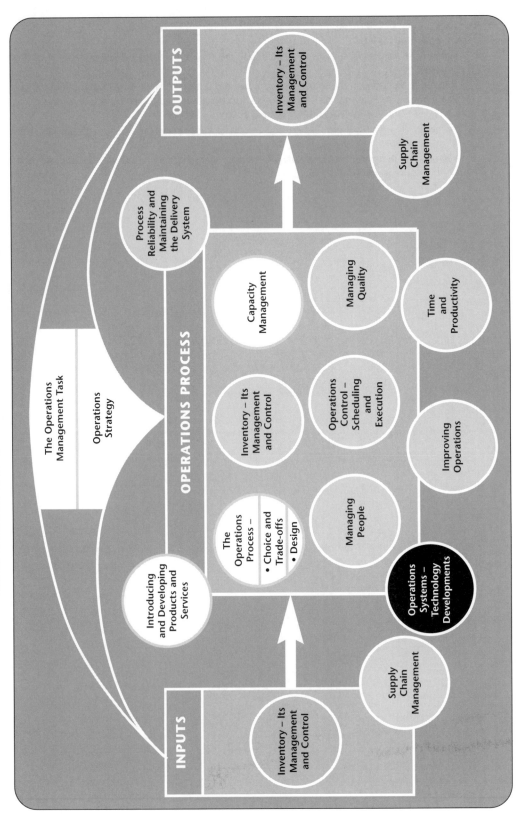

Operations Systems – Technology Developments

Chapter overview

The period since 1950 has witnessed significant developments in the systems used by companies in the provision of products and services. Many of these involve computer applications to the fundamental tasks within the operations process and have taken the form of hardware and software improvements and the essential links between the two.

Although several of these developments have been referred to elsewhere in the book, the purpose of this chapter is to provide an outline of the more important ones as a way of offering an overview of these changes both in themselves and how they link to one another. In terms of layout, the chapter is divided into two parts. The initial sections are orientated towards developments in manufacturing while service applications are reviewed in the second half of the chapter, as shown below:

- **Technology applications in manufacturing** concern both the software (systems and procedures) and the hardware (products and processes) dimensions of a firm. These range from computer-aided design (CAD) through to a whole range of computer-aided manufacturing developments.

- **Technology applications in services** describe the general uses made in basic activities such as data processing, transmission, storage and presentation. In addition, this section illustrates specific uses in a wide range of service fields from education and healthcare to leisure and travel.

TECHNOLOGY APPLICATIONS IN MANUFACTURING

The application of technology within the manufacturing sector has been in progress for centuries. Examples such as hand tools and ways to move products such as the wheel and simple lifting gear come readily to mind. With the Industrial Revolution, developments quickened and have further accelerated since the mid-1900s. The nature of these changes reflects the technologies on hand and the widespread use of computers. Information technology has not only continued the pace of change but also widened its base. Some of the key applications are now described in the following sections. To help you take on board these developments they have been grouped together under the headings systems and procedures, and process and product technologies.

1. Technology applications in systems and procedures

This section deals with the applications of technology to the procedures and systems used in all phases of manufacturing from design through to production.

Computer-aided design

Computer-aided design (CAD) concerns the use of computerized processes in designing and testing new products or modifications to existing products. In this way it is a generic phrase covering the technology applications in several phases of the design process, as illustrated below.

Computers were first used to mechanize the draughting phase – detailed drawings of what is to be made. The similarity of tasks and the repetition of the basic elements of draughting made this activity an ideal place to start. Since then, developments include interactive graphics with full three-dimensional capabilities and, with the advent of microcomputer architectures and large data storage facilities, an increasing use in design for both engineering analysis and automated drawings.

The central hardware of any CAD system is the graphics workstation, the important elements of which are illustrated in Exhibit 7.1. This is supported by a range of software that includes design, draughting and engineering analysis applications.

Design and draughting

Available as two- and three-dimensional systems, CAD software fulfils the physical production of drawings that would be based on corporate standards established within the database.

With three-dimensional systems, wire frame or solid modelling systems are available with spin-off advantages in marketing, training and other general purposes. The advantages include:

- improves response time to customers' initial and modified requirements
- reduces costs for creating and maintaining drawings
- supports the need for simplification, the use of standard components, and forms an integral and important part of value engineering/value analysis initiatives
- eliminates the more mundane facets of the draughting task
- facilitates adherence to corporate norms and procedures
- provides accurate and easily accessible records to support future requirements.

Exhibit 7.1   *Graphics workstation for a CAD system*

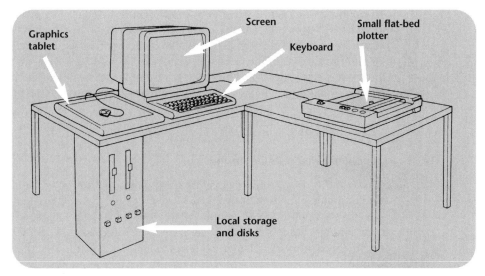

Source: Schofield, N 'Strategies for acquiring and building integrated CAD/CAM systems' (unpublished).

Engineering analysis

Product development in the past has been a lengthy and often expensive phase in the design process. Designers, having to cope with the unknown, have reduced uncertainty by a combination of modelling, analysis, prototype building and the over-specification of component and material requirements in order to address the range of possibilities at this early stage. Modifications have also typically led to a lengthy and often expensive phase within the total design process.

The development of engineering analysis software has led to cost and lead time reductions as it is now possible to undertake 'what if' studies as an integral part of the procedure. This relates to fundamental questions of form, fit and function and involves assessments on aspects such as strength, stress, material content and weight. To provide a further link between the customer and the sale, Caterpillar, the American construction machinery and heavy equipment maker, has introduced a software package with extensive colour graphics and 'exploded' shots to give customers a close-up of the working parts of the equipment that they buy.

With an increasing need to respond quickly to consumer demand changes, the key advantages derived from CAD concern reductions in cost and response time. In fact, in many organizations it is the latter that can often be the more relevant gain and which should be given equal weight when evaluating investments in this area of a business.

Rapid prototyping

Rapid prototyping takes a CAD file, converts it to hundreds of layers and builds a prototype from these. The result is shorter lead times of up to 80 per cent. For example, the computer mouse producer, Logitech, used rapid prototyping to produce a mouse in 10 days for a meeting with IBM, one of its major customers.[1]

Laser measurement

Developments in laser measurement have increased the level of precision achieved by processes to the extent that the need for subsequent processing has been significantly decreased. Known as micro machining, the equipment works accurately down to 10 nm (10 millionths of a millimetre) using diamond tips no bigger than the point of a knife. The result on cycle times is significant. For example, the parabolic antenna on the radio telescope near Zermatt in Switzerland has a span of 3 m and would typically take several weeks of polishing to attain the desired degree of precision. Using a laser-based milling machine, one segment of the antenna was completed to specification in a few hours.

Computer-aided manufacturing

As CAD is the generic phrase covering technology application in the design procedure, computer-aided manufacturing (CAM) serves the same role in manufacturing. It concerns the application of computerized processes to help integrate the production of parts through computer-controlled automatic processes. In both CAD and CAM, computerized processes relate to both individual stages within the total design or manufacturing process and the link between the stages themselves. As with the previous section on CAD, this section on CAM describes the parts (the developed applications) while recognizing that the link between the parts will typically offer a greater set of benefits (a fact highlighted by the section on computer-integrated manufacturing).

Computer-integrated manufacturing

Computer-integrated manufacturing (CIM) is an umbrella term that refers to a total interpretation of design, engineering, manufacturing and the planning and control

Case example 1

Since the early days of printing, the technology used to transfer ideas, information and images to paper has been fundamental to the advances made throughout the last few centuries. From the woodblock printing developed by the Chinese to the movable type pioneered in Europe by Johannes Gutenberg and William Caxton, the printed word has been at the centre of education, culture and entertainment.

The advent and use of computing power is bringing about changes as significant as those in earlier times. Now that sound, text and pictures can be handled digitally, printing companies are changing the very way they work. One area of development is in the pre-press activity from design creation to the scanning of images, the manipulation of text and pictures before they are put onto film and the page creation ready for printing. Software enables sophisticated artwork to be completed leading towards on-demand colour printing and, with the introduction of new printing technology, shorter runs are now economical. Also, the digital format allows the information to be changed as necessary or customized to target markets. The outcome is short-run, short lead time colour printing and, as the investment costs fall, the offering is becoming widespread.

Case example questions

1.1 What are the advantages of these developments to the customer?

1.2 What do you think might be the concerns of printers with these technology changes?

procedures used within an organization through the application of complex systems. In many continuous processing industries this level of integration has already been achieved because of the nature of the product and process involved. CIM seeks to move the manufacture of discrete parts (rather than homogeneous parts as in, say, oil refining) towards this level of integration.

Typically, investments in computer applications are one-off, designed in isolation of one another and resulting in 'islands' of automation. The need to link these is an essential step in order both to reduce the resulting problems and to harness the potential benefits of interfacing these with each other and within a total system. CIM involves the interpretation of the various piecemeal applications into a coherent whole.

In the early 1960s some experts predicted that most manufacturing would be computer integrated by the 1990s, often referred to as the 'factory of the future'. That forecast has not been met and reality is still a long way off. CIM is an industry-driven technology, with each sector conditioned by its own particular needs, experiences and circumstances. For all sectors, however, adapting computerized technology takes time, investment and a commitment by everyone. It often involves fundamental changes to existing systems, controls and skill requirements. The levels of financial investment and the time-consuming nature of these decisions bring their own levels of risk and often result in a cautious approach being taken. One outcome is that the integrating role potential provided by CIM is often the feature that is overlooked, being perceived as less essential, a fact that reduces the potential gain from investments, while contributing to the existing reluctance to invest and a tendency for caution.

2. Product and process technology applications

Whereas the last section dealt with system and procedure applications, the software, this part of the overview looks at technology applied to products and processes, the hardware.

Automation

Automation is nothing new. Improvements in manufacturing based on increasing levels of automation (from the use of gravity to sophisticated robotics) have been a feature of engineering activity and have underpinned many of the substantial productivity improvements made since the Industrial Revolution.[2] Thus, the use of appropriate forms and levels of automation is, and always has been, a critical feature when designing a process.

What is new, however, is the fusion of computing with control and machine technologies to produce systems that are both highly productive and flexible. Some of the different forms in which machines or other mechanisms can do the work conventionally performed by people are now described. Many of these applications fall within the generic description 'automation' as you will see when you read through the section.

Transfer mechanisms

The introduction of transfer mechanisms into processes has developed from traditional, power-driven conveyor and gravity roller concepts into a range of machines that transfer a product from step to step at each end of which operations are performed automatically.

Mechanization

Varying forms of mechanized aid have been developed and designed into processes. These involve power-driven fastening devices with magazine feeds, quick locating and grasping devices for machines, strip feeders into stamping or punching machines, vibrating/rotating hoppers to feed components into automated machines, automated welding and jointing, assembly of products, automated product finishing, testing and materials handling including the use of automated guided vehicles (AGVs). All replace human effort either in part or in whole. Normally, they are specially designed to provide one or a few operations at the most.

Numerical control

The use of computers has led to a number of major improvements within the field of automation and the move towards the complete, automatic control of a process. This progression is described in Exhibit 7.2 which shows three levels of automation culminating in the integration of a large number of machines or processes.

The move towards the automatic control of a process has been provided in the form of a series of coded instructions, and because mathematical information is the base used, the concept is called numerical control (NC). An NC machine refers to the operation of machine tools from numerical data stored on paper or magnetic tape, tabulating cards, computer storage or direct information. Thus, NC is the operation of machine tools and other processing machines by a series of coded instructions.

It was first developed in the 1950s by the Massachusetts Institute of Technology whose work was sponsored by the US Air Force to improve the manufacture of jet aircraft. The principal objectives were cost reduction and the repeatability of work requiring very close tolerances. The original NC machines used cards or punched tape with semi-skilled labour to load and unload a machine.

Recent NC machines no longer receive their instructions from a punched tape or card but from a computer. A system that has a computer controlling more than one machine tool is known as direct numerical control (DNC). The NC machine tools are linked to a common computer memory with access to all data being provided on request. Computer numerical control (CNC) systems, on the other hand, use a minicomputer to

Exhibit 7.2   *Different levels of automation and the corresponding machine configuration*

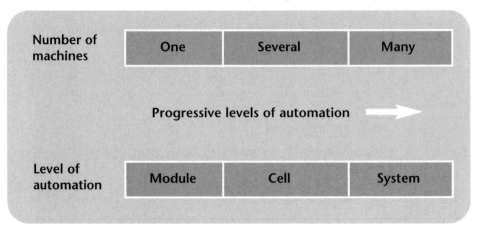

perform NC operations stored in the computer memory. This minicomputer may be used as a terminal to accept information from another computer source or by direct input. For example, dial control may be used to input dimensions for each workpiece.

An NC program is a means of machine control that initially (and most importantly) defines the relative position of the tool to the workpiece. The list of instructions that forms the program establishes feeds and speeds and normally includes adaptive control to sense operational variables such as torque, heat, vibration, material condition, tool wear or breakage and other machining conditions, and then adjusts the speeds and feeds accordingly.

A further development from the NC concept is the machining centre. This has a magazine storage for more than 100 tools on a permanent or semi-permanent basis that can be selected and used as programmed. Centres can start and stop machines, select and return tools to the magazine, insert them into a spindle, index the table and then mill, drill, bore, ream, tap and contour (with some operations being completed at the same time) in line with the programmed requirement.

In all the NC developments one important feature is their link to the CAD engineering database referred to earlier. The transfer of the design and processing information into the CAM procedure will further enhance the growing advantages of NC applications.

Within the context of Exhibit 7.2, an NC-based machine would be an example of a module. On the other hand, a cell would typically contain a small number of interconnected NC-based machines often with some level of automated loading and unloading. In some instances, the machines are in a semicircular arrangement to facilitate a robot to perform the materials handling function; for example see Exhibit 7.3(a). Other configurations may be linear with the transfer of parts from one machine to another provided in a number of ways as shown in Exhibit 7.3(b).

Co-ordinating measuring machines

Automating to reduce costs is one facet of the drive to increase competitiveness, but an equally important part of this automation initiative concerns quality conformance. NC-based equipment offers an important step in this direction. Also direct applica-

Exhibit 7.3   *Examples of cell configurations: (a) semicircular; (b) linear*

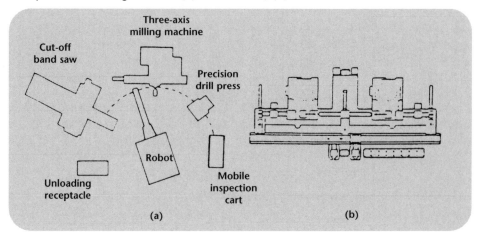

Source: Open University (UK).

tions to improve the level and reduce the costs of quality control are increasing and one estimate suggests that by the late 1990s more than 50 per cent of inspection systems in manufacturing had vision capabilities. Cameras are currently used to check joints and welds and to take measurements, and where accurate manufacture is essential then co-ordinate measuring machines (CMMs) are available.

CMMs are computer-controlled machines that can be programmed to go through a routine set of measurements for solid objects. Using a probe at the end of an arm that registers when it touches an object's surface, the machine switches to the next dimensional check and thus, by following a programmed path, can undertake the measurement of complicated parts machined to close tolerances.[3]

Companies have developed ways to use CMMs in flexible manufacturing system (FMS) cells and to link them to CAD systems to generate CMM programs as a byproduct of the computer-based design system.

Flexible manufacturing systems

A flexible manufacturing system (FMS) links the work of a number of cells and/or individual modules (see Exhibit 7.2). It is a larger version of a cell and hence will typically require some form of automated transport to link the parts of the system together. These often include a combination of automated guided vehicles (AGVs) and conveyors (see Exhibit 7.4).

The first FMS was developed in the 1960s by Molins, but it was not until the advent of inexpensive and powerful programmable control in the early 1980s that the growth

Exhibit 7.4   *Layout of the flexible manufacturing system at R. A. Lister*

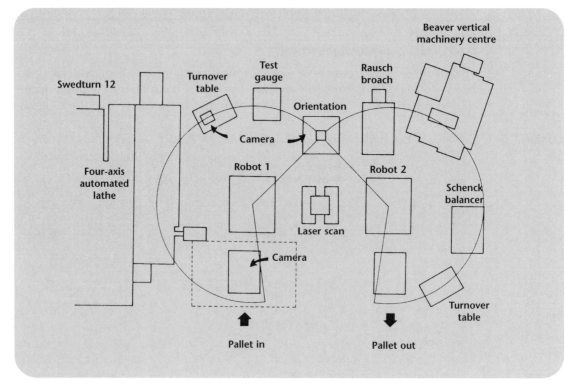

Source: Open University (UK).

Exhibit 7.5   *Spot welding robots – Ford Fiesta assembly line, Dagenham (UK)*

Source: Ford Motor Company (UK).

in applications took place. As with other forms of NC-based applications, the gains inherent in these developments come from linking different operations with built-in tool change capability supported by automated workpiece transfer. Thus, aspects of the manufacturing task such as inventory levels and production control are now completed within the module, cell or system before the workpiece is transferred to the next stage.

On the other hand, FMS installations are expensive and complex systems that require adequate utilization levels and appropriate manufacturing infrastructure provision and developments in order to be successful.

Two factors that affect the sophistication level of these system applications are the difficulties that suppliers experience in working at the forefront of technology, and in determining customer requirements. The result is a shift away from complex, multimachine systems to simpler alternatives.

Robotics

Robots are machines that can perform human-type operations. They are a form of programmable automation designed to undertake highly repetitive tasks. Initial applications were often to undertake heavy, dangerous or unpleasant work where the financial benefits for such investments were of secondary importance.

Robots, as with other forms of programmable automation, do as they are told and, as yet, are not sufficiently intelligent to make judgements. The absence of sensory data, adequate control mechanisms and sophisticated programs incorporating artificial intelligence have limited the principal use of robots to repetitive tasks such as welding, paint spraying, palletizing, the loading/unloading of machines and assembly-related operations – see Exhibits 7.5 and 7.6 for examples of typical applications.

Improvements in the areas of path control, sensing devices and manipulative dexterity are increasing the opportunities for robot applications. However, as shown in Exhibit 7.7, the number and growth rate of applications differ from one country to the next.

Exhibit 7.6   *Robots at work – Land Rover, paint shop 21*

Source: Land Rover, Solihull, UK.

Exhibit 7.7   *Comparative data for selected countries – robot densities and market size (1994)*

Country	Total robot stock	Robot density[1]
Australia	2 416	22
France	15 632	40
Germany	66 817	88
Italy	28 386	63
Japan	412 961	277
Korea	30 199	104
Singapore	3 299	93
Spain	6 944	27
Sweden	4 986	63
Russia	23 000	18
United Kingdom	9 958	19
United States	77 108	42

Note

1. Robot density is the number of robots per 10 000 persons employed in the manufacturing industry.

Source: United Nations/Economic Commission for Europe (UN/ECE) World Robotics (1998).

A computer-controlled robot system has three major components (see also Exhibit 7.8):

■ the mechanical structure (linkage or manipulator)
■ an actuating or drive system to power the manipulation
■ a control system.

Exhibit 7.8   *Major components of a robot system*

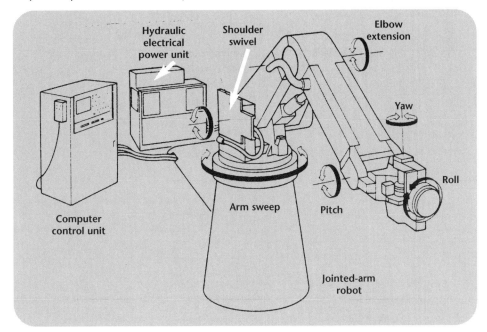

Source: Dooner, M and Hughes, J *Structure and Design of Manufacturing Systems*, Open University (UK).

The degree of sophistication within a system can be defined as being at two levels. A level 1 robot is one where the system cannot be modified through the result of a feedback and control process that senses the external environment. Thus, all aspects of the task must be explicitly specified in advance. On the other hand, level 2 robots are systems that can be modified based on adaptive feedback and a control process that senses the external environment through some type of transducer. The result is a robot that can perform some tasks without having to specify explicitly all aspects in advance. Thus, in Exhibit 7.9 the ability to transport and manipulate an object falls within level 1 robotics, a factor that is reflected in the major areas of application (for example material handling, machine loading, spraying and welding). The ability to use external sensing for feedback control relates to level 2 robotics and allows applications in the areas of machining (involving tool positioning), assembly and inspection tasks especially where visual information is used to identify the part, to determine its location and to have the robot move into position and grip the part appropriately.

As expected, level 1 robots are more limited in their application, but nonetheless have many uses within manufacturing. By building in attachments to provide the equivalent of the manual function, the use of robots has shown a marked increase in the last 20 years. Many versions exist and some of the principal types of hand application are given in Exhibit 7.10.

Exhibit 7.9 *Major categories of robot applications in manufacturing and the capabilities generally required within each application*

Major application area	Examples within the area	Capabilities required to perform application		
		Transport	Manipulation	Sensing
Material handling	Parts handling	✓		
	Palletizing	✓		
	Transporting	✓		
	Heat treatment	✓		
Machine loading	Die cast machines	✓	✓	
	Automatic presses	✓	✓	
	NC milling machines	✓	✓	
	Lathes	✓	✓	
Spraying	Spray painting		✓	
	Resin application		✓	
Welding	Spot welding		✓	
	Arc welding		✓	
Machining	Drilling		✓	✓
	Deburring		✓	✓
	Grinding		✓	✓
	Routing		✓	✓
	Cutting		✓	✓
	Forming		✓	✓
Assembly	Mating parts		✓	✓
	Acquiring parts		✓	✓
Inspection	Position control			✓
	Tolerance checks			✓

Exhibit 7.10 *Some principal types of hand applications for level 1 robots*

Hand types	Built-in applications
Magnetic	Photocell detectors
Vacuum	Television cameras for inspection
Spray gun	Microswitch sensors
Welding gun	
Hook(s) for heavy objects	
Extra-long finger(s)	

As future sales will need to be justified on investment grounds, then several things need to happen:

■ Continued reduction in robot prices, including the development of fixed price kits of parts for add-on conveyors and feeders to allow appropriate configurations to meet new needs at low costs.

■ Improved robot simulation, with easier built-in, off-line programming. This enables a user to reprogram a robot for a new application without taking it out of commission.

■ The need for suppliers to abandon systems work. The ideal would be for suppliers to sell the equipment in modular form and so allow a company to organize the application to meet its own requirements without the added costs associated with current levels of systems support.

As labour costs continue to rise at a faster rate than the costs of robots, and as the flexibility of robots is improved and simplified, then the viability of robotics applications will continue to increase.

Case example 2

Robots are taking on more varied roles in the electronics industry and for a range of reasons. While the classic advantage is to reduce cost, practical considerations such as quality conformance are increasingly key issues. For instance, a semiconductor plant today needs to be 1000 times cleaner than an operating theatre in a hospital, which leads to the growing use of vacuum working by the chip makers and the need for robot not human inputs.

In disc drive assembly, robots are used widely because the intricacy of the work and rising quality standards pose problems for manual workers. In printed circuit board manufacturing quality conformance and cost reduction are driving companies to automate, particularly those competing with low-wage regions of the world.

Not all the tasks performed by robots in the electronics industry are difficult. In semiconductor manufacture, robots carry out undemanding tasks such as loading and unloading silicon wafers from the various processes but in an environment where human presence is undesirable – a slight brush of an eyebrow would create a cloud of dust sufficient to close down the production lines. As a result, every semiconductor maker uses robots.

The same is true elsewhere. The most automated disc drive factory is Matsushita Kotobuki Electronics' (MKE) facility in Japan. The manufacturing arm of Quantum, MKE daily makes 50 000 disc drives using 400 people and 150 robots.

2.1 What are the advantages and disadvantages facing electronic product manufacturers in the use of robots?

2.2 While MKE uses many robots, Seagate (Quantum's main competitor) has facilities in Taiwan and Singapore where it produces about the same number of disc drives each day with a workforce of 25 000 and robots only where absolutely essential. Why?

Automated warehousing

The application of computers in warehousing has been undertaken for many years with the number of fully automated warehouses in the UK estimated at over 200. It is based on an automatic storage and retrieval system using stacker cranes under computer control. The system identifies each arriving pallet using bar code technology; the operators need only to key in the details and the system does the rest. For example, Frigoscandia's fully automated cold storage distribution warehouse in Bristol was built with 5600 spaces, uses stacker cranes fitted with microprocessors that are controlled by the warehouse's supervisory computer. The computer also operates a stock control system and uses critical path analysis to minimize crane movements.

Automated warehouses in a production set-up are based on principles similar to those in distribution although often linked to the AGV system used in the plant. Thus, an AGV will deliver goods for storage to a load station from where a stacker crane will automatically pick up and transfer them to a given location. All instructions come from a warehousing control system that, in turn, is linked to its counterpart in manufacturing. The benefits include reduced labour costs, the elimination of paperwork, improved utilization of floor space, highly accurate inventory records, reduced damage and controlled inventory turnover.

Reinforced ceramics

In terms of industrial applications, the desirable characteristics inherent in ceramics of hardness, chemical stability and heat resistance are nullified, to a large extent, by a lack of toughness. Ancient urns do not corrode as they lie under the sea or are buried on land, but break. One result has been that the use of ceramics has been passed over even where metal alternatives are in short supply and more costly. The reason is that ceramics are not traditionally strong enough.

Developments from the late 1980s onwards have successfully combined ceramic with aluminium. This has led to a reinforced material that is providing greater strength and a lighter alternative, critical in the aerospace and automotive industries. For example, avionic chassis for US military aircraft are now moulded as a single piece and weigh only one-third of the aluminium alternative. Also, the improved strength/weight ratio allows smaller parts than before to be moulded.

Semisolid metals

Semisolid metal (SSM) casting works on the principle that alloys move gradually from a liquid to a solid state over a range of temperatures. Within that range is a semisolid state with a consistency similar to that of butter. With SSM casting, a semisolid slug or bar of alloy is squeezed into a die or mould and cooled in the desired shape.

The resulting castings are free of gas bubbles and so can be heat treated or welded and used in applications hitherto restricted to premium casting or forged components. Also, the SSM process involves lower heat levels than those used in liquid die casting which leads to less shrinkage, faster cycle times and shorter cooling times. The outcome is cost (closer tolerances result in less post-casting machining) and process time gains. All in all, cost reductions of 10 to 50 per cent are realized depending upon component complexity.

TECHNOLOGY APPLICATIONS IN SERVICES

The application of automation in service businesses is part of the progression that has followed the growth of this sector. In a labour-intensive industry the opportunities to increase productivity through timely and appropriate investments are widespread. Some of these are of a general nature while others are specific to one or more types of service business as explained below.

1. General technology applications

Clerical, administrative and secretarial service support all types of business and are not unique to one sector. The application of microtechnology to the transmission of data and speech has introduced significant opportunities to improve the efficiency of all businesses. The basic tasks within this wide range of activities relate to:

- collecting, processing, analysing, storing and retrieving data
- transmitting spoken and written messages
- composing, preparing and distributing documents
- presenting, discussing and assimilating information
- co-ordinating activities within agreed timescales.

These activities have always formed the basic tasks within clerical, administrative and secretarial activities, but the application of technology to some of them has changed their nature, altered the role of those providing these services, and enabled quicker and more accurate support to be available.

Collecting, processing, analysing, storing and retrieving data

Computers that store data in a way that facilitates access while reducing the time required at each step of the procedure have been used increasingly in all sectors. Although one principal benefit is the cost reductions involved, there are other significant advantages such as reduced space and faster retrieval. For many companies, the problem is paper. Before the widespread use of technology in the 1990s it was estimated that over 1.3 trillion (million million) documents were created in the USA alone – enough to paper the Grand Canyon almost 110 times. About 95 per cent of company information is stored on paper – and it takes up space. With quick access required, this normally requires storage on-site which adds cost.

Technological developments in the form of documentation image processing (DIP) are transforming data processing, storing and retrieval. The theory of DIP is simple:

information is stored and transmitted electronically. The advantages are significant. At Western Provident Association, the Bristol-based private medical insurance company, central filing took up 25 per cent of floor space while between 25 and 35 per cent of all salary costs was dedicated to managing records. The introduction of DIP has begun to yield significant benefits.

The combined use of CD-Roms to store information and a pen-based computer to access it is allowing information to be stored, retrieved and transferred quickly and efficiently. For example, car insurance assessors have data on the most popular cars stored on a CD-Rom. When evaluating the damage to a car, a pen-based computer allows simple access by pointing to the parts of the car to be replaced with all relevant information then being transferred and collated onto a relevant file for assessing the claim and agreeing the repair costs involved.

At the other end of the technology spectrum is bar coding. A bar code is a set of bars and spaces of various widths which are unique to an item. The information contained includes the key details necessary to recognize the item together with information such as quantity, price, location and any other relevant to its description and subsequent identification or retrieval. The information is stored on a computer and read on the item by an optical scanner. The use of bar codes is truly universal even though in the past it has been restricted by the amount of information that can be squeezed onto a label; often as little as a single identification number. The advent of two-dimensional (2D) bar codes has increased by one hundred fold the amount of information that can be stored and transmitted. This has opened the way to a simple but extensive support system in a whole range of applications. For example, NASA is using a 2D bar code system to improve its method of identifying spare parts in the space shuttle. This system enables NASA to bypass steps where a person would manually transfer serial numbers, thus reducing the risk of human error.

Transmitting spoken and written messages

The application of solid state electronics to telephone systems has enabled a range of developments to take place that have reduced the inconvenience of being unable to make contact with the person concerned, the task of redialling, the opportunity to redirect calls, hold discussions with several people at one time, to receive a signal when another call is waiting, and to leave and receive recorded messages. In addition, message exchange systems allow users to call their own numbers and receive any recorded message thus facilitating communication between two people on the move who do not have a high level of administrative support.

Further developments to speed communications and to reduce the need to travel while providing essential contact with colleagues, customers and suppliers are provided by the growing (and in some instances, already widespread) use of fax machines, e-mail (see below) and video conferencing. The supercharged PCs accompanying these developments means that executives can converse while their PCs exchange data – the need for face-to-face meetings is declining.

At a lower technology level, managers use tape recording machines to dictate memos and letters, and to draft reports so eliminating the need for dictation and the corresponding duplication of effort. Audio facilities also mean that the taped material can be transposed to a hard copy format with little error while decoupling the manager and support staff thus allowing each to work more effectively and efficiently.

Composing, preparing and distributing documents

Mailing lists can be stored on computer and, linked to a capability to prepare standard letters with customized changes, can offer personalized letters and mailing shots as a by-product of the system.

The ability to transmit written messages using the telephone system in the form of a telex has been supplemented by the capability to transmit facsimiles of written documents quickly and accurately down telephone lines to locations throughout the world. The 'fax' system scans a document, converts the images to electronic impulses, and sends them across telephone lines to the receiving facsimile machine which converts the images back to an identical hard copy of the original. In 1980, fewer than 20 000 facsimile machines were operating in the USA. By 1989 there were 2 million and by the late-1990s experts predicted that this number will have more than doubled.

Developments to overcome some of the barriers to using personal computers are being sought to facilitate their use still further. Software packages to recognize hand-written characters are already developed.[4] The final hurdle will be voice recognition both for comprehending voice commands and for speech-to-speech dictation. Developments are on the way and companies are already signalling progress.[5]

Presenting, discussing and assimilating information

Technology is resulting in widespread changes to the way in which information is presented and assimilated. One fundamental development has been the growing availability and use of CD-Roms. Their use in general knowledge provision and as a data source for professional and leisure activities is widespread and continues to grow.

The convergence of the computer, broadcasting and publishing industries into the multimedia sector has led to changes in the role of newspapers and magazines and one, which some believe, will lead to their demise in the next decade. Some publishers in the wake of these changes are proactively generating new formats. For example, *Newsweek* has a quarterly, interactive CD-Rom video magazine. Other developments include computer services tied to magazines covering areas such as homes, gardens and auto mechanics, while computerized newspapers will not be long in coming. On-line electronic services are springing up everywhere and a growing number of proprietary on-line databases are available which subscribers can access. For example, British Telecom offers a range of services from a daily recipe to weather reports and the up-to-date position on selected sporting events, while in the USA there are more than 2000 commercial databases offering a range of professional services. These include stock price quotations, full texts of major foreign newspapers and local regulations and legal opinions for the needs of solicitors and lawyers. The facility to search for homes using a television programme and telephoning system to seek further detailed information including mortgage arrangements is also a growing feature of selling houses in the USA.

2. Specific technology applications

Besides the general technology applications described above, different levels of technology application have been taking place in several parts of the service sector. Some of these are specific to or predominantly developed for one part of the sector, while others have a more universal application. Driven principally by productivity gains, these developments have also allowed decisions to be made about the location of back office and front office tasks within a business's service delivery system. The main applications within parts of the service sector are described below. However, there are overlaps which, in many instances, have not been highlighted.

Education

The introduction of automated equipment into the process of learning has provided a new range of options for those involved. For children it offers the opportunity to pace the speed of learning to their own capabilities while freeing a teacher to attend to individuals needing assistance. For adults, it presents similar opportunities allowing them, for instance, to use the journey time constructively by listening to taped programmes. Furthermore, it enhances the learning process by extending the use of visual aids: a medium which is generally acknowledged to increase levels of knowledge retention. One example of this is the growing use of interactive videos. Optical discs are used to store sound, video images, text and graphics with which trainees interface enabling them to control the pace of their learning, make choices by mouse pointer and get feedback. Advantages include higher levels of learning success, more flexible learning, a sharp reduction in learning time and lower training costs.

In some areas of learning, sounds can be prerecorded ensuring the highest quality reproduction. Language learning provides a classic example where the use of audio material can help in developing correct intonation and accent. In addition, recording the learner's own correct version of a particular item of learning (for example to improve spelling or to increase a person's foreign language vocabulary) has been found to increase the progress of those with learning difficulties.

Finally, simulators have been developed to allow on-the-job training by creating virtual reality in a 3D format. Uses of this include the training of junior surgeons in the growing field of keyhole or laparoscopic surgery, the technique of inserting a camera and surgical instruments down tubes into the human abdominal cavity. Since its introduction in the mid-1980s, operations have been revolutionized and this technology is now widespread throughout the world. But this development requires surgeons to develop new skills. A 3D anatomical simulator enables junior surgeons to practise minimally invasive surgery in a real world.

Financial services

The introduction in the 1930s of cheque sorting machines was the first example of automation within the banking industry. Since then, banks have been automating increasingly throughout their operations. In the back office, electronic funds transfer systems (EFTSs) move monies electronically between different bank accounts. Direct payroll deposits, instant credit analysis and automatic teller transactions are all services made available through an EFTS.

In the front office, automatic teller machines (ATMs) enable customers to withdraw cash, make deposits and check their account balances without the help of bank employees. This not only improves the speed of service and reduces the administrative support within the back and front office but it also enables these basic services to be provided 24 hours a day throughout the year.

The use of credit card systems to replace cash and cheque-based payments is extensive and growing. This move towards a cashless society has been further enhanced by the introduction of electronic cash systems such as Mondex. These 'smartcards' have a microchip for storing electronic cash. A card's chip is loaded with money through special cash dispensers or by using telephone lines to access a bank account. The money is transferred between cards by special wallets and their use is ideal for services using pay machines and other developing technologies such as pay-as-you-watch television.

Financial services are also using computer-based support to help automate several tasks. Trust administration and portfolio management are examples where automation is helping to improve the level of service while reducing administrative costs. The transfer of stock exchange dealings throughout the world's major finance cities was a well-publicized event in the late 1980s. This now enables share price quotations to be given on demand, has lengthened the period of stock dealings within a centre while in effect linking the markets to form the equivalent of a globally based activity.

Although the spending by banks on electronic-based services has grown at a compound annual rate of 150 per cent in recent years,[6] it has still not provided a clear lead over the non-banking players and could yet be eclipsed. The competition in some banking services from outside is growing and, for the most part, is technology-led. Retailers have long been competing in the field of credit. Now they are competing head-to-head in other financial services as fundamental as retail banking. Other threats to traditional banks are also coming from IT companies. As much of the work in the financial sector concerns transactions, transmission is a core activity that leads to the form of competition being based on technology.

Health care

Technology applications in the field of health are extensive. The types of application together with examples to illustrate the wide-ranging use of technology within this large and growing part of the service sector are outlined below:

- **Diagnostic** – including scanners, endoscopes, clinical test analyses, home diagnostic tests, foetal monitoring and electrocardiography. For example, at Kochi Hospital in Japan, computerization produces results of tests from the pathology department within a maximum of 26 minutes, while laboratory staffing costs have been cut by 50 per cent. More recent applications concern telemedicine. To provide the full range of specialist medical support on a local community basis is impractical. In the USA, for example, there are an estimated 35 million people who live in medically underserved areas. Using video-conferencing, consultants are able to provide specialist advice for patients in remote areas. The benefits of these developments have also been extended to provide international links to help treat rare and complicated conditions.

- **Survival** – for example intensive care and coronary care units.

- **Illness management** – including pacemakers and renal dialyses.

- **Prevention and cure** – such as computerized instruments to measure health risks, organ transplants and the use of probes and lasers in surgery. An example of the latter is stereolithography. By combining laser technology with medical tomography scans, precise 3D models of a patient's bone structure can be created enabling surgeons to tackle operations that might otherwise be too risky to undertake. Also, the application of virtual reality systems is gaining acceptance in several areas of medicine from helping the rehabilitation of people who have suffered traumatic brain injuries to reducing the stress levels of dental patients who wear a headset to watch a film or music video while undergoing treatment.[7]

■ **System management** – for example ranging from hospital and medical records, access to biomedical data for research and teaching through to financial records. In El Camino Hospital near San Francisco a computerized operational care system enables doctors to access patient's medical records upon referral and to write up the necessary orders even before admission. The results include shortening the average patient stay by a full day and an estimated saving on record-keeping time of eight hours per 34-bed ward per nursing shift.[8] In the UK's National Health Service, as elsewhere, the growing concern to reduce the cost of healthcare in an environment of finite financial resources has meant a long, hard look at efficiency. It now matters how much treatments cost and whether they are effective. The change in approach has been introduced under the banner of resource management that involves healthcare professionals in management decision-making and captures relevant data to review existing activities, practices and approaches to help consider effective and efficient alternatives. The new systems collect data (for example, how much resource a patient has cost during a given period) and enables these details to be reviewed as well as comparing costs for similar treatment both within the same hospital and within hospitals in other parts of the country.[9]

Information system improvements also mean that transactions (for example orders for blood tests) are now keyed in at source and with all associated data becoming instantly available from any terminal, including back at a patient's family doctor's practice; paperwork is minimized at all stages of the process.

Case example

3

The falling costs of telemedicine are increasing its use and availability. It concerns the transmission of medical data and images between medical centres. It makes specialists available to regions or countries that lack a particular expertise and improves services to remote areas. The system works by digesting and compressing images of patients' X-rays, magnetic resonance imaging (MRI) and computerized tomography (CT) scans. These are sent down telephone lines and in the course of a few minutes expert advice is provided. The advantage is that the system depends on ordinary telephone lines and so can support doctors and patients most likely to need this type of service support.

Video-conference is also growing. Video connections save long round trips for patients while diagnosis of a wide range of medical problems can be completed in this way. Even psychiatric patients are interviewed using video links, according to the Department of Telemedicine at the University of Tromso, Norway.

Case example question

3.1 What are the benefits of the use of telemedicine within the diagnostic phase of a healthcare service delivery system?

Hotel and catering

The use of automation within the hotel industry is increasing. The provision of lifts and escalators to move people and materials has long been in place. Back office applications now include food preparation, dishwashers, automatic laundry and ironing machines, and automatic clean-up, vacuum, washing and waxing machines. In the front office, investments are being made in automated reservation, message and morning-call systems as well as electronic key and lock systems.

In addition, a range of information-based systems are apparent in this growing part of the service industry. The applications relate to both the back and the front office and are described as evolving through four stages:

- Clerical computer applications used for accounting, payroll and to maintain reservation records.

- Administrative computer applications, including food and beverage control, inventory control, guest histories, reservations and planned maintenance procedures.

- The provision of information to assist tactical decision-making. This will enable managers to include in their decisions information on consumer tastes, tour operator schedules and link-ups, and money market fluctuations.

- Strategic decision-making is the final phase where the computer will be used to identify markets, plan products and services, schedule capital requirements, recommend manpower needs, allocate resources optimally to different business activities and suggest what kind of operations processes should be used in the highly automated kitchens.

Leisure and travel

Whether it is as old as gambling or as recent as international business travel, technology is enhancing the delivery of a whole range of services in the leisure and travel industry.

- **Gambling** relies heavily on off-course betting outlets for a large part of its revenue. To help improve customer service, interactive touch-screen videos are being introduced in betting shops. These systems cover all sports for which betting is available and, using a touch-screen facility, selections are made, odds are advised and bets placed. The systems also provide background information to help selections such as form details, riders and trainers for race meetings.

- **International business travel** for the busy executive means long days and lost sleep. Any way, therefore, to reduce the overall length of a journey brings welcome relief and tangible benefits. Smart card technology at a number of airports in the USA and Canada have gone some way to bypassing one frustrating aspect of these journeys, waiting to be cleared at immigration. Known in the USA as Inspass and in Canada as Canpass, the new cards allow those travellers enrolled in the schemes to check themselves through immigration and customs in a couple of minutes. The self-service system is built around fingerprint (Canpass) or hand geometry (Inspass) recognition and, when the two match, an automated gate swings open and the pass holder walks through. Other countries interested in employing the scheme include Germany, the Netherlands and the UK with the aim of coming up with a standard card for all those involved.

Smart card technology is starting to replace the traditional bus ticket in a growing number of urban transport systems around the world. Hong Kong introduced smart cards across all forms of public transport in the late 1990s. London Transport is doing the same for both bus and underground or metro travel.

Smart cards are the same size as a credit card, but their extra thickness contains a silicon chip that stores and processes information and an internal aerial that transmits data to a reader. This development allows the card to store much information such as details of fares including discounts to encourage journeys at off-peak times and to link overground and underground services. The cards do not need to be swiped and so the reading is quick and not subject to the faults that come with card wear and tear. For transport operators, records of journeys completed on the facilities of different providers can be made allowing accurate revenue allocations, while the types of journey passengers make means services can be adjusted accordingly.

Case example question

4.1 Using these examples and that in the section on 'international business travel', what are the principal benefits of these developments in the respective service delivery systems?

■ **Sound reproduction** had its last major breakthrough in 1925 when modern speakers were launched. With the advent of compact discs in the 1980s, distortion has been virtually eliminated from audio recordings. The weakest link now became the sound speaker itself. That was until the recent development of hypersonic sound that allows big, boxy loudspeakers to be replaced by ones smaller than the palm of your hand. Existing electromechanical speakers use electrical signals to vibrate a thin diaphragm, creating sound waves in all directions. Using quartz crystals, hypersonic sound emits a pair of ultrasonic sounds that when they interact create a sound which is better than that given by speakers costing thousands of dollars.

Restaurant and food services

Being tied to the kitchen sink has never had much appeal. The use of technology, however, is increasingly taking out some of the manual tasks while other applications are improving customer service. Automatic ovens, food processors, drink dispensing machines and disposal systems are illustrative of back office applications. The increasing versatility of vending machines has offered improved service to the general public, while frozen food/microwave systems enable hot food choices at all times of the day and night.

Transportation

No matter which way you travel the concerns are the same – safety, avoiding hold-ups and getting there on time. Technology applications to improve these dimensions within all forms of transportation have been high on the agenda list over the last few decades. In parallel, the need to cut costs and improve several dimensions of customer service in more competitive markets has also driven the increased use of automation in all forms of transportation – air, rail, road, water and pipeline.

■ **Air** – the increased use of computer-based control systems in modern aircraft covers all aspects of the workings of an aeroplane through to autopilot capability. On the ground, computer-based controls monitor the intricate traffic patterns and complex airline schedules. Meanwhile, support systems use many forms of automation and computer-based systems including reservations, check-in, baggage conveyancing and security surveillance.

■ **Rail** – administrative tasks such as ticket sales, seat reservations and the entry and exit from stations have long been in place. On the track side, automated switching terminals, signalling and computerized rail car tracking systems form the core of the network.

■ **Road** – the management and control of roads have used automated equipment in the form of traffic signals and motorway, tunnel and bridge toll systems for many years. Although government investment in roads has been high, the increasing congestion on city streets and many trunk roads and motorways has, in most developed economies, been a growing phenomenon in recent years. To help meet this, car systems to alert drivers to road congestion ahead have been introduced. The devices (increasingly being installed as a standard fitting in top-of-the-range cars) provide traffic congestion graphics and news information for an annual subscription. With the UK currently experiencing hold-ups twice a day and each trapping some 5000 motorists, it is estimated that being linked into systems can save users up to 2½ hours a month.

In a similar vein, car navigation systems that tell you not only where you are, but where to go and how to get there are gaining ground. As they become easier to use (the next systems will include a synthesized voice for instructions) and lower in cost, demand is taking off. By the year 2000 the car-navigation market in Japan alone is estimated at 2.2 million units. Not only of practical value to professionals in all sectors, taxi companies are installing them to help interpret passengers' less precise directions as well as giving them confidence that chosen routes are not unduly long.

■ **Water** – to keep a ship afloat costs an estimated $18 000 a day. Faster turnarounds, therefore, are a major priority. The use of computers to manage and control ports and to load and unload ships has been vital to their survival, as the following example illustrates.

Wholesale/retail trade

Technology applications in the wholesale and retail sectors have long been in evidence. Security tagging to deter shoplifting is one of the early examples and has been singularly successful in reducing losses of this kind. It is now widely used but may be not as far as the approach illustrated in Exhibit 7.11! More recent technology applications, however, concern the recording, retrieval and use of information on point of sale activity. Bar coding and more recently smart tags are consequently having widespread applications in the wholesale and retail trade. As explained earlier, a bar code is unique to a product and the information contained in the code includes a product's description, lot number, quantity/size, location and price. The bar code system facilitates changes to variable data such as location and price by simply

Case example

5

Singapore is one of the world's busiest container ports. On average a vessel arrives and departs from the port every three minutes. At any one time, 700 ships are in port, 60 000 containers are in the dock compound and 6000 trucks enter or leave port every 24 hours. Technology is vital to combat Singapore's land and labour shortage problems, to keep costs down, improve port efficiency and handle the complex scheduling task and daily activity. An integrated computer system controls container movement from the freight forwarding agent to the hold of the ship. A database containing sailing times of vessels, length of delivery schedule en route and space availability is checked against a container booking with details of content, weight of goods and ship required. Entry into the port is automated and vehicle clearance takes on average 45 seconds. Agents use transponders on the top of containers to register arrival. Cameras read the container numbers, the driver flashes his identification disc against a magnetic screen and, at the same time, the container is weighed. In less than a minute the driver receives a computer readout detailing where he should wait for a crane to unload his container. At the same time crane operators and dockside prime mover drivers receive computerized messages on where and when to pick up a container, on which ship to load it and the sequence in which the containers should be loaded. Retrieving containers from the store reverses the procedure. By the year 2000, it is estimated that annually Singapore will handle 15 million TEU (twenty-foot equipment units) containers. One key to its growth is the investment in technology to provide a fast turnaround of ships. It can do this better than elsewhere, being able to turn around a ship carrying 1000 TEUs in less than twelve hours.

Case example questions

5.1 Detail the service delivery system from agent to the container ship leaving Singapore.

5.2 Identify the technology applications in each part of the delivery system and explain the principal gains that have been made by these developments.

changing the information file for that product, a quick, low-cost operation. A bar code can be printed directly onto a product or its packaging or can be printed onto a label for fixing at an appropriate stage in the manufacturing process.

At a supermarket checkout, the sales assistant uses an optical scanner to read the bar code on the product. The price is automatically recorded on the sales till while inventory records are updated.

Recent developments aimed at speeding up the retrieval of data are known as smart tags. These are radio frequency transponders containing silicon chips. For distributors, this will enable them to communicate via satellite to a stock-keeping tag attached to a container of goods anywhere in the world. This will trigger a communicating link to tags on smaller trading units (for example boxes) and then to individual products. For wholesalers and retailers the same facility will apply, allowing an instantaneous update on inventory at all locations. In addition, these will also be a major plus regarding shoplifting. Small enough to fit in the cap of a lipstick, the smart tags can be read in boxes and could be used to trace stolen goods anywhere in the world.

Other applications relate to intelligent price tags on items such as food and clothing. The aim is to build into the tag the cooking and washing programmes so that when placed into the microwave or washing machine, the transmitter will do the rest.

Exhibit 7.11 *Technology helps to deter shoplifting. He will probably think twice in future!*

Source: © Roger Beale.

Utilities and public services

Utilities and public services describe a diverse group of activities including electricity, gas, communications, refuse collection, armed forces, libraries, social security departments, hospitals, fire service, legal system, tax offices, customs and excise, and postal delivery services. In addition to the clerical, secretarial and other more general applications described earlier, automation takes many forms within this diverse sector. Examples include library lending services with electronic-based checking, disposing and recording procedures, military warning systems, computer-based missile systems, automatic incinerary facilities, electronic fighting equipment, heat-sensing devices and power generation stations.

Credit cards

Perhaps the most widely recognized technology application in the banking and finance world has been the use of credit cards to transact purchases. This has seen significant growth within developed economies over the last two decades to the point that in 1997 Visa alone allowed access to credit at over 12 million merchants around the world. One result of this widespread use is that credit card transactions have, to an increasing extent, replaced the branch as the prime link between customers and their bank. As the use of cards grows, both in terms of the number of customers having cards and the range of transaction types covered, then the impact they will have on the shape of banking will increase. Further developments of integrated computer chips will add more functions to a card while reducing the need for branches. Furthermore, such chip developments will lead to cards that will provide customers with information on when, where and how the card was used. A personal terminal or chip reader attached to a home personal computer would enable a customer to download information on recent transactions. Surfing the Internet, shopping via virtual reality, selecting goods and paying for them with a credit card would be possible from home at any time.

Account management

Recording, storing and accessing documents and other relevant information on customers as part of the essential task of managing accounts is time-consuming and costly. Document image processing and workflow automation are increasingly being used. In this IT application, all information is screened in or entered as word processing files. This allows the storing and accessing of documents on screens instead of as paper files. Original documents (other than, for example, property deeds in the case of mortgages) are no longer kept. Other benefits include automatic customer listings to help in the task of managing and improving control from accounts exceeding agreed overdraft limits to handling arrears, signalling higher than normal transactions and highlighting further sales opportunities with selected customer groups.

Cash transactions

Automatic teller machines (ATMs) characterize developments in banking. A common sight in high streets, at large supermarkets and in retail outlets, they not only reduce costs within the service delivery system but also importantly allow customers access to cash at all times.

However, even with the advent and widespread use of ATMs, handling cash transactions costs banks and other financial institutions billions of pounds a year. To meet this basic need yet reduce the cost of its provision has led to the development and introduction of electronic cash systems. The potential for reducing costs is very high. As a recent analysis revealed, worldwide some $8.1 trillion cash transactions are made in a year and of these 22 per cent (or some $1.8 trillion) involve purchases of less than $10. To meet this requirement in a more cost-effective way, cash cards have been introduced. These are plastic cards with a microchip for storing electronic cash. The card's chip is loaded with money through special cash dispensers by using telephone lines to access a bank account, modified ATMs or cash-to-card terminals. The intention is for these cards to displace currency, especially coins, in low-value cash transactions for goods and services such as newspapers, car parking, pay phones, vending machines, pay-as-you-watch TV and other developing technologies.

CONCLUSION

Computer-based applications have underpinned many of the recent developments in manufacturing and service systems. The intention is to incorporate operations technology with management/business technology. Operations technology is concerned

Case example 6

A medium-sized insurance company handling 15 000 claims and issuing 300 000 policies a year introduced document image processing and workflow automation. The results have been speedier claims handling, a halving of paper and telephone costs and an expansion in the business without moving to bigger offices.

All documents and records are now stored on the system from incoming correspondence, diagrams and photographs to brief details of telephone calls. Once scanned in, original documents are kept for seven days simply as a precaution. The only documents kept longer are those that might be needed in court.

Now, when staff log in each day, the system lists the tasks due on specific claims. They can review the entire history of a claim, while daily reminders to undertake the priority tasks means that claims are handled much more quickly. The result is lower costs and faster processing of applications and claims.

with the process that makes products or provides services. Management/business technology deals mainly with the flow of information essential to the effective planning, control and management of the conversion process. Their increasing integration is helping to bring about vital co-ordination within organizations and the benefits that accrue.

It is essential, however, to recognize the key features underpinning these initiatives and to ensure that they characterize the nature of the activities within an organization. These include:

■ **The need for the initiatives to be business-led**. System developments are not an end in themselves. Both the stimulus for and the specification of these initiatives must be to meet the needs of a business. The business objectives, as translated through an appropriate operations strategy, need to provide the parameters in which the developments should take place.

■ **The initiatives should be multi-disciplinary in nature**. The opportunities offered by systems improvements and the mix of hardware and software developments require an integrated response best provided by a multi-disciplinary approach. A combination of line executives and relevant specialists ensures that not only are the technical knowledge inputs provided but also that rigorous testing takes place in terms of the complex nature of reality. Unless solutions embody the application/evaluation loop (see Exhibit 1.4) then the constraints and needs of reality will not be adequately recognized. Furthermore, it is essential that the proposals form a coherent whole in order to avoid the serious limitations and potential inadequacies of piecemeal developments.

■ **The initiatives should be action and change orientated**. The success of systems development needs to be measured by the resolution of problems or realization of opportunities. Implementation should be made on a continuous basis and the practicality of improvements needs to form the ultimate test. A report, no matter how comprehensive, is not a measure of success. Action and change need to be the sole goals of these initiatives.

It is most important that organizations place systems improvements within the context of their business needs. Major changes have too often been specialist-led and panacea-driven.[10] Organizations need to develop business-based strategies that can then provide the direction for developments. As emphasized in Chapter 2, investments in the operations function are both large and fixed by nature. It is essential, therefore, that a business understands what it is buying to ensure that the opportunity for systems development is maximized.

SUMMARY

The role of operations is to use technology to support an organization's markets and customers. While engineering was the principal technology development in the period from the Industrial Revolution up to the mid-nineteenth century, IT has increasingly added to the technological thrust and contribution since that time.

This chapter has described some of the key developments in both the manufacturing and service sectors. These are, as you will have seen, wide-ranging in their applications and providing all or some elements of cost reduction, reduced lead times or the ability to meet a wider range of products and services.

Managing the interface between these developments and their use within an organization is a key operations management task. Bringing many of them together in this chapter enables them to be handled in a comprehensive way and avoids the need to detour into technical explanations elsewhere in the book. I trust you found the illustrations a fascinating and absorbing look into the extensive and varied range of technology applications.

Discussion questions

1. Visualize a holiday abroad. Assuming that you are flying to your destination, travel by car to the airport and use the long-stay car parking facilities, identify the technology applications from when you leave home to boarding the aircraft.

2. When you next go to the supermarket identify the technology applications that are used in the store. What are the gains involved?

3. In June 1989, the *Daily Mirror* was the first tabloid newspaper to use a bar code. Broadsheets resisted longer, partly because the inclusion of a code cut into valuable front page editorial space. The last paper to fall into line was the *Financial Times* that printed a bar code in the bottom left-hand side of the front page from late 1991. The universal use of bar codes in newspapers was brought about in part by increasing pressure from retailers to print bar codes – the campaign even included a threat not to stock newspapers without codes.

   Why did retailers put so much pressure on the newspaper companies to include a bar code on the front page?

Discussion questions (cont'd)

What are the potential advantages and disadvantages for newspaper companies to make this move?

4. In what circumstances will robots have the advantage over using people and vice versa?

5. The sales ordering process for a wine merchant is a core activity. Complex pricing structures (with up to 80 prices – 40 for both a bottle and a case), varying outlets from retail to warehouse and up to 5000 product lines reflecting the types of product, vintages and bottle sizes have to be handled by the systems in place. Identify the key dimensions of the operations task described above and where technology applications would be usefully applied.

6. Are pan-European mobile telephones a business necessity? Give three examples where their use would be essential in operations.

7. Farmers are using US navigational satellites in orbit 12 000 miles above the earth to beam down data on each field. How would this help operations to meet the basic tasks of improving grain and crop yields in increasingly price-sensitive markets?

8. What will be the impact of new information technologies on the operations managers' role?

9. Crime across Europe is becoming more sophisticated. Too often when police move in to arrest drug dealers or terrorists they find drugs or arms and radio scanners but no bad guys. What technology developments do you think are being introduced to improve police operations within countries and across Europe?

Notes and references

1. Baxter, A 'Making it quickly into metal', *Financial Times*, 15 July 1993, p. 18.
2. Chapter 15 provides basic approaches to improving operations and thus overlaps the applications referred to in these sections.
3. BS6808 *Co-ordinate Measuring Machines* gives users the measurements they should take, the directions of travel to use and the readings at the probe tip they should obtain if they follow the guidance.
4. Forenski, T 'Coming up with the write stuff', *Financial Times*, 25 Oct. 1994, p. 13.
5. Booth, SA 'Super-charged desktop PCs', *World Traveller*, April 1996, pp. 25–8.
6. Houlder, V 'High street dinosaurs wake up', *Financial Times*, 29 Jan. 1996, p. 11.
7. Cole, C 'Seeing is relieving', *Financial Times*, 22 Feb. 1996, p. 18.
8. 'Computers streamline care in hospitals', *Sunday Times*, 7 May 1989, p. F5.
9. Gooding, C 'Recovering well after surgery', *Financial Times*, 23 Jan. 1992, p. 16.
10. Discussed in more detail in Terry Hill, *Manufacturing Strategy; Text and Cases*, 2nd edn (Basingstoke: Macmillan, 2000).

CHAPTER EIGHT

The content and planning of this book: an overview of what is involved, what has been addressed so far and what is covered in this chapter

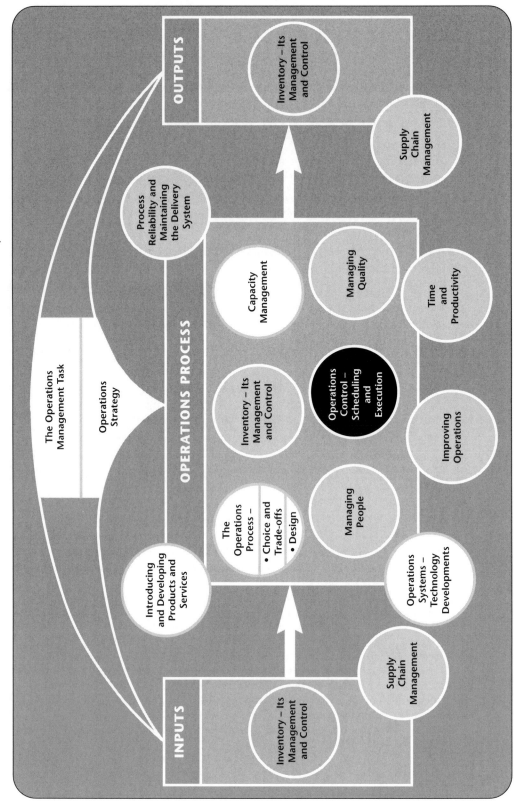

Operations Control – Scheduling and Execution

Chapter overview

This chapter is concerned with the short-term control, scheduling and execution tasks and the systems appropriate to each choice of process and type of business. In summary, the chapter deals with the following topics:

- **Overview and interface** – these short, initial sections overview the aspects of operations planning and control and detail the interface between these phases.

- **Operations control – scheduling and execution** – the factors that influence the design of appropriate systems precede a detailed explanation of the basic tasks involved in operations control.

- **Operations scheduling systems** are reviewed and the fit between the principal systems of bar charts, network analysis, materials requirement planning and just-in-time are discussed.

- **Materials requirement planning (MRP)** is then explained in detail with examples to illustrate how MRP works.

- **Manufacturing resources planning (MRPII)** is introduced and how it evolved from MRP is explained.

- **Just-in-time (JIT)** is now discussed and a detailed explanation of this control system is provided together with the philosophy underpinning this approach.

- **Optimized production technology (OPT)** is explained and how it fits into and supplements control systems is reviewed.

- **Enterprise resource planning (ERP)** is outlined and its link into and extension of MRP is discussed.

INTRODUCTION

The task of a business is to sell its goods and services in the marketplace and then provide them through its operations function. To do this, it invests in the primary facilities of buildings, processes, people, systems and procedures. The problem confronting most organizations is how best to meet both the needs of their markets and the performance targets (for example, output and efficiency) that a business places on its operations function. On the one hand, they are the basis of sales revenue, while on the other they underpin the cost structure and very success of the organization.

One cause of this conflict arises from differences in the nature of the two activities. While markets are inherently unstable, the operations function needs to be kept as stable as possible in order to achieve the levels of performance (for example, those regarding utilization, output and costs) essential to the success of a business. To cope with these differences organizations invest in a number of ways to cushion the operations core from the instability of their markets (see Exhibit 8.1). One such investment is in appropriate operations and control systems, the subject of this chapter.

To provide goods and services, organizations invest in the necessary processes. However, investment concerns not just process hardware. It also consists of any change to the operations system that improves an organization's capability to meet customer requirements. Thus, as illustrated by Exhibit 8.1, investments to cushion the demands that an unstable market places on the desired stability of the operations core take several forms. Long-term capacity planning was discussed in Chapter 6. Inventory is the subject of Chapter 10. This chapter concerns operations control – the scheduling and execution phases in Exhibit 8.2. (Exhibit 8.2 is, in fact, Exhibit 6.6 that has been reintroduced here to give an overall picture on planning and control.)

In total the planning, scheduling and execution tasks cover an extensive set of procedures to help reflect forecast and actual demand in terms of capacity and capability. Such procedures cover a wide planning horizon that spans the strategic through to the tactical decision-making levels. These dimensions of planning and control were first introduced in Chapter 6 and are repeated here to reinforce the links between these key phases:

Exhibit 8.1   *Cushioning the operations core from the instability of the market*

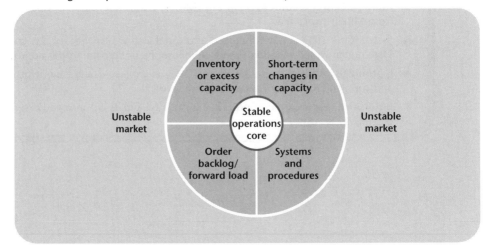

Exhibit 8.2 *Operations planning and control systems*

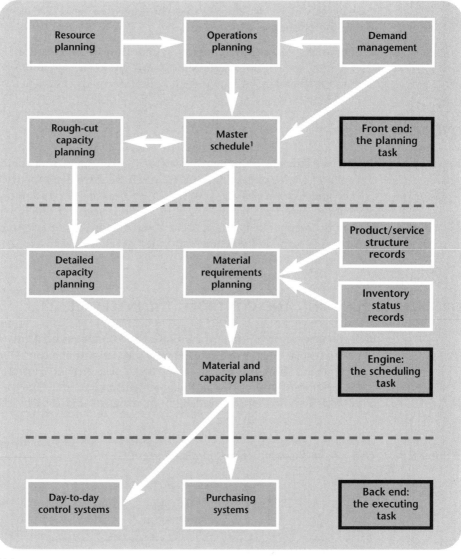

Note

1. Referred to in manufacturing planning and control systems as the 'master production schedule' or MPS.

Source: Adapted from Vollman, TE, Berry, WL and Whybark, DC *Manufacturing Planning and Control Systems*, 4th edn, Irwin/McGraw-Hill, (1997), p. 69.

■ **Long-term operations planning** is a corporate strategic issue looking (depending on the business) up to five or more years ahead and is dealt with in Chapter 6. It aims to provide the capacity requirements necessary to meet the sales forecasts that underpin an organization's long-term objectives by planning for capacity changes in line with major shifts in existing products and services and to meet plans for new products, services, technologies and markets.

■ **Medium-term or rough-cut planning** is for periods up to two years ahead (again depending on the business) and details how demand will be met from available facilities which, in principle, are considered to be at a fixed level. This is also covered in Chapter 6.

■ **Short-term operations control, scheduling and execution** is responsible for executing and controlling the short-term, day-to-day operations activities to ensure that customer demands are met and resources used effectively.

OVERVIEW

Exhibit 8.3 provides a simple overview of the key steps in operations planning and control and relates back to Exhibit 8.2 when we discussed capacity. It represents the essence and sequence of the tasks that organizations need to undertake in order to calculate (if orders are known ahead of time) or assess (if orders are not known and have to be forecast) demand, translate these calculations or assessments into material and capacity plans and schedules, and then develop ways to execute requirements on a short-term, day-to-day basis.

OPERATIONS PLANNING AND CONTROL – THE INTERFACE

Before looking at the operations controls tasks in more detail, it will be useful to spend some time explaining the interface between the planning and control phases of a system.

A glance at Exhibits 8.3 and 8.4 shows that a planning and control system is designed to take a forward look at demand requirements and identify the implications for and constraints imposed by the availability of materials and capacity. This broad picture

Exhibit 8.3   *Overview of the main phases in planning and control*

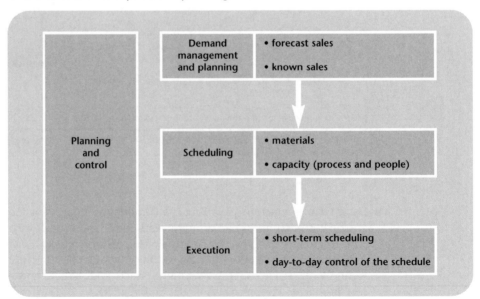

alerts a company to problem areas in the future and to recognize the decisions that need to be addressed and the investments (if any) and timescales involved. It is then able to plan for future sales levels accordingly as the lead times for adjusting capacity and purchasing materials are within the time frame of the forward-looking review.

As the time for completing an order draws closer handling these same dimensions and requirements moves the plan to the scheduling and execution phase. Part of this phase is again to review demand, capacity and material requirements but at a more detailed level (see Exhibit 8.4). This results in material and capacity plans over the short term that take the form of detailed schedules in terms of process allocations, staffing levels, material purchases and deliveries. This creates the operations' response to meeting customer demand, with the day-to-day control and purchasing systems in place to help manage and execute the task.

Exhibit 8.2 shows the pivotal role of the master schedule (or MPS, see Exhibit 8.2) within an operations planning and control system. Its key task is to take actual or forecast orders and translate these into demand statements for operations – process capacity, staff levels and material requirements. At the long-term and rough-cut planning stages it provides information in a form that operations needs to assess capacity and identify any investments to reflect anticipated changes in volumes or

Exhibit 8.4 *Aspects of the demand and capacity review by phase in the operations planning and control system*

Aspects of demand and capacity reviews	Phase in the system		
	Planning	Scheduling	Execution
Timescales[1]	Although the length of time will be business-specific, it will always be long relative to the other phases of planning and control in a business	The scheduling task may be up to several weeks ahead (some car plants, for instance, fix the master schedule up to six weeks ahead), but the execution phase will typically concern one or two weeks at most	
Role	To provide a forward look and to identify problem areas relating to the timescales of the review	To establish and agree the actual orders to be completed and the detailed plans involved. In service companies where demand is met on a daily basis (for example, retail outlets, restaurants and hospital emergency units) patterns of past demand (for example, time of the year and day of the week) will be reviewed to help identify anticipated customer requirements	
Nature	Broad-brush picture and long planning horizons	Detailed reviews identifying capacity and material provision from one or two weeks ahead down to an hour-by-hour level in some sectors (for example, staff schedules in call centres are often determined on a half-hourly basis)	

Note

1. This dimension is always specific to a business. Building a large manufacturing plant compared to buying and refurbishing an existing retail outlet will often be years compared to months, weeks or even days.

MK Electric manufactures and distributes wiring devices, circuit protection and cable management systems and services most of its distributors and retail customers ex-stock from a central warehouse that, in turn, is supplied by manufacturing facilities. The latter hold no stock. All marketing, sales and sales order processing were carried out centrally.

In the past, forecasts used to pass through a central manufacturing planning group that scheduled material deliveries to the factories and agreed production schedules. When reviewing the increasingly poor on-time performance of the business (only 30 per cent of the top 200 lines were delivered within the 10-day target and another one-third took over 30 days to fulfil) the company found that:

■ product promotion and sales incentive programmes were not included as part of the sales forecasts

■ operations was principally measured on its productivity and efficiency performance, the targets for which it tried to meet while trying to match sales patterns and short-term customer demands and schedule changes

■ sales knew nothing of operations' plans and offered ex-stock delivery even when there was no stock in the warehouse.

One key problem in all of this was demand planning. To improve the accuracy of this key phase in the procedure, organizational and systems changes were introduced. Central planning was disbanded and replaced by teams comprising marketing, sales and operations. The teams had responsibility for demand planning with direct access to sales and marketing and used historical data, information on current sales levels and knowledge of promotional activity to improve the accuracy and timing of the essential forecasts of demands.

1.1 What were the principal weaknesses of MK Electric's original approach to demand planning?

1.2 What factors did MK Electric change in this procedure, and why?

product/service mix. In the same way, the master schedule provides operations information that not only enables the scheduling task to be completed but, in turn, feeds the day-to-day control and purchasing procedures that underpin the execution phase of a system. As you will deduce from this description, and as explained in the last section, a planning and control system starts off as a broad-brush statement of known or anticipated demand and capacity and results in a detailed schedule of staffing lists, process allocations and purchase orders for a day or sometimes as little as a half-hour period.

OPERATIONS CONTROL – SCHEDULING AND EXECUTION

Operations control concerns meeting the short-term, specific demands placed on the process or delivery system. It comprises the scheduling and execution phases of the control task as overviewed in Exhibit 8.2 and detailed in Exhibit 8.4. Within the context of the long-term and rough-cut planning activities described earlier, demand needs to be translated into operations' requirements both in terms of the capacity (the staff and processes to complete the tasks) and materials to complete the products and services required. Its principal activities are to create the instructions and plans to undertake the tasks necessary to meet customer orders and to ensure that all the requirements to make the products or provide the services are available as and when needed.

Not all companies require the same operations control system. Factors that influence the choice and design of the system include:

■ **Product/service complexity** – the complexity of the product or service directly impacts the choice and design of the scheduling system. Service businesses offering a limited and narrow range often provide a service within the delivery system as a single transaction. Neither the customer nor information is thus required to be processed at a second stage and that simplifies the scheduling task. At the other extreme, scheduling a range of multi-step products or services completed in different parts of the total delivery system will result in the need for a more complex scheduling system.

■ **Special vs standard products and services** – bound up with the last point, another factor that affects the nature and type of operations control systems is whether a product or service is a special or a standard. In the case of the latter the steps to complete the task are known. This creates the opportunity to develop a system to manage scheduling and execution. Where products and services are specials then typically a control system is less detailed and relies on the skilled staff that provide the products or services also to undertake the day-to-day scheduling tasks.

■ **Choice of process** – linked to the last two points is the choice of process. This reflects the nature of a business in terms of volumes, order sizes and markets, and the operations scheduling system will reflect these differences as will be illustrated later.

■ **Internal span of process** – the extent to which a company makes or provides internally the parts that comprise the products or services it sells will directly affect the complexity of the operations scheduling task. The more it purchases from outside, the simpler will be the task of scheduling the steps of the internal process. Similarly, the more it purchases from outside then the greater the orientation of the execution phase towards purchasing and supplier management.

■ **Decisions on demand and capacity reconciliation** – the decisions taken by a business regarding the management of demand and capacity will directly affect the complexity of the scheduling task. The more demand and capacity are managed, the easier will be the scheduling task and its execution.

OPERATIONS CONTROL – BASIC TASKS

An operations control system comprises three distinct but integrated activities designed to manage and execute requirements:

■ **loading** – determining the capacity and volumes at each stage in a process. This step will include assigning tasks to work centres or staff groups
■ **sequencing** – deciding on the order in which jobs will be completed at each stage in the process
■ **scheduling** – involves allocating a start and finish time to each actual or forecast order

This section gives further detail on these three activities as part of setting the background for the rest of the chapter that describes the types of operations control systems in use.

Loading

Loading concerns determining the capacity and volumes at each stage in a process and assigning jobs/tasks to a part of the process (for example, work centre or person). As explained in Chapter 6, for planning purposes capacity plans need to be based on the net amount available. Staff only work for a given period while processes, although theoretically available for 24 hours a day on each day of a week, are often intended to run for less than the 168 hours per week maximum. In addition, the normal scheduled time needs to be adjusted for necessary, known reductions such as set-up times, personal and relaxation time for staff and maintenance, as well as an allowance for unknown reductions such as breakdowns, absenteeism and training.

Within this task there are two principal approaches to loading operations – finite and infinite loading:

- **Finite loading** allocates work to an agreed upper limit. Examples where this applies include appointment systems for dentists, restaurants, hospital outpatient departments and hairdressers. Booking passengers onto scheduled airline flights falls into this category, but also provides an example of how an operations control system also handles uncertainty. In this instance, airlines will overbook flights as a way of coping with passengers that have confirmed tickets but who fail to turn up for the flight. As no-shows, as they are called, are not penalized then airlines overbook flights. The overbooking of a flight to take account of the anticipated no-shows can be as high as 15 per cent. The rationale for this overbooking decision is to avoid less than full flights in times of high demand. The downside is handling the occasions when flights are overbooked and 'dead heading' has to be implemented. As airlines deliberately overbook then the known outcomes include those times when more passengers turn up for a flight with confirmed reservations than there are seats. How to handle this is then built into the operations control procedures.

- **Infinite loading** places no limits on accepting customers' orders. Examples include accident and emergency care units in hospitals, fast-food restaurants and banks. In these businesses customers accept that at busy times queues will be longer. But, the operations system responds to situations by developing a capacity provision that can adjust its level up or down in line with changes in demand as they occur. For example, in banks additional teller positions open as queues lengthen and are closed as queues shorten. Also, in times of major accidents off-duty hospital staff are asked to report to work to meet the resulting higher levels of patient treatment and care.

Sequencing

When orders are received or customers arrive, the decision on which jobs to be completed at each stage of the process or which customers to serve first needs to be made. This activity is termed sequencing. Prioritizing rules are often used to help in making such decisions, and include:

■ **Customer due date** – typically customers' required delivery (or due) dates form the basis of the operations schedule. Where customers' requirements are processed as and when they are received (for example, in a fast-food restaurant, bank, post office or retail outlet), then the 'schedule' reflects a customer's position in the queue. In businesses where customers order ahead of time then the sequencing within the operations control system reflects the relevant due date.

■ **Customer priority ranking** – operations will sometimes alter the position of an order or customer in the schedule due to the importance attached to the customer involved – for example, the relative value (£s) of business a customer places with the company. Other factors that may lead to a change in schedule position include remedying a service failure or faulty product.

■ **Minimizing set-ups** – in some manufacturing processes sequencing the order in which products are made has a significant impact on loss of productive time through set-ups. As you can imagine, in injection moulding, the length of time needed to change from one colour of plastic to another will vary depending upon the two colours involved. Thus, when sequencing colour changes many companies move progressively from light (for example, white and yellow) to dark (for example, dark blue and black) colours for this reason. Similarly, the time to change the setting on a machine will vary by product sequence. In order to minimize total lost productive time due to set-ups, decisions on the operations schedule will reflect these factors.

■ **First in, first out (FIFO)** – some businesses schedule customer requirements in exactly the order in which they enter the service or production system. The examples given earlier in the section titled 'Customer due date' apply here. Other examples include mail order companies, applications for driving licences, passport applications and most high customer contact service systems where booking ahead of time is not a feasible option. Passenger air terminals use a FIFO system for checking in passengers. However, the British Airways (BA) system for handling business class travellers at London Heathrow Airport's Terminal 4 uses a mixed system. Recognizing that business travellers are often short of time when arriving for flights, BA staff check the flight times of each passenger entering the check-in queue. If in their opinion a passenger would be pressed for time if processed by normal check-in procedures and existing queues, BA staff reroute these through two check-in desks designated for such passengers. In that way, the system has been designed to provide a supplementary subsystem to bypass the normal service delivery provision so that the needs of all passengers can be met.

In a similar way, an accident and emergency unit in a hospital will treat patients in line with the seriousness of their condition and then on a FIFO basis. To help in this, the on-duty medical staff assess the seriousness of a patient's condition into life threatening, serious but not life threatening, and routine. Within these categories a decision on priorities may still be made with the FIFO principle then being used within these bands.

Scheduling

A schedule is a detailed timetable allocating a start and finish date to each order while taking into account the sequence in which they will be completed. An integral part of this concerns the short-term capacity and materials management tasks as shown in

Exhibit 8.2. The scheduling and execution of the orders in a system is thus concerned with determining when to start jobs in order to meet delivery requirements and to manage and control these orders through the process.

In some businesses such as rapid-response service operations where customers arrive in an unplanned way, the scheduling of orders is linked to the arrival of customers within the service delivery system. The key short-term control tasks in such businesses concern material purchasing and capacity planning. The detailed scheduling task is an inherent part of the system with the server/customer interfacing in stimulus/response mode.

Even so, the task of matching short-term capacity with uncertain patterns of demand creates a difficult task that companies alleviate by reshaping demand and varying capacity through the whole of the activities described in Chapter 6.

Many businesses are, however, faced with a more complex scheduling task due to some or all of the factors detailed earlier and concerning product/service complexity, choice of process, internal span of process and decisions of demand and capacity reconciliation.

OPERATIONS SCHEDULING – SYSTEMS

The remainder of this chapter describes the systems used to schedule and manage operations. You will see as you go through this section that, as products and services differ in terms such as complexity (the number of steps involved to make a product or provide a service), the one-off or repetitive nature of demand and the range offered, then the system will differ to reflect the task on hand. The simpler the task, the simpler the scheduling system that can be used. In fact, in some businesses the level of system-based scheduling will be low. Whereas capacity and materials will be scheduled against expected levels of demand, hour-by-hour control will be exercised on an as-needed basis. Take for example a café on a main street that has a limited number of seats inside but space for more on the outside pavement or sidewalk, and also offers a takeaway service. The fresh food requirements will reflect the day of the week and time of the year. Staffing will be scheduled in line with each hour of a day and decisions taken regarding the preparation of some food (for example, salads and sandwich fillings) in pre-peak time periods. Staff training to handle the various tasks (for example, fresh coffee maker, toaster and hot foods) will facilitate staff movement during busy times. Then, within these dimensions (that is, actual staff capacity scheduled by each hour, the quantity of fresh food ordered, the amount of food prepared ahead of time and level of staff flexibility) decisions on who does what will be handled by a combination of allocating principal tasks to staff supplemented by an *ad hoc* reallocation depending upon the level of demand during the day. Attempting to schedule in a more detailed way would be inappropriate as being able to forecast daily demand would depend on factors such as the weather, level of passing trade and pattern of regular demand in a service business where demand needs to be met as quickly as possible and queue lengths kept short.

In other businesses, the level of operations scheduling will be more detailed as the system is more manageable in that customer orders are not of the short-duration demand profile described above. Even so, some scheduling systems are simpler than others but adequate to meet the control requirements of the operations system involved. We will start off by describing the easier systems and then move onto ones that meet the needs of more complex operations tasks.

1. Bar charts

One of the simplest methods of operations control is a bar chart. In essence, this method shows the elements of capacity (for example, process or staff) on the vertical axis and represents time as a bar on the horizontal axis – see Exhibit 8.5. Selecting the appropriate dimension of time (for example, hours, days or weeks) will reflect the nature of the operations system to be scheduled. Exhibit 8.5 uses weeks as this best suited these scheduling needs. Often in professional companies there would also be a calendar running horizontally to show the schedule against actual dates as an aid, in this instance, in scheduling consultant availability against client requested start times for new assignments. Finally, a description of the task (in the example provided by Exhibit 8.5, this is the name of the client) is added to the chart.

Bar charts are also used to schedule and control more complex operations systems, particularly where choices can be made. Exhibit 8.5 represents an overview of consultant allocations to clients. Within each assignment, the various elements would be covered by the team of consultants allocated to that job. The lead consultant would typically control the allocation of tasks to other staff to reflect skills and experience, individual loadings and completion times. Exhibit 8.6 shows a bar chart to represent this. You will see from this that it covers some of the tasks identified at the start of the assignment. Other tasks will be identified as the assignment continues and these will be introduced into the schedule of work and allocated a team member(s), an estimated time to complete and a start and finish date. Typically, a weekly review would check progress. The bar chart would then be updated in terms of the work completed with any revisions to the schedule being incorporated at the review meeting.

Some products and services comprise several steps with each of these completed by a different part of the processes or delivery system. Again bar charts are used to schedule these jobs through the system to meet the required delivery dates. A bar chart identifies and helps to resolve potential capacity problems, provides short-term control over the progress of work and allows a business to assess whether or not operations is able to take on additional customer orders within existing capacity levels and

Exhibit 8.5   *Part of a bar chart representing assignment allocations to management consultants*

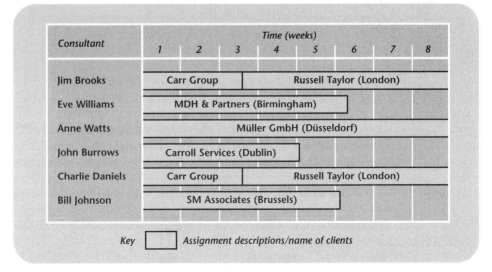

Exhibit 8.6 *Bar chart for scheduling the initial tasks in a consultancy assignment following the day 1 introductions and client discussions*

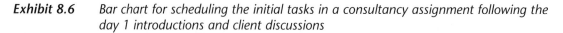

delivery timescales. Exhibit 8.7 provides part of a schedule showing jobs loaded on different processes within the sequence necessary to complete the task. You will see from this that the items comprise a number of steps that, in turn, need to be completed on different processes. The resulting task is more complex and includes the need to determine priorities between jobs that require the same process to complete one or more of the necessary steps.

Exhibits 8.5 to 8.7 show the use of bar charts to manage scheduling requirements of differing complexity in terms of variety and detail. The use of IT-based systems would typically be used to manage such systems. In many businesses, the demands on and requirements of operations control lead to other systems being used to meet these more difficult control tasks. The sections that follow describe these.

2. Network analysis

Businesses involved in making products of such size or construction that they cannot be transported after completion, or providing services that can only be undertaken at a client's premises, will often use a project process to undertake the work involved (see Chapter 4). If a project contains only a few activities a bar chart or even an informal scheduling approach can be adopted. However, most projects are complex and involve many interrelated activities necessitating the development of a formal plan and the use of IT-based systems.

The one-off or infrequent nature of these tasks militates against the use of the more traditional scheduling and progressing methods described later. As a result, control systems under the heading network analysis were developed, the principles of which are now described.

Exhibit 8.7 *Part of schedule using a bar chart and showing orders against machine processes on a timescale*

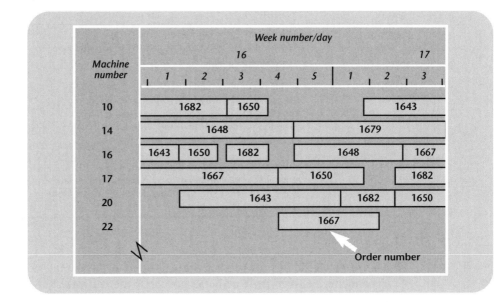

General aspects of network analysis

The first task in network analysis is to determine the level of detail on which the activities to complete the task will be based. Often in large projects an overall network will be developed with subnetworks provided to give control at a more detailed level. When this has been agreed, the activities that have to be completed will be listed.

All the activities listed at the start should represent the total task. By building a network, the task to be completed is stated as a series of activities all of which have to be completed for the task to be finished. The key is to draw the network so that the activities are shown in the order in which they have to occur. To do this it is necessary to establish for each activity, the other activity or activities that have to be completed before it can start. This is called dependency. One or more activities will, however, be independent of any other activity being completed before they can start. These are obviously the ones that are completed at the beginning (although in complex networks some independent activities may not be started at the beginning, as explained later). When these independent activities have been completed (an event) then any activities that can only start when these are complete can now commence, and so on. In this way the network is developed. Those activities that follow others are said to be sequential, while those that can be completed at the same time as others (that is, they are independent) are said to be parallel. The language and symbols used in constructing networks are provided in Exhibit 8.8.

Scheduling by network analysis

When constructing a network the steps to follow are:

Exhibit 8.8   *The principal building blocks used to construct networks*

Type	Description	Symbol
Activity	Activities are tasks that have a time duration. At the start and finish of each activity there will be, in network language, an event	⟶
Event	Events occur instantaneously and state that the preceding activity or activities is (are) now complete and other activities that depend on their completion can now start. As it is instantaneous it has no time duration	◯
Dummy activity	Dummy activities are used in two ways ■ an aid to drawing a network, as will be shown later ■ a way of extending the dependency of one or more activities to other activities	- - - -▶

■ **Planning** – establish all the activities or steps to be completed, determine the dependency between these activities and draw the network.

■ **Scheduling** – apply to a network any limiting factors such as time, cost and the availability of materials, equipment and staff. These factors will often necessitate the redrawing of parts of a network to accommodate the constraints they impose.

■ **Controlling** – is the task of obtaining feedback during a project to ensure adherence to the plan, and to update the plan in the light of any changes that occur.

Planning

The first task when constructing a network is to establish and list all the activities necessary to complete a project and at the level of detail already agreed (earlier we mentioned that networks can be used to provide a control system to overview a project as well as providing control at a much more detailed level). This step is invaluable as part of the overall control of a project. Following this, it is necessary to determine which activities depend upon which other activities being completed before they can start; this is described as dependency. The final task is to draw the network. Several examples that result from the completion of these tasks are provided later. The symbols used throughout were explained in Exhibit 8.8, and the following general guidelines will prove useful when setting about the task of drawing a network:

■ all activities start and end with an event
■ an activity is a time-consuming task
■ an event is instantaneous; its occurrence means that all activities entering that event sign have now been completed and, therefore, all activities leaving that event sign can now be started
■ any number of activities can go into and out of an event
■ activities, wherever possible, should go from left to right
■ activities occurring on the same path are sequential and are thus directly dependent upon each other

Exhibit 8.9 *Introducing the use of a dummy activity*

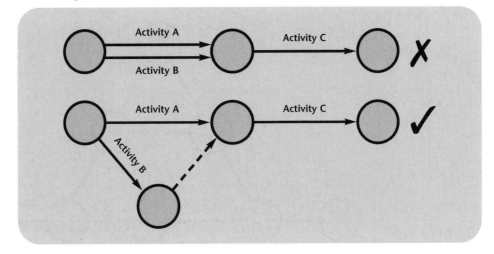

■ activities on different paths are termed parallel activities, are independent of other sets of parallel activities and can, therefore, take place at the same time

■ dummy activities are used in two ways:
  – as an aid to drawing a network. As such they form part of the set of conventions to be followed. One of these conventions is that two or more activities cannot leave one event sign and enter the same end event sign. In order to accommodate such situations dummy activities are used (see Exhibits 8.9 and 8.10)
  – as the way of extending the dependency of one or more activities to other activities (see Exhibit 8.11).

The role of a dummy activity is to facilitate the presentation of networks and to extend the dependency function to other, relevant activities which is the essence of the network concept. Dummy activities are not time-consuming (the time involved is already registered with the original activity), hence their name.

To explain, the following example lists the activities to be undertaken to complete a task and indicates those activities on which an activity is dependent. Therefore, Activity B cannot start until Activity A has been completed and so on.

Activity	Activities on which it is dependent
A	–
B	A
C	A
D	B
E	B
F	C, D
G	E
H	F, G

Exhibit 8.10   *Network representing the task above*

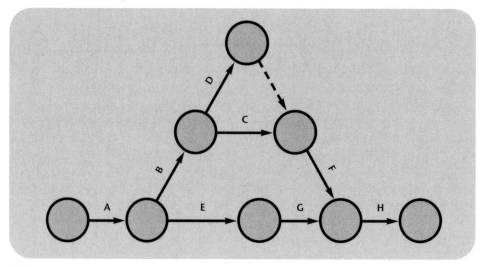

Notes

Activities A, E, G and H are examples of sequential activities.
Activities B, C, D and F are parallel to activities E and G.

The resulting network is shown as Exhibit 8.10. It starts with Activity A as this is the only activity that does not depend upon any other activity before it can start. Then the rest of the activities are built into the network to represent the statement of the task.

Scheduling

The next step is to schedule the network. This involves applying limiting factors such as time and cost to the network. In the example presented as Exhibits 8.11 and 8.12 the activities are given for the production of an educational cassette with the number of days it takes to complete each activity. All the tasks, unless specified, are completed by the consultant running the business. Note that the time units in which duration is expressed must be common for all activities, should reflect the task on hand and can be in hours, days, weeks or even months. From this information the resulting network is shown as Exhibit 8.12.

There are three further points to note from this exhibit:

■ Activity descriptions, often abbreviated, are written above the line of the arrow symbol. It is important where possible to avoid using references (often difficult with a computer program) because it makes the reading of the network laboured and may lead to mistakes being made.

■ The time duration for an activity is written below the line of the arrow.

■ The event signs (known as nodes) have been used to provide additional information. This is explained in Exhibit 8.13.[1,2]

Earliest start time is calculated from the beginning of a network by cumulating the time units of all sequential activities. It expresses the earliest time by which any

Exhibit 8.11 *The activities involved in preparing an educational cassette*

Activity		Duration (working days)
1.	Client briefing	4
2.	Write draft 1	7
3.	Await client approval of draft 1	5
4.	Write draft 2	6
5.	Await client approval of draft 2	5
6.	Create the production script (PS)	3
7.	Await client approval of the PS	2
8.	Produce the cassette tape of the PS	5
9.	Book studios	1
10.	Confirm studio booking	1
11.	Send script to the actors	1
12.	Actors prepare the scripts	2
13.	Complete artwork roughs	1
14.	Await client approval of artwork roughs	5
15.	Send artwork roughs to artist	1
16.	Fine artwork and typesetting by artist	10
17.	Check fine artwork and photocopy	2
18.	Send copy of artwork to three printers	1
19.	Await quotations of printers re artwork	3
20.	Accept printer's quotation	1
21.	Send artwork and confirmation to the printer	1
22.	Artwork printed	10
23.	Send artwork prints and cassette tapes to a duplicating house	1
24.	Tapes duplicated and matched to artwork prints	10
25.	Deliver to client	1

Notes

1. This list describes the sequence of tasks involved in the production of an educational cassette for a client. The consultant engaged in this work was able to vary his working week by working the odd Saturday or Sunday in order to meet any necessary deadlines, but this is to be regarded as the exception rather than the rule. However, for the purpose of this task, any parallel activities requiring the consultant's time should be regarded as not being able to be completed at the same time. All times are given in whole days even though some activities may only take a few minutes.
2. The numbering of the activities is for reference purposes only.
3. The earliest the studios can be booked is following Activity 3.
4. Once Activity 6 is complete, Activities 10 and 11 can start.
5. Artwork roughs can be completed after Activity 3 is complete.

activity leaving a particular event can start. Where two or more activities enter an event then the activity to finish last will establish the earliest start time for any subsequent activities. Thus, in Exhibit 8.12, two activities enter Event 20. Activity 'Tape production' between Events 16 and 20 would result in an earliest start time of 33 + 5 = 38 days. However, activity 'Print' between Events 19 and 20 results in an earliest start time of 41 + 10 = 51 days. Consequently, as activity 'Send tape and artwork to duplicating house' depends on all activities entering Event 20 before it can

Exhibit 8.12 Network for the activities given in Exhibit 8.11 for preparing an educational cassette

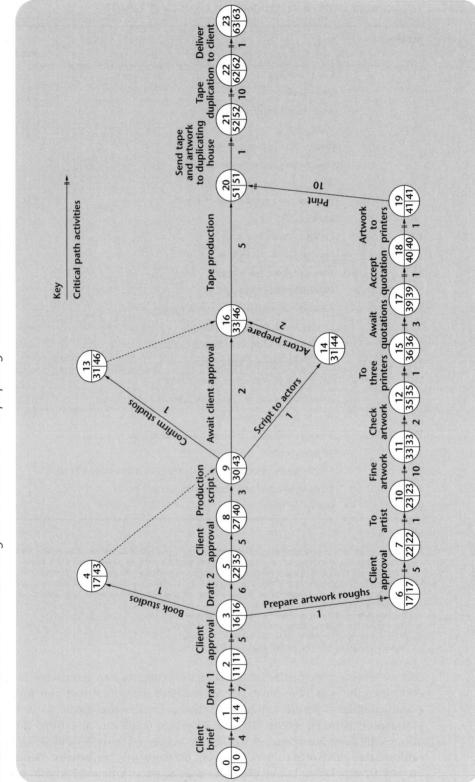

start then it will be the 51 and not 38 days that is entered in the left space of Event 20. The final event sign of a network contains the planned finish time for the project – for example, 63 days in Exhibit 8.12.

Latest finish time is calculated from the end of a network. The same cumulative time as that entered in the earliest start time segment of the final event node is entered in the latest finish time segment of that node – for example 63 in Exhibit 8.12. Then, the duration of activities is successively subtracted from this finish date and entered into the appropriate event sign. Where two or more activities back into one event, then the earliest of the cumulative times will determine the latest finish time for all previous activities.

For example, look at Event 9 in Exhibit 8.12. Activities from Events 13 and 14 back into this event. While the calculation for the former would be 45 days, it is the 43 days resulting from the Event 14 to Event 9 calculation that is recorded as the start/finish time for activities entering Event 9. The reason is that unless the latest finish time requirement of 43 days is met at this point in the network, additional time to that planned will be added to the sequence of activities starting with the one between Events 9 and 14.

Critical path analysis – of essential interest in scheduling is the minimum length of time it will take to complete a project. This is determined by critical path analysis. To do this it is necessary to find the longest path through a network and this represents the critical path. Each task on the critical path, moreover, is called a critical activity because delays to any of these activities will increase the overall length of a project. The critical nature of these tasks is also shown by the fact that the earliest start and latest finish times recorded in the series of events on the critical path are the same. For these activities there is no flexibility; if the start of any activity is delayed, the project will be delayed. The critical path is then marked in one of several ways, see Exhibit 8.12 for example.

When activities do not fall on the critical path, some delay will have no effect on the completion time for a project. The extent of the delay before the overall time is affected is the difference between the earliest start time and the latest finish time less the activity duration. This is known as total float or slack[2] and is usually entered on the network diagram as part of the information necessary for the controlling phase of a project.

Exhibit 8.13   *Explanation of the information contained in an event node*

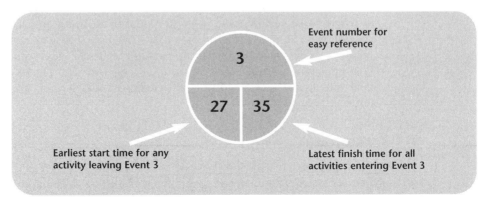

Controlling

A network is a control mechanism. Information on the tasks completed and delays anticipated or incurred needs to be fed back so that a network can be updated. Knowledge of these changes and the impact they have on a project as a whole are essential for three important reasons:

■ It is a prerequisite for effective control.

■ Throughout the life of a project, decisions need to be made on the best course of action to take in the light of changing circumstances. Networks readily help managers to appreciate the impact of delays. In turn, this allows them to consider, in advance, the action to take with knowledge of the impact on aspects such as cost and completion dates, rather than taking decisions in a crisis situation with insufficient time to evaluate alternative courses of action.

■ Out-of-date networks soon fall into disrepute and managers stop using them.

The details discussed so far form the basis for network analysis and have introduced the concepts of scheduling the limiting factors and the task of controlling a project as it progresses. It is not intended here to go into further detail. But, there are some important points of which an operations manager should be aware:

■ The examples provided are intentionally simple. Network analysis is normally used for complex tasks consisting of many interrelated activities.

■ Although one-off projects are the most frequent type of tasks for which network analysis is used, it is also applied to tasks that will be repeated. Its purpose in these situations is to establish the best way to complete the interrelated activities involved, and this is then used on future occasions. The production of an educational cassette is an example of this application (see Exhibits 8.11 and 8.12).

■ In complex project applications, there are usually several sets of constraints that need to be accounted for within a network. This chapter refers to the use of critical path analysis (CPA). However, there are many more applications that provide for the more sophisticated requirements of complex one-off projects. These include PERT (programme evaluation review techniques), resource levelling and precedence diagrams.[3]

■ An important safeguard to incorporate into any network is the concept of target or key dates. These are established at the end of different phases within a project and at which times reviews take place. In addition to being an integral part of the control phase, it helps prevent float or slack from one phase in a project being used up at an earlier stage. If this is not carefully controlled then projects can use up float prematurely and create a situation in which the end phases have little or no float and hence several critical paths emerge with sets of activities becoming unnecessarily critical.

3. MRP and JIT

The two most widely used forms of operations control to help manage more complex operations systems are materials requirement planning (MRP) and just-in-time (JIT) planning and control. Both MRP and JIT have extended definitions and roles that will be explained at the end of the relevant section.[4] The purpose here is to introduce these two major systems before explaining them in full within their own separate sections that follow later.

Operations control systems start with a statement of demand. In businesses where demand is for special (that is, do not repeat) products and services, the nature of the control system will reflect this significant factor. As explained earlier in Chapter 4 (and specifically as shown in Exhibit 4.14), the operations control and scheduling task will be undertaken by the person responsible for meeting a customer's requirements. This person would often use a bar chart or network to schedule the tasks involved – for example, see Exhibit 8.6.

Where a business provides standard products and services (and also where a business sells technically complex products and services with many steps and stages), it needs to use scheduling systems that can handle the control requirements involved. Two of the more widely used systems in such circumstances are MRP and JIT.

As stated earlier, all operations control systems start with a statement of demand. The key dimension to managing and controlling operations in situations where the products and services are standard (as well as complex specials as explained earlier) is to recognize the principle of independent and dependent demand:

■ **Independent demand** describes products and services for which the pattern of demand does not directly relate to the use of any other item. Examples include finished goods and services.

■ **Dependent demand** describes products and services for which the pattern of demand is directly linked to the use of other items, for example parts that go into products. Thus, such items do not need to be forecast but can be calculated.

In a fast-food restaurant, daily demand for each type of burger, fries and other items on the menu would be classed as being independent. The demand for burgers, buns, other ingredients and packaging would be classed as dependent. Similarly, the oil and packing for fries would have a dependent pattern of demand and, thus, as with all such items, do not need to be forecast as they can be calculated.

With these principles now in place let us turn our attention to MRP and JIT.

4. MRP

The role of an operations system is to translate demand into statements of capacity (staff and/or process) and materials requirements in terms of how much and when. For products and services that have an independent pattern of demand, the statement of demand for those products and services will be the starting point for the control system. In make-to-order (MTO) businesses, the products and services, known as customer orders, will have been received beforehand. In make-to-stock (MTS) businesses the statement of demand may comprise both known orders and forecast requirements or solely the latter.

MRP[5] is a system that determines the final products and services (in terms of which ones and the volumes involved) a company will provide during a future period and then specifies the necessary operations inputs to that demand. MRP is then used to manage the material and capacity needs where demand for items is dependent. For example, the demand for engines, wheels, body panels and other parts that go into a car assembly is linked to the demand for cars. To determine the number of engines, wheels, body panels and other parts we have first to determine the number of cars to be built in different time periods and then calculate the requirements for all dependent items.

Before the advent of MRP, most operations control systems relied on models (such as order point) for managing materials inventory (see Chapter 10) for items with both an independent and dependent pattern of demand. These systems frequently resulted in situations where there was simultaneously too much inventory of some items and too little inventory of others. The reason for this was that these systems:

■ failed to take advantage of the fact that demand for dependent items can be calculated and does not, therefore, have to be forecast
■ looked to the past when determining how much to order and when; they assumed that the future would be like the past and used this information to generate forecasts for items that, in turn, drove operations schedules
■ were based on replenishing stock depleted by past schedules and not to meet the needs of current and future demand.

To remedy these deficiencies, MRP was developed. The first task, as always, is to determine the future demand for all independent items. For each final product or service an MRP system contains a recipe (or bill of materials in systems language) of the inputs necessary to make one unit. It then simply multiplies the number of finished products or services by the recipe. This results in a statement of the gross requirements to meet forecast demand. Any existing inventory of dependent items will then reduce the final requirement to give a net requirement figure.

What makes MRP attractive is that it is straightforward, makes sense and is practical to use. Reality brings issues of uncertainty (for example, suppliers' adherence to requested delivery dates and actual internal capacity matching the plan) but the fundamental logic offers many advantages over past approaches. With the context in which MRP was developed having been set, let us now look at MRP in more detail.

Overview of an MRP system

MRP looks at known and/or forecast future requirements and uses these and other information to determine demand for end products and services and to generate statements of the materials, components and subassemblies necessary to complete these. It is known as a 'push' system (as opposed to a 'pull' system, such as JIT, described in the next section) in that statements of requirements are made in line with agreed delivery dates and these are stimulated at the start of the process in line with relevant schedules. In this way, the necessary materials, components and subassemblies are pushed into the process. In order to keep inventory as low as possible and the associated inventory control task as simple as possible, the dates on which orders are due (referred to as due dates) are checked to ensure that materials are available. Materials are then 'pushed' through the process to meet due date requirements. The advent of low-cost computing offered companies the opportunity to plan and control complex operations processes in an orderly way by using MRP principles. As explained earlier, MRP relies on the fact that the demands for all materials, components and subassemblies are dependent upon the demand for finished products or services. For such items only one forecast is necessary. It must be made at the highest level (that is, where the item has an independent demand pattern) and from which all other demands can be calculated. The principle on which this operations control information system is based is one of planned requirement, hence its name. Requirements for all dependent items are thus calculated based on the known and/or forecast demand for the independent products and services in which they are used.

The demand for independent items is determined from known and/or forecast orders modified by any existing inventories and forms a schedule of operations requirements or master schedule normally for one or more time periods. This then becomes the input into MRP which, by means of a parts explosion, calculates the requirements for all dependent items.

The elements of an MRP system

Chapter 6 dealt with capacity and introduced, as Exhibit 6.6, an overview of the planning, scheduling and execution elements of the operations control task. This overview was reintroduced earlier in this chapter as Exhibit 8.2. A glance back at Chapter 6 and Exhibit 8.2 will remind you that the tasks involved in the planning phase were discussed as part of the issues addressed on capacity. These front-end requirements need to be completed no matter what type of control system is chosen to manage the operations scheduling task. Whether a company selects, for instance, JIT or MRP, the phase concerning long-term planning and the translation of demand into a commitment by the company to make or provide an agreed mix of products or services has to be undertaken. Without a statement of what to make or provide (a master schedule) then operations cannot function. How a business then schedules and executes the operations control task will depend upon the system it chooses to use and the basis of that choice should reflect its own business needs and characteristics.

An MRP system takes the master schedule information and translates it into relevant operations tasks as shown in Exhibit 8.2. It is a general model of a control system depicting MRP as the scheduling function on which it is based and provides details of the inputs and outputs of the system. As shown in this outline, the MRP system consists of several elements – the inputs, the package itself that carries out the calculations and the output reports. The general model depicted here may differ in terms of the content and descriptions used, depending upon the organization and the products or services in question, but it is important to appreciate the purpose of these elements in order to understand the basis on which MRP is structured. At the top of the outline is the master schedule highlighting the key role that it plays within a planning and control system, and this is where we will start.

Master schedule

The master schedule is a management commitment to produce or provide certain quantities of finished products or services in particular time periods. To do this it takes statements of demand (both forecast sales and known orders) and tests them against statements of capacity and resources (rough-cut capacity plans and short-term elements of capacity) for the same period(s). The result is an anticipated schedule of finished products and services. As such, it is a statement of operations output and not of market demand. That is, the master schedule is not a forecast and should not be confused with such. Sales forecasts are a major input into the master scheduling function. However, by taking into account capacity limitation as well as the desire to utilize capacity fully, the master schedule will optimize these requirements when forming its statement of what is to be produced or provided. In this way the system highlights problems and the master schedule resets levels to match capacity, so forming an important and core communication link between sales and operations. It is a schedule and thus states requirements in terms of product/service specifications (for example, part numbers or product/service descriptions) for which bills of materials exist. The detailed schedule produced drives the MRP system that, in turn, drives the operations and purchasing records and procedures.

The master schedule thereby has a key role in the control system that leads to an agreement between marketing and operations on what to produce or provide and the financial implications that derive from these decisions. To perform this task well, accurate information is essential. This requirement includes inventory records, the quantity and timing of current operations schedules, outstanding purchase orders, up-to-date bills of materials that reflect changes and clear information about existing customer requirements, current orders and sales forecasts.

A master schedule is created for each item using known customer orders, sales forecasts and a knowledge of operations capacity. It is likely that the schedule will contain a major proportion of firm customer orders in the more immediate time periods and will be based mostly on forecasts in the later periods of the planning horizon as shown in Exhibit 8.14. The length of the planning horizon is determined by calculating the operations lead time for an item (materials lead time plus process lead time) and adding a period of time to allow the purchasing function visibility over the future so that price and delivery advantages can be secured (see Exhibit 8.15).

Exhibit 8.14   *Master schedule for a given product at a point in time*

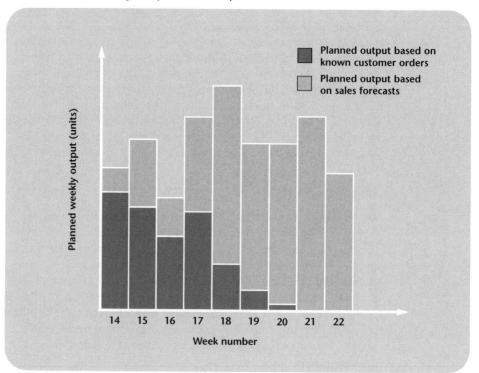

Exhibit 8.15 *Elements of the planning horizon*

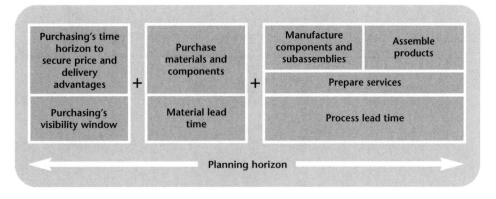

For many companies, the resulting planning horizon will be several months. It would, therefore, be impractical not to allow changes to the master schedule particularly for time periods well into the future. One method of controlling changes to the master schedule is to split the planning horizon into time zones, each of which has different rules concerning acceptable levels of change (for example, see Exhibit 8.16).

As shown in Exhibit 8.2, the master schedule forms part of the 'front end' of a planning and control system, whereas MRP is at the centre (the 'engine' phase) of a system. Its primary purpose is to take the period-by-period demand statements for the specific products and services that are contained in the master schedule and produce a time-phased set of subassembly, components, material and capacity requirements to meet these. An MRP package completes these calculations at each level and so converts the master schedule of independent demand statements of finished products and services into planned orders for dependent demand parts. To do this it requires recipes or 'bills of materials' information (including relevant specification change data) for relevant products and services, together with 'inventory status data' in order to make any necessary adjustments. In this way it provides the link between the front

Exhibit 8.16 *Rules concerning the level of change allowed to the master schedule at different times on the planning horizon*

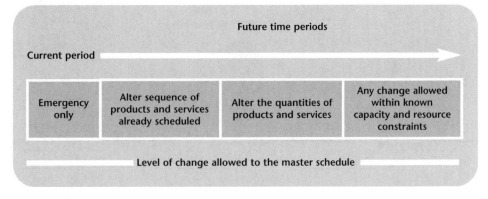

Exhibit 8.17 *Photographs of an EIW 20 mm gland as detailed in Exhibit 8.18*

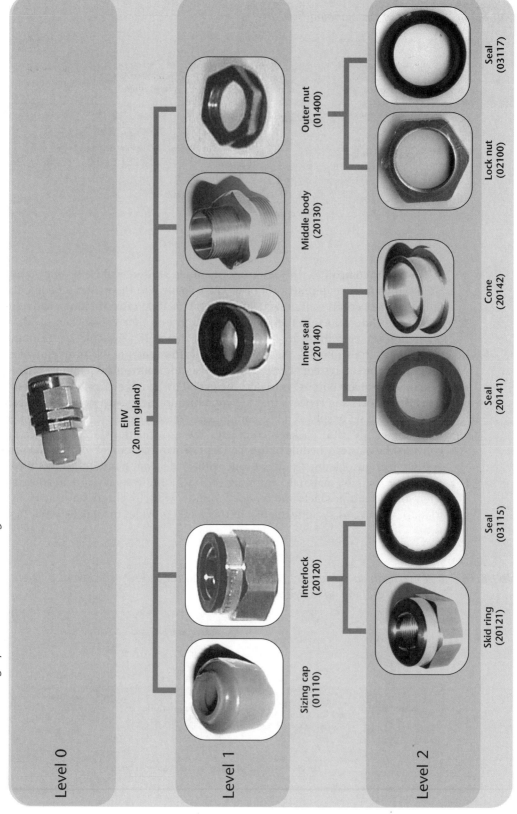

Level 0

Level 1

Level 2

EIW
(20 mm gland)

Sizing cap
(01110)

Interlock
(20120)

Inner seal
(20140)

Middle body
(20130)

Outer nut
(01400)

Skid ring
(20121)

Seal
(03115)

Seal
(20141)

Cone
(20142)

Lock nut
(02100)

Seal
(03117)

Source: Remora Electrical Limited, Sheffield (UK).

end of a business (demand forecasts and known customer orders) and the tasks to be completed by operations. Now let us move on to explaining two of the elements within an MRP system as depicted in Exhibit 8.2.

Product/service structure records

Product/service structure records provide information on materials and components (the bill of materials) and how each product or service is made (the routing file). The bill of materials (BOM) is a file or set of files that contains the 'recipe' or formula for each finished product or service (see Exhibits 8.17 and 8.18). The recipe consists of information regarding the materials, components and subassemblies that make up each finished product and service and is held on what is often known as a product/service structure file. In addition, a parts master file contains all the standard information about each item including part number, description, unit of measure, process lead time, materials lead time, purchase order quantities, buffer stockholding and inventory data.

Depending upon the complexity of the product/service structure, there will be a number of levels within a bill of materials. The end item itself is termed level 0. The components (subassemblies, parts and materials) that together make the end item will be listed in the parts explosion and designated level 1. Any level 1 components that have themselves a components list will, in turn, be exploded as level 2 and so on. This explosion would then be completed for all components across all products and services. The requirements for each component would be accumulated plus any indepen-

Exhibit 8.18 *The bill of materials for an EIW 20 mm gland*

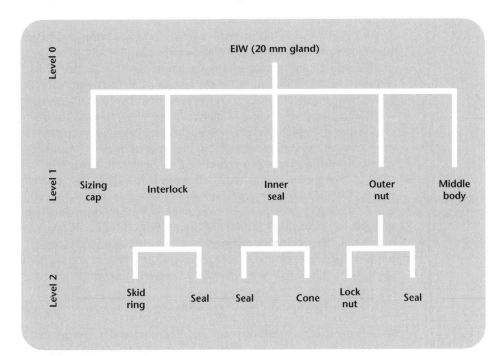

dent demand for a component (for example, spare parts) and these would then be added together (that is, treated by the system as one order quantity) to provide delivery plans. Using delivery and product lead times, a release schedule for each order to meet final assembly is then determined.

It is frequently preferable to identify a component requirement with the higher-level part or end items for which it is to be used. This is known as pegging and provides a partial listing that identifies, at a desired level of detail, where requirements come from and are to be used. This is helpful when rescheduling.

The routing file provides information on the preferred sequence of operations to be undertaken to complete the components, subassemblies or service. It will also specify other possible routings. These would be suboptimal to the preferred routing and only used when necessary.

Inventory status records

The inventory status file records all transactions and inventory balances. The transactions are mainly receipts and issues. Adjustments to recorded balances will also be made as a result of inspection reports identifying rejects and physical inventory checks revealing balances different from that on file. As the required degree of control varies, the level of detail at which inventory records are kept will also vary. Where greater control is required then the work-in-progress (WIP) inventory condition may be separated into a number of different stages within the total process. This enables relevant components and subassemblies to be monitored from one predetermined stage (or even operation) to the next.

As with product service structure records discussed in the last section, the main requirements of inventory status information are accuracy and timeliness. They are critical to the running of an MRP system and their absence would undermine the very usefulness of the output reports that form the basis of the operations and purchasing plans.

For organizations with diversified products and services, MRP is practical only with some form of data processing. Without this aid it would normally be too difficult to recalculate requirements for complex assemblies with each change in the schedule. MRP provides a control and information system to help co-ordinate operations decisions concerning finished goods, material/component and WIP inventory levels and the scheduling and rescheduling of materials and components through operations to final assembly and inspection. It does this by time-phasing requirements by quantity, based on a due-date planning system for higher-level items. The independent/dependent demand principle explained earlier in the chapter, is at work here. Higher-level item (that is, final products or services) demand is calculated using known and/or forecast orders. The due dates for these are also recorded in the system and recorded by the master schedule. As dependent items, the materials, components and subassemblies necessary to meet these higher-level items, both in terms of quantity and delivery (or due) dates, are calculated (referred to as time-phased requirements). Any changes in terms of quantities or due dates are fed into the system and the time-phased requirements are recalculated. Accurate product/service structures and inventory records are a key requirement of the system.

There are two approaches to recalculating MRP plans:

- **Regeneration** – previous plans are discarded and a new master schedule is calculated at the beginning of each time period. Each time the master schedule of forecast requirements for the independent items is exploded into the gross requirements for dependent items. Available inventories are then deducted and net requirements form the new planned orders for dependent items.

■ **Net change** – here, only changes from the last master schedule are exploded down through the bill of materials until a component is reached that is unaffected by the change.

The MRP system

As shown in Exhibit 8.2, the master schedule, inventory status and product/service structure records comprise the inputs into an MRP system. Exhibit 8.19 shows the master schedule for 20 mm gland, EIW. This schedule was completed for Period 7 (hence the firm programme in that period) with a forward look for Periods 8 and 9.

This schedule is then exploded by the bill of materials for EIW and the firm requirements are netted down by existing levels of relevant components and subassemblies (see Exhibit 8.20). This shows the gross and net requirements for 20 mm gland, EIW. To help you follow the calculations completed in Exhibit 8.20, notes on the columns are now provided:

■ **Inventory** – the current inventory holding (# units).

■ **Scheduled receipts** – the quantity (# units) of an item already scheduled to be received during Period 7. This could be from a supplier (for example, as with cone ring) or a subassembly made internally but currently in WIP waiting to be completed (for example, as with outer nut and inner seal – see Exhibit 8.18).

■ **Gross requirements** – the quantity required without taking account of any inventory. Note for EIW 20100, the gross requirement in Exhibit 8.20 is taken from the master schedule (Exhibit 8.19) – that is, 6000. Thereafter, the gross requirement of (say) outer nut 01400 is the net requirement for EIW 20100 (that is, 4860) and so on. Here again, reread the footnote to Exhibit 8.20 regarding common parts.

Exhibit 8.19 *Master schedule for 20 mm gland, EIW in Period 7 with a forward look at Periods 8 and 9*

Product – 20 mm gland, EIW			
Period	7	8	9
Forecast sales	5500	6000	7000
Forecast end of period stock	1250	1400	1500
	6750	7400	8500
Opening stock	950	1250	1400
	5800	6150	7100
Firm programme	6000*		

Note

* Any known orders for delivery in Period 7 would be noted and taken into account when determining the 'firm programme' quantity. If an export order for 1500 EIW had been received in Period 7, the 'firm programme' quantity would probably be adjusted upwards to take account of this. The reason is to ensure that the forecast end of period stock of 1250 units would be achieved by the end of Period 7.

Exhibit 8.20   *Gross and net requirements for 20 mm gland EIW for Period 7*

| Part | | Inventory | Scheduled receipts | Requirements | |
Description	Number			Gross	Net
EIW (20 mm)	20100	1 140	–	6 000	4 860
Sizing cap	01110	3 500	5 000	4 860	–
Interlock	20120	700	–	4 860	4 160
Skid ring	20121	300	1 000	4 160	2 860
Seal	03115	600	1 000	4 160	2 560
Middle body	20130	1 500	–	4 860	3 360
Inner seal	20140	1 250	–	4 860	3 610
Seal	20141	–	2 500	3 610	1 110
Cone	20142	–	2 000	3 610	1 610
Outer nut	01400	5 000	10 000	4 860	–
Lock nut	02100	6 400	–	4 860	–
Seal	03117	12 900	–	4 860	–

Note

Part numbers 01110, 03115, 02005, 01400, 02100 and 03117, as the above quantities suggest, are common to other products. Hence the larger 'inventory holding' and 'scheduled receipt' quantities recorded here. Therefore, as explained in the text, the MRP system would aggregate the demand for these parts and undertake a similar calculation to that above to determine total requirements.

■ **Net requirements** – the quantity required when inventory and scheduled receipts are taken into account.

A key element of the MRP system is the gross to net explosion. This is the procedure for translating product requirements into component part requirements while taking existing inventories and scheduled receipts into account. Only the requirements net of any inventory or scheduled receipts are considered, as shown in Exhibit 8.20. Thus, the gross to net relationship is not only the basis for calculating appropriate quantities but also the communication link between part numbers.

You will see from these explanations that the outputs from an MRP system underpin the concept of dependent demand. To calculate the latter, bills of materials, inventory status and scheduled receipts are all necessary. The concept of dependent demand is often called the fundamental principle of MRP as it produces the way to remove uncertainty from requirement calculations.

Outputs from MRP

Looking back at Exhibit 8.2 you will see the principal outputs from an MRP system. They comprise different levels of reports and executive instructions to make or purchase items. The initial outputs concern material and capacity statements and planned order releases for made in-house or purchased parts. As shown by the headings used in Exhibit 8.2, the MRP outputs are initially plans and not committed actions. As plans are easier to change it is important not to convert plans into actions any earlier than necessary. Eventually, the plans become actions covering purchase orders, operations orders and reschedule notices.

The headings and details in Exhibit 8.2 provide sufficient understanding of what is contained in and the role of the different outputs highlighted. These together with the overview in this section should provide you with a clear understanding of what is involved.

5. Evolution of manufacturing resources planning

As mentioned earlier, the role of materials requirement planning has been expanded into manufacturing resources planning. As both these titles share the same abbreviation, materials requirements planning is referred to as MRPI and manufacturing resources planning as MRPII.

MRPII has evolved to encompass not only the planning and control of operations and materials but other areas of a company. This approach is intended to provide a planning and monitoring system for all the resources of a business including operations, marketing, finance and technical support. The organizational needs that stimulated this development include:

- **The need for integration** – in today's dynamic business environment integrating different parts of a business brings major gains. The integration of these various parts ensures that all aspects of a business are taken into account when reaching an effective corporate decision. One principal facet of MRPII is an integrated system with one database used by the whole business according to individual functional requirements. This then allows the resources controlled by individual functions (for example, inventory and capacity in operations and cash-flow controlled by accounting and finance) to form part of the corporate decision-making process. A single database reduces inconsistencies, facilitates updating and allows multi-functional perspectives to be taken into account.

- **Time-based-competition** – increasingly important order-winners in many markets include shorter lead times. More sophisticated information technology systems provide timely and essential data to managers to help support customers' changing demands and to respond more quickly to decisions and enquiries in a more informed manner.

- **Multinational and multi-international communications** – many companies currently support their markets using a national and international provision. Data embracing the whole supply chain enable operations executives to better co-ordinate worldwide operations and purchasing activities. Satellite-based communications displaying real-time information from around the world enables operations to respond to changes and react quickly even in widely dispersed systems and operations locations.

Powerful computer-based systems with large storage capabilities enable expanded MRPII systems to support the wide-ranging needs of companies in terms of real-time data and comprehensive reviews. Information on corporate activities and resources is updated continuously and this has led to decisions being made on the basis of the business as a whole and with current information providing an up-to-date picture.

6. JIT control system

The advent of low-cost computing enabled the widespread use of MRP systems in the planning and control of different processes and conditions. The systems that went before were typically characterized by confusion and disorder supported by expediting and involving constantly changing priorities. By comparison MRP offered a well-ordered system reducing the need to reschedule frequently. However, an alternative approach to the operations control task that originated in the Japanese automobile industry and has since gained much support in other industrial countries and types of businesses is known as the JIT system. Whereas MRP is a plan–push system, JIT is demand–pull (see Exhibit 8.21).

The JIT operations system is relatively simple, requires little use of computers, and in some sectors can offer far tighter levels of control than computer-based alternatives. The idea is to produce and deliver goods and services just in time to be sold, subassemblies just in time to be assembled into finished goods, services and parts just in time to go into subassemblies, and purchased materials just in time to be transformed into parts.[6] The purpose is for all materials to be in active use within the total process. In this way materials are then always a productive element within the operations system which avoids incurring costs without corresponding benefits. Thus, the JIT system is based upon the concept of producing small quantities just in time as opposed to many alternative philosophies that are based on making inventory to optimize process capacity utilization or 'just in case' it is required.

With the continued spread of JIT systems many varieties or hybrids of this approach are being developed. Unfortunately many of these developments purport to being something that they are not, mainly because those involved have not recognized the concepts of which JIT is based. Consequently companies have introduced apparent JIT initiatives without understanding, examining and explaining the often significant modifications necessitated by these alternatives if they are to work. In some instances the concept has been so changed that the potential advantages of JIT throughout the supply chain are not forthcoming.[7] In order to explain the concept of JIT this section outlines the principles involved and against which JIT proposals should be measured.

JIT control systems are based on the principle that each part of the total operation (suppliers as well as a company's internal processes) delivers to the next stage the exact

Exhibit 8.21 *The direction of orders and flow of the operations process in an MRP and JIT system*

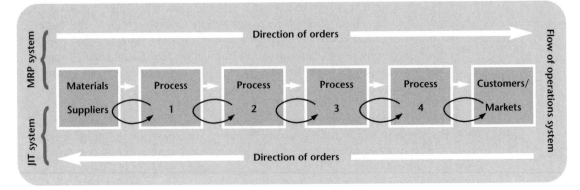

quantity needed for the following period's requirements. The period involved varies. In some instances the quantities equate to one day's requirement and in others, deliveries may be made several times each day. This means that each stage in operations receives sufficient parts from the previous stage just in time to enable it to complete a given quantity. In turn, it meets the exact requirements of the subsequent stage in the process, again on a JIT basis. The more deliveries during a day, the less inventory will be in the operations process. The number of deliveries is typically not the same between all stages. Factors such as length of set-up time, the physical size of the parts and, in the case of suppliers, the distance involved will affect this decision. However, the procedure used to call for an order quantity is similar. Parts, components or materials are delivered from one stage in a process to the next in agreed quantities and in a designated container, together with a card or document relating to that part. When a container of parts, components or materials is taken to be used, the card (the most well-known system is *Kanban*, which means card in Japanese) or similar signal is sent to the previous stage in the operations system. This signal now authorizes that part of the system to make an agreed order quantity. In turn it uses materials, components and subassemblies and this triggers its own signal to the previous part of the process and so on. In this way, all parts of operations supply the next stage just in time.

As mentioned above, for suppliers the frequency of deliveries is bound up with the distance between locations and the physical size and value (£s) of the parts involved. Normally, the longer the distance, the greater the physical size and lower the value (£s) of a part, the less frequent will deliveries be made. To facilitate increasing the number of deliveries and hence reducing inventory, suppliers are encouraged to build smaller facilities close to a plant. In the Ford car plant at Dagenham (UK), passenger seats for the Fiesta are made by the supplier (Johnsons Controls) in line with the assembly schedule. Although the supplier's factory is off-site it is connected to the assembly line by an overhead conveyor system that transports the seats directly onto the assembly line to match exactly the build programme of the car plant. Some suppliers to the Nissan car plant in Washington (UK) are within a few minutes' delivery time. To keep inventory as low as possible, deliveries are made every two hours throughout the day. To ensure delivery times are met, Nissan has agreed three different routes for suppliers' vehicles to take. These need to be used in a preferred order thus providing alternatives in cases of difficulty.

Case example ● 2

Nissan's JIT system developments include synchronizing supplier deliveries with its own car assembly programme. One such link is between Nissan and Sommer Albert, a French-owned carpet and trim manufacturer that has a satellite plant 3 km away from the car factory. As each car starts its journey through Nissan's manufacturing system, a special coding tag triggers a message to Sommer that specifies which of the 120 variations of carpet and trim is needed for that particular vehicle, a factor that reflects colour, right or left-hand drive, engine size and option selection. At Sommer the correct requirement is selected, (including carpet, parcel shelves and boot linings) trimmed and finished before being stacked in sequence and loaded on a vehicle in reusable carriers. On arrival (and that can be as many as 120 times a day) the driver takes the sets straight to the assembly line.

Case example questions

2.1 Why is a car plant particularly suited to JIT scheduling systems?

2.2 What developments in this example have been important in making the system work?

2.3 What advantages and disadvantages would be inherent in these arrangements?

To allow these exact deliveries to be met, end-users need to fix their own output programmes which then cannot be altered within the lead times of suppliers. Only with this certainty of requirements can a JIT control system be introduced and maintained where inventory is kept to a minimum at all stages of a supply chain.

The last section outlined how a JIT control system works. The main features of JIT systems and some prerequisites for its introduction are now summarized:[8]

■ It reverses the flow of information concerning parts and materials so that each stage calls off requirements from the previous stage as needed.

■ WIP inventory is kept to a minimum.

■ Bottlenecks need to be eliminated and process downtimes reduced to a minimum. As WIP is now minimized, the cushion of inventory is no longer provided. Process uncertainty, therefore, has to be kept to a minimum.

■ Changeover or set-up times, need to be reduced so that smaller order sizes become practical. For example, the set-up time for a hood and fender stamping operation was estimated by Toyota for typical parts as follows: USA 6 hours, Sweden and Germany 4 hours and Toyota's time 0.2 hour.

■ As a result of the last point, the operations system can handle smaller quantities on a more frequent basis as the relationship between set-up time and run length is maintained.[9]

The concept is very appealing. However, there are several prerequisites if it is to be achieved:

■ It is most suited to high volume, low variety and repetitive operations situations.

■ It must be end-user driven. The business making the final products and services must take responsibility for instigating this development and liaise with its suppliers accordingly.

■ Operations schedules must be firm. As the material is not available in the system (the desired state in JIT), then scheduled quantities cannot be increased.

■ Suppliers must be geographically close to customers thereby enabling regular deliveries to be made. Where the geographical distance is not short, frequent deliveries of small quantities are not feasible. Larger amounts at longer intervals will be the alternative and inventory will result.

Key factors for this system to work effectively are stable schedules (that is, call-offs are fixed and cannot be changed inside the material lead times of a supplier's supplier) and developing close relationships with suppliers. In many companies, however, the impact of the inherent instability of markets and a lack of close liaison with suppliers are more typically the operations situations that control systems have to handle. JIT although desired is often introduced or demanded. One typical result is that end-users do not keep schedules stable yet require JIT support from suppliers. The result is that suppliers hold inventory with all its attendant costs.

Achieving JIT

JIT advantages include the pursuit of zero inventories. The gains associated with inventory reduction are typically large and comprise two major elements. The reduction in inventory itself and the cost of managing the inventory and other aspects of operations associated with materials control. Reduced inventory has implications for cash, space, insurance costs, loss through damage and obsolescence and so on. No inventory also means no control requirements and the attendant overhead costs in managing materials. In fact, these latter gains often outweigh the former.

One key difference between MRP and JIT is the switch from using order quantities as the basis for loading onto the control system to one using throughput rates. In so doing, JIT replaces the time-based principle of MRP (that is, loading is in line with due dates) with a rate-based one (that is, loading is in line with throughput rates that trigger the system to replenish the next stage in the process). To achieve this switch, several changes need to be made, as follows.

Physical changes

There are several physical changes that need to become an inherent part of the process. These include:

■ **High volume, low variety demand** needs to underpin operations. This justifies the investment involved and allows the creation of a series of processes that are as near to the coupled nature of a line process as possible. The fact that JIT was first developed in the automobile industry was not by chance. These operations conditions provide some of the prerequisites (especially high volume) necessary for JIT control systems. Ways of developing this high volume requirement include product simplification in terms of range and standardization and the use of mix mode assembly to allow the manufacture of more products on a process, thus increasing the volumes involved.

■ **Set-up reduction** to allow order quantities to be reduced. In a line process there are no set-ups. Where processes require to be reset when a different product is to be made, then reducing set-ups allows smaller order quantities to be loaded.[9] This is necessary to enable components, subassemblies and final assemblies to be made in line with demand and to be unaffected by the length of time it takes to reset a process.

■ **Layouts** are changed so that the flow of products follows a consistent pattern in terms of preferred routing (see Exhibit 8.22).

■ **Operations arrangements** are often based on autonomous cells, each responsible for its own tasks and the supply to and from adjacent cells.

■ **Balanced flow of materials** throughout the processes.

Exhibit 8.22   *Simplified operations unit controlled by a JIT system*

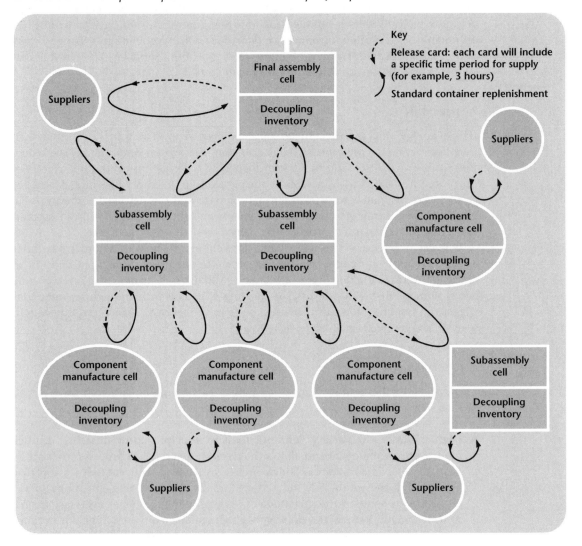

■ **Preventive maintenance programmes** (see Chapter 12) normally support JIT initiatives to help remove the causes of uncertainty and waste especially in conditions of minimum inventory holdings.

■ **Standard containers** to hold predetermined quantities are used to fix material levels and as part substitute for a control system and paperwork-based procedures.

■ **Improved quality conformance** through the process. This would be based on the use of statistical control techniques (see Chapter 9) and results in lower costs and the elimination of stoppages and inventory to cover process uncertainties.

Employee involvement

The role of staff in the process is also radically changed in the following ways:

■ Broader, day-to-day role in terms of job content. This includes cross-training regarding the tasks in a cell and often involves indirect work such as improving operations and scheduling. This not only improves the quality of the task but also means that when there is no active work to complete (in JIT the authority to make an order quantity must be received before work can commence) then staff can do control and evaluating tasks which are now forms of 'legitimate' work. However, in more traditional systems, when there is no scheduled work to do, then the choice is between making inventory and recording 'excess' labour hours.

■ As part of the last point, employees assume responsibility for the quality conformance checks completed during the process (see Chapter 9). This includes responsibility for stopping the process if a quality defect is discovered. The increased involvement of workers is also designed to use their knowledge to improve the system as part of the drive for continuous improvement. Exhibit 8.23 offers an amusing comment on this issue.

Control system changes

JIT impacts all areas of scheduling but principally within the operations and purchasing systems. These have already been overviewed. A more detailed description of how a JIT control works now follows.

The objective of a JIT system is to ensure that all materials in the process are active. In order to do this, steady schedules need to be supported by a drive towards shorter set-up times so that appropriate quantities of parts can be delivered to each stage of the process. To enhance the basic quantity factor, standard containers designed to hold agreed quantities are introduced. Lastly, a card-type system (*Kanban* was mentioned earlier – other systems have their own signal, for example 'action plate' at Nissan and 'DOPS' at Honda) forms the basis of all transactions. This document is the authority to

Exhibit 8.23   *JIT brings a change in attitudes, or else (smiles)!*

produce, and only on receipt of it can work be started. Exhibit 8.22 provides an outline chart illustrating materials flow in a simplified manufacturing business. The last module in this illustration is the final assembly cell which makes the end product. In a demand–pull type material flow system, final assembly will withdraw a standard container of work from a small quantity of decoupling inventory (see Chapter 10). Part of this transaction includes sending the release card to the previous, appropriate cell. In turn, this latter cell is now authorized to make a standard quantity of components or subassemblies. To do this it withdraws, from its own small quantity of decoupling inventory, a standard container of components/subassemblies. Again as part of this transaction, this cell also releases a card to its material supplier as illustrated in Exhibit 8.22.

By striving continuously to reduce set-ups and WIP inventory, the operations system is simplified in control terms, requires less inventory material to support transactions and has fewer interprocess dependencies. As a result, inventory levels continue to decline and the basis of control is simplified still further.

However, given the unstable nature of the marketplace described in Exhibit 8.1, to achieve the high level of stability necessary to underpin a JIT system the 'operations core' has to be effectively cushioned. This is achieved in three principal ways:

- **Schedules are fixed** – that is, what is to be produced cannot be changed within the lead time it takes to make alterations to material purchases. This factor relates to one of the prerequisites listed earlier that such systems need to be end-user driven.

- **Finished goods inventory** is held. Thus, when demand is lower than output, inventory will be created to sell in a later period (known as capacity-related inventory – see Chapter 10). Exhibit 8.24 shows the inventory holding at a Mitsubishi outlet in California. The finished goods inventory at the time totalled 284 2-cwt vans of standard design over a given range of colours.

- **Or, companies adopt a make-to-order approach** which means that products are only made on receipt of an order and will result in an order backlog or forward load preceding the delivery system. Now the system works on known orders and material is scheduled accordingly. Most European car makers produce on a make-to-order basis and hence are able to use JIT control systems.

Exhibit 8.24　　*Finished goods inventory at a Mitsubishi outlet in California*

From these general requirements it can be deduced that JIT applications are suitable for the regular schedules of repetitive manufacturing and not for the irregular work demands associated with one-off, low volume batch processes providing the needs of markets with uncertain and intermittent demands. As highlighted earlier (for example, Chapter 4) these issues need to be addressed when considering which control system best reflects the characteristics of a particular business. It is equally important to recognize that a company may require more than one type of operations control system to meet the needs of its different markets.

Finally, there are also a number of prerequisites to be met at the operating level in order to support the conceptual base of the JIT system. These include:

- **Level schedules** – schedules must be level. That is, within a given period, daily workloads need to be equal.

- **Frozen schedules** – schedules must be frozen over a time period. To do this a company should be able to use the final assembly schedule as the master schedule. This, in turn, necessitates getting the cumulative process lead times sufficiently short to eliminate the need for parts holdings at an intermediate level.

- **Fixed routings** – routings must be fixed to allow schedules for parts to follow closely the final assembly schedule. As process times are fixed then all schedules can work in tandem with one another.

- **Frequent set-ups** – a large number of set-ups will be completed each day to support the basis of making only as required. Consequently, set-ups must be very short.

- **Order quantities** – order quantities for parts must be small and fixed in size.

- **Quality conformance** – quality levels must be high to reduce rework and to increase the certainty of both capacity provision and schedules.

- **Process breakdowns** – processes must function. This requires diligent preventive maintenance to reduce breakdowns.

- **Labour utilization** – the principle of labour utilization should not be the basis on which schedules are determined. In turn, this requires that those involved are trained to cope with a wide range of tasks (including indirect work) in order to provide the necessary flexibility to meet both a wide range and times of no work being called for.

- **Employee involvement** – employees must participate in making improvements in order to monitor the existing system to ensure that quality conformance levels are maintained in the short term and to achieve continuous improvements in the future. The goal is, therefore, correct rather than hurried work.

7. JIT – A philosophy of operations management

The introduction and development of JIT within businesses often comprise a set of approaches that are integral to the success of its role as an operations scheduling system. This overall approach is referred to by some advocates of JIT as a philosophy in that it provides a set of steps, approaches and techniques to help manage operations.

In the management of operations, many of these techniques are now in general use as stand-alone approaches and form part of several other areas of development such as total productive maintenance and continuous improvement which are dealt with in Chapters 12 and 14 respectively. The set that typically forms an integrated part of JIT is now briefly reviewed.

Asset emphasis: inventory versus process

One driving force for many businesses in the past was the high utilization of fixed assets. Given the period prior to the mid-1960s when in most sectors, world capacity was less than world demand, high utilization of fixed assets (such as processes) was the way for a business to maximize its output and profit. This view continued to be held even in sectors where the imbalance between capacity and demand had been reversed. JIT challenged this view by trading off the objective of high utilization of processes for lower levels of inventory, as shown in Exhibit 8.25.

The advantages of material scheduled on a JIT basis are not restricted to those associated with the investment and cash benefits inherent in lower inventory. There are additional and sizeable gains concerning an easier scheduling task, simpler and less expensive systems and controls and lower overhead costs to manage the material system. The downside is that, as products are only made on an as-required and JIT basis, spare process capacity typically exists throughout the system.

Improvement through exposing problems

Integral to the JIT approach is a philosophy designed to deliberately expose problems and to use this as a vehicle for improvement. Exhibit 8.26 illustrates a classic example. This shows how excessive inventory (in the form of water depth) allows the delivery system (in the form of a ship) to operate with a whole range of problems going undetected. It creates a situation where management is unaware of the type and size of the inefficiencies that exist in the operations system and the improvements that need to take place. By reducing inventory (water) levels, the problems (depicted in Exhibit 8.26 as rocks) are exposed, the ship will now founder (management is alerted to issues) and the areas for improvement are highlighted. Within the JIT philosophy there is a desire to expose problems with such events being viewed as sound management practice in that only then can areas for improvement be identified. In more traditional approaches, problems are viewed as being a sign of inefficient management, are not deliberately sought and often covered over (for example, the role and origin of excess inventory as depicted in Exhibit 8.26). The opportunity to identify areas for improvement is thereby lost.

Incorporating indirect activities into the remit of direct staff

In traditional organization approaches, direct staff are employed to undertake direct work. Thus, direct staff only make products or provide services. The results of this traditional philosophy include:

■ In circumstances where there is no demand for a product or service, operations managers either have to make inventory or record direct staff as an excess cost (that is, not working). Most corporate performance measures make the latter less preferable than the former.

Exhibit 8.25   *The different orientation of traditional and JIT approaches*

Aspects		Traditional	JIT
		Approaches	
Focus		Make so as to keep processes and staff working. Objective is high utilization	Make only when needed. Objective is low inventory
Use of inventory[1]	cycle	Large order quantities to reduce the impact of set-ups on net available capacity	Make as little as possible – reduce set-ups or leave processes pre-set until the next order quantity arrives
	decoupling	Allow processes to make to and draw from WIP inventory. This decouples the dependency of processes and allows them to operate independently of one another	Minimize inventory between processes. This increases their mutual dependency and the need for co-operation and procedures to co-ordinate throughput
	overall	Make inventory just in case it is needed	Make inventory just at the time it is required
Operations emphasis		Process throughput speeds. Inventory facilitates high process utilization and high efficiency objectives	Set-up reductions or to hold excess capacity to allow small order quantities to be scheduled and low inventory levels to be maintained

Note

1. These types of inventory are explained in Chapter 10.

■ The experience and capability of direct staff is limited to making products or providing service. The involvement of direct staff in indirect activities such as scheduling, quantity conformance and improvement is not an integral part of their role, and consequently is not provided for as part of their job nor seen as part of their contribution to a business.

One element of the JIT philosophy is to increase the involvement of staff, particularly in areas such as first-line maintenance, day-to-day scheduling, quantity conformance and the drive for continuous improvement. (These aspects are dealt with in more detail in relevant chapters.) This is supported by appropriate training and by incorporating indirect tasks into the role of direct staff with the new mix of work being reflected in the time allocations and expectations concerning performance and output of those involved. This approach not only secures the contribution of all staff in areas such as continuous improvement but also eliminates the 'make inventory' or 'no work' scenario identified earlier. If there is no direct work on hand, staff now have legitimate indirect tasks to undertake.

Exhibit 8.26 *Excess inventory covers over problems that are consequently not exposed and dealt with*

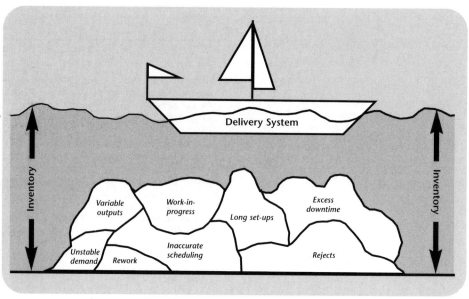

Eliminating waste

Waste is any activity that does not add value. One of the cornerstones of the JIT philosophy is to identify and reduce or, where possible, eliminate waste that occurs throughout the operations system. Examples of waste include the following.

Inventory

The drive to reduce inventory has already been highlighted. The benefits of lower investment, the release of cash to be used elsewhere in a business, the simplification of systems and reduced costs of associated control bring significant gains to a business.

Movement

The unnecessary movement of materials and people results in unproductive activity and introduces uncertainty into a system. While the waste element is easy to visualize what is often not appreciated is how common this is in operations systems and the size and extent to which it occurs. Changing layouts to reduce movement and improving systems and procedures to eliminate the need to check, ask questions or fetch necessary materials that should have been on hand are common improvements that result in significant gains.

In addition, unnecessary movement similar to the examples above also introduces uncertainty into a system. The additional time taken and when these instances will occur are unknown and introduce elements that cannot be incorporated into a system other than on an *ad hoc* basis.

Lead times

One by-product of waste is that operations lead times are extended. Unnecessary movement has already been highlighted. Other causes include:

■ **Waiting time** – material in the operations system that is not being worked on results in delay and additional lead time. See the throughput efficiency index calculation given at the end of this chapter.
■ **Set-ups** – long changeover times increase lead times.
■ **Process failures** – equipment breakdowns introduce delays and lengthen lead times.

Set-up reduction

The relationship between how long it takes to set up or make ready before work can begin and the length of time the order quantity takes to complete is often a core issue in operations. The ratio between these two activities is carefully monitored, particularly where capacity is in short supply.

In order to make products as required and on a JIT basis implies making smaller quantities on a more frequent basis. Reducing set-up times allows this to happen while keeping the ratio between these two elements at an acceptable level. A one-hour changeover to make an order quantity equivalent to six hours of processing time offers the same ratio as a 10-minute changeover and an order quantity taking one hour.

Set-up reduction underpins the opportunity for smaller quantities to be made more often. Alternatively, excess process capacity offers the same opportunity to make small order quantities in that processes can remain unchanged as they are not required to make alternative products or changeovers can be completed at times when a process is not being used.

8. Optimized production technology

Much attention has been given in the last decade to a proprietary system called optimized production technology (OPT). The development comprises two parts. The first is the conceptual base of the system and the second is the software package (OPT/SERVE) which supports the system itself.

OPT's main impact concerns scheduling. In essence (although OPT does possess other inherent contributions) it is a sophisticated control system based on finite loading procedures that concentrate on a subset of work centres. The finite loading of the bottleneck processes within operations is at the heart of this system and the software package uses an algorithm developed by Eliyahu Goldratt to accomplish the finite loading.

The basic philosophy underpinning OPT is not only important in itself but also in helping to understand some major issues in the management of an operations function.

In essence OPT addresses the following issue. To achieve the most profit from a given set of resources it is necessary to maximize the flow through and not the utilization of those resources. Throughput is limited by processes with inherent capacity constraints. These are known as bottlenecks. Thus, it is necessary to control the inputs into the operations process (that is, the amount of work scheduled into operations) in line with these constraints. The level of throughput that bottleneck processes can handle will determine the amount that can be completed and made available to sell. Companies, particularly in the past, often adopt a policy of maximizing the utilization of all available resources. Where this policy is adopted the result is that a business will generate part-completed work at some stages in the process that cannot be worked on at other stages (that is, the bottleneck processes) because of a lack of capacity. The result is WIP inventory.

Loading in line with the available capacity at bottleneck (or scarce resource) processes enables companies to maximize the flow of work to achieve maximum saleable output. Leading on from this, OPT prioritizes attention on increasing capacity at these bottlenecks by improvements such as set-up reduction and improved process yields. Creating more capacity at these processes leads to increased saleable output and greater profits.

In line with these central features the OPT literature highlights other points to reinforce the logic and provide direction on the action to follow. These include the following:

- The aim of a company should be to balance flow and not capacity. Reducing bottlenecks will increase total flow through the system thus releasing the potential capacity of other non-bottleneck processes.

- As a consequence of the above, an hour lost at a bottleneck is an hour lost for ever, but an hour saved at a non-bottleneck is of no consequence. Thus, saving set-ups at a bottleneck increases capacity and throughput, while additional set-ups at a non-bottleneck do not affect output but do minimize WIP inventory.

- The transfer order quantity may not, and often should not, be equal to the order quantity processed. This recognizes the fact that a company needs to determine order quantities at a bottleneck process with a view to both reducing the number of set-ups and hence increasing available capacity (the concept of cycle inventory – see Chapter 10) and then reducing the order quantity it transfers to the next process in line with demand rather than to maximize the utilization of subsequent processes. Thus, the process order quantity should be recognized to be variable not fixed.

- When determining schedules, capacity issues and priorities need to be considered at the same time and not separately.

9. Theory of constraints

The principles underlying the OPT philosophy have universal applicability. Consequently they can be used to enhance many existing control systems as well as providing useful insights into the more effective management of the operations function both in manufacturing and service companies. To this end, the general use of the concepts introduced in the last section on OPT is encapsulated in the term 'theory of constraints' (TOC), where a constraint is anything that limits an organization's ability to improve. Constraints can be physical (for example, process capacity or resource availability) or non-physical (for example, procedures or systems) in nature. It is the effective management of these constraints that makes this approach such a useful tool in managing operations as well as other functions. The six-step process below can help managers get the most out of an organization's resources:

1. Identify a system's constraints, whether physical or non-physical.

2. Ascertain those that affect the overall throughput of that part of the organization (the idea of bottlenecks and non-bottleneck processes described earlier).

3. Decide how best to get the most possible within the limits imposed by the current constraint.

4. Avoid keeping non-constraint resources busy as this produces unneeded work that sits in the form of WIP or part-completed tasks.

5. Evaluate a system's constraints and take actions to reduce the effects of these constraints such as reducing existing capacity losses, increasing available capacity and offloading demand or parts of demand to another part of the operations system. It is important here to make everyone aware of these constraints and their effects in order to focus attention on the problem and solutions.

6. Where constraints are relaxed in Step 5, go back to Step 1.

10. Enterprise Resource Planning

Enterprise Resource Planning (ERP) systems are designed to provide the information backbone to cope with the complexities of modern business and the global nature of today's markets. They provide a seamless integration of all the information that was previously dispersed through a company and turn it into a tool that managers can use. This includes supply chain information, customer information, human resource information, finance and accounting information and management reporting information (see Exhibit 8.27).

The attraction of ERP systems has its origins in the problem it is designed to solve – the fragmented information systems in organizations. As businesses become larger, more complex and widely dispersed managers typically have to cope with incompatible information systems and inconsistent operating practices that are frustrating, time-consuming and costly.

Exhibit 8.27   *ERP system: common central database providing information to meet the needs of diverse company functions and activities*

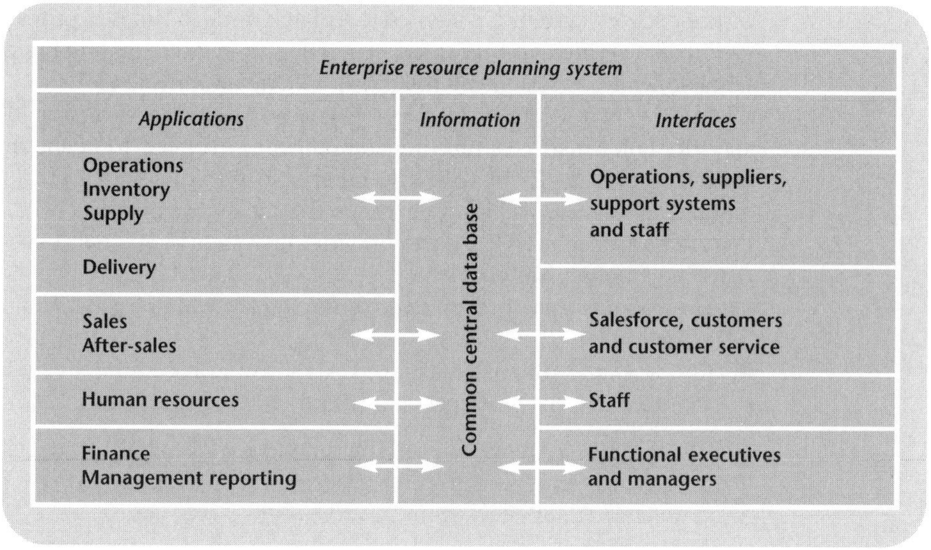

ERP can trace its origins back to the materials requirement planning (MRP) systems that gave control of operations processes. MRP became MRP II with the addition of more supply chain activities, such as distribution and other related activities in a business. These developments then broadened into ERP to take in financial control, human resource management and the international and diverse activities and locations that characterize today's companies.

Companies collect, generate and store vast quantities of data but in most instances this is undertaken by separate computer systems that cannot talk to one another. Each of these so-called 'legacy' systems provides invaluable support for the individual functions, business units, regions, factories or offices for which they were developed. The source of this disconnect is simple – IT developments have been undertaken in businesses over many years. The initial choice would have reflected specific sets of needs and, while the decision was sound in itself, it was taken, understandably, to meet the requirements on hand. This piecemeal growth of IT accepted the inherent lack of system interfacing, and the need to start again with a common system postponed until some later, often unspecified, time. The growing internationalization of business and the flurry of take-overs and mergers in the last 20 years has heightened the size of the incompatibility problem.

The developments in IT and the obvious impact that e-business is producing has brought to the fore the need to introduce systems using a common data base. ERP fulfills such a need. The other main driver behind ERP installations is the growing desire by companies to re-engineer their business activities to respond to market challenges (see Chapter 14 where re-engineering is discussed).

So, how would an ERP-based system work differently? Let's say that a Milan-based sales team for a USA-based software house prepares a quotation for a customer. With an ERP system, basic information about the customer's requirements would be entered and a formal contract, in Italian, would be produced specifying the product configuration, range of applications and locations involved, lead times concerning pre-application review, development phase, installation, post-development support, training and price. After contract discussions any modifications would be made on the system and quotations would be updated as required. When the customer accepts the quotation, the order is recorded in the system, credit checks are made and all aspects of the delivery system are advised. Feedback on lead times is provided, capacity allocations are verified and recorded, schedules are revised, materials are ordered and the whole operations system is brought up to date and into line.

An ERP is a generic solution. Therefore, unless a company decides to design specific, tailor-made features and modules it will need to adapt the way its organizations works to fit in with the enterprise system logic. The ERP, due to its all-embracing nature, will impose its own way of working on a company's strategy, culture and structure. Thus, the underlying systems logic will have to be accommodated by an organization.

The benefits that companies are enjoying are wide-ranging. Examples include:

■ Autodesk, a leading US maker of CAD software reduced delivery lead times from a two-week average to 98 per cent of orders being delivered in 24 hours.

■ IBM's Storage Systems reduced the time to re-price all its products from 5 days to 5 minutes, the time to deliver a replacement part from 22 to 3 days and the time to complete a credit check from 20 minutes to 3 seconds.

■ Fijitsu Microelectronics reduced order fill time from 18 to 1½ days and halved the time to close its financial records to 4 days.

■ Owens Corning replaced its total of 211 existing systems with an ERP system. This coordinates order-management, financial reporting and its diverse, world-wide supply chain. It is now able to track finished goods inventory daily in all parts of its delivery systems and has cut spare parts inventory by some 50 per cent.

However, as with all applications, success is bound up with fitting the system to the business needs, including its strategic positioning. Two areas of concern are being signalled by companies both of which reflect the size of ERP undertakings.

■ **Failed or out-of-control applications** – the cost of ERP projects in larger organizations runs from $50m to over $500m. The issue, however, is not just the investment costs but the fundamental nature of such a sizeable development. Fox Meyer Drug, a US pharmaceutical company, alleges that its ERP system installation helped drive it into bankruptcy. Mobil Europe spent hundreds of millions of dollars on its ERP system only to abandon it when it merged with Esso/Exxon. Dell Computers found that its ERP system did not fit its new, decentralized management structure. Dow Chemicals spent 7 years and almost $0.5bn implementing a mainframe ERP system and then decided to start all over on a client-server application.

■ **ERP systems: standard versus customized offering** – clearly ERP systems offer substantial benefits. However, with past IT systems organizations would first decide on what the business needed and choose a software package that would support these needs. They often rewrote large portions of the software to provide a better fit. With the size (investment and timescale) of ERP systems, the sequence is reversed. The business often needs to be modified to fit the system. ERP systems will enable a company to operate more efficiently. In some instances, however, the system's assumptions will run counter to a company's best interest. For example, a company, by developing a system that enabled it to shorten lead times by circumventing formal procedures, had increased sales that also attracted a premium price. If after installing an ERP system it had to follow less flexible procedures, its source of competitive advantage may be at risk.

In more general terms the adoption of the same ERP system by companies in the same business sector also raises concerns. How similar can a company's information flows and processes be to those of its competitors before its source of differentiation is undermined? Similarly, for companies competing in price-sensitive markets, ERP system investments raise similar but different strategic issues. With the cost of ERP applications being so high, the eventual savings need to be rigorously assessed and weighed carefully against the investments involved. In some instances, companies may find that not going down the ERP system route may offer a cost advantage over competitors that do.

Just having good data does not mean that a business will improve. To gain the most out of ERP systems companies need to recognize the full business implications. Organizations may have good reasons to change. They may have struggled for years with incompatible information systems and may see ERP as a quick fix. However, before moving forward organizations need to address key questions:

■ how might an ERP system strengthen our competitive position?

■ what will the system's effect be on our organization and structure?

■ do we need to extend the system across all functions, across all regions or only implement certain modules and reflect differences in need with differences in approach?

Because of an ERP system's profound implications for a business, off-loading responsibility to IT specialists is not only irresponsible but risk-taking of the highest order. ERP systems must fit business needs and the way an organization works. There is no one right answer. For instance, take Monsanto and Hewlett-Packard. After studying the data requirements of each business unit, Monsanto managers placed a high priority on achieving the greatest possible degree of commonality across the whole business even though they knew it would be difficult to achieve and to standardize fully on more than 85 per cent of the data used would not be possible. At Hewlett-Packard, a company with a strong tradition of business unit autonomy, applications specific to each part of the business were developed. With little sharing of resources the estimated investment is over $1bn, but autonomy, a recognized corporate strength, has been preserved.

CONCLUSION

Operations strategy has been highlighted throughout in terms of its role to support a company's markets by meeting the requirements of the order-winners and qualifiers for which it is solely or jointly responsible. One key part of this support is provided by the operations control system and its essential role in the effective and efficient provision of products and services.

Operations control links market demands with the necessary capacity and materials requirement, and contributes to the flow and control of products and services through the system. This part of operations will impact key dimensions in many markets such as delivery speed and delivery reliability. Selecting how best to provide this function is, therefore, a core operations management task. Alternative systems have been explained in the previous sections. Approaches to fulfilling this essential task are, however, characterized by a number of problems.

1. Lack of integration

It is essential that the products and services, the processes and delivery systems for providing them and the system(s) to control them are developed as integrated parts of the one task. Controls are, however, often developed independently of key dimensions of operations. The inherent weakness of inadequate systems can be reduced by adaptation and good management. But they will continue to be inadequate where these developments have not been integrated into the other functions of operations that impact key issues such as delivery reliability and delivery speed.

2. One control system to support diverse sets of needs

Many organizations implement a single control system to meet the diverse needs of its various markets. A preference for single solutions, a desire to keep investment and

Exhibit 8.28   *Operations control systems and process type*

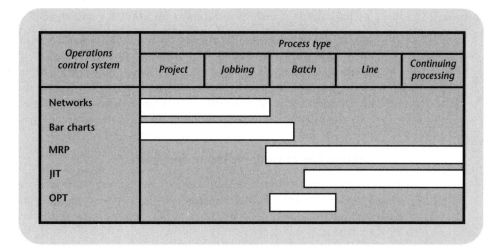

running costs as low as possible and a failure to recognize that different processes and business needs require different control systems (see Exhibit 8.28) are some of the reasons why this frequently happens. One result is that the control system deliverables do not match and support the wide range of needs, demands and characteristics of a typical business.

3. Suboptimal applications

Attracted by the benefits associated with alternatives, companies implement a control system without ensuring that it fits their needs or that the prerequisites for its introduction are in place. JIT control systems provide a classic example of this. Whereas in Japan, companies only apply JIT to control operations with certain characteristics, the allure of the benefits of JIT has led to suboptimal applications by Western companies.

■ **Japanese view** – the term 'just in time' is used very strictly in Japanese companies and recognizes that its use is ideally related to supporting markets characterized by stable volumes and where the product mix is known well in advance. Delivering JIT means planning in plenty of time.[10] Furthermore, when Japanese managers refer to the approach embodied in the term 'just in time' they prefer to speak of the JIT philosophy embodied in the Toyota production system that spawned the development of the JIT system.

■ **Western view** – although displaying the appropriate characteristics of high volume and stable product mix, Western companies have introduced JIT control systems without creating the environment for this to be developed in its optimum form. Two of the more critical dimensions essential to the introduction of a JIT system and its drive to reduce inventory throughout the supply chain and which Western companies often fail to provide are:

  – Not fixing forward schedules. As a consequence, the end-user, while requiring JIT response from suppliers, still retains the 'right' to change call-offs within material lead times. The only option for a supplier to meet such schedule changes in terms of quantity and/or delivery date is to hold inventory, thus undermining the underlying principle of minimizing inventory throughout the supply chain.

– As explained earlier, for Japanese companies JIT embodies approaches to technical dimensions and people that are integral to its successful introduction and outcomes. In some Western companies the tendency (often driven by the greater corporate influence exerted by accountants relative to operations) has been to fix on the spectacular WIP reductions (that are a consequence not a cause) and overlook the technical and people change prerequisites to bring this about.[7]

4. Selecting the most appropriate approach

All too often, companies seek solutions rather than concentrating on understanding situations and problems. One outcome of this is that companies introduce control systems inappropriately or in a form that fails to reflect the needs and characteristics of their business:

■ OPT – companies often introduce OPT as a systems solution to a capacity problem. An alternative (and often by far the best) is to recognize constraints as issues of capacity and flow and address them as such rather than tackling them with a computer program.[11] Increasing capacity, re-engineering and rerouting products are engineering alternatives to the IT approach advocated by OPT. Invariably, the engineering and operations-based solutions are simpler, quicker to bring about and less expensive to implement and maintain. Selecting OPT is often presented as an off-the-shelf solution that does not require an understanding of the issues and alternatives involved.

■ Companies introduce approaches unaware that often modifying the system variables will better reflect the characteristics of their operations system and supply chain. For example, lead times on fixing schedules need to reflect a company's own reality. Japanese car companies vary considerably on the length of notice given to suppliers and the confirmation intervals during the period from the forecast projections several months ahead through to the finalized schedule. There are no fixed intervals. Details reflect the reality that suppliers can provide.

■ The control task itself is characterized by and needs to reflect and embrace several major factors including:

– The complexity of the link between products/services and processes/delivery systems in terms of dimensions such as total volumes, customer order size, product/service range, complexity of the task, whether the product/service is repeated (a standard) or not (a special) and the process chosen to complete the tasks involved.

– The level of certainty in demand forecasts, capacity provision, product/service supply and prior knowledge of the task.

– The organizational decision on how to cope with the imbalance between demand and capacity and the amount and timing of the approaches (for example, inventory and excess capacity) taken.

– The overriding organizational style, level of development in the delivery system and the degree of maintenance or development of the control system over time.

5. Providing relevant control statements and reports

Finally, the system needs to provide relevant control statements and reports to help operations executives manage the function and assess how well it is both supporting customers and meeting the internal, efficiency-based needs of the business. Typical statements and reports include the following.

Delivery performance

- Per cent of orders (by line item) delivered on time or within the timescale targets set by the business, including the number of instances when queues exceeded target lengths in retail-type outlets.
- Per cent of times customers requested lead times were agreed – the dimension of delivery speed.
- Number and nature of customer complaints.
- Throughput efficiency index to assess delays in the delivery system:

$$\frac{\text{Total process lead time}}{\text{Actual time to complete}}$$

- Order backlog/forward load assessment to review the demand and capacity situation within the process at a point in time and shown as a trend:

$$\frac{\text{Average \# orders waiting to be processed}}{\text{Average \# orders processed in the period}}$$

Efficiency

Measures around utilization and efficiency were provided in Chapter 6 (on capacity) and Chapter 13 (on productivity) respectively. In addition, variance reports need to be prepared to show actual staff, material and total costs incurred compared to budgets and identifying areas for review.

Quality conformance

The various measures of quality conformance are outlined in Chapter 9.

Inventory

Checking inventory levels using the causal analysis approach are explained in Chapter 10.

The measures, supplemented by additional reports reflecting other key issues within a business, need to form an essential by-product of an operations control system. The scheduling of products and services provides inherent information that is relevant to many key aspects of operations. Capturing these as an integral part of the control system is critical in itself and also provides essential insights into how well the delivery system is meeting the demands of a business and needs of its markets, thereby reinforcing the essential role of the control system within operations.

SUMMARY

In many markets, meeting the on-time delivery needs of customers is a prerequisite for getting and staying on a customer's short list, and providing this qualifier is a key operations management task. While the need is the same in all organizations, the way to schedule operations to meet this requirement differs from business to business and needs to reflect those dimensions that alter the control task and alter the control system design. These include the complexity of the product or service, whether the products and services are specials or standards, the choice of process to provide the products or services, how much of the process is undertaken in-house and the extent to which an organization manages the demand and capacity interface.

A control system comprises three distinct but integrated activities:

- loading – determining the capacity and volumes at each step in a process and the assignment of tasks within a system to work centres or task groups
- sequencing – deciding on the order in which jobs will be completed at each stage in the process
- scheduling – the task of allocating a start and finish date to each order.

The main section of the chapter then introduced the alternative scheduling systems that are available, explained these in detail and illustrated their use with examples. If you recall these were:

- Bar charts – recording capacity (for example, process or staff) against a timescale. Exhibits 8.5–8.7 provided illustrations of their application.

- Network analysis – organizations often use this method to plan, schedule and control complex, one-off tasks. The simple example in Exhibit 8.10 is then followed by the more complex task in Exhibit 8.12.

- MRP and JIT – two of the most widely used systems to schedule standard products and services are MRP and JIT. Referred to as a push and pull system respectively, these two systems are explained in detail and also how they differ is explained (for example, refer to Exhibits 8.21 and 8.25).

All operations control systems start with a statement of demand. Known a~d/or forecast sales are translated into statements of demand which in scheduling language

SUMMARY (cont'd)

is referred to as a master schedule. A glance back at Exhibit 8.2 confirms the pivotal position of the master schedule and its linking role between the planning and scheduling phases of a system.

One other key reminder at this time is the principle of independent and dependent demand. Whereas assessing demand levels by known and/or forecast orders is the fundamental task for independent demand items, requirements for dependent items can be calculated as they are directly related to the pattern of demand of the independent items to which they relate.

Once the master schedule for a product or service is established then the scheduling task of determining material requirements and process/staff capacities can be completed. These, in turn, provide the inputs for the day-to-day execution of the plan. Detailing the MRP and JIT systems then completed this section.

Next we introduced OPT and explained its finite scheduling role in refining existing control systems, with the final section addressing the developments in ERP systems outlining benefits and concerns and highlighting the key dimensions to ensure successful applications. The conclusions provided an overview of the various systems described throughout the chapter, related these one to the other in Exhibit 8.27 and highlighted some key concerns when selecting, developing and maintaining the systems that form the basis of the operations control and scheduling task.

Discussion questions

1. Each week nurses are assigned to different parts of a hospital. For one department the number of nurses required for each for the next six weeks is estimated as follows:

Period	Mon	Tue	Wed	Thu	Fri	Sat	Sun
0600–1000	15	15	15	15	15	10	8
1000–1400	18	15	18	15	18	10	8
1400–1800	15	15	15	15	15	10	8
1800–2200	10	10	10	10	10	6	4
2200–0200	5	5	5	5	5	3	3
0200–0600	3	3	3	3	3	3	3

Discussion questions (cont'd)

Agreements with the nurses' union requires that staff work a continuous eight-hour shift for five consecutive days followed by two days' rest.

(a) How many full-time nurses are needed to meet the staff levels detailed above?

(b) How many hours of overstaffing exist when you compare the number of staff called for in question (a) to the minimum establishment levels given in the above table?

(c) How many full-time nurses would be needed to meet the above schedule if the five consecutive days rule was relaxed so that the two days off in each seven-day week could be taken at any time including as single days?

2. A small business consultancy company has three specialists in one area of its work. Furthermore, each of these three is further specialized to undertake certain phases of an assignment. Jim Brown handles phase 1, Anne Dewar, phase 2 and Jean Holden undertakes phase 3.

Details of the work to complete each of these assignments together with agreed completion dates is given below. In all cases, the phases need to be completed in the order 1, 2 and then 3.

Client	Phase			Agreed completion (# days[1])
	1	2	3	
McCanley	10	16	8	49
Williams	3	9	16	46
Beattie	12	10	10	45

1. Calculated from day 1 as the start date.

The three consultants can complete other, non-fee-paying work during the period.

Using day 1 as the start date, draw a bar chart to schedule the above tasks in order to meet the agreed completion dates and release each consultant as early as possible to take on other fee-paying work when their part of these three jobs has been completed.

3. Give an example of a business that would use a push and one that would use a pull operations control system. Explain your choice and briefly describe how the system would work.

4. What is the difference between independent and dependent demand? Give two manufacturing and two service examples to illustrate your answer.

5. Under what conditions should a company refuse a customer order that it is technically able to provide?

6. Your local dry cleaner always specifies a two-day lead time, no matter what items of clothing you take in to be cleaned. Suggest reasons why the outlet is able to do this and how it works.

Discussion questions (cont'd)

7. Describe a service application where the principles of the theory of constraints can apply.

8. A piece of equipment requires the following times to manufacture:

Activity	# days	Activity	# days
1. Purchasing	15	5. Assembly	7
2. Fabrication	5	6. Controls	6
3. Hydraulics	5	7. Test	3
4. Electronics	18	8. Packaging	1

Each of the activities must be completed sequentially except that fabrication can be started 10 days after purchasing begins and the hydraulics and electronics steps can be completed in parallel. Draw a bar chart for this job.

9. If in question 8 above, the hydraulics and electronics steps could also be started 10 days after purchasing begins, draw a network for this job and calculate the critical path.

10. In operations, priorities manifest themselves in a conflict between meeting customers' lead times and due dates, and the productivity and efficiency goals of the operations system staff. Discuss and provide examples to illustrate your points.

Notes and references

1. In more complex networks, the event node often contains more information.
2. Strictly speaking, 'float' and 'slack' are not the same, and in complex networks it may be important to distinguish between them. In many instances, though, this would not be a worthwhile exercise.
3. The following books treat network analysis in depth and provide the more detailed information and analyses often used in the control of complex projects: Burman, PJ *Precedence Networks for Project Planning and Control* (Maidenhead: McGraw-Hill, 1982); Moder, JJ *et al.*, *Project Management with CPM and PERT with Precedence Diagramming* (Van Nostrand Reinhold, 1983): Burke, R *Project Management and Control*, 2nd edn (John Wiley, Chichester, 1993); Meredith, JR and Mantel, S *Project Management: A Managerial Approach*, 3rd edn (John Wiley, New York, 1995) and Lockyer, K and Gordon, J *Project Management and Project Network Techniques*, 6th edn (Pitman, London, 1996).
4. The extension of materials requirement planning is, in fact, into manufacturing resource planning. As both have the same initials their abbreviated forms are referred to as MRPI and MRPII respectively.
5. Materials requirement planning is also referred to as MRPI. The reason why is explained in the section 'Manufacturing resources planning'.
6. One of the earliest statements providing this definition comes from Schonenberger, RJ *Japanese Manufacturing Techniques: Nine Hidden Lessons in Simplicity* (New York: Free Press, 1982), p. 16.

7. An example is where end-users require suppliers to provide materials and components just in time but do not fix their own schedules correspondingly. They demand JIT supply which can only be met by suppliers holding inventory. However, the JIT system is designed to reduce inventory in all parts of a supply chain. For this to happen, end-users need to play their part by creating the conditions where this can happen. Fixing their own schedules within material lead times is part of the necessary conditions. Without this prerequisite when end-users change their requirements suppliers in such situations can only meet JIT supply by holding inventory.

8. For further information and details on JIT systems refer to Harrison, A *Just-in-Time Manufacturing in Perspective* (Prentice-Hall, London 1992) and relevant chapters in Vollman, TE, Berry, WL and Whybark, DC *Manufacturing Planning and Control Systems*, 4th edn (Irwin/McGraw-Hill, Burr Ridge, IL, 1997).

9. If a 30-minute set-up is reduced to 10 minutes then the order quantities to be loaded can be reduced to one-third while maintaining the ratio between length of set-up and length of run time.

10. A thoughtful review of JIT systems is provided by Roy Westbrook in his article 'Time to forget just-in-time? Observation on a visit to Japan', *IJOPM*, Vol. 8, No. 4, pp. 5–21.

11. Ibid., p. 19.

Further reading

Ames, BC and Hlavacek, JD *Market-Driven Management* (Irwin/McGraw-Hill, Chicago, 1997).

Bennett, D and Forrester, P *Market-focused Production Systems* (Prentice-Hall, Hemel Hempsted, 1993).

Davenport, TH *Working Knowledge: How Organizations Manage What They Know* (Harvard Business School Press, 1997).

Hammer, M and Champy, J 'Reengineering the Corporation', *Harper Business*, New York (1993).

Hill, T *Manufacturing Strategy: Text and Cases* (Macmillan, Basingstoke, 2000).

Vollman, TE, Berry WL and Whybark, DC *Manufacturing Planning and Control Systems*, 4th edn (Irwin/McGraw-Hill, Burr Ridge, IL, 1997).

CHAPTER NINE

The content and planning of this book: an overview of what is involved, what has been addressed so far and what is covered in this chapter

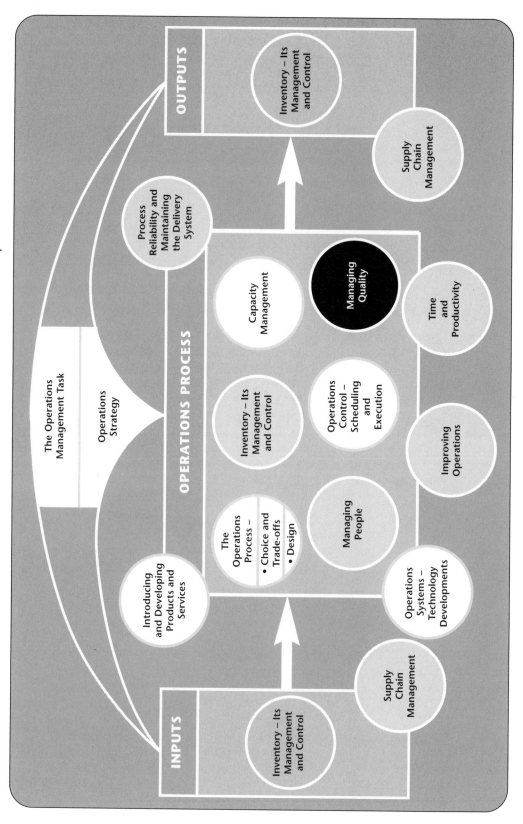

Managing Quality

Chapter overview

The quality of the products and services provided by a business is an important concern to both an organization and its customers. While the cost of quality calamities can be high in themselves, customer confidence in the level of quality will have a significant impact on a company's overall prosperity in terms of future levels of demand and the long-term success of the business. To ensure that quality levels meet market requirements, issues concerning quality need to be resolved at the corporate level and be seen to form an integral part of an organization's objectives, strategies and tactics. This is not easy to achieve, but unless addressed at the top it will, as in many organizations, be decided lower down in a business due to the day-to-day need at the operational level to achieve output levels, efficiency and other yardsticks, and to meet delivery promises.

In view of the fundamental importance of meeting quality requirements in a business environment where customers' expectations regarding the quality of the products and services they purchase have changed noticeably in the last 20 years, then the need to manage quality is increasingly critical to the overall success of any business. This chapter covers the issues and aspects of quality for which operations is responsible. In particular, it addresses the following topics:

- **What is quality and why is it important?** The opening section of the chapter clarifies definitions and positions the importance of quality within the context of the overall business.

- **Quality conformance** concerns the consistent meeting of product and service specifications and operations' key role in achieving this.

- **Quality principles** help summarize the key facets of managing and controlling quality.

- **Quality philosophies** – the principal contributors to the improved management of quality are discussed in detail to provide the foundation and context for the more detailed sections of the chapter.

- **Tools and techniques** – this section outlines the main tools and techniques used to help analyse causes and provide ways to improve the management of quality.

> ## Chapter overview (cont'd)
>
> ■ **The operations process: quality management in practice** – where to undertake quality reviews and the approaches to be used are explained and covers purchasing, operations process and output reviews.
>
> ■ **Six-sigma quality** – the goal of reducing the level of defects to 3.4 per million transactions – is being embraced by companies as part of the way to maintain and grow share in the competitive markets of the new millennium.
>
> ■ **Formalizing the search for quality** – the need to set and meet national and international standards has seen the development of government and non-government-sponsored initiatives to help formalize the search for quality. The ISO 9000 series, Malcolm Baldrige Award and the European Quality Award are discussed.
>
> ■ **Total quality management** – the concepts and approaches underpinning total quality management are explained and its role in fulfilling the quality mandate is discussed.

WHAT IS QUALITY AND WHY IS IT IMPORTANT?

Meeting, or better still exceeding, customers' expectations is a core task of a business. The growing awareness of the importance of the dimension of quality performance was stimulated in the 1970s and 1980s by the improvements made and sustained in Japanese companies and the impact that the resulting improvements had in terms of increased sales and market share. The quality movement that followed accelerated the introduction of a range of philosophies, approaches, tools and techniques.

Part of this increased awareness also led to the word 'quality' being used to reflect a wide range of dimensions. A first step for us, therefore, is to clarify, from an operations management viewpoint, the meaning of quality and to define the dimensions to be addressed later in the chapter.

What is quality?

From an operations perspective, quality concerns consistently meeting customers' expectations. This, in turn, embodies decisions around specifying expectations and then consistently meeting these specifications for the products and services involved.

■ **Product/service specification** – the issues around product/services mix and design were covered in Chapters 1 and 3 respectively. Determining customers' needs and embodying these in the design specifications of the range of products and services on offer is the first step in meeting the quality requirements and managing their provision.

■ **Quality conformance** – consistently meeting the product and service specification is referred to in operations as quality conformance. For a customer, quality provision, therefore, combines the two elements of the specification itself and its consistent provision – see Exhibit 9.1. A glance at this exhibit highlights the interrelated nature of the quality offering. The link between these elements needs always to be

Exhibit 9.1   *The quality offering*

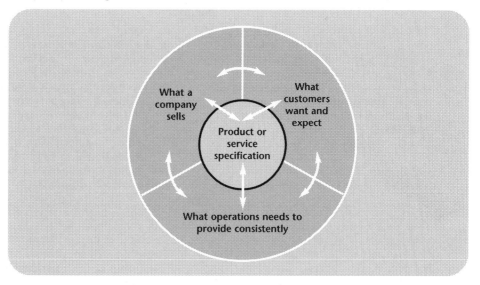

tested and the level of fit assessed as an ongoing part of managing the quality offering. Gaps between the different elements need to be monitored and managed.

The specification on offer reconciles customers' needs and expectations with what a company sells. Companies need to determine proactively the specification on offer. In so doing, it is essential to take into account customers' expectations on the one hand, while on the other, positioning themselves within the markets in which they wish to compete. The reconciliation of these elements in the product/service specification offered is a key strategic decision and the issues involved were discussed earlier in Chapter 3. It needs to be managed proactively as the outcomes determine the markets in which a company wishes to compete and, by definition, those in which it does not wish to compete. The phrase 'a customer is always right', therefore, only relates to a company's chosen markets and the sets of customer needs and expectations that comprise them. Continuously monitoring existing and potential customers' needs and expectations, competitors' offerings and potential changes to existing product and service specifications is an essential task in the management of quality. Rigorously assessing how well operations consistently provides what is offered completes the quality offering provision.

Why is quality important?

The last section has, in part, already addressed the question of the importance of quality. What a company sells, a customers' needs and expectations and consistently providing the product and service specifications on offer represent the essence of a business and will determine the growth and success of an enterprise. Recognizing the interrelated nature of these parts of the task and ensuring that the essential dialogue and feedback are sustained alerts a company to what it is doing well, where it needs to improve and the actions it needs to take. The importance of continuously reviewing the quality offering (see Exhibit 9.1) is a core task as Case examples 1, 2 and 3 illustrate.

Case examples

1

The US-based Hampton Inns chain decided to offer guaranteed refunds to any customers dissatisfied with their stays for any reason. Guest surveys showed that the policy was pretty persuasive and the cost/benefit calculations revealed that additional sales revenues ($) brought in by the programme were almost 11 times that of the refunds paid out. An added bonus for the company was higher staff morale. With all staff being empowered to grant refunds, job satisfaction rose, while staff turnover fell from 117 to 50 per cent in a three-year period. The refund programme also helped to identify the aspects of service that most annoyed guests. One of the biggest in the Embassy Suites' part of the company's hotel chain was a lack of irons and ironing boards and the delay involved between request and provision. The company ran some numbers and found that providing an iron and board in every Embassy Suite room totalled less than $0.5m. It eliminated the problem while taking out the service staff costs incurred in taking irons and boards from room to room.

2

Zebra Technologies Corporation, a US maker of bar code printers, had earned a reputation as a manufacturer of high-quality, top-of-the-line printers. The company saw a lot of sales potential in the low-end segment of this market, but had two concerns. First, it might affect its top drawer image while second, it might cannibalize its existing product line. Its solution was to introduce a basic, no frills version at a 25 per cent lower selling price. It was slower, could not print on different types of materials and, most importantly, could not be upgraded. The result – total sales went up by almost 50 per cent and as margins on the new product matched those on the original line, so did profits.

3

United Parcel Services (UPS) had always assumed that on-time delivery was the paramount concern of its customers. UPS's definition of service quality centred almost exclusively on meeting its delivery promise – for example, all next-day packages had to be delivered by 1030 hours the following morning. So too did operations' priorities and measures – elevator times and the delay in customers answering their doorbells was measured and included in schedules. UPS even shaved the corners off delivery van seats to help reduce time. In addition, surveys confirmed customers' satisfaction with its reliable delivery performance. The problem was that UPS did not ask customers what they wanted. When questions were broadened to address needs and expectations the biggest surprise to UPS management was that customers wanted more interface with drivers. If they had more time to chat, customers could get some practical advice on shipping. The result – the company now encourages its drivers to visit customers along with sales staff and allows drivers thirty minutes each day to spend at their discretion to strengthen customer ties and bring in new sales. The programme costs UPS over $4m in drivers' time but additional sales are many times higher.

Case example questions

1. Review these three cases and identify the elements of the quality offering that the companies changed or improved.

2. What benefits did these companies and their customers receive and what disadvantages or costs were involved?

QUALITY CONFORMANCE

Quality conformance means providing products and services to specification and constitutes operations' quality-related task. As Exhibit 1.6 illustrated, most offerings combine elements of both products and services and a specification needs to be provided for all these. But what often happens is that whereas the predominant element of an offering is recognized and specified, the supporting product or service element receives insufficient attention and results in being inadequately defined. In markets that are increasingly competitive companies are now more alert to these issues and, as often the support elements can be significant factors to ensure repeat business, the total offering is defined and specified with the provision of all elements forming part of measuring performance.

The steps involved in the quality conformance procedure are outlined below. As products and service constitute a number of characteristics, then each characteristic will need defining and controlling as part of meeting the specification of the product or service in total.

1. Quality characteristics – definition

Separating the task of specifying a product or service from that of consistently providing the detailed elements involved was made to identify and highlight the different functional responsibilities within the quality offering. The first step then is to determine the characteristics that make up the product or service to be provided.

As you would anticipate, many of the characteristics that make up a company's products and services will form part of the specification at the design stage. These explicit characteristics are invariably the core of what is provided. But, as highlighted earlier, the total package also includes implicit services (for example, level of attention and recognition of regular customers by restaurant staff) and supporting structural facilities (for example, the quality of the table linen, porcelain, cut glass and cutlery in the same restaurant). A glance back at Chapter 3 will refresh your memory on these points.

2. Quality characteristics – measurement and control

The characteristics that make up the specification need to be defined, wherever possible, in such a way that the dimensions involved can be measured and controlled. This involves taking a general quality characteristic, such as appearance, and breaking it down as much as possible into its constituent elements. For example, taking the restaurant example above, then appearance would be a dimension within all facets of the service delivery system. But appearance, as such, is difficult to measure. To enable measurement and control to be undertaken then 'appearance' would need to be separated into elements that, in themselves, could be more easily measured – see Exhibit 9.2.

The characteristics that describe quality are grouped into two sets:

- **Variables** can be measured on a numerical scale, such as weight, length and time. Examples of variable measurements are the dimensions of parts and components or the length of time to serve a customer.

- **Attributes** are measured by using the qualitative conditions of a process. These can be based on judgement or checks without detailed measurement. For example, pass/fail such as a go/no-go gauge that indicates that an item has failed to meet the specification without taking an exact measurement.

Exhibit 9.2   *An example of redefining a general quality characteristic into constituent elements using the service delivery system of a restaurant*

Dimension	Some elements of 'appearance' in the service delivery system of a restaurant
Explicit service	■ Minimizing delays at different stages in the service delivery system. For example, to greet guests, to take pre-dinner drinks orders, to offer menus and to take orders for dinner ■ Food ingredients – for example, freshness by food type, and size of portions ■ Food presentation – factors such as layout on a plate, spacing and colour combinations
Implicit service	Regular guests: ■ Identified by name ■ Staff advised ahead of time ■ Table preferences noted and allocated
Supporting structural facilities	■ Table spacings ■ Table layout ■ Glassware and cutlery checked and polished with a dry cloth

From the quality characteristics that can be measured, those to be measured are then selected and a standard is set against which actual performance is checked. What is deemed acceptable has to be agreed in terms of level and frequency. For example, customers should not queue longer than three minutes, 95 per cent of the time.

When setting quality levels, the decision has to take into account:

■ where in the operations process to check conformance to the quality standards
■ how to undertake the check(s).

Where to check

Within the operations process there are a number of possible points where quality checks could be made. The scope is wide as outlined in Exhibit 9.3. While decisions concerning where to check need to be related to each operations situation, the choice will need to reflect cost and technical considerations. Examples of applying tools and techniques to check quality conformance in the operations process are given later in the chapter.

■ **Cost considerations** fall into two sets. The first is the inspection costs involved and the second is the cost of allowing defective items (product) or errors (service) to pass on through a process. The optimal number and location of these points are achieved when the total of these two sets of costs is at a minimum. The assessment of these costs, especially the latter, is not easy and tends largely to be one of judgement. The costs involved are those at each stage in the process plus those for correcting errors and defective items. Thus, selecting inspection points before relatively high-cost parts of a process are started or where error correction would become substantially more expensive or not cost-effective, become important factors when making this choice.

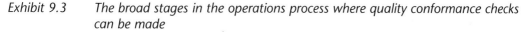

Exhibit 9.3   *The broad stages in the operations process where quality conformance checks can be made*

The process in a manufacturing company

Procurement	Receiving	Operations	Finished items	Installation
Purchased items Vendor rating	Incoming quality inspection	Conversion and assembly processes involving several quality activities	Test and inspection of finished items	On-site installation and test

The service delivery system

Procurement	Receiving	Operations	Service and delivery completed	
Purchased items and services Vendor rating	Quality checks on purchased items and services	Process to provide the service and requiring several quality activities	Inspect level and quality of intended provision	Service consumed by customer

■ **Technical considerations** include making checks before stages in a delivery process where one of the following conditions might be involved:

- previous defects or problems might afterwards be concealed
- where checking is difficult
- after which rectification or recovery is difficult
- where functional responsibility changes
- the point where the provision and consumption of the service take place.

How to check

Having decided where to check, the next step is how many products or services to check. If we wished to guarantee that the quality level was being attained the first reaction may be to say 'let's check everything'. In theory this should ensure that no substandard product or service is allowed to proceed through a process. In reality this approach has major limitations:

- it is expensive
- lead times are increased
- when people are involved in the checking or monitoring it leads to errors
- deterioration may result from excessive handling.

These limitations give rise to the concept of acceptance sampling. Most acceptance inspection procedures are based on the principles of statistical inference by which conclusions are drawn about the characteristics of a large batch of products or services, by inspecting very carefully a small sample from that batch. Any acceptance sampling plan, however, may lead to a wrong judgement – this is known as sampling risk and, together with approaches to sampling, is discussed later in the chapter.

Case examples

4

In 1982, the US healthcare products group, Johnson & Johnson faced a dilemma. An extortionist tried to wring money out of the company by contaminating capsules of its Tylenol painkiller with cyanide. Seven people died. While the US government pondered what to do and before the media had time to put the company on the defensive, Johnson & Johnson recalled all Tylenol products at a cost of $100m and loss of short-term sales. But, it emerged with consumer confidence enhanced and quickly regained its leadership of the painkiller market.

5

In 1995, Philip Morris recalled all its Marlboro cigarettes from the US market fearing they could harm smokers' health. It turned out that a batch of filters had become contaminated with a chemical that caused coughing and sneezing. As with Johnson & Johnson, Philip Morris went to great lengths (including full-page newspaper advertisements and a free inquiry service). The recall cost £200m and was believed to contribute to the increase in Marlboro's market share that followed.

6

In 1999 Coca-Cola finally admitted its products going into some European markets (particularly Belgium) had been tainted by two separate incidents – the accidental injection of 'defective' carbon dioxide gas into some cola and the outside of soft drink cans being contaminated by a fungicide used to treat wooden shipping pallets. But the admission came only following many days of Coca-Cola assuring consumers that its products were safe and during which time dozens of children were hospitalized following complaints of stomach cramps, dizziness and vomiting. Coca-Cola's plan was a partial withdrawal of its products that was met by the governments of Belgium and Luxembourg banning the sale of all Coca-Cola products, with some major supermarkets (for example, Carrefour in France) unilaterally removing all Coca-Cola products from their shelves to avoid confusion. Coca-Cola also earned the hostility of the media with its trademark polar bear doubled up in pain and another retitling the company's name to 'Coca-Colic'. Coca-Cola's response was similar to that of Perrier, the French producer of sparkling water. In 1990, Perrier reacted slowly and grudgingly when traces of benzene were found in its products. At first reluctant to act, it was eventually forced to recall every bottle at a cost of $200m and suffered a tarnished reputation.

Case example questions

1. Describe the reaction of these four companies to the quality conformance problems they each faced.
2. What type of criterion was quality conformance in these four companies and how did it affect their markets?
3. What role would operations have in each situation? Give details to explain your points.

3. Identify causes of below-standard quality and seek improvements

The checks made to ensure that the specification is being consistently met will record instances of below-standard quality and identify causes. By recording quality failures the more common reasons will form the basis for prioritizing improvements. A more proactive response by operations managers typifies the current approach to controlling quality. Failure is seen as a guide to process improvement rather than a negative criticism of the delivery system. This more enlightened response captures the inherent benefits that come from failure and uses it as a signpost to correcting faults and thereby improving the quality offering.

QUALITY PRINCIPLES

It will help at this point to summarize the key principles in managing and controlling quality. This will reflect on the issues covered so far and also link into the next parts of the chapter. This section lists four key principles in quality management and highlights the benefits of consistently meeting customers' needs. The sections that follow then cover philosophies, tools and techniques and implementation.

1. Meet customer requirements

As explained in the last section, consistently meeting customer requirements is at the core of quality conformance. Requirements originate with the customer, result in an understanding and agreement on the specification and necessitate the consistent meeting of these needs. At the same time, companies also have requirements that suppliers must fulfil if the quality offering is to be met. In that way quality is a three-dimensional proposal – a company, its suppliers and its customers.

2. Error-free work

Error-free work sets the standard for how often a customer's requirements are met – the need to consistently meet the product or service specification. There is only one standard for which to aim – right first time and every time. This does not mean that errors will not occur. What it does mean is that adopting an attitude that errors are OK is not acceptable.

This approach to quality requires that the question 'why?' is always asked when an error occurs. The cause needs to be identified and changes made to keep the error from happening again.

3. Manage by prevention

One of the first issues on which an organization has to decide is whether its basic philosophy is to adopt a reactive or proactive approach to managing quality. In the former the emphasis is towards detection with the aim to prevent faulty work being passed onto subsequent processes and so minimize the costs involved in rectification, scrap, returned or rejected products or services, reimbursement, compensation and, most importantly, non-repeat business. The alternative is a prevention-orientated approach to quality control, allocating resources to provide products and services right first time.

To manage by prevention means that quality must be built into work. It cannot be inspected in or repaired in. It must be built in! The principle of prevention is that work is managed in a way that keeps errors from happening. Emphasis on prevention will result in more consistently meeting customer requirements. Identifying what could go wrong and why leads to preventive action and back-up plans.

4. Measure by the cost of quality

Measure by the cost of quality means reducing the cost of doing business by eliminating errors. The sets of costs concern detecting and correcting errors on the one hand and preventing errors on the other. For most companies, the largest costs are associated with detection and correction. Doing things right the first time and every time reduces costs. Measuring quality costs prioritizes improvements and tracks progress.

Investing resources in identifying causes and preventing errors will reduce overall costs. However, in time these prevention costs need also to be reduced. Analysing and assessing how the measurement, detection, correction and prevention are undertaken with the aim of reducing costs in itself becomes a key task in managing quality.

QUALITY PHILOSOPHIES

During the 1980s concerns about competitiveness stimulated many companies to a new interest in quality. The growth in market share by Japanese and other Far East companies leading up to and during this period was impressive and much of the gain was on the back of a markedly superior quality performance.

The principal quality contributors at this time were W Edwards Deming, Joseph M Juran and Philip B Crosby. All were active consultants and writers in the field, with many years of practical, business-based experience. At the time of their mutual impact in the West, Deming and Crosby were in their eighties and Juran was in his sixties. Each had a distinct orientation although, and understandably so, they all argued the same salient points. Deming saw quality as a management responsibility that required fundamental change and a long-term (three to five years) time frame. Juran, on the other hand, centred much of his argument on the cost of quality and used data to shock management into action. Finally, Crosby looked to make an impact in a few months and, in that way, stir management into action. Now let us look at those three world-renowned contributors on quality in more detail.

Deming

W Edwards Deming was widely credited with leading the Japanese quality revolution. He exposed Japanese managers from the 1950s onwards to the fundamental concept of variance reduction through the introduction of tools and techniques such as statistical process control (SPC) which will be dealt with later in the chapter. He envisaged quality as an organization-wide activity rather than a technical task for quality specialists.

His early life was with the US Department of Agriculture as a mathematical physicist during which time he was exposed to the theories and practices of statistical science and statistical control. Following the Second World War, Deming visited Japan in 1946 as a representative of the Economic and Scientific Section of the US Department of War. With its manufacturing base destroyed by the US Air Force, Japanese managers listened intently on how to rebuild their manufacturing processes based on quality systems. Beginning in 1950, thousands of Japanese managers attended Deming's courses on statistical process control.

Recognizing Deming's important effect on the performance of manufacturing firms, Japan created the Deming Prize in 1951. This annual award recognizes a company or individual for active contributions to the development of quality management tools or to the spread and implementation of quality improvement programmes.

Deming summarized his views on what management must do to improve quality in his 14 points for management[1] and these are summarized below.

1. **Create constancy of purpose towards improvement of product and service**
   His call was to managers at all levels in an organization to promote a clear vision of the firm, its customers, its methods of delivering value and the role of quality in that provision. He stressed the need for managers to change from a preoccupation with the short term and to build for the longer term and focus on efforts to reduce unnecessary variance in a system.

2. **Adopt the new philosophy**
   Mistakes, defects, rejects, shoddy materials, inadequate training, ineffective supervision and poorly motivated managers are unacceptable. Putting procedures and systems right is essential. To survive and grow requires managers to accept the need for continuous change and innovation.

3. **Cease dependence on mass inspection**
   Planning 100 per cent inspection, Deming argued, is planning for defects and a recognition that the process cannot consistently meet the specified requirements. Such an approach comes too late and is ineffective and costly. The orientation of effort needs to be on process improvement to eliminate errors and rejects.

4. **End the practice of awarding business on the basis of the price tag alone**
   Price has no meaning without a measure of the quality being produced. The focus must change from the lowest initial cost of material purchased to the lowest total cost. Management must establish new guidelines, and long-term relationships with fewer suppliers need to replace short-term, multi-sourced approaches. Working together will lead to the lowest total cost position.

5. **Improve constantly and for ever the system of production and service provision**
   Waste must be reduced in every part of the system by never-ending improvement. This will not come, however, from measuring the defects but by measuring the process. Quality needs to be built in at every stage, starting with design and then increasing uniformity in the process to reduce variation and waste. Putting out fires is not a form of process improvement. Using data, adjusting the process and observing the effects is the way to improve.

6. **Institute training**

   Training must be reconstructed and centred clearly on the concepts of acceptable work and then management needs to remove any inhibitors to achieving good work.

7. **Adopt and institute leadership**

   The job of management is not supervision but leadership and should concentrate on improving the quality of the product and service.

8. **Drive out fear**

   Fear to speak out inhibits people from taking sensible actions. The results are costly. People must be encouraged to ask questions, report problems, express ideas and come up with solutions.

9. **Break down barriers between staff areas**

   People in research, design, sales, procurement and incoming materials need to know the problems encountered with various materials and specifications in operations. Each function must change from optimizing its own contribution and instead replace it with a team-based approach for corporate advantage.

10. **Eliminate slogans, posters and exhortations**

    Exhorting people through slogans and posters is superficial and fails to bring the long-term benefits of sustained improvement. Posters and slogans never helped anyone to do a better job. Management should, instead, ensure that people have the right tools and training to do the task and improve the process.

11. **Eliminate work standards and numerical quotas**

    Quotas focus on quantity not quality. Over time attempts to meet reasonable quotas lead to complacency since workers achieve their goals and need do no more. As a result, the inherent room for improvement is lost. Quotas, therefore, distract from the drive to continuously improve.

12. **Remove barriers that rob people of pride in their workmanship**

    Within operations systems there are inherent barriers and obstacles to good workmanship. Barriers that hinder pride in one's work must be removed including not knowing what constitutes good work, supervisors motivated by quotas, below-standard materials and out-of-line processes.

13. **Encourage education and self-improvement for everyone**

    Continual training keeps people up to date with new developments, design and process changes, new tools and systems and innovative techniques. Because quality and productivity improvements reduce staffing levels, people must be trained and retrained. All training must include basic statistical techniques.

14. **Take action to accomplish the transformation**

    To accomplish these steps top management needs to create a structure to drive forward the other thirteen points on a continuous basis. Top management's actions communicate the true importance of quality throughout the firm and they need to lead by example. Managers, and not staff lower down an organization, are the key to achieving continuous improvement.

Deming used his 14 points for management to highlight and underscore the central role of managers in bringing about essential improvements in quality conformance levels and productivity. He saw managers, and not staff lower down an organization, as the real obstacle, pointing out that 85 per cent of quality problems could be traced to management actions and failures. He also recognized that implementing these 14 points would put a strain on managers' skills and determination. As a first step, therefore, he advocated that companies should address the five 'deadly diseases' as he called them.[2]

1. **Lack of constancy of purpose.** Once a company commits to quality improvement it cannot permit any variation in the message. Quality conformance has to be judged by absolute and not relative standards. It is better to protect the investments in a business by working consistently towards process, product and service improvements.

2. **Emphasis on short-term profits.** The pursuit of short-term profits defeats the constancy of purpose. It encourages short-term thinking and short-term actions and sacrifices long-term growth.

3. **Performance evaluations and annual reviews.** Most organization have systems by which a manager's performance is rated annually. Such annual reviews nourish short-term performance, rivalry and politics and militate against long-term improvements. What is basically wrong with this approach is that it does not focus on leadership to help people.

4. **Mobility of management.** In many organizations managers are moved to other roles or other parts of the same overall business every two or three years, it is argued as a way to broaden and develop and invariably becomes a clear signal that a person is on the promotion ladder. Lack of regular movement is interpreted as a failure signal. The downside of this common approach is lack of tenure and an understandable lack of commitment to long-term improvement. In fact, it is well argued that if you are not going to be there to see through development then it is better for a manager not to undertake major improvement programmes in the first place.

5. **Running a company on visible figures alone (counting the money).** While visible figures are important it is essential to take account of other factors when assessing performance. Maximizing figures to reflect good performance emphasizes the short-term and also underpins several of Deming's other 'diseases'.

Deming's belief that an uncompetitive business was due to the 'failure of top management to manage'[3] was central to his argument and the changes he advocated on how to manage. Quality and productivity were not to be traded off against each other. Rather, improved productivity needed to be recognized as a by-product of improved quality and of doing a job right the first time. Management needed to take the lead in changing the systems and processes that generate current problems. The changes needed were often fundamental and corporate-wide. For example, to ensure consistent quality of incoming materials and purchased items meant developing long-term relationships with vendors and working with them to maintain and improve quality. Similarly, management needed to substitute the 'low price' brief for buyers and to train its own staff in statistical control techniques to create data as part of assessing quality and identifying improvements. This typified the long-term and fundamental nature of the change he advocated that needed to be made.

Juran

Joseph M Juran defined quality as 'fitness for use'. That is, users should be able to expect that a product or service would provide what they needed or wanted to do with it. His work on quality spanned over thirty years and included twelve books. His contribution to the ideas and approaches on quality management centres on five themes that are now explained.[4]

Definitions of quality

Rather than defining quality in terms of specifications and conformance, Juran described it as fitness for use (as explained above) that has the following five major traits:[5]

1. **Quality of design** reflects the suitability of a design concept and specification for its intended use.

2. **Quality conformance** reflects how well an actual product or service achieves the intentions of its design.

3. **Availability** relates to the absence of problems that could affect a product or service's use. Reliability or the probability of a breakdown and the ease of maintenance and repair affect the availability factor.

4. **Safety** concerns the threat of harm to a user.

5. **Field use** represents the condition of a product or service when it reaches a customer and depends on aspects such as packaging, storage, field support and maintenance.

To achieve fitness for use Juran developed a comprehensive approach to quality that spans a product or service's entire life from design, through vendor relations, process development, operations control, test, distribution, customer relations and field service. All aspects were carefully analysed to include the impact of each part or component on the elements comprising fitness for use and leading to solutions to those most critical to the performance and safety of a product or service. A whole range of statistical methods were used in this analysis and also for setting realistic improvement targets and quantifiable goals.

Cost of quality

Juran's analytical methods led to improvement targets with built-in tracking to monitor the implementation programme. However, these statements were in the language of operations, such as defect rates and per cent occasions not to specification. Recognizing that top management would not be inherently interested in these dimensions of a business problem, Juran developed the concept of the cost of quality (COQ). This system related quality to the common denominator of money, the language of top management. It stated quality in terms of the costs associated with defective products or services – the costs of making, finding, repairing or avoiding errors or defects. To help focus attention further, all costs were allocated to four categories:[6]

1. **Internal failure costs** that result from the detection of quality failures before shipment to customers. These include scrap, rework, reinspection, yield losses and disposal.

2. **External failure costs** that arise from finding defects after despatch to a customer, such as complaint adjustments, the return of materials, warranty claims, handling complaints, field service support or repairs.

3. **Appraisal costs** associated with assessing the condition of products, materials and services. These include incoming inspection, product/service and process/delivery system checks, quality assurance/control staff and support costs and the purchase and maintenance of test equipment.

4. **Prevention costs** that result from activities to prevent defects including quality planning, new product/service reviews, process control, data collection and analysis, reporting and improvement activities.

In most companies, internal and external failure costs account for 50–80 per cent of COQ. When these are converted into money top management usually sits up and takes notice. COQ not only provides cost-based information but also improvement targets for quality programmes. With guidelines for investment and an assessment of the benefits involved, companies launch quality programmes until additional investments do not provide acceptable returns.

Quality habit

Juran's ultimate goal for a quality programme was for the company as a whole to be totally involved and committed to a process of continuous improvement. Slogans, posters and exhortations would not result in the necessary level of change. As with Deming, Juran identified that the key to bringing about such a fundamental shift was management action. An unwavering focus on the need for better quality should develop into a quality habit that was based on objective results and the lessons to be learned from the process and outcomes of these activities and tasks. To help a company develop this quality habit, Juran advocated a four-stage process:

1. **Goals** – establish specific goals for the organization
2. **Plans** – detail plans for reaching these goals
3. **Responsibilities** – assign clear responsibilities for undertaking these plans and achieving the set goals
4. **Rewards** – base rewards on results.

Quality offensive

To achieve and maintain a successful quality management programme, Juran proposed a three-stage offensive for improving quality.

1. Breakthrough projects

In the early stages of a quality improvement programme when failure costs greatly exceed the sum of appraisal and prevention costs, there would be many significant opportunities for breakthrough projects aimed at chronic problems (see Exhibit 9.4). The approach identified is based on a COQ Pareto analysis (the vital few concept introduced earlier), gaining management's support for the programme of change and underpinning the activity with the goals, plans, responsibilities and rewards sequence

Exhibit 9.4 *Juaran's sporadic and chronic quality problems*

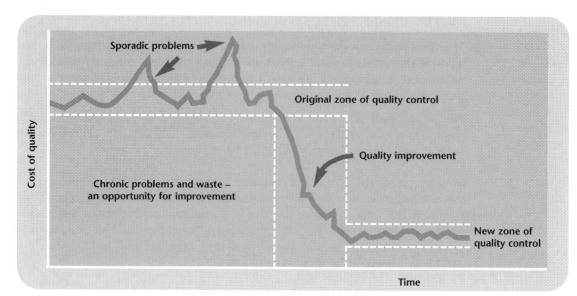

Source: Adapted from JM Juran and FM Gryna *Quality Planning and Analysis* (New York: McGraw Hill, 1993), p. 10.

introduced in the last section. Juran claimed that as over 80 per cent of quality problems were under the jurisdiction of management, involving relevant staff throughout, identifying the key people to successfully implement proposals and using appropriate authority to overcome resistance to change were essential.

2. Control sequence

After successive breakthrough projects, a company reaches the optimum level of quality, the bottom level of the COQ curve as shown in Exhibit 9.5.

An organization then needs to introduce a control sequence to maintain its gains – see Exhibit 9.4. The ongoing feedback loop involves choosing an objective to control, defining the measures to use, setting standards, measuring performance and introducing a reporting system. Current underperformance or gaps created by introducing new standards leads to action programmes.[7] This control sequence is also used to handle sporadic problems (see Exhibit 9.4).

Juran's approach ran from vendor selection and review through to customer service. Its comprehensive nature and the rigour associated with the breakthrough and control phases described here led Juran to advocate the need for quality control engineers, and for this function to be involved in all phases of a programme.

3. Annual quality programme

Juran used the annual quality programme as the principal vehicle to involve top management. This gives objectives for management, reinforces the quality habit and ensures that complacency does not set in.

Breakthrough sequence

Introduced in the last section, breakthrough projects identify actions directed towards achieving major leaps in quality levels. To facilitate this Juran advocated a sequence of steps to be followed, the effective application of which absolutely requires prior management acceptance of the responsibility for improvements. The steps involved are:[8]

1. **Proof of need.** The first step is recognizing that a fault in the current process needs an immediate response. This proof of need is underscored by demonstrating that the costs of not changing exceed the costs of the change itself. Using costs introduces a simple but powerful denominator that is readily understood by all and needs no explanation.

2. **Project identification.** To concentrate improvement efforts, specific projects are used to focus attention and become catalysts for change. Breakthroughs start with project identification with people working on proven needs and clear problems. Careful choice needs to concentrate on projects with large and highly visible pay-offs.

3. **Organizing for improvement.** The successful completion of projects needs infrastructure in place at two levels – a steering group and a diagnostic group. The former is composed of staff from several departments and defines the programme, suggests problem causes, lends authority to the activity, helps overcome any resistance to change and implements the improvements. The diagnostic group is made up of quality professionals and line managers with the task of allocating resources, analysing problems, identifying improvement, setting out a programme of change and agreeing a timetable for implementation. To undertake this step successfully the following phases need to be completed:

Exhibit 9.5   *Minimizing the costs of quality*

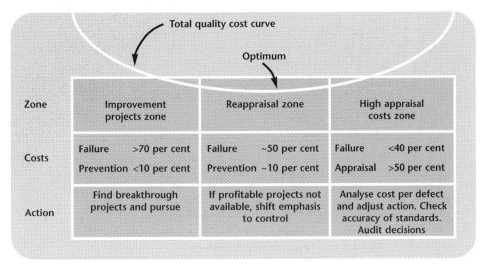

Zone	Improvement projects zone	Reappraisal zone	High appraisal costs zone
Costs	Failure >70 per cent Prevention <10 per cent	Failure ~50 per cent Prevention ~10 per cent	Failure <40 per cent Appraisal >50 per cent
Action	Find breakthrough projects and pursue	If profitable projects not available, shift emphasis to control	Analyse cost per defect and adjust action. Check accuracy of standards. Audit decisions

Source: Adapted from JM Juran and FM Gryna *Quality Planning and Analysis* (New York: McGraw Hill, 1993), p. 26.

■ **Analysis.** The diagnostic group studies symptoms, develops hypotheses, tests alternatives and identifies a problem's true causes. In so doing it separates defects into those that are within an operator's and those that are in management's control. To be in an operator's control, a problem has to meet three criteria – operators know what they are supposed to do, have the data to understand what they are actually doing and are able to regulate their own performance. Using past and current data and conducting experiments lead to proposed solutions.

■ **Overcoming resistance to change.** An essential element of any change programme is to identify the key people involved. Including them from an early stage and then preparing them for both the technical and cultural aspects of change is an essential next step.

■ **Implementing and maintaining the changes.** Overviewing the cost of the problem, looking at alternative solutions and associated costs/benefits, reviewing the steps to be taken and highlighting the changes involved need to be presented to all involved in appreciating, implementing and maintaining the programme. The final challenge is to maintain the changes and prevent any return towards old procedures, processes and habits. Consolidating improvements is a key task and will be enhanced by establishing new standards, increased training, developing new control systems with reliable warning signals, statistical techniques and feedback loops and introducing relevant performance measures.

Crosby

Philip B Crosby is the third major influence on quality management. As with Deming and Juran he addressed his message to top management, proposing that quality management provided a viable strategy for corporate survival and growth. Further, Crosby denied that a firm had to make large investments to improve quality. He asserted that a quality management programme would lead to such a level of savings that it would pay for itself; ultimately, 'quality is free'.[9]

The goal of quality improvement was zero defects, to be achieved through prevention rather than after-the-fact inspection. The key to quality improvement, he believed, was to change top management's thinking. Management needed to establish a higher standard of performance and communicate these expectations throughout all levels of the company. Zero defects was possible, but needed to be a management standard and not simply a motivational programme for employees. To help managers understand the size of their quality problems, Crosby provided the following ideas and approaches.

Cost of quality

In most companies, Crosby estimates that the cost of quality is between 15 and 20 per cent of sales. Identifying the size of the problem arrests management's attention, illustrates the opportunities for profitable improvement and gains corporate support for a quality programme.

Absolutes for quality management

Crosby identified the fundamental elements of an effective quality management system and called the following four laws the absolutes for quality management:

1. **Quality is conformance to requirements, not goodness.** Crosby required only one definition of quality – when the goods or services meet or exceed customers' expectations. Management must ensure that everyone understands these requirements and then provide the tools and systems to allow this to happen.

2. **Quality management is based on prevention.** Successful quality management begins with an analysis and evaluation of current processes. The analysis needs to use essential statistical tools to identify all the opportunities where quality problems could disrupt a process. The elimination of these opportunities then leads to the prevention of quality problems.

3. **Zero defects is the performance standard.** Effective quality management sets a goal of zero defects. Such an aim creates a corporate environment that accepts no errors and promotes systems and procedures designed to eliminate defects.

4. **The price of non-conformance.** To make quality a corporate issue, the cost of failing to meet conformance to requirements needs to be measured and expressed in money terms, the language of top management. The high cost of quality motivates top management to become involved with subsequent improvement programmes. The investments in training, improved product/service and process design, and better supplier relations are, in turn, the price of conformance.

Quality management maturity grid and 14-point programme

To help identify a company's position on the dimension of quality management, Crosby introduced a maturity grid for corporate self-assessment. It identified five states of quality awareness as summarized in Exhibit 9.6. For each of the five stages, Crosby also examined the status of the quality function, the problem-solving procedures used, the reported versus actual costs of quality and the actions taken.

Once companies had positioned themselves on the maturity grid, they could introduce Crosby's 14-point programme for quality improvement (the subject of the next section). This emphasized prevention over detection and concentrated on changing corporate culture rather than on analytical or statistical tools. The goal should always be zero defects, with leadership a top management task and quality professionals providing a lesser though important role as facilitators, co-ordinators and trainers as well as offering general and specific technical support. Crosby's 14-point programme is now outlined.[10]

1. **Management commitment**. Managers must be convinced of the importance of quality and demonstrate a clear commitment to improvement throughout the organization by aligning actions, policies and priorities to improving quality.

2. **Quality improvement team**. The quality improvement programme needs to be supported by a multi-functional team that reports directly to top management. Its role should include establishing quality-orientated policies, involvement in educational activities and co-ordinating and supervising changes in corporate culture.

3. **Quality measurement**. Quality measures need to be introduced that are meaningful and relate specifically to areas needing improvement. They need to relate to all functions and address key dimensions.

Exhibit 9.6   Crosby's quality management maturity grid

Categories of quality		Stages				
		1. Uncertainty	2. Awakening	3. Enlightenment	4. Wisdom	5. Certainty
Management understanding and attitude		Fails to recognize quality as a corporate issue	Supports quality management in theory but does not allocate resources	Embraces quality management and actively supports it	Participates personally and provides leadership in quality activities	Recognizes quality as necessary for corporate survival and growth
The organizational status of the quality function		Quality limited to the operations and technical functions and largely comprises inspection and checking activities	Quality leader appointed but otherwise activities remain similar to those in Stage 1	Quality function reports to top management and its leader actively involved in company management	Quality manager is a top management appointment and activities reorientated to prevention	Quality manager is on the board of directors. Prevention now the main activity and zero defects the management goal
Approach to handling problems		Fire-fighting approach. Symptoms, not causes addressed	Teams established to resolve problems but still short term in nature	Problems resolved in an orderly fashion and involves corrective action	Problems identified at an early stage and preventive action taken	Problems are prevented at the design and development stage
Cost of quality as per cent of sales	reported	Unknown	5 per cent	8 per cent	6 per cent	2–3 per cent
	actual	0–40 per cent	18 per cent	12 per cent	8 per cent	2–3 per cent
Quality improvement actions		No organized activities	Actions based on exhortation and short term in nature	Implements the 14-step programme	Continues the 14-step programme	Quality improvement is a regular ongoing activity
Overview of corporate position on quality management		'We don't know why we have problems'	'Do we always have to have quality problems?'	'Management's commitment and quality improvement programme is resolving our quality problems'	'We routinely prevent quality problems from occurring'	'We no longer have quality problems, we know why, and we aim to do better'

Source: Adapted from PB Crosby, Quality is Free (New York: McGraw-Hill, 1979), pp. 32–3.

4. **Cost of quality evaluation**. The programme collates the price of both non-conformance and conformance. This forms part of the essential guide to prioritizing action in line with different opportunities for improving quality.

5. **Quality awareness** needs to be promoted and co-ordinated throughout the company. Raising awareness among employees of the need for quality conformance and the cost of non-conformance is essential.

6. **Corrective action**. Opportunities and ideas for action are brought to the supervisory level and resolved there if possible. The team takes any remaining problems to higher levels for action.

7. **Zero-defects planning**. Managers need to plan the move from corrective action to achieving the goal of zero defects.

8. **Employee education**. Early in the quality programme all staff need to be trained in the principles of quality management and relevant tools and techniques.

9. **Zero-defects day**. Crosby recommended scheduling a particular date as zero-defects date. This signals a company's new standard of zero defects and the start of its move towards this new goal.

10. **Goal setting**. To achieve zero defects, a company needs to turn commitment into action by setting goals that represent progress towards this target. Not only do these guide action but they also guide performance measurement and evaluation.

11. **Error cause removal**. A quality programme should encourage staff to identify and report any problems that prevent them from producing error-free work. Everyone should take responsibility for identifying and correcting problems and preventing them recurring.

12. **Recognition**. A programme should include public, non-financial appreciation for all those whose actions have helped achieve or exceed a firm's quality goals and objectives.

13. **Quality councils**. Crosby recommended forming a quality council comprising quality professionals and team leaders who should meet regularly to share experiences, problems and ideas.

14. **Do it all over again**. To highlight the never-ending process of quality improvements the final step returns the programme to the beginning to start the process again. This renews a company's commitment to quality and will bring a new round of quality improvement opportunities and gains.

Quality vaccine

To help make quality management an integral part of an organization's activities, Crosby introduced the concept of the quality vaccine. This idea describes a corporate quality state that improves the overall health of a firm by addressing and correcting many of its problems. The major components of Crosby's quality vaccine are illustrated in Exhibit 9.7 and are now reviewed.[11] Corporate integrity represents the honest commitment to improve performance and satisfy customers in the most effective way. The concept embodies a firm's policy commitment to offer products and services that are right first time, every time. The second component, communications,

Exhibit 9.7   *Major components of Crosby's quality vaccine*

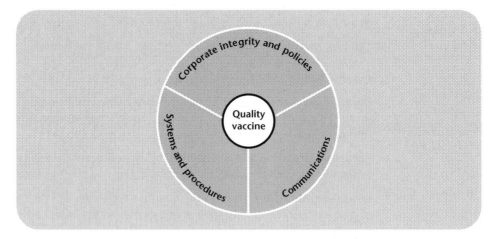

represents the flow of information through the whole supply chain. It emphasizes the need for regular exchanges of information on quality problems, performance, progress and related issues. The final element is the systems and procedures designed to maintain the new quality management environment.

TOOLS AND TECHNIQUES – GENERAL ISSUES

The key to good quality lies in good management, a point central to the views of all the main contributors to improving quality. Management has the responsibility and has to give the lead in changing the systems and processes that create the quality problems. A key part of this provision is to train everyone how to use the tools and techniques to enable the quality offering to be consistently met. Sound quality management relies heavily on contributions from empowered staff and, in turn, this requires access to appropriate tools.

The tools and techniques used in quality management are based on analysis and statistical approaches to measure and improve the level of quality in a company's processes and delivery systems. These tools indicate how well operations is consistently meeting the agreed specification of its products and services and, in turn, identify the source of any problems.

Case example   7

Bill Conway (Nashua Corporation) made this point most effectively to some top management visitors from Ford. He started the meeting with a challenge. 'Suppose I ask two of you successful vice-presidents at Ford to enter a contest. The winner will win a trip around the world for his whole family. I know that both of you are totally motivated and dedicated by virtue of your exalted positions at Ford. The contest is to see who can drive a nail into this wall. One of you will get a hammer, the other nothing but management encouragement. Who do you think will win?' The answer was obvious. Motivation and management support and encouragement are important, but employees having the correct tools is essential.[12]

In general, these tools and techniques fall into those used in the design phase and those used in the process:

■ Design tools help staff to develop new products and services that incorporate the needs and expectations of customers into the specification while reducing or preventing quality problems inherent in the design itself. Similar tools and techniques are used in the design of the process to achieve the same ends of reducing or preventing problems in the way products or services are provided. A glance back at Chapters 3 and 5 will remind you of the approaches used and the advantages, disadvantages and outcomes of their use.

■ Process tools enable staff to assess the conditions and capabilities of existing processes in relation to meeting set standards. These help detect problems that require intervention and regain any lost control within a process or delivery system.

To apply design and process tools and techniques, data are required. In general, the tools help staff to draw pictures of the process. These highlight trends or provide indicators of actual or potential quality problems. As mentioned earlier, process conditions can be measured using variable or attribute data. Variable data measure quantifiable process conditions. They can be counted and allow absolute or comparative positions to be established. A glance at Exhibit 9.8 illustrates the point.

A receiving department checks incoming products by taking a sample of 40 from each delivery. If there are four or less (≤10 per cent) defects the delivery is accepted. With five or more defects, the whole delivery is rejected. By this method, 12 of the 15 deliveries in Quarter 1 (see Exhibit 9.8) were accepted and three were returned to the supplier – an acceptance rate of 80 per cent. In this example, the number of defects provides variable data because it can be arranged in ways to allow comparisons to be made. For example, the early part of Quarter 1 showed a high percentage of rejects compared to the latter part of the same three month period. Furthermore, when deliveries were rejected the percentage of defects was relatively high, between 15 and 25.

Exhibit 9.8   *Data on 15 deliveries in Quarter 1*

Delivery date	# defects per batch of 40 units	Decision: accept (✓) or reject (✗)
3 Jan.	6	✗
6 Jan.	2	✓
11 Jan.	10	✗
24 Jan.	4	✓
3 Feb.	7	✗
17 Feb.	0	✓
19 Feb.	3	✓
28 Feb.	3	✓
3 Mar.	2	✓
6 Mar.	2	✓
12 Mar.	1	✓
18 Mar.	1	✓
24 Mar.	3	✓
26 Mar.	4	✓
30 Mar.	4	✓

In contrast, attribute data, as explained earlier, measure qualitative conditions of a process such as go/no-go or, in this instance, the accept/reject decision in column 3 of Exhibit 9.8. Comparisons using attribute data provide limited insights. For example, without column 2 in the exhibit, the differences in the number of rejects for each delivery would not be available. A delivery has either been accepted with 10 per cent or less rejects or rejected with in excess of 10 per cent rejects.

Variable and attribute measures are, however, linked and, from the simple example in Exhibit 9.8, it can be seen that knowing what data will provide the insights required is essential when designing process controls.

PROCESS TOOLS AND TECHNIQUES[13]

Exhibit 9.3 outlined the stages in the operations process where quality checks could be made. This section describes the tools and techniques available to undertake these checks. As you will see, some of them have been introduced and described in other chapters and are, therefore, only included here by a brief statement with appropriate references.

Companies use these tools and techniques to evaluate how well processes and systems consistently meet the product and service specifications and hence the expectation of their customers, identify problems and their most likely causes and assess the effect of corrective actions. These tools and techniques provide different and complementary analyses and so using a combination of these provides greater insights and more information by which to manage and control quality.

1. Pareto principle

The size and importance of problems, causes or other aspects of quality will vary and often the relationship between their relative frequency will reflect what is known as the Pareto principle or 80/20 rule (explained in more detail in Chapter 10). The 80/20 rule indicates that, say, 80 per cent of the total quality problems identified would be the result of 20 per cent of the total number of causes.

In managing quality, a Pareto analysis would begin by listing the quality problems identified and recording the number of times these occurred. Additional information such as the costs (for example, rectification or reject) associated with each problem would also be kept. Over a given period data would be collected and the number of occurrences or total costs involved would be identified for each problem. Placing the

Exhibit 9.9   *Pareto analysis of reasons for flight departure delays due to an airline's own systems and procedures*

Problem	Per cent incidences	Cumulative per cent
Accepting late passengers	39	39
Waiting for tug push back	24	63
Waiting for fuelling	14	77
Late weight and balance sheet	9	86
Cabin cleaners take longer than scheduled	8	94
Waiting for food services	4	98
Other	2	100

highest (either number of occurrences or total costs depending on which dimension was perceived to be the more relevant) at the top of the list, the second highest next and so on (see Exhibit 9.9) gives a Pareto listing. A Pareto analysis thus highlights where a company should start its improvement efforts. Beginning with those at the top will bring a higher return than starting lower down the list.

2. Checklists

A checklist is a simple, widely used tool to collect data in a form that records the size and other dimensions of quality (and other) problems. Exhibit 9.10 provides an example for a retail outlet. You will see from this that a number of problems were chosen to be reviewed. By using the five-bar gate method of recording, each occurrence is logged and totals calculated. You will also see from this list that the 80/20 rule applies where two of the five problems account for 71 per cent of the total problem occurrences. (This also illustrates that the phrase 80/20 is one indicating relative size and not exactness.) Looking at these in more depth would be the place to start.

3. Cause and effect diagrams

Also known as fishbone (due to their shape) or Ishikawa charts (named after the person who developed this tool),[14] cause and effect diagrams (also discussed later in Chapter 13) identify potential causes and help to direct problem-solving and data-collection efforts towards the most likely causes of observed defects.

These diagrams are built up from a problem statement through to detailed causes using the following steps:

■ **Problem statement**. Analysis of the symptoms and causes yields the problem statement. In turn, this then becomes the label for the root effect arrow as shown in Exhibit 9.11.

■ **Major causes**. The second step is to identify major categories of causes. These are then drawn at an angle to the root effect arrow. For example, 'airport' and 'personnel' in Exhibit 9.11.

Exhibit 9.10   *A checklist of the frequency of problems at a retail outlet during a busy weekday*

Problem	Frequency	Total	Per cent total
Shelf display differs from bar code record	1111 1111 1111 1	16	14
No goods on shelf	1111 1111 1111 1111 1111 1111 1111	34	29
Goods out of stock	1111 1111	10	8
Length of checkout queue exceeds target	1111 1111 1111 1111 1111 1111 1111 1111 1111 1111	49	42
Items returned faulty	1111 111	8	7
Total		117	100

Exhibit 9.11   *Cause and effect diagram used to ascertain the cause of flight delays*

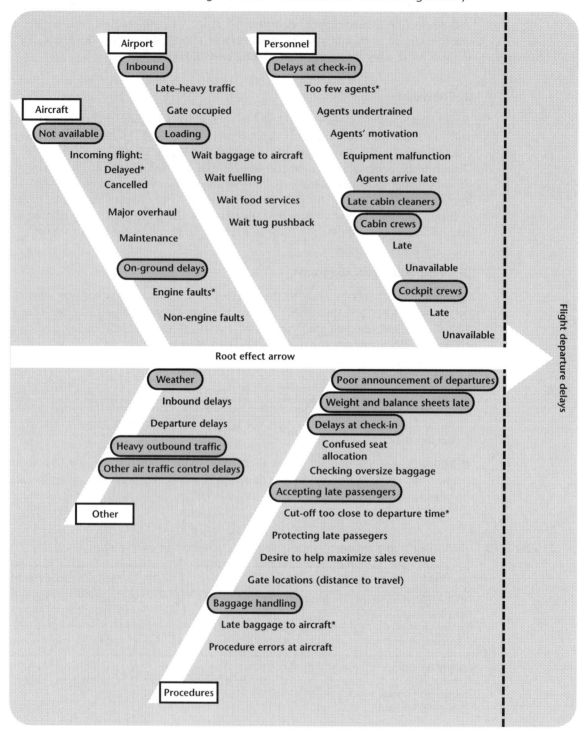

■ **Detailed causes**. The next step is to list all the detailed causes within each of the major categories. For example, 'weather' and 'other air traffic control delays' under the major cause 'other' in Exhibit 9.11.

■ **Principal causes**. The final step is to identify the principal causes within the list of detailed causes as a guide as to where to look first. For example, Exhibit 9.11 indicates these with an asterisk.

Sumitomo Electric has developed the use of cause and effect diagrams by adding the following refinements:

■ For each cause, two coloured cards are introduced. One records details of facts and the other details of ideas.
■ Any number of 'fact' cards are placed on the left of each cause. These contain data and issues relating to a particular cause.
■ In the same way, any number of 'ideas' cards are placed on the right of each cause and these contain suggestions for improvements.
■ All 'fact' cards are first reviewed as part of the problem clarification stage before moving onto 'ideas' cards that address potential improvements.
■ All cards are initialled by the contributor allowing for explanation, questions and greater clarity.

4. Process mapping

One key process tool for improving quality is to record the existing process. Charting the sequence of steps and clarifying what goes on at each step is an important analysis. As this is covered extensively in Chapter 13 then further explanation is not provided here. By turning to this chapter, however, you will be able to review the different types of process maps and charts available and which ones are used where.

5. Scatter diagrams

Collecting data is one step, identifying why a variable happens turns data into information from which insights result. One way of doing this is to construct a scatter diagram. This tool illustrates graphically the relationship between two variables. It reveals relationships between pairs of variables (known as a bivariate relationship) such as the number of errors per day and the length of an operator's experience or the number of training days received. Exhibit 9.12 shows a scatter diagram illustrating the relationship between the percentage of defects and the length of a production run. You will see from this that as the run length increases, the percentage of rejects decreases and this decline follows a consistent pattern.

6. Sampling

To ensure that the level of quality is consistently met then 100 per cent inspection should, in theory, ensure that below-quality products or services are not allowed to proceed through the process. Technology developments, particularly in high volume manufacturing processes, have enabled this to be undertaken as an integral part of the system. For example, checking the weight of, or liquid level in, a container provides a simple pass/reject mechanism ensuring that a pack contains the required amount.

Exhibit 9.12   *Scatter diagrams graphically illustrating the relationship between per cent rejects per run and the run length (hours)*

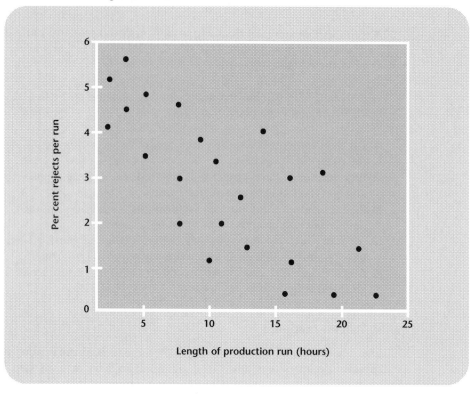

Where, however, inspection is undertaken by people, then as explained earlier in the chapter, there are in practice major limitations. Checking becomes monotonous and errors creep in, it is costly, it takes longer and where testing would make a product unusable (for example, lighting fireworks to see if they work) then sampling is a practical alternative.

Where 100 per cent inspection is not an integral part of the operations process, the limitations above give rise to the concept of acceptance sampling. Most acceptance checking or inspection procedures are based on the principles of statistical inference by which conclusions are drawn about the characteristics of a large quantity of products or services, by inspecting very carefully a small sample from the total. Any acceptance sampling plan may lead to a wrong judgement. This, as explained earlier, is known as sampling risk and is covered later.

There has been much written about the subject of sampling and the methods are so well refined that it is not necessary to understand the mathematical principles involved. Also, tables are available to show the inferences that can be drawn from the different sampling procedures and outcomes. (Should you wish to review these aspects in more detail then suggested readings are included at the end of the chapter.)[15]

When using the concept of sampling, the following principles must apply:

■ The sample has to be either truly random or stratified (that is, the samples are chosen so as to be representative of the operations provision over the time period involved).

- The sample size needs to relate to the size of the order quantity involved to ensure that what is checked is sufficiently representative of the whole.

- The identity of the bulk lot from which the sample has been taken should, where possible, be preserved. After all, a sample has no meaning in itself; it is the bulk lot that is important.

7. Acceptance sampling plans

There are several types of acceptance sampling plan that may be used. In each instance, the plan is designed to ensure that products or parts of a service do not pass to the next stage in the process if an unacceptably high proportion of the batch or order quantity is outside the quality limit. Some of these different plans call for a single sample and others for double or multiple sampling to be taken from the total quantity being processed. The plans may also differ in the way the items in the sample are checked. Some of the more important differences are examined here. In practice the plans used are rarely designed from first principles but more frequently are based on one of several already published.

Acceptable quality level (AQL)

AQL is the maximum per cent defective (or the maximum number of defects per 100 units) that, for purposes of acceptance sampling, can be considered satisfactory as a process average. Thus, when a value of AQL is determined for the quality characteristic being checked, providing the average number of defective items is not greater than the agreed AQL, then the great majority of the lots inspected will be accepted.

Sampling risk

The phrase 'great majority' was used above because no sampling scheme is perfect. There will be the risk that an unacceptable batch will satisfy the AQL and, therefore, be accepted (known as the consumer's risk) and, similarly, that an acceptable batch fails to meet the AQL and, therefore, is rejected (known as the producer's risk). The way to reduce this risk is to take a larger sample, with 100 per cent sample plans being the upper limit where, theoretically, no risk is taken.

Economics of sampling

The consumer's and producer's risks referred to above both incur costs. In the former they are the costs associated with passing defective products or services through the process. In the latter, they are the unnecessary checking, rework and administrative costs involved as the batch or order quantity is, in fact, acceptable. Thus two sets of costs are involved at each inspection point in a process – those associated with making the check and those relating to the sampling risk. Clearly, the level of inspection to apply is that at which the sum of these two sets of costs is at a minimum. However, in practice it is difficult to assess these costs and so what constitutes the minimum sum is judgemental. It is important, though, that the concepts described here are appreciated and form the basis of that decision.

Sampling scheme

A sampling scheme contains a range of sampling plans and procedures and the results of inspecting one or more samples are used to assess the quality of a batch or order quantity and help determine whether or not to accept it.

Each sampling plan states the sample size to be taken in relation to different batch or order quantity sizes and the decision criteria to be used for accepting or rejecting a batch. The sample sizes are based on the mathematical theory of probability and will not be covered here.

Earlier, the limitations surrounding a 100 per cent inspection procedure were discussed. While the concept of sampling holds true in most situations, there are times when 100 per cent inspection is necessary, for example where safety is of the utmost importance.

Single sampling plan

This plan is essentially a go/no-go procedure. The sampling size related to the batch or order quantity is determined and the acceptable quality level is applied. Only if the number of defective items (products) or errors (services) meets the AQL criteria is the batch or order quantity accepted.

Double sampling plan

A double sampling plan introduces another option to the single plan above. The example shown in Exhibit 9.13 requires a sample of 100 to be taken from an order quantity of a known size. If on the first sample of 100 the number of defects or errors is two or less then the whole batch is accepted on the first sample. Conversely, if the number of defective items or errors is seven or more, then the whole batch is rejected on the first sample. If, however, the number of defective items or errors is between three and six then a second sample of 100 is taken. If the cumulative number of defective items or errors from both batches is seven or less then accept it, if eight or more then reject it.

Multiple sampling plan

The principle of the double sampling plan can be extended into a multiple sampling plan. This too uses not only the AQL concept but also the unacceptable quality level (UQL) concept. This latter relates to the percentage defective level at which the batch or order quantity would be rejected. As in the case of double sampling plans, there is a yes, no and don't know situation. A first sample is taken which is usually smaller than in a single sampling plan. If the number of defective items or errors is between the accept and reject areas then further samples are taken until the cumulative results of the multiple samples fall into either the accept or reject category (see Exhibit 9.14).

Exhibit 9.13 *Double sampling plan*

Sample		Number of defective items or errors	
#	Size	Acceptable quality level	Unacceptable quality level
1st	100	≤2	≥7
2nd	100	≤7	≥8

Exhibit 9.14   *Multiple sampling plan*

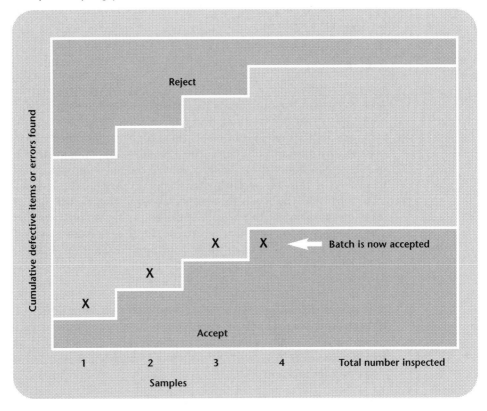

Sequential sampling plan

A sequential sampling plan is similar to a multiple plan. The sample size is one, with the results normally plotted on a graph. The sampling is repeated until the graph contains sufficient information on which to reach a decision.

Normal, tightened and reduced inspection

Normal inspection is defined as that used where there is no reason to think that the quality of a product or service differs from that specified. Inspection is tightened or reduced when the results of normal inspection indicate that the quality of the lot is worse or better than specified.

THE OPERATIONS PROCESS – QUALITY MANAGEMENT IN PRACTICE

Having explained the important, general aspects of quality management, this section looks at the major stages in the operations process and the types of quality checks to apply and tools to use. Several of the techniques explained earlier (for example, the Pareto principle, checklists, cause and effect diagrams, process mapping and scatter diagrams) will be used as part of a general approach to managing quality. This section will identify the more quality-specific tools while recognizing that the more general techniques will invariably form part of the overall approach used to manage quality.

Earlier in the chapter the question 'where to inspect?' was introduced. This section now reviews in more detail the issues of where to check and some of the principal tools used at each stage.

1. Purchasing

The ever higher per cent of total costs that purchased items constitutes increases the need to control their quality. In operations, machines, equipment or people convert material from one form to a more developed form. In machining processes, the process is subject to variation. In non-machining processes, adjustments by an operator can be made only within certain limits. Thus, the material being fed into a process must fall within certain limits of variability to enable the machining or non-machining process to convert it into the required new state. To do this the level of quality must be predictable and the levels of variance assessed and agreed. But for this to happen suppliers must first be told what is wanted. If they do not know then they will not be able to supply at the necessary level of quality. Hence a precise specification is needed, and the first step is to explain what is required in terms of variables and attributes, as outlined earlier. The use of a purchasing specification is most essential where the items or services:

- are expensive in themselves or are bought in large quantities
- relate to the essential function (product) or essential attribute (service) to be provided by what is sold
- will cause difficulties and expense in the process if they are below the product or service specification.

To help maintain desired quality levels it is essential to buy materials or services from reliable suppliers. While there are other important considerations such as cost and delivery reliability that will form part of this choice, these are not discussed in this section.

The quality of purchased components and materials is rooted in the process of suppliers. A company will not receive the required quality if the methods used by its suppliers are not capable of consistently meeting the agreed specification. It is, therefore, important that an evaluation of procedures is established for suppliers that provide materials or services critical to the process and end-product or service. This will usually contain three distinct phases. The first is vendor appraisal that is completed before placing an order and is designed to assess the ability of a supplier to deliver goods and services at the required level of quality. The second concerns supplier evaluation which is designed to vet a supplier's control of quality when an order has been given, and the goods and services supplied. The final phase is that of supplier rating which monitors the actual performance of a supplier.

Checking purchased items and services

Where the maintenance of quality levels is critical to the end-product or service, organizations typically insist on monitoring a supplier's processes and quality control procedures. A classic example of this is the aviation industry. Civil and military aircraft companies have developed sophisticated quality assurance procedures to meet the high safety requirements of many of its components and equipment purchases. Tracking the origin of materials and evaluating and monitoring suppliers' processes forms part of their supplier controls. Similar checks are increasingly being introduced in the service sector. For example, companies purchasing consultancy services will interview the consultants themselves as part of the selection process. In the same way, companies contracting out the supply of executive education will interview those providing direction and also require to see first hand the teaching faculty in a classroom or other learning environment as part of their decision-making procedure. However, most organizations limit themselves to checking items or services once they have been purchased. Understandably, as items become more complex, then so do the inspection procedures. In many instances these checks may be no more than a quantity count as, for example, with office supplies. Yet even where an organization wishes to check the characteristics of a product or service it will not usually inspect each one: the costs of doing so are just too high. Thus, the inspection agreed with a supplier has to contain not only what is intended to be the quality level but also how it is to be judged and measured and the level of imperfection that is acceptable (see earlier in the chapter). Where some level of imperfection is permitted, then sampling is the basis on which to proceed.

Consequently, the principle of acceptance sampling will be applied in this situation. The design of any sampling plan is a trade-off between sampling cost and risk. To help in this choice, a useful way of depicting the relationship is provided by plotting an operating characteristic (OC) curve (see Exhibit 9.15). Each OC curve is associated with a particular sampling plan and it shows how well an acceptance plan discriminates between good and bad batches or order quantities. Exhibit 9.15 explains how a particular acceptance plan operates, but as each acceptance plan relates to a particular situa-

Exhibit 9.15   *General relationships of an OC curve*

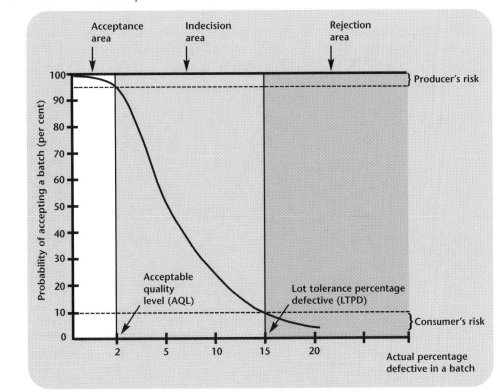

tion, then each OC curve will usually be uniquely designed, offering different choices between sample size and the acceptable number of defects – see Exhibit 9.16.

In Exhibit 9.15 the OC curve must meet the following conditions:

Acceptable quality level (AQL)	2 per cent
Lot tolerance percentage defective (LTPD)	15 per cent
Producer's risk	5 per cent
Consumer's risk	10 per cent

Let us remind ourselves of what these factors mean:

■ AQL is the desired quality level at which the probability of acceptance would be high.
■ LTPD is the rejection quality level at which the probability of acceptance would be low.
■ Producer's and consumer's risk are the probabilities of good order quantities (at AQL) being rejected or substandard order quantities (at LTPD) being accepted.

A curve that passes through the two specified points AQL and LTPD can be found by trial and error or by using tables.[15] This example shows not only the power of the plan to discriminate between good and bad batches or order quantities but also the extent of the risk of accepting bad batches and rejecting good ones. The question now is, 'How can managers modify acceptance plans in order to minimize this risk?' The most obvious way is to increase the sample size. Exhibit 9.16 shows the effect of this

Exhibit 9.16   *OC curves for different sampling sizes*

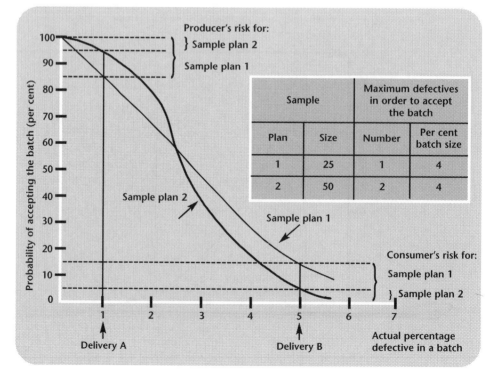

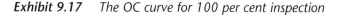

Exhibit 9.17   *The OC curve for 100 per cent inspection*

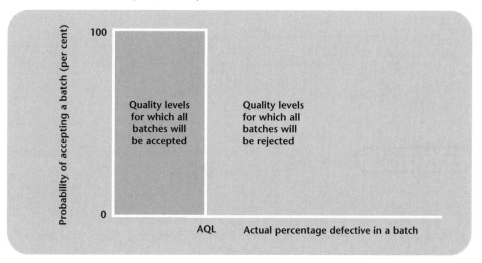

and the larger discriminatory power of the sample size, as shown by comparing sample plans 1 and 2 against two deliveries, delivery A with 1 per cent actual defects and delivery B with 5 per cent actual defects. It can be seen clearly from the figure that sample plan 2 reduces both the consumer's risk and producer's risk. As it is consumers who are most concerned about the degree of acceptable risk inherent in the application of sampling plans to incoming inspection, then it is they who not only set the AQL but also the steepness of the OC curve. As illustrated in Exhibit 9.16, this is related to the sample size, for although the maximum percentage allowable for acceptance was the same at 4 per cent of the sample, the increase in sample size resulted in a steeper curve. Exhibit 9.16 also illustrates the probabilities of accepting a delivery if sample plan 1 or 2 were adopted. Where the actual percentage defective in a batch was only 1 per cent (as in delivery A), then the probability of accepting the batch increases; where the actual percentage defective in a batch was 5 per cent (as in delivery B) then the probability of accepting this batch decreases.

An OC curve, therefore, is a graph showing what any particular sampling plan will be expected to do in terms of accepting or rejecting batches. Although any sampling plan can be used without understanding its operating characteristics, it makes sense that the quality assurance function of any organization should be able to compare one sampling plan with another to help establish appropriate quality controls. As the selected AQL is the dividing line between good and bad batches, the ideal system would be one in which all batches whose quality was better than the AQL were accepted, and all whose quality was worse, rejected. This, of course, is only possible with 100 per cent inspection (see Exhibit 9.17). Sampling, being the alternative to this method, will not provide this level of discrimination and means that the vertical line shown in Exhibit 9.17 will have to run at a slope as shown in Exhibits 9.15 and 9.16. Which OC curve to choose balances risk and cost. The closer the OC curve fits the slope of the curve in Exhibit 9.17 then the lower the risk but the nearer to 100 per cent inspection and the costs associated with this form of checking.

2. Processing and the delivery system

The way a process or person performs is independent of the product or service. To manage and control quality, therefore, it is necessary to know what the process will do, is likely to do or, better still, what it is doing. Furthermore, processes do not make identical but merely similar products or services. Variability is inherent in a process or delivery system and the need to appreciate this is an important first step in managing process quality.

Case example 8

As the financial services sector becomes more competitive companies are analysing what they need to do to maintain and grow share in a market characterized by overcapacity. Take the Royal Bank of Scotland (RBS) which made a surprising discovery when it decided to measure how much customer satisfaction dictated future buying intentions. It divided its customers into three categories:

■ those with a problem that was not resolved
■ those with a problem that had been efficiently dealt with and
■ those whose experience with the bank had been problem-free.

Predictably, those still dissatisfied were the ones least likely to buy any more of the bank's services. But, the surprise was that those customers with settled grievances were the most likely to buy RBS products in the future. In approximate terms the percentage of customers who will purchase from the same supplier shows 40 per cent for the dissatisfied group, 60 per cent for the problem-free group and 80 per cent for the settled grievances group.
And this picture is broadly consistent across most similar studies: keeping customers happy is not simply a wise move to help retain existing business but a way of increasing future revenues from the same sources.

Case example questions

8.1 Why do you think the 40:60:80 ratio described above consistently reflects customer attitudes re future purchases?

8.2 How should companies manage this aspect of service quality to best reflect customers' responses to getting things right?

In process control, information is received on what is happening in a process or delivery system and so distinguishes between those quality changes resulting from the natural variations of the process or delivery system (referred to as assignable causes) and those resulting from some new, persistent influences on the process (referred to as random causes). This distinction is fundamental to controlling process quality and allows corrective action to be taken only where it is necessary. To do this effectively, it is necessary to:

■ use the knowledge of what has been happening in the process
■ differentiate between assignable and random changes in quality, and
■ determine the causes of any random changes and rectify them.

Control charts

While acceptance sampling of a completed order quantity is an important part of managing quality, other forms of control are necessary to help prevent worsening levels of quality conformance going undetected until after the products or services have been completed.

To measure what is going on requires checks to be made at points in a process or delivery system. Where and how to complete these checks can vary as follows:

■ **Where** – at predetermined points in a process or delivery system or 'patrol' checks involving routine or random visits to several stages in a process or delivery system.
■ **By whom** – undertaken by independent quality control staff or those responsible for making the product or providing the service being monitored.

Except where automatic 100 per cent checking of products is built into a manufacturing process, decisions on the 'where' and 'by whom' checks need to be taken. The dimensions affecting where to check were covered earlier. The recognition that controlling quality works best where the person responsible for making a product or providing a service is also responsible for meeting the specification needs to be reflected in these decisions. In this way, managing quality is based on the principle that the person responsible for a process also has to measure the process, monitor quality movements and rectify the process or delivery system as needed.

One important way to measure quality is using control charts that record outputs from the process while it is taking place. For the most part they can be used to control both variables and attributes of repetitive processes.

■ **Control charts for variables** – typically, the process mean or average is established and acceptable levels of deviation agreed. These have two sets of limits: warning (or upper and lower control) limits which form the band of usual variation, and action limits which form the band of unusual variation – see Exhibit 9.18.

Exhibit 9.18   *Control chart for variables*

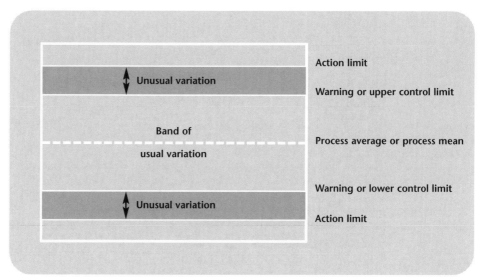

■ **Control charts for attributes** – as attribute measures of quality are obtained by an acceptable or unacceptable classification, then an exact measure of the process is not taken. Consequently, to control attributes through the use of control charts, sampling is used as shown in Exhibit 9.19. The control chart measures the actual item or number of defectives in a sample that, when plotted, show any variation in the process for which corrective action needs to be taken.

■ **Cumulative sum charts** – a control chart is a clear way of presenting data. However, it is based on checking specific observations independently from one another. Cumulative sum (cu sum) charts, on the other hand, take into account past data and, by incorporating these into the chart, allow trends to be more clearly shown than in control charts.

The cu sum chart is devised by establishing a reference value for the process that is usually the process mean. An actual reading is then made and is subtracted from the reference value. This result is then plotted. The next reading is similarly calculated but is then added to the previous result and then plotted. In this way, slight changes in the process can be detected, for if the mean value increases there will be a rise in the cumulative sum level. Similarly, a downward slope will mean a decrease in cu sum, while a horizontal graph will show stability in the data.

Statistical process control

The increasing competitive pressure to produce higher quality products or provide higher quality services has brought about changes in attitudes and expectations.

Exhibit 9.19   *Control chart for attributes*

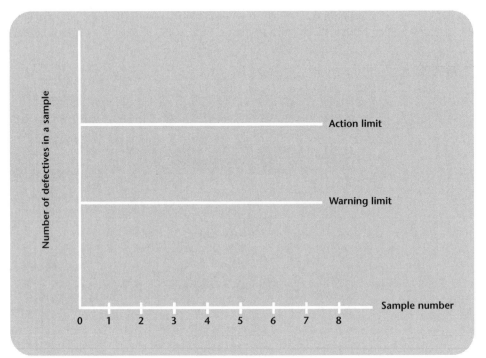

Coupled with these changes has been a greater use of statistically based tools to create data as the basis for analysing problems and identifying causes. The use of statistical process control (SPC), incorporated within the responsibilities of those completing the task, is increasingly being employed to help achieve these necessary and significant improvements. Only through monitoring the process on a continuous basis (for example, using charts similar to Exhibits 9.18, 9.19 and 9.20) can quality levels be systematically improved by checking the outputs from a process or system and making any necessary adjustments on an ongoing basis.

It is important to recognize that the purpose is not to achieve a position where all sample points are within limits and close to the average. If this prevails, it is usually a sign that the proactive use of this approach has not been recognized. The Shewhart rule for a process in control is to have two-thirds of the points within the limits and one-third of the points outside the limits.[14] The dual purpose of SPC includes the need to change the control chart limits in such a way as to achieve the Shewhart result. The next step is to change the process, thereby bringing all the points within the new limits and then begin the cycle again with the overriding aim of continuously reducing variability by systematically improving process capability. Remember, the purpose is to reduce variability and thereby improve quality.

Building the responsibility for quality conformance back into the job of the person responsible for making the product or providing the service and supporting these responsibilities with appropriate training and top management's active and continued support are essential to achieving and maintaining quality improvements. As emphasized earlier, quality is not free but the return on investment is most attractive.

Exhibit 9.20   *Control charts in a call centre*

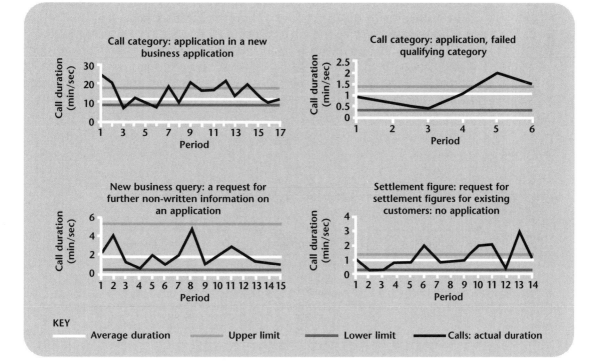

3. Outputs

The final stage concerns the control of quality at the end of a process, including delivery and installation where appropriate. In make-to-stock situations, inspecting finished items will usually form an integral part of the system. For products of high value there will usually be a 100 per cent inspection on certain functional aspects of an item. As with ongoing inspection, the first step will be to prepare a specification based on appropriate variables and attributes and then detail the inspection procedures to be followed. With less expensive items, a sampling plan is more appropriate and would be based on the same factors as those discussed earlier under purchased items and services.

In make-to-order organizations, decisions similar to those described in the last paragraph will prevail. In addition, with high-value items or in the case of large organizations including governments, strict procedures concerning quality checks will form part of a contract and will be undertaken by the customer. From the viewpoint of customers, you are now a supplier and the tools and procedures discussed in the section under 'Purchasing' will form part of their approach.

SIX-SIGMA QUALITY

The drive to improve existing levels of quality conformance has been encapsulated in the mandate of six-sigma quality. In the late 1980s Motorola's Semiconductor Products Division laid down for itself the six-sigma challenge: that is, 3.4 defects per million transactions or virtually error-free output. And it set the goal of achieving ±6 sigma capability in all phases of the business including product design, manufacturing, sales and services. Most companies currently fall well short of that. Typical processes generate about 35,000 defects per million which sounds a lot (and is a lot!) but is consistent with the defect levels of most successful companies – in statistical terms this constitutes three and a half sigma (see Exhibit 9.21). Other companies are also recognizing the competitive advantages of setting quality conformance goals that will change the rules of the game. (Issues concerning continuous improvement are covered later in Chapter 15 which also includes a section on benchmarking – the approach of setting best-in-class corporate goals – and the idea of changing the rules of the game.)

Exhibit 9.21 *Specification limit and corresponding percentage good quality and # defects per million*

Specification limit	# defects per million	Per cent good quality
±1 sigma	697 700	30.22
±2 sigma	308 700	69.13
±3 sigma	66 810	93.32
±4 sigma	6 210	99.37
±5 sigma	233	99.98
±6 sigma	3.4	99.99

9

Jack Welch, General Electric's Chairman and Chief Executive Officer, has set a corporate 'goal of becoming, by the year 2000, a six-sigma quality company, which means a company that produces virtually defect-free products, services and transactions'. As he outlined in his address to GE's 1996 and 1997 Annual Meetings: 'Three- to Four-Sigma quality is typically 10–15 per cent of revenues. In GE's case, with over $70bn in revenues, that amounts to some $7–10bn annually, mostly in scrap, reworking of parts and rectifying mistakes in transactions. So the financial rationale for embarking on this quality journey is clear.

'But beyond the pure financials, there are even more important rewards that will come with dramatically improved quality. Among them: the unlimited growth from selling products and services universally recognized by customers as being on a completely different plane of quality than those of your competitors... Six-Sigma will be an exciting journey and the most difficult and invigorating stretch goal we have ever undertaken. The magnitude of the challenge of going from 35 000 defects per million to fewer than 4 defects is huge. It will require us to reduce defect rates 10 000 fold – about 84 per cent for five consecutive years... [But] we want to make our quality so special, so valuable to our customers, so important to their success that our products and services become their only real value choice.'

Case example questions

9.1 What will be the key tasks for GE to reach its year 2000 goal?

9.2 How will this change the competitive factors in its markets and what will be the strategic advantages that will result?

FORMALIZING THE SEARCH FOR QUALITY

To meet the increasing importance of consistent quality conformance in today's markets, companies have highlighted the dimension of quality management within their own organizations. As quality conformance levels in one organization are affected by the ability of its suppliers to meet the specification of the products and services they deliver, then knowing how well suppliers are able to consistently conform to these standards is a key element of managing quality.

To this end, many large organizations (for example, international companies and governments) have, for a long time, set up their own system of approving suppliers. These approval procedures assess potential suppliers as a whole and their operations function's ability to meet the volume and specification requirements in particular. The growing awareness of the need to improve quality has led directly to the introduction and use of national and international programmes that formalize systems for evaluating the capability of any organization to consistently design, provide and deliver products and services to specification. ISO 9000, the Malcolm Baldrige National Quality Award and the European Quality Award are the three widely used programmes to help formalize the search for quality, and are now reviewed.

ISO 9000

Established in 1947, the International Organization for Standardization (ISO) is a non-government body to which over 100 countries subscribe. Its role is to secure international agreements on key topics and then publish these as international standards.

The ISO 9000 series is a set of worldwide standards that detail the requirements for an organization's quality management systems. The series, adopted in 1987, defines internationally accepted standards for business quality. They provide a framework that governs the activities and procedures for managing quality that customers expect of a supplier to demonstrate its effective control of its processes. Most countries have their own equivalent, if not identical, standards,[16] but accept ISO 9000 as the internationally recognized and accepted certification.

ISO 9000 comprises five documents that list a whole range of standards that have to be met to gain certification.[17] Third-party assessment of a company's quality standards is undertaken and, following registration, is audited regularly. ISO 9000 certification thus assures customers that a company has designed and is managing its processes to assure delivery of products and services to specification. But, as the Dilbert cartoon points out, certification is not a cosmetic exercise (see Exhibit 9.22).

Exhibit 9.22   *ISO 9000 certification – what it is and what it isn't!*

Source: Copyright © Scott Adams

An overview of the ISO 9000 series of standards is now provided:

- **ISO 9000** 'Guide to selection and use' details how to use the other standards in the series and is essential to the correct interpretation and application of them. It also has three subset documents (ISO 9000–2, 9000–3 and 9000–4) that give among other things, guidelines to the use of ISO 9001, 9002 and 9003.

- **ISO 9001** specifies design/development, operations, installation and servicing. It has 20 clauses covering the following:

management responsibilities	inspection, measuring and test equipment
quality system	inspection and test status
contract review	control of non-conforming product
design control	corrective action
document control	handling, storage, packaging and delivery
purchasing	quality records
purchaser supplied material	internal quality audit
product identification and traceability	training
process control	after-sales servicing
inspection and testing	statistical techniques

- **ISO 9002** covers circumstances where an organization is responsible for assuring the product or service quality during the course of provision or installation only. This part has 18 of the 20 clauses above excluding 'design control' and 'after-sales servicing'.

- **ISO 9003** contains specifications for final inspection and test. It is used when conformance to specified requirements can be assured solely at final inspection and test and contains 12 elements of those listed above under ISO 9001.

- **ISO 9004**, as ISO 9000, is a guide to good quality management practice. It gives more detail than ISO 9001, 9002 and 9003, contains reference to a number of quality aspects (for example, quality risks, costs and product service liability) that are not covered to the same level as in ISO 9001, 9002 and 9003 and places considerable emphasis on the satisfaction of customer needs and requirements. As with ISO 9000, it has three subset documents (ISO 9004–2, 9004–3 and 9004–4) that give guidance and comprehensive overviews for establishing and implementing a quality system for services, the application of quality management for processed materials and for implementing continuous quality management within an organization respectively.

Malcolm Baldrige National Quality Award

The Malcolm Baldrige National Quality Award was a response by the USA to the competitive challenges facing businesses in the early 1980s. A US government mandate for a national study on productivity led, in part, to a recommendation by the National Advisory Council for Quality and the American Productivity and Quality Center that the US government should sponsor a national quality award. In 1987 this was established and renamed after Malcolm Baldrige (the Secretary of Commerce at the time who was a strong advocate of this step) following his accidental death in July of that year.

The Baldrige Award, as it is now referred to, seeks to recognize and encourage quality and productivity improvements by:

- stimulating companies to attain excellence in quality
- recognizing outstanding companies and helping disseminate experience and best practice regarding quality and its impact on corporate performance
- establishing guidelines for organizations on the assessment and management of quality
- gathering information on how to manage for superior quality by changing corporate cultures and practices.

The award is administered annually by the National Institute of Standards and Technology, and the process involves an independent review by outsiders, on-site visits and judges' reviews. The award examination defines seven categories against which an applicant's performance is evaluated. Exhibit 9.23 lists the categories, items and assigned weights for 1999 and a glance at this clearly shows the emphasis placed on business results which account for 450 of the 1000 total points awarded. The scoring system reflects three different aspects:

Exhibit 9.23   *Baldrige Award – 1999 criteria for performance excellence*

Categories and items	Points	Value
1. LEADERSHIP		
■ organizational leadership	85	
■ responsibility and citizenship	40	**125**
2. STRATEGIC PLANNING		
■ strategy development	40	
■ strategy deployment	45	**85**
3. CUSTOMER AND MARKET FOCUS		
■ customer and market knowledge	40	
■ customer satisfaction and relationships	45	**85**
4. INFORMATION AND ANALYSIS		
■ measurement of organizational performance	40	
■ analysing organization performance	45	**85**
5. HUMAN RESOURCE FOCUS		
■ work systems	35	
■ employee education, training and development	25	
■ employee well-being and satisfaction	25	**85**
6. PROCESS MANAGEMENT		
■ product and service processes	55	
■ support processes	15	
■ supplier and partnering processes	15	**85**
7. BUSINESS RESULTS		
■ customer-focused results	115	
■ financial and market results	115	
■ human resource results	80	
■ supplier and partner results	25	
■ organizational effectiveness results	115	**450**
TOTAL POINTS		**1000**

■ Approach   – appropriateness of methods
             – effectiveness of methods
             – evidence of innovation

■ Deployment – use of the approach by all work units

■ Results   – current performance
             – demonstration of sustained performance.

The three applicant groups are manufacturing, service and small business (less than 500 staff) and up to two winners in each group can be nominated each year.

European Quality Award

In 1988, 14 leading West European companies formed the European Foundation for Quality Management (EFQM) and by the year 2000 it had over 850 members.

One of EFQM's core objectives is to recognize quality achievement and to this end it launched the European Quality Award (EQA) in 1992. Each year participating companies initially apply for their own national award and the top firms from each country go into the EQA competition. The scoring system reflects the 'approach', 'development' and 'results' aspects as outlined under the section on the Baldrige Award. The EQA also has categories and a total of 1000 points are awarded with weight reflecting the levels of importance and emphasis, as shown in Exhibit 9.24.

Exhibit 9.24   *European Quality Award: categories and weights*

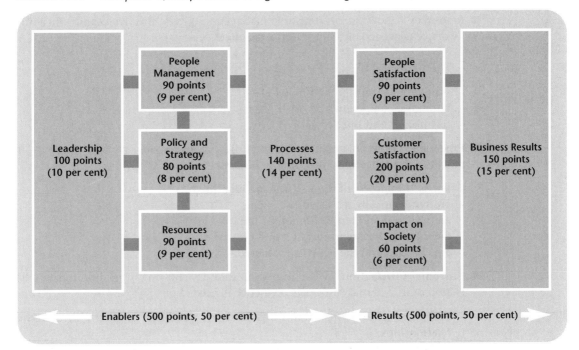

The nine elements shown in Exhibit 9.24 are defined by the EFQM as follows:

■ **Leadership** – how the behaviour and actions of the executive team and all other leaders inspire, support and promote a culture of total quality management (TQM). Evidence is needed of how leaders:

- visibly demonstrate their commitment to a culture of TQM
- support improvement and involvement by providing appropriate resources and assistance
- are involved with customers, suppliers and other external organizations
- recognize and appreciate people's efforts and achievements.

■ **Policy and strategy** – how an organization formulates, deploys, reviews its policy and strategy and turns them into plans and actions. Evidence is needed of how policy and strategy are:

- based on information that is relevant and comprehensive
- developed
- communicated and implemented
- regularly updated and improved.

■ **People management** – how an organization releases the full potential of its people. Evidence is needed of how people:

- resources are planned and improved
- capabilities are sustained and developed
- agree targets and continuously review performance
- are involved, empowered and recognized
- and the organization have an effective dialogue
- are cared for.

■ **Resources** – how an organization manages resources effectively and efficiently. Evidence is needed of the sound management of:

- financial resources
- information resources
- supplier relationships and materials
- buildings, equipment and other assets
- technology and intellectual property.

■ **Processes** – how an organization identifies, manages, reviews and improves its processes. Evidence is needed of how processes:

- key to the success of the business are identified
- are systematically managed
- are reviewed and targets are set for improvement
- are improved using innovation and creativity
- are changed and the benefits evaluated.

■ **Customer satisfaction** – what an organization is achieving in relation to the satisfaction of its external customers. Evidence is needed of:

- customers' perceptions of the organization's products, services and customer relationships
- additional measurements relating to the satisfaction of the organization's customers.

■ **People satisfaction** – what an organization is achieving in relation to the satisfaction of its people. Evidence is needed of:

– the people's perception of the organization
– additional measurements relating to people satisfaction.

■ **Impact on society** – what an organization is achieving in satisfying the needs and the expectations of the local, national and international community at large (as appropriate). This includes the perception of the organization's approach to quality of life, the environment and the preservation of global resources, and the organization's own internal measures of effectiveness. It will include its relations with authorities and bodies that affect and regulate its business. Evidence is needed of:

– society's perception of the organization
– additional measurements of the organization's impact on society.

■ **Business results** – what an organization is achieving in relation to its planned business objectives and in satisfying the needs and expectations of everyone with a financial interest or stake in the organization. Evidence is needed of:

– financial measurements of the organization's performance
– additional measurements of the organization's performance.

TOTAL QUALITY MANAGEMENT

The evolution of quality management stimulated, at least in part, by the impact of the demand by customers for higher quality conformance levels and the increasing competitiveness in world markets has resulted in the need to address quality management in all aspects of a business, including customers and suppliers. This development is known as total quality management (TQM).

TQM requires that the principles of quality management are applied in all aspects of and at every level in an organization. It is a company-wide approach to quality management with improvements being undertaken on a continuous basis by everyone. It thereby embraces the collection of management theories, approaches, tools and practices that help an organization reap greater profits by increasing product/service quality and decreasing costs. It requires a broadening of outlooks and skills, an innovative approach to improvement, a more sophisticated application of quality management tools and approaches and an increased emphasis on people and their involvement. The process extends to suppliers and customers and the activities will include a marked orientation towards customers and their needs.

You will see by these statements that TQM is a philosophy and set of guiding principles for managing an organization, and, as such, embodies several key elements that are now summarized:

■ **Commitment and leadership from the top** – as with many approaches, the belief and commitment by those at the top of an organization coupled with the leadership to make these changes happen are critical to the success of a TQM initiative. Without the allocation of resources and time, and a clear statement of the priority that needs to be given to this initiative, then TQM will not succeed.

■ **Planning and executing the programme** – TQM represents a major shift in approach and changes of this nature and magnitude need to be well planned and their execution carefully managed. Features include:

  – integrated into the rest of a business
  – part of the long-term execution of strategy within an organization
  – linking functions and ensuring that co-operation is improved
  – quality dimensions are built into product and service design as well as processes and delivery systems
  – move to a proactive approach to quality management in all aspects of a business
  – quality dimensions need to be part of the way performance is measured.

■ **Using tools and approaches** – to support and develop a process of continuous quality improvement an organization will need to use a selection of quality management tools and approaches. Their use is designed to identify problems, facilitate improvements, implement solutions and sustain the new ways of working.

■ **Education and training** – to achieve the last requirement, organizations need to provide the necessary levels of education and training for all concerned. These need to cover a general awareness of quality management concepts, skills and attitudes that address the philosophy of continuous improvement and the changes in personal, functional and organizational behaviour involved. A formal programme of education and training needs to be arranged on a timely and regular basis to help people improve their approach and contribution to improvement initiatives. Such programmes introduce new approaches to resolving problems and new attitudes to change. They need to be recognized as an investment in people that increases their ability, and helps them fulfil their overall role together with an associated range of short- and longer-term benefits in terms of greater efficiency, higher levels of market support and sales revenue growth.

■ **Involvement and teamwork** – one key to the successful introduction and maintenance of TQM within an organization is the involvement of people and increased co-operation through greater teamwork. Managers need to release the capabilities and skills of those working in their areas and empower people to seek and make improvements in their area of responsibility. People have to be encouraged to undertake initiatives especially given the managerial approaches that typified past organizations. Involvement is also further enhanced by teamwork. For without it, it is difficult to gain the commitment and participation of people across and throughout an organization.

■ **Measurement and feedback** – there is a need to provide positive feedback and recognize and reward achievement. People must not only see the results of their actions and endeavours but also see that their improvements really count and contributions are recognized by the organization. This requires regular feedback and constant support. For TQM to be successful, the results of improvements need to be proactively and extensively communicated to all involved.

  Part of this communication needs to include results against key internal and external targets, including internal and external benchmarking. This enables true measures to be made and will, in turn, identify gaps and help develop new improvement programmes.

■ **Culture changes** – for many organizations TQM is a marked style change from past approaches. Underpinning the success of these initiatives, therefore, is a need to change attitudes, behaviour and working practices throughout an organization. Key areas include:

   – responsibility for one's own quality
   – improvement as being an integral part of everyone's job
   – the whole organization and those working in it need to be focused towards meeting the needs of customers
   – suppliers and customers need to be part of the improvement process
   – mistakes should not be seen as reasons for criticism, but as opportunities to correct processes thereby eliminating error situations in the future.

CONCLUSION

The evolution of quality management has, to some extent, come full circle. In pre-Industrial Revolution times, skilled craftsmen were responsible for both undertaking tasks and ensuring that they were completed to specification. The Industrial Revolution saw the advent of high volume requirement and with it the separation of the

Exhibit 9.25   *The evolution in managing quality, changing characteristics and switch in orientation*

Inspection	Quality control	Quality assurance	TQM

• Checking work after the event
• Identifying sources of non-conformance
• Taking corrective action
	• Self-inspection
	• Quality planning and procedures
	• Use of basic statistics
	• Quality manual
	• Use of process performance data
		• Develop quality systems
		• Use of quality cost data
		• Quality planning
		• Use of statistical process control
		• Involve non-operations functions
			• Teamwork
			• Employee involvement
			• Process management
			• Performance measurement
			• Involves:
			  – all operations
			  – suppliers and customers

	Changing characteristics and switch in orientation	
• Compliance to specification • Blame culture • Internally focused • Process-driven		• Continuous improvement • Involvement • Ownership of issues • Empowerment of people • Externally focused • Customer-driven

making or providing task from the responsibility for ensuring that specifications were met. One outcome was that inspection was performed by non-producers and completed after the work was finished. However, since the 1970s systems for monitoring and managing quality have been evolving rapidly as illustrated by Exhibit 9.25. Since this time simple inspection activities were first replaced or supplemented by quality control, then enhanced by quality assurance developments with many organizations now working towards TQM that returns the responsibility for quality conformance to those who have the task of providing the product or service. While TQM embraces other key dimensions such as involvement with suppliers and customers, the progression described in Exhibit 9.25 concerns core responsibilities and attitudes towards the key competitive dimension of meeting product or service specifications. In this way, TQM signals the need for the mutual co-operation of everyone in an organization and associated business processes with suppliers to provide products and services to specification and to meet customers' needs and expectations.

The role of quality conformance within the set of competitive dimensions that relate to the markets of most organizations is clearly recognized. And the response of operations to the provision of this key requirement has appropriately raised the profile and changed attitudes to the key task of managing quality throughout organizations.

SUMMARY

The quality of products and services is fundamental to the success of organizations. The dimension of quality for which operations is responsible is that of conformance and how best to manage this aspect of quality was addressed in this chapter.

The specification on offer reconciles customers' needs and expectations with that which a company sells and provides. The interrelated nature of these dimensions constitutes the quality offering as depicted in Exhibit 9.1. How to undertake these tasks in terms of defining the quality characteristics and their measurement and control, where to check, how to check and the need to identify causes of below-standard quality levels and seek improvements was explained in detail.

As part of providing the background of and context for the topic of managing quality, a number of quality principles were introduced and explained. These were:

■ **meet customer requirements** – the core of quality conformance
■ **error-free work** – only one standard to aim for – to be right first time, every time
■ **manage by prevention** – adopting a proactive approach to managing quality leads to prevention rather than the detection of faulty work
■ **measure by the cost of quality** – the key measure is the cost of doing business – doing things right the first time reduces costs in the task of meeting customers' needs and expectations.

A review of the principal quality philosophies and approaches was the topic of the next section and a detailed summary of the work of Deming, Juran and Crosby and their contributions to this field was provided. Then followed a section covering general issues and the specific tools and techniques used including the Pareto principle or the 80/20

SUMMARY (cont'd)

rule, the use of checklists, cause and effect diagrams, process mapping, scatter diagrams, sampling and acceptance sampling plans.

With the background issues in place and an introduction about where and what to do, the task of managing quality in practice was addressed. This began by looking at the purchasing function and the appropriate checks and approaches to be used to control the quality of purchased items and services. This section introduced the aspect of OC curves and their use with different sample sizes. Then followed a look at how to measure quality in the processing and service delivery system stages of operations. Control charts were introduced and their use with regard to variables and attributes was explained. The concept of statistical process control was then addressed and an example of its use in a call centre formed part of the review. The final part in this section concerned the control of quality at the end of a process, including delivery and installation where appropriate. Here, the nature of the items would influence how quality was controlled – for example, whereas high-value items may attract 100 per cent checks, inspecting less expensive items would more typically be completed by a sampling plan.

The growing awareness of the need to improve quality has led to the introduction and use of national and international programmes that formalize systems for evaluating the capability of an organization to consistently design, provide and deliver products and services to specification. The three most widely used programmes (ISO 9000, the Malcolm Baldrige National Quality Award and the European Quality Award) were explained in detail.

To conclude the chapter, the evolution that has taken place in managing quality and the change in orientation that parallels these developments is summarized.

Discussion questions

1. The table below lists data concerning the errors in an account management function in the financial services sector.

Error type	Frequency in last period	Estimated costs involved (£s)
A	40	12 500
B	4	2 800
C	33	36 000
D	56	15 500
E	22	7 500
F	12	5 750
G	16	23 000
H	28	116 000

Discussion questions (cont'd)

Prepare two Pareto lists – the first based on frequency and the second on estimated costs. Comment on these rankings.

2. Draw a fishbone diagram to represent why your car might be two hours later than the promised completion time at an auto service centre.

3. To assess part of its service delivery system, a fast-food chain undertakes regular checks on certain elements of the system. One such check at an outlet revealed the following control data:

Aspects	Product freshness (minutes)	Queue length (# customers)	Time to serve (# minutes)	Cleanliness Floor (# items)	# tables not cleaned
Upper control limit	7.0	8.0	3.0	10	6
Average	3.0	4.0	2.0	5	4
Lower control limit	1.0	2.0	0.5	0	0
Sample #					
1	6.5	3.0	1.5	8	3
2	4.5	7.0	3.0	6	5
3	5.0	6.0	3.0	2	1
4	3.5	2.0	1.5	4	5
5	2.0	8.0	1.5	3	4
6	6.0	5.0	2.0	7	6
7	3.0	6.0	3.5	9	3
8	2.5	10.0	1.5	12	8
9	6.0	4.0	1.0	2	1
10	6.5	3.0	2.5	4	0
11	5.5	2.0	2.5	6	2
12	1.5	9.0	3.5	8	4

Notes

- Product freshness
  - length of time (to the nearest half-minute) since any of the next to be used main item products were made. Any product made eight or more minutes before is discarded
- Queue length
  - number of customers waiting: assessment above was made on all customer queue lengths in the service delivery system
- Time to serve
  - worst and best times in a ten-minute period for a selected server to serve a customer (to the nearest half-minute)
- Cleanliness
  - floor: number of items (for example, food, packaging and cutlery) on the floor; tables: number of free tables that have not been wiped down since the last customers left.

Draw a control chart for each of these four aspects. What are your comments on what you found?

Discussion questions (cont'd)

4. Discuss the advantages and disadvantages of staff recording their own performance data in the form of a control chart and analysing the outcomes for the delivery system for which they are responsible.

5. An operations manager records the daily output and number of rejects on a bag making line that runs for a single eight-hour shift with occasional overtime on a Saturday. The data for the last 40 days are given below.

Day #	Day	Output (# bags)	Rejects	Day #	Day	Output (# bags)	Rejects
1	Mon	2040	24	21	Wed	2440	36
2	Tue	2210	28	22	Thu	2290	30
3	Wed	2090	34	23	Fri	2180	26
4	Thu	2235	20	24	Sat	2260	31
5	Fri	2050	14	25	Mon	2095	37
6	Sat	2240	32	26	Tue	2080	19
7	Mon	2080	39	27	Wed	2290	22
8	Tue	2280	34	28	Thu	2260	38
9	Wed	2260	30	29	Fri	2125	41
10	Thu	2260	41	30	Sat	–	–
11	Fri	2150	38	31	Mon	2235	37
12	Sat	2290	18	32	Tue	2140	38
13	Mon	1970	29	33	Wed	1985	24
14	Tue	2285	41	34	Thu	2195	31
15	Wed	2265	26	35	Fri	2180	37
16	Thu	2160	32	36	Sat	–	–
17	Fri	2165	37	37	Mon	2165	41
18	Sat	2365	20	38	Tue	2265	37
19	Mon	2100	26	39	Wed	2280	44
20	Tue	2190	24	40	Thu	2165	39

- What tools would you use to manage this process?
- What does the data analysis tell you?
- What management action should be taken?

6. Casual Elegance is a mail order business in clothes for the younger business man and woman. From time to time customers complained about errors in their orders – wrong style, wrong size and so on. The company wishes to keep order errors to less than 2 per cent. To check how well the system was working a sample of 50 orders was taken several times over a representative period with the following results:

Discussion questions (cont'd)

Sample #	# orders OK	# orders problem	Sample #	# orders OK	# orders problem
1	50	0	11	47	3
2	47	3	12	50	0
3	49	1	13	45	5
4	48	2	14	48	2
5	48	2	15	47	3
6	46	4	16	46	4
7	50	0	17	48	2
8	50	0	18	50	0
9	49	1	19	50	0
10	48	2	20	49	1

- What type of control chart is appropriate for checking the process capability of the ordering operation?
- Construct a control chart using these data. What observations can you make about the process?

7. Explain what is meant by acceptance sampling. Give an illustration for each of the sampling plans included in this chapter.

8. The evolution in how best to manage quality has been described as follows:

Product reliability ⟶ Process reliability ⟶ People reliability ⟶ Total quality management

Discuss.

9. What are the advantages and disadvantages of 100 per cent inspection?

Notes and references

1. These 14 points are explained fully in W Edwards Deming's book *Out of the Crisis* (Cambridge: Cambridge University Press, 1986).
2. Ibid., Chapter 3, pp. 97–148.
3. W Edwards Deming, *Quality Productivity and Competitive Position*, Cambridge, MA: Center for Advanced Engineering Study, Massachusetts Institute of Technology, 1982, p. i.
4. Also see the following articles written by Juran that provide an overview of his thinking, approach and concepts: 'Japanese and Western quality: a contrast', *Quality Assurance*, Vol. 5, No. 1 (March 1979), pp. 12–17; 'Product quality – a prescription for the West: Part I: Training and improvement programmes', *Management Review* June (1981), pp. 9–14 and 'Part II: Upper management leadership and employee relations', *Management Review*, July (1981), pp. 57–61.
5. Artemis March, 'A note on quality: the views of Deming, Juran and Crosby', in *Readings in Total Quality Management*, Harry Costin (ed.), (New York: Harcourt Brace, 1994), p. 143.

6. Refer to Joseph M Juran and Frank M Gryna, Jr *Quality Planning and Analysis*, 3rd edn, (New York: McGraw-Hill, 1993), pp. 16–19.

7. The description of this control sequence is based on Joseph M Juran *Managerial Breakthroughs* (New York: McGraw-Hill, 1964), pp. 183–7.

8. This summary is adapted from Juran and Gryna, op. cit., pp. 47–52.

9. This assertion was captured in Crosby's book entitled *Quality is Free* (New York: McGraw-Hill, 1979).

10. Based on ibid., pp.

11. Based on ibid., pp.

12. Taken from Keri R Bhote *Strategic Supplier Management: A Blueprint for Revitalising the Manufacturing–Supplier Partnership* (New York: American Management Association, 1989), p. 168.

13. Chapter 5 covered process design and introduced tools and techniques to improve the provision of quality conformance in the delivery system. A glance back at this will be useful here.

14. Ishikawa, K *Guide to Quality Control* (New York: Quality Resources, 1985), pp. 18–29.

15. For details on sampling, see Dodge, HF and Romig, GH *Sampling Inspection Tables – Single and Double Sampling*, 2nd edn, (John Wiley & Sons, London, 1959); Duncan, AJ *Quality Control and Industrial Statistics* (Irwin, Burr Ridge, 1974); Montgomery, DC *Introduction to Statistical Control*, 2nd edn, (John Wiley & Sons, London, 1991); and Owen, M *SPC and Business Improvements* (IFS, 1993). In the UK, the British Standards Institute provide a range of suitable sampling plans, with explanations on how to use them. They include OC curves, AQLs, single, double and multiple sampling plans and cover both attributes and variables – see BS 600 (1991, 1993, 1994 and 1996) and BS 6002 (1993 and 1994).

16. For example,

- Australia   AS3900
- Belgium   NBN X50
- Denmark   DS/EN 29000
- Germany   DIN ISO 9000
- Malaysia   MS 985
- Netherlands   NEN 9000
- South Africa   SABS 0157
- Sweden   SS-ISO 9000
- UK   BS 5750

17. See Rabbit, JT and Bergh, PA *The ISO 9000 Book* (White Plains, NY: Quality Resources, 1993) for a detailed review.

Further reading

Bank, J *The Essence of Total Quality Management*, Prentice Hall, London (1992).

Bounds, G, Yorks, L, Adams, M and Ramsey, G *Beyond Quality Management: Towards the Emerging Paradigm*, McGraw-Hill, NY (1994).

Breem, M, Jud, R and Pareja, PE *An Introduction to ISO 9000*, Society of Manufacturing Engineers, Reference Publication Division, Dearborn, MI (1993).

Brown, SA *Total Quality Service*, Prentice Hall, Scarborough, Canada (1992).

Dale, BG (ed.) *Managing Quality*, 2nd edn, Prentice Hall, Hemel Hempstead (1992).

Dean, JW Jr and Evans, JR *Total Quality: Management, Organization and Strategy*, West, Minneapolis/St Paul, MN (1994).

Evans, JR and Lindsay, WM *The Management and Control of Quality*, 3rd edn, West, Minneapolis/St Paul, MN (1996).

Gervin, D *Managing Quality*, Free Press, NY (1988).

Imai, M *Kaizen: The Key to Japan's Competitive Success*, Random House, NY (1986).

Kehoe, DF *The Fundamentals of Quality Management*, Chapman & Hall (1996).

Logothetis, N *Managing for Total Quality*, Prentice Hall, London (1992).

Montgomery, DC *Introduction to Statistical Control*, 2nd edn, John Wiley & Sons, NY (1991).

Oakland, JS *Total Quality Management*, Butterworth-Heinemann, Oxford (1993).

Oakland, JS and Followell, RF *Statistical Process Control: A Practical Guide*, 4th edn, Butterworth-Heinemann, Oxford.

Porter, LJ, Oakland, JS and Gadd, KW *Evaluating the Operation of the European Quality Award Model for Self-assessment*, CIMA Publishing, London (1998).

Ran, H '15 years and still going…', *Quality Progress* (July, 1995), pp. 57–9.

Reichfield, FF and Sasser, WE Jr 'Zero defections: quality comes to services', *Harvard Business Review* (September–October, 1990), pp. 105–11.

Stahl, MJ *Management – Total Quality in a Global Environment*, Blackwell, Cambridge, MA (????).

Teboul, J *Managing Quality Dynamics*, Prentice Hall, London (1991).

Zeithanil, VA, Paraswamann, A and Berry LL *Delivering Quality Service: Balancing Customer Perceptions and Expectations*, The Free Press, NY (1990).

CHAPTER TEN

The content and planning of this book: an overview of what is involved, what has been addressed so far and what is covered in this chapter

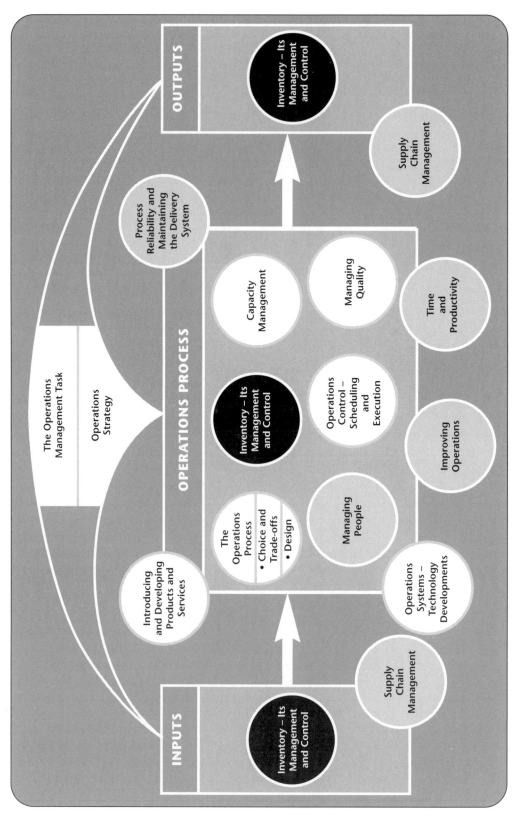

Inventory – Its Management and Control

Chapter overview

The reasons why inventory management and control is a key operations task is that it is large (£s), helps operations to run smoothly and efficiently and effects the supply of goods and services to customers.

In Chapter 6 we dealt with capacity, the capability to make products and provide services. This chapter is on inventory. It concerns the management and control of the materials that go into the products and services at different points in the conversion process. As Exhibit 1.1 illustrated, these include the inputs (materials, components and services) into the conversion process, the part-finished items (products, customers or information) in a process (called work-in-progress inventory) and the outputs (finished items) from a process to be sold or supplied to customers (see Exhibit 10.1). These relationships are also clearly illustrated in the overview at the start of this chapter. This shows inventory in the three phases of operations – inputs, operations process and outputs. You will see from this and Exhibit 10.1 the presence of inventory throughout operations.

As the flow of materials into and through the process differs from the pattern and rate of customer demand, then inventory will form or be held to cushion the operations core from these changes. How much inventory there is will depend upon the relative rates of demand and supply. To illustrate this, Exhibit 10.2 depicts the relationship between the rate of supply, rate of demand and the level of inventory using the analogy of a water tank. In this example, the rate of inflow and outflow of water will directly affect the level of inventory in the tank which depicts the conversion process. Why inventory is kept, the level of inventory involved and its management and control are dealt with in this chapter which will cover the following sections:

- **Corporate attitudes** – inventory, though typically sizeable in balance sheet terms, tends not to be a priority task within a business.
- **Role, types and functions of inventory** – the forms and functions of inventory are explained and the division between corporate and operations inventory is defined as part of the way to effectively manage this important asset.

Chapter overview (cont'd)

■ **Managing and controlling inventory** – the two sections that cover these aspects of inventory are separated into general and specific issues. The general issues highlight the different functional attitudes to inventory, the impact of inventory on profit levels, inventory cost structures and corporate issues around service levels, lead times and supplier relations. The specific issues cover the independent/dependent demand principle, Pareto principle, the use of economic order quantities and how reorder levels are calculated and used.

■ **Inventory decisions** – the key questions to be addressed in the management of inventory are what and how much to hold and to order. The approaches to follow and concepts to use in answering these key questions are explained in detail.

■ **Inventory systems and analysis** – this section explains the different systems to manage inventory and goes on to give a detailed review of analysing inventory by cause and using this as the basis for reducing levels.

Exhibit 10.1   *The flow of materials and position and types of inventory*

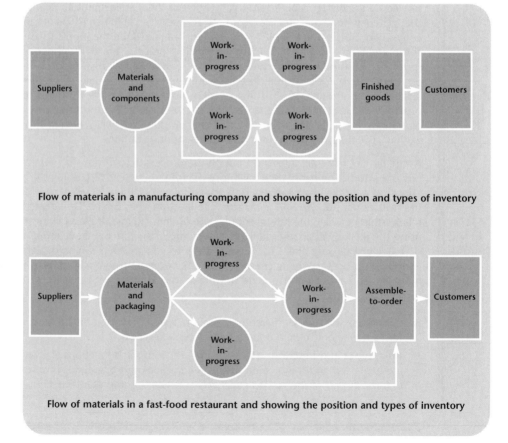

Flow of materials in a manufacturing company and showing the position and types of inventory

Flow of materials in a fast-food restaurant and showing the position and types of inventory

Exhibit 10.2 *The rate of supply and demand, and the level of inventory depicted as the inflow, outflow and water held in a tank respectively*

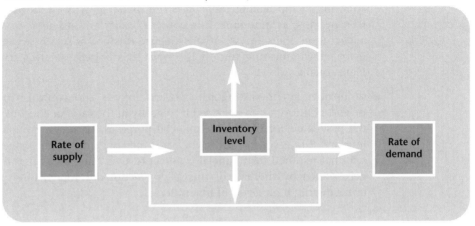

CORPORATE ATTITUDES

The way an organization uses its funds and then manages and controls these investments is a key executive task. A glance at the balance sheet of any organization will show that inventory typically represents a sizeable part of its working capital and, as such, needs to be efficiently managed and controlled. Although the size of the inventory holding in many organizations is significant in itself and also in relation to other assets, the key task of inventory management and control is typically not allocated sufficient resources or given adequate executive attention. While decisions to use funds for plant and equipment purchases are usually carefully judged and monitored, the efforts to manage and control inventory levels normally come too late. Increases in inventory invariably happen first and a company becomes concerned about controlling them later. A case, too often, of closing the stable door after the horse has bolted.

Although investments in equipment/processes and inventory are both sizeable, typically the former is better managed than the latter. There are several reasons as to why this is so, including the following:

■ Inventory is an inherent part of a company's operations. When output exceeds sales, purchases exceed output, or purchases exceed sales inventory increases. Thus changes to the level of inventory are a consequence of a company's day-to-day activities, but are usually not specifically addressed each time these events take place. With equipment purchases, however, the investment is a one-off event and invariably made following a conscious decision to address a particular proposal to buy an item of equipment. Control in this instance is easier to effect.

■ Inventory all looks the same and there are normally large but acceptable quantities of it; more of the same is not easy to detect. However, new equipment, no matter how small, draws attention, questions and thereby control.

■ The control of inventory investment needs to be ongoing. Plant investment on the other hand is a one-off decision and over a period is often not so demanding of management's time.

■ Inventory control is often not seen as part of the task of senior executives. It has no qualities or characteristics that give it inherent attraction or bring it to the attention of top management. It is not dynamic. It is a task of day-to-day detail seen by most as mundane. The content, issues and discussions on inventory all appear to be the same. As a consequence it is not normally an agenda item for a management meeting (unless the horse has bolted) whereas fixed asset investment usually is.

■ Companies fail to distinguish between records and control. Consequently, the inventory information provided is typically in the form of a record – a statement of the past often for historical, financial purposes. However, companies mistakenly interpret this as control data, whereas it merely expresses the value of inventory in a format required for financial statements. One outcome is that ongoing controls necessitated by the size of this asset are not developed, often contributing to unnecessarily high levels of inventory.

INVENTORY – ROLE, TYPES AND FUNCTIONS

What is the role of inventory and why do organizations hold it? Before answering this question, let us first discuss what we mean by inventory. In the context of this chapter it concerns those materials or services that directly or indirectly form part of the ongoing task of making the products or delivering the services that an organization sells or provides. It comprises the inputs, services or materials used, any part-finished items (products or services) and those items that are complete and held awaiting their sale. On the other hand it does not comprise the equipment or fixtures and fittings (for example, the tables, chairs, tablecloths, napkins, cutlery, plates, dishes and glasses in a restaurant) needed to make products or provide services. These are the fixed assets of a business and do not form a direct part of what it sells.

Perhaps the easiest way to explain and illustrate these differences is to ask you to reflect on the inventory you keep and why you keep it. You hold stocks of food and other items which you use as part of day-to-day living. In addition, you have other assets such as cooking equipment and clothes which are used and reused as part of your everyday routines. The former is used and replenished while the latter items are purchased and consumed (that is, the function they provide is used) over a much longer period. This chapter concerns the management and control of a company's equivalent of the stocks of food and other consumables you keep. And, just like you, they need to make decisions about which items to hold, how much of each item (that is, inventory) to carry, when to replenish stocks and how much to buy at any one time.

Before addressing the question of the management and control of inventory let us first consider its role, the types of inventory and the functions they provide.

General role of inventory

The underlying purpose of inventory is to uncouple the various phases of the process or service delivery system and thereby allow each to work independently of the other parts. Hence, keeping food in the kitchen allows you to prepare a meal without first having to shop. However, in reality there are many other issues and dimensions involved. For example, you may only need fresh milk for your breakfast coffee but you have to buy milk in large quantities as prescribed by the retail store from which you buy it. Similarly, you may buy a larger box of food or more than the one item that you need for a meal as the direct result of a price deal offered by the food store. These dimensions of inventory management will be addressed later, but need to be recognized early on. First, however, let us explain the different types of inventory there are and look at the functions they provide in more detail.

Types of inventory

There are two principal categories of inventory:

- **Process-related inventory** – comprises items directly used in making the products and providing the services sold by an organization. Thus, the wheels, subassemblies, windscreens, engines and other parts that go into a motor vehicle are examples of process-related inventory. The ingredients to bake bread and pastries would similarly form part of the process-related inventory for a bakery as would the foodstuffs to prepare meals in a restaurant. All items going into the products or services from raw materials through to packaging come within this category.

- **Support inventory** – in addition to the process-related inventory described in the last section there are items that are not an integral part of the product or service produced but are essential to the overall running of any organization. These are known as support inventories. For instance, maintenance and office supplies are examples in the car assembly and bakery examples given earlier. Cleaning materials for kitchen utensils, ovens and the like are examples for the restaurant.

Generally, organizations with activities centred on products or manufacturing processes have more inventory and need to develop more controls and systems than do organizations where the product/service mix is orientated more to the service end of the product/service continuum described earlier in Exhibit 1.6. This is because the fewer process-related materials that are involved then the less inventory there will be in the system to control. For example, in a bank the service is consumed as it is generated and the process material content is negligible. In fact, the forms and other paperwork used in a bank's delivery system are examples of support inventory described above. While in all organizations the control of support inventories is an important task, more emphasis will normally be given to process-related inventories because of their greater importance to the business as they both are an integral part of the product and service and also represent a much higher investment. And this is so in both manufacturing and service organizations. Where the product or service sold is less labour intensive, inventory management will be more important. Retail shops, for instance, have substantial inventories essential to their business. Similarly, hospitals will carry large amounts of inventory from plasma and drugs to supplies of linen and foodstuffs.

Finally, within the process-related inventory there are the three categories consisting of raw materials and components, work-in-progress and finished items. How they link to the stages in the process and a brief explanation of each is given in Exhibit 10.3. These categories provide an essential insight into the management and control of inventory and will feature throughout the rest of the chapter.

Exhibit 10.3   *Process stage and types of inventory*

Process stage		Inventory	
		Process-related	**Support**
inputs	raw materials	Inputs into the process or delivery system used to make the product or provide the service. Include raw materials, services, bought-out parts and components	Supplies that are not central to the products or services provided. They include maintenance and office supplies and consumables such as cleaning materials
in-process	work-in-progress	Partly completed items in the process waiting to go into the next stage. Include subassemblies and partly prepared items such as foodstuffs awaiting cooking	
outputs	finished items	Outputs of the process. Inventory in its finished form waiting to be sold. Include items to be sold in a retail store, baked bread and pastries in a bakery and manufactured items to go to an end-user in either the manufacturing or service sectors	

Functions of inventory

Why does an organization invest so much in inventory? Why does it exist and what is the return? Earlier, the underlying purpose of inventory was identified as one of uncoupling various phases of the process or service delivery system. This is a common, overall function, but there are also important advantages that relate more to one type of inventory than another. Using the categories explained earlier, some of the principal reasons are outlined in Exhibit 10.4. Note how they differ from one inventory category to another.

As you read the detail in Exhibit 10.4 you will notice that some advantages relate to operations' issues while others relate to the business as a whole. To help identify these different functions it is helpful to categorize them into two broad types of inventory each of which comprises a number of subfunctions. These two types are known as corporate and operations inventory. While the latter directly helps operations to undertake its basic tasks, the former covers inventory that is held to provide advantages for other parts of an organization – hence the phrase corporate inventory! These two categories and their assorted subcategories are useful ways to help in the management and control of inventory and will be used in some of the sections later in the chapter. They identify the basic function being provided by clusters of inventory and so help to evaluate the impact on inventory levels of actions taken and decisions made within a business and the specific roles that different types of inventory provide.

Corporate inventory

Corporate inventory is that inventory which does not provide an operations function. The types of corporate inventory are numerous and reflect the nature of the organization involved. One dimension of corporate inventory is, however, a common

Exhibit 10.4   *Overview of the role of different types of inventory*

Raw materials and bought-out-parts inventory allows an organization to:

- cater for the variability of supply
- take advantage of quantity discounts or market prices
- provide parts holdings which could in future be in short supply due, for instance, to anticipated supply problems
- as a form of investment when price increases are anticipated
- reduce overall lead times

Work-in-progress inventory helps maintain the independence of stages in the process by, as explained earlier, uncoupling the steps involved. This leads to:

- orders being easier to schedule
- stabilizing the different output rates at each part of a process
- reducing the total delivery lead time to supply customer demands
- facilitating higher utilization of plant, processes and labour

---

Finished-goods inventory with which an organization can:

- provide fast, off-the-shelf delivery
- achieve a steady delivery of goods to customers in the face of intermittent production or supply
- cope with fluctuations in demand, particularly in the case of seasonal products
- provide an insurance against equipment or process breakdowns and, in some instances, against suppliers' strikes

---

feature – in total, these categories typically account for 20–25 per cent of the total. Examples of these types include:

- sales inventory to support customer agreements
- sales inventory owing to actual sales being lower than forecast sales
- corporate safety inventory due to the uncertainty of supply (for example, in anticipation of national or international strikes)
- purchasing inventory incurred to take advantage of quantity discounts
- marketing inventory to support a product or service launch
- inventory to reduce lead times as a strategic response to market needs; this can be held at the raw material, work-in-progress or finished goods stages, or at all three.

Operations inventory

Regardless of whether the operations inventory under review is at the raw material, work-in-progress or finished goods stage it may be further described as one or more of decoupling, cycle, pipeline, capacity-related or buffer inventory. Each of these fulfils a specific function. Exhibits 10.5 and 10.6 illustrate the inventory functions and how they relate to both the category of inventory and the particular choice of process involved. An explanation of these five types of operations inventory and the two related exhibits is now provided.

- **Decoupling inventory** separates one process from another. Thus, a product or service is worked on at one stage and from there it goes into work-in-progress from which the next stage in the process draws the work as and when required. In

Exhibit 10.5　*Inventory functions related to different categories of inventory*

Inventory function	Inventory category		
	Raw materials	Work-in-progress	Finished goods
Decoupling		✓✓✓	
Cycle		✓✓✓	
Pipeline		✓✓✓	✓
Capacity-related		✓✓	✓✓✓
Buffer[2]	✓✓	✓✓	✓✓✓

Notes

1. ✓ = Degree of function typically provided.
2. Buffer concerns variation in supply or demand around the average and essentially to cover instances where supply delays or actual levels of demand are higher than average. However, where inventory is held because of reasons such as uncertainty of supply then it should be identified under a relevant category within corporate inventory.

Exhibit 10.6　*Inventory functions in relation to jobbing, batch and line processes*

Inventory function		Inventory category		
		Jobbing	Batch	Line
Decoupling			✓✓✓	
Cycle			✓✓✓	
Pipeline		✓✓	✓✓	
Capacity-related:	work-in-progress		✓	
	finished goods		✓✓	✓✓✓
Buffer:	raw materials		✓	✓✓
	finished goods		✓✓	✓✓✓

Note

✓ = Degree of function typically provided.

this way, decoupling inventory allows processes to work independently of one another thereby facilitating scheduling and enhancing the level of efficient working of each stage. In jobbing there is no decoupling inventory as the skilled person will progress a job on a continuous basis. Similarly, in a line process there is no need for decoupling inventory as the line itself is a set of coupled processes. An apparent exception to this which you may raise is where inventory is used to decouple the dependency of one part of a process from the preceding part by providing an inventory which can be used in the case of machine breakdowns or yield uncertainty. When such inventory is held it is not due to the line process itself, a factor which is illustrated by the absence of a tick in Exhibit 10.6. Thus, where this exists it should be recognized as corporate inventory under the category 'process or yield uncertainty'.

Decoupling inventory is predominantly found in batch processes. As explained earlier, inventory in this category decouples one process from the next, allowing them to work independently and separating otherwise dependent parts of the total operation. The emphasis is on the material or customer (for example, a patient in a hospital) waiting for the process (for example, the hospital consultant) so that the process itself can work most efficiently. The principle is, therefore, that the customer, information or material waits for the process.

In the same way inventory typically decouples steps in the total supply chain. For example between producer, warehouse, distribution centre and retailer.

■ **Cycle inventory** relates to the decision to make a quantity of products or to process a quantity of services (referred to as an order quantity or lot batch size) that reflects dimensions such as the time to complete a set-up compared to the order quantity processed or size of customer demand. The rationale behind using cycle inventory in the operations system is to reduce the set-up costs and avoid process capacity losses. In jobbing there is little need for this function as the skilled person will set up for each job individually and is often making an order quantity of one. Similarly, cycle inventory is a function which a line does not require as it is continually set up to manufacture an agreed range of products and processes these one at a time. As shown in Exhibits 10.5 and 10.6, cycle inventory is a feature of batch processes where set-up or make-ready tasks are an inherent feature of this choice. The principle here is that by processing two or more customers, information requirements or products at a time, the costs of setting up the system are spread, thereby reducing the set-up costs per unit.

■ **Pipeline inventory** (also referred to as transit inventory) concerns the inventory support where companies decide to subcontract one process to an outside supplier at some time during the total operations process lead time. This can be part way through the operations process or at the distribution stage. Examples during the process include a dentist subcontracting the manufacture of a crown for a patient's tooth, a doctor having blood sample analyses completed off-site and a manufacturer having the finishing processes (for example plating and painting) completed by a subcontractor.

All the inventory associated with this decision is classed as pipeline. A decision to subcontract one operation within line processing would be unfeasible and, therefore, does not happen. However, in both jobbing and batch many companies decide to subcontract a particular operation during the process and, in so doing, create pipeline inventory in support of that decision. Decisions to subcontract despatch at the end of the operations process will incur pipeline inventory holding as part of making this decision.

■ **Capacity-related inventory** – one way to cope with anticipated sales is to plan operations in line with sales forecasts. This, however, often leads to situations of peak capacity requirements involving overtime, recruitment of additional labour or the holding of spare process capacity. Another way is to plan some sort of level operations programme, stockpiling inventories in the low sales periods for selling in the high sales periods. This concerns the use of capacity-related inventory which transfers work from one time period to the next in the form of inventory, and provides one way of stabilizing operations capacity in an environment of fluctuating sales levels.

A city-centre sandwich bar will prepare the fillings and garnish for is products in the hours before its peak demand periods around lunchtime. Some outlets also prepare the completed products ahead of time. Fast-food outlets do the same and thereby use work-in-progress and finished-goods inventory to transfer capacity in low demand to high demand periods. Similarly, the seasonal demand for fireworks to celebrate national festivals and toys and gifts for the peak period at Christmas are also accommodated, in part, by capacity-related inventory.

■ **Buffer inventory** relates to the basic fact that average demand, by definition, varies around the average. In order to cope with those situations where demand exceeds the average, businesses hold buffer inventory. The function of this inventory holding, therefore, is to help protect the process core (see Exhibit 9.1) against unpredictable variations in demand levels or supply availability. The higher the service level set by a business or the lower the level of stockout risk it is willing to endure then the higher the size of buffer inventory it must carry. However, as explained in the footnote to Exhibit 10.5, inventory held that exceeds buffer levels falls into the category of corporate inventory.

MANAGING AND CONTROLLING INVENTORY – GENERAL ISSUES

This and the next section concern some general and specific issues regarding the management and control of inventory. Their purpose is to provide essential context in which these tasks have to be implemented and to set the scene for the section that follows where the detailed tasks in the management and control of inventory are explained.

1. Functional attitudes towards inventory levels

One factor influencing the size of the inventory investment is the pressure applied by the various functions within a business, each of which will have a different view of what is a desirable inventory level (see Exhibit 10.7). The result is a conflict of views over where the company's funds should or should not be invested.

2. Inventory and its impact on profit levels

So far this chapter has looked at inventory as a part of working capital. However, it is not just in this form that pressure is applied to inventory levels. Consider the situation facing managers where a company is going through a period of reduced sales. It is difficult to shed costs quickly in the short term by reducing either variable or fixed costs. Such a course of action would normally be expensive. On the other hand, if all the overhead costs are carried by a level of throughput set in line with the current, lower sales activity, the profits for that period would be considerably reduced. Instead, management often decides to carry over some of the costs from the current to a future

Exhibit 10.7 *General preferences of three key functions towards the level of holding by type of inventory*

Type of inventory	General preference by function		
	Finance/ accounting	Operations	Sales
Raw materials	Low	High	Indifferent
Work-in-progress	Low	High	Indifferent
Finished goods	Low	Indifferent	High

period. It does this by using spare capacity to make products for stock or to undertake work (for instance, research work or the development of current or new services) for which there are no sales but for which it is anticipated there will be sales in the future. In this way, a proportion of the costs from one time period can be legitimately absorbed into the inventory value of that period and carried forward to a future period when the work-in-progress or finished-goods inventory is sold. Thus costs incurred in one time period are transferred to a future time period in the form of inventory, as the value of the inventory includes the associated direct and overhead costs involved.

One result of this action is that profit will not fall as much as it would otherwise have done and the value of the company will be held more in check. With an upturn in sales, the inventory will be sold, the associated costs of the inventory incurred earlier will be recovered.

If the upturn in sales does not come about, then a company will often be reluctant to sell the excess inventory at a low price in order to recover at least some of the investment. Such action would usually lead to further reduced profits and a further reduction in the value of the company. This aspect of inventory can, therefore, frequently result in organizations operating with too much inventory and yet being reluctant to remedy the situation.

3. Inventory cost structures

The management of inventory is, in part, to provide the roles of inventory on the one hand, and control the cost of inventory on the other. One important prerequisite to undertake this task is understanding the make-up and structure of the associated costs of the inventory investment. These are now discussed:

- **Cost of an item** concerns the cost of buying or producing the individual items held in inventory. Volume often reflects on the cost of an item as quantity discounts can be secured for purchased items and services, and non-variable costs such as over-heads can be spread over the greater number of items produced.

- **Ordering and set-up** costs relate to the ordering and provision of a given quantity. Any costs associated with arranging and providing products or services fall into this category. They include order preparation and placement, monitoring the order, transport, receiving, and invoice reconciliation and payment.

- **Carrying costs** concern the costs of holding inventory. These include the cost of the inventory investment itself, the storage costs including space and insurance, and the costs of deterioration, obsolescence and losses that occur during the period in which the inventory is held awaiting its use in the process or sale to a customer.

- **Stockout costs** reflect the economic consequences of running out of stock. This concerns the lost profit on a particular sale and any loss of customer goodwill occasioned by the late or non-delivery of a product or service.

4. Corporate issues

At the corporate level in organizations there are a number of key decisions that affect the competitive stance of a business and which, in turn, impact inventory requirements. These include the following:

■ **Service levels** are statements concerning the targets set by a business with regard to meeting the demand and expectations of its customers. Those concerning shorter lead times and product or service range support will have a direct impact on the levels of inventory to be maintained. The impact on inventory of agreed targets must not only be recognized but assessed as part of a company's review of its competitive positioning and the role that inventory investment makes in meeting these.

■ **Lead times** are directly affected by decisions concerning whether a company:
   – makes to order (MTO)
   – assembles to order (ATO), or
   – makes to stock (MTS).

Progressively, lead times are reduced as companies move from MTO to MTS with an increasingly larger part of the product or service being undertaken before a sale is made. Part or all of the task is made ahead of the sale thereby reducing the lead time required to fulfil a customer order.

■ **Supplier relations** concern the level of co-operation between customers and their suppliers. This entails not only accurate and timely information with regard to demand schedules but also a mutual understanding of the products and services and the processes involved in both organizations. As suppliers are, in fact, part of the total supply chain customers need proactively to involve them in order to help reduce materials in the system. These issues are addressed in detail later in Chapter 11 which covers supply-chain management.

MANAGING AND CONTROLLING INVENTORY – SPECIFIC ISSUES

The last section highlighted some of the general issues regarding the management and control of inventory. This section looks at the more specific issues relating to several aspects of the task. Introducing them in this way allows you to understand the issues involved and then when the approaches to managing and controlling inventory are discussed these can be referred to as and when they form part of executing these tasks.

1. The independent/dependent demand principle

The starting point for the management and control of inventory is customer demand. Companies translate their forecasts of demand into statements of operations requirements, for example, the capacity and materials needed. In order to manage the latter, companies also use the principle of dependent/independent demand.

Dependent demand items are the components or materials used in a process to make a product or provide a service. They are, therefore, dependent on the number of final products or services sold. Hence, a car company will need five wheel rims and tyres (including the spare) for each car it makes. The quantity of these and other parts directly relates to the number of cars made. The wheel rims, tyres and other components and materials are classed as dependent and can be calculated based upon the number of final products (in this instance, cars) scheduled to be made. Similarly, a fast-food restaurant would calculate the number of fillings, buns, frozen french fries and other items based on its forecast of each type of meal to be sold. Items for which demand is linked to the use of other items are, therefore, said to have a dependent pattern of demand.

Independent demand items, on the other hand, are the final products made or services provided. They are said to be independent because they are neither a function of nor are they linked to the demand pattern of other items. Thus, in our earliest examples the demand for cars and meals would be classed as being independent. Thus, where the pattern of use for an item does not relate directly to the use of any other item it should be treated as an item with an independent pattern of demand.

The choice of inventory management system reflects whether an item has a dependent or an independent pattern of demand, as will be explained later. The key difference here to remember is that with independent demand items, the number of products or services is either known (that is, orders have already been received) or has to be forecast. With dependent demand items, the number can be calculated.

2. Pareto analysis[1]

As highlighted elsewhere, the size and importance of items will vary and often the relationship between the relative value or importance of a range of items will typically reflect what is known as the 80/20 rule. A review of inventory will show that it is no exception to this principle.

The 80/20[2] rule concerns the phenomenon that, for example, with regard to inventory, 80 per cent of the inventory value will be held in 20 per cent of the items in stock. Given this relationship then, consequently, most of the effort in managing inventory should be concentrated in the areas of high value in order to maximize the control exercised to minimize the inventory held.

Where to direct this major effort is easily derived from a Pareto analysis based on the annual requirement value of each item. For each item of inventory two facts are needed: unit value and annual usage. The product of these two figures is known as the annual requirement value (ARV).

The inventory items are then placed in order, largest ARV first, then the next largest and so on. Exhibit 10.8 lists a representative sample of 30 items in order of decreasing ARV. Such a list would be typical in many organizations. Because of the wide range of ARVs it would not make sense to spread the effort of inventory control equally over each part. Pareto's 'vital few' and 'trivial many' idea, or the 80/20 rule, applies here, as illustrated by Exhibit 10.9.

From this summary it can be seen that 74 per cent of the total ARV is accounted for by as little as 23 per cent of the total items held in inventory. This approach to inventory control is further extended into the ABC analysis. Here, the high ARV items are classed as A items, the middle range as B items and the low ARV as C items (Exhibit 10.10). Once this has been accomplished (bearing in mind that the ARV for an item may change over time and so, therefore, would its classification) the approach used to control items in each of these categories will differ to reflect the varying levels of inventory value.

It stands to reason that A items should be controlled and checked, and requirements calculated in order to keep inventory levels in line with forecast usage. It is worth the clerical and management costs involved. C items, on the other hand, would be managed with less control and effort as explained later in the chapter.

Exhibit 10.8 *A representative sample of 30 inventory items listed in order of decreasing annual requirement value (ARV)*

Part number	Unit value (£)	Annual usage (units)	Annual requirement value (£) Actual	Annual requirement value (£) Cumulative
303-07	58.50	6 000	351 000	351 000
650-27	2.46	80 000	196 800	547 800
541-21	210.00	500	105 000	652 800
260-81	164.11	450	73 850	726 850
712-22	2.39	25 000	59 750	786 400
054-09	5.86	10 000	58 600	845 000
097-54	136.36	300	40 908	885 908
440-18	17.30	2 000	34 600	920 508
440-01	337.35	100	33 735	954 243
308-31	136.20	200	27 240	981 483
016-01	12.89	2 000	25 780	1 007 263
305-04	45.30	475	21 518	1 028 781
155-29	38.02	500	19 010	1 047 791
542-93	62.91	300	18 837	1 066 664
582-34	32.08	500	16 040	1 082 704
323-34	71.30	200	14 260	1 096 964
412-27	23.01	600	13 806	1 110 770
540-80	24.76	500	12 380	1 123 150
137-29	12.31	1 000	12 310	1 135 460
401-53	30.64	400	12 256	1 147 716
418-51	168.86	65	10 976	1 158 692
418-50	168.80	65	10 972	1 169 664
390-02	17.47	500	8 735	1 178 399
037-41	24.05	200	4 810	1 183 209
402-50	22.00	600	4 400	1 187 609
900-01	41.64	100	4 164	1 191 773
543-61	15.10	200	3 020	1 194 793
900-11	46.80	50	2 340	1 197 133
003-54	11.41	200	2 282	1 199 415
691-30	0.41	5 000	2 050	1 201 465

3. Economic order quantity and economic lot size

One of the fundamental decisions in inventory management concerns how much to order in the context of what quantity will result in the lowest total cost. The order quantity decision, therefore, needs to relate the various costs involved in placing an order and carrying inventory to the quantity ordered. The economic order quantity (EOQ) and economic lot size (ELS) models address the question of how much to order to minimize the total cost of holding inventory.

The formulas to arrive at the quantity to be ordered to minimize total variable costs are given below.

$$EOQ = \sqrt{\frac{2zC_s}{cC}} \quad \text{for instantaneous replenishment}$$

or

$$ELS = \sqrt{\frac{2zC_s}{cC} \times \frac{p}{p-d}} \quad \text{for replenishment at rate } p$$

Exhibit 10.9   *Summary of the items given in Exhibit 10.8*

Percentage of total items		Percentage of total ARV
	23	74
	44[1]	21
	33	5[1]
Total	100	100

Note

1. Figures have been rounded up

Exhibit 10.10   *Pareto curve of the cumulative ARV for the thirty items listed in Exhibit 10.8 and analysed into ABC categories*

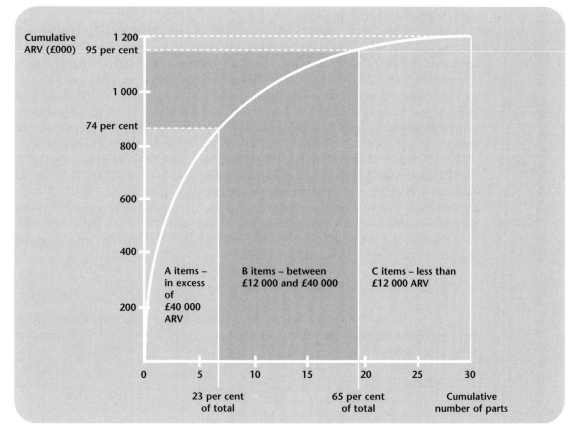

where z = total annual usage, C_s = cost of placing an order, c = unit cost of the item, C = carrying cost rate per year, p = production provisioning rate (units) per day and d = demand rate (units) per day.

However, it is important to note that these models make the following simplifying assumptions:

■ the rate of demand is constant
■ costs remain fixed
■ operations and inventory capacity are unlimited.

Despite the fact that these assumptions are fundamental to the basis of the models and would seemingly restrict their use, they provide useful guidelines for ordering decisions even in operating conditions that depart significantly from these assumptions.[3]

4. Reorder levels

A key question to be addressed by inventory systems for the various items involved is when and how much to order. In some situations the decision is in response to another event. For example, ordering dependent items is typically linked to a decision to make or provide the independent item to which they relate. The same goes for companies working on a make-to-order basis as explained earlier. Here, the customer order triggers the other decisions.

In other situations companies need to deal with the question 'When should an order to replenish inventory be placed?' Assuming that a company does not wish to run out of inventory then the level at which it must reorder is calculated by multiplying the time it takes to get an order into the company from an outside supplier (the lead time) by the number of units used of this particular item during the same period. Thus, if the delivery lead time for an item is one week and the weekly usage is 100 units then the reorder level (ROL) is $1 \times 100 = 100$ units. Ideally, the time to place an order is such that the last item of inventory is used as delivery of the next order for this item is made.

But the rate of usage will vary with demand, and may often vary considerably. In calculating the ROL, average figures are used based upon historical data. However, the pattern of demand will vary around the average and it is the incidence of above average usage that will result in being out of stock. To avoid a stockout it will be necessary to carry inventory to cater for the higher than average demand during a lead time. This extra quantity is called buffer inventory as explained earlier. Hence, the ROL calculation can now be modified as follows:

ROL = average usage in a lead time + buffer inventory

So far we have discussed stock levels without stating what they mean. As the example below illustrates, physical stock levels need to be adjusted for both allocations and stock on order.

Item 746B
Actual physical stock	125
Less allocated stock	38
Available stock	87
Plus stock on order	100
	187

ROLs are normally based on available stock figures. Stock allocations are ignored in these calculations where they relate to time periods in the future such that they will not affect inventory levels within the material lead time. Similarly, stock on order is taken into account when defining available stock with regard to future allocations and purchase order decisions.

INVENTORY DECISIONS

Inventory comprises the process-related (that is, materials and components, part-made items (work-in-progress) and finished items) and corporate cateories introduced earlier. For both these categories decisions on inventory concern:

■ what items to hold in stock
■ how much to hold
■ when to order
■ how much to order.

The answer to these questions will relate to the general and specific issues covered in the last two sections as well as other agreements with customers and suppliers and any internal decisions made within a business. One of the most fundamental factors affecting the decisions to be made, systems to use and approaches to follow is the independent/dependent demand principle explained in the last section. This factor is reflected in the following sections that address these questions.

Before relating in detail the general and specific management and control of inventory issues covered in the two preceding sections to the questions what and how much inventory to hold and when and how much inventory to order, it will help if we outline typical approaches to these issues that companies adopt. This will provide an overview and give an idea of what will be the possible outcome to these questions for different inventory types. A detailed discussion on the issues that companies need to take on board and the different approaches to managing and controlling inventory that can be used will then follow.

1. **Process-related inventory** – companies that make ahead of demand will base material requirements on anticipated levels of sales for the independent demand items they provide or in line with known orders to be delivered at a later date or a combination of the two. This making-ahead-of-time response can be met by finished items, part-made items (work-in-progress), materials and components, or a combination of all three types of inventory.
   Now let us address the question what and how much to hold:

   ■ What to hold – companies will decide to make products or complete services ahead of time for a number of reasons. Often, known orders or scheduled call-offs against customer contracts will be made or provided in advance to ensure that due dates are met. Similarly, inventory to meet future demand peaks, known seasonality patterns or to level out operations capacity requirements over a period are practical inventory responses used by companies to manage these different circumstances. As part of these decisions the 80/20 rule will often be employed to help guide a company as it attempts to balance the level of inventory investment with the level of support for its markets and customers and/or the costs in operations as it adjusts capacity to meet varying levels of demand. Corporate issues such as agreements with customers to hold certain items in stock will also influence this decision.
   Now let us look at dependent demand items. In principle, these need not be made until the relevant independent demand items are required. However, companies often carry inventory of dependent demand items for reasons such as

safety (to guard against uncertainty of supply), buffer (to reflect the variance within suppliers' delivery time), as well as economic order quantity benefits, purchasing discounts, reduced transaction costs and the like. Holding dependent demand item inventory to gain lower costs and improve a company's ability to support its markets and customers makes for sound management practice.

■ How much inventory to make ahead of time – the answer to this question will typically need to reflect not only the assemble-to-order (ATO) or make-to-stock (MTS) decision (that is, the more an MTS position a company takes the greater the value of inventory created versus the shorter operations lead times that result) but also dimensions such as the 80/20 rule that helps identify the trade-offs between investment and inventory size, corporate agreements with customers on inventory support levels, and the like. Calculations concern issues such as reorder points while buffer inventory requirements will also form part of these decisions. Details of these factors and others are given in subsequent sections.

■ The when and how much to order questions will reflect issues such as demand profiles, the lead times involved and range of corporate agreements. Issues that are covered in subsequent sections include demand forecasts and scheduling horizons (that is, what a company expects to sell and the lead times involved), reorder levels that reflect how much will be sold or required in the time it takes to replenish the inventory used, economic order quantities that aim to arrive at the lowest cost provision alternative and so on.

2. **Support inventory** – companies will often need to have these support items (for example maintenance and office supplies) to hand and, therefore, need again to address the questions of what and how much inventory to hold and when and how much to order. Issues here concern unit costs, purchase lead times, impact of delays on a business or the work of a function, level of uncertainty in locating and acquiring parts, and similar factors. More often in the past, individual functions have made their own rules regarding support inventories. But, as the size of overhead functions and the growth in technology-based systems used within these functions have increased, the need for a wider range of system support inventory items has grown. As these are also individually more expensive, the result is that inventory values have increased and the opportunity to manage and control these to secure sizeable cost and lead time advantages is available.

With this overview now in mind, the factors affecting a company's response to these questions are now addressed.

What items to hold in stock

The factors affecting the decision on what items to hold in stock will include the following:

Make-to-order, assemble-to-order or make-to-stock

A major factor influencing the decision what to hold in stock is whether a company selects a make-to-order, assemble-to-order or make-to-stock response to meeting customer needs.

■ **Make-to-order (MTO)** businesses are usually involved in the provision of special (that is, will not be repeated[4]) products and services. In addition, some companies decide to meet demand for standard (that is, repeat) items only on an MTO basis. Either way, an MTO response means that inventory will not be held either as part-finished or finished items. What may be held in stock are the materials and components that form all or part of an item.

■ **Assemble-to-order (ATO)** businesses are those that part-finish an item beforehand and then complete it on receipt of an order. The stage of part-completion reflects the associated value of inventory and process lead time reduction that results. Fast-food restaurants prepare beforehand the individual items in the range (for example, french fries and different types of burgers) and then assemble-to-order customers' requirements. Similarly, top restaurants part-prepare some food (for example, desserts and vegetables) ahead of time.

■ **Make-to-stock (MTS)** business are those that complete or purchase items ahead of demand and then meet orders from finished goods inventory. Examples include all retail outlets and manufacturers making finished goods. Others such as newspaper shops can only sell this way – if a newspaper is not available then the sale is simply lost.

80/20 rule

As explained earlier, the 'vital few' and 'trivial many' phenomenon is a characteristic of inventory. Based on this, companies often decide to hold inventory of low annual requirement value items based on the principle of setting purchasing costs against inventory holding costs.

Independent/dependent demand items

Decisions to hold items in stock are affected by whether or not they fall within the independent or dependent demand categories. As explained earlier, the former are end items and are more open to choice concerning whether or not to hold them in stock – for example, some of the corporate inventory types. However, as the usage for dependent items is linked directly to the demand for independent items then there is no requirement to hold inventory for these until the decision is made to provide relevant independent items. Decisions to otherwise hold inventory for dependent items will be due to gains such as those associated with the economic order quantity and economic lot size rationale or for corporate reasons as discussed earlier and also set out in the next section.

Corporate inventory

Companies often hold inventory for non-operations reasons. Classic categories include customer agreement and corporate safety stock.

■ *Customer agreement inventory* is where a company agrees to hold a given level of inventory at all times in anticipation of a customer order or call-off. This may be provided on a consignment stock[5] basis and held on a customer's own premises.

■ *Corporate safety stock* is held due to the uncertainty of supply. For example, to guard against national or international strikes or in anticipation of a general national, regional or world shortage.

Illustrations of corporate decisions on inventory that reflect the nature of a company's business or to meet market needs are now provided.

How much stock to hold, and how much and when to order materials

The three issues of how much stock to hold and how much and when to order materials are an integral set of decisions and so are addressed together. The factors that affect these questions include some of those discussed in the last section 'What to hold' as well as others that are specific to these key questions.

Demand forecasts and scheduling horizons

Key factors in answering these three questions are demand forecasts and the scheduling horizons determined by a business. In part this will reflect the nature of a company's markets as explained earlier.

Make-to-order – special products and services

Companies providing special products and services will use customer orders already received (known as order backlog or forward load) together with forecast sales profiles

---

Case examples

1

Retail outlets need to hold inventory in order to sell products and also to display the extent and nature of a range of goods. Where the purchase price is low or where a lack of stock will lead to a lost sale (for example, a newsagent or food store) then the policy will be to hold inventory in line with forecast sales and will reflect demand fluctuations. Where the items are of high value (for example, a suite of furniture, china dinner service or set of cutglass tumblers or wine glasses) then examples of the range (typically those that sell the most) supported by fabric choices, catalogues and the like will be the basis for what is held in stock.

2

Restaurants hold the basic food and other ingredients in stock and part- or fully prepare food in line with the menu and anticipated sales of the various menu options. The extent to which materials are part-prepared will reflect the level of choice provided, and the speed of service offered or expected by customers.

3

A company selling a range of household items used two approaches to holding inventory of its products. Category 1 products were made in anticipation of sales and on a make-to-stock basis. Orders for a category 2 product were allowed to go into arrears and then a quantity of a product would be made that covered:

Case examples (cont'd)

3

(a) outstanding sales orders
(b) sales orders received during the process time to make the order quantity
(c) inventory to cover a given number of weeks of future sales.

When the quantity was made, outstanding orders in (a) and (b) above would be met. Future sales would be met from the finished goods inventory that remained. Eventually the company would go into an outstanding order position for its category 2 products and the procedure outlined above would be repeated.

Case examples questions

1. What is the role of inventory in these three illustrations?
2. Explain in detail how inventory would be used in each delivery system.

to estimate capacity and to determine material requirements. How much and when to order the necessary materials will be in line with the size and start dates of the orders on hand. In some instances, particularly where expensive materials are involved, customers, as part of the contract, will provide materials on a 'free issue' basis (that is, a customer buys the materials and has them delivered to the supplier). Companies will often stock some non-specific materials that are in general use for a number of products and services and replenish these in line with the forward orders that a business has on hand. For materials that are specific to an order, companies will normally purchase quantities in line with customer order requirements. An exception to this is where minimum order quantities are imposed by a supplier and these exceed the materials required to meet a specific customer order. In such instances the minimum order quantity will need to be purchased. Companies should then build the total cost of this minimum order quantity into their price calculations for an order and hold the balance in stock where there is a possibility of future use. Balances so held should be recorded as having a zero value and thereby ensure that any gain is only registered when it happens. (This is based on sound accounting practice. However, although the book value of such inventory is zero, the physical items are in stock and will need to be managed and controlled in the normal way.)

Standard products and services

Where companies supply standard products and services then decisions on how much stock to hold and how much and when to order materials is influenced by a number of factors, of which demand forecasts, make-to-order or make-to-stock decisions and operations scheduling horizons are key.

As outlined earlier, companies providing standard products and services can do so using a make-to-order or make-to-stock approach. Using make-to-order as the basis for scheduling means that companies provide products and services only in line with actual customer orders or contract call-offs and the timing and quantity of materials required are thereby known and built into the scheduling procedure. This then becomes the essential mechanism for managing and controlling inventory.

Companies choosing to provide products and services on a make-to-stock basis convert sales forecasts of demand into statements of operations requirements as explained in Chapter 8. These operations requirements are then converted into schedules and material call-offs identifying which and when materials are needed. In this way, the scheduling system ties in the aspects of capacity and material requirements to forecast demand and arranges the timing of these to meet future sales.

To help in managing these decisions companies use a number of approaches to help control the different categories of inventory, that is materials/components, work-in-progress and finished items. These approaches are now discussed.

Reorder point

As explained earlier, companies use the principle of reorder levels as the basis for deciding how much stock to hold and when to reorder. This system can be used for finished items as well as for raw material and component inventory holdings.

The logic of an order point system is to trigger the reorder of a part every time the inventory level of that part falls to a predetermined level. As illustrated by Exhibit 10.11, the timing and quantity of the reorder take into account the usage in the lead time plus the agreed buffer inventory to take account of above-average usage. Using the example as an illustration, then the reorder level is the sum of the average usage in the lead time (1 × 100 = 100 units) plus the extra inventory to cater for the above-average demand during a lead time (estimated here as 25 units). Exhibit 10.11 illustrates the control of an individual part through an order point system. The three cycles in this example show different levels of usage during the lead time, although the pattern of

Exhibit 10.11 *The control of an individual part through an order point system*

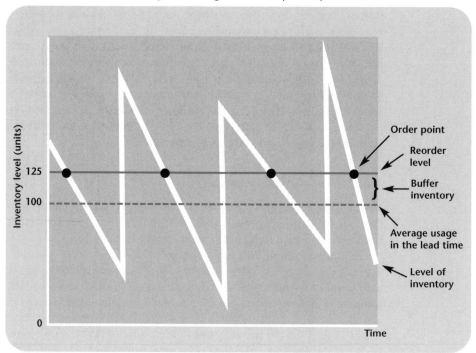

usage has been simplified (it would not normally be so regular) and the actual lead times are shown as being more consistent than typically experienced in reality.

However, this illustration shows the importance of recognizing that only usage patterns after the reorder level is reached are of consequence in terms of stockouts and for this reason the period following an order point is known as 'being at risk'.

Let us explain this important point more fully. Demand patterns above a reorder point will only result in inventory falling to this level either more quickly or more slowly than average depending upon whether actual demand is higher or lower respectively. As far as potential stockouts are concerned, this phase in demand is not a factor. However, above-average demand patterns experienced after a reorder point has been reached are a direct factor as to whether or not stockouts occur. Above-average demand will result in a stockout if the amount of buffer inventory is insufficient to cover the level of actual demand experienced. Hence the term 'being at risk'. Exhibits 10.12 and 10.13 illustrate these points. In Exhibit 10.12, above-average demand is followed by a period of below-average demand, whereas in Exhibit 10.13 the reverse demand patterns are shown and their impact on inventory levels and stockouts is illustrated.

Finally, a reminder that the illustrations of the reorder point model have been kept simple without invalidating the principles involved. In all three examples, material lead times have been assumed constant and usage patterns have been shown as being regular. In practice these factors (and especially usage patterns) will typically vary during a period.

Exhibit 10.12 *Higher than average demand above the reorder level followed by below-average demand*

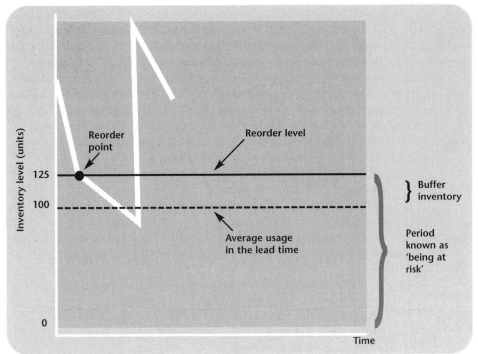

Exhibit 10.13 *Below-average demand above the reorder level followed by higher than average demand and the resulting stockout*

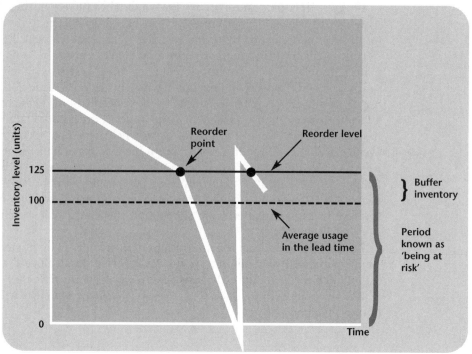

Buffer inventory

The function of buffer inventory is to provide a safeguard against periods of above-average demand and thereby avoid or reduce the number of stockouts. Where there is sufficient information, buffer inventories can be calculated using basic statistics. The first step would be to calculate average usage for an item and the standard deviation of usage around that average. For example, assume that an item has an average weekly usage of 100 and is normally distributed with a standard deviation of 12 units. By applying normal curve theory (see Exhibit 10.14) the individual weekly usage would be within two standard deviations either side of the average for 95 per cent of the time (the mathematical explanation of this is not given here, but for those interested it will normally be available in any textbook on inventory control). Of the 5 per cent of the time that usage does not fall within two standard deviations, half can be expected to be less than average and half to be more than average. Now, the organization is concerned only with instances where usage is above average, therefore it can expect that only for 2½ per cent of the time would usage exceed the average plus two standard deviations. That is 100 + 2(12) = 124. In this situation, if the reorder level was set at 124 then a stockout would not be expected more than 2½ per cent of the time or one time in 40 occasions.

Calculating buffer inventory in this way, however, should normally apply to A and possibly some B items (see Exhibit 10.10). In these instances the high annual requirement value and resulting impact on inventory levels would make the time and cost worth while. For other B and all C items, buffer inventory levels would be determined using much cruder methods.

Exhibit 10.14 *Normal distribution curve showing the average weekly usage of 100 units and two standard deviations (SDs) either side of this average*

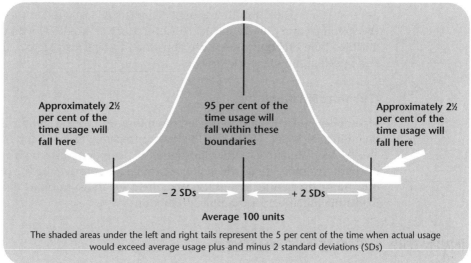

Approximately 2½ per cent of the time usage will fall here

95 per cent of the time usage will fall within these boundaries

Approximately 2½ per cent of the time usage will fall here

− 2 SDs   + 2 SDs

Average 100 units

The shaded areas under the left and right tails represent the 5 per cent of the time when actual usage would exceed average usage plus and minus 2 standard deviations (SDs)

Service levels

A further measure that may be used to gauge the level of customer support is the service level. The level of service that an organization wishes to maintain can be established and the level of buffer inventory needed to yield acceptable service levels can be calculated. One commonly used way of expressing service levels is given below.

$$\text{Service level (per cent)} = \frac{\text{\# customers served without delay}}{\text{Total orders received}} \times 100$$

To approach this requirement from the opposite perspective, companies can determine the risk of a stockout they are prepared to accept. This is also known as the protection level and is the equivalent of $100 \times (1 - \text{probability of a stockout})$. Protection levels can thus be established and the level of buffer inventory to provide these levels can be calculated.

Economic order and economic batch quantities

The economic order quantity (EOQ) and economic batch quantity (EBQ) or economic lot size (ELS) models were explained earlier. They are, as their titles suggest, directed towards helping to determine the quantity that would give the lowest total cost outcome. Although these models are built on a number of simplified assumptions they are useful in providing guidelines on how much to order or provide.

Other companies use different criteria for arriving at the order quantity to be processed. For example, a company making high specification, reproduction furniture limited its order quantity to that which equated to no more than two days of work for their operators. To this company, limiting the amount of time on the same piece of furniture would support job interest and help ensure that conformance to the very high specification demands of its product range would best be met.

Consignment stock

As explained earlier, consignment stock describes inventory held at a customer's premises that is not paid for until it is used. Suppliers typically retain the responsibility for checking inventory levels and replenishing stock as needed. In these instances, how much to hold on a customer's site and when to replenish are based on actual usage and agreed minimum stock levels.

Corporate inventory

Many of these latter approaches are often directly influenced by corporate decisions on a range of issues. Those classified as 'customer agreement' and 'safety' stock have already been explained. Other illustrations of corporate inventory include purchase-discount inventory (that held at above-normal levels to acquire the price discounts on offer) and marketing inventory (that held at above-normal levels to support a marketing initiative; for example, promotions).

INVENTORY SYSTEMS AND ANALYSIS

The models and approaches described so far to help in the control of inventory have simplified the size of the problem. Coping with thousands of stock items, supplied by many different suppliers and supporting the needs of numerous customers, results in a complex and dynamic operations task. To cope with this level of complexity operations managers need to do several basic tasks. First, they need to recognize that the level of control to be provided reflects the ARV of an item. Second, they need to select and develop a control system in line with existing systems (for example, operations scheduling) and the nature of the item itself (for example, dependent versus independent items). Finally, they need to undertake checks on current inventory levels to verify the system, test how well it is working and to identify changes in working practices, customer demands and other business issues and how they impact on inventory. The sections that follow address these issues.

1. Inventory systems

Companies use a variety of systems to help manage and control inventory. Which to use will reflect the nature of their business and will take into account the issues discussed earlier. The sections that follow list these key points and discuss the approaches used to control both corporate and operations inventory.

Background issues

A company's choice of inventory control system should be made within the context of the type of business involved and the appropriate level of control to be exercised. Some of the key issues have been highlighted throughout the chapter and include the following:

■ **Operations scheduling systems** interface with the control of inventory. The translation of customer orders into operations requirements has already been mentioned and Chapter 8 addresses these issues in detail. The aspect of inventory control is an integral part of the material schedules that form part of the operations control system. High volume, make-to-stock businesses (for example, motor vehicles) typically use just-in-time (JIT) systems that dictate material call-offs and help control and maintain low levels of inventory.

Where companies adopt a make-to-order policy for the scheduling of standard products and services then actual customer orders and call-offs will trigger the operations schedule that, in turn, activates the demand for materials. For those companies that use a make-to-stock approach for scheduling operations then they will use one of the systems described in a later section.

■ **Dependent demand** items are, by and large, calculated in line with requirements for independent demand items as described earlier. This approach is typically supplemented for low ARV items by simple systems which are low cost to manage and control and designed to ensure no stockouts. These are explained in a later section.

■ **The 80/20 rule** should determine the level of control that companies provide. The selection of appropriate systems for low ARV items is, as explained in the last section, concerned with keeping the management and control costs low yet ensuring that stockouts are avoided. Calculating and ordering small quantities of these items would not make sense. For high ARV items the reverse is true.

Corporate inventory control

In most companies some 20–25 per cent of inventory is held for corporate rather than operations reasons. So far, 'customer agreement', 'safety', 'purchasing-discount' and 'marketing' inventory have been described. There are several other categories and explanations of these are provided later.

The control of this inventory is specific to its provision. Based on the value involved, companies will need to evaluate the investment in terms of its size and return (what advantages and functions the inventory provides). Each category will need to be assessed item by item. The approach to be followed is described more fully in the later section entitled 'Causal analysis'.

Operations inventory control

Operations inventory typically accounts for 75–80 per cent of the total. This inventory exists for operations reasons and provides a number of the functions described earlier. This section describes the systems used to control operations inventory. You will see when you read this section that several of the aspects and issues introduced earlier in the chapter are included. This will, therefore, enable us to refer to them without going into detail. Should you wish to refresh your understanding of these points then references will be given to where they are in the chapter.

Continuous review systems

In a continuous review system the stock position is monitored after each transaction (that is, continuously). When the stock drops to a predetermined level (or reorder point) a fixed quantity is placed on order. Since the order quantity is fixed, the time between orders will vary in line with the different levels of demand. The continuous review system is also referred to as a fixed-order quantity system (or Q system for short). Exhibit 10.11 provides an example using this principle and shows the following characteristics:

- a fixed quantity (that incorporates the economic order quantity principle) is placed on order
- the material lead time (the time between an order being placed and its delivery) is deemed to be the same
- the gap between orders will vary in line with the different levels of demand.

The calculation of the reorder level, as explained earlier, is the average quantity used in the lead time plus buffer inventory to cover the likelihood and extent of above-average usage. Another factor to be taken into account in this calculation is any variation in material lead times. If this varies then these above-average length of lead times would need to be factored into the reorder level calculation.

Periodic review systems

While the virtue of the continuous review system is that it can make use of economic order quantities, monitoring and checking inventory levels continuously (even when using suitable, computer-based systems) is time consuming and expensive. An alternative and similar approach is the periodic review system, also known as fixed-order period system (or P system for short). In a periodic review system, the stock position is reviewed at fixed intervals and a reorder quantity is placed that constitutes the difference between the actual and target inventory level. The target level is set to cover demand until the next periodic review plus the delivery lead time. As usage varies so the amount ordered will vary and hence one disadvantage of this system is that the economic order quantity principle cannot be used.

Using P and Q systems in practice

Both P and Q systems together with modified versions of them are widely used for the management of independent demand items. The choice between the two is not an easy one and will be made on the basis of management practices as well as costs. Conditions, however, that favour the use of one system as opposed to the other include the following:

- **Timing of replacement inventory** – when orders must be placed or material delivered at specified intervals then a P system should be used. Weekly deliveries of items to a retail store would be an example of this condition.

- **Multiple item shipments** from the same supplier would follow a P system in order to secure the gains of consolidating items into a single shipment and the resulting reduction in delivery and paperwork costs.

- **Inexpensive items** not maintained on inventory records should use a P system. Low-value items such as fasteners (for example, nuts, washers and bolts) could be stocked in bins and periodically checked and replenished to a given target quantity. No records of use or receipts of inventory would be made in keeping with the low-cost management needs of such items.

- **Expensive items** are best managed using a Q system that helps keep inventory to a minimum. To safeguard against stockouts, P systems require higher buffer stocks which makes them less suited to expensive items. The increase in costs associated with Q systems and the management of higher ARV items, is justified by the greater control provided and associated lower inventory levels that result.

In practice, hybrid systems are developed with a mixture of P and Q inventory rules. One such hybrid is the optimal replenishment system. Here inventory is checked both on a quantity and time basis. Either of these factors will highlight the inventory items for review, but an order is placed only if the inventory level has reached the point where the economic order quantity would be required.

Supplementary systems and approaches

In addition to the systems described above, companies use a number of supplementary systems and approaches to manage different inventory requirements. Three of the more common requirements are now explained:

1. **Managing low ARV items**. The costs involved in managing and controlling inventory can be high. For low ARV independent and dependent items we need systems that ensure no stockouts but are not costly to maintain. Two of the more commonly used systems that provide this low-cost requirement are now described:

   ■ **Single-bin systems** involve filling up a shelf, bin or tank periodically. Examples are shelves in retail outlets, small-part bins in repair shops and fuel tanks in petrol or gas stations. These are examples of P systems with the size of container the target level of inventory. Individual records of receipts and usage would normally not be made. Control is provided by checking expected usage levels over a period compared to the level of purchases made during this time.

   ■ **Two-bin systems** comprise inventory held in two bins or two containers. The one in current use is open and the second is sealed. When the first container is empty, the second is opened and this act triggers a replacement order. This is a Q system with the quantity in the second container equal to the reorder level. As with single-bin systems, records of individual transactions are not kept with control provided by period checks similar to those described for single-bin systems.

2. **Seasonal demand**. Demand patterns for many businesses have a seasonal element. As explained in Chapter 6, some companies alter capacity to meet these changing requirements. Where companies can make products in one period to sell in the next, then meeting seasonal demand by using capacity-related inventory is an alternative to changing capacity levels. While the downside of using inventory is the investment and cost involved, advantages include maintaining a stable and experienced workforce and avoiding the costs of training and lower productivity levels associated with temporary staff.

   Where companies use capacity-related inventory as one way to balance fluctuating demand levels with the decision to maintain level output, it is important for them to establish the different ratios between the standard hour content of inventory and its overall value. Calculating the ratio between inventory value and standard hour content will enable a company to elect to produce for stock those items with the most favourable ratios. In this way it will be able to absorb 'spare capacity' for the lowest inventory value increases. Exhibit 10.15 provides an example of this approach. Representative items from a company show the inventory value (column 3) and also the number of standard hours required to make the item (column 4). Dividing the inventory value by the standard hours to make an item gives the value of inventory made per standard hour used (column 5). In low-demand periods companies can then absorb the overcapacity in operations but restrict inventory value increases. Let us look at Exhibit 10.15 to see how it works. While item E180 has a unit inventory value of £25.80 it in effect uses 6.3 standard labour hours to produce each item. Consequently its inventory/labour ratio is only £4.10/hour. On the other hand, E150 and WD162 both have unit values less than E180 at £13.50 and £18.65 respectively. However, their inventory/labour ratios are significantly higher than that for E180 at £19.30/hour and £23.30/hour respectively. Thus, using this calculation as one factor in planning inventory at times when capacity is greater than sales will enable companies to keep inventory increases to a minimum while using effectively the capacity on hand.

3. **Limited shelf-life items.** Some products have a limited life. This could be due to the shelf life of the item itself or products that are linked to major events – for example, companies designing and making products for the Olympic Games in Sydney in 2000.

2. Inventory analysis

Inventory is an integral part of business activity. It is an asset that helps companies in the provision and sale of goods and services. Recognizing that an organization needs inventory and that this investment is costly, the more pertinent question concerns 'Is the amount of inventory necessary?'

We have already reviewed the systems and procedures from which companies choose to best meet their inventory management needs. As with all systems these will have to be developed and improved to provide sound controls and ensure that the inventory levels are kept to a minimum while providing the benefits and functions inherent in these investments.

To evaluate how well systems are working and to highlight aspects that need to be checked companies should also analyse inventory as part of this review process. In many businesses the recording and valuation of stock lead to statements which separate total inventory into the categories of raw materials and components, work-in-progress and finished goods. Typically this is done once or twice a year in line with the need for the accounting function to prepare a profit and loss account and balance sheet. While this analysis meets these requirements it provides little information useful to management in their task of evaluating inventory. The insights on inventory provided by the categories raw materials/components, work-in-progress and finished goods concern the state and position of material within the system. In other words, material has not been processed (raw materials and components), the processing of material is now complete (finished goods) or the material is somewhere between these two positions (work-in-progress). But, while this is adequate as a basis for assessing the value of inventory, it fails to provide the key insight to help manage and assess inventory levels – that is, why is it there? To provide this insight companies need to undertake a review of inventory to determine why it is there, or what caused the inventory.

Causal analysis

It is not necessary to undertake this task at the same time for all the inventory held. Parts can be reviewed at different times and the first step is to select a portion of the

Exhibit 10.15 *Inventory/labour hour ratios: establishing the ratio between the value of inventory (WIP and/or finished goods) and its work content (standard hours) as a means of setting priorities in times when available capacity exceeds levels of demand*

Products		Inventory value (£s)	Labour content (standard hours)	Inventory made per standard labour hour used	Product rankings – to minimize inventory value (£) increases per standard hour of labour used	
Reference	Inventory	Per unit		£ p	WIP/ finished items	Overall
WB674		66.05	13.2	5.00	2	3
WA321		35.50	2.6	13.70	8	13
WC193		32.85	3.2	10.30	5	10
WB280	work-	21.15	4.1	5.20	3	4
WB055	in-	19.00	1.4	13.60	7	12
WD162	progress	18.65	0.8	23.30	10	18
WD610		6.35	0.4	15.90	9	16
WB405		4.25	0.9	4.70	1	2
WE350		3.54	0.4	8.90	4	8
WC184		1.15	0.1	11.50	6	11
G163		150.10	10.1	14.90	7	15
D114		122.50	8.0	14.20	6	14
A195		93.75	3.2	29.30	9	19
B680	finished	65.00	12.5	5.20	2	4
B008	items	33.60	5.5	6.10	3	6
D710		28.00	2.9	9.70	5	9
E180		25.80	6.3	4.10	1	1
E150		13.50	0.7	19.30	8	17
B160		11.50	1.3	8.80	4	7
D109		6.75	0.2	33.75	10	20

inventory holding for review. Inventory is then reviewed asking the question, why is it there? The answers are then categorized into:

■ one of the many categories of corporate inventory that exist
■ one of the five functions of corporate inventory that were explained earlier.

In addition, the position of the inventory in the operations process is recorded. Position here identifies the stage through which it was last processed and the stage it is waiting to enter. Also, where inventory is recognized as providing more than one category or function then the value of the holding is split equally between the categories or functions provided and recorded as separate entries.

In this way a picture of inventory is developed that shows clusters of inventory by category or function and stage in the operations process. Large clusters are then

Case examples

4

Corporate inventory – support inventory for a customer was found to be running at the equivalent of three weeks of sales. This was due to an agreement with the customer to hold finished-goods inventory at a given level. On reviewing the current position it was found that weekly sales of this item to the customer had reduced but the inventory holding had not been recalculated. Whereas the original agreement was to hold two weeks of sales, the inventory equivalent had not been recalculated to reflect this lower sales position. Discussions with the customer also included revising the agreement. The overall result was that the level of customer support inventory was reduced to one week of sales at current levels.

5

Operations inventory – a review of inventory highlighted a large cluster of inventory awaiting to enter a given process. The resulting analysis led to the purchase of an additional process as it was found that there was insufficient capacity at this stage. The alternatives to handling this bottleneck were considered, but as the process investment costs were low it was decided that purchasing additional equipment was the most effective solution.

checked to see why they exist. This allows the rules and procedures involved to be reviewed and modified where it is considered that such changes would still meet the relevant corporate or operations needs but would reduce the amount of inventory involved. This approach is based on the recognition that changing the rules that allow inventory to be made will reduce the level of stock entering the system and thereby lower inventory holdings.

Let us consider two examples, one involving corporate and the other, operations inventory.

CONCLUSION

Inventory is a significant asset in most organizations. Its effective management, therefore, is a key task within the auspices of operations. But controlling inventory is far from easy. It involves a complex set of decisions due to the many forms inventory takes and functions it provides. In addition, inventories are the result of functional policies within an organization as well as the short- and long-term decisions in purchasing, operations and sales. There is, therefore, a need for the corporate perspectives of inventory to be exercised at the highest level as well as the detailed control systems and procedures to be used lower down in an organization. Furthermore, the all-embracing and interrelated nature of this investment necessitates that its provision and control are shared by all concerned.

The task facing operations then is to ensure that the amount of inventory held is necessary in terms of the functions provided. Often, particularly in the past, the level held included quantities and types which brought questionable gains. This chapter has detailed the ways in which inventory can be effectively managed and controlled. All facets provide part of the answer. As Oliver Wight's parody on John Godfrey Saxe's poem 'The blind man and the elephant' illustrates, choosing the combination that meets the needs of a situation is a key management decision:

It was six men of management
To learning much inclined
Who discoursed on production control
And the answers they did find –
From experience, and the lessons
That reward an inquiring mind.

'Order to mins and maximums',
The first was heard to say,
'You'll have neither too much nor too little
When production's controlled this way.'

'But the answer lies in the forecast',
Said the second in line,
'Just anticipate your sales,
And everything will be fine.'

'I doubt it' said the third one,
'You've forgotten the EOQ.
With balanced setups and inventories,
What problems can ensue?'

The fourth one said: 'Use order points
To get the desired control.
When you order materials soon enough,
You'll never be "in the hole"'.

'But you really need a computer.'
Said the fifth – 'PC's a dream
With loads run from last week's payroll cards
And exception reports by the ream.'

Said the sixth, 'Materials management
Is a concept to which I'm devoted –
Instead of learning production control,
I've escaped by getting promoted.'

So study each book and seminar,
Attend every one you can, sir!
You'll find a thousand experts –
Each with PART of the answer![6]

SUMMARY

Inventory is not only sizeable in asset terms but is also complex to manage and control. On the one hand companies wish to keep the investment as low as possible, while on the other inventory is an integral part of a company's activities and central to the workings of its process and delivery system. It is in this context that inventory needs to be efficiently managed and controlled.

One overriding principle that featured throughout the chapter was that of distinguishing between independent and dependent demand items. As usage rates of the latter are linked to the demand levels of the former then dependent demand item requirements can be calculated and scheduled in line with levels of the demand rates for the independent items to which they relate.

This principle of calculating requirements for dependent demand items is central to managing and controlling this type of inventory. However, as explained in the chapter, it may make more sense for a company to hold inventory of some of these dependent demand items at a level that is not tied to a calculated rate of requirement. Reasons for severing this link are to do with issues of overall cost. For items that have a low unit cost (for example C items) it may lower total unit cost (price per unit plus related inventory costs) to buy in quantities that exceed demand patterns. Buying or making in large quantities will almost always lower the actual cost per unit and such items lend themselves to the use of systems such as two bin type controls that are simple to operate and inexpensive to manage, thereby lowering total unit costs still further.

The approaches to managing and controlling independent items need to reflect the several issues and dimensions that were introduced and discussed throughout the chapter. Upfront will be the choice, where available, between make-to-order, assemble-to-order and make-to-stock approaches. In make-to-order businesses, material and work-in-progress inventory will reflect the delivery dates and delivery system requirements of the products and services provided. Items when finished will go straight to customers. Where items are part made and then assembled or finished in line with customer orders and where items are made-to-stock, what and how much is made and when and how much to order, need to take into account issues such as the 80/20 rule, corporate inventory commitments, reorder point, buffer inventory requirements and economic order quantities.

The key throughout, and as explained elsewhere in the book, is fitting the decisions to the characteristics and requirements of an organization. Knowing the alternatives that can be used and incorporating relevant dimensions into the decision-making process should always form the basis of the management and control outcomes. The objectives of the chapter include providing you with these essential dimensions and help you understand the alternative approaches that can be used to effectively manage and control this sizeable asset.

Discussion questions

1. How does inventory contribute to the value-adding activities of a firm? When should inventory be considered a symptom of waste?

2. What are the types of material inventory you would find in the following businesses?

   - a retail pharmacist
   - a petrol station
   - a coffee bar
   - a stone and gravel extraction company

3. What activities add to the cost of inventory and which functions are responsible for incurring them?

4. What aspects of the delivery system in service companies need to accommodate their inability to convert capacity into inventory?

5. How realistic are the assumptions of the EOQ model? Why is this model still being used in both textbooks and businesses?

6. Describe the difference between independent and dependent demand and give two examples of each for a pizza restaurant.

7. Explain the ABC classification system and detail its advantages.

8. Referring back to Chapter 8, how does JIT influence inventory holdings?

9. Textet Computing sells software through the Internet. With each purchase, the company includes a computer manual and currently it is rethinking whether it should outsource the preparation of these manuals or continue to make them inhouse. Below are the cost estimates for the options:

Outsourced	– total cost of £0.50p per manual
Make in-house	– variable cost per manual £0.30p
	– annual fixed costs of £7500

   - Which alternative has the lower total cost if annual demand is 30 000 copies?
   - At what annual volume do these alternatives have the same cost?
   - Textet Computing estimates that its sales of software next year will increase to 55 000 units. The outside supplier will drop the price per manual to £0.43p on these volumes. At what quantity are the cost of making in-house and the cost of outsourcing at £0.43p equal?

10. Choose one manufacturing and one service company and extract the following information from their latest balance sheet:

    - inventory or stock
    - each category of fixed assets
    - total fixed assets

    Compare your findings to the observations made in the early part of this chapter.

Notes and references

1. In 1906, Vilfredo Pareto observed that a few items in any group contribute the significant proportion of the entire group. At the time he was concerned that a few people in a country earned most of the income. The law of the significant few can be applied in many areas, including inventory. Pareto, V *Manual of Political Economy* (Kelley Augustus, 1969).
2. The 80/20 relationship implied in the rule is only intended as an indication of the size of the actual figures involved, as shown in Exhibit 10.10 and also in Exhibit 4.6.
3. The limitations of the EOQ model are further discussed in Schönenberger, RJ and Knod, EM *Operations Management and Continuous Improvement*, 5th edn (Irwin, Burr Ridge, 1994).
4. Special products and services are either ones that will not be repeated or the time gap between one order and the next is so long that investments (including inventory holding) will not be made.
5. Consignment stock is where inventory is held at a customer's site but is not invoiced until used. The customer houses and manages the physical inventory but typically the responsibility for replenishing what is used remains with the supplier.
6. Plossl, GW and Wight, OW *Production and Inventory Control: Principles and Techniques* (Englewood Cliffs, NJ: Prentice Hall, 1967), p. 190.

CHAPTER ELEVEN

The content and planning of this book: an overview of what is involved, what has been addressed so far and what is covered in this chapter

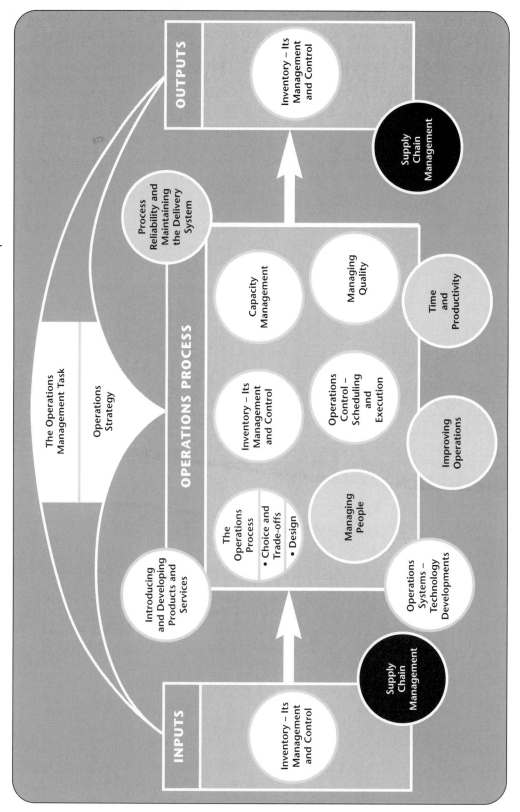

Managing the Supply Chain

Chapter overview

Companies rarely, if ever, own the resources and activities to make a product or provide a service from start to finish, including delivery to customers. Consequently what to make or provide internally and what to buy are key operations management decisions. Furthermore, whether a company makes or buys an element of the eventual product or service it sells, it needs to manage effectively the internal and external phases of the supply chain, both in terms of parts and as an integrated whole.

Increasingly businesses must recognize that they are at the centre or hub of networks of materials and information flows. These flows extend from the customer interface through operations to the building of relationships with suppliers. The operations role, however, is not just the integration and management of the parts of the supply chain but also the constant reviewing and alignment of these closely linked networks to better meet the changing needs of its markets and help achieve the sales revenue and profit goals of the organization. This chapter addresses these tasks and in particular covers the following:

■ The question, what is a supply chain? is addressed to provide clarity for you regarding the aspects covered in the chapter.

■ Managing the supply chain and what is entailed is overviewed and the synchronization of the business dimensions involved is explained.

■ To make or to buy and the reasons for making these choices are discussed in detail. This section also explains why these decisions are often made in practice together with a comprehensive review of the advantages and disadvantages of these alternatives.

■ Other options to making or buying are introduced, including joint ventures and non-equity-based collaborative arrangements.

■ The section on managing the supply chain gives a detailed review of the issues involved such as the impact of globalization, the need to incorporate uncertainty, customer/supplier dependence and different types of supplier relationship developments.

Chapter overview (cont'd)

- The origins and evolution of supply chains introduce the section on developing supply chains. This section also highlights the changes that need to be embraced by managers to secure these important developments. These include effective consumer response, the increasing use of IT, the impact of e-commerce and strategic partnering.

- The section on process tools to help in managing supply chains highlights sourcing as a core task and how to develop the supplier base including supplier selection.

- Distribution and transportation systems reviews the alternatives of rail, road, air freight, water and pipelines.

WHAT IS A SUPPLY CHAIN?

If you reflect on any purchase that you make there will be a series of steps between the origin of the product or service in question and your use or consumption of it. The series of steps involved are known as supply chains. Organizations will typically undertake some of these steps themselves while buying in earlier steps in the form of materials and services and contracting other organizations to undertake the later stages, for example distribution to the end-user in a retail outlet. Exhibit 11.1 provides an overview of a supply chain for a sandwich bar and a company making consumer products. As the exhibit footnotes highlight, the number of tier 1, tier 2 and tier 3 suppliers and customers shown is to illustrate the stages and interconnected characteristics of supply chains. As you can imagine, there will be a varying number of tiers of suppliers and customers, depending on the complexity of the product or service and a varying number of suppliers and customers in each tier that would reflect not only the complexity factor but also how much of a product or service was provided in the internal operations phase and how much was bought in from outside. This constitutes the make-or-buy decision, a factor discussed in a later section.

Most of the book is concerned with managing the internal operations process that transforms inputs into outputs (see Exhibit 1.1 and the examples given in Exhibit 1.2), while this chapter concerns managing those parts of a supply chain at each end of the internal operations process.

SUPPLY-CHAIN MANAGEMENT

The challenges of managing the supply chain are considerable. It requires a shift away from traditional functional models towards managing a set of integrated processes that encompass several key dimensions of a business as illustrated in Exhibit 11.2.

Exhibit 11.1   *An example to illustrate the supply chain for a high street sandwich bar and a manufacturer of consumer goods*

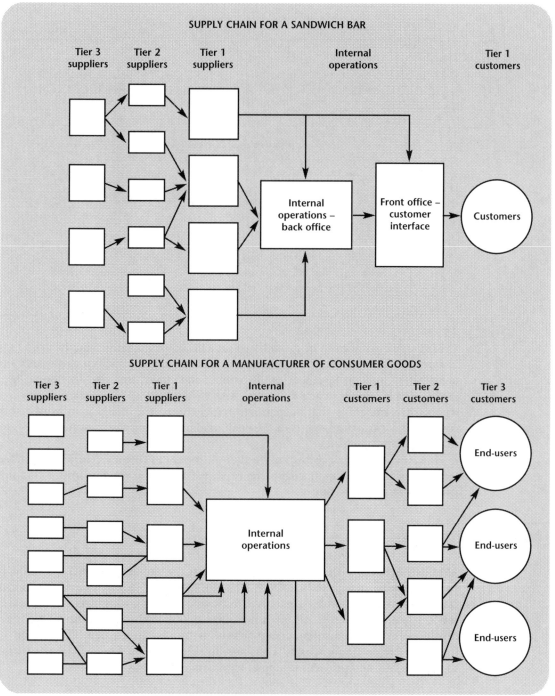

Notes

1. The above diagrams are not to scale and the number of customers and suppliers are illustrative.
2. For the manufacture of consumer goods example, the tier 1 customers would be wholesalers and the tier 2 customers would be retailers.

Exhibit 11.2 *Managing the supply chain and synchronizing the business dimensions involved*

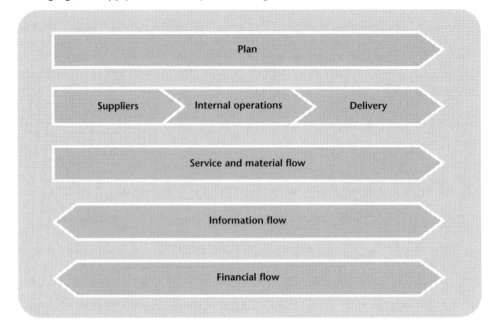

Developments need to be made based on a vision of the entire supply chain that, in turn, needs to reflect the market needs of the company as well as the efficient organization and management of all parts of the chain itself. By developing integrated supply chains, companies are able to respond to the opportunities and competitive pressures that increasingly characterize the markets in which they compete by restructuring parts of the chain and developing the information systems that underpin these parts.

However, before proceeding any further on the issues that are central to the effective management of supply chains, we need first to look at the reasons for choosing whether to make or to buy.

TO MAKE OR TO BUY

Although in theory every product or service can be provided internally or bought from outside, in reality the choice is far more restricted. In many instances, organizations have no real alternative than to outsource materials, components, products or services due to barrier of entry reasons such as not having the in-house technical capability or the unjustifiably high levels of process investment that would be involved. This section discusses the factors to be considered when deciding whether to make or buy and provides examples to illustrate decisions.

Retaining core technologies of the business

Most companies choose to keep in-house those processes that represent the core elements of their business. For example, companies that make their own products will invariably retain in-house the assembly-onward end of the production process. Similarly, many service firms wish to retain the process that constitutes the ultimate link with customers. For example, in the mid-1990s NatWest Bank pondered on the decision of whether or not to subcontract the service processing end of the retail and corporate banking sectors (for example, voucher and cheque processing and account management). In the past these back-office activities had always been an integral part of the in-house banking service, but now options to subcontract were available. In the end, NatWest decided to retain these activities in-house. One major factor in this decision was NatWest's desire to retain this stage in its service delivery system as it provided a direct link with its customers and the company did not wish to subcontract this essential element of the banking service.

Strategy considerations

Make-or-buy decisions need to be made within the strategic context of a business. The order-winners and qualifiers (for example, price, delivery reliability, delivery speed and quality conformance) that relate to a company's markets and that affect make-or-buy decisions need to be reflected in such actions and their outcomes. For example, Dell Computer Corporation developed the capability to assemble personal computers quickly in response to customers' orders, but found that this potentially competitive dimension was constrained by component suppliers' long lead times. However, other companies alert to key market-related issues incorporate these into their make-or-buy and sourcing decisions. For example, Lego, the privately owned Danish manufacturer of building kits and other toys has for years concentrated its production in Europe and the USA, arguing that this best satisfies its design and quality conformance requirements. And Lego is not alone in basing decisions on strategic rather than cost alone factors. For example, Motorola's decision to set up cellular phone production in Germany and Benetton's decision not to source garments in the Asian Pacific but to retail local suppliers that would meet the fast response needs of its supply chain, a critical supporting factor for its fashion-based marketplace.

A key factor then is how current and future positions on the make-or-buy continuum impact operations' ability to support those market criteria for which it is solely or jointly responsible. Similarly, issues concerning relevant process and product technologies need to be considered as explained in the last section.

Whether or not a company makes in-house, supply-chain performance regarding relevant order-winners and qualifiers will directly impact a company's ability to retain customers, grow share and make money. The issues involved will be addressed in detail in the later section on managing the supply chain where the fundamental nature of this decision is clearly highlighted, fully discussed and appropriately illustrated.

Impact of products/service and process technologies on span of process

The earlier sections highlighted situations where companies retained relevant product, service or process technologies. In cases where there is a significant increase in a related product or service technology the very opposite can happen. Where a company applies new technology developments to its existing products or services or on the introduction of new, if similar, products or services into its current range, it may find itself without the in-house capability to meet all of the new and more complex technology requirements. The result is that it buys in the technology in the form of components or materials for products and the expertise in the form of customer or information processing for services.

Products and service volumes

Companies faced with sets of demands for products and services that have different volume levels may consider buying out one set of demands for which it may not wish to develop the in-house process. Examples of this include a manufacturer of engine parts for agricultural and diesel trucks. When the low volume spares demand in a product's life cycle was reached the company increasingly outsourced the components involved. Similarly, an upmarket ladies' clothes outlet undertakes minor garment changes to meet customers' needs, whereas all the more complex modifications to adjust a garment to the specific size requirements of a customer are sourced from outside specialists.

The globalization of world trade

Trade barriers across much of the world have declined sharply. It is estimated, for example, that the average tariff by 1990 stood at 7 per cent or less than one-fifth of the level in 1960. This has made global manufacturing more commercially feasible. One outcome is the reduced need for many overseas plants. Markets that previously demanded local production facilities because of high tariff levels can now be supplied by imports. A good example of this is the Australian automotive sector. In the ten years to 1997, tariffs on imported cars dropped from 57.5 to 22.5 per cent, while imported cars rose from 15 to about 50 per cent of the market.[1] Domestic car plants (for example Nissan) have already started to close.

THE REALITY OF MAKE-OR-BUY DECISIONS

The previous sections identified some of the principal reasons that may form the basis of make-or-buy decisions. In reality, many companies approach this critical task and base the strategic decision involved on reasons that are less rational and seldom sound. The more common of these are as follows.

History – continuing yesterday's decisions

Make-or-buy decisions taken at one moment in time are often not reconsidered at a later date. Inertia, a reluctance to add additional executive tasks and avoiding possible short-term problems militate against taking appropriate reviews. Once made, make-or-buy decisions often remain unchallenged.

The dominance of cost and technology arguments

The format used to address the question whether to make or buy is typically centred on the issues of technology and cost. The initial consideration is whether or not a company has the process technology to make a component or product. Where the technical capability is not already in-house, the automatic response is often to buy from outside.

Where process technology is not a barrier, the next consideration is the cost of provision. While a most important dimension in itself, a make-or-buy decision taken without considering the requirements of markets and corresponding order-winners and qualifiers such as delivery speed, quality conformance, ability to ramp up and deliver on time, will lead to inappropriate conclusions and have a potentially damaging impact on a firm's short-term, let alone long-term, strategic position.

ADVANTAGES AND DISADVANTAGES OF MAKING AND BUYING

The previous sections introduced some of the important perspectives, issues and context concerning make-or-buy decisions. These next sections outline the benefits of making or delivering internally and also the advantages and disadvantages of outsourcing.

Benefits of vertical integration or making or providing more in-house

All make-or-buy decisions bring a mix of internal or external benefits and costs. In particular, decisions on vertical integration (or making or providing more in-house) offer a company a number of inherent competitive advantages that are linked to increased knowledge of markets and technology, improved control over its environment and increased opportunity to support the characteristics of its markets. These include:

■ **Improved market intelligence** – this increases a company's ability to forecast more accurately trends concerning key aspects of a business from demand patterns to cost changes.

■ **More readily available technological innovations and options** – this enables companies to share technology initiatives, increase opportunities for collaboration and facilitates the transfer of experience within the one organization or between groups of companies.

■ **Increased control over relevant aspects of a firm's competitive environment** – these opportunities can take the form of backward integration to reduce dependency on suppliers and forward integration to help gain market penetration or acceptance.

■ **The provision of low-cost opportunities** – this is accomplished by generating internal demand and thereby contributing to high volume requirements and their associated low-cost potential. Japanese companies such as Fujitsu, Hitachi, Mitsubishi, NEC and Toshiba have progressively outcompeted their competitors (particularly their US rivals) partly through the high level of integration that characterizes their businesses. The highly integrated Japanese semiconductor manufacturers are able to make their products at substantially lower costs than their competitors elsewhere in the world. One key reason for this is the high volume base created by internal corporate demand. These Japanese giant zaibatsus make semiconductors along with everything else. The result is that Japan currently has 50 per cent of the world semiconductor market.

Benefits of outsourcing

On the flip side of this key decision are the benefits to be gained from outsourcing. These primarily concern cash, costs and technology and include the following:

- **Freed resources** – buy decisions reduce or more often eliminate the associated resources necessary to provide the component, subassembly, final assembly service or technical capability involved. One result is that resources are freed, making funds available to be used elsewhere in a business.

- **Reduced operating costs** – with less being made internally the process technology requirements and associated support are reduced together with the management and control tasks that typically accompany operations.

- **Easier to control costs** – with buy decisions, the dimension of cost control is simplified to one of a supplier's unit price. Although contract negotiations demand their own set of skills, the task of cost control for the materials, components, subassemblies or assemblies involved is, in itself, simplified.

- **Superior design** – suppliers can often provide superior designs or improved specification of services than organizations can using their own internal resources. Examples include car radio specialists and bakers supplying rolls and croissants to restaurants.

- **Market perception of sound design** – purchasing from suppliers renowned for providing high specification items can lead customers into attributing a similar view of high specification levels to a company's own products and services. For example, microcomputer users purchase small manufacturers' products in part based on the knowledge that they are assembled using components from the world's best suppliers such as Intel and Sony.

- **Access to capacity** – meeting demand surges or known peaks in demand within certain markets is often made easier by being able to access suppliers' capacity. Within limits companies can use suppliers' operations processes and other elements of their supply chains as alternatives to holding excess capacity, increasing capacity in the short term through overtime working and carrying inventory.

- **Up-to-date technology** – where a supplier's specialist capacities are accompanied by high volumes, investment in more recent technologies and operations capabilities is justified. Conversely, suppliers' customers will also reduce the risk of having underused technical investments and being exposed to the likelihood of out-of-date technologies.

- **Access to world-class capabilities** – purchasing from selected vendors creates the opportunity to source from potentially world-class capabilities. It gives access to the technologies and expertise that make up a provider's primary business.

- **Increased focus on own core tasks** – the reverse side of the last point, it allows a company to increase its attention, in terms of development time and investment, on its own primary business and associated core tasks.

Disadvantages of outsourcing

To some extent the disadvantages of outsourcing are the inverse of the benefits discussed in the last section and include:

- **May lose control of important capabilities** – outsourcing brings with it the possibility of losing control of key capabilities. For example, dimensions such as quality conformance, delivery speed and delivery reliability are now, in part, within the processes and systems of suppliers. Managing the whole supply chain, as discussed later, becomes an increasingly important priority for the operations function.

1

Fender International, the US-based manu-facturer of world-famous electric guitars such as Stratocaster, Squier and Guild, set an objective to double market share in Europe, the Middle East and Africa. Part of its strategy to achieve this was to commit to a 'positive retailer experience' that included a condition that when a retailer took a guitar out of its box it must be playable. Whereas this requirement was already being met in the USA, the distribution networks and multi-carrier deliveries to 22 countries in Europe and a further 10 in the Middle East and Africa seemed an insurmountable obstacle. Discus-sions between Fender International and UPS Worldwide Logistics overcame all that. Operations are now centred in the UPS European Distribution Centre at Roermond in the Netherlands, where Fender guitars are received from manufacturing sites around the world and then tuned up by professional and amateur musicians listening in through a small amplifier prior to final distribution. All guitars from standard models to some of the most expensive and élite guitars in the world are now inspected by players before being sent to customers. UPS also handles the return of damaged guitars for repair and the central facility manages inventory for the whole region. This has, in turn, led to lower inventories in the whole supply chain, shorter distribution lead times and enabled Fender to get closer to distributors, retailers and customers. One unexpected outcome is that many distributors are ordering products that they never ordered before.

Case example questions

1.1 What was the significance for Fender International of the guitar tuning provision offered by UPS?

1.2 Why do you think distributors are now ordering products that they never ordered before?

■ **Reversibility** – the decision to subcontract is invariably irreversible. This is partly due to a reluctance to reconsider and then change direction on previous outsourcing decisions coupled with the stepped nature of such a change in terms of buying in technical capability and expertise from a zero base.

■ **New management skills** – managing a supply chain requires different, and often more demanding, skills than those to handle the in-house operations process. Often, and particularly in the past, purchasing and related functions within a busi-ness have been allocated Cinderella status with corresponding levels of resource and management talent. Integrating the essential links within a supply network requires skills of a high order to secure the essential contribution to meeting the needs of a firm's markets.

ALTERNATIVES TO THE MAKE-OR-BUY OPTION

The discussion so far has implied that the choices on offer to companies must involve an ownership or non-ownership option. Either organizations invest in operations capabilities or they outsource their requirements. However, where greater control is considered necessary companies should include the following alternatives in their list of options:

Exhibit 11.3   *Responses to the question 'Are joint ventures a viable alternative?'[2]*

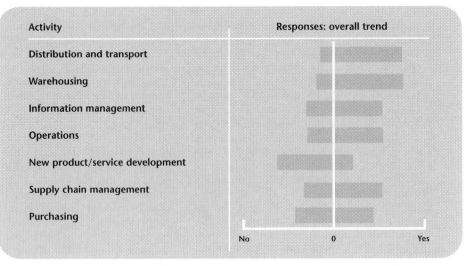

Joint ventures

Companies often have to exploit opportunities particularly in areas such as applied technology and research. Where two or more organizations have similar needs and can benefit from combining, a joint venture is a sensible alternative.

Joint ventures are separate entities sponsored by two or more actively involved organizations. Because joint ventures draw on the strengths of their owners, they have the potential to tap into the synergy in such a relationship and the improved competitive abilities that should accrue. Since the late 1970s, the number of joint ventures has increased substantially particularly in the communication systems, IT and service sectors. As Exhibit 11.3 shows most companies see joint ventures as a viable alternative and one that, in most businesses, will increase.

Joint ventures should not be seen or used as a convenient means of hiding weaknesses. If used prudently, such ventures can create internal strengths. They can be resource-aggregating and resource-sharing mechanisms, allowing sponsoring firms to concentrate resources where they possess the greatest strengths. Exhibit 11.4 provides a list of reasons for forming joint ventures that have been classified into operational and strategic advantages. As you will see from this list, joint ventures not only share investment but can provide direction and help create fresh opportunities.

Non-equity-based collaboration

Companies unwilling or unable to cope with joint venture arrangements can resort to an appropriate form of non-equity-based collaboration to meet their needs. These collaborations provide the means of establishing co-operative working arrangements that need a long-term base if the collaboration is to yield meaningful and useful results. Such arrangements include:

■ Research and development consortia to enhance innovation and exploit results.
■ Cross-marketing arrangements to provide opportunities such as widening product and service offerings and sharing distribution channels.

Exhibit 11.4   *Reasons for forming joint ventures*[3]

	Advantages

Strategic	■ Strengthen current strategic position:
	  – pioneer developments into new segments
	  – rationalize existing segments
	
	■ Pre-empt competitors:
	  – facilitate access to new markets and customers
	  – support market share growth
	  – gain access to global markets
	
	■ Augment current strategic position:
	  – create and develop synergies
	  – technology and skill transfers
	
	■ Widens product/service range

Operational	■ Share investment and risk
	
	■ Process capacity sharing:
	  – increased utilization
	  – avoids process/skill duplication
	
	■ Sharing facilities in other parts of the supply chain; for example, distribution channels and outlets
	
	■ Increases technological know-how by:
	  – facilitating information exchange
	  – potentially creates critical mass in areas such as research and development
	  – broadens expertise for example in IT systems
	
	■ Help retain key staff:
	  – increased job scope
	  – improved job opportunities

▓ Cross-operations agreements to share capacity especially in peak demand times, provide vertical integration opportunities and transfer technical know-how in areas such as IT systems.

▓ Joint purchasing activities to enhance buying power.

▓ Joint provision of other support facilities including staff and executive development and recruitment.

MANAGING THE SUPPLY CHAIN

The make-or-buy decision is not only critical in itself but it also governs the size and nature of the supply chain and the resulting management tasks. However, whether a company makes or buys the need to effectively manage the whole supply chain has increasingly been recognized as a key executive role and one that directly impacts a company's ability to compete in its chosen markets. The task of managing the in-house or internal phase of the chain is addressed throughout this book. This chapter deals with the key issues and approaches that relate to managing the external parts of the supply chain.

The concept of a totally integrated supply chain – from material producer through to end customer – is bringing great changes to the way businesses operate. Increasingly companies no longer compete just with each other but rather they compete through their supply chains. To bring this about companies need a supply chain that is managed as an integrated whole to secure maximum support for the competitive factors in their markets and that is underpinned by responsive and adaptive systems and procedures. This, in turn, requires meaningful collaboration and fuller relationships to provide the essential basis for co-operation and joint developments.

SUPPLY-CHAIN MANAGEMENT ISSUES

In the 1980s companies turned their attention to fixing their operations problems, but few addressed total supply-chain costs and other dimensions such as lead times. By the early 1990s firms started to realize the need to shift emphasis. With shortening product and service life cycles, more customer choice and reducing lead times set

Exhibit 11.5   *Outsourcing in the supply chain continues to grow[4]*

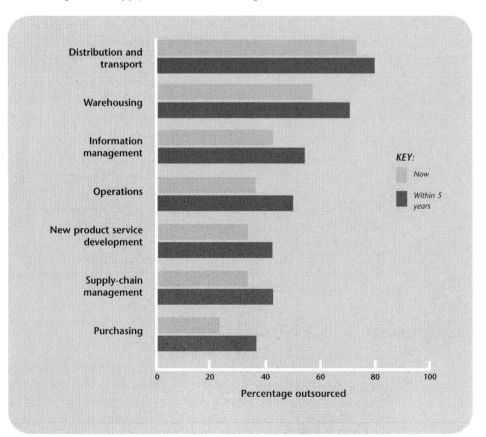

within the context of growing world competition, it became essential to review the supply chain as a whole, identify opportunities and manage these improvements. As most companies expect outsourcing to increase in future years (see Exhibit 11.5) then the need to manage the supply chain effectively has to be high on the corporate agenda. Whether you make or buy the responsibility for managing the whole chain can no longer be ignored as often in the past. Some of the key management issues involved are now discussed.

Globalization

With trade barriers easing, markets opening up and technology developments facilitating access to markets, the globalization of business activity has accelerated. Two key issues result from this – a widening choice of suppliers and the need to manage the global supply chain that emerges.

The growing manufacturing base of regions and countries such as Eastern Europe, the Far East, Mexico and South America has received high exposure. Similarly, the growing IT capability of countries such as India and the availability of satellite communications allows the outsourcing of data processing and computer programming even where meeting short lead times is essential.

There is an increasing emphasis on global capability. In order to take full advantage of this opportunity companies need to manage the processes and interfaces involved. It is essential to avoid the scenario of gaining advantage in one phase of a supply chain and losing the benefits in the next. Key to this is globalizing total customer relations from design through logistics to the end-user.

Incorporating uncertainty

Today's markets are characterized by shortening product and service life cycles and stiffening requirements for all aspects of customer service. Against this background, large companies are characterized by complexity as clearly illustrated by a review of the different markets they serve, the ever-widening product or service range provided and the multiple suppliers of materials, parts and services.

The real management problem within this complex network is, however, the uncertainty that characterizes it. But many companies still treat this task as if it were predictable. The planning and scheduling systems inadequately incorporate demand uncertainty. They are designed as if certainty rather than uncertainty was the reality with which they had to cope. And, as today is increasingly less predictable than in the past, this leads to situations of unnecessary inventory and high obsolescence. To illustrate, data on the percentage of mark downs within US department and speciality stores is given in Exhibit 11.6. The levels since 1970 have risen dramatically.

Furthermore, all this is in the context, on the one hand, of IT developments such as electronic point-of-sale scanners that provide up-to-the-minute data on customer buying patterns and, on the other hand, manufacturing improvements concerning the production of smaller order sizes. But at the same time, the drive to meet customer requirements has typically widened product/service ranges dramatically even in industries that traditionally have not been considered fashion-driven. For example, the annual number of new product introductions in the US food industry rose from some 2000 in 1980 to about 20 000 in the mid-1990s.

Exhibit 11.6   *Rising level of mark downs in the retail sector*

Year	US department store mark downs as a percentage of dollar sales
1970	8
1989	17
1997	20

Source: Financial and operating results of department and speciality stores, National Retail Federation (USA).

But new product or service introductions have two adverse side effects:

■ Average life cycles are reduced that, in turn, shorten the relative duration of the more stable phase of demand in relation to the less certain initial and end phases.

■ Total demand is spread over more stock-keeping units (SKUs) leading to increased difficulty in forecasting sales for a larger number of items. (Stock-keeping unit is the phrase used by all products and services that have a different code number in a company's system.)

Overall the result is growing unpredictability that increases the need to manage each phase of the supply chain and the interface between them. As highlighted earlier, Dell Computer Corporation having shortened its own assembly lead times in response to the delivery speed requirements of its customers found itself constrained from meeting these needs by the long lead time of its component suppliers.

Customer/supplier dependence

The relationship between customers and suppliers is influenced by the level of dependency of the one with the other – see Exhibit 11.7. Where customers and suppliers are positioned will impact potential relationship options, as explained in the next section.

Types of supplier relation

Part of the make-or-buy decision is how best to structure relationships with suppliers. Customers can position themselves in a number of ways within the constraints of dimensions such as the 'dependence factor' introduced in the last section. Characteristics of these different types of supplier relationships are now reviewed.[5] Which one a company should choose needs to reflect the characteristics of the materials or components involved and of the marketplace in which a company operates.

■ **Trawling the market** – here suppliers are held are arm's length with a growing amount of business completed using computerized interaction. For example, General Electric (GE) in the USA is increasingly purchasing more components over the Internet where it posts details of parts electronically and prequalified vendors then quote for the contract. Here, there is little face-to-face interaction and the key order-winner is price. Delivery on time and quality conformance are qualifiers and form part of the listing prerequisites. Gains also include reduced processing costs – for example, GE quotes a 90 per cent reduction using this method of purchasing

Exhibit 11.7 *Customer/supplier dependence*

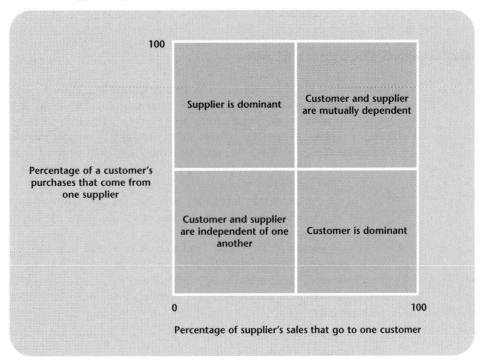

compared to traditional paperwork procedures. Finally, this phase may entail placing a significant amount of business with competitors.

■ **Ongoing relationships** – these involve establishing medium-term contracts with suppliers, developing relations in terms of information sharing and require sound management by customers.

■ **Partnerships** – involve long-term contracts characterized by the extensive sharing of information and increased trust. For example, since 1988 the US car maker Chrysler's average contract length with suppliers has more than doubled.

■ **Strategic alliances** – the trend in sourcing is towards strategic alliances that are characterized by the increased depth and breadth of the whole customer/supplier relationship. A prerequisite of more co-operative relationships is a dramatic reduction in the supplier base and a recognition by customers of the fact that their costs, quality conformance levels and lead times are partly within the processes of their suppliers. For example, Xerox has reduced its suppliers from over 5000 to about 400, while Chrysler in the mid-1990s saved more than $0.5bn from supplier-generated ideas.

Strategic alliances are marked by long timescales, extensive sharing of information, increased trust, joint development of products and processes and the intent to work together over an extended period. Boeing has strategic alliances with GE, Rolls-Royce and Pratt & Whitney, partly to reduce the financial risk of new aeroplane programmes and partly to cope with the complex technical interfaces between engines and airframes that have to be designed in conjunction with each other.

■ **Backward integration** – the final step is to change from relationship to ownership. This leads to the full sharing of information and the transfer of goals and culture.

DEVELOPING THE SUPPLY CHAIN

The goal of supply chain management is to link the market, distribution channel, operations process and supplier base such that customers' needs are better met at lower costs. As highlighted earlier, while many companies began fixing their operations problems from the early to mid-1980s, few addressed the total cost of ownership. By the early 1990s, progressive companies had begun to realize the need to refocus from 'fixing' manufacturing to addressing how to better manage the supply chain, a fact confirmed by a 1996 European-based survey. This identified that 88 per cent of the companies reviewed had been carrying out significant overhauls of supply chains and saw supply chain management as the focus for improvement in their overall performance.[6]

But we should have learned from history that little ever changes. In 1929 Ralph Borsodi observed that in the '50 years between 1870 and 1920 the cost of distributing necessities and luxuries had nearly trebled, while production costs had come down by one fifth… what we are saving in production we are losing in distribution'.[7] The same scenario exists today.

Origins and evolution of supply chains

The origin of organizations in the twenty-first century is rooted in functional management and control with the subsequent result of split responsibilities. The outcome is fragmented supply chains with an emphasis on vertical rather than horizontal processes as illustrated in Exhibit 11.8.

For most companies, developing a supply chain is a multi-phased task. It starts with integrating the steps within the internal supply chain as illustrated in Exhibit 11.9.

Exhibit 11.8 *Phase 1 – typical, initial position of functionally fragmented supply chains with built-in delays/inventory, vertical reporting structures and systems, and the separation of suppliers, operations and customers*

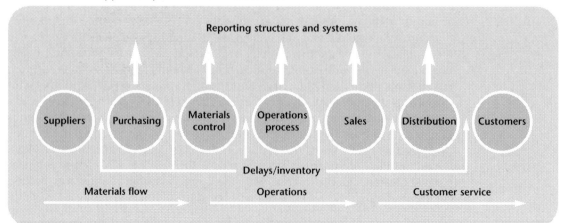

Exhibit 11.9   *Phase 2 – integration of the supply chain activities within a business*

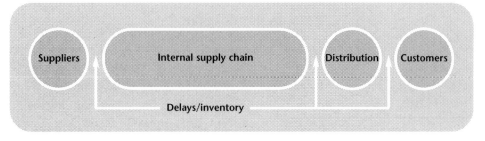

This internal co-ordination emphasizes the horizontal nature of the processes inherent in the basic tasks of procurement through to finished goods provision and forges co-operation between the steps to create an integrated whole and the opportunity to reduce costs and delays on the one hand and improve responsiveness to customer needs on the other.

The next step concerns co-ordinating activities between businesses. As shown in Exhibit 11.10 this stage involves recognizing additional facets within the supply chain (for example, tier 1 and tier 2 suppliers and stages in the distribution channel) in order to ensure that these form part of the collaborative development between supply chain partners.

The final phase is to synchronize the planning and execution of activities across the supply chain (see Exhibit 11.11). This requires partnership and strategic alliance arrangements that will include the transfer and access of data between businesses from design through to order fulfillment, call-offs and delivery schedules. Traditional roles and responsibilities will change dramatically with suppliers at times taking responsibility for design on the one hand through to the internal supply chain deciding how much and when to ship goods to customers, on the other – refer back to Exhibit 11.2.

The principles underlying these changes have their origins in the recognition that the whole and not solely the internal phase of a supply chain is the basis for today's competition. Given the extent and nature of the support for markets that is provided by operations then aligning the supply chain provision with the requirements of agreed markets needs to be a central feature of strategy implementation. Key issues that result include:

■ **Overcoming the barriers to integration** – functions within organizations and organizations themselves create barriers to integration. Viewing the supply chain as

Exhibit 11.10   *Phase 3 – collaboration across the supply chain by co-ordinating activities between businesses*

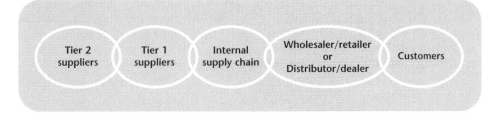

Exhibit 11.11 *Phase 4 – the synchronized and real-time planning and execution of activities across the supply chain*

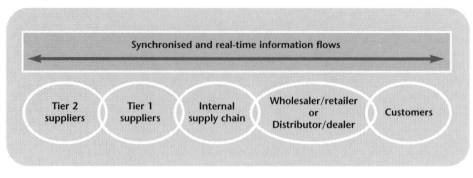

a whole is a prerequisite for rethinking how best to provide market support through the entire supply chain and overcoming these inherent obstacles.

■ **Responding to short lead time** – delivery speed is an order-winner or qualifier in many of today's markets. Customers are seeking to reduce lead times and the strategic support of suppliers has to match these quick response demands. To do this reliably requires developing lean logistics and managing the supply chain as an integrated whole. A study completed by Ernst & Young and the University of Tennessee in the late 1990s showed that with outsourcing average order cycle times fell from 6.3 to 3.5 days.[8]

■ **Eliminating costs** – an integrated approach lowers costs by reducing inventory, simplifying procedures, eliminating duplication and other non-value-added activities together with associated overheads. Viewing the supply chain as a whole enables processes and procedures to be structured with the associated gains of reduced time and cost. In the same Ernst & Young and University of Tennessee study[8] outsourcing in participating businesses led to average logistics costs and average logistic assets falling by 7.8 and 21.6 per cent respectively.

■ **Moving information, not inventory and delays** – non-integrated approaches have built-in delays comprising time and inventory. By moving information, delays are reduced and subsequent parts of the chain can match real-time needs rather than using inventory to provide against uncertainty and the unknown.

One parallel to lean supply chain management is provided by the revolutionary changes brought to high peak climbing by Reinhold Messner. As the example below explains, the 'direct alpine approach' he introduced changed the 'conventional mountaineering strategy' (one based on 'massive amounts of support including extra oxygen') to one using 'little equipment and no oxygen support to reach the top'. Messner argued that under the conventional approach, the slowest man set the pace, whereas his goal was 'speed of execution' – the final assault was made 'by himself, or with one other person in a single day'.

2

Reinhold Messner, the Italian climber, is one of the great sports heroes of Europe. His claim to fame is not so much that he climbed all 14 of the world's highest peaks, his primary achievement is that he introduced a totally new way of climbing – the direct alpine approach – which uses little equipment and no oxygen support to reach the top.

Conventional mountaineering strategy is based on massive amounts of support, including extra oxygen, thought essential for climbs over 25 000 feet. Men such as Sir Edmund Hillary and Chris Bonington relied on hundreds of guides who carried food, oxygen and other supplies; an American expedition to climb Everest in 1963 included 900 porters trudging up the mountain with 300 tons of equipment.

Messner argues that under this strategy, the slowest man sets the pace. His goal is speed of execution. Although assisted by guides up the base of the mountain, Messner usually makes the final assault by himself, or with one other person, in a single day. He scaled the north face of Everest solo, without oxygen – one of the most severe mountaineering challenges ever attempted.[9]

ASPECTS OF CHANGE

Underpinning the developments set out in the last section are a number of changes that need to be secured if the desired supply chain management improvements are to be realized. The most important of these changes are now discussed.

Effective consumer response

There is more to supply chain management than hard-nosed procurement and tight controls over inventory levels. While effectively managing the supply chain concerns eliminating delays and reducing resources along the way, the orientation of such improvements needs to be towards more effective consumer response where market requirements, and not traditional dimensions such as cost reduction, underpin priorities and direction.

The result fosters closer relations with fewer suppliers. The greatest challenge is working both the internal and external dimensions of the chain in line with the needs of agreed markets. The key to making this happen is attitude and information, the topics of the next two sections.

Changes in attitude

Relationships with suppliers have a history where co-operation was not the way in which customers behaved. Absolute control over aspects such as design and scheduling, pitting suppliers against each other and ruling by threat and fear are being abandoned in favour of long-term relationships often with single suppliers. Companies are also bringing suppliers on board much earlier in the design process, seeking technical help and contributions and even inviting suppliers to help in identifying future products and services.

To underpin these changes customers are reviewing the way they handle suppliers and the level of co-operation involved. The trend towards greater co-operation goes hand in hand with a more proactive style as illustrated in Exhibit 11.12.

Increasing use of IT

Since the early 1960s four major stepped changes in information technology developments have transformed the way that companies have conducted business, and each wave of technology has radically altered the supply chain that links suppliers through to end-users.

Exhibit 11.12 *Phases in changing customer attitudes to suppliers*

	Changing customer attitudes to suppliers
Threat and fear	Traditional stance. Perceptions based upon: ■ customer dominates the relationship with suppliers ■ suppliers respond to demands ■ customers pitted against each other ■ underpinned by the threat of the purchases being given to other suppliers on the one hand and a supplier's fear of losing the contract on the other
Reward	First steps towards co-operation and moving from a reactive to a proactive stance. Characterized by elements such as: ■ fewer suppliers ■ long-term contracts ■ customer is proactive in building a relationship with suppliers
Collaborate	Progressive move towards fuller and more co-operative relationships the pace of which is set predominately by the customer. Evolution through a series of steps such as: ■ customer identifies improvements that a supplier can make ■ customer provides support and resources (for example, technical capability) to undertake improvements ■ customer gives actual help to improve suppliers' capabilities including training a supplier's staff ■ customer starts to take into account the processes of its suppliers when designing products and services so as to help them improve their support ■ customer focuses attention on tier 2 suppliers as a source of improving tier 1 suppliers' support (see Exhibit 11.10)
Integrate and synchronize	The final step is to integrate activities achieving benefits typically associated with ownership – the concept of virtual ownership. Based upon mutual respect and trust these include suppliers' access to real-time information with customers harmonizing their suppliers' work and synchronizing their support. These changes range from: ■ access to design-related information and responsibility for product/service design ■ suppliers' responsibility for deciding when and how much to ship

The initial phase of information technology application was based on mainframe computers, began in the early 1960s and continued to be the dominant technology until the early 1970s. Business applications included material requirements planning and manufacturing resource planning (MRPI and MRPII respectively). These enabled companies to standardize and systemize the day-to-day tasks in operations and parts of the supply chain. As a result, companies developed functional expertise supported by systems design based on the tasks of relevant functions.

The second phase was based on personal computers (PCs) that began in the 1970s and continued well into the 1980s. PC applications like word processors, spreadsheets and presentation software facilitated communication across functional boundaries. PCs also resulted in the power of computing being in the hands of employees, and businesses built on this opportunity by focusing on the development of cross-functional processes that brought benefits that were both functional and overall business in origin.

The third phase of computer-based IT applications is based on network computing. Starting in the mid-1980s it continues to have a dominant influence on how companies are managed and business is conducted. Network computing, customer/supplier applications, electronic data interchange (EDI), point-of-sale response and other forms of electronic mail are reducing the costs of handling information and transactions while speeding up information exchange that allows real-time systems and responses to be developed while leveraging the efficiencies of functional expertise (phase 1) and cross-functional business processes (phase 2).

Case examples

3

Caterpillar, the giant US earth-moving equipment manufacturer, has developed electronically based systems that identify ahead of time when equipment needs servicing. An electronic message is relayed to the Caterpillar centre which, in turn, informs the local dealer and sends the necessary parts to complete the servicing requirement. Dealers agree appropriate dates with customers and, when the parts are received, complete the specified work.

4

GAP, a US-based apparel company, is currently achieving 14 inventory turns a year while also being able to change the stockholding in all its outlets 13 times per year and on the same day. The data requirements and real-time systems that underpin these arrangements include accurate inventory data, electronic point of sale (EPOS) facilities and synchronized logistics.

The fourth phase is e-commerce based on the Internet and world wide web. Providing a universal infrastructure, the Internet facilitates the interchange of information between businesses by not only reinforcing existing trends of co-operation but also helping companies to consider their supply chains as a whole and one in which their role is to manage and orchestrate process priorities and performance. By fostering better communication and interchange of information between companies,

Case example　5

E-commerce presents some businesses with promising new opportunities, while posing a significant threat to those that ignore it. Many sectors have seen the increasing and competitive impact of the Internet. For those ready to adapt to the new technology it represents an opportunity to rethink all aspects of order fulfilment, from order entry to distribution. One company that is building on its current history of excellent supply-chain management is Dell Computer Corporation. Dell uses supply-chain management to continuously improve its direct model that is underpinned by sound supply-chain integration as follows:

- Dell purchases components on a just-in-time (JIT) basis thus benefiting from the latest (that is lowest) component prices.

- Dell only makes to order – no resources are committed until a customer order is received.

- By holding little inventory Dell is able to respond to component developments quickly and without incurring inventory losses through obsolescence.

- Short component lead times also allow Dell to meet the delivery speed characteristics of its market with minimum inventory investment.

Dell continues to develop and improve the capabilities of its supply chain in several ways. For example, by 1999 the Dell web site was generating daily revenues of more than $14m, an increase from about $2m at the start of 1998. The web site makes on-line ordering quick and convenient by allowing customers to specify the product features they want, and by instantly giving them a price quote.

In the corporate sales market Dell has also created 'Premier Pages' that are web sites dedicated to corporate clients that can be accessed by a client's authorized employees to research, configure and price PCs before purchase. Each web site page holds client-specific data such as preferred configurations and prices. The development increases order accuracy and simplifies Dell's order-entry processes. The cost of buying PCs is greatly reduced. For example, in 1999 the Ford Motor Company estimated that Premier Pages had saved it about $2m.

Case example questions

5.1　Explain how Dell integrates its supply chain.

5.2　How does the Dell web site feature in these integrative developments?

5.3　How was the Ford Motor Company able to save $2m in 1999 by using Dell's Premier Pages?

this phase enables fully integrated processes between businesses, not only customers to suppliers but also between suppliers.

One of the lasting effects of these technology applications is that they have facilitated the breakdown of barriers from cross-individuals to cross-corporations – see Exhibit 11.13.

The rapid growth of e-commerce has, however, brought with it some concerns that originate both from the delivery system that underpins the system and from the speed of its use within commercial activities and transactions:

Exhibit 11.13   *The evolving role of IT in managing a supply chain*

Phase	Aspects of change
1. Cross-individuals	Broke down barriers between functional experts themselves and between these and the executives responsible for managing core parts of a business, particularly operations
2. Cross-functional	Facilitated links between functions by requiring and helping the interchange between different parts of the same business
3. Cross-businesses	Impact on the way companies conduct business by removing barriers within an organization and between parts of the immediate supply chain
4. Cross-corporate	Continued the cross-corporate changes by facilitating co-operation of businesses within a supply chain including tier 2 suppliers

■ **Fraud** – the annual report of the Fraud Advisory Panel (the UK Government's Serious Fraud Office) estimated that fraud could be costing £5bn a year and is likely to increase. US data from the National Consumers' League supported this trend. Its reports showed that incidents of Internet fraud had increased from 1280 in 1997 to 7750 in 1998.

While the cartoon provided as Exhibit 11.14 depicts the humorous side of fraud (but no doubt equally concerning if you were the parent!), the implications are suitably highlighted.

■ **Vulnerability** – the level and nature of vulnerable outcomes inherent in the growing use of the Internet are being highlighted in a series of incidents throughout the world. Richard Tomlinson's (the former British Intelligence Officer) disclosure of British Secret Service names is well exposed in Exhibit 11.15.

■ **Focusing on non-value-added activities** – increasingly companies have focused attention on minimizing non-value-added activities while providing information and communication tools that allow employees to focus on the value-added and strategic activities within a business. As firms reduce non-value-added activity they redirect those newly released resources to the value-added and strategic dimensions of their business. For example, companies are increasingly using electronic intranet catalogues that enable office staff (the actual consumer) to order non-operations goods (for example, office supplies and computer software) directly from agreed suppliers. Not only does this break down barriers but also eliminates non-value-added activities such as data re-entry and checking, thus allowing more time for purchasing staff to focus on their value-added activities such as developing supplier relations and contract negotiations.

Strategic partnering

The need to be more competitive has led to a major drive to partner with other companies in the supply chain. As stressed in the earlier section on 'Changes in atti-tudes', customer/supplier relations continue to undergo major changes where the

Exhibit 11.14 *A more humorous look at fraud on the Internet*

© Roger Beale

Exhibit 11.15 *A vulnerable side of the Internet!*

© Roger Beale

goal is to synchronize activities to the point where virtual integration is achieved (see Exhibit 11.12).

The extent to which this can be secured is not only constrained by the parties involved but also by the stage in a sector's evolution. For example, in the early days of the computing industry the major players had no option but to build the infrastructure necessary to produce all the components and parts a computer needed. They had little choice. As the industry grew, more specialized companies developed to produce specific components. This allowed new entrants a choice. As Michael Dell (founder of Dell Computers) explained, 'as a new start-up, Dell couldn't afford to create every piece of the value chain. But more to the point, why should we want to? We concluded we'd be better off leveraging the investments others have made and focusing on delivering solutions and systems to customers... It's a pretty simple strategy', Michael Dell continued, 'but at the time it went against the dominant "engineering-centric" view of the industry. The IBMs, Compaqs and HPs subscribed to a "we-have-to-develop-everything" view of the world. If you weren't doing component assembly you weren't a real computer company.'[10]

Strategic partnering is based on a conscious decision that sees its ultimate goal as virtual integration. This seeks to incorporate other parts of the supply chain as if they are part of one's own business – a long way from the not uncommon stance of outsourcing parts of a business that were, in fact, problem areas that a company could not fix.

On the delivery end of the chain, companies work with their customers to better understand their needs. In some partnerships, retail stores are sharing point-of-sale data to help suppliers better meet market trends and changes. On the sourcing end of the chain, suppliers are delivering more frequently, keeping consignment stock in a customer's warehouse (and only invoicing on use) and managing the replenishment cycle to reflect usage, while helping to optimize their own schedules. While the customer frees up resources, the supplier has longer-term customer commitment, a barrier from competition that reduces sales and marketing effort and provides firm data on which to plan and schedule operations and its own suppliers.

Case example   6

In 1989 Calyx and Corolla, a US-based company, pioneered the delivery of fresh cut flowers direct to customers from the growers. Using Federal Express (FedEx), customers' orders are relayed to one of only 25 suppliers (the flower growers) who assemble the chosen bouquet from one of 150 SKUs. Within the supply chain FedEx visit all suppliers to train their staff on the best ways to pack the flower arrangements and ensure that the delivery phase of the chain synchronizes with the work schedules and product availability of individual growers. Direct supply results in the flowers lasting nine to ten days longer than competitors' product offerings. For Calyx and Corolla, this not only results in a no-inventory arrangement but the delivery speed and quality conformance advantages allow the company to price its products at a 60 per cent premium. Sales revenues in the period 1992–98 have grown from $10m to $25m.

Case example questions

6.1 How has Calyx and Corolla synchronized its supply chain?

6.2 What advantages has the company gained from these developments?

PROCESS TOOLS WITHIN SUPPLY-CHAIN MANAGEMENT

So far we have addressed the important issues concerning whether to make or to buy and managing and developing the supply chain that results. This section now looks at some of the key tools used in managing the supply chain and addresses the key areas of suppliers and logistics.

Sourcing

Within the context of managing the supply chain, relations with suppliers will be critical and will raise some compelling managerial issues that need to be addressed and resolved. As emphasized throughout this chapter, managing operations entails the key component of the supply chain and a recognition that operations has to reach beyond its own capabilities and resources and look to suppliers to help add value to customers. Good suppliers then are more than providers of goods and services, but need to be recognized as an invaluable resource, making a direct contribution to an organization's success. Looking at supply chains creates the appropriate context for this to happen. Making it happen requires the necessary systems to be in place and appropriate action to be taken. The key elements involved are now discussed.

Developing the supplier base

An appropriate and adequate supplier base, like other functions within a company, is an essential resource. The trend towards fewer suppliers changes the emphasis to one where evaluation and selection are key dimensions and providing adequate supplier resources, while using significantly fewer suppliers (for example, Xerox reduced its supply base by over 90 per cent) allows the potential gains of smaller numbers to be realized.

This dimension of sourcing starts with a knowledge base of potential suppliers with current evaluations on performance. Sources of supplier information include:

- In-house supplier information files concerning material and service range, delivery reliability performance, quality conformance record, ability to handle long-term growth as well as short-term demand uplifts and an evaluation of the technical and managerial capabilities of key areas and executives.

- Supplier catalogues – a catalogue library helps promote general background information and highlight potential sources of relevant materials and services.

- Trade registers, directories and journals – registers (for example Kompass Publications) provide not only technical but other important, general background on potential suppliers while trade journals give current information on suppliers that are specific to the technical areas that a journal covers.

- Trade exhibitions – provide opportunities to discuss general and specific sourcing dimensions with potential suppliers while assessing their technical and professional offerings.

- Professional colleagues – purchasing executives often use their professional colleagues whose judgement they respect both to suggest and assess possible suppliers based on their own experience.

Supplier selection – internal review mechanisms

While purchasing and supply executives have the ultimate responsibility for supplier selection, companies approach this task in a number of ways. These include giving the task to the supply management team alone, using cross-functional teams and putting together commodity teams to source and manage a group of similar products or services. Cross-functional and commodity teams typically consist of buyers, process engineers or specialists and schedulers. The difference between these two is that while commodity teams tend to manage ongoing arrangements that cover a given range of services and products, cross-functional teams are often put together at specific times and tend to handle specific tasks.

Supplier selection – evaluation

From the long list of potential suppliers companies need to evaluate prospective providers. The dimensions that need to be considered in this evaluation process include:

- overall viability of the potential supplier organization particularly regarding its financial condition including credit ratings and resources to grow in the future

- review technical know-how to assess the ability of a supplier to meet the product or service specifications on the one hand, and its potential for matching or contributing to future technical changes on the other

- assess managerial capabilities and attitudes towards undertaking self-initiated developments and improvements, desire to meet customer needs and the willingness to move towards partnership arrangements over time

- evaluating operations helps assess technical capability and current capacity to support anticipated levels of demand and a supplier's plans to meet future growth

- a check on how well a supplier currently meets the relevant order-winners and qualifiers of its customers' markets will help provide valuable insights into its support for your own markets.

Supplier selection – process

When companies have established a short list of potential suppliers the next step is to decide which of these will be selected. The preliminary survey stage would have already checked on the points raised in the last section. Selecting which suppliers to work with now moves to a more in-depth phase where the dimensions covered in the last section are checked in the following ways.

Site visits

By visiting the facilities of potential suppliers the sourcing team can obtain first-hand information regarding the adequacy of key dimensions such as technical capabilities, operations capacity and management's technical know-how, attitude and orientation. Specific aspects to check include:

- attitude and stability of the top and middle management teams
- level of process and equipment investment

■ competence of the technical and operations management teams
■ morale of staff at all levels
■ willingness of a potential supplier to work with the buying organization and its top management's goals regarding the eventual level of customer/supplier relations
■ current major customers
■ internal measures used by the potential supplier to evaluate its own performance, appropriateness of the measures chosen and its actual performance over the last several months.

In addition, the degree of professionalism demonstrated by a potential supplier's team in handling the visit and the level of internal staff involved will help in assessing the overall calibre of the company's executives and the importance attached to the visit.

Checking specific capabilities

During this process, checks also need to be made to assess whether a potential supplier is able or, more importantly, has had experience in providing the capabilities that are specific to a customer's needs. These include:

■ Quality conformance – ISO 9000 registration and records together with any similar registrations with other customers.

■ JIT capability – experience in providing JIT schedules for customers.

■ Short-term capacity increases – the extent to which a potential supplier is able to increase capacity in the short term and an assessment of the approach to be adopted and a check on how feasible this support would be.

■ Inventory support – an evaluation of potential consignment inventory and customer-specific inventory arrangements that could be accommodated.

■ Future growth – the potential of the supplier to increase capacity to match anticipated growth in future demand and a check on the approach that would be followed and, where possible, an illustration of similar past or current support for other customers.

■ Technical support – the extent to which the potential supplier could liaise in the future on the technical aspects of the purchased items and services.

■ Partnering – both an attitude and feasibility check on how developments towards partnering in the future may evolve.

Selecting the supplier

In many instances, one prospective supplier is so obviously superior to the others on the short list that selection is a very simple decision. In other instances, however, the choice is not so clear-cut. In these instances a weighting system can greatly help in the decision process. Using such a weighting system calls for three tasks:

■ agreeing the selection criteria
■ weighting each criteria to reflect the level of importance in the selection process
■ rate each potential supplier on all the selection criteria.

Exhibit 11.16 *An illustration of the weighted-factor rating approach to supplier selection*

Factors		Weights		Potential suppliers			
				A	B	C	D
Order-winners and qualifiers	■ delivery on time	60		50	60	60	50
	■ delivery speed	80		40	40	70	50
	■ quality conformance	40	250	40	35	35	35
	■ price	30		30	30	20	30
	■ after-sales technical support	40		30	30	35	30
				(190)	(195)	(220)	(195)
Operations	■ current capacity	20		20	20	20	20
	■ ability to increase capacity in the short term	10	80	0	0	10	5
	■ meet long-term growth requirements	50		30	40	45	40
				(50)	(60)	(75)	(65)
Technical	■ level of technical staff provision	50		40	45	45	40
	■ staff technical know-how	30	100	25	25	30	25
	■ future contributions to developing products and services	20		10	10	15	15
				(75)	(80)	(90)	(90)
Corporate	■ managerial and financial standing of the organization	70	70	50	50	60	60
				(50)	(50)	(60)	(60)
Totals		**500**		**365**	**385**	**445**	**410**

Exhibit 11.16 provides an example of this approach. However, as you would imagine, the factors and the weightings shown in this illustration would need to reflect the particular requirements of specific supplier evaluations. Consequently, both the factors used and the weights awarded would change accordingly. In this example, the market-related dimension has been heavily weighted to reflect the key contribution of suppliers within the strategic role of operations.

Maintaining the supplier base

These last sections have addressed the tasks involved in developing the supplier base by selecting suppliers to meet the needs of a business. Another important dimension of sourcing concerns maintaining the existing supplier list. In many ways the procedures and checks used in supplier selection will form the basis of the evaluation process for existing suppliers. The critical difference between the two procedures is the ongoing relationship with a supplier, the first-hand knowledge of a supplier's performance and the opportunity to measure a supplier over time thus replacing estimates and opinions with hard data and facts.

What should be measured and evaluated will be similar to that provided in the Exhibit 11.16 illustration while again needing to reflect the particular requirements of each supplier. The ongoing relationship that exists, however, provides an opportunity to change the style and method of evaluation rather than what is measured. Key changes include:

■ Agree with the supplier the performance measures with an explanation of why and how they will be used.

■ Both customer and supplier need to keep records of performance and meet regularly to discuss trends and improvement opportunities. Keeping separate records will reveal any discrepancies, thereby allowing these differences to be identified and corrected, while the need for both parties to record performance keeps these dimensions at the top of their respective corporate agendas.

■ Regular meetings should not only cover current levels of performance but also provide an opportunity to inform each other of known or possible changes that could affect customer requirements or supplier performance.

DISTRIBUTION AND TRANSPORTATION SYSTEMS

Distribution is a key element in the management of a supply chain. For some manufacturing companies, distribution and transportation costs can be as high as 20 per cent of the total. For service companies involved in the distribution of retail items such as catalogue sales, the percentage of total costs can be even higher. In one year, LL Bean (the US-based merchant) despatches 11 million packages or an average of 650,000 each week. At peak times, the company fills a 40-foot trailer every 20 minutes.

Distribution and transportation costs depend largely on where a company is located relative to its customers and the means of transportation selected. Consequently, while distance is a factor so also is the transportation selection which reflects issues of lead time, volume and, for some businesses, the physical nature of the product. For example, oil and gas are typically transported using pipelines due to both the physical nature of the product and the volumes involved between one part of the supply chain and the next. Thus, oil from oil well and oil field to refinery will be piped, as will gas from extraction site to processing and distribution network. However, oil products such as petrol and diesel will be taken to petrol or gas stations by road tanker.

The five principal commercial modes of transportation are rail, road (trucking), water, air and pipeline. The options have different pricing structures and speed factors and the typical mix in a developed economy is shown in Exhibit 11.17. Note, however, that some of these relative positions would change if the distance travelled was lengthened or shortened.

Rail

Railways are best suited for transporting low-value, high-density, bulk products such as raw materials over long distances. Examples include coal, minerals and ores. Although fast between points, the total lead time for rail transportation is significantly lengthened by the before and after phases of the rail travel itself.

Exhibit 11.17 *Commercial modes of transportation compared on the dimensions of price, speed and percentage of goods moved*

Price per tonne/mile*	Low	Pipeline and water	Rail			Road	Air	High
Speed, door to door	Slow	Water	Rail	Road		Air	Pipeline	Fast
Per cent of total goods moved	High	Rail	Road		Pipeline	Water	Air	Low

Note

* Price per tonne mile = 1 tonne of freight carried 1 mile.

Road

Providing flexible point-to-point service and delivering small loads over short to long distances makes road transport the most used way of moving freight. In more developed economies, road haulage systems are extensive and the service provided is typically fast, reliable and less prone to damage than some alternatives. The growing use of articulated vehicles (in which the trailer detaches from the front, pulling unit) and containers allows vehicle loading to be completed while the front, pulling unit (and high investment part of a truck) can be used elsewhere.

With greater emphasis being placed on reducing inventory in a supply chain, the need for orders to be delivered on time and without damage is becoming essential. Carriers are now a critical link in supply chains and the need to match the short lead time, delivery reliability and quality conformance requirements are paramount.

Airfreight

Recently the number of airfreight carriers that carry relatively small packages (for example, UPS, Federal Express and DHL) has been increasing. Using both passenger and airfreight flights, goods travelling by air is the fastest growing transportation segment. The types of product shipped by airfreight tend to be lightweight or small. Examples include medical supplies, electronic components, perishable products such as flowers, fruit and vegetables and documents.

The advantages of airfreight are speed and reliability. It is an efficient and economical way to transport high-value, lightweight products, important documents or skilled people over long distances, particularly where the destination is overseas. However, air transport is so much more expensive than alternatives that it is cost-prohibitive for most products. Furthermore, the collecting, handling, loading, unloading and delivery adds to the point-to-point overall time, making it not much quicker than road haulage for shorter distances of up to 500 miles.

Water

Carrying goods by water is one of the oldest means of freight transportation. Inland the system of waterways may include rivers, canals and lakes. In addition, there is coastline and sea travel across the world's oceans.

As Exhibit 11.17 indicated, while water transportation costs are low it is also the slowest form of shipping goods. In addition, inland water transportation is tied to a fixed system of river and coastal ports that serve as terminals and distribution points. It is particularly suited to moving heavy bulk items such as raw materials, ores, grain, chemical, mineral and petroleum products. For international shipping, water is the only option for transporting these latter types of product as airfreight is unable to handle them.

Transocean shipping companies have developed intermodal transport systems in order to reduce overall point-to-point delivery times and lower handling costs. They combine trucks, railroads and ships with container systems being at the heart of these developments. Here, standardized containers are packed at the point of origin, loaded onto trucks, reloaded either onto rail flat cars or directly onto a container ship with the process in reverse at the other end of the journey. And throughout the journey the goods never leave the container.

Pipelines

Pipelines are used to transport liquids or gases from one point to another. For example, crude oil and natural gas are piped from an oil field to refineries (for example, there are over 150 000 miles of crude oil pipelines in the USA) and petroleum products such as petrol and diesel from refineries to tank farms. For example, ExxonMobil has pipelines taking aviation fuel to Heathrow Airport from its refinery at Farley near Southampton on the south coast of England.

Other uses include carrying water (probably the most common use) and transporting slurry products (for example products that have been pulverized and transformed into liquid form such as kaolin (china clay) and coal). Once the latter products arrive at their destination the water is then removed leaving the solid material. Although characterized by high initial investment, pipelines are economical because they carry materials over terrain with which other forms of transportation could not cope (for example the Trans-Alaska and North Sea oil pipelines) and, once in place they have a long life and are low cost to operate.

E-COMMERCE

Although introduced in relevant sections earlier in the chapter, the impact of e-commerce demands additional coverage particularly within the context of supply-chain management.

The spread of electronic commerce (e-commerce), both in selling direct to consumers and business-to-business (often referred to as e-business), dealings with suppliers and customers creates the potential for building more efficient and effective supply chains. Other constraints (such as capacity, material supply, material lead times and inventory) apart, the opportunity to improve the way companies do business has been no less than dramatic. At the very least it speeds up transactions, slashes costs and promotes inter-business co-operation, fostering a recognition that suppliers are part of a company's strategic resource. At its most potent, e-commerce allows companies to make or provide products and services to order rather than against a sales forecast while also increasing the extent to which customers can configure what they buy. But, to deliver the commitment requires control over the supply chain to ensure that fulfilment matches promise. A stark example of this was provided by the high profile problems that Amazon.com and other online providers had in failing to meet the Christmas 1999 levels of demand.

Thus, e-commerce transforms a supply chain into a demand chain in which the core activity of the system is not to fill a warehouse, but to deliver to a customer. The well-known exponent of this approach is Dell Computers and earlier examples have already illustrated this. Dell builds all its products on a make-to-order (MTO) basis, with about $20m of business a day transacted on the internet. MTO in the Dell sense changes the place in the supply chain where stock is held. In MTO mode, operations needs to be prepared for every eventuality and this requires excellent partnerships with suppliers based on sharing information and fast deliveries. There can be no inter-functional or inter-business silos. The intermediaries in a supply chain not only need to exchange information, but increasingly move to inter-working mode. Having such links and working practices in place makes it possible to enhance customer support. On the one hand, customers can track the progress of their orders in the systems of its suppliers while, on the other hand, suppliers can proactively anticipate delivery requirements without waiting for an order. In addition, suppliers can also gain access to other suppliers in the chain, allowing them to track the entire process.

Putting internet-based information in front of consumers is transforming the supply chain in the pharmaceuticals industry. In the USA, unlike Europe, companies are allowed to advertise their products. Drug information via the web is a fast and effective way of communicating details of approved products. Patients can find out about new treatments quickly and become more proactive in the treatment phase of illness. For example, SmithKline Beecham's new treatment for diabetes, Avandia, outsold rival products in its first six months on the market.

Establishing close supplier links can also help boost sales. For the UK supermarket, J Sainsbury, special promotions account for about 10 per cent of sales revenue. But planning promotions is difficult, particularly if it concerns perishable goods. To help overcome these problems, Sainsbury built a web-based, supply-chain planning and collaboration system, that allows suppliers and buyers to work through every detail of a product promotion in advance and to track its success in real time.

Companies are also changing emphasis regarding IT supply-chain investments from cost-cutting to sales revenue growth – see Exhibit 11.18. The Dell and SmithKline Beecham examples earlier illustrated this. Similarly, Chrysler recognized that car-

Exhibit 11.18 *Main goal of IT investment*

Period	Goal (% total)	
	cost-cutting	sales revenue growth
1991–92	69	31
1996–97	37	63
2001–02	20	80

Source: The Economist survey of electronic commerce (1998).

purchasing decisions were perceived by many consumers to be tedious. As a result, in 1996 it started an online system for customer purchases. This first year resulted in $900m in sales and by the year 2000 the estimate was $15bn.

As sales revenue growth adds value to a business, current e-commerce developments are reflecting this potential core contribution. Whereas currently e-commerce typically allows customers to order from a specified range of goods, increasingly customers will be asked 'What is your need?' The need for supply chains to be able to cope with exceptions is the next phase of development. To do this the supply chain will move from a passive to a more dynamic mode, responding to customer demands, advising if it has the capability to meet the requirement, at what price and in what lead time. The impact that such developments will have on the supply chain will require fresh approaches to how products and services are managed in operations.

CONCLUSION

Traditional management approaches and organizations can stand in the way of an integrated supply chain. Many companies still operate with structures that typically lead to the functional optimization of dimensions of performance. Within this format there are only functional links between key parts of a supply chain and, with the absence of an integrating mechanism, functions work and plan separately and in line with their respective priorities. At best, these priorities may be inconsistent while at worst they may be incompatible. The result is potential internal conflict putting an organization's ability to meet customer requirements at risk. Furthermore, similar problems can arise between a company and its suppliers on the one hand and with its customers on the other.

The extended enterprise

The conflicts described in the last section can be resolved first by internal supply chain co-operation and liaison and second by extending these developments to suppliers and customers, thus forming an integrated supply chain. Known (as you can visualize) as the extended enterprise, here planning is shared and execution processes are integrated. Where this is achieved, the supply chain now begins to truly encompass the business from tier 2 and tier 1 suppliers to tier 1 and tier 2 customers.

The transfer of a product or service from one stage in a business to the next (the internal phase of a supply chain) or from one business to another business (the external phase of a supply chain) simply represents a supply chain. A supply chain is integrated when all the steps are co-ordinated to manage costs and inventory levels while maintaining customers' on-time and lead time delivery requirements. Process integration is achieved through practices such as collaborative planning and vendor-managed inventory that are jointly defined by all supply chain participants.

Embracing technical developments

An earlier section emphasized the need to recognize technology development opportunities. The ability to move information across the supply chain through IT systems is giving a new perspective to the dimension of integration. Similarly at the point of customer interface, e-commerce is providing the opportunity not only to change the point of sale procedure but also to create an opportunity to increase sales. Empowering customers leads to more sales for a number or reasons, including:

- Companies are able to sell additional services by giving customers and potential customers more information on the services or products on offer.
- Eliminating steps helps conclude a sale and reduce delivery lead times.
- Customers have more insight into what is on offer thus increasing choice.
- Increased choice and introducing new ideas and opportunities leads to more sales as customers buy more – one dimension of which is humorously depicted in Exhibit 11.19.

Competing at the level of supply chains

An earlier section emphasize the need for organizations to recognize that firms increasingly compete at the level of the supply chain. As highlighted earlier, Dell's failure to work with suppliers prevented the company from being able to support the shortening lead times of its customers. Similarly, the delivery problems that Boeing, the world's number one aircraft maker, experienced in the late 1990s not only resulted in lost revenue but also in customers turning to competitors. To build a large passenger jet such as a 747, 767 or A320 you need about 6 million parts. That is complex in itself. But in addition, between 1992 and 1999 Boeing had increased production from 228 to 620 aircraft per year while reducing delivery lead times from 36 to between 8 and 12 months. During this period Boeing, however, failed to ensure that suppliers could handle these critical changes in activity. The result was that it

Exhibit 11.19 *Some unforeseen consequences of e-commerce*

© Roger Beale

could not get the parts to build the aircraft. While its sales were booming, the company had failed to develop its supplier base to meet the new task and fell well behind on its delivery schedule.

Managing the supply chain for competitive advantage

Markets evolve and what is important to customers needs to be identified and then form the basis of functional strategies. Recent research[11] confirms the trend away from price to other operations factors. The increasingly important role of the supply chain in delivery advantage is clearly marked as shown in Exhibit 11.20.

Furthermore, as the trend towards outsourcing is increasing (see earlier Exhibit 11.5) then the need to manage this task in the future will be a significant part of the operations management role.

Exhibit 11.20 *Potential factors for market differentiation: identifying the order-winners (per cent of responding companies)*

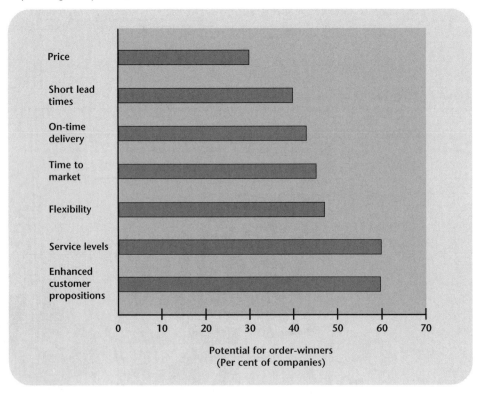

SUMMARY

A company's decision whether to make or buy is tied up with a range of factors from core technology and strategy considerations through to the greater opportunities that have come with the globalization of world trade. In reality, however, companies often fail to address and re-address this decision in line with both the internal and customer-facing dimensions that affect the key outcomes that result.

But, whether a company makes or buys, the need to manage the supply chain that results – and how well this key task is undertaken – is an important priority within operations, and its impact on the business as a whole is increasingly and appropriately a high profile corporate task.

The alternatives to the make-or-buy option, such as joint ventures and non-equity-based collaboration, complete the introductory phase of the chapter. The orientation then switches to supply-chain management issues and developments. These sections detail the origins and evolution of supply chains (in particular, refer back to Exhibits 11.8 to 11.11) before outlining the key aspects of change. These include effective consumer response, changes in attitude from the classic stance of threat and fear through collaboration to integration and synchronization (see Exhibit 11.12) and the increasing use of IT.

The next section addressed the areas of sourcing, supplier base development, supplier selection and evaluation and how to maintain the supplier base. Then followed a detailed review of alternative distribution and transportation systems and comparisons between rail, road, airfrieght, water and pipeline alternatives.

The final section on e-commerce built on the earlier IT section. Its inclusion here was to highlight the dramatic impact those developments are having and will continue to have on supply-chain management not only in direct consumer selling but also in business-to-business dealings.

Discussion questions

1. What factors should be taken into account when taking make-or-buy decisions? Illustrate your answer with examples from both a manufacturing and service organization.

2. Under what circumstances would you consider that each of the following would be advantageous to a company:

   - single sourcing
   - multisourcing

   Use both a manufacturing and service organization to illustrate your views.

Discussion questions (cont'd)

3. Given the increasing importance of environmental concerns, how would a company incorporate these issues into the make-or-buy process? Give two examples to illustrate your views.

4. How will e-commerce continue to impact the supply chain?

5. Using the web site for an online supplier such as Amazon.com, detail the delivery system involved and list the benefits to the consumer.

6. List two firms that you think have achieved competitive advantage through vertical integration. Explain why and give illustrations to support your views.

7. What benefits do suppliers receive from developing closer ties with major customers?

8. A major company decides to move to a more collaborative stance with a supplier. What would be the first key changes it would need to take? What possible initial responses might be made by the supplier?

Notes and references

1. Tait, N 'Handling the Sourcing Decision: Lowest Cost is Not Always the Answer', *Financial Times*, 15 October 1997, p. 13.
2. PricewaterhouseCoopers 'Shaping the Value Chain for Outstanding Performance: Meeting the Challenge of Global Supply Chains' (1998), p. 6.
3. Developed from Harrigan, KR 'Managing Joint Ventures – Part I', *Management Review*, February 1987, p. 29.
4. Based on PricewaterhouseCoopers (1998), p. 6.
5. Tait, N (1997), p. 13.
6. Economist Intelligence Unit and KPMG Management Consultants' Report entitled 'Supply Chain Management: Europe's New Competitive Battleground', 1996.
7. Borsodi, R 'The Distribution Age', D Appleton & Co (1929).
8. As reported in Allen, E 'One-stop Shop is No Cure-All', *Financial Times*, 17 June, 1999, p. 16.
9. Bleeke, JA 'Peak Strategies', *McKinsey Quarterly*, Spring 1989.
10. Margretta, J 'The Power of Virtual Integration: An Interview with Dell Computer's Michael Dell', *Harvard Business Review*, March–April, 1998, p. 74.
11. PricewaterhouseCoopers (1998), p. 4.

Further reading

Bhote, KR *Strategic Supply Chain Management*, American Management Association, New York (1989).
Burt, DN and Pinkerton, RL *Strategic Proactive Purchasing*, American Management Association, New York (1996).

Child, J and Faulkner, D *Strategies for Cooperation: Managing Alliances, Networks and Joint Ventures*, Oxford University Press, Oxford (1998).

Gattorna, JL (ed.) *Strategic Supply Chain Management*, Gower, Aldershot (1998).

Gattorna JL and Walters DW *Managing the Supply Chain: A Strategic Perspective*, Macmillan Business, London (1996).

Lamming R *Beyond Partnership: Strategies for Innovation and Lean Supply*, Prentice Hall, London (1993).

CHAPTER TWELVE

The content and planning of this book: an overview of what is involved, what has been addressed so far and what is covered in this chapter

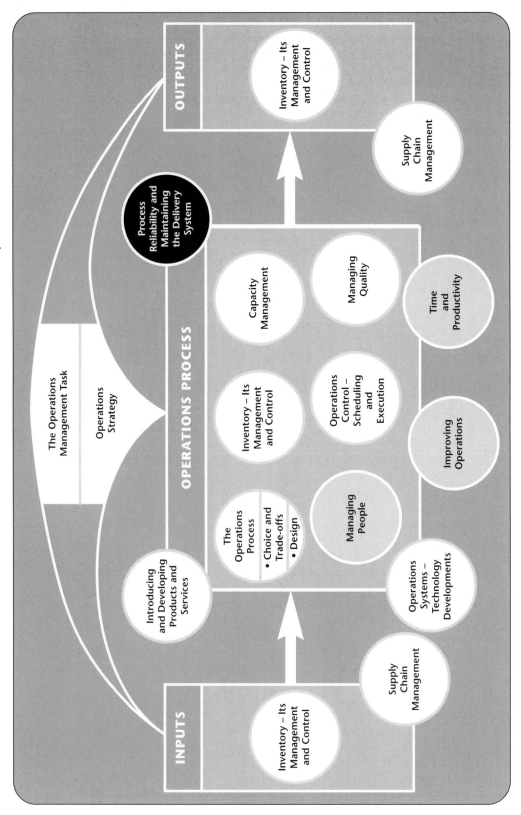

Process Reliability and Maintaining the Delivery System

Chapter overview

As part of the need to lower costs, reduce lead times and improve the availability and format of data, investments in processes and systems will continue to be made and are likely to increase in the future. Rapid advances in technology, many of which were highlighted earlier in Chapter 6, have led to more opportunities to invest in both the hardware and software parts of the operations process. The technology dependence, however, is changing in form with the increasing use of electronics (for example microchips) in both the working and control of process equipment and IT-based systems applications. One outcome of this is the changing nature of maintenance provision. For example, while stand-by processes will tend not to be financially viable through reasons of investment and obsolescence, stand-by controls or other types of process support units will prove to be justified. This pattern of investment, however, has led to a growing need in most organizations to recognize the continued importance of and to reconsider their approach to the management of the maintenance function. This chapter outlines the important maintenance decisions and illustrates the types of controls and tasks that maintenance managers should address, as part of the overall operations function. In particular, it covers the following sections:

- **Process reliability and checking for failure** – this section introduces the issue of process reliability and outlines ways of assessing and measuring failures, how to establish the rate of failure and process reliability as well as ways to calculate mean time between failures and process availability measures. It concludes with an introduction on how to identify levels of failure, failure analysis and ways to improve a system.

- **Maintenance and terotechnology** – explains the broader concept of terotechnology and positions maintenance of the delivery system within this context.

- **Maintenance** – the concept and task introduces the area by highlighting the increasing investment by businesses in equipment and technology and the subsequent key role of maintenance within operations.

> ## Chapter overview (cont'd)
>
> - **Types of maintenance** explains the alternative approaches to maintenance, how they differ one from another and the need to match type with requirement in order to ensure best fit.
> - **Planned maintenance** is discussed in more detail due to the fundamental role provided by this approach.
> - **Other policy issues** are listed and discussed. These range from the options of outsourcing maintenance provision to systems and controls and the style of management to be considered.
> - **Total productive maintenance** is described in detail and the reasons why this approach is increasingly being adopted are explained.
> - **Energy management** – introduces a key area of costs that typically comprises part of the maintenance function's contribution to the overall business.
> - **Managing maintenance** – outlines some of the developments to help assess and manage this function.

One of an organization's basic tasks is to provide products and services in line with customers' needs and expectations. Central to this provision is the operations process. Preceding chapters have already highlighted some important dimensions that can affect this role, for example:

- **Chapter 3** covered the introduction and development of products and services and included issues around failure that resulted from the design itself.
- **Chapter 6** discussed the key role of managing capacity and introduced its links to delivery of products and services fast and on time.
- **Chapter 8** addressed the task of scheduling operations and highlighted its key role within the delivery system of meeting the needs of customers.
- **Chapter 9** covered quality management and identified the key link between this task and meeting customers' specifications and expectations.
- **Chapter 10** concerned managing inventory and how this dimension of operations impacted capacity alternatives and delivery on-time performance.
- **Chapter 11** introduced the dimension of supply-chain management and explained its role in managing the total process to meet the needs of customers.

All of these dimensions contribute to and can impact on how well an organization meets its customer requirements. This chapter adds to this issue by introducing the aspect of process reliability and, in particular, the approaches used to maintain the delivery system.

PROCESS RELIABILITY – MAKING A SYSTEM FAIL-SAFE

The concept of integrating fail-safe mechanisms into a process in order to reduce failures is increasingly being used in manufacturing and service systems. The introduction of *poka-yoke* (*poka* meaning inadvertent errors and *yoke* from *yokeru* meaning to prevent) as part of the operations improvement methods used by Japanese companies has emphasized these developments and highlighted the benefits to be gained. The principle underpinning these approaches stems from the fact that people and processes can make errors. Consequently, if situations in which errors take place can be eliminated then this is often the best way to reduce failures. Making a system fool-proof by introducing mechanisms that counterbalance potential failures with a signal of some kind is the basis of *poka-yoke* developments.

Examples of *poka-yoke* devices are now provided to illustrate the principles and highlight how they work. You will see from these that they are designed into the process or service delivery system itself and also to fail-safe servers or customers as they interface with the system.

Process and service delivery system illustrations

- in-process gauges on filling lines to check the quantity in each pack by weighing or measuring the fill levels in each container
- limit switches on machines that allow the process to start only if the part to be processed is the correct one
- positional gauges that check that a part is correctly positioned before allowing a process to begin.

Server-related illustrations

- hospitals use different size tubes to dispense (say) blood and food, thereby eliminating mistakes
- automatic dispensing machines that ensure that correct quantity of a product (for example soft drink) is delivered
- bar code readers at supermarket checkouts reduce pricing errors at a till
- in hospital operating theatres, instruments in preformed trays are used to allow a count back at the end of an operation to eliminate potential errors
- the outline of tools in a machine shop allows tool placings to be identified and to highlight tools not replaced at the end of a job.
- multi-stack filing cabinets that only allow one drawer to be open at a time. This prevents serious accidents where cabinets may overbalance forward if two or more drawers were open simultaneously.

Customer-related illustrations

- the days of the week are stamped on capsule packs to enable a person to double-check their routine
- similarly, colour coding of tablet dispensers help particularly elderly patients to avoid mistakes in self-administering their drug treatments
- the main light switch in aircraft toilets is triggered by the door closure thus avoiding embarrassing situations
- beepers on telephones are used to signal that a hand set has been replaced correctly and, therefore, that batteries will be charged
- similarly, telephone handsets not replaced correctly will emit a loud signal to draw the user's attention to this fact.

- go/no-go bag checks are used by airlines to allow passengers to self-check the size of the hand luggage they wish to take on board.

PROCESS RELIABILITY – CHECKING FOR FAILURE

Reducing or even eliminating process failure is high on the agenda of most businesses as they strive to improve the reliability of their processes. For some organizations process failure is critical, even life-threatening as in the failure of aircraft in flight or prolonged power cuts to emergency and intensive care units in hospitals.

While there is always the possibility of a process failing, it is essential to recognize that:

- Some failures are not as critical as others, and this factor needs to be reflected in the time and effort allocated to managing a process.

- Managing failure is a key part of the operations task. That failure will occur is a given. What is important is to manage and control failure in line with the consequences that failure brings.

Assessing and measuring failure

One key issue in assessing the reliability of a process is measuring failure and the principal ways of doing this are now explained:

- **Failure occurs over time** – failure is a function of time. For the most part, the longer the life of a product the more likely it is to fail. However, this is not always the case. Products often reflect three stages where the likelihood of failure differs: where this occurs this phenomenon is known as the bathtub curve (see Exhibit 12.1). However, surveys show that less than 10 per cent of all equipment has a bathtub profile. Electronic equipment has an infant mortality profile, but over 50 per cent of all equipment has a pattern of failure that is uniform and linear, a fact that makes the statistical calculation of the time of failure very unreliable. Because of this, planning maintenance (as explained later) becomes a key factor in reducing failure and maintaining the reliability of a process.

Similarly, delivery systems based on human capabilities as in many service processes often show patterns of deterioration that are more to do with staff complacency and lack of management interest and control than other factors. As you can imagine, the pattern and level of failure in these types of service delivery system would tend not to be uniform and consequently the reliability of the process would need to be monitored in such a planned way as to check for potential deterioration.

- **Rate of failure** – as the name implies, failure rate is the number of failures that occur in a given period or as a percentage of the total number of products produced or services provided. For example, a banking system could be measured by the number of errors in a period, while a mail order company may check the number of errors as a percentage of the total orders received:

Exhibit 12.1 An illustration of a bathtub curve (note the shape of the curve in this example, hence the name)

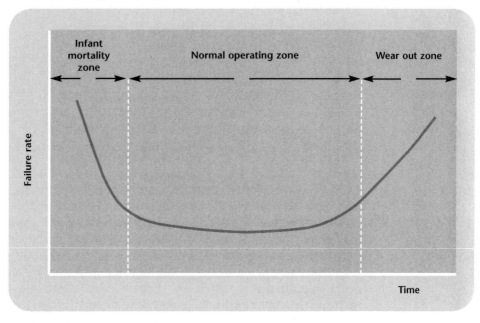

$$\text{Failure rate} = \frac{\text{number of failures} \times 100}{\text{total produced or service transactions completed}}$$

$$\text{Failure rate} = \frac{\text{number of failures}}{\text{operating time}}$$

■ **Process reliability** – the reliability of a process or delivery system is a measure of how well it performs. Where a system has two or more stages then the reliability of each step will affect the overall reliability of the process. For example, a mail order process involves three steps and the processes involved and the current reliability of each step is given below:

Steps	*Reliability*
■ Customer order checked	
– Accurate and goods requested are available }	0.980
– Order amended where goods not available }	
■ Items picked and collated	0.935
■ Items packed and sent to mail routing	0.990

If any of these steps is completed incorrectly the order will not be delivered correctly or within guaranteed timescales. Thus, the reliability of the total system is:

$$\text{Reliability of the system} = 0.980 \times 0.935 \times 0.990$$
$$= 0.907$$

You will see from this example that the reliability of the system at 0.907 is markedly less than any of the individual parts of the process. Hence, the more interdependent steps there are in a process the lower will be the reliability of the total system.

■ **Mean time between failures** – an alternative way to measure the failure of a system is the mean time between failures (MTBF) which is calculated as follows:

$$MTBF = \frac{operating\ hours}{number\ of\ failures}$$

Thus, if an ATM at a bank averages three failures every two weeks the MTBF would be:

$$MTBF = \frac{21\ days \times 24\ hours}{3} = 168\ hours$$

■ **Process availability** – a process is not available to work if it has either failed or is being repaired following failures. To calculate process availability you need to know the MTBF for a process and also the mean time to repair (MTTR) which is the average time taken to repair the process or equipment from the time it fails to the time it is again in use.

In the last example, the bank was reviewing alternative ways to increase the availability of ATMs. Currently, the MTTR was 7.5 hours which made the availability:

$$Availability\ of\ an\ ATM = \frac{168}{168 + 7.5} = 0.957$$

Option 1 to increase availability was to reduce the interval of regular servicing which would increase the MTBF to 194 hours. Option 2 was to improve the speed of response time in the existing repair contract, thus lowering the MTTR to 5.0 hours. Which would be the better option?

$$Option\ 1 \qquad Availability = \frac{194}{194 + 7.5} = 0.963$$

$$Option\ 2 \qquad Availability = \frac{168}{168 + 5.0} = 0.971$$

Option 2 consequently will improve availability more than option 1.

Identifying levels of failure

The issue of managing quality has already been covered in Chapter 9. This section is a short overview to help identify ways of proactively checking the delivery system to identify failures that have occurred and need attention.

■ **In-process checks** – ascertaining whether the process is maintaining the required level of quality conformance can be undertaken in several ways. These include checking with customers on how well a service is progressing (for example, verifying with customers in a restaurant that the food and service are of an acceptable standard at each stage during a meal) or by undertaking point-of-departure interviews with customers as they are about to leave the service delivery system. In manufacturing, checks using control and SPC charts help monitor processes as explained earlier.

■ **Overall checks** – asking customers to discuss aspects of a delivery system can also be made at other times than when they are in the process itself. For example, complaint cards, feedback sheets and questionnaires can be mailed to solicit views about the products and services provided; focus groups of customers brought together to discuss specific products and services or the delivery system in general are often used to gain insights into where failures have occurred or may occur; similarly telephone surveys are used to identify all aspects of products, services and delivery systems including points where failures may occur or have occurred in the past.

Analysing failures

One important activity in this quest for establishing process reliability levels is analysing the failures that have been experienced. At the one end of the spectrum are large-scale accidents or disasters such as airline crashes and major oil tanker spills, especially close to land. At the other end of the spectrum is the systematic analysis of complaints by companies as part of their way of ascertaining failures and identifying their source or origin.

One analytical way of undertaking these types of checks is failure mode, effect and criticality analysis (FMECA). This approach analyses each potential failure in a system in the light of the probability of occurrence and categorized as to its probable effect on the successful operation of the system. The three elements of FMECA are:

■ Failure mode analysis – a study of the system to determine how likely it is that a failure will occur.

■ Failure effect analysis – a review of the possible failures and their likely effects.

■ Failure criticality analysis – a check on the potential failures in a system and the consequences of these in terms such as affecting the product or service quality conformance, the impact on delivery reliability or speed performance and systems breakdowns.

Each potential cause of failure is assessed and quantified in terms of these three perspectives and the outcomes are prioritized. Corrective action then follows to reduce or eliminate potential failures. The main steps in the FMECA procedure are:

■ list all parts of the system under review
■ identify all possible ways in which each part of the system could fail, known as the failure modes
■ for each failure mode, ascertain the causes and also the effect on the current system
■ rate the probability of each cause in a given period, the seriousness of an occurrence and the possibility of detecting failure on a scale of 1 to 10
■ calculate the criticality index by multiplying together the three ratings and use this to rank the importance of failures
■ identify corrective action to reduce the criticality of factors.

MAINTENANCE AND TEROTECHNOLOGY

The necessary importance of reviewing physical assets in terms of investment and cost has led to the concept of terotechnology, defined in BS3811 (1993) as:

> A combination of management, financial, engineering, building and other practices applied to physical assets in pursuit of economic life cycle costs.[1] Its practice is concerned with the specification and design for reliability and maintainability of plant, machinery, equipment, buildings and structures, with their installation, commissioning, operation, maintenance, modification and replacement and with feedback of information on design, performance and costs.[2]

Although there is little that is new about each of these activities and ideas, the concept of terotechnology highlights the need to focus attention on the gains to be made by co-ordinating their interrelated functions. How these important aspects relate to one another needs to be understood. The introduction of terotechnology (from the Greek *terin* meaning to watch over) is designed to concentrate awareness on this important concept and to help to promote and apply it appropriately throughout an organization.

Whereas maintenance is the largest aspect of terotechnology, and that on which the rest of this chapter concentrates, many activities at earlier parts of the business cycle, such as design and purchasing, can significantly affect maintenance costs and effectiveness. For example, the co-ordination necessary to identify that a modified design may lead to reductions in maintenance costs is typical of the gains to be made by reviewing activities on a wider perspective and in a co-ordinated way. When reading this and other chapters it is important, therefore, to consider the part and whole issues discussed in Chapter 1.

MAINTENANCE – THE CONCEPT

In most developed countries, gross national product continues to increase markedly faster than population growth. In all sectors this is largely the result of replacing manual operations by technological innovation. One result of this trend is a need for companies to become increasingly equipment conscious and to build this perspective into the way in which they manage operations. This will contribute to improving many key dimensions of a business. These include avoiding unnecessary equipment investment, ensuring the maximum use of existing equipment, enhancing the throughput and usage rates of processes, reducing the costs of energy and limiting the environmental side effects through innovations in equipment and improving the methods of their use.

These tasks are solely or partly provided by sound maintenance practices. Current costs of this provision are high and typically far outweigh the purchase of new equipment. A survey in the 1990s revealed that the UK spent £14bn annually on maintaining equipment worth $80bn, while spending on new equipment was only £4.3bn. With maintenance typically adding some 8–12 per cent to operations costs it is not surprising that improving the practice and management of this function has become a major factor in the drive to improve aspects of the corporate agenda such as increasing productivity, reducing costs, improving on-time delivery performance and shortening lead times as part of the need for fast response. To secure these opportunities companies need to manage and co-ordinate their maintenance activities both in terms of the efficiency (internal) and effectiveness (external) dimensions. The direct costs of spares and labour and the indirect costs of unplanned equipment failure, secondary damage, unplanned overtime, output loss and excess spare parts offer significant saving opportunities. In addition, good maintenance practice needs to emphasize the role of equipment reliability within the wider corporate context. Several of the order-winners and qualifiers relevant to a company's agreed markets are based in part on the reliability of its processes. The increase use of just-in-time agreements also makes it essential to ensure that all equipment is available when needed and called for within the operations plan.

MAINTENANCE – THE TASK

All physical facilities are susceptible to failure through breakdown, deterioration in performance through age and use, and to obsolescence due to improvements in technology. The resulting impact on costs and market-related order-winners and qualifiers has already been highlighted. Reducing the likelihood of these features occurring involves considerable expenditure. If the sole objective was to reduce instances of failure, deterioration or obsolescence, then the investment and expense involved would eventually exceed the actual costs of allowing the status quo to exist. Achieving a balance has to be addressed and determined. Each situation will be different. Some processes and systems will require more sophisticated maintenance support than others, while increased investment in the process will, in turn, increase the need to sustain high levels of utilization and guarantees on availability.

The starting point for a sound maintenance programme, therefore, is to have a clear understanding of what maintenance tasks have to be undertaken. Only then is it possible to specify the staff needed to do the work, the spare parts necessary to support it and the systems required to manage and control the programme.

The maintenance function encompasses a wide range of responsibilities in different organizations.[3] Although the prime task usually concerns keeping the operations process in good working order, there are other important responsibilities that fall within its total function (see Exhibit 12.2). The list given in the exhibit is not exhaustive but is typical of the set of tasks frequently placed under the control of this function, if only as a matter of convenience.

Although maintenance involves the range of responsibilities referred to in Exhibit 12.2, the rest of this chapter will concentrate on those functions directly concerned with the operations process. At times other areas will be referred to, but it is not intended to address comprehensively the management issues involved in these. The four areas listed below are key considerations in the sound management of the maintenance function and will be discussed in detail in the following sections.

1. Determine which parts of the process are to be maintained.

2. Decide between the different types of maintenance that could be employed and agree when maintenance should take place.

3. Consider the various policies available to an organization, including repair or

replacement, the use of internal or external personnel and a centralized or decentralized approach to maintenance provision.

4. Develop procedures, systems and performance measures to help manage and control these activities.

WHICH PARTS OF A PROCESS TO MAINTAIN

A prerequisite of determining the scope of the activities to be provided is to list all items that need to be maintained. The list should include not only equipment in the process but also other equipment, transport, building and structures in line with the range of activities set out in Exhibit 12.2. This list will comprise the physical asset register and provide details of each item including:

1. A unique reference number for identification and often coded to show location and function.
2. Description – make, model, age and modifications.
3. Location.
4. Details of major components or parts to include any items common to other equipment, and inventory holdings.
5. Comments upon the critical nature of the equipment to the process.

The maintenance task will vary depending upon the number and complex nature of the equipment involved. Take British Airways (BA) for example. In the year 2000 it had about 300 aircraft. The fleet ranges from Concordes, Boeing 747s, Boeing 767s, A320s and A319s flying international routes to turbo-props island-hopping on Scottish domestic services. To keep these flying while conforming to the exacting safety and service quality

Exhibit 12.2   *Typical maintenance activities*

Area of responsibility		Typical activities
Buildings and structures		To provide extensions, modifications and repairs to all buildings and structures, including grounds
Support-function provision		To arrange the re-layout, modification, and non-equipment provision and repair in office and administrative functions
Utilities		To maintain and provide supplies of all utilities including power, light, gas, water, steam, heating, air conditioning, pollution, sewage, refuse disposal and general housekeeping
Plant and equipment	repair	To maintain (including re-layout) all items of plant equipment both in the operations process and in the support functions
	essential work	To design and manufacture, to complete major modifications and to install equipment. To manufacture auxiliary equipment (for example tools and jigs) for new and existing equipment
Safety		To ensure that the necessary safety requirements are met, including the provision of mechanisms to reduce the likelihood of accidents

standards it sets, BA employs over 9000 engineering staff worldwide and annually spends some £600m on engineering services and maintenance. The maintenance schedule, moreover dominates an aircraft's working life as the following example shows.

Case example 1

An aircraft's early life is dominated by its engineering and maintenance requirements. Its flight pattern for months ahead is planned to ensure it is back at base in line with its maintenance schedule. In practice, its flight programme is so well organized that only in exceptional circumstances does an aircraft even come close to the legally permitted limits on the number of flying hours between overhauls.

An aircraft's working life is punctuated by a rigid succession of maintenance schedules based on the number of hours it has flown. These checks are frequent and become progressively more thorough as the airmiles mount. In brief, the schedule is as follows:

■ **pre-flight inspection** by ground engineers and flight crew before take-off

■ **every day** a small engineering team carries out a more detailed inspection including electrics, tyre pressures, oil and hydraulics as well as investigating and rectifying all small problems reported during the previous day's flying

■ **every 150 flying hours** (about 2 weeks*) a series of scheduled checks are completed.

Typically this is between scheduled flights and at night

■ **every 1000 flying hours** (about 3 months*) a full 24 hour check is made

■ **every 18 months** the regular maintenance is supplemented by a major overhaul (called an Intermediate Check in BA) which involves 120 engineers spending a week or more on the aircraft

■ **after 24 000 flying hours** (about 4 to 5 years*) an extensive overhaul is completed (called a Major Check in BA). The aircraft is out of service for one month while a large team of engineers virtually dismantle the entire aircraft to carry out a rivet-by-rivet inspection of the entire airframe. Not only do engines and surfaces come off for inspection or replacement but also any necessary major structural work is undertaken such as replacing main undercarriage units, renewing skin panels and replacing fuselage frames

* These figures are typical for a big jet flying on international routes.

DIFFERENT TYPES OF MAINTENANCE

A company may undertake its maintenance function in a number of ways. The most effective method will vary depending upon the item concerned and its importance in the operations process. The mix will vary from one facility to another and will depend upon the goals of the maintenance provision, the nature of the facility and the type and age of the processes involved. The essential provision, however, is to make them part of a co-ordinated approach by introducing the key element of planning. Approaches may include a mix of the various forms of maintenance to meet the particular requirements and conditions of the task on hand. These various types of maintenance are now described.

Reactive maintenance

Reactive maintenance repairs equipment as needed and undertakes emergency maintenance as required. The systematic identification of parts of the process that need, or may need, to be replaced or maintained is not a feature of this approach.

This form of maintenance is also known as 'breakdown' maintenance which, as the name suggests, concerns repairs being carried out after a failure has occurred. This approach may be a consequence of problems occurring even though other types of maintenance are in place to prevent unscheduled and unanticipated equipment failures from happening.

However, some companies deliberately use reactive maintenance as part of their overall approach to carrying out the maintenance task. This is particularly so for equipment where this method has advantages (for example where the impact of breakdowns on other parts of the organization or on support for its markets is relatively small) or where there is a significant variation in the rate of deterioration which makes such equipment less responsive to the benefits of periodic inspection. There are also occasions when a machine will continue to be operated even though maintenance is known to be needed. This derivation of reactive maintenance is described as 'run to failure' where, for instance, the value of production resulting from an extended manufacturing run may outweigh the maintenance costs incurred following failure.

However, the reactive approach can still be planned in nature. When breakdowns occur maintenance teams are allocated to the problem and their role is to respond quickly and make the necessary decisions to minimize the effect of the breakdown on the operations system. In many instances, temporary repairs may be made so that the process can function again as soon as possible. Permanent repairs would then be made at a later and more convenient time.

Preventive (or scheduled) maintenance

Preventive or scheduled maintenance is carried out at predetermined intervals or corresponding to prescribed criteria (for example equipment hours worked) and is intended to reduce the probability of failure or the performance degradation of an item. Its objective is to reduce the probability of breakdown by replacing worn components at set intervals. The replacement interval is usually based on the mean failure time of certain components. However, in critical areas such as aircraft maintenance, replacement and maintenance schedules are typically specified by a legal or government body. Planned activities can range from simple inspections and adjustments to full overhauls.

Condition-based (or predictive) maintenance

Condition-based maintenance concerns preventive maintenance initiated as a result of knowledge of the condition of an item that comes from routine or continuous monitoring.[4] It often involves a procedure of systematic inspection (especially of key parts or those that are expensive either in themselves or to replace) and can be undertaken to identify instances where maintenance could be performed either earlier or later than the regular preventive maintenance schedule dictates.

In addition, this planned procedure can also enable ongoing checks to be made on the effectiveness of a preventive maintenance schedule and thus enable it to be fine-tuned where necessary but without incurring the disadvantages that would accrue from the original schedules.

Condition monitoring or predictive maintenance involves taking a set of measurements to indicate the operating condition of each process, machine or item of equipment. This 'wear out' profile then enables maintenance to be scheduled shortly before the failure is anticipated.[5] Over time, the profile changes and so constant monitoring needs to be completed to enable companies to ensure that the interval between maintenance activities is as long as possible without risking excessive failure.

Stand-by equipment

The provision of stand-by equipment for all or part of a process is another potential element of an appropriate maintenance plan. It will typically be used where the cost or risk of breakdown is extremely high. Thus, it offers an alternative to paying for a high level of maintenance in order to reduce the impact of breakdowns. In addition, back-up equipment can be an effective alternative to use where time constraints demand that planned maintenance is undertaken in normal working hours. However, as mentioned at the beginning of the chapter, it is less likely to be a viable alternative for core processes on account of the high investment involved. Its use is more likely to be as a cover for support services such as compressed air, water, other utilities and control units.

Stand-by equipment does not take the place of regular maintenance but serves as an insurance policy for equipment that can seriously disrupt the process or delivery system if it breaks down. However, if stand-by equipment is provided it is important to ensure that it is fully operational. Where possible it is advisable to run the equipment at regular intervals.

If several pieces of equipment are identical, then one stand-by unit can serve this function for all on-line processes and result in a substantially lower-cost provision. Examples of this include generator and compressed air equipment to support the processes within a manufacturing plant. Other examples include BA which maintains a fully serviced, ready-to-fly Concorde as a stand-by aircraft for every transatlantic flight to and from London. In this way BA is able to guarantee its premier flight programme.

Corrective maintenance

Corrective maintenance involves making improvements to existing equipment, in addition to its general upkeep through other types of maintenance, with the aim of eliminating problems at source. It is intended to change the design of the equipment in such a way that the failure no longer occurs, or, if it does, in such a way that the failure no longer matters.

Equipment upgrades

Upgrades can form part of an overall approach to maintaining equipment. This involves redressing or modifying equipment to achieve one or both of the following:

■ to increase process reliability
■ to facilitate repair.

Data from other maintenance activities will invariably provide key indicators on which to base an updating programme. In many instances, these upgrades also form part of a larger decision to enhance a process in terms of its technical capability and/or throughput speeds.

PLANNED MAINTENANCE

As emphasized at the start of the last section, different approaches to maintenance are needed for different equipment or even for different parts of the same equipment. For example, consider on-site vehicles used in the construction industry. Changing the engine oil and undertaking a general service at fixed intervals are forms of preventive or scheduled maintenance. Items such as brakes and tyres are checked for wear on a regular basis and changed before they become defective, a form of condition monitoring. Headlights are probably a run to failure item, whereas replacing pneumatic tyres detailed in Chapter 4 are forms of equipment upgrades to reduce the high number of punctures, the problems caused to work schedules and overall costs. The underlying concept underpinning these examples concerns determining which type of maintenance to use for each part of the task. Planned maintenance is the term used to describe this approach.

As the above example illustrates, while planned maintenance does not advocate one approach compared to another, it does emphasize the need to determine the maintenance provision so that it is organized and carried out in a conscious manner. Thus, while reactive maintenance and condition monitoring are two ends of the maintenance provision continuum both can contribute appropriate planned responses as part of a company's overall approach to maintenance.

In developing planned maintenance, important decisions need to be taken that concern the approach and extent of planned maintenance and mix of types to be used. Thus, decisions are based on conscious choices that need to be reviewed regularly in order to check the appropriateness of current approaches.

Planned maintenance programmes yield a range of benefits including:

■ The minimizing of maintenance costs – plans can be made and material and spare parts ordered in line with the plan.

■ Maintenance can be completed when it is convenient to the operations process thus minimizing losses in capacity.

■ The loss of capacity is also reduced as maintenance tasks can be planned with the minimum of time lost during normal working hours.

■ Minimum material and spare parts inventory can be achieved, with levels of inventory in line with planned requirements rather than in anticipation of possible breakdowns.

■ Increasing the opportunity to use contract maintenance more effectively, as work of a similar or specialized nature can be planned to be completed at the same time thus reducing the higher costs associated with one-off jobs.

■ A reduction in maintenance overtime working following the reduction in emergency repairs associated with increased planning.

■ The disruption that accompanies emergency work will be less extensive.

■ The need for stand-by equipment can be reviewed and the trade-off between the reduced incidence of emergency breakdown and the costs associated with stand-by equipment can be reassessed.

A common misconception about planned maintenance is that it is a high-cost alternative. However, even setting aside the capacity gains associated with this approach, the actual maintenance costs are also typically lower compared to an unplanned approach. Furthermore a key management task is to check continuously the costs of providing the current planned maintenance programme and to seek lower-cost alternatives. This is achieved by comparing current costs with those which would have been incurred if alternative mixes of the different types of maintenance had been chosen. This checking and rechecking lead to selecting different approaches to the various elements of the overall maintenance task as conditions and alternatives change.

One outcome of a research programme completed over a 30-year period from the mid-1960s led to the development of a process known as reliability centred maintenance (RCM).[6] This helps refine approaches within a planned maintenance programme by establishing a sensible framework for making choices. It starts with the premise that failures are a cause for concern only because they have consequences. Sometimes these consequences only cost money to repair while others interfere with operations; in the most serious cases they can lead to environmental incidents or fatalities.

Clearly, the more serious the consequence of a failure, the more time and effort should be spent trying to prevent it occurring. RCM is a decision-making framework to help companies to reflect an evaluation of the failure consequences in their selection of which type of maintenance to choose. What equipment must do (together with the desired standards of performance) summarizes the part that the equipment plays within an overall business both in meeting its appropriate performance targets and the external view of the business by its customers and company at large. Examples of the benefits gained from an RCM programme are provided in Exhibit 12.3.

The key step is to agree on what the company is trying to prevent when it undertakes planned maintenance. This is then followed by assessing the consequences of each failure. Depending upon the nature and severity of the consequences, the final step is to select the most appropriate type of maintenance for dealing with the failure.

A planned maintenance programme concerns identifying and agreeing what needs to be maintained, the type of maintenance to be employed and the frequency and timing of the schedule. However, it is easy to let the schedule of planned maintenance work slip because of pressures from the operations function, emergencies and other work of a high priority. Inevitably, if this slippage is not checked then the benefits of planning are lost and total costs will rise. It is necessary to agree a sensible schedule and then to adhere to it. However, a regular review of the programme content is necessary. This often leads, in the light of experience, to some decrease or exclusion of parts of the programme while introducing or increasing the frequency of others. RCM and other reviews will be the basis of these changes.

In establishing the maintenance programme, short- and longer-term plans will be determined with each task allocated throughout the period. A planned approach will not only ensure that all the items are included but also provide for a fairly even workload across the maintenance function on both a short- and long-term basis. This evenness will aid capacity, overtime, purchasing and overall costs.

Exhibit 12.3   *Examples of the benefits results from using RCM*

Source of benefit	Examples
Improved plant availability and reliability	■ Automotive wheel plant trebled output per-man per-shift in a 6-month period ■ Emergency shutdowns of a main boiler were eliminated for 3 years with savings of over $11m ■ Plant efficiency increased from 68 to 98 per cent in the first month
Environmental integrity	At an effluent treatment plant, the time after every major start-up when environmental hazards could possibly occur, was reduced from one hour to zero
Safety	The aviation industry recorded a reduction in crashes per million take-offs caused by equipment failure from 40 in 1960 to 0.3 in the early 1990s
Increased efficiency	■ Maintenance schedule completion rates improved from 50 to 100 per cent in a toffee-making plant ■ In a steel mill, all fixed-interval overhauls were eliminated

OTHER POLICY ISSUES

In addition to the decisions concerning the nature and extent of the planned maintenance activities, there are other issues of policy that concern the maintenance provision. These decisions include the following.

Internal or external personnel

The decision whether to provide the necessary maintenance personnel or facilities internally or externally is based primarily on cost and technical know-how. Often a combination of the two will be the most suitable arrangement. When the needs are irregular or require very high technical know-how, maintenance will usually be contracted to outside firms. For instance, organizations frequently contract out their maintenance requirements on elevators and computers while for other specialist equipment, such as photocopying and telephones, maintenance forms part of the rental agreement. With supplies such as inks and lubricating oils[7] there is a growing trend to have the supplier provide technical support as part of a contract. In cases such as ink, suppliers often have their own staff on a customer's site as part of the contract. Such decisions are relatively straightforward.

The more difficult decisions on provision are associated with the mainstream maintenance tasks – the operations processes. Where the technical know-how is not available within an organization (for example when new equipment is purchased) then external maintenance services are often used initially. However, an organization will normally wish to build up its internal skills because of the high downtime costs associated with these processes. It will do this through training courses supported by sound documentation, the development, where possible, of self-diagnostic facilities into the equipment and the use of diagnostic tools and instruments to enhance visual checks (for example, vibration monitoring equipment). In situations where the internal maintenance expertise is available, problems of demand peaks for these capabilities will be eased through planned maintenance and other forms of forward planning, and will be supplemented by overtime working or buying in from outside on an as-needed basis.

Centralized or decentralized maintenance

Maintenance may be organized on a centralized or decentralized basis. With centralization, all the workers are in one location with work being allocated as the need arises. In a decentralized set-up, the workers are located in different geographical areas and with responsibilities more or less confined to those areas. Advantages of centralization include:

- improved utilization of the workforce (especially specialists) and equipment
- more able to balance maintenance capacity to fluctuating workload demands
- allows more centralized control (for example one manager, centralized systems, and more control over capital work)
- better training and the employment of specialists can be justified.

Advantages of decentralization include:

- faster service, with travelling time reduced
- improved continuity from shift to shift
- greater knowledge of the particular processes
- improved supervision with reduced geographical area of working.

Group or individual replacement policies

Some components are increasingly prone to failure as they age. Sudden failure creates more difficulty than wear and tear. Therefore, where a large number of identical low-cost items fall into this category, then a group replacement policy becomes feasible. At the other end of the scale, individual replacement applies to a single item that is replaced when it fails. Several types of policy are possible, for example to replace:

- only failed units as they fail
- only failed units periodically
- all units (both good and failed) periodically
- failed units as they fail and all units periodically.

Which method is chosen will be determined by the critical nature of the item. For instance, a policy of replacing all units (both good and failed) periodically may be feasible for certain light bulbs in a building but not for electronic components or relays in a critical part of the process. To help in making this decision, three zones in the operating life of an item need to be identified and then used to determine which policy should be followed (see Exhibit 12.1):

- 'Infant mortality', the initial failure period.
- Normal operating life – if a component survives the initial failure period, then the chances of failure tend to be low for a time.
- Last, the wear-out zone, where the probability of failure rises sharply, peaks and then falls. The shape of the curve must be discovered by testing.

Replacement parts inventory

Replacement parts carry the same costs as those outlined in Chapter 10. On the other hand, the costs of failing to have a part available when needed can be considerable. As a first step, it is important to classify the parts to be stored.

Spare materials and parts

■ *Critical parts* – some spare parts are considered to be critical for a number of reasons, including:
- – essential to the process, in that shutdowns would occur if they were not available;
- – the purchasing lead items are long;
- – there may be safety or pollution hazards if the part is not replaced quickly.

■ *Normal parts* – refers to items used frequently in maintaining a process.

Equipment and tools

Equipment and tools refer to portable plant used by maintenance personnel in carrying out their tasks.

An analysis of spare materials and parts and equipment and tools will normally reveal a sizeable investment. However, a check needs to be made on the purpose and importance of these items and then an ABC analysis established to distinguish the level of control to be used for the various categories of parts. These steps will ensure that a distinction is made between those items that need to be held in stock, and those that do not. Of those that do, the large cost items are to be controlled as described in Chapter 10.

Computerization of records

As part of the drive to reduce costs and improve the accuracy of records, computers are used in this function as elsewhere in organizations. Particular applications include asset registers and recording systems, such as for costs and spares. Companies changing to computerized procedures, however, need to be aware of the problems associated with these conversions:

■ The inaccuracy of existing records.

■ As maintenance needs to be available throughout the working day, there will often be times when the administrative support is unavailable. All staff, therefore, will need to be conversant with the proposed system.

TOTAL PRODUCTIVE MAINTENANCE

A coherent theme throughout several chapters has been the need to involve people in the development and implementation of key activities at all levels in an organization. The area of maintenance provision is no exception. At the core of total productive maintenance (TPM) is the need to involve people to help to improve equipment effectiveness and this feature will be discussed in more detail in a later section. The format, introduction and development of this approach need to form part of the policy decisions that make up a company's overall maintenance provision.

The Japanese Institute of Plant Maintenance defines TPM as a system of maintenance covering the entire life of equipment and involving everyone from the top to the bottom of an organization. The approaches to maintenance described earlier in the chapter were recognized as implying that they were principally, if not exclusively, the concern of the maintenance function. It was recognized that while an organization was concerned with prevention it was more concerned with the productive output of the equipment or process. Hence the switch from the word 'preventive' to 'productive'. Furthermore, and as part of a wider move to increase employee involvement, it is also recognized that operators are in the best position to note the first signs of a problem and that assigning them to complete some aspects of maintenance would not only reduce the overall costs of maintenance but also increase their overall involvement in the productive output of a unit. Hence the inclusion of the word 'total'.

TPM can only be built on a sound maintenance programme encompassing the issues and alternatives outlined earlier. It requires a planned approach to maintenance which will identify the type of maintenance to be used. The distinguishing principles that guide a TPM programme are:

■ Staff must always strive to improve equipment effectiveness based on constant attention to detail and aimed at solving problems by identifying causes rather than just treating symptoms.

■ Routine care needs to be carried out as part of the job. A literal translation of the Japanese term is 'parlour factory' suggesting that the working environment should be as clean and tidy as the home.

■ Operators are recognized as being in the best position to monitor equipment performance. Their involvement in and responsibility for its continuous monitoring improves performance and increases their role in the checking and enhancement tasks within the overall maintenance function.

■ Skill development is based on transferring suitable maintenance tasks to operators and using breakdowns and other problems as learning opportunities thereby increasing operator understanding and ownership.

As with other employee involvement applications, the potential of a company's equipment is being released through the potential of its employees. In effect, TPM is uncovering the 'hidden factory' trapped behind process and equipment inefficiencies. However, given that business-wide TPM can take years to fully implement it is important to recognize the major phases in a successful TPM application:

■ An introductory phase that includes an awareness study, pilot programmes, plant clear-and-clean exercises and developing analytical techniques such as problem solving.

■ The second phase is to bring all sections up to 'best practice' by using agreed approaches across all areas and at all times.

■ Phase three is designed to raise overall performance by developing the capability of employees, equipment and processes. This requires employees to become increasingly proactive in searching for new ways to improve equipment effectiveness.

Exhibit 12.4   *Examples of the benefits resulting from the introduction of TPM*

Company and product	Breakdowns per month reduced			Productivity		OEE %[2]		
	From	To	Period (years)[3]	Current indexed on previous year[1]	Period (years)	Now	Before	Period (years)
Dynamic – book covers	18	3	5	125	2	75	55	3
Gunze – clothing	707	15	2	120	2.5	85	71	3
Sekisui – chemicals	200	10	4	150	4	100[4]	100[4]	4
Daikin – air conditioning	250	5	6	200	6	88	65	6
Toshiba – lighting	387	33	4	247	4	88	71	4

Notes

1. Indexed figures have been based on the previous year's performance.
2. OEE stands for overall equipment effectiveness and is covered in detail in the final section of this chapter.
3. Period (years) indicates the length of time over which the improvements were gained.
4. Data available only in this form.

- The final phase is labelled 'striving for zero losses'. Although unattainable in a practical sense, its purpose is to set targets as an essential facet of the improvement process.

The benefits of TPM are marked as the results in Exhibit 12.4 testify. As with other employee involvement initiatives, time and staying with the task are prerequisites for securing large and sustainable gains.

ENERGY MANAGEMENT

A significant part of the maintenance task concerns energy management in terms of its storage, conversion, distribution and utilization. The increasing use of automation and IT systems within operations and other departments in a business is placing even greater emphasis on this function.

To successfully manage energy the following tasks need to be addressed:

1. **Assessments and targets** – the first task is to undertake an energy audit to determine the actual amount of energy used in each part of an installation. Once completed, usage targets can be set within the different parts of a building or process.

2. **Energy use** – the second aspect concerns the level of efficiency at which energy is used. The overall drive in businesses to improve overall efficiency has led to

Hoechst Trespaphan's Swindon (UK) plant makes polypropylene film for labelling and packaging products for the food industry. In the early 1990s, the company restructured its plant into six units each with a dedicated shift team with all units supported by a separate maintenance team. Training and cross-skilling has increased staff flexibility and helps keep all the processes running in a business where capacity is having difficulty matching demand.

At the time of these changes, the plant averaged 300 breakdowns per month together with equipment deficiencies that affected quality conformance levels. The high level of automation in the plant included integrated process control so when one item of the plant fails the whole line stops. In addition, the planned preventive maintenance schedule required each line to stop one day in every 12

weeks. The outcome of all this was that the uptime level of the plant was only 78 per cent.

The introduction of TPM first examined bottleneck processes and set the basis for future improvements and activities including eliminating set-up failures, increasing through-put speeds (for example the speed of the main film slitting machine was doubled), stopping leaks on feed pipework, the reintroduction of routine checks, finding the root cause of minor problems and the immediate implementation of low-cost improvements.

The plant is now zoned and shift teams select projects within their areas. Regular audits monitor progress and improvements are significant. But TPM is a long journey. Overall equipment effectiveness (OEE) is now a principal measure, and while significant gains have been made 69 per cent is a long way off the 85 per cent posted by world-class performers.

Case example questions

2.1 What were the key steps in bringing about the improvements in this plant?

2.2 Why has OEE replaced process up time as the principal measure used at Hoechst Trespaphan?

increasing attention being given to overhead costs. In energy terms this concerns reviewing rates of usage, reducing losses and the possibility of reclaiming and recovering certain forms of energy such as heat.

3. **Energy management system** – the final task concerns installing a system to manage and control each form of energy from electricity through to compressed air. The main components of an energy management system include:

■ sensors to monitor existing conditions, for example, controls to measure inside and outside temperatures, lighting requirements and humidity levels
■ direct digital controllers that activate or shut down the system depending upon the information received from the sensors
■ a network to link the digital controllers
■ supervisory terminals to inspect the information, including the automatic display of faults.

The installation of energy management systems in the USA currently exceeds £2bn. While those in Europe are at about half that level the recognition that these investments concern not only cost savings but form an integral part of employee working conditions and a company's green agenda is increasing corporate awareness of the overall benefits to be gained.

MANAGING THE MAINTENANCE FUNCTION

The management task in maintenance is similar to that for other functions – the planning and control of work against realistic standards both in terms of capacity and costs and measuring performance against these.

Measuring workloads

The next chapter outlines ways of measuring the capacity requirements and utilization levels in a function. One of these, group capacity assessment (GCA) is well suited to the task of determining maintenance capacity requirements compared with a function's current workload. It also enables management to monitor workload fluctuations and to adjust capacity as required.

In addition to the GCA method of establishing times for maintenance tasks, the universal maintenance standards (UMS) scheme is also available. This is similar to analytical and comparative estimating as described in Chapter 13. In UMS, a large number (200–300) of benchmark jobs are chosen as being representative of the maintenance work involved. Each of these is directly observed and the method checked. An analysis is then completed for each element using methods time motion (MTM) values, and times for completing each element are then determined.[8]

From this analysis, a table of about 20–30 elements is constructed. All other work is then analysed, and, with the aid of the benchmark jobs, the elements of each job are matched to this table and time standards are then established.

Planning maintenance

By introducing a TPM approach companies are able to separate maintenance tasks both into time frames (daily through to annual tasks) and maintenance staff/ operator allocations.

The first step, therefore, is listing all the maintenance work to be undertaken, the frequency of the schedule and to which category of staff it will be allocated. Maintenance calendars then need to be devised to cover the scheduled times that eventually result in annual, monthly, weekly and daily plans. From these, detailed schedules are drawn up for each item of equipment (see Exhibit 12.5), each department and each section within a department. These will, in turn, be translated into monthly and weekly calendars of work to facilitate ordering spares and balancing capacity over a period of time.

Measuring performance

A key factor in managing a maintenance function is to agree the key measures to help gauge and monitor performance. Below are some of the more important measures used.

Exhibit 12.5 *Part of a maintenance plan for a zinc plating unit*

Unit / Location	Maintenance			Parts		Assigned to	Year												Remarks
	Task	Period (weeks)	Total hours (# staff)	Used	Costs (£s)		Month												
							1	2	3	4	5	6	7	8	9	10	11	12	
Pump / Circulation pump	Over-haul	26	16 (2)	–	–	M		/					/						
Outer pump	Over-haul	52	100 (2)	–	–	M													
Valve	Replace sealing gasket	52	30 (4)	Sealing gasket	640	M	X								/				
–	Tighten	13	16 (2)	–	–	M&O		/		/			/			/			
Electricity supply / # 2	Replace roll	4/5	9 (2)	Roll	200	M	X	/	/	/	/	/	/	/	/	/	/	/	
Bearings																			

Notes:

1. M = maintenance. O = operations.
2. / denotes plan. X denotes completed.

Internal departmental performance measures

These should include:

■ The level of effective performance by relating the hours of maintenance work produced to clocked hours in the department. This shows the amount of work produced per hour.

■ Actual tasks completed compared to the plan in terms of the hours of work involved. This helps to assess overall performance and checks the maintenance support for operations during a given period.

■ Total hours of work by each type of maintenance as a percentage of the total maintenance hours. This measures the actual types of maintenance used to the level set in the plan and helps assess how well the function is managing its maintenance response.

Operations-related measures

These should include those that assess the cost of maintenance support overall and those that measure trends in the key areas of improvement. For example:

■ Checking the number of maintenance hours worked with the number of direct hours worked in operations helps assess trends in the relative size of maintenance support. Comparing maintenance costs (including hours, materials and overheads) with the value of the products and services completed in the same period would provide a similar check.

■ Relating the number of breakdowns both in terms of occasions and time lost to the number of operations hours worked would provide an insight into the success of reducing this element of maintenance. However, where a run to failure type of maintenance had been chosen, these incidents should be shown separately and would not form part of the trend review.

■ Safety-related measures such as the number of days lost through accidents help highlight this important aspect of work and the joint role of operations and maintenance in driving these incidents down to zero.

Overall measures

These help to set the maintenance contribution within the context of the overall business. For example:

■ Overall equipment effectiveness (OEE) is one of the most widely used measures. How it is calculated and used is illustrated in Exhibit 12.6. This measure combines both maintenance and operations performance and can be calculated for individual items of equipment, a section or the business as a whole.

    Initial OEE figures for a typical company are in the 40–50 per cent range, while world-class performers post 85 per cent and above. This offers much scope for improvement and sizeable benefits to organizations that continue to manage their way to the high levels similar to those shown in Exhibit 12.4.

■ Checking on the relative cost of maintenance is provided by expressing maintenance cost as a percentage of sales revenue. Although this will be affected by changes in the make-or-buy decision, adjusted trends help to provide a valuable, overall measure.

Exhibit 12.6   *Overall equipment effectiveness – its derivation and use in terms of measurement and target setting*

Week	Availability %		Performance %		Quality %		OEE %
1	84	×	92	×	96	=	74
2	89	×	88	×	97	=	76
3	86	×	90	×	94	=	73
4	83	×	91	×	98	=	74
Average	86	×	90	×	96	=	74
Best of the best	89	×	92	×	98	=	80

Case example   3

One hundred and twenty miles north-east of Aberdeen in Scotland, Forties Alpha is one of BP's platforms extracting oil from the North Sea. At 25 years old it is a declining asset. Around 1980 the oilfield was delivering its peak daily output of 150 000 barrels of oil, while today with reserves falling and more and more water being dragged up with the oil from under the sea bed, Alpha's potential is down to around one-third its peak.

While full capacity is out of reach, equipment efficiency had eroded production output in the early 1990s to about 50 per cent of potential. At that time, BP concentrated its efforts on controlling and improving the visible operational costs (people, maintenance, overheads and material) of the platform.

What received little, if any, attention were the hidden costs of lost opportunities that continued to erode the platform's business performance. These hidden costs induced water management cutbacks, unplanned shutdowns, restart losses, safety and technical integrity, water content in the product, poor work environment and a lack of staff flexibility. All were factors affecting overall efficiency.

The platform's five-shift complement of 75 technicians and supervisors went through a TPM training programme. The first project, to review the platform's system for disposing of the water dredged up with the oil and which reduces oil production, identified 143 improvements. When these were implemented the throughput of the water disposal plant increased by 80 000 barrels a day while one water treatment unit was able to handle 45 000 rather than the previous 20 000 barrels per day. The knock-on effect of this was that the platform's OEE rose from 29 to 63 per cent in the first six months of the TPM project. Asset care was more diligently carried out because the need for it was clearly understood.

These improvements were complemented by the cultural benefits that resulted – stronger teamwork, a proactive approach to maintenance, all-round increased knowledge of processes and procedures and the resolution of problems. Technical information, knowledge, routines and experiences were all shared. As a result, problems were resolved rather than given a quick fix. The impact on the business as a whole became the context in which problems, improvements and descriptions were reviewed.

Case example questions

3.1 Why do companies such as BP typically concentrate their efforts and measure their performance on operational costs such as people, maintenance, overheads and materials?

3.2 To what did the TPM programme switch the focus of the platform's attention?

3.3 What was the key to the success of its TPM initiative?

CONCLUSION

For organizations to secure essential increases in productivity requires the combined efforts of all functions. The increased use of technology has resulted in maintenance making a major contribution to the effective efforts in most businesses. Furthermore, the increasing introduction of JIT scheduling arrangements and the growing importance of delivery reliability and delivery speed places increased emphasis on equipment and processes being available in line with schedules or customer needs.

As a result, the role and activities within the maintenance function have changed in recognition of and to meet these new requirements. For example:

■ To help reduce the growing cost of maintenance, organizations are considering the maintenance dimension much earlier in investment decisions in recognition of the importance of post-installation costs as an essential factor within investment appraisal procedures.

■ As part of the importance to support delivery needs while keeping inventories low, high and guaranteed levels of equipment availability are essential.

■ Where equipment does fail, then process support becomes a vital role. Quick and effective response to process problems and breakdowns is an increasingly important task. On site, well-trained staff are needed to support core processes, while those companies using control systems often supplement their own in-house capability by establishing computer links to outside specialists to help diagnose problems through the use of computer-based control systems.

The need to reduce costs has also led companies to reduce total manning levels within maintenance and to compensate for the loss of skill areas by increased training of staff and changes in working practices through teamwork approaches based on multi-skilling principles and the increased use of operators to take on appropriate routine maintenance tasks – the concept of TPM.

As part of this development, companies are also increasingly involving the maintenance function in the later stages of installation and throughout the commissioning phase of equipment as the first stage of training and also to provide the opportunity to identify possible modifications to help simplify process support in the future.

All organizations will continue to invest in technology at an increasing rate in order to reduce costs and improve response times in terms of data provision, control and decision making. It is important for organizations to recognize the consequences of this. Maintenance managers need to bring top management's attention to these important perspectives before the technology decisions are made. Furthermore, with investment, growth, the need for supporting specialists will also increase. It is essential, therefore, that the management of the company's physical resources is at the appropriate level and that the controls to ensure that this is so are installed and developed.

SUMMARY

The reliability of the delivery system is a key factor in operations as it impacts both the internal and external (or market-related) tasks in managing this function:

■ Internal tasks including cost targets, assessment of capacity which, in part, will need to take into account the reliability of the process, and inventory management that similarly will need to reflect the level of uncertainty of a process in terms of the level of inventory it will carry.

■ External tasks that concern on-time and fast delivery requirements and, in which, process reliability will be a key factor.

The first section of the chapter addressed the issues around process reliability and introduced ways of checking for failure. The ways to assess failure were discussed

SUMMARY (cont'd)

including rate of failure, process reliability and process availability measures. This section also covered ways to identify levels of failure and how to analyse failures as a way of improving process reliability.

This part of the chapter also introduced ways used to improve the reliability of a process by introducing fail-safe mechanisms as an integral part of the systems design.

The remainder of the chapter then addressed ways to maintain processes and the management tasks involved. The opening sections clarified meanings and terms and identified the different types of maintenance – reactive, preventive, condition-based, use of stand-by equipment and corrective maintenance before leading onto a major section on planned maintenance.

The final major section highlighted the key issues in managing the maintenance function. Areas covered included measuring staff workloads, planning maintenance tasks and ways to measure performance.

Discussion questions

1. The radio alarm clock you recently purchased needs three elements all to be working for it to provide the alarm in the morning. The reliability of these three elements are as follows:

Element	Reliability
Clock	0.96
Alarm switch	0.94
Radio	0.98

   What is the probability that the alarm will ring in the morning?

2. Identify three *poka-yoke* examples used in service delivery systems. Classify them into process, service and customer-based applications as described and illustrated in this chapter.

3. A major European bank has 2378 automatic teller machines (ATMs) in the UK. When an ATM has a machine or software failure, the system controlling an ATM would trigger an automatic call-out to NCR who are contracted to provide a back-up maintenance service to the bank. Last year the total number of 'auto-calls' to NCR was 19 738. What was the average mean time between failures for an ATM?

   In addition, there are several occasions during a year when ATMs run out of cash. This is particularly so when national holidays fall on a Monday or around major holiday periods such as Christmas and Easter. If these cash-outs are added to the auto-calls, the total for last year is now 22 115. What now would be the mean time between failures?

Discussion questions (cont'd)

4. How does planned maintenance differ from the other types of maintenance outlined in the section entitled 'Different types of maintenance'. What are the underlying principles that distinguish planned maintenance?

5. Analyse the maintenance work completed on your car in a 12-month period and classify each activity into its relevant category.

6. A photocopying outlet has several machines, three of which are under heavy demand during most days. The mean time (operating hours) between failures (MTBF) and minimum time (hours) to repair (MTTR) for these machines are as follows.

Machine reference	MTBF	MTTR
3	80	4
5	100	2
8	75	4

What is the availability for each of these three machines?

7. For the three machines in Question 6, the company would be able to change the maintenance and service contracts with the following outcomes:

| Machine reference | Revised | |
	MTBF	MTTR
3	95	3.5
5	130	2.0
8	85	3.0

If the cost to complete these improvements was similar one machine to another, which machine would you improve first?

8. Why is stand-by equipment usually not a sound part of providing maintenance? Give two examples where stand-by equipment would be an essential provision?

9. The photocopying machine in a solicitor's office has the following performance data during a six-week period:

Week	Availability %	Performance %	Quality %
1	80	90	93
2	74	88	96
3	82	92	97
4	83	91	92
5	76	87	94
6	78	89	93

Discussion questions (cont'd)

Calculate the overall equipment effectiveness

- for each week
- as a six-week average
- the best of the best in this period.

Notes and references

1. Life cycle costs are defined as the total costs of an item throughout its life including initial, maintenance and support costs.
2. *Glossary of Terms used in Terotechnology*, BS3811 (British Standards Institution, 1993) No. 1101 and *Guide to Terotechnology*, BS3843 (British Standards Institution, 1992), Part 2.
3. The maintenance function is usually either an engineering or an OM responsibility. This will depend on aspects such as the size of the organization and the nature of its products/services. Exhibit 1.3 illustrates this function as part of the operations task. In other organizations it may report to the V-P Research and Develement or, more normally, to the V-P Engineering.
4. Also see Holder, R 'Why condition-based monitoring offers solid bottom line results', *Works Management*, March (1996), pp. 18–19.
5. These issues are discussed in an article by Bates, A 'Effective strategies deliver plant reliability', *Works Management*, July (1996), pp. 45–9.
6. This approach is reviewed by Moubray, J in an article entitled 'Reliability centred maintenance: making a positive contribution to asset management strategy' in *A Guide to Best Practice Maintenance Management*, Part 1 (Shell Oils publication, London 1996).
7. See, for example, Raynes, M 'Outsourcing: the way to solve your lubricating problems' in *A Guide to Best Practice Maintenance Management*, Part 2 (Shell Oils, London 1996).
8. MTM is a widely used predetermined motion time standard. This form of measurement is covered extensively in Chapter 13. Suffice here to say that with MTM, predetermined times for operations are used that have been built up through research and analysis, and issued as tables.

Further reading

Davis, R *Productivity Improvements Through TPM*, Prentice Hall, Hemel Hempstead (1995).

Nakajima, S *Introduction to TPM; Total Productive Maintenance*, Productivity Press, Cambridge, MA (1988).

Senju, S (ed.) *TQC and TPM*, Asian Productivity Organization, Tokyo (1992).

Takahashi, Y and Osada, T *TPM: Total Productive Maintenance,* Asia Productivity Organization, Tokyo (1990).

Womack, JP, Jones, DT and Roos, D *The Machine that Changed the World*, Rawson Associates, New York (1990).

## part four

Improving Operations

CHAPTER THIRTEEN

The content and planning of this book: an overview of what is involved, what has been addressed so far and what is covered in this chapter

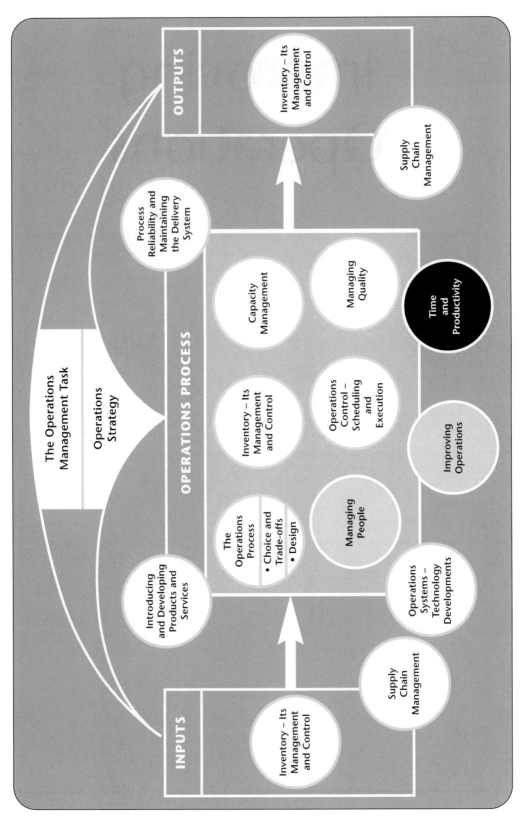

Time and Productivity

Chapter overview

This chapter addresses two important dimensions that are central to managing operations:

- **Time** – measuring how long a job should take.
- **Productivity** – measuring the outputs from a system in relation to the inputs that go into their creation.

On reflection you will clearly recognize the link between these two aspects of operations as the measurement of time will invariably form part of measuring the outputs and inputs (the numerator and denominator respectively) of the productivity calculation.

The layout of the chapter reflects both the link between these two aspects by incorporating them in the same chapter and the separate perspectives involved by addressing each in its own section. First we will discuss the aspect of time, with the section on productivity coming later. An overview of the aspects covered in the chapter are:

- **Why time is the common denominator of operations management** with illustrations to highlight this issue.
- **Measuring the content of work** – measuring work sets out to answer the question, how long should a job take? This section overviews the approach to follow.
- **Approaches to measuring work content** – as jobs are different then the approach to measuring jobs will also differ. This section illustrates how the approaches to measuring short repetitive tasks, long non-repetitive tasks and techniques to measure capacity utilization and requirements differ and gives examples of each.
- **Productivity** – what it is and what, in general terms, it measures.
- **Productivity and efficiency** are compared to help distinguish between these two dimensions that are used to evaluate the results of improvement.
- **Approaches to measuring productivity** are discussed and the difference between single and multi-factor measures and the use of added value is explained.

Chapter overview (cont'd)

■ **Ways to improve productivity** are outlined and the link between these and the next chapter on the ways to improve performance in operations is established.

■ **Service applications** – with the growing importance of the service sector in the more advanced economies, the need for and ways to secure productivity improvements in service businesses are discussed.

TIME – THE COMMON DENOMINATOR IN MANAGING OPERATIONS

The two dimensions used by a business to control its activities are time and money. Time is the basis for tasks such as planning, estimating, costing and payment systems, and money is the basis for trading, accounting and financial reporting.

Whereas the money dimension is primarily explained through accounting and finance, it is through operations management that an understanding of the time dimension may be gained. It is essential, therefore, that operations managers fully understand how work may be measured and are able to choose the most appropriate method of measurement to meet a given requirement. This section explains these aspects of the task. Furthermore, operations managers must understand both the time and money dimensions in themselves and ensure that the translation from one to another is both accurate and appropriate. For, whereas operations is managed on a time base, the costs associated with products, services, customers and investments will be reported in terms of money.

This opening statement explains that operations uses time as the common denominator for assessing, controlling and managing many of its activities. The question is, why? To explain let us use a number of examples.

Example 1 – Conform

A glance back at Exhibit 6.2 shows that the nine products made on day 1 of that week all had different standard times. Therefore, to use the quantity of products made as the measure of how good a day was or as the basis to calculating capacity requirements would be of little value. Making 100 of product reference 2766 at 3.0 standard minutes each is not the same as making 100 of product reference 1229 at 36.0 standard minutes each.

Example 2 – Heath Motors

Heath Motors makes three small electric motors for a wide range of applications. As in Example 1, to use the quantity of products as the basis for calculating capacity requirements or to assess weekly performance would not provide a meaningful approach to these and other dimensions of operations as the examples in Exhibits 13.1 and 13.2 illustrate.

Using quantity as the basis for assessing output, then Exhibit 13.1 shows that week 1 appears to be a much better period than week 2. The factor missing from this assessment is how long it takes to make each different motor. When these data are introduced (see Exhibit 13.2) it can be seen that, in terms of hours, the output for weeks 1 and 2 is very similar.

Example 3 – John Michael

For the owner of John Michael to determine how many hairdressers would be required or to assess the output of a day based upon the number of customers served would be misleading. As with earlier examples, the time it takes to dress a customer's hair will differ in line with what the service entails. A dry cut, wash and cut, and wash and style will take different times to complete. Yet again, the factor of time needs to be included when calculating capacity, scheduling appointments, measuring performance and determining costs.

MEASURING THE CONTENT OF WORK

The purpose of measuring the content of work is to establish the time for a qualified worker to complete a specified job at a defined level of performance.[1] In other words, measuring work sets out to answer the question, 'How long should this job take to

Exhibit 13.1   *Heath Motors – output in terms of units produced for two different weeks*

Week	Electric motor type	Quantity produced	
		#	Total
1	HM 40	100	
	HM 60	100	440
	HM 80	240	
2	HM 40	480	
	HM 60	200	830
	HM 80	150	

Exhibit 13.2   *Heath Motors – output in terms of hours produced for the two different weeks*

Week	Electric motor type	Quantity produced (#)	Time per product (hours)	Hours produced	
				#	Total
1	HM 40	100	0.5	50	
	HM 60	100	1.5	150	1160
	HM 80	240	4.0	960	
2	HM 40	480	0.5	240	
	HM 60	200	1.5	300	1140
	HM 80	150	4.0	600	

Exhibit 13.3 *The reasons for and objectives of measuring work*

With the continuous improvement approaches described in Chapter 14, measuring the content of work plays an essential role in tasks such as to:

- eliminate ineffective time, with work content determining the extent of possible improvements
- allow comparisons of alternative methods to be made
- balance work members in a team
- determine an adequate workload for a person

As a basis for:

- planning and scheduling work
- estimating and costing
- staff and staff-cost control
- payment and reward systems
- estimating future capacity requirements both in terms of labour and equipment
- establishing delivery promises

complete?' And, as the time dimension is the basis for managing most key operations activities, then establishing times and knowing what the statements used to express time comprise are essential operations management tasks.

Before describing the approaches used to provide this information it is useful to first understand the reasons for and objectives of measuring work, see Exhibit 13.3.

Measuring work

The simplest way to measure work is to time how long a task takes. However, the reality of work does not lend itself to such a simple method. In particular, there are three dimensions that can make a significant difference to the time it takes to complete a job. These are listed in Exhibit 13.4, together with the ways used to account for these factors.

The procedure to measure the work content of jobs

The steps to measure the work content of jobs are explained below with a brief explanation of what is involved. The alternative ways to measure and establish the content of a job are then explained in more detail.

Select, record and analyse the job

Which jobs to measure are selected for reasons similar to those given earlier and range from continuous improvement, the planning and scheduling of work through to establishing delivery lead times (see Exhibit 13.3). Recording what is involved in the work selected, agreeing the method to be used and analysing what the work entails are then the next steps to complete before deciding how best to measure the task(s) involved.

Measure the job and establish the time

There are a range of ways to measure jobs. Which is the most appropriate needs to reflect two principles:

Exhibit 13.4   *Factors affecting the time to complete a task and approaches to overcoming these factors*

Factors affecting the length of time to complete a job	Approaches used to account for these factors
Different methods may be used to complete a task	The time to complete a task is based on an agreed method. A revised method would require a new time
The time taken directly relates to the speed and effort of the person doing the task	Variations in speed and effort are accounted for when assessing how long it takes and adjustments are made to account for such differences. This is known as 'rating'
Some tasks are more strenuous or difficult than others and require more time for a person to rest and recover	All observed rest time is excluded from the initial assessment of how long a job takes. This 'net' time is later increased uniformly to include an allowance for rest and personal needs in line with the type of job being undertaken

■ The level of measurement accuracy required.

■ The expression of the time taken will vary from job to job. Short, repetitive tasks will normally be expressed in minutes and parts of minutes. Long jobs (for example, undertaking a management consultancy contract and building an oil tanker) will normally be expressed in weeks and parts of weeks.

To reflect these factors the approaches to measuring work are divided into those for short, repetitive tasks and those for long, non-repetitive tasks. These are described more fully in a later section.

Check that the measurement is accurate

Before the times for a job can be used it is essential to complete studies to check that the calculations have been correctly made so that their use will lead to sound decisions.

APPROACHES TO MEASURING WORK CONTENT

As explained earlier, this section provides more detail on the approaches to measure the work content of a task. It is in three parts to help you recognize that different jobs require different approaches and to recognize which approach would be the best in a given situation.

Approaches to measure short, repetitive tasks

As a general rule, the techniques used to measure short, repetitive tasks will be chosen to provide accurate information expressed in minutes and parts of a minute. The reason for this is fundamental to the task itself – as it only takes a short time to complete but will be completed on numerous occasions, the time taken to complete the task needs to be measured accurately.

The techniques most commonly used to provide this level of accuracy are time study and predetermined motion time standards. The first of these will be described in more detail and will include the procedure to establish a 'standard time'. This will provide a sound basis for understanding how to measure the content of work. The other approaches will then be described in less detail.

Time study

As providing a more accurate time is needed for work that is short duration and repetitive in nature, the job under review is broken down into elements enabling the time involved for each element to be more accurately assessed. When undertaking this type of measurement, the elements of work are further identified as being either:

■ *repetitive* – occurring regularly in every work cycle or once in a given number of cycles

■ *occasional and contingency* – occurring irregularly and, though not directly part of the job on hand, are part of the general working conditions, for example, discussing work with a supervisor.

When the job is being studied there will typically be activities other than the work elements described above. These will be either periods of rest or tasks not directly to do with the job under review (for example, undertaking work on another job). These are duly recorded but are set to one side. An allowance for rest is added later but the activities that are unrelated to the job being reviewed are simply excluded from the calculations.

To establish how long to do a job under time study a trained person measures the time taken to complete each element observed, while at the same time assessing the speed and effectiveness with which the person undertaking the task is working. Often the recording part of this procedure is completed by videoing the work. This facilitates the person doing the job to become involved and the time element is easily and accurately established. Assessing the speed and effectiveness of a person is known as rating and takes into account a person's speed of movement, dexterity and consistency of application. Rating is based on a numerical scale of which there are three in use known as 60–80, 0–133 and 0–100 and each serve the same purpose.

The role of rating is to allow the observed times for elements to be adjusted up or down to reflect the speed at which a person is working. In that way times are established based on a common rate of working (for example, at 100 on the 0–100 scale).

So far we have identified that in time study applications, a job is broken down into elements, each element is measured and the time taken to complete an element is then adjusted by the rate at which the person observed was working. The same elements of work are measured on several occasions (ideally at least three different people on three different occasions) to provide an average. This is known as the basic time or normal time. A basic time is calculated for each element of a job to which is then added a percentage to cover occasionals and contingencies and also an allowance for rest to reflect the need for relaxation and personal time and to compensate where the work is more strenuous or demanding to undertake. The various elements are then added together and the total is known as the 'standard time' to complete the job under review. To help you put this description together, the procedure described here has been summarized in Exhibit 13.5 and illustrated in Exhibit 13.6.

Exhibit 13.5   *The steps to establish a standard time for a job using time study*

Step	Description
1	Select the task to be reviewed
2	To facilitate the accurate measurement of the task, it is broken down into the following elements: ■ repetitive ■ occasionals and contingencies These elements then become the basis on which the measurement is made
3	A person undertaking the task is observed and the time taken to complete the various elements is recorded. Often videoing is used to complete this step. Work not directly to do with the job under review is identified but excluded from the final calculations
4	At the same time that each element of a job is being measured, the rate the person undertakes these tasks is assessed
5	At the end of the study the time recorded for each element of work is adjusted up or down to reflect the lower or higher rate compared to an agreed norm. On the 0–100 scale, this 'norm' is usually the rate of 100. The observed time adjusted for the recorded rating is known as the 'basic time' or 'normal time'
6	To the basic time is added an allowance for occasionals and contingencies (work to be done but not specific to any particular job) and rest. The result is called the 'standard time'
7	The respective elements are then totalled together and this becomes the standard time for the job reviewed

Predetermined motion time standards (PMTS)

The essence of time study is to time and rate the task by direct observation. However, from the genesis of time study the concept of having predetermined times for operations was recognized. Several effective systems have been devised that replace observations by highly detailed method study in order to analyse and classify the motions used. Tables of predetermined times for each classified motion are drawn up, and thus the total time for an operation can be calculated by adding together the predetermined times of its constituent parts. Later developments of PMTS systems provide higher-level data that provide times for complete tasks (as opposed to the motions comprising a task) and this enables the time for a job to be calculated more quickly.

Synthetics

In the same way that PMTS systems provide predetermined times for basic operations, synthetic times can be built up from previous time studies carried out in an organization. In this way, times for completing part or all of a task can be calculated from numerous past studies, and used to build up the time to complete a range of similar work at a defined level or performance.

Exhibit 13.6 *The details in Exhibit 13.5 shown diagramatically*

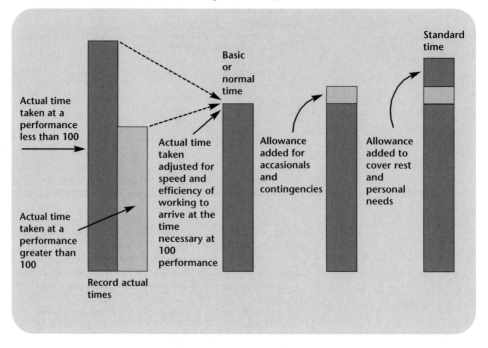

Normally, these times would embody higher-level data and cover much longer parts of a task than basic human movement. For example, dust a chair, paint one running metre or window frame or make an outer carton.

Approaches to measure long, non-repetitive tasks

Many tasks have a long work cycle and will often occur infrequently. For such, time study and PMTS are not cost-effective ways of measurement. It is more appropriate to use one of the following forms of estimating.

Estimating

This form of measurement involves an 'assessment of the time required to carry out work, based on a knowledge and experience of similar types of work'.[2] This assessment is made on the total job without a breakdown into elements (Exhibit 13.7) and is thus dependent upon the knowledge and experience of the evaluator. In making an assessment, the evaluator will often use historical times in an informal way.

Analytical estimating

This is a refined form of estimating, in which 'the time to carry out elements at a defined rate of working is estimated partially from knowledge and practical experience of the work concerned and partially from synthetic data'.[3] When using this technique the work is broken down into suitable elements and the times for these are either esti-

Exhibit 13.7 *Types of estimating that may be used to determine the time to be allocated to completing a particular task*

Task	Estimating	Analytical estimating	Comparative estimating
Office Cleaning	An estimate of the time it would take to empty all the waste bins, vacuum clean and dust the office under review would be made. This would be based on the estimator's own past experience of similar work	The tasks involved in cleaning the office under review would be broken down into smaller parts, for example: Emptying 10 waste bins Dusting 10 desks Dusting 10 chairs Dusting 20 filing cabinets Dusting 50 metres of skirting board Dusting 10 window ledges Dusting 5 doors Vacuum cleaning 150 square metres of carpet with a high level of furniture congestion The next step is to complete an estimate for each of these parts. The individual estimates would be added to give an overall time to complete the cleaning of this office. Again, the times should be based on the estimator's own past experience of similar work	From past experience of cleaning offices, a number of job categories would be compiled by the estimator. These would be chosen to reflect the different time bands of the work undertaken (see below), and one or more benchmark jobs would be selected as being representative of each band. When selected, each benchmark job would then be analysed in greater depth, and a detailed study would be completed to check that the time band to which each job had been allocated was appropriate. A full description of the individual tasks involved for each job would also be recorded and filed for later use: Time band (hr) Benchmark job(s) 0–½ Partner's office, 8 Southall Gardens ½–1 Purchasing department, AB Imports, Floor 4, Bradley House 1–1½ Drawing office, Markham, Roberts & Co. 1½ –2 General office, Housing Department, Bursley DC 2–3 Main open plan office, British Energy, West Midlands And so on. All future jobs would then be compared to each benchmark job and, usually, the midpoint of the time band for the job to which it was most similar would be allocated and used in all the appropriate calculations

mated or taken from synthetic data (see Exhibit 13.7). Although more time-consuming to apply than estimating, it is normally more accurate.

Comparative estimating

This is a further development of estimating in which the time taken for a task is evaluated by comparing the work involved with the work in a series of similar tasks. This method is based on the principle of using categories of work, where jobs are not given precise times but are placed in a time band (for example, two to three hours – see Exhibit 13.7), and the use of benchmark jobs on which comparisons are based. These latter jobs are chosen as being representative of a time band, and their times are based on a primary method of work measurement (for example, time study). The use of benchmarks makes for a speedy evaluation by slotting tasks into broad bands of time.

Techniques to measure capacity utilization and requirements

In many situations it is important both to measure the extent to which existing capacity is being used and to be able to monitor utilization in the future. The techniques available to produce this information are described here.

Activity sampling

Activity sampling involves making random observations over a representative period of time to provide information on:

- capacity utilization of the facilities or persons employed on a task or in an area
- the average time taken to complete a common task.

Applications of these techniques include operations areas with several pieces of equipment, warehousing, and administrative or technical units. In each, an assessment of utilization or an average time taken can be established.

The overall time spent on a specified activity is deduced from a number of random observations. Owing to the limitations inherent in sampling, an error is introduced. The size of this error can be calculated statistically. For this purpose, a 95 per cent confidence limit is considered to give sufficient accuracy, and is built into the following formula:

$$N = \frac{4P\,(100 - P)}{L^2}$$

where N = number of random observations, P = percentage occurrence of the particular activity being reviewed, and L the level of accuracy required. For example, if through observation or pilot study a personal computer (or other piece of equipment) is estimated to be unused say 35 per cent of the time, the number of observations required to determine the actual percentage of time unused to an accuracy of ± 5 per cent, with 95 per cent confidence in the answer would be:

$$N = \frac{4(35)\,(65)}{5^2} = 364$$

Conversely, it may be that a study has been completed, and the level of accuracy obtained at 95 per cent confidence limits needs to be ascertained. The following equation would be used:

$$L = 2 \times \sqrt{\frac{P(100 - P)}{N}}$$

For example, of the percentage of time that warehouse staff were not working was 10.1 per cent of the time observed and the number of observations totalled 6500, the level of accuracy at 95 per cent confidence limit would be

$$L = 2 \times \sqrt{\frac{10.1(89.9)}{6500}} = 0.7$$

So, the warehouse staff were not working between 9.4 and 10.8 per cent of the time. If there were 20 staff observed, then the capacity needed to cope with present through-puts could be reduced by some 10 per cent.

So far the activity sampling study has revealed the percentage of time an activity has happened during the period of observation. To assess how long on average a task took, the percentage of time observed when staff were doing the task is first established in the way described here. A period of time (for example, day or week) is then studied to determine on how many occasions the task was completed (for example, orders dispatched, invoices processed or units produced). If during an eight-hour day, four staff were employed 65 per cent of their time on dispatches and completed in that period 180 dispatches, then the average dispatch time can be calculated as follows:

$$\frac{65 \text{ per cent} \times 4 \times 8 \text{ hours}}{180 \text{ dispatches}} = \frac{1248 \text{ minutes}}{180} = 6.9 \text{ minutes per dispatch}$$

Information provided in this way enables operations to establish the capacity required to handle the throughput observed during the period studied. Whether this is a normal load can be checked by comparing (say) the number of dispatches completed within the observed period with the number of dispatches completed in a reference period in the past. This reference period is chosen to represent a period of normal working over a given time (for example, three months).

When capacity required to handle a normal workload has been established, then monitoring throughput against capacity levels on a regular basis can be put into effect. This is achieved by comparing (say) the weekly net hours available (that is, total hours less rest and personal time) in a finished goods warehouse with the amount of work completed in the same period (for example, the number of dispatches made, deliveries received, stock checks made and paperwork processed), the times for these activities having been established through activity sampling. Where work was not seen during the sample (for example, tasks completed on a monthly basis only) then estimates of the time taken to complete these tasks are established.

This comparison enables management to monitor any throughput changes and their effect on, in this instance, the warehouse, and enables them to come to better decisions on whether to increase or decrease capacity on a temporary (through overtime or by making an internal transfer) or permanent (adding staff or natural wastage) basis.

Group capacity assessment

Group capacity assessment (GCA) provides a basis for controlling staffing levels in indirect areas where more rigorous forms of work measurement are more difficult and expensive to apply. The first task is to establish times (that a trained person is expected to achieve on a day work basis without allowance for rest) for all the major tasks in a particular department. This is accomplished by using an appropriate form of work measurement. For example, time study, synthetics, activity sampling or analytical estimating. In sensitive situations, a video recording is made, and the number of completed work cycles counted in that period. An average time is then established.

While this information is being generated, the number of tasks completed in the department each day is being recorded. The average number of tasks completed in this period is calculated and extended by the time allowed. The number of people required (making due allowance for rest and personal needs) can then be established.

As in activity sampling, the capacity required is agreed, and changes are monitored in the future. This is done by totalling the number of tasks completed each day, extending these by the agreed time and calculating the total labour content of the work done that day. This is compared to the hours worked during that day, and an 'efficiency percentage' is calculated. These daily controls are monitored at department level, with weekly controls for each department being provided for the next level of management.

Clerical work improvement programme

Banks and other high volume service sectors (for example, insurance and other parts of the financial sector) often monitor staff requirements through a programme similar to that described under GCA, but specific to their own organization. One example is the clerical work improvement programme (CWIP) that measures staff requirements for different administrative units and centres. Synthetic times are established for the range of activities undertaken. One common approach is to video the tasks and then afterwards use the tape to observe and calculate the times for elements of work. Standard times (an allowance being added to the observed time to cover occasionals, contingencies, rest and personal needs) are then established and used to calculate times for existing and future jobs. Typically, all times are verified by observing the tasks being completed, where possible, at a number of locations.

The assessment of staff needs is primarily based on the number of transactions completed. Daily volumes are recorded (normally as an automatic by-product of the system) and continuously reviewed over a 20-day period. Four-weekly reports would form the basis by which a company monitors capacity and helps to control costs.

Exhibit 13.8   *Approaches to measuring work – some typical service applications*

Approaches to measuring work	Some typical applications
Time study, PMTS and synthetics	Maintenance schedules (for example, vehicles, aircraft and equipment) Cleaning services Secretarial and clerical tasks services and word processing Administrative functions
Estimating, analytical estimating and comparative estimating	Maintenance schedules Restaurants – back and front office operations Hotels – back and front office support services Consulting assignments Design services
Activity sampling	Warehousing and stores provision Equipment utilization Call centres Supermarkets – back and front office activities
GCA and CWIPs	Banking and financial services Administration Secretarial services and clerical tasks Warehousing and stores provision

SERVICE APPLICATIONS

The service sector in many economies is large and continues to form the largest employment sector for a nation's workforce. Couple this with the typically large overhead provision within all sectors and managing white-collar staff effectively in terms of capacity, costs and other key functions is an essential task.

The last section examined some of the approaches that are successfully used in the service sector, while Exhibit 13.8 provides a summary of likely applications to illustrate the widespread nature of these opportunities and to help identify others within different functions and organizations.

CONCLUSION

As time is the common denominator in managing many of the key tasks in operations, then understanding the alternative approaches to measuring time and recognizing which alternative is the most appropriate to use is fundamental to an operations manager's role. Determining capacity requirements, setting realistic throughput targets and evaluating performance are core tasks. With typically 70–80 per cent of people and costs falling within the remit of operations then controlling and managing these large resources in line with budgets and customer needs is central to the overall success of a business.

Also, given the need to reduce costs and improve all dimensions of performance, then evaluating and choosing alternatives is an essential part of securing the improvements necessary for the short- and long-term success of a business. Measuring time is a key facet of this task and provides essential dimensions of the need for continuous improvement in operations, the subject of Chapter 14.

PRODUCTIVITY

As explained at the start of the chapter, this separate section now deals with the aspect of productivity. You will see from the very first exhibits (see Exhibits 13.1 and 13.2) the link between the two aspects is clearly visible. Now let us turn our attention to the important dimension of productivity.

The prosperity of nations and organizations alike is recognized as being dependent upon their comparative productivity. At a national level, the relationship between the level of output per hour in the manufacturing sector from 1960 to 1998, the share of world trade in manufactured goods and the gross domestic product per capita for five more advanced economies is clearly shown in Exhibits 13.9, 13.10, and 13.11 respectively. Productivity, then, is a most useful comparative measure at a national, sector or individual business level to provide comparisons between relative performances and to measure trends over time. This section explains productivity and some of the ways in which it is measured.

Exhibit 13.9 *Trends in output per hour in manufacturing for selected countries 1960–98 (1992=100)*

Country	1960	1970	1980	1990	1995	1998
Belgium	18	33	65	97	109	122
Canada	41	59	75	95	108	112
France	23	46	71	99	114	128
Germany	29	52	77	99	111	127
Italy	20	37	44	93	114	114
Japan	14	38	64	95	109	121
Netherlands	20	39	70	99	120	133
Sweden	28	53	74	95	122	137
United Kingdom	30	43	54	89	107	105
United States	53	62	94	98	115	127

Source: Monthly Labor Review, Bureau of Labor Statistics, US Department of Labor, August 1999

WHAT IS PRODUCTIVITY?

What then is productivity? In general terms, it expresses the relationship between the outputs from a system and the inputs which go into their creation, as shown below:

$$\text{Productivity} = \frac{\text{Output}}{\text{Input}}$$

Exhibit 13.10 *Share of world trade in manufactured goods for selected countries, 1980–96*

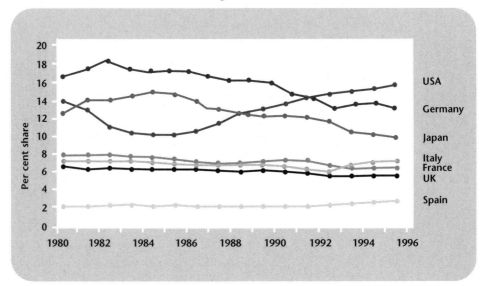

Source: OECD and UK Department of Trade and Industry.

Exhibit 13.11   *GDP per capita for selected countries (US = 100), 1980–96*

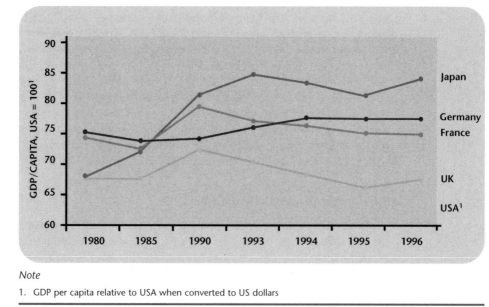

Note

1. GDP per capita relative to USA when converted to US dollars

Source: OECD.

An increase in productivity, therefore, can be secured by changing either or both the numerator or denominator of this simple equation. However, it follows that an increase in output itself does not necessarily mean an increase in productivity unless there has been a less than pro rata increase in inputs.

PRODUCTIVITY AND EFFICIENCY

Part of your task in understanding the field of operations is to assimilate the technical differences between the concepts and dimensions that make up the field. One key difference concerns that between productivity and efficiency, the explanations for which follow:

■ **productivity** measures the amount of input required to achieve a given output or, expressed the other way, the amount of output resulting from a given input

■ **efficiency** measures how well resources have been used by comparing actual output with the expected or standard output that should have resulted from the use of these resources and will be addressed in more detail in the next chapter.

$$\text{Efficiency} = \frac{\text{Actual output}}{\text{Expected or standard output}}$$

APPROACHES TO MEASURING PRODUCTIVITY

Single and multi-factor are the commonly used measures of productivity. As an example of single-factor measurement, labour productivity typically measures output per hour. Total factor productivity, on the other hand, includes not only labour but also other inputs such as processes, energy and materials. All productivity measures are exposed to a number of indirectly acquired sources of improvement. For example, technological change, and the increasing skill base and know-how of people would, in themselves, typically lead to an increase in productivity in related areas but may not appear to be directly associated with the improvement. However, as a measure to reflect trends and compare performance, productivity is a simple and effective way of providing these insights. Examples of single and multi-factor measures are now provided.

Single-factor productivity measures

■ **Labour productivity** is the most commonly used measure and relates output to hours worked (see below). Its universal application derives from several factors including that it is easy to calculate and the like-for-like dimension of labour both within and between nations, sectors and businesses, a factor illustrated earlier in Exhibit 13.9:

$$\text{Labour productivity} = \frac{\text{Output (£s)}}{\text{Hours worked}}$$

■ **Process productivity** measures the value of the outputs produced in relation to the process time involved:

$$\text{Process productivity} = \frac{\text{Output (£s)}}{\text{Process time (hours)}}$$

Another means of evaluating process productivity is to compare the value of goods sold (£s) to the fixed asset investment in the processes under review.

Multi-factor productivity measures

The single-factor dimensions of the labour and process measures of productivity provide one view of a total picture and when using them, this needs to be borne in mind. However, by using a multi-factor measure of productivity, certain of these problems will be overcome.

Multi- (also called total) factor productivity includes not only labour inputs but also some or all of the costs of capital, energy, materials and other purchased services:

$$\text{Multi-factor productivity} = \frac{\text{Output (£s)}}{\substack{\text{Costs (£s) of labour, capital, energy,} \\ \text{materials and other purchased services}}}$$

This measure provides an improved framework for assessing the whole of operations and gives a basis for analysing productivity changes due to substituting or improving one or more of the factors involved.

Added value

One useful refinement to measuring productivity is to relate factors to added value. The latter refers to the value added to a product or service by a business and is, therefore, the difference between sales revenue and all material and service costs incurred to make those sales. These costs include materials and components, stationery, subcontract and any other elements of material or staff costs purchased from outside a business (see Exhibit 13.12):

$$\text{Added value} = \begin{array}{c}\text{Sales revenue less materials}\\\text{and service costs purchased}\\\text{from outside a business}\end{array}$$

Thus, over the period being reviewed, the added value measures the wealth produced by a unit. The added value index (AVI) is also a useful overall measure because it relates the added value to total employment costs (for example, salaries, pensions and national insurance contributions). It is calculated as follows and is often expressed as a percentage:

$$\text{Added value index} = \frac{\text{Total employment costs}}{\text{Added value}}$$

The ratio is a valuable measure of operations management's performance because, unlike profit, it is less affected by factors outside a manager's control (for example, inflation) and because it focuses on a fundamental aspect of management's task, that of being responsible for employee productivity.

AVI measures operations by relating the current AVI against a previously agreed standard, with a lower figure indicating an improvement in this ratio. Added value reward schemes are also used by some organizations.

Exhibit 13.12 *Added value in relation to bought-out materials/services and to sales*

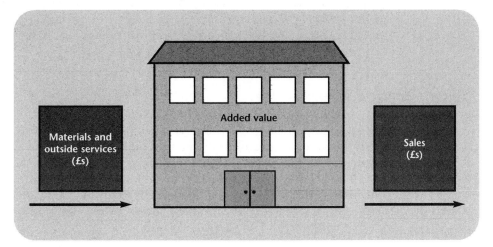

Exhibit 13.13 *Approaches to improving productivity and some of the trade-offs involved*

Aspects	Approaches		
	Scientific	Technical	Operational
The cost of providing the necessary facilities and staff to complete these activities	High	⟶	Low
The potential for improving productivity	High	⟶	Low
The length of time to yield the productivity gains	Long	⟶	Short

WAYS TO IMPROVE PRODUCTIVITY

There are three levels at which productivity improvements can be made:

■ **scientific**, involving research leading to new knowledge in, for example, materials, processes and IT chips
■ **technical** which comprises the adaptation or application of new scientific knowledge to replace existing ideas or to introduce new ways to complete tasks
■ **operational** where the aim is to develop procedures that make the best use of technical developments.

In terms of productivity improvements, the activities at the scientific and technical levels provide the principal increases. However, they will also be more expensive to fund, and take much longer to bring to fruition than activities at the operational level where the investment is relatively inexpensive and yields quick, though less significant, results (see Exhibit 13.13). Consequently, many organizations have solely pursued productivity improvements at the operational level. The methods adopted, however, vary. Some improvements come through experience, trial and error or ingenuity. Other ways of studying work have been developed that provide a systematic approach to investigating existing methods and to developing and implementing improvements as ways to increase the productivity of existing resources. Chapter 14 introduces many of these approaches and provides examples of how and where they may be used.

SERVICE APPLICATIONS

The growing importance of the service sector within more developed economies places increasing emphasis on the need to improve productivity in this sector. Past trends indicate that, even in the USA which is often regarded as the most developed of all service sectors, productivity improvements lag behind. Exhibit 13.14 shows that whereas manufacturing productivity has been increasing year on year since the mid-1980s, total business (excluding farming) productivity in the USA has been declining

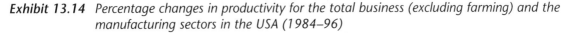

Exhibit 13.14 *Percentage changes in productivity for the total business (excluding farming) and the manufacturing sectors in the USA (1984–96)*

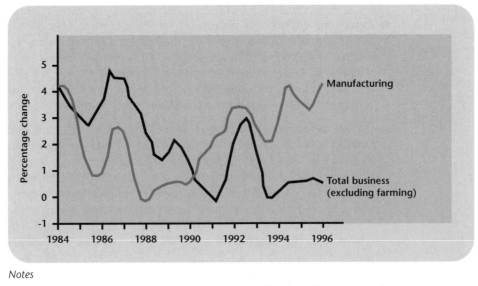

Notes

1. The graph represents the percentage change year over year based on a four-quarter moving average.

Source: US Labor Department.

year on year and that suggests that service sector productivity has also been actually declining over the same period.

The need to improve and measure productivity in service businesses (and the white-collar/service dimension in goods-producing firms) is a significant and necessary task. As the service element of economies grows, then productivity in this sector has an increasing bearing on the living standards of nations.

It is important, therefore, to accomplish this in an effective way. In so doing, organizations should remember and incorporate lessons from the past and recognize the expectations and abilities of the staff involved. Essential to the successful introduction and maintenance of approaches to measuring and improving productivity are the following:

■ **Involve those concerned** – the failure of companies to involve the blue-collar workers in the past led to resentment and resistance at the time, an attitude which sometimes prevails even today. The success achieved by other nations (for example, Japan) has, in part, been based upon appropriate high levels of involvement. Including people in the process needs to be undertaken as early as possible, particularly in service industries where procedures are less rigid and the outputs less tangible. Discussing the purpose of the measures and their ultimate use will allay fears, reduce resistance and match the expectations of incumbents concerning levels of responsibility and their role in the interpretation of the service and in managing and improving the delivery system.

■ **Establish the purpose** – starting with the goals of the organization, measures should be developed to fit relevant targets. Congruency between measures and objectives ensures relevance of effort, and consistency and coherence of purpose. In the service sector this linkage is normally inherently less defined than its goods-producing counterpart.

- **Determine appropriate measures** – be aware of using existing output/input ratios as this approach brings with it the potential problem of modifying, at a later date, a measure which is not fit for purpose. The approach should be to determine first the outputs, then the inputs and lastly the ratios. This will first enable the different factors to be assessed independently of one another, then later assessed within the relevant measures. Defining each part separately simplifies the task.

- **Output measures** – by electing to define outputs first, the more difficult and important factor in the equation is addressed without introducing additional complexity. As output measures are often difficult to determine directly, surrogate measures are sometimes used. It is most important, therefore, to involve those concerned in such decisions to ensure that what a measure is intended to accomplish is understood and is deemed suitable. This avoids unduly emphasizing non-critical factors which, if achieved, may distort what constitutes good performance. Group consensus not only reduces this possible outcome but also creates the opportunity to refine measures over time.

- **Input measures** should be chosen to reflect the task. Choices between single and multi-factor measures were discussed earlier and some illustrations are given in Exhibit 13.15. When choosing which inputs to use, the need to relate them to the output measures must also be appreciated. One aspect to consider here is the appropriate time base of the input(s) compared to the output(s) involved. Thus, clerical staff inputs may be measured in hours or days, whereas a research department would be more appropriately described by the numbers of people or salary bill.

Exhibit 13.15 *Examples of single and multi-factor productivity measures relating to five businesses*

Organization	Single-factor measure	Multi-factor measure
Law firm	$\dfrac{\text{\# briefs filed}}{\text{Lawyer}}$	$\dfrac{\text{\# briefs filed and court attendances undertaken}}{\text{Lawyer}}$
Bookshop	$\dfrac{\text{\# customers served}}{\text{Full-time equivalent staff}}$	$\dfrac{\text{\# customers served, deliveries handled and despatches sent}}{\text{Full-time equivalent staff}}$
University	$\dfrac{\text{\# student contact hours}}{\text{Faculty member}}$	$\dfrac{\text{\# student contact hours, research assistants supervised (hours) and administrative tasks (hours)}}{\text{Faculty member}}$
Consultancy firm	$\dfrac{\text{\# consultancy days billed}}{\text{Total consultancy days available}}$	$\dfrac{\text{\# consultancy days billed, training undertaken (days) and administrative tasks (days)}}{\text{Total consultant days available}}$
Engineering design firm	$\dfrac{\text{\# design projects completed}}{\text{Engineering staff days}}$	$\dfrac{\text{\# design projects completed, tenders submitted and site visits undertaken}}{\text{Engineering staff days}}$

■ **Ratios** – the last step in defining the measures is to select the ratios. The multiples on hand will be many. Some factors to consider in general terms, as well as to do particularly with service applications, include:

  ■ Keep the number of measures small and focused. Avoid any measures that are not central to a review.

  ■ Select measures with the following characteristics:
    – data are readily available
    – reflected performance is understood by all concerned
    – some control is exercised by those being measured.

  ■ Measures for one function are compatible not only with other parts of an organization but also with the corporate measures in use.

■ **Revise** – implementing a productivity measurement system is not a one-off project. In service industries particularly, changes in mix, the continuous reinterpretation of tasks, the application of technology and changes in organizational goals will bring about short- and long-term implications for a business and the best measures to evaluate performance and improvement. Periodic revision needs to be built into the system both in relation to productivity measurement in particular and as part of an ongoing, corporate review in general.

CONCLUSION

While factors such as national resources will play a major part in determining a country's level of wealth, the prosperity of a nation and the living standards enjoyed by its people are also bound up with productivity. If you stop to consider, the standard of living enjoyed today by many of the more advanced economies has its roots in the primary (mining and farming) and secondary (manufacturing) sectors' productivity gains over the last several decades. The improvements secured in these areas of the economies of many nations have been significant.

The increasing importance of service industries in the more developed economies has switched the spotlight onto the need to improve productivity in this sector. Only in this way will the improvements in national prosperity and individual living standards be sustained. Current overall performance, as shown in Exhibit 13.14, points to a current failure to meet these expectations. In part this may be explained by a failure in some elements of the service sector to acknowledge this essential task. However, there are other parts where this need has been fully recognized. Often this goes hand in hand with the increasing move of services from a sheltered to a traded environment, a factor often enhanced by the progressive privatization in many countries of large service industries that had historically been developed and managed in the public or government domain. The results, as Exhibit 13.16 illustrates, can be as dramatic as many of the earlier gains in the primary and secondary sectors.

A glance at this exhibit shows that all ten countries now provide a three-minute international telephone call at a price that is significantly less than that charged in 1989. In fact, while the average price for all these countries was £2.99 in the late 1980s, it had fallen to 0.84 by 1998. (As the figures in Exhibit 13.16 do not take into account inflation in the period then the reduction in prices are, in real terms, even more pronounced.) Underpinning these significant decreases was a parallel improve-

Exhibit 13.16 *Comparative prices for a three-minute international telephone call for selected countries (1989–98)*

Country	Price (£s) for a three-minute international call				Index 1998 (1989 = 100)
	1989	1994	1997	1998	
Australia	2.65	1.61	1.27	1.22	46
Belgium	3.73	2.00	1.36	0.92	25
Canada	2.22	1.30	0.66	0.65	29
France	2.02	1.68	0.99	0.52	26
Germany	4.04	2.30	1.13	1.13	28
Italy	5.39	2.74	1.14	0.94	17
Netherlands	3.26	1.98	1.15	0.80	25
Sweden	N/A	1.68	0.75	0.79	47
UK	1.74	1.08	0.62	0.40	23
USA	1.89	2.06	1.03	1.02	54

Notes

1. N/A = not available.
2. Sweden's 1998 index is based on 1994.

Source: 'International Communications Price Survey' by the National Utility Services Ltd.

ment in productivity driven by a combination of technology investment and continued improvements in all areas of telephone provision.

The need for and benefits that accrue from sustained productivity improvements are central to the continuing prosperity of nations, whatever their level of development. Bringing this about is a central feature of operations management and some of the ways and approaches that can be used are addressed in Chapter 14.

SUMMARY

The fundamental nature of time in managing operations is often overlooked or not fully recognized. Assumptions are typically made about the origins and appropriateness of this fundamental input into key operations activities such as cost data, capacity calculations and work schedules. Functions in a business use the data and assume them to be accurate and a sound basis on which to undertake calculations and make decisions.

The chapter started by illustrating why time needs to be an essential part of assessing, controlling and managing many of the activities within operations. Specific illustrations of the role of time in key activities was then provided. The section that followed outlined the procedure to measure work so as to provide the context for the next sections.

With an understanding of the essential role of time in so many aspects of operations management, the approaches to measuring the content of jobs were reviewed. At the start the need to recognize that the time taken would need to reflect the agreed method,

SUMMARY (cont'd)

take account of how effectively the work was completed and provide allowances for rest and personal needs was emphasized. This was then followed by a description of the principal approaches used and the types of work where they were most appropriate to determine the question, how long should this job take to complete?

The second major topic of the chapter addressed the aspect of productivity. The national as well as corporate dimensions provided context and background before introducing the definitions of productivity, the difference between this measure and that of efficiency and the perspectives provided by value added calculations.

The final section addressed the ways to improve productivity and the key role of service sector improvements in sustaining the productivity gains made in the primary and secondary sectors particularly during the last century.

Discussion questions

1. The owner of a photocopying outlet wishes to know how busy the receptionist is in the front office. The observations based on random sampling made so far are below.

| | # times receptionist | | Total # |
Day	busy	no work	observations
1	20	4	24
2	14	3	17
3	28	5	33
4	16	2	18
5	32	8	40
8	25	6	31
9	18	4	22
10	30	9	39

If the owner wants an answer that has a 95 per cent confidence limit with an accuracy of ±4 per cent, how many observations are needed?

2. What is the difference between basic or normal time and the standard time for a job?

3. A worker assembled 15 units in 60 minutes during a time study. The analyst rated the worker at 90 on the 0–100 scale. The allowance for occasionals and contingencies, rest and personal time totals 18 per cent. At the standard rating of 100 calculate the

   ■ basic or normal time for this assembly
   ■ standard time for this assembly

Discussion questions (cont'd)

4. The manager of Oils and Tyres wishes to establish a standard time for an oil change. Jim Beswick completed 32 oil changes over a period of time and in a total of 260 minutes. Jim is the best mechanic at the outlet and was rated at 115 on the 0–100 scale. The rest allowance is 12.5 per cent. Calculate the standard time for an oil change.

5. Reflecting on questions 2 and 3 above, how does the process of rating normalize the eventual standard time?

6. What are the advantages and disadvantages of using output per staff hour as a measure of performance?

7. How does efficiency qualify productivity measures?

8. What are the advantages of using a video as opposed to a person to help calculate the length of time to complete a job?

9. Why does an operations manager need standard times?

Notes and references

1. Definitions of work measurement are provided in the British Standard 3138 (1992).
2. Ibid.
3. Ibid.

CHAPTER FOURTEEN

The content and planning of this book: an overview of what is involved, what has been addressed so far and what is covered in this chapter

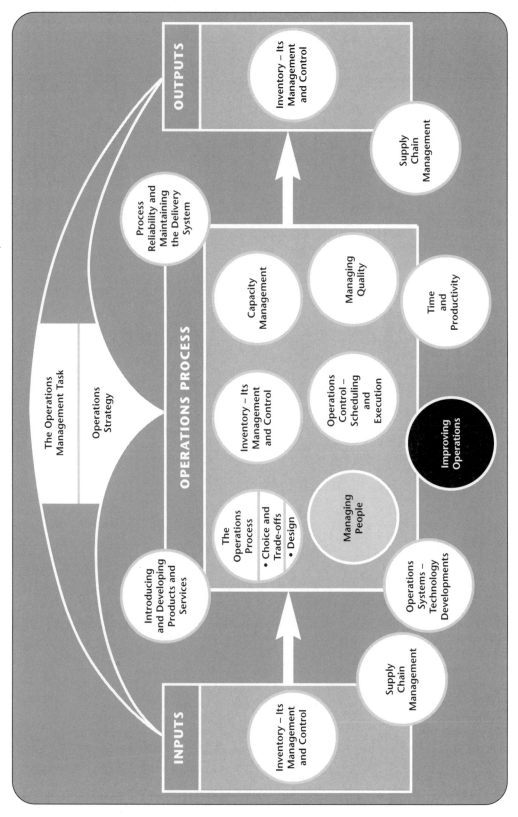

OUTPUTS

Inventory – Its Management and Control

Supply Chain Management

OPERATIONS PROCESS

The Operations Management Task

Operations Strategy

Process Reliability and Maintaining the Delivery System

Capacity Management

Managing Quality

Time and Productivity

Inventory – Its Management and Control

Operations Control – Scheduling and Execution

Improving Operations

The Operations Process
• Choice and Trade-offs
• Design

Managing People

Introducing and Developing Products and Services

Operations Systems – Technology Developments

INPUTS

Inventory – Its Management and Control

Supply Chain Management

Improving Operations

Chapter overview

Operations managers are responsible for the conversion process that transforms the material, labour, capital and other inputs into the required goods and services (see Exhibit 1.1 and also the book overview across). To do this they need to establish the processes involved, the facilities to be used and the procedures and systems to be followed. This will cover many aspects including product/service range, level of capital investment, utilization of materials, labour and capacity, the expectation of productivity at all stages in the system and the management and control of these resources to meet the needs of the market and the corporate objectives of the business. But the task does not finish there. An operations manager's role also includes the need to improve the processes, delivery systems and other aspects of operations on an ongoing and continuous basis as an inherent part of the overall job.

In the previous chapter we covered the different ways to establish how long a task takes to complete, the uses that the dimension of time provides, and the evaluation and measurement of productivity as an overall gauge of how well a nation, sector or organization is performing over time and in comparison to others. This chapter concerns the task of improving operations. It explains the different methods and approaches that can be used to help undertake this key activity and, in particular, covers the following:

- **Measuring performance** – what to measure, setting targets and standards (including benchmarking) and setting the improvement agenda.
- **Stepped versus incremental improvements** – identifying the difference and relative contributions made by undertaking improvements that are stepped (or large) in nature and those that comprise small, incremental gains. The link back to the levels of productivity improvements in the last chapter will also be established.
- **Continuous improvement** – the notion to undertake improvements on a continuous basis will be discussed and the merits inherent in this approach will be explained.
- **Approaches to making improvements** – the ways to review how tasks are undertaken will be explained in detail and examples used to illustrate the different approaches described.

> ## Chapter overview (cont'd)
>
> ■ **Employee involvement** – whereas the last section reviewed the content of what to do, the aspect of how to undertake these reviews and the key dimension of involving those staff responsible for the aspects of work being examined is introduced. This aspect is explained in greater detail in Chapter 9 under the heading Total Quality Management (TQM).

MEASURING PERFORMANCE

The maxim 'what gets measured gets done' is singularly true. The reason for this is simple. If data are collected to measure an aspect of operations performance, then how well that dimension is being achieved will be noted, monitored and reviewed. As a consequence, performance levels will be highlighted and the attention given to that task will result in time and resources being allocated to maintaining or improving that aspect of operations.

One of the key dimensions then of reviewing performance is to select which aspects to measure and why. With this agreed, the next step is to set the standards to be met within agreed timescales. Here we are concerned with what to measure and setting the standards. The rest of the chapter deals with how to bring about the required improvements.

The ways to measure productivity were introduced in the last chapter. These comprised general reviews that give an overview and facilitate comparisons between the overall performance of nations, sectors and organizations. This section looks at the different measures that may be used, highlights the need to separate the strategic and internal dimensions of operations and introduces the role of benchmarking in setting standards and agreeing targets.

Strategic versus operational dimensions of performance

Chapter 2 emphasized the strategic dimension of operations and highlighted the need to recognize the external as well as the internal tasks of the operations function. Exhibit 14.1 lists some of the dimensions for which it is solely or jointly responsible and is based on Exhibit 2.6. A glance at these shows a mix of the strategic and operational. The purpose of this list and subsequent narrative, however, is not to identify when a dimension would be strategic rather than operational but to provide an overview of the range and nature of the measures that may be used to help evaluate the performance of the operations function. You will also note from the list that most are not new; they have been used by companies for many years. What is new is the importance attached to them. These measures truly drive the operations process, replacing the traditional cost accounting and variance reporting procedures of the past.

Price

Monitoring and/or reducing costs is an inherent operations task whether or not price is an order-winner within a market. As up to 70 per cent of costs are typically incurred

Exhibit 14.1 *Operations task and some relevant performance measures*

Dimension	Task	Performance measures
for which operations may be solely or jointly responsible		
Price	Maintaining and/or reducing costs	■ labour cost per unit ■ material yield ■ unit overhead cost ■ efficiency (also known as effective performance) ■ experience curves
Quality conformance	Making products/ providing services to specification	■ defects as a percentage of total units made or service transactions completed ■ customer complaints – number and percentage of total sales ■ warranty claims – number and value (£s) ■ scrap levels – percentage of material costs and value (£s) ■ customer satisfaction scores
Delivery speed	Matching customers' requested lead times	■ meeting customers' requested lead times – number agreed and as a percentage of total customers ■ operations lead times – trends ■ queue lengths – actual versus target during selected periods
Delivery reliability	Delivering orders on time	■ percentage of orders delivered on time – line item review ■ orders part-delivered – number and percentage of total
Product/service range	Supporting the products or services on offer	■ stock-keeping units (SKUs) – number and trends ■ inventory holding – value (£s) by each product ■ 80/20 review – sales value (£s) related to inventory held (£s) by product or service
New product/service introductions	Reducing the operations phase involved	■ rate of product or service introductions – number and trends ■ lead times – actual and trends by product/service category
Demand spikes	Match demand with inventory and/or short-term capacity increases	■ monitor overtime and inventory costs ■ measure effective performance in high demand periods against non-peak levels

by operations then effective cost control is essential. That materials and overheads typically account for upwards of 80 per cent of total costs is reflected in the suggested measures. One measure listed in Exhibit 14.1 does, however, require some explanation.

Efficiency was introduced in Chapter 13. This measures actual product/service output with that expected, or standard output, as it is called. Using time as the common denominator (a theme of Chapter 13) then both the numerator and denominator are expressed in minutes, hours, days or even weeks, whichever is the most appropriate unit of measurement. The illustration given as Exhibit 14.2 is the result of extending the output of individual tasks by the standard time to complete each task and comparing this total with the total hours worked in the distribution warehouse involved. It is typically (as here) expressed as a percentage. Reflecting back to Chapter 13, all tasks would be given a standard time, that is, that which a company would expect an average-skilled and trained person to be able to complete the task on hand. As the time would include an allowance for rest then one hour of work should result

Exhibit 14.2 *Calculating the weekly efficiency for distribution warehouse staff*

Task description	Standard minutes per task	# completed	
		tasks	standard minutes
Check customer order details (including labels) pick order and label each carton	6.5	892	5798.0
Load orders onto vehicle	40.0	21	840.0
Unload incoming vehicle and put away products	115.0	11	1265.0
Stock take one-third of locations (monthly)	210.0	–	–
General duties (sweeping and cleaning)	180.0	1	180.0
Meetings (including general information and continuous improvement reviews)	340.0	1	340.0
Total	–	–	8423.0

		Normal	Overtime hours	Total
# hours worked	– Sue Gibbons	35.0	1.5	36.5
	– Alec Carpenter	35.0	–	35.0
	– Jill Sawyer	35.0	1.5	36.5
	– Anne Roper	35.0	–	35.0
	– Total	140.0	3.0	143.0

$$\text{Efficiency} = \frac{\text{\# standard minutes produced}}{\text{\# hours worked} \times 60 \text{ minutes}} \times 100$$

$$= \frac{8423}{8580} \times 100 = 98.2$$

in the equivalent of one hour's worth of tasks. Hence the effective performance expectation would be 100 per cent. The example in Exhibit 14.2 is for a distribution warehouse with four staff each working 35 normal hours per week.

Experience curves

Evidence clearly shows that as experience accumulates, performance improves and experience curves are the quantification of this improvement.[1] The basic phenomenon of the experience curve is that the cost of providing a product or service falls in a regular and predictable way as the total quantity increases and Exhibit 14.3 provides a general illustration of this principle.

The price of a product or service always declines after its initial introduction as it becomes more widely accepted and available. However, it is not so commonly recognized that cost also follows a remarkably consistent decline. The pattern is that costs (in constant £s) decline by a consistent percentage each time cumulative unit output is doubled. The sources of these improvements are not only the result of reduced

Exhibit 14.3 *A general illustration of the experience curve principle and showing cost/volume or price/volume relationships expressed on both a linear and log-log scale*

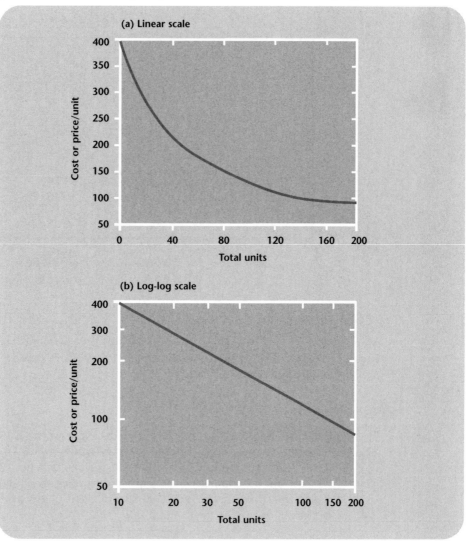

labour costs due to learning curve benefits. In fact, the real source of the experience curve effect comes from organizational improvements. The importance of calculating the extent to which the opportunity to reduce unit costs has been achieved is an important measure, particularly where markets are or will become price sensitive. The characteristic decline in cost or price per unit was established by the Boston Consulting Group's (BCG) work in the 1960s and early 1970s as between 20 and 30 per cent for each doubling of cumulative output. Reflecting this rate of decline, experience curves are expressed in percentage terms; thus an 80 per cent experience curve slope means that each time output doubles the cost or price per unit will be 80 per cent that of the previous output, and so on. Exhibit 14.4 provides an example for a large voucher processing centre. A glance at this will show the consistent reduction in unit processing costs over the period from 1994–99.

Exhibit 14.4   *Experience curve – voucher processing centre (1994–99)*

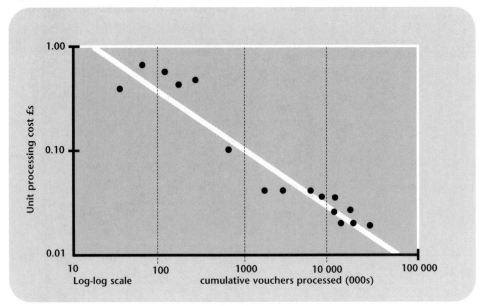

Quality conformance

Much is said on this issue in Chapter 9. The task in operations concerns making a product or providing a service to specification. The measures suggested in Exhibit 14.1 are largely self-explanatory.

Delivery speed

The trend in customers' expectations regarding delivery is towards shorter lead times. Operations' task is to meet these requirements. The initial measure under this section in Exhibit 14.1 concerns the extent to which operations matches customer requests. This signals how often a company's customers are required to extend their lead times to those which the company can offer. Checks on meeting agreed delivery dates are a measure of delivery reliability.

Delivery reliability

Having agreed when products or services are to be delivered, being on time is the measure to test how well this is provided. One key element of this measure is that only where all items on a customer's order are delivered by the agreed date should an order be considered as being on time, hence the 'line item review' element of the first measure.

Product/service range

As markets become increasingly different then product/service ranges will tend to widen to reflect this trend. Developing a capability to cope with this dimension becomes part of the operations task. Measuring increases in product or service range needs to be supplemented by monitoring how operations meets this requirement – for example, through holding inventory.

New product/service introductions

New products and services are the life blood of an organization. Reducing the time it takes to develop and introduce new products and services is a key element in this core activity. Monitoring operations' role in this total provision is the key measure here.

Demand spikes

Demand is rarely predictable or uniform. For many businesses how and how well operations copes with supporting this is an important measure in assessing this dimension.

Benchmarking

Benchmarking, the practice of comparing business practices and performances between companies, has become a widely adopted approach across all sectors. It provides a systematic way of identifying, measuring and setting improvement targets in key areas of performance against competitors, especially those recognized as market leaders.

Benchmarking is part of a continuing need to improve operations. Knowing both the competition's and your own performance is core to this approach, as Sun Tzu (a notable Chinese general) reflected in 500 BC:

> Know your enemy and know yourself and in a thousand battles never be in peril.

And the results that come from this combined approach are testimony to its effectiveness:

Rank Xerox (Europe)
- manufacturing costs halved over 15 years
- inventory down to 40 per cent in the same period

BP Chemicals (Belgium)
- productivity up by 50 per cent in 5 years

IBM (Germany)
- productivity in non-manufacturing areas up by 30 per cent in 3 years.

Benchmarking is concerned with the search for best practice. It presents the 'what' rather than the 'how' (the subject of later sections in this chapter). Thus, companies are presented with targets not solutions. For benchmarking to be successfully implemented, some key elements need to be in place:

- **Rigour** – targets need to be set high enough and continually reviewed.

- **Overcoming disbelief** – in the initial phases of this process companies often need to convince themselves that they can do better and the benchmark performances are achievable. The closed mind syndrome has been and still is a characteristic obstacle to change, as these quotations bear testimony:

  'Everything that can be invented has' (Head of US Patent Office, 1889)
  'There is a world market for fifteen computers' (IBM Chairman, 1945)
  'Japan is not likely to become a world leader in aerospace' (SBAC Report, 1989).

■ **Accountability** – measuring performance and ensuring improvement requires everyone to become responsible for checking, identifying and implementing the changes necessary to bring this about.

■ **Manageable task** – although the underlying aim of benchmarking is to set targets 'outside the box' it is essential to make the targets achievable. As the process is on-going when targets are met, new ones get set. The need for companies to assess

Case examples

1

Sheffield City Council (UK) introduced a new geographic information system in the mid-1990s. By inputting Ordnance Survey sheets and details from more than 1350 information maps on property holdings, road details, 'street furniture' (such as road signs, and traffic lights) it has significantly reduced the time to answer queries. For example, 1 day instead of 4 weeks to undertake a land and property deed search and 30 seconds to give information on any property or parcel of land. Planning temporary diversions and modifying existing route options similarly takes minutes, while assessing the impact on school numbers by altering catchment areas can be reviewed and refined almost at will.

2

Applying established methods of quarrying of stone to underground mining has revolution-ized productivity in South African gold fields. A synthetic-covered steel cable, studded with industrial diamonds saws through the rock face cutting away the ore in large chunks. At $290 a metre it is expensive. But it can operate 24 hours a day, requires less labour and minimizes the amount of waste rock mined by eliminating many of the 900 000 blasts the gold mines in South Africa currently make every day.

3

Japan's large electronics makers hit by reces-sion and the strong yen are struggling to revi-talize their operations by changes in organization and cutting the number of sections and overheads. Sony, for example, recently reduced the number of divisions and departments by 25 per cent and reorganized its manufacturing and marketing groups into eight internal companies. Matsushita Electric Industrial, the country's largest consumer electronics maker, cut its administration staff to 70 per cent of its previous level by relo-cating surplus employees to marketing positions.

4

McDonald's fast food chain is renowned for its lean operations including the use of customers to provide capacity, tight portion control and fast service. But the drive to reduce costs is not only limited to its core tasks. By analysing elec-tricity costs on a half-hourly basis, reviewing this provision and proactively seeking alterna-tive suppliers, McDonald's has taken £1.4m from its £18m electricity bill for England and Wales. A separate deal for Scotland has led to savings of more than 30 per cent.

Case examples question

Review the four examples given here. How are the first three examples stepped and why is the McDonald's example classed as incremental?

themselves against externally derived standards is at the heart of benchmarking. Identifying 'best-in-class exemplars' is a key step and examples often need to come from a number of company classifications, including:

- internal: other parts of the same organization
- direct competitors
- companies in the same sector, but not direct competitors
- latent competitors
- companies outside the industry.

How companies have used different sources to provide targets is provided in the examples that follow:

- Rover Cars (UK) halved its test times after benchmarking against Honda
- Lucas Verity (USA) cut the number of shop floor grades fourfold after a review against a German competitor
- British Rail (UK) reduced the time taken to clean a train to eight minutes after benchmarking British Airways
- GE Capital (USA) aimed by the year 2000 to achieve six-sigma quality (3.4 defects per million operations) in its financial services sector following IBM's lead.

STEPPED VERSUS INCREMENTAL APPROACHES TO IMPROVEMENT

Improvements come in many forms. One key difference concerns the extent of the change and resulting improvement. The alternatives are referred to as stepped and

Exhibit 14.5   *The different patterns of improvement resulting from stepped versus incremental change programmes*

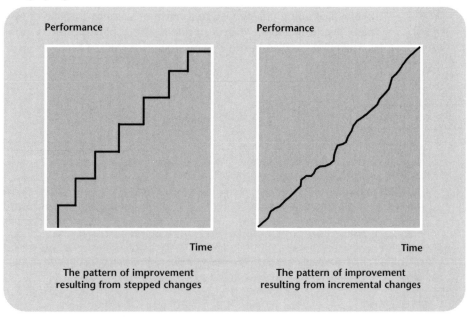

incremental, thereby signalling different approaches to bringing about different levels of change.

Stepped improvements result from major changes to existing practices and normally involve large investments (see Case examples 1–3).

Incremental improvements, on the other hand, comprise smaller but more frequent steps. The philosophy here is to undertake small improvements on an ongoing basis with the continuous nature rather than the size of improvements holding the key to achieving and sustaining change programmes over time (see Case example 4).

Exhibit 14.5 reviews the pattern of performance resulting from stepped and incremental change. The picture is self-evident but helps highlight the different approaches to bring about necessary improvements. However, for most companies combining these two approaches makes most sense and will typically provide the best way to achieve and sustain improvement over time (see Case example 5).

To help evaluate which approach to use and when a combination of the two would be more suited to the needs of an organization, Exhibit 14.6 summarizes some of the key differences that would form part of the decision on which approach better suits the needs of a business.

CONTINUOUS IMPROVEMENT

The last section highlighted different approaches to securing improvements. This section discusses the importance of fostering an approach to improvement that recognizes the necessity, as well as the sense, of implementing improvements on an ongoing basis. In this way, the drive towards improvement becomes a never-ending journey. Being better than the day before by encouraging everyone within an organization to identify and act on opportunities for improvement is at the centre of the continuous improvement philosophy.

Often, as you would anticipate, continuous improvement goes hand in hand with incremental change. But it does not set any conditions on the size of improvements, thereby not ruling out stepped improvements as a by-product of the activity although these, while being identified in the context of continuous improvement, would normally be handled in the way outlined in Exhibit 14.6.

Case example 5

Porsche AG's sales fell from a 1986 high (including 30 000 in the USA alone) to less than 13 000 cars in 1993, pushing the small German car maker to the brink of collapse. As profits fell and losses of up to DM250m were incurred the challenge was to transform a company steeped in laborious craftsmanship into an efficient and profitable competitor. The key has been a mix of stepped and incremental change. The workforce was reduced by 34 per cent over the next four years. In addition, introducing lean operations methods also led to an inventory reduction of over DM100m and production time down from over 120 to 80 hours with a further 20-hour reduction the goal in the next two years. Meanwhile, in purchasing the number of suppliers has been reduced from 900 to just 300, while in design 36 per cent of parts in the latest version of the 911 are identical to those in the new Boxster.

Exhibit 14.6 *Features of stepped and incremental approaches to improvement*

Features	Stepped	Incremental
	improvement	
Level of investment	Large	Small
Basis of improvement	Technology	Systems and procedure reviews
Relative time frame	Long term	Short span
Nature of task	One-off, additional large project	Continuous, inherent part of day-to-day activity
Involvement	Few, led by specialists	Many, with all staff contributing
Maintaining the gains	Self-sustaining improvements are inherent in the investment	High level of maintenance necessary to sustain gains and to make future improvements

Kaizen is a Japanese name for a formal system to promote continuous improvement. Masaaki Imai has described the approach in detail[2] citing the system as an important basis for the success of many leading Japanese firms. He highlights, as fundamental to *kaizen*, the need for everyone in an organization to be involved in the philosophy and reality of continuous improvement. It begins with the notion that an organization can only assure its long-term success when everyone actively seeks ways to identify and implement improvements as part of their approach to work. In this way, it keeps people thinking about the current processes, systems and structures. Understanding the system and procedures, continuously reflecting on how well they work and the source of the problems that occur help spot improvements and creates an environment for ongoing developments as a by-product of day-to-day activity.

The nature of continuous improvement highlighted by *kaizen* is explained by three guiding principles:

■ **Process reviews** – the basic unit for analysing a system in *kaizen* is to review the processes involved. This analysis would concern, for example, a review of the process for providing or the process for designing a product or service.

■ **Success comes from people** – successful *kaizen* programmes rely on people's knowledge and insight of the systems and procedures involved and their ability to identify improvements. High levels of skill, employee participation and corporate support for implementing improvements are key factors in bringing success, as Case example 6 illustrates.

■ **Constant need for change** – a successful *kaizen* programme depends on everyone feeling the constant need for change and never accepting the current process, however good, as being adequate. Complacency is avoided. Feeling the need to improve, seeking out improvements and implementing the changes that result are the basis on which this approach is built – successful change programmes need to concentrate on outcomes and not the process.[3]

Case example ⟩

6

In part of his study of the problems at IBM, Paul Carroll identified that in IBM's software development function, quality, at the time of the review, was measured by the number of lines of code written per day. The more lines, the more the function was deemed to be productive. When IBM and Microsoft combined to review certain programs, a Microsoft developer took an existing IBM code requiring 33 000 characters of space and rewrote it using only 200, thereby reducing the time to read into memory and process the code to $\frac{1}{160}$th of the time. From a professional viewpoint such action was considered by IBM managers to be 'rude'. Other Microsoft developers then rewrote other parts of IBM's code to make them smaller and faster. IBM's managers' complaints then went further – according to their measurements, Microsoft had not been pulling its weight. In fact, using lines of code as the measure, Microsoft was actually doing 'negative work'.[4]

The encouragement in Microsoft for staff to identify and implement improvements was in marked contrast to the bureaucratic style which, at the time, pervaded the IBM organization. The results speak for themselves.

Case example question ⟩

6.1 Use this example to illustrate the three points guiding continuous improvement.

The contrast between more traditional approaches in organizations to an environment that encourages and recognizes the need and benefits of continuous improvement is provided by Case example 6.

APPROACHES TO IMPROVEMENT

This section looks at ways to improve current processes and systems. Before looking at these it is useful to place them within the context of an overall procedure, thus providing you with an overview as well as the tools and approaches from which to select to help undertake the necessary analysis.

The Deming Cycle

The Deming Cycle is also called the Deming Wheel or the PDCA Cycle (from the sequence plan–do–check–act, as shown in Exhibit 14.7). This series of linked activities is used to examine processes and systems and helps to identify opportunities for continuous improvement.[5]

■ **Plan** – the start point is identifying a problem or selecting an aspect of the current process or system that can be improved. This step is critical, for where and on what the investment of time and money is spent will be the basis for the gains that follow. The work needs to be of lasting benefit and can be at different levels. On the one hand, the areas of improvement can be in line with the market-related priorities set within an organization. On the other hand, the improvements can relate to

Exhibit 14.7   *The Deming cycle*

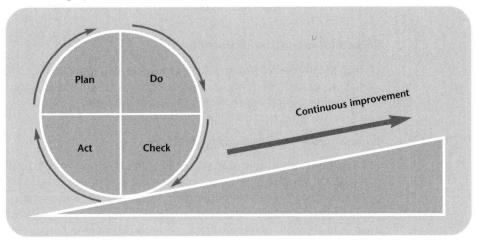

any areas where benefits can be secured. While the former are set within the strategic direction of an organization, the latter concern the equally important need of improving the efficiency of the internal activities of a company.

Having selected the areas for improvement, the way forward is to record all the relevant facts about the present work, examine these critically using a number of the tools and techniques discussed later in the chapter and then develop ways to improve the current process or system.

■ **Do** – having formulated the plan, the next step is to implement it. By involving those with responsibility for the area of work being reviewed, acceptance of the improvements tends to be an integral part of the activity. Sometimes, however, the outcomes will also necessitate improving existing skills and the training requirements that go hand in hand with such changes need also to be identified and arranged.

■ **Check** – the principal activities of this step are to monitor and check the results of the improvement(s). They include ensuring that the improvements identified are in place and the anticipated gains are forthcoming. Performance measurement is an integral part of this step as this facilitates the checking and quantifies the improvement. Reasons for any shortfall are also examined.

■ **Act** – in the final stage, information is collected and reviewed and any necessary corrective action is taken. This step is also designed to ensure that the improvements made are maintained. Periodic checks both monitor the progress achieved and ensure that the process or system is now running as intended. Finally, this step allows adjustments to be made as part of the overall improvement initiative and in line with the continuous nature of the approach.

TOOLS AND TECHNIQUES FOR IMPROVEMENT

This section explains the various tools and techniques that can be used as part of the improvement process. In turn, you will see that this has been separated into three further subsections to help you understand the issues involved and how they fit together to form an overall approach to the improvement process.

Recording process and procedures

Having identified the problem area or step in the process to be improved, the next stage is to record the processes and systems involved. Here, there are two different ways of addressing the issues and procedures involved.

Business process re-engineering (BPR)

BPR is a more radical approach to bringing about improvement. In all but the smallest organizations, systems and procedures have always been carried out laboriously across a number of fragmented functions or specialist departments. These include product/service design, marketing, operations and accounting. Each has its own hierarchy and vertical communication and reporting system through which the requirements pass on their way to the next stage that is performed by another part of the business. Ways of bridging these structures have been sought over the years from permanent matrices through to project teams and task forces. Business re-engineering goes one step further. It transforms processes by reconfiguring them into ones that flow permanently across the relevant departments with the tasks performed at the appropriate (often, organizationally, at a low) level. This involves delayering structures and breaking up existing functions and then reconstructing them around the redefined task and processes.

In essence, it seeks to develop processes that meet the needs of and provide the highest value for customers. Its aim is to achieve dramatic improvements in critical areas of performance and its radical nature stems from the approach it adopts to secure these. Underlying the BPR approach are two key dimensions:

- Operations should be organized around the total process that adds value to customers and not around the functions and activities that form the value – adding activity. In turn, a review of operations should similarly be based on the process rather than the functions providing the various parts.

- The analysis should begin, not with the existing process, but with the outputs from the process that customers want. The next step then is to develop a process or system that delivers these outputs.

Since BPR was championed in the early 1990s,[6] it has been successfully used in many companies including Ford, IBM, Kodak, Bell Atlantic, Astra-Merck, Xerox and Taco Bell. However, like many of the tools and techniques advocated to help improve processes, BPR is not new. Both Henry Ford and Alfred P. Sloan (General Motors) as early as the 1920s[7] used this approach to make cars. What is new is the fact that companies are rethinking the approaches to bring about fundamental change and looking for ways of doing it.

Business process re-engineering (or more accurately described by some as core process redesign) advocates a fundamental rethink of the core processes from customer need or expectation through to the delivery process to bring this about. The principles involved are described below:

Case examples

7

Ford Motor Company reviewed its accounts payable function with the aim of reducing it from 500 to 400 staff. Ford was enthusiastic about its plan until it looked at Mazda with an accounts payable staff of only five people. A review found that Ford's purchasing department placed an order and copied it to accounts payable. On receipt of the items or materials, goods inwards did the same. When the vendor invoiced, accounts payable had to find and reconcile the three documents. Checking, queries and investigations (in all, accounts payable had to match 14 data items) led to delays and the need for a lot of staff and cost. Now there is 'invoiceless processing' where checks are automatic. Also, if goods are received and there is no record then they are returned. As for invoices, customers are told not to send them – Ford pays on receipt of goods.

8

Mutual Benefit Life handled customer application through a series of linked but independent steps taking the paperwork from one department to the next:

- credit checks
- quote
- rating
- underwriting
- document preparation

Typical process times of 5 to 25 days with delays, checking and rechecking throughout the procedure. A relook linked databases, swept aside job descriptions and made case managers responsible for an application from start to finish. No more file hand-offs, no more backtracking and no more delays between stages. Turnarounds can now be completed in as little as 4 hours and typically take 2 to 5 days. And this with 100 less staff and each core manager handling twice the number of applications as before.

9

Taco Bell, the US fast-food chain with a Mexican menu, looked radically to improve its performance. At the time, each outlet had its own kitchen and prepared food on site. This took up space, reduced the customer seating area, increased overhead costs and lengthened service lead times. Starting with its customers, Taco Bell found that they did not want extensive facilities and children's play areas but placed great emphasis on good food served hot and fast at an affordable price. The conclusion reached was that outlets should switch from making food to retailing food. The 'K-Minus' system replaced existing kitchens with smaller food preparation areas where staff, in response to customers' orders, assembled the various menu items from food (for example, meat, corn tortilla shells and beans) prepared centrally and delivered to the various outlets. In addition to savings on outlet running of $87m, the re-engineered process brought additional benefits including improved quality control, higher staff morale and lower staff turnover, in part, through eliminating the drudgery of food preparation and savings on outlet running costs.

10

Sony, the Japanese consumer electronics company, rethought its current structure in the mid-1990s and decided to reorganize to improve corporate decision-making by reducing management layers. It cut the number of divisions and departments from 580 to 450 and reorganized its operations and marketing group into eight separate, internal sections. Each section head now had design, operations and marketing reporting in the same structure.

Case examples (cont'd)

11

Western Provident Association (WPA), a UK-based health insurer, improved productivity by almost 50 per cent by introducing BPR. For example, processing an application previously involved 7 staff and 28 days. It now involves 1 person and takes 4 days. This includes reviewing the medical history, setting up the policy and arranging the collection of insurance premiums. In the old system that took 28 days a file was worked on for only 45 minutes. Like many companies opting for BPR, WPA combines image processing and workflow software to speed up re-engineered procedures. Image processing captures a complete image (including signatures and graphics) of a document on a computer. Work flow software automatically forwards the document image onto the relevant worker handling the next stage. Looking at targets that a business wants to reach (in WPA's case, shortening processing lead times and reducing costs) BPR then works backwards to achieve this.

Case examples question

1. Using these five examples, identify the BPR-based changes made.

■ **Impact statement** – summarizes the costs and implications of maintaining the current process.

■ **Redesign the process** – this step includes the need to rethink current procedures and should embody several key dimensions around the need to merge parts of the process, often in a fundamental way. Examples include some of the following which represent options, some of which overlap:

– the stages of generating, processing and using data should be embodied, wherever possible, in the same step of the procedure, the maxim being those who use the output of a process should perform the process
– put the decision-making step where the work is performed and build controls into the process; merging the checking and action steps reduces overall control costs
– look to link geographically dispersed resources and seek the benefits of size by managing them as one centre even when they are located in different areas.

The benefits of a fundamental redesign of a company's core processes bring with them stepped changes in performance, as the following examples illustrate. Such benefits are not, however, forthcoming without securing major changes in staff attitudes and corporate response. As the opening remarks intimated, BPR entails major upheaval inside existing organizations that typically brings with it resistance built around internal politics, organizational status and human inertia.

Tools for mapping process sequences

One key step in the improvement process is recording an existing process. There are a number of ways to chart the sequences and these provide different levels of detail and show different aspects of a task. The recording of a process is facilitated by clarifying activities under the five headings explained in Exhibit 14.8.

■ **Outline process charts** – the two principal activities in a process or procedure are operations and inspections. These charts give a valuable overview of the work being reviewed, with the minimum of recording effort, by showing the sequence of only the main operations and inspections involved. They are usually completed at the start of an investigation into a department or function to help decide the further areas for study. Against each main operation and inspection, a brief description is shown together with the time taken if available (see Exhibit 14.9).

■ **Material or information flow process charts** – these record what happens to material or documents in the process or procedure being studied. They amplify an outline process chart by showing all operations and inspections as well as the movement, delay and storage or filing of the materials or documents involved (see Exhibit 14.9).

Exhibit 14.8   *Symbols used to complete process charts and their different meanings*

Symbol	Activity	Used to represent	
		Material or information	**Person doing the task**
○	Operation	Material, product or information is modified or acted upon during the operation	Person completes an operation or task. This may include preparation for the next activity
□	Inspection	Materials, product or information is checked and quality, quantity or accuracy is verified	Person checks and verifies for quality, quantity or accuracy at this stage in the process or procedure
⇨	Transport	The material, product or information is moved to another location without being part of an operation or inspection	Person moves from one position to another as part of the process or procedure without being part of an operation or inspection
⊃	Delay	Temporary storage or filing of an item. Not recorded as 'in store' or filed and not requiring authorization for its withdrawal	Person unable to complete the next part of the task
▽	Storage	Controlled storage, governed by authorized receipt and issue; document filed and retained for future reference	Not used
⊡	Combined activities	To show activities performed at the same time or a person completing two tasks at the same time	

Exhibit 14.9 *Relationship of charting techniques showing the relative level of detail and illustrating their differences*

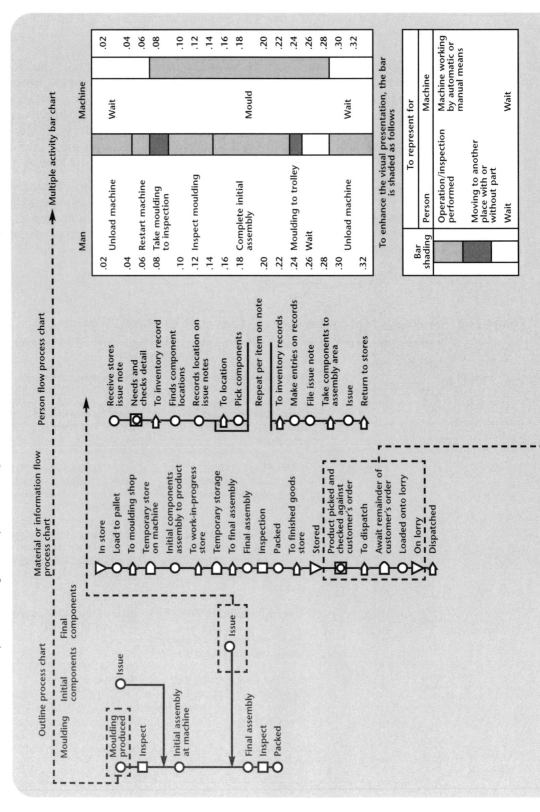

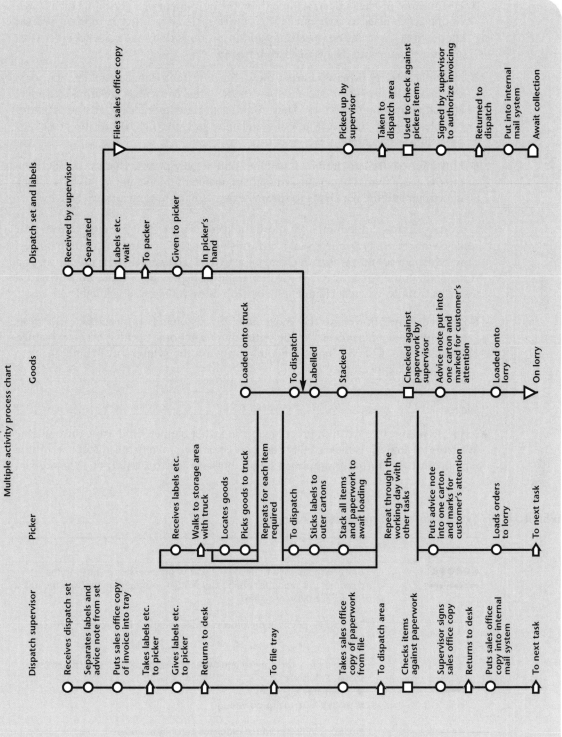

Multiple activity process chart

■ **Person flow process charts** – these show the movement of a person who has to go from place to place to carry out a task. As with material or information flow process charts, they show all the operations and inspections that take place together with any movements and delays (see Exhibit 14.9).

■ **Multiple activity process charts** – these show the interrelated activities of persons, equipment, materials or documents with the latter particularly relating to clerical and administrative activities. They record, on a common scale, all the activities completed in the task and how they relate to one another within the process or procedure (see Exhibit 14.9).

■ **Multiple activity bar charts** – as with multiple activity process charts these show the interrelated activities of persons, equipment, materials or documents but have a time dimension and use bar charts to show relevant lengths of time for each activity.

As the examples in Exhibit 14.9 show, the level of detail is significantly greater for some charts. For the operations manager, the most useful is often the outline process chart which gives an overview of the main activities. This can then be used to agree a work programme for future investigations and also provide a framework to guard against situations where a change in detail will cause problems elsewhere.

■ **Service maps** flowchart the movement of customers, information and tasks through the service process. While sometimes using some of the symbols explained in Exhibit 14.8, service maps predominantly use the symbols in Exhibit 14.10 to chart what happens.

Video

As an alternative to charting a process, videoing what happens and using the outcome as a basis for analysis is increasingly being preferred. Improvements in video recording equipment have not only simplified its use but also led to significant reductions in

Exhibit 14.10 *Symbols used in drawing service maps*

Symbol	Explanation
●●●●●● ●●●●●●●●●●●	*Line of visibility* used to divide the part of the operations visible to the customer (including telephone and written communication) from the rest of the service delivery system
△	*Fail points* – points in the process where there is a high level of service failure
⟹	*Service paths* – the optimal and 'when things go wrong' service paths are shown as follows: ■ optimal service path ■ path where things go wrong
(P)	*Problem* – indicates where problems occur in a process
⟨D⟩	*Dialogue* – indicates where customer interface with the delivery system takes place

cost, both in terms of the initial investment and subsequent applications. Its advantages over methods of charting include:

■ **Level of accuracy** – it provides a complete record of the activities that take place, especially where the task itself is complex.

■ **Facilitates analysis** – the medium of a picture record facilitates subsequent analysis, both in terms of access and skill/experience levels of those involved.

■ **A visual record of events** can be reviewed by all concerned and on any number of subsequent occasions. In addition, it allows all concerned to participate in the examination of activities.

■ **Acceptability** – by taking away the element of human interpretation and presenting a more neutral approach to the activities under review, those involved more readily accept the record of events (the camera shows it as it is) and acknowledge their participation in the procedure, leading to improved ways of working.

Tools for identifying problems

As explained in the last section, mapping provides an overview of a process to help understand what happens, where duplication occurs and where potential improvements exist. This section concerns tools and techniques to help identify what causes the problems experienced in a process.

Cause and effect diagrams

These were first introduced earlier in Chapter 9 and are also known as fishbone diagrams (from their shape – see Exhibit 14.11) or Ishikawa charts after Kaoru Ishikawa who first developed this tool.[8] This approach provides a mechanism to help solve problems by identifying the causes and effects involved. The example in Exhibit 14.11 is the outcome of an investigation into a company's problem of being unable to supply products to specification to meet the requirements of the high speed production lines of one of its customers. Excess processing waste was clearly identified, involving a minimum annual loss of over $40 000 in addition to the serious problem of failing to achieve acceptable levels of delivery reliability. The detailed and systematic analysis provided by the cause and effect diagram enabled the company to review the causes and identify several areas where improvements were needed and could be made.

Why-why reviews

These offer another way to identify the causes of problems. The approach is to start with the problem and ask why the problem occurred. The reasons are recorded. Then, the process is repeated by asking of each reason why it had occurred. These reasons in turn, are recorded and so on.

Tools for generating improvement ideas

The charting/recording stage described in the last sections comprises a review of the process but also embodies the need to identify improvements. Most people, because of their training and background, are good at analytical thinking. On the other hand,

Exhibit 14.11 An example of a cause and effect diagram

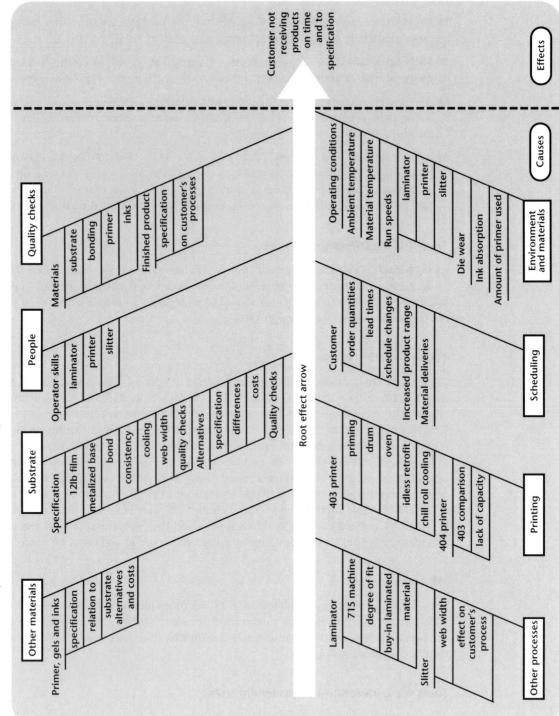

few are good at divergent or creative thinking, either on its own or in combination with analytical approaches. Barriers are set up, either consciously or unconsciously, that prevent the growth of ideas. These restrictions come from a number of sources:

- self-imposed limits to possible solutions
- an inherent belief that there is one right answer
- fear of being wrong
- conformity to behaviour norms
- unwillingness to challenge the obvious.

Analytical approaches restrict imagination, and continuous evaluation puts the brake on ideas outside apparent norms or perceived boundaries. Creative thinking, on the other hand, is the process of relating ideas or things that were previously unrelated. By consciously suspending judgement and evaluating ideas at a later stage, the mind is given the opportunity to think laterally rather than being constrained within the vertical dimension associated with analytical approaches.

The stages involved in creative thinking are:

1. *Preparation* – collecting the known facts, defining the problem in different ways and restating/clarifying the problem.
2. *Generation* – concerns the need to generate ideas, both in themselves and as a stimulus to creating other perspectives.
3. *Incubation* – leaving the problem in the subconscious state as a way of creating new thoughts, the process of bisociation.
4. *Insights* – linking ideas to possible solutions.
5. *Evaluation* – analysing all the facts on which to base evaluations of the possible solutions.

Stages 1 and 5 are based on analytical approaches, whereas the other three are based on creative thinking. The key in this procedure is the deliberate separation of the phases involving the creation and evaluation of ideas. Completing stages 2, 3 and 4 is best done in groups, with the aim of creating quantity not quality of ideas. By creating large numbers of ideas, new ideas are sparked off. To help achieve this, the following rules apply:

- *Suspend judgement* – criticism of ideas is not permitted. Evaluation comes after the creative stage. Bringing these two phases together will lead to implied criticism and a reluctance to contribute. The key is to discourage self-evaluation from entering the process.
- *Freewheel* – wild ideas are deliberately fostered as they lead to better results.
- *Cross-fertilize* – at set stages, give participants the task of combining and improving on the ideas of others.

To help in the generation of ideas a number of techniques may be used including:

- *Brainstorming* – 6 to 20 people take a problem and, working under the rules 1 to 3 above, seek solutions. All ideas are written so as to remain visible throughout. Typically, the five stages listed earlier form the basis for using this technique.

■ *Reverse brainstorming* – this asks, of an idea which is being considered, 'In how many ways can this idea fail?'

■ *Attribute listening* – this technique lists the main attributes of the idea or object and them examines how it can be changed.

■ *Forced relationships* – this approach seeks to list the ways in which ideas or objects can be combined.

EMPLOYEE INVOLVEMENT

To introduce and maintain an effective continuous improvement programme requires that employees are involved in all phases, agreeing the aims of the programme, delivering the results and implementing the ideas. The commitment of all concerned is fundamental and involvement is the way to ensure this happens. In fact, the very term 'continuous improvement' goes hand in hand with employee involvement. As emphasized elsewhere, using the capabilities and experience of everyone in an organization is an essential part of successfully developing and growing a business. The approaches used are covered extensively in Chapter 15. The purpose of this short section is to underscore the essential nature of this dimension of managing successfully an operations function.

CONCLUSION

Most of the approaches described in this chapter have been around for a long time and have comprised the content of books in the field of operations over the last 50 years. The significant change in recent years is a recognition in operations that the approaches adopted need to form part of an overall philosophy rather than a list of alternatives. The result brings two major changes:

■ The approaches chosen need to build on one another and form part of a coherent way to bring about change.

■ Improvement does not end with implementation. The hallmark of successful improvement is the stress placed on the continuous nature of the task. The aim is to move closer all the time to an absolute ideal by making small beneficial changes throughout the process and infrastructure of the operations function.

Many chapters of this book address ways of achieving improvements. What follows is intended to reflect important features of this core activity, not complete in itself, but designed to provide linkage, with more extensive coverage provided elsewhere in the book.

Eliminating waste

A key dimension of improvement is the elimination of waste. Excesses in all forms are unnecessary and costly. F. Cho (Toyota Motor Company) provides a concise definition of waste as 'anything other than the minimum amount of equipment, materials, parts and workers which are absolutely essential to production'. The aim is to strive to achieve this ideal by introducing continuous improvement throughout a range of activities. Because services tend to be labour-intensive, many of the improvements concern changing the activities and roles of people. However, other key areas of waste reduction come from activities such as improving housekeeping and the immediate environment in general.

Improved design

Costs, quality conformance and product/service range are an integral part of design. In fact, the ease with which operations can meet the requirements of these dimensions is inherent in the product/service design itself. Early involvement in the design procedure and designing for operations are key facets of the corporate improvement process.

Jidoka – quality at source

Introduced in the early 1950s by Taiichi Ohno, *jidoka* is based on the philosophy that all staff should be personally responsible for the products they make or services they provide. In the car assembly plants *jidoka* push buttons were introduced and all employees are authorized to stop the line for reasons of quality, safety or pace of the line. This overt mechanism facilitates the drive for quality at source – stopped production concentrates the mind on putting things right. The same levels of concern need to form part of the continuous improvement drive.

Process redesign

A continuous and rigorous re-examination of how products, services and information are delivered needs to be made. Of concern is not just cost – delivery speed, delivery on time and quality conformance are often of a higher priority in today's competitive markets.

Involving people

To support these approaches, companies need to involve people extensively both within and outside the organization. Work needs to be restructured in terms of increased participation, involvement, responsibility/authority links and job interest. This leads to environments where continuous improvement can flourish as an integral part of the way an organization works.

Companies need to adhere to the principle of employing people for their heads as well as their hands. This has not always been the case, especially in the West. As Konosuke Matsushita explains, 'Your firms are built on the Taylor model; even worse, so are your heads. With your bosses doing the thinking, while the workers wield the screwdrivers, you are convinced deep down that this is the right way to run a business. For you, the essence of management is getting the ideas out of the heads of the bosses into the hands of labour'.[9]

Similar differences in approach are to be found in supplier relations. Many US and European customers still manage their suppliers in terms of contract placement by threat and fear – the you-need-us-more-than-we-need-you syndrome. They fail to appreciate that win/lose situations are a poor base on which to build mutually beneficial relations. Suppliers need to be recognized as partners in terms of design, quality, cost and delivery improvements. As customers generally hold the power, then they must initiate sound and mutually beneficial relations with suppliers. As a partnership, both sides need to contribute. Win/win situations need to be developed in order to compete successfully in today's global markets.

As the service sector becomes more important it is essential that organizations in their quest for better performance not only recognize the benefits but also the opportunities to realize these by adopting a philosophy of continuous improvement. As product quality and manufacturing productivity were a central feature of the 1980s, then service quality and productivity was a major theme of the 1990s. Attitudes to improvement, however, need to be developed. Without this core activity many firms will, at best, underperform while, at worst, will miss out altogether.

SUMMARY

Reflecting the important strategic and short-term aspects of performance in the measures used within operations is an essential dimension in managing this function. For, as the opening sentence of the chapter highlights 'what gets measured gets done'. To help provide context, Exhibit 14.1 overviews some of the relevant dimensions, tasks and performance measures that effect operations followed by explanation and examples.

How to improve operations and the key role of continuous improvement is then introduced, highlighting alternative approaches including the Deming Cycle and business process re-engineering. The tools and techniques used in the continuous drive for improvement follow, including those for mapping process sequence, for identifying problems and for generating ideas.

The final short section reinforces the key role provided by employee involvement and also serves as a link to the next chapter that specifically deals with the core task of managing people.

Discussion questions

1. A retail outlet offering a range of high specification women's clothes wishes to develop relevant performance measures. Suggest those that you consider appropriate.

2. Explain the difference between stepped and incremental change programmes. What are the advantages and disadvantages of each?

3. Develop a cause and effect or fishbone diagram to explain lengthy service at a restaurant.

Discussion questions (cont'd)

4. Draw an outline process chart when arranging a holiday for which the hotels and flights are directly booked by you.

5. Why is the video gaining widespread use in the field of continuous improvement?

6. Company A achieves 85 per cent experience curve gains while Company B achieves gains of 80 per cent. Company A's first unit cost was £200 while Company B's was £240.

- How much will the 128th unit cost for each company?
- When will Company B's unit cost match that of Company A?

7. Why is there actual conflict between management and staff over productivity levels? What actions can operations managers take about it?0

8. Use the Deming cycle approach to suggest and implement improvements to the library lending delivery system.

Notes and references

1. The compilation of the experience curve is detailed in *Experience and Cost: Some Implications for Manufacturing Policy*, Harvard Business School paper 9-675-228 (1975). Also, see Ghemerant, P 'Building strategy on the experience curve', *Harvard Business Review*, Mar–Apr (1985), pp. 143–9.

2. Masaaki Imai *Kaizen: The Key to Japan's Competitive Success*, New York: Random House (1986).

3. Schaffer, RH and Thomson, HA in their article 'Successful change programs begin with results', *Harvard Business Review*, Jan–Feb (1992), pp. 80–9 emphasizes the need to evaluate change programmes by an assessment of the true worth of their outcomes.

4. This example is taken from Carroll, P's book *Big Blues: the Unmaking of IBM*, New York: Crown, (1995), p. 101.

5. Deming, WE *Out of the Crisis*, Cambridge, MA: MIT Centre for Advanced Engineering Study (1986), pp. 88–9.

6. In particular, Michael Hammer in his article 'Re-engineering work: don't automate, obliterate', *Harvard Business Review*, Jul-Aug (1990), pp. 104–12 and with Champy, P in their book *Re-engineering the Corporation*, New York: Harper Business (1993). Also see Davenport, TH and Short, JE 'The new industrial engineering: information technology and business process redesign', *Sloan Management Review*, Summer (1990), Vol. 31, No. 4, pp. 11–27.

7. See, for example Ford, H *Today and Tomorrow*, Cambridge, MA, Productivity Press (1988).

8. Ishikawa, K *Guide to Quality Control*, White Plains, NY: Quality Resources (1985), pp. 18–29.

9. Matsushita, K 'Why the West will lose', *Industrial Participation*, Spring (1985), p. 8.

Further reading

Dixon, JR, Nanni, AJ and Vollman, TE *The New Performance Challenge: Measuring Operations for World Class Competition*, Homewood, IL, Dow Jones-Irwin (1990).

Hall, RW, Johnson, HT and Turney, PBB *Measuring Up: Charting Pathways to Manufacturing Excellence,* Homewood, IL, Business One Irwin (1991).

Holland, M *When the Machine Stopped*, Boston, MA, Harvard Business School Press (1989).

Johansson, HJ, McHugh, P, Pendlebury, AJ and Wheeler, WA III *Business Process Reengineering: Breakpoint Strategies for Market Dominance*, Chichester, John Wiley & Sons (1993).

Kobayashi, I *Twenty Keys to Workplace Improvements*, Portland, Productivity Press (1995).

Pisano GP and Hayes RH *Manufacturing Renaissance*, Boston, MA, Harvard Business School Press (1995).

Senge PM *The Fifth Discipline: The Art and Practice of the Learning Organisation*, London, Random House (1990).

The Productivity Press Development Team *5S for Operators: 5 Pillars of the Visual Workplace*, Portland, Productivity Press (1996).

Womack, J, Jones, D and Roos, D *The Machine that Changed the World*, New York, Macmillan (1990).

## part five

Managing People

CHAPTER FIFTEEN

The content and planning of this book: an overview of what is involved, what has been addressed so far and what is covered in this chapter

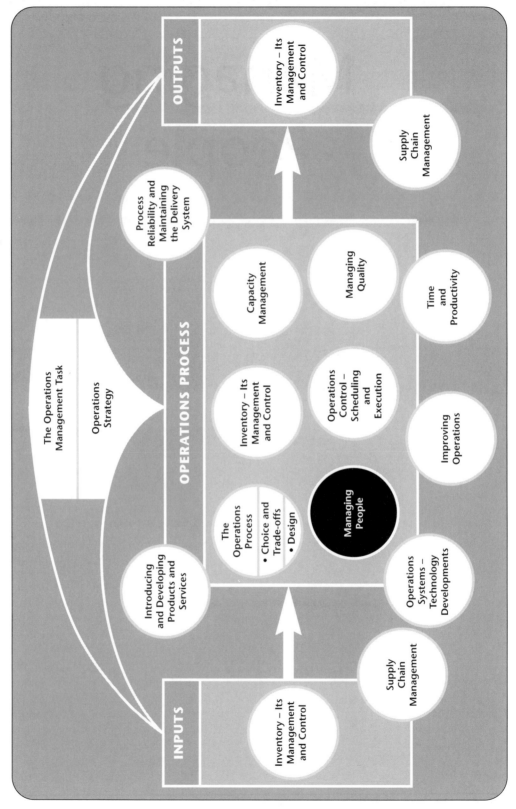

Managing People: The Key Resource in a Business

Chapter overview

Operations managers must meet the challenge of creating an environment that helps people develop their full potential, where people care sufficiently to want to do a good job and the needs of both the people and the business are met within the workplace. Progressive companies have long since recognized the key role of people in the continued success of a business and, therefore, the need to safeguard and nurture their human capital.

Managing 60 to 70 per cent of those employed is a large dimension of the operations management role. Furthermore, this difficult assignment competes for attention with all the other operations tasks and priorities. But, the sound and responsive management of human resources in an organization is essential for long-term success. Whereas companies are able to control materials, design business processes and develop procedures to a level that will almost guarantee that the product or service specification is met, the role and contribution of people in the delivery system are essential to ensure this provision. To develop and maintain delivery systems that consistently meet customers' requirements and expectations, companies have to recognize the need for and embody the dimension of employee commitment into their design and delivery. Only in this way can processes be consistently maintained and developed to meet the increasingly competitive nature of today's markets.

As late as the 1970s, many operations managers took the narrow view of the nature and extent of people's contribution in the delivery system – that of completing the physical tasks involved in product and service provision. The role of people in the planning, improvement and evaluation of processes was neither recognized nor required. Why this was so, the change in managing people that is being adopted and the nature of their contribution in today's organizations is discussed in the rest of the chapter. In particular, the following aspects are covered in detail:

■ The opening section highlights the size and nature of changes in the workplace and illustrates these by dimensions such as the increasingly competitive nature

Chapter overview (cont'd)

of markets, employee attitudes to work and their commitment to organizational goals, the higher technical content of jobs, the pace of change particularly regarding shorter product or service life cycles, the relative insecurity of employment and the worldwide sourcing of products and services.

■ Contributing to the context–setting nature of the first part of the chapter, general definitions used in describing the job of work are provided. These include job content that establishes the scope and depth of work, job satisfaction and motivation and how these differ, job performance and the role of management in creating an environment where the ingredients of skill and attitude can coexist to enhance performance.

■ A further part of the scene-setting for this chapter is provided by the section outlining managerial philosophies of work. These include the use of specialists, the tendency to control from a distance and the specialization of labour. Each dimension is discussed and how it impacts the current work structures is explained.

■ The final section in this opening part of the chapter outlines the traditional approaches used in managing people. These include job enlargement, rotation and enrichment.

■ The orientation of the chapter then switches to the principles of organizational and workplace design. The aspects covered in the former include the learning organization, what it involves and what it can deliver; developing a change-orientated organization and the cultural and behavioural shifts involved; the changing role of managers in terms of creating conditions where people want responsibility, will learn and hence manage themselves such that they maximize their contribution to an organization as well as their own learning.

■ The trend towards flatter organizations is introduced and the changes it brings to organizational design are discussed.

■ The aspect of workplace design covers the dimensions of employee involvement and empowerment and the different forms it can take; job redesign in terms of current job profile and the increasing move towards increasing the scope of work to include elements of planning, doing and evaluating.

■ The role of training and development in bringing about these changes is then highlighted and the additional areas outside the technical dimension of work are outlined.

■ The move towards flexi-working and job-sharing arrangements is introduced and examples of the schemes used in organizations are explained.

■ The final area is that of ergonomics, and the workplace, environmental and behavioural factors are introduced.

Finally, given the importance that has been attached to this critical aspect of managing operations you may wonder why the chapter addressing the topic of 'managing people' has been left to last. As you will no doubt have gathered from these opening remarks, lack of importance is not the reason, far from it. Positioning this chapter here serves two purposes:

Chapter overview (cont'd)

■ The people issue has been addressed in many chapters within this book, as and when it was pertinent – the chapters on managing quality, continuous improvement and maintenance illustrate this point to good effect. The positioning of this chapter at the end of the book then allows the issues raised in other chapters to be pulled together and placed in the context of this specific chapter on managing people.

■ Management comprises the dimensions of content and style. Content in that operations management comprises a number of related topics that address specific issues and requirements within the overall role. Style concerns how managers undertake these tasks. Having addressed the key topics in operations management (the content dimension), now is the appropriate time to turn our attention to the way the whole role should be undertaken (the style dimension).

CHANGES IN THE WORKPLACE

As economies, societies and technologies develop, then attitudes, expectations and other dimensions that concern the workplace will also change. An inherent requirement within a business is to recognize and anticipate how these developments will affect the nature of work, the changing roles of those involved and how best to manage the people within organizations as they evolve. This section sets out the principal changes that have and are taking place in the workplace so as to set the scene and provide context for the later sections that address approaches and developments to the ways of managing people.

Increasingly competitive nature of markets

The increasingly competitive nature of markets has been highlighted throughout the book, and the strategic role of operations concerns supporting the market-related order-winners and qualifiers for which it is solely or jointly responsible. In many markets, the order-winning and qualifying criteria that relate to operations are becoming more important in terms of both retaining and growing market share. In such circumstances the ability of managers to organize resources to meet these needs is paramount. Central to this provision are the people that work in operations, and how they are managed and motivated is increasingly important to the eventual outputs. Managing an organization's human resources to meet the needs of a business while allowing and encouraging the people involved to attain their full potential is a critical operations management role. As markets become increasingly competitive the contribution of everyone to help an organization meet these new challenges is essential. Part of the way to bring this about lies in the structure of work, how well people are motivated to do a good job and the involvement of people in the continuous improvement of all aspects of the operations task and work environment.

Employee commitment

As economies develop, people's attitudes to work and the inherent commitment they have to an organization's goals often change. While organizations retain many people who are self-motivated, for whom work is challenging and who wish to complete tasks as well as possible, there are many who need to be induced to work well. This is not really surprising. Many people go to work for reasons based on custom and necessity. Also, the job opportunities open to many rarely afford a wide choice and are, by and large, prescribed by education, experience, physical and mental abilities, personality and chance. Consequently, many take on jobs that, after a time, tend to become repetitious and dull.

The ability to inspire the emotional and intellectual commitment of people needs to be high on the corporate agenda, and a critical skill that operations executives have to develop and apply. Although the operations task is typically seen as being inextricably bound up with technology, processes, materials and other tangible dimensions of the task, managing people is not only sizeable (operations executives manage those directly involved in the delivery system as well as a range of support staff) but critical to the operations task and overall success of a business. Consequently, improving people's jobs, creating opportunities for them to influence and improve their working environment and linking their contributions to business outcomes must be provided and sustained.

Technical content of jobs

While the increasing use of technology developments in the workplace has increased the technical dimensions of some jobs, for many jobs the technical content has declined. And, this trend will continue, for it forms the basis of the productivity improvement so essential to becoming and remaining competitive in current and future markets, a factor that, in turn, maintains and improves a nation's living standards. Where the technical content has grown, the improved technology leads to improved processes with fewer but better educated people for whom the motivational needs must be recognized and met. On the other hand, for those people where the technical content of work has declined the downside is that the inherent interest that this provides is lost. To compensate for this loss, other ways to motivate people need to be sought and introduced.

Pace of change

Organizations also have to deal with the issues discussed so far in an environment of change. The increasingly competitive and turbulent nature of today's markets was highlighted in an earlier section. In addition, reducing life cycles, the global nature of markets, the relative insecurity of employment and the worldwide sourcing of products and services add to the dynamics of the business environment in the twenty-first century.

The information superhighway and related technologies are also changing work roles and organizational relationships. Beepers and mobile telephone systems empower people to interact with others, including customers, outside the formal reporting structures of organizations. Teleworking requires different management skills and staff responses to work. Technology-based provision of services such as call centre arrangements is changing the roles of functions as well as individuals.

Innovations such as these will need to be accommodated within revised organizational structures and are challenging operations managers in the new millennium. The pace of change is not easy to live with, but those companies that develop organizations that accept change as a way of life and progressively involve people in better serving their customers and developing and improving their delivery systems will succeed in the future, as the San Diego Zoo development illustrates.

Case example ❱ **1**

Until recently at the San Diego Zoo, the wild animals were not the only ones plotting their escape. Many employees felt as if they were in cages, too. Though their cages were figurative, not literal, the effect was the same: the employees felt as if they were trapped in rigid, dead-end jobs, without the power to make a difference.

In an effort to raise the quality of life for both animals and employees, zoo management decided to radically restructure the way the zoo saw itself. Instead of a place that merely displayed wild animals, the San Diego Zoo transformed itself into an organization that could delight its customers by creatively educating visitors about the animals and their habitats.

Zoo officials got rid of traditional cages and spent millions of dollars to create 'bioclimatic zones' where the animals could feel at home. The employees of each zone were organized into work teams to brainstorm ideas for making the zoo a better place to work as well as for delighting and educating visitors.

At two of these zones, Gorilla Tropics and Tiger River, the work teams began to function as separate organizations, with team members or immediate supervisors making almost all the decisions on hiring, vacations and budgets. 'It is like managing your own business here', one team member explained.

Not all employees were immediately enamoured with the new arrangement, however. Some cynically saw the work teams as a way for management to squeeze more work out of them. But even the sceptics came round eventually, and now almost everybody agrees that the zoo is a better place to work.

Employees were not the only ones to benefit from the restructuring. Many senior managers at the zoo are also top-notch curators, but the pressure of day-to-day decision-making had kept them too preoccupied to pursue their true vocations. With the work teams now handling most of these operating details, the curators can focus on their areas of expertise.

As for the animals, one can only assume they are much happier, too.[1]

GENERAL DEFINITIONS

It will be helpful at this stage to check the definition of some general terms used when discussing work and jobs. This will provide the purpose of clarifying meanings, introducing concepts and serve as a prerequisite to developing ideas on how to go forward.

Job content

Job content establishes the scope and depth of work. Job scope is the range of operations required to be completed in the job. Thus, a job with narrow scope means that it contains few operations and will tend to be highly repetitive. A widening of job scope implies that the range of operations to be completed is increased horizontally. This increases the variety of the work performed and reduces monotony, but does not

Exhibit 15.1   *The elements of job depth and job scope that form the content of a job as illustrated in the two jobs A and B*

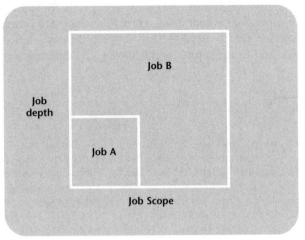

increase the responsibilities within the job, or the depth of the work involved – see Exhibit 15.1 that illustrates how the content of job B is greater than job A on both the dimensions of job scope and job depth.

Job depth refers to the degree of responsibility people have to plan and organize the work for which they are responsible. It concerns the level of control that they have over their own working environment. Thus if people have no influence over the planning of their work and have to carry out the plans of others, the job depth is low. Therefore the assembly line worker whose rate of working is controlled by the pace of the line and who carries out the tasks planned by others has a low job content (both low scope and low depth).

Similarly, an audio/copy typist who is required to prepare a narrow range of work to an agreed layout and format has low job content.

Job satisfaction and motivation

Job satisfaction and motivation are not synonymous. Job satisfaction reflects a person's attitude to the job and the level of interest it holds. This results more in increased organizational loyalty and commitment than in increased performance. Motivation, on the other hand, concerns the desire to perform well which could lead to increased effort and a higher performance. The distinction between aspects of work that lead to satisfaction or dissatisfaction and those that motivate people was well drawn by Hertzberg.[2] He emphasized the difference between those factors that led to dissatisfaction if not maintained (referred to as hygiene factors) and those that prompted motivation (referred to as motivators). Factors such as physical conditions, security, pay and relationships were put forward as hygiene factors, while aspects of work such as job growth, responsibility and achievement were classed as motivators. The important insight presented by these perspectives is the distinction between the factors that motivate people and those that make them dissatisfied. Motivation, therefore, plays an intermediate role between satisfaction and performance, for even a satisfied person will only tend to meet performance standards when adequately motivated.

Job performance

Job performance is dependent not only upon the level of motivation that exists but also upon a person's ability. For good performance standards to be achieved and sustained, it is essential that both skill and attitude form the ingredients of the work situation.

Job performance is a product of skill and attitude. It results from the job and behavioural characteristics being brought together in the work situation. Unless both these aspects are reviewed, therefore, results will be less than adequate.

MANAGERIAL PHILOSOPHIES OF WORK

Some of the principal philosophies of work that have influenced Western business cultures are now outlined. It is not intended that this should be an exhaustive list but it aims to provide a basis for later discussion on important features in work design.

Control through specialists

With growth, companies become more complex and they handle this increased complexity by splitting the organization into parts and controlling these parts in the form of functions. In addition, they also introduce specialists with a brief to improve relevant functions by developing and improving procedures, systems and activities within the broad area of their specialism.

One result of this division into parts and the creation of functions and specialist departments is that activities that were once completed in one part of an organization, are housed under the control and auspices of the specialist function. This has taken place for several reasons:

- the view, often held by organizations, that all activities of a similar nature should be under one function
- an executive function's (such as operations and sales) willingness to shed some of its total task
- a specialist function's inclination to grow the size of its department.

This development has, in turn, led to a number of problems:

- Developments in a specialist field have often outpaced the understanding of those managers responsible for the executive functions in which the specialist advice and developments will be applied. Hence, the eventual users and custodians of technology have difficulty in participating in discussions on the technology in question, both in terms of technical fit and appropriateness of application.

- Some tasks best performed in an executive function are now performed elsewhere.

- Ownership of the development and maintenance of the systems and procedures is typically seen by an organization to be part of the specialist function's responsibilities. This view is compounded by the fact that the staff necessary to complete the development and maintenance tasks are available only in the specialist departments.

Control from a distance

Invariably, the controls and procedures have too often been designed and installed from a distance. The approach has been one of analytical detachment from the reality of the function or business concerned, with the solution based upon some theoretical view of what should take place rather than developing the controls and procedures around what really happens.

Specialization of labour

As volumes increase, the move towards higher volume processes has also brought with it the design of jobs based on specialization. Higher investment in the delivery system, also underpinned by higher volumes, has often further reduced the technical content of a job and presented a simple, repetitive task at each step in the process.

This basic concept has been central to increasing the effectiveness of delivery systems and has made a significant contribution to the growing prosperity of nations and the high standard of living now available to most industrialized communities. However, these potential gains in productivity are only realized by the sound control of resources, continuous improvement and the effective management of people. The sections that follow describe traditional approaches to undertaking the managing people aspect of this role and the key principles of organizational and workplace design that impact this task.

TRADITIONAL APPROACHES TO MANAGING PEOPLE

Some of the traditional approaches employed to overcome the managerial philosophies to work described in the last section are now discussed. Again, the purpose of this (as with the last) section is, in part, to provide essential context when addressing the issue of how to manage people effectively while also introducing relevant approaches and concepts to help undertake this key role.

Job enlargement

Job enlargement increases the scope of a job by adding to the number of operations to be performed by a person. This type of increase is horizonal in nature. The advantages of such a structural change are to increase the variety of both the work to be completed and the skills to be used, and to provide the opportunity for a person to be responsible for a set of tasks that constitute, where possible, an identifiable programme of work.

Job rotation

Sometimes it is not possible to enlarge jobs as a way of increasing their intrinsic interest. Also, in many service organizations certain jobs have to be performed throughout the normal day or over a 24-hour period – for example, the checkout counter in a library or supermarket, and the night shift in fire, police and hospital services. In the first example the task is monotonous but does not lend itself to enlargement. In the second example, although parts of the work often include areas of greater responsibility than the tasks completed during the other parts of each working day, the unsocial nature of the shift makes it undesirable to most people. In circumstances like these, job or shift rotation is used periodically to change the job assignments or times of working. In either case, the redesign of the job is not an available alternative.

Job enrichment

Whereas job enlargement widens the scope of the job, job enrichment also increases the job depth giving people a greater responsibility to organize and control the work that has to be done. For meaningful control to take place, the necessary information on which to base sensible decisions must be made available to those now responsible for making decisions. In addition, the organizational climate necessary for a successful change of this kind must be provided by all concerned. In the early stages, at least, there will be many in an organization who will view job enrichment as including a measure of role reversal and that leads to an erosion of their own responsibilities.

Changes in working schedules

In more developed economies there is typically a debate on the need for a reduced working week. To meet this preference, certain developments have been introduced as a step towards this end. The first of these is a working week comprising the normal weekly hours but worked over four days to allow a longer weekend. This is common practice in night-shift working. The second is the introduction of flexitime that allows employees a certain amount of freedom in selecting their hours of working. The basis for a flexitime arrangement is that each person is required to be at work during certain 'core' hours, but at other times an employee can choose, within certain procedural agreements, the pattern of working for a particular day or week.

PRINCIPLES OF ORGANIZATIONAL DESIGN

The next two sections introduce some key principles that need to be incorporated in organizational and workplace design. Several of these principles have been appropriately included in earlier chapters to illustrate their application to particular areas of a business. These two sections discuss these points in general while also introducing other key issues that concern the management of these issues in today's environment.

This section reviews some key aspects that need to form part of the way that organizations are managed in general and operations is managed in particular. These concepts and approaches form part of the way that progressive companies design their organizations and develop their people to help meet the demands of today's markets while creating environments that provide those involved with the opportunity to contribute fully to the needs of a business.

The learning organization

The underlying argument and rationale for improving and adapting to change is easy to recognize and overwhelming in its proposition. But designing and developing an organization that helps individuals as well as the business as a whole to embrace and adapt to change is as difficult as it is logical. Organizational commitment to such fundamental tasks is a prerequisite for success but often this is neither recognized nor forthcoming. Peter Senge puts forward the view that organizations, like individuals, can suffer from learning disorders. Learning disabilities are tragic in children... but are no less tragic in organizations, he observes.[3] Because of these disorders, few organizations live even half as long as a person – most die before the age of 40. Senge's view of learning organizations includes a framework for understanding why some organizations are unable to develop team-based management styles that can adopt a proactive attitude towards and an acceptance of the necessity for change. He highlights the need for organizations to embrace change as an ongoing feature of today if they are to grow and prosper.

But, these capabilities are not ones that are inherent in organizations. They need to be built into the structure and developed on an ongoing basis. Management teams do not start out great but learn how to produce extraordinary results. Teams and organizations that learn faster than competitors can gain a competitive advantage. Creating a learning organization is not only fundamental to long-term success but cannot be purchased or created as the need arises. It can only be developed over time and those organizations that have embraced change and nurture and reinforce these attitudes and environments can create a sustainable advantage over their competitors.

To create an organization that can 'truly learn', Senge puts forward five essential dimensions:

■ **Systems thinking** highlights the need in a learning organization to understand and work at the 'big picture' level in order to evaluate developments and prioritize actions. The Gestalt approach to learning emphasizes the need for organizations to understand the whole to better understand the parts, and firms need to develop a process for seeing the big picture as part of the way to provide context in which events, issues and developments are placed and evaluated.

■ **Personal mastery** involves a reciprocal relationship between individuals and an organization. Developing the emotional and intellectual needs of people and directing their energies towards achieving personal goals and development targets will both enhance themselves as individuals as well as enhancing their contribution to the organization in which they work.

■ **Mental models** highlight one way in which individuals learn and carry forward experience and learning from the past into their current way of working. Deeply ingrained assumptions, generalizations and paradigms influence the way individuals see the world in general and the work environment in particular and influence approaches to current ways of completing tasks and making changes. Mental models often form barriers to personal development and organizational change. People in learning organizations must have open minds that are receptive to the need for change, are willing and able to recognize and assess their own perceptions and can address the underlying assumptions that underpin their own mental models in order to reduce or remove any barriers that are inherent in the way they think about and review situations and opportunities.

■ **Building shared vision** involves developing common views of the future that 'foster genuine commitment and involvement rather than compliance'. But developing a shared vision needs to be in the context of an organizational structure where employees are truly empowered and learning takes place throughout.

■ **Team learning** emphasizes the need for people to develop the capabilities to set aside assumptions and stereotypes and address issues and problems in such a way that individuals, teams and the organization as a whole can learn and develop.

Developing a change-oriented organization

As competition increases the need for organizations to anticipate the need for change is paramount. Whereas a competitive environment helps sharpen awareness, companies have to be on the lookout not only for competitive threats but also opportunities to proactively change to keep ahead.

A change-accepting culture stimulates and reinforces awareness of development opportunities by creating an environment where experimentation is encouraged without recrimination. You will recall that in Chapter 9 on quality management, one of Deming's 14 points for management urges organizations to drive out fear as a prerequisite for change.

Similarly, Senge lists as one of the 'laws of the Fifth Discipline' that there should be 'no blame' within organizations in order to encourage and stimulate a proactive response to change from inside companies. Too often managers create an environment that discourages individuals from proactively challenging current approaches and practices. The ensuing risk-averse culture is, at best, unproductive and, at worst, promotes political infighting to safeguard individual and functional boundaries. 'Turf protection', which refers to functions safeguarding the existing status, activities and responsibilities of staff in their part of a business, is the unproductive outcome.

Using external threats to prevent organizations becoming complacent can, however, be a constructive development. For example, Bill Gates, when he was CEO of Microsoft, frequently e-mailed staff to alert them to the ongoing threat of competition thereby helping to prevent complacency. In the same way, some organizations encourage staff to think 'outside the box' by making this activity an integral part of their work. For instance, 3M require researchers to spend 10 per cent of their time on personal ideas that are not a part of the formal corporate research and development agenda. Post-it notes are one example of the outcome of this corporate initiative.

The changing role of managers

As with executives who manage other functions, operations managers are responsible for two distinct sets of activities:

■ to organize, manage and control those areas of a business for which they are responsible – the internal dimension
■ to develop and improve performance in operations with regard to the order-winners and qualifiers for which operations is solely or jointly responsible – the external, customer-facing, strategic dimension.

The first step is to separate the strategic directing tasks from those of managing and controlling the internal sets of responsibilities that concern making day-to-day, short-term events happen. With this separation complete, it is then necessary to recognize that managers do not manage people. On the contrary, people manage themselves. What executives manage and influence is the context and environment in which people work. The management task then is to think through the structure and systems of an organization (that is, the way an organization works) in order to create the values, expectations and environment in which people can manage themselves more effectively.

The essential role of managers is to create conditions where people want responsibility, will learn and hence manage themselves in a way that maximizes their contribution to an organization as well as their own personal development. One result is that it makes the decision and action phases part of the same set of responsibilities. To bring this about, managers have to recognize their role change from one of making decisions to one of communicating a vision and getting people to see their own behaviour, to own their own problems and to be responsible for putting things right.

To do this managers have to think through their own role and relationships as well as the roles of others. People interpret roles from their past experience of organizations and the sets of responsibilities, areas of decision-making and status associated with roles and titles. Similarly, what a manager says or asks questions about has a symbolic as well as a literal meaning. At the very least what a manager asks questions about signals or implies interest, but typically most interpret such questions as pointing to an area of concern inferring responsibility and ownership – the symbolic dimension. The activities in which managers get involved (for example meetings) have the same two sets of meanings. Similarly, if managers answer the questions posed about an aspect of a business then they are perceived as owning the problem and consequently the decision-making role within that area of a business. Defining the areas of responsibility and boundaries for taking ownership of problems and solutions is part of the environment-setting task of managers, and a prerequisite for empowering people within an organization.

Flatter organizations

In the more developed economies most organizations make extensive use of specialists to run a business. The typical approach adopted by companies has been to create specialist functions to supply to the main functions in a business such as operations expert advice, guidance and help in various relevant areas.

One outcome of the extensive use of specialists is organizations with too many layers. The results are reviewed in Exhibit 15.2 that illustrates the changes with number of layers of management from the 1900s to the early part of the twenty first century. The need to reduce the layers in most organizations is essential. However, companies need to undertake this critical task with care. Avoiding across-the-board reductions is most important as this approach assumes that existing structures will be appropriate in a reduced form. Reshaping organizations is a job for a scalpel and not an axe. Reducing the size of and reshaping organizations have to be in line with business requirements. They need to start with the business and build up from the bottom as well as down from the top. Past approaches have often been top-down only and this has merely added to the existing layers. Reshaping an organization has to take into account the role of functions, establish the responsibility for decisions and boundaries of authority, and agree on which overhead tasks are completed centrally and which are allocated to those that provide the organization's products and services. This approach ensures that truly specialist activities are left for specialists to provide, while all other activities are undertaken by those functions and people that provide the products and services involved.

Exhibit 15.2 *Number of levels with a typical expansion at different times*

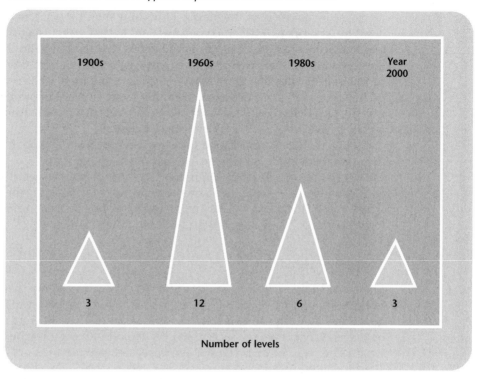

A business-related approach, therefore, enables a company to develop its organization in line with its needs and the opportunity to change the perception of who does what at all levels in a firm. In this way, the role of managers, the need to empower people throughout an organization and where tasks are best undertaken can reflect the needs of the business in the increasingly competitive nature of today's markets.

PRINCIPLES OF WORKPLACE DESIGN

Superior performance is ultimately provided by the people in an organization. Appropriate infrastructure in the form of procedures and systems is essential, but the capabilities that enable an organization to best support the order-winners and qualifiers of its markets are those that come from people. These capabilities include the skills, technical know-how, ability to solve problems and make decisions, capacity for learning and motivation to make these happen. Also, what makes it difficult for an organization to match the people capability within another organization is the time to bring this about and the necessary mind-set changes involved. As discussed in the last section, creating an environment in which people can more effectively manage themselves is difficult and involves long timescales. The purpose of this section is to introduce some of the important dimensions in workplace design and highlight some of the issues involved.

Employee involvement and empowerment

Employee involvement is the process of pushing information, knowledge and power down to appropriate levels in an organization. In that way it is a management initiative designed to increase employee information about, and commitment to, the organization. However, the idea of employee involvement is not new. Columella, a Roman agriculturalist, reflecting on the ways of managing his estate workers, wrote in AD 100: 'Nowadays I make a practice to call them [his estate workers] into consultation on any new work... I observe they are more willing to set about a piece of work on which their opinions have been asked and their advice followed'.[4]

Clearly, Columella understood the impact on the level of worker commitment by involving them in the decision-making process from the start.

Over the last 30–40 years, companies have increasingly recognized that involving people in aspects of work other than the prime role of completing their principal tasks is essential if the abilities of all employees are to be harnessed to help improve the overall business. These have taken a number of forms as follows:

Suggestion schemes

These encourage staff to come up with ideas that, on the one hand, may lead to tangible savings, while on the other, make an improvement on the way something gets done. Results, in terms of the average annual number of suggestions per employee, vary as does the success rate, but typically an organization can expect up to 20 ideas per year for each 100 staff employed and adoption rates of over 25 per cent. However, in the 1990s, Toyota recorded success rates far in excess of these norms with 48 suggestions per employee per year and an adoption rate of 96 per cent. To succeed, suggestion schemes need to meet the following criteria:

■ They must be carefully planned and provided with the resources and management backing to sustain them over the long term.

■ They require constant promotion. Linking them to other regular events helps. For example, Richer Sounds, a UK-based hi-fi chain, funds a monthly brainstorming session for the teams working in each of the company's stores and the venue is each team's local pub.

■ They should be fun. For example, tee-shirts and coffee mugs with appropriate logos for all who contribute. Also, schemes can be enlivened with short-term campaigns based on themes such as customer care, energy savings or the environment.

■ Suggestions must be handled quickly and efficiently. If staff get a good idea and get excited they should not wait more than a day or two at most for a response, and a decision should be made within a week. Also 'not adopted' rather than 'rejected' reduces the demotivational aspect of a turndown.

■ Suggestions should be rewarded. Although views vary on the extent and type of the reward, one-off payments tend to average about 20 per cent of the annual savings that result.

Quality circles

These comprise structured, voluntary work groups of around six or eight people from a particular work area. Typically meeting for about one hour on a weekly or fortnightly basis, they address and resolve work-related problems that the groups themselves have selected. Those taking part are trained in new skills, such as problem analysis, as well as developing their all-round abilities such as working in groups, problem solving and implementing change. Quality circles are a means of giving employees the opportunity to do something positive about the problems and issues they face, rather than just making suggestions for others in the organization to consider. They are based on the philosophy of making more effective use of an organization's most valuable asset, its people. The role of a group is to identify and select problems over which they have jurisdiction, while solutions that fall outside their remit are put forward as suggestions for change. Although generally having limited power, groups typically are able to fix certain problems that fall within their scope of activity.

The origins and development of quality circles have their roots in Japanese businesses. Many of the early problems facing Japanese companies concerned quality-related issues and this led to the approach being termed 'quality circles' whereas, in fact, the problems addressed concern all aspects of work.

Job redesign

Organizations are introducing extensive job redesigns so that employees use a variety of skills, often in teams. Under this development, staff have considerable freedom in deciding how to do the necessary tasks. Furthermore, work is designed to involve elements not directly associated with providing the products or services such as aspects of planning, scheduling and evaluation.

As mentioned earlier, organizations have appointed specialists and established specialist functions as an essential part of the structure to improve control and undertake developments in a business. The brief for these specialist groups has been to improve relevant parts of an organization by developing procedures, systems and activities within the broad area of their specialism. This has typically led to activities that originally were undertaken by line or executive functions (such as operations) being separated out and housed under the control and auspices of a specialist function – see Exhibit 15.3.

The downsides of this approach were discussed earlier. In addition, such developments result in activities that are not central to the expertise provided by a specialist area actually being undertaken by that function on the basis that the tasks fall within a broad spectrum of similar tasks and consequently would be best handled by having them report into and be completed by the same part of the organization. For example, the tasks undertaken by a purchasing department typically include supplier-related roles, contract negotiation, placing purchase orders and arranging for goods and services to be brought to site when needed. The rationale for such a grouping is that they form part of the total purchasing role. Such developments are then reinforced by structures that typically create distinct reporting lines that reinforce the provision of an activity from the direct user as shown in phase 2 in Exhibit 15.3.

The disadvantage of these arrangements is that whereas the first two tasks listed in the purchasing example above fall within the area of a purchasing specialist, the other two tasks would be better undertaken by and also fall within the responsibility of the

Exhibit 15.3 *Typical phases in the evolution of specialist functions in an organization*

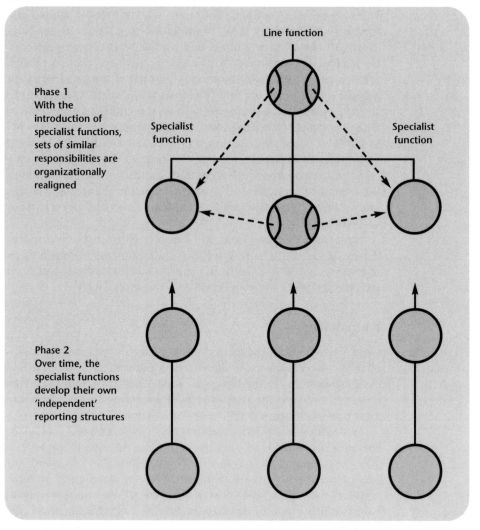

function wanting the goods and services. For, in this instance, what products or services are required and when the products or services are needed is best known and is best undertaken by the user. A central provision of these latter tasks results in additional procedures, additional communications and the potential for errors.

In most Western companies the decision concerning who does which tasks results in operations staff completing the doing task (that is, providing the product or service). But work comprises the three separate elements of planning, doing and evaluating. As shown in Exhibit 15.4 and as intimated in earlier sections of this chapter, these three parts of work have been separated and typically report in different functions within an organization. The rationale for this is a by-product of the use of specialists and the development of support functions within a business. Exhibit 15.4 is, therefore, an extension of phase 2 in Exhibit 15.3. It illustrates a typical structure and shows the separation of important parts of the whole task into different func-

Exhibit 15.4 *The separation of the three facets of work and the gap between their reporting structures created by the organizational set-up*

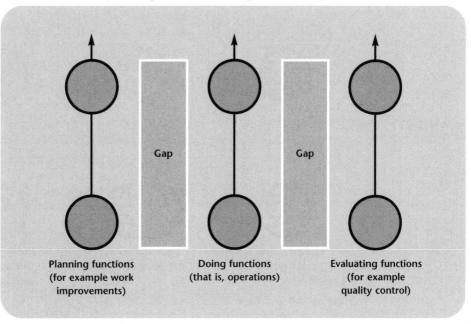

Planning functions (for example work improvements)

Doing functions (that is, operations)

Evaluating functions (for example quality control)

tional responsibilities that report in different systems and the inherent gap that results between the reporting lines of these three intrinsic parts of work.

Consequently, it has led to a situation where the inherent contribution of those responsible for providing the products and services to activities such as continuous improvement and the day-to-day scheduling of work has been lost and the essential link between the responsibility for providing products and services and checking the quality conformance of the product or service involved has been severed.

As implied by the earlier comments on what constitutes work, organizations need to build back aspects of planning and evaluating (see Exhibit 15.4) into the providing role undertaken by operations. Exhibit 15.5 illustrates how appropriate planning and evaluating activities (presently completed by specialist support functions) should be reassigned to those currently responsible for providing the products or services (that is, operations). Such actions lend support to the arguments put forward earlier and also provide a tangible, common-sense illustration of the effect this can have. Such actions switch activities so that they now form part of the task undertaken by those responsible for completing the products and services, thus facilitating productivity improvements, the day-to-day scheduling of work and consistent conformance to specification, while at the same time creating greater job interest for all concerned. On the one hand it releases specialists from undertaking non-specialist tasks, while on the other it gives those who provide products or services the responsibility for all three dimensions that make up meaningful tasks by broadening their activities and so allowing them to plan and evaluate the work they carry out.

The example of purchasing was given earlier. Exhibit 15.6 includes this as well as other functions to illustrate possible reallocations of activities from specialists to those who complete the products or services involved.

Exhibit 15.5　*Incorporating into the providing tasks appropriate planning and evaluating activities*

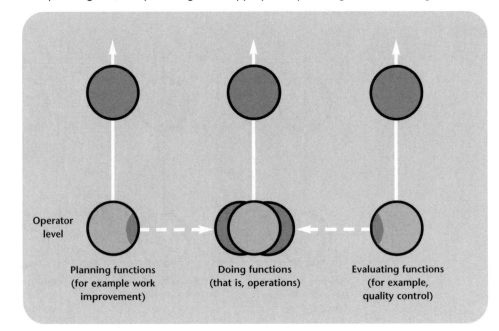

In addition to the significant empowerment and involvement gains that come from increasing job scope by including indirect activities (that is, tasks that are not concerned directly with the provision of products and services) into the role of product and service providers, there are two further key advantages that, in themselves make sense:

■ Decisions on day-to-day scheduling and the checking of products and services against specification are best completed at the point where the products or services are provided. For it is here that the up-to-date position is known and the time gap between finding faults and correcting the delivery system is shortest.

Exhibit 15.6　*Examples of activities better undertaken by specialists and those better undertaken by those providing the products and services*

	Activities that are best undertaken by	
Aspect	**Those providing products or services**	**Specialists**
Purchasing	Placing orders or calling off deliveries of product or service against contracts	Supplier selection, supplier relations and contract negotiation
Operations planning, control and scheduling	Short-term operations control and day-to-day scheduling	Long-term planning and capacity planning
Quality assurance and control	Quality control including inspection at all stages in the delivery system	Quality assurance including the development of sampling plans, customer reviews and material tests

■ Where staff only undertake activities directly concerned with providing products and services, then at times of low demand there are no alternative, indirect or non-providing tasks for them to undertake. The available choice is to make inventory or incur non-value-adding costs.

Given these sets of gains then many companies are reallocating activities previously completed by overhead staff to the role of providers of products and services. Now these latter staff have a mix of work that is more rewarding, reflects more appropriately the demand patterns and customer expectations in today's markets and the costs of which are met by the reductions in overhead staff that follow.

Staff training and development

Implied, if not explicit, so far has been the need for these changes to be underpinned by extensive training and staff development. This provision is essential for three key reasons:

■ The developments described here will entail changing from an environment and experience base comprising limited job scope and where taking the initiative to contribute ideas or make changes would not typically have been encouraged.

■ The need for training and development would not be confined to the necessary dimension of technology but would also need to involve new skills in the planning and evaluating activities that work would now comprise.

■ These new ways of working would also require skills that concerned the change in style and approach involved. Group working, analysis, decision-making and implementation skills typify the areas that training and development would need to address.

Flexi-working and job sharing

To help create conditions that meet the needs of organizations and also the needs of their staff, companies are turning to other work arrangements and packages that better fit the availability of their staff or provide people with more choice.

Flexitime

This offers staff an opportunity to adjust their working day to meet their domestic or social life patterns on a permanent or as-needed basis. In essence, staff contract to be at work in what are described as core hours. While being at work the core hours cannot be altered, the hours before and after core time can be. These, as the name suggests, are called flexi hours. Such arrangements allow staff to change the start and finish time of a day or work additional hours on certain days that can be used to take time off at other times, thus allowing them a measure of choice over when they work. The principal purpose is to help staff manage both their work and home commitments – unlike the humorous interpretation given in Exhibit 15.7. In most schemes, the totalling and balancing of hours is made over a period of several weeks and allows for plus and minus balances to be carried forward within agreed limits.

Exhibit 15.7   *Perhaps not the desired intention of flexible working arrangements!*

Flexible benefit schemes

These require staff to take part of their salary as cash but allow them to use the rest to buy extra benefits. For example, PricewaterhouseCoopers, a large UK accounting firm, gives staff a reward package comprising a notional salary and benefits entitlement. At least 80 per cent of salary must be taken as cash but the rest can be used to purchase benefits. In the PricewaterhouseCoopers' scheme the range of benefits includes:

- up to 10 days extra holiday
- childcare vouchers
- sports and leisure club membership with discounts
- pension plan
- luncheon vouchers usable at 30 000 outlets with 6 per cent discount
- leased car scheme
- substantial savings on group medical, dental and personal accident insurance.

Job sharing

This provides the opportunity for typically two people to meet the requirements of a job. These arrangements are usually on a 50/50 or 40/60 share basis.

Ergonomics

Ergonomics is primarily concerned with how the human body fits with its environment. Reviewing and matching the physiological aspects of job design to the person doing a job contribute to greater productivity while reducing fatigue and avoiding conditions that may lead to physical strain and other types of health risks. Sometimes referred to as 'human factor engineering', ergonomics designs the interface between people and the physical aspects of the workplace such as seating, desks and equipment and also determines the environmental aspects of the job including temperature, lighting and noise levels.

■ **Workplace factors** are the aspect of ergonomics that concerns detailing the interface between the physical attributes of people and the workplace. The dimensions reviewed relate to features such as reach, relative heights of equipment to body positions such as seating to monitor dials or use of PC screens. The purpose is to design workplaces that reduce strain and fatigue over a working day while eliminating conditions that could lead to physical injury over time.

■ **Environmental factors** cover aspects of work that also impact job performance and could affect people's long-term health. Specified and supported by comprehensive occupational health and safety legislation, ergonomics lays down conditions concerning the temperature, lighting and noise levels for a variety of working environments.

■ **Behavioural factors** highlight the role of these dimensions in effective workplace design. These factors link personal motivation and commitment to work design and build on to the change principles discussed earlier. Key factors include providing a meaningful set of activities that constitute a whole task, embodying aspects of planning, doing and evaluation within teams and establishing relationships, allowing staff to contact internal and external customers.

By combining these factors companies are able to design workplaces that improve productivity, motivate people, encourage involvement and provide safe and stress-free environments.

CONCLUSION

The challenge to create a working environment that helps people to develop their full potential, want to do a good job and contribute fully to improving all aspects of work is central to the role of operations management. To bring this about will require businesses to fundamentally rethink their approach to organizational design and the structure of work.

One key to this is involving and empowering people. This, however, means more than employee participation. Even where companies delegate authority and resources this does not, by right, lead to empowerment. Attempts to empower people from above will fail. The emphasis on empowerment needs to shift to providing the opportunity for staff at all levels to exercise increasing influence over themselves. The giving of power itself without providing support in the form of training and direction will result in failure.

Where empowerment does exist leads to power and control being exercised by individuals. Giving people more control over their own actions results in them accomplishing more and increasingly taking initiatives to get things done.

Creating the conditions where people are responsible for a meaningful set of activities is a key factor in these developments. This, however, can only be achieved with a fundamental reappraisal of work and organizational structures. Essential factors to making this happen include:

- **Self-managed teams** are not only responsible for given tasks but are capable of making and implementing their decisions and are held accountable for results.

- **Sharing information** highlights the need for people to have full information about all elements of the job and performance figures. Without full information, teams cannot be held responsible for their performance as they do not know the dimensions of the company's problems.

- **Creating autonomy** is essential and needs to be developed. To help do this, structure needs to be built into these arrangements as it enables people to handle the uncertainty they feel when trying out new behaviours. As teams evolve, more autonomy can be created, and this is essential to the sound and full working of teams.

However, these developments are dependent on how well people and, in particular, organizations learn. People, like businesses, need to be continually reinvented. But self-learning is not easy. 'It is no accident', Senge concludes 'that most organizations learn poorly. The way they are designed and managed (and) the way people's jobs are defined... create fundamental disabilities'.[6] However, progressive companies have been addressing these issues of change as they recognize the key role that people play within the success of organizations. The outcome of such changes will help companies to capitalize on their key resource – the people within the business.

SUMMARY

Creating an environment in which people can fulfill their potential and one that meets both their needs and those of the business is a key operations management role. This in itself presents a task that is difficult and made the more complex by the fast-changing nature of today's business in terms of market needs, level of employee commitment and the technical content of jobs.

General definitions concerning jobs set the scene while managerial philosophies of work and traditional approaches to managing people completed the introduction.

The orientiation of the chapter then switched to the need for companies to create change-orientated business environments that, in turn, bring implications for the current role of managers and the traditional shape of organizations. Then followed core section of the chapter that introduced developments such as employee involvement and empowerment and a range of key dimensions from staff training and development through to issues such as flexi-working, job sharing and ergonomics.

Discussion questions

1. Name some factors that fall into the hygiene and motivator categories. How may these differ for blue and white collar workers?

2. Using Exhibit 15.1 and the accompanying narrative, give two illustrations of manufacturing and service jobs that illustrate the difference between job depth and job scope.

3. Why are companies increasingly building indirect tasks into the remit of those staff priarily responsible for making products and providing services?

4. How are job satisfaction and motivation different? Illustrate your answer with an example.

5. Why, in the past, did companies build organizations based on 'control through specialists' and 'the specialization of labour'?

6. Can all jobs be enriched successfully? Illustrate your answer with examples.

7. Why is it imperatve that businesses turn themselves into learning organizations?

8. What are the advantages and disadvantages of job enlargement, job rotation and job enrichment? Give an example in operations where these would be beneficial and an example where it would be better not to employ these approaches.

Notes and references

1. Jacob, R 'Absence of management', *The American Way*, February (1993).
2. Hertzberg, F *Work and Nature of Man*, Cleveland: World Publishing Co. (1966).
3. Senge, PM *The Fifth Discipline*, New York: Doubleday (1990), p. 18.
4. Columella as quoted in Saskin, M 'Changing toward participative management approaches: a model and methods', *The Academy Review* (1976), pp. 75–86.
5. Senge, op. cit., p. 18.

Further reading

Bratton, J and Gold, J *Human Resource Management*, Macmillan Business, Basingstoke, UK (1999).

Gates, B and Collins, H *Business @ the Speed of Thought: Using a Digital Nervous System*, Penguin Books, London (1999).

Gibson, R (ed.) *Re-thinking the Future*, Nicholas Brealey Publishing, London (1997).

Grief, M *The Visual Factory: Building Participation Through Sharing Information*, Portland, Productivity Press (1991).

Lawler, EE, Mohramann, SA and Ledford, GE *Employee Involvement and Total Quality Management*, Jossey-Bass, San Francisco (1992).

Marchington, M, Goodman, J, Wilkinson, A and Ackers, P *New Developments in Employee Involvement*, Manchester School of Management, University of Manchester Institute of Science and Technology. Employment Department Research Studies No. 2 (1992).

Nilles, J *Managing Telework*, John Wiley & Son, New York (1998).

Ortege, B 'In Sam we trust; the untold story of Sam Walton and how Wal-mart is devouring America', *Times Business*, Random House, New York (1998).

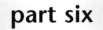
part six

Case Studies

Berwick Carpets plc

Berwick Carpets plc (BC) manufactures and sells tufted and woven carpets and carpet yarn. Although part of an international group of companies, it is managed as an independent business responsible for its own marketing, manufacturing and investment requirements. It ranks about tenth in size in the industry with current sales revenue of £100m. In common with the remainder of the carpet industry, it has over the past 15 years experienced a shift in the balance of sales towards tufted and away from woven carpets.

The manufacturing facilities consist of a spinning mill and both a tufted and woven carpet facility. While the spinning mill is on a separate site, carpet manufacturing processes are in the same location as the sales and other functions of the business. The tufted and woven carpets, however, comprise two separate divisions, and this case study concerns the tufted carpet division (TCD).

THE PRODUCTS

Unlike many UK carpet companies, BC has held its sales levels for tufted carpet over the past three years. It makes a range of carpet qualities and Exhibits 1 and 2 show these in three grades and the average manufacturing costs of a typical product. The company's marketing strategy has been to provide products in the top segment of each of the grades shown in Exhibit 1. Hence, each of the grade 1 carpets is at the top of the grade 1 range, and so on. Details for sales up to the current year are given in Exhibit 3, together with the forecasts for the end of the next year, which have been based upon the upturn in actual sales in the second half of the current year and known orders in the first two months of next year.

RAW MATERIALS

Each carpet is offered in a range of colours and is made from either a spun polypropylene, nylon or spun-woollen base. The colours offered and raw materials used are

This case study was written by Terry Hill (Templeton College, University of Oxford) and KHA Negal. It is intended as the basis for class discussion and not as an example of good or bad management. © AMD Publishing.

Exhibit 1   *Grades of tufted carpet*

Grade	Tufted carpets
1	Marble, Grenoble, Firenza, Barcarole, Casino
2	Maltese, Gazelle, Baroque, Barbary
3	Dalmatian, Royalty, Centurion, Lotus

Notes

1. Grade 3 is the highest quality of carpet.
2. Contract carpets are one-off carpets designed to customer specification and sold direct to the customer (for example hotels, house and office block builders and cinema chains). Invariably, they are made from non-standard colours, and often in material qualities not used on the standard range of carpets.
3. All non-contract carpets are sold to retail shops.
4. On contract carpets, one problem is judging the required yarn delivery to meet the order. Excess yarn is difficult to use while under-production constitutes failure to meet a customer's contract.

Exhibit 2   *Manufacturing costs for a product that is typical of all grades of carpet*

Aspect	Percentage of total manufacturing costs
Direct labour	7
Direct materials	81
Manufacturing overhead[1]	12
	100

1. 'Other' overhead is included at a later stage in the costing procedure.

Exhibit 3   *Actual sales of tufted carpets for the last three years and forecast sales for the next 12 months*

Grade	Carpet	Actual sales[1]			Next year's forecast[1]
		Current Year −2	Current Year −1	Current Year	
1	Marble	1423	1321	1457	1400
	Grenoble	76	35	30	20
	Firenza	38	6	4	4
	Barcarole	24	4	2	4
	Casino	59	35	36	55
	Total	1620	1401	1529	1483
2	Maltese	42	46	45	50
	Gazelle	213	225	166	150
	Barbary	54	52	64	180
	Baroque	202	268	286	250
	Total	511	591	561	630
3	Dalmatian[2]	–	28	57	100
	Royalty	106	84	108	130
	Centurion	184	134	168	230
	Lotus[2]	–	–	16	100
	Contract	7	11	28	160
	Total	297	257	377	720
Total		2428	2249	2467	2833

1. All figures are in square metres (000).
2. Dalmatian was introduced in current year −1 and Lotus will be introduced at the end of the current year.

Exhibit 4   *Raw materials and colour range offered*

Grade	Carpet	Number of colours	Raw material		
			Spun polypropylene	Nylon	Spun-woollen
1	Marble	26	✓		
	Grenoble	8	✓		
	Firenza	(see note)		✓	
	Barcarole	(see note)		✓	
	Casino	(see note)		✓	
2	Maltese	(see note)		✓	
	Gazelle	15	✓		
	Barbary	7			✓
	Baroque	12	✓		
3	Dalmatian	10	✓		
	Royalty	(see note)		✓	
	Centurion	20			✓
	Lotus	(see note)		✓	
	Contract	Unlimited	✓	✓	✓
Material delivery lead times (weeks)			2	6	6

Note

1. These carpets are made from nylon which is delivered in a natural colour and dyed on site to meet a whole range of colours. The dyeing process takes one day.

given in Exhibit 4. Both polypropylene and nylon are man-made, while wool is a natural fibre. Consequently, there is a relatively high incidence of faults in the spun-woollen yarn deliveries (see Exhibit 4). Without raw material inventory in the appropriate colour, faults in a yarn delivery will lead to failure to meet a customer's delivery promise. This problem is invariably the case on contract carpets where the yarn colour(s) involved will be customer-specified. If faults go undetected and the yarn enters the process, then the additional costs associated with substandard carpet and the further impact upon delivery delay can be considerable.

Raw material inventory is valued at about £450 000 with work-in-progress standing at a further £250 000.

PRODUCTION PROCESS

The process lead time is between two and five days. Each carpet goes through some of the common processes and these are shown in Exhibit 5. Carpets can be delayed between one process and the next without affecting the quality of the carpet. All carpets are tufted (that is, the primary backing cloth for the carpet is fed underneath a needle carrying the yarn. At predetermined intervals, the needle passes through the backing cloth and a looper on the underside retains a loop of yarn beneath the cloth). After several other processes, the carpet has its secondary back put on by the backing plant. This can be either jute cloth which is stuck to or latex foam which is applied to the reverse side of a carpet.

Exhibit 5   *Production processes by carpet quality*

Grade	Carpets	Production process							
		Tuft	Yarn dye and dry[1]	Repair[2]	Print[3]	Steam	Shear	Steam[4]	Back
1	Marble	✓					✓		✓
	Grenoble	✓					✓		✓
	Firenza	✓	✓		✓		✓		✓
	Barcarole	✓	✓		✓		✓		✓
	Casino	✓	✓		✓		✓		✓
2	Maltese	✓	✓				✓		✓
	Gazelle	✓					✓		✓
	Barbary	✓					✓		✓
	Baroque	✓					✓		✓
3	Dalmatian	✓		✓			✓		✓
	Royalty	✓	✓				✓		✓
	Centurion	✓		✓		✓	✓	✓	✓
	Lotus	✓	✓				✓		✓
	Contract[5]								

Notes

1. Yarn dye and dry is only for nylon-based carpets.
2. Repair – all carpets are inspected after tufting. If a repair is necessary it is completed on the tufting machine except in the case of Dalmatian and Centurion where any repairs are completed on a separate frame.
3. This printing process is to apply dye-resistant chemicals to these carpets.
4. Only the top quality grade 3 carpets go through the steaming process before and after shearing.
5. Contract carpets go through different processes depending upon the raw material. Polypropylene is as for Gazelle; nylon, Royalty and woollen, Centurion.

SPUN-WOOLLEN YARN DELIVERIES

On deliveries of spun-woollen yarn, the number of faults experienced on a delivery reduces the tufting process, because of delays involved, to about two-thirds of its standard throughput. It is estimated that for every square metre of yarn tufted there will be, on average, one yarn break due to faulty yarn.

In addition, because of the different materials (yarns) and the different carpet qualities involved, not all tufting machines can be used to make all carpets. Exhibit 6 shows the range of tufting machines, the average weekly, potential output and the carpet types for which the machines can be used.

Dyeing and drying are processes only used on nylon yarn which is purchased as a natural shade. After tufting, nylon-based carpets are then dyed and dried, a process called 'piece dying'. The dye house currently works a 40-hour week and can produce in a single shift sufficient dyed yarn per week to make 10 000 square metres of carpet.

The shearer crops the tip of each tuft as a cylinder lawn mower trims grass. The length of yarn removed by the cut can be adjusted on the machine. The pre- and post-steaming processes take place before and after the shearer. They are, however, only used for Centurion and to ensure that the tuft is presented in the way to yield the best quality results. The shearing machine is currently utilized for about 65 per cent of its time.

Exhibit 6   *Tufting machine average output*

Tufting machine	Carpet type	Average weekly output (square metres)
1	Dalmatian	5 500
	Contracts	3 000
2	Casino	10 000
	Barcarole	10 000
	Firenza	10 000
3	Royalty	7 000
4	Centurion	4 000
	Lotus	4 000
5	Baroque	10 000
	Contracts	8 000
6	Marble	15 000
	Grenoble	20 000
	Maltese	10 000
7	Marble	15 000
	Grenoble	20 000
	Maltese	10 000
8	Gazelle	12 000
9	Grenoble	20 000
	Barbary	10 000

Notes

1. Centurion outputs on machine 4 can vary between 3000 and 5000.
2. Contracts on machine 5 can vary between 6000 and 10 000.
3. Dalmatian on machine 1 can vary between 4000 and 7000.
4. Woollen contracts are completed only on machine 1 and both polypropylene and nylon on machine 5.
5. Not all tufting machines are run throughout a week. The output figures above express the potential levels of output and not the actual, as machines are run in line with sales demand.
6. The output figures above show alternative figures depending upon the carpet type. Hence machine 1 can produce either 5500 m²/week of Dalmatian or 3000 m²/week of Contract carpet.
7. Carpet types can only be made on the machines shown above. In a very few instances it may be possible to make a carpet on another machine, but it would result in lower throughput figures and a significant increase in faults.

The backing plant is currently running on a 24-hour basis over five days with weekend overtime where necessary. The skills required for this job are difficult to find and consequently three eight-hour shifts are not feasible. Also, an agreement with the local trade union restricts the total hours which can be worked over a 12-month period. Average output from this process is some 45 000 square metres per week. This figure takes into account average maintenance, breakdowns and changeover times. The number of working weeks available in a year is 46 when account has been taken of the annual shutdowns and bank holidays.

LABOUR FORCE

Of the 220 directs employed at BC, some 70–80 work on the production processes described in the case. In total, there are about 350 employees on this site. Exhibit 7 gives the breakdown of gross pay for a direct worker. Bonus payments are made in direct proportion to output and do not relate to the hours worked. The payments made vary depending upon the weekly output and are shown in Exhibit 8. In the current pay discussions, the trade unions are requesting, among other things, a higher incentive payment for output. They argue that the current actual bonus earnings are reducing and that a productivity-linked payment increase through the incentive scheme would make sense all round.

Exhibit 7   *Composition of gross pay for a typical direct worker*

Payment	Percentage of total gross pay
Basic	75
Overtime	10
Bonus	15
	100

Exhibit 8   *Standard production hours for different carpets and bonus payments*

Grade	Carpet	Standard hours to produce 100 square metres
1	Marble	4.1
	Grenoble	3.0
	Firenza	5.1
	Barcarole	5.1
	Casino	5.1
2	Maltese	5.4
	Gazelle	4.5
	Barbary	6.8
	Baroque	4.9
3	Dalmatian	6.8
	Royalty	5.9
	Centurion	8.5
	Lotus	4.8
	Contract	Varies depending upon the yarn

Bonus payments

Weekly output (square metres)	Bonus payment per thousand square metres (£)
Up to 30 000	1.00
31 000–40 000	1.30
41 000–50 000	1.70
51 000 and over	2.00

THE FUTURE

BC's marketing strategy is to continue to produce the present range of carpets and also to start to build up the business in the contracts market. Currently, 50 per cent of all contract carpets are made of spun-woollen and it is expected that this composition of sales will remain the pattern for the future. If it does change, then it is anticipated that it will show an increase in spun-woollen yarns of up to a further 10 per cent.

Contracts is a very cost-competitive market, but one where very large repeat orders may be earned by a successful supplier. BC intends that this area of the market will provide an important area of sales growth. BC's all-round success, however, has been built on its growing reputation as a manufacturer of quality carpets. It recognizes quite clearly that this is the basis for both its current and future strategy in the marketplace.

British Airways: Customizing the Service

As the world changes so the service requirements of customers change. For British Airways (BA) the need to match and anticipate such changes has increased in recent years as the general overcapacity within the passenger airline industry has led to growing competition on many of its prime routes. Foremost of these are trans-Atlantic flights that carry corporate and business executives to and from Europe and North America. By the late 1990s BA found itself losing first and business class passengers to rival airlines that were transferring capacity from Asia to trans-Atlantic routes while reducing fares to increase sales and grow market share.

With the hangover effects of BA's problems in the late 1990s (such as the three-day cabin crew strike in 1997 and the problems associated with its decision to sub-contract its in-flight catering facilities and provision) still around, profits had fallen sharply and BA's share price halved.

Meeting competition head-on is not new to BA. Its rise from being an airline not well-regarded by most and making losses more times than it was in profit to becoming the most profitable airline in the world was acknowledged as an example of sound business management. Central to this metamorphosis was orientating its staff and systems to customers and their needs partly built on the Putting People First initiative launched in 1983.

To keep ahead British Airways continued to consult passengers to help identify improvements to the service it offered. In the mid 1990s it unveiled a new and very different approach to in-flight service. Cabins were redesigned, and the passenger service offering was redesigned as well. Whereas previously the emphasis had been on an efficient but slightly homogeneous service, the pendulum had swung back the other way; now the emphasis was on customized, personalized service that attempted to cater to each passenger's individual needs.

At the heart of the changes was the concept of customer focus. In Club World, the change process began with a customer consultation exercise. The results were good – but not great. The service was perceived as being acceptable, and indeed comfortable within the limits of the space provided, but it was also seen as predictable. Rather than seeing this result as confirmation that the existing service offering was working, BA chose to see it as a sign that change was needed.

This case study was written by Terry Hill (Templeton College, University of Oxford). It is intended as the basis for class discussion and not as an example of good or bad management. © AMD Publishing.

The first task was to redesign the environment as far as possible, to ensure passenger comfort (although, of course, without compromising safety). The major focus here was on seating arrangements. On the principle of 'if you don't do it on the ground, why do it in the air?', designers sought for a seat design that would give the maximum possible comfort. The result was a cradle seat, designed to give full-body support. Features of the new seat included lumbar supports that adjusted individually to fit the passenger's preferences; a much wider footplate; a cushion that provided support behind the knees; an adjustable leg rest extension that again could be suited to the height of the passenger; and an adjustable headrest that included wings to support the head while a passenger slept. Overall, the new design increased the pitch (the distance between one seat and that of the seat in front) from 40 to 50 inches while improving the level of recline to 140°.

Along with the physical design there was a change in the manner and mode of service delivery. BA consulted cabin crews as well as passengers, and found that the former, like the latter, wanted a more personalized service. Cabin crew also found the previous service predictable, and wanted to be able to offer a more 'spontaneous' service to passengers. Putting the wishes of both crew and passengers into effect, British Airways Club World now concentrates on letting passengers in effect design their own service. For example, on overnight trans-Atlantic flights the emphasis was on allowing customers to rest and get as much sleep as possible. Passengers were offered both blankets and sheets to make them feel more as if they were tucked up in bed. While in the morning, unlike the old system where passengers were awakened and served breakfast at a standard time before landing, passengers wake in their own time. As and when they wake, cabin crew offer each a mug of coffee and a choice of croissants or other breakfast foods. Passengers could now wake up more or less in the fashion they are used to at home.

Breakfast was not the only meal to undergo change. The scaled-down cutlery formerly in service has been replaced with full-sized knives and forks, again to emphasize the familiar. Lunch and dinner have always been flexible, with passengers able to opt for just one or two of the three courses, but now another dimension was added; passengers who feel hungry between meals can quite literally 'raid the larder'. Chocolate, fruit, biscuits and cheese are available on short flights, while on longer flights, pies, sandwiches and other snacks are ready for passengers who wish to help themselves. Again, the aim is to create a comfortable atmosphere reminiscent of a passenger's own home. Being able to help themselves rather than waiting for meal times or asking for service improves the passenger's sense of being in control.

The changes in Club World in the mid-1990s were mirrored by design and service changes in first class. Here the designers went further in making use of existing space. On 747s, for example, the number of first class seats was reduced from eighteen to fourteen. The regimented rows of seats were broken up to give greater privacy. Those on the edges of the cabin now sit alone, while those in the centre can sit side by side with a travelling companion, or be screened for greater privacy.

Not content with repositioning the seats, the designers went further. Each seat, which resembles a deep bucket chair, has a small 'visitor's seat' attached to the foot. In an atmosphere specifically designed to resemble a small sitting room, passengers can sit together and have a drink, chat or discuss business for as long as they like, then go back to their original seats. The 'visitor's seat' then converts into an extension to the main seat, and the whole ensemble can be converted easily into a horizontal bed, allowing passengers on overnight flights the chance for a real night's sleep.

The same flexibility was extended to food service in first class. Set meal times were abolished; an extensive menu was provided and passengers order and eat when they wish, after the fashion of a restaurant.

But in markets with overcapacity (as is the case with passenger airlines) the need to stay competitive and to continue to anticipate or meet the needs of customers is on-going. As a result BA is continuously trying to keep one step ahead of its rivals. To this end, BA made a whole series of changes starting in the period 1999/2000 to reinforce its position and differentiate itself from its rivals on dimensions other than price.

BA's promise to its customers at this time recognized 'that simply getting through the airport and onto the plane is not always a hassle-free experience'. To this end BA declared its intent to make a customer's journey 'as smooth as possible, from check-in to aircraft seat and beyond'.

Underpinning these changes was BA's Putting People First Again programme that was intended to link back to and build on developments in the early 1980s. Launched in 1999, all BA's 62 000 staff underwent an intensive customer service course that involved staff from different parts of the company evaluating each other's attention to passengers.

In addition, BA also introduced more executive lounges (over 75 in Europe alone) modelled on a Mediterranean style (and named Terraces) incorporating coffee, fruit juice and wine bars together with Combiz facilities providing telephone, fax and plug-in laptop capability.

Other facilities were also made available. Showers are on hand for long-haul passengers to freshen up. On the return journey to London from the east coast of the USA, customers can now eat dinner (for first class passengers this includes a waiter and silver service provision) before they fly from Washington, JFK, Newark, Philadelphia, Detroit and Boston airports. Cutting out breakfast is also an option, thereby making even more time to sleep. Instead of eating before you land, breakfast (as well as a shower and clothes pressing service) is available in BA's arrivals lounges. Open from 4 am to 7 pm, with a full English breakfast available until 12 noon.

But development did not stop there. In March 2000 BA introduced beds in business class – a quantum leap in comfort for the business traveller. With a click of a button the seat turns into a flat 1.83m bed. By July 2000 this will be standard on all New York flights and then routes such as Tokyo, Hong Kong and Los Angeles will be added. The refitting is scheduled to be completed by 2002.

All of these developments are an integral part of BA's overall strategy. Concentrate on premium, high-yielding travellers, focus on point-to-point traffic rather than uneconomic routes that transfer passengers onto more lucrative long-haul flights. Underpinning this plan has been BA's shift in its long-haul fleet to smaller aircraft. It has been replacing 747s with smaller 777s and shedding a few rows of backpackers (economy tickets sold to cut-price travellers) pushes up yields.

This strategy plays to BA's strengths. It already has a brand with which business executives identify. And, London Heathrow and London Gatwick are BA's backyard, with a 43 per cent share of available capacity between Heathrow, its main hub, and the USA. While some passengers may not care which airport they go through to and from the USA, most executives have some business in London. Flying directly to Heathrow and Gatwick with fast and frequent rail services to central London (four times an hour to and from Heathrow, dedicated rail track avoiding delays and a journey time of a little over 10 minutes) reduces total travel time before and after the flight.

As BA recognizes, its customers' time is a 'precious commodity'. Its aim is to demonstrate its intent to offer 'the highest service specification as well as helping to streamline the travel process of its customers'.

Caltrex Engineering

Sales, profit and cash targets are a high priority in terms of our corporate performance measures. Recent efforts, particularly with our existing large customers, and the contract with a new large customer in Germany have resulted in a sales growth which keeps us well on target for this year. The improvements in manufacturing have lowered costs and the shedding of some low price work and the growth of higher margin sales will, in turn, ensure that our profit forecasts will be met. The third leg of these key measures is cash, and one critical facet of this [explained Bob Murray, CEO, Caltrex Engineering] concerns our inventory levels. Hence this review. As a first step we have undertaken a number of analyses to gain some insights into why the inventory levels are high and to help us consider the actions to take to reduce them.

BACKGROUND

Caltrex Engineering manufactures seals for a wide range of applications in the aerospace, automotive and general industrial sectors. It is part of Lambrin Industries, a US-based group of companies which comprises a wide range of businesses including electronics, electrical engineering and mechanical equipment. Based in New Jersey, Lambrin currently has sales revenues of $16.5bn.

MARKETS

Caltrex manufactures and sells a range of products customized to meet the specific needs of a wide range of customers. 'As you would guess, the seals are specific to one application and the materials and shapes involved are typically specified by the customer concerned', explained Mike Daley, vice-president of marketing. 'Our business, however, is very much at the engineered end of the seals market involving expensive materials, high specification designs and with quality conformance an

This case study was prepared by Terry (Templeton College, University of Oxford) and AJ Hill (UMIST). It is intended for class discussion and not as an illustration of good or bad management. © AMD Publishing.

Exhibit 1   *Manufacturing process*

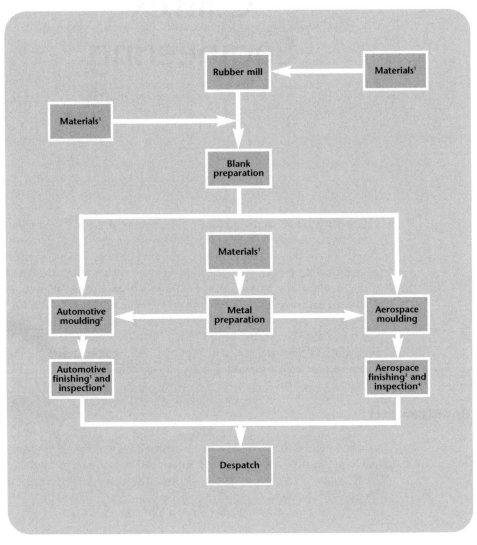

Notes

1. Materials indicate an outside supply.
2. Automotive moulding includes general industrial sectors.
3. Finishing can be either internal or external.
4. All inspection is completed internally.

essential requirement. Orders for these customized products', Mike continued, 'vary from sector to sector and within a sector. The principal sales patterns, however, are contracts with scheduled call-offs, orders placed on a regular basis (although the frequency will vary markedly) and those that allow little predictability. The latter include orders for most spares.'

Mike went on to explain that this was a make-to-order business in that products were only made in response to orders and scheduled call-offs. The main customer sectors were aerospace, automotive and industrial. Over the last year, manufacturing had been split into two areas to reflect the differences in these markets. However, to provide some association with the past, areas retained the names aerospace and automotive whereas, in fact, sales in the aerospace unit comprised orders from automotive customers and vice versa.

MANUFACTURING

Process

All products go through the same set of processes. As Exhibit 1 shows, the materials from which seals are moulded are either further processed in the rubber mill or, in the case of the material used in injection moulding, are delivered directly from an outside supplier. At the blank preparation stage, the material is formed into smaller, pre-cut sizes, known as blanks. These vary in size depending upon the dimensions of the final seal. One blank is prepared for each seal irrespective of its size. Once prepared, blanks go straight to the moulding areas or are held in the blank stores awaiting call-off by a moulding area.

The seal is often moulded around a metal component to form the final product. In these instances, the metal components are made by outside suppliers to the exact specification of customers' drawings and despatched to Caltrex in line with agreed schedules.

The next stage is moulding. Material blanks and metal components, where required, are sent to the moulding areas. The seals are then moulded in either the aerospace or automotive moulding areas in line with manufacturing schedules.

Following moulding, the seals are then finished which typically involves separating out the formed product from the rest of the blank. Whereas finishing for all aerospace parts is completed internally, automotive seals are finished by out-workers. (Out-workers are trained staff who work at home with products being delivered to and collected from them on a regular, often daily, basis.) All finished parts are then inspected internally and packed at this stage. Completed seals then go to despatch to meet customer orders, or go into finished goods inventory awaiting customer call-offs.

Planning and control

Production is planned one month ahead to meet customer orders scheduled for the following month (see Exhibit 2). To balance the trade-offs between the length of change-over times and the size of the production runs (in terms of time taken), manufacturing order quantities (MOQs) have been calculated and these become the length of a production run unless the actual customer requirement is greater (see Exhibit 2). 'There are times, however, when production is scheduled for call-offs two months ahead', explained Sam Isaacs, vice-president of operations. 'This is where it suits manufacturing to make in one period to meet sales in the next. Most of the time, though, we make in line with the following month's demand.'

Exhibit 2   *Work-in-progress inventory, planned production, MOQ and other data for parts within the moulding, finishing and inspection areas for a representative sample of products*

Part #	Position within production process		cost per part (£s)	Moulding # units			Customer schedule (# units) planned call offs		Last 12 months' sales (# units)
	last	next		inventory at 31 May	planned production in June	MOQ	June	July	
00042	AU14	EF	0.09	258 300	250 000	50 000	250 000	250 000	1 750 000
05891	EF	AUIN	0.71	40 760	–	10 000	20 000	20 000	200 000
14567	AU4	IF	0.52	52 100	–	50 000	20 000	–	300 000
37148	AU6	IF	1.24	2 110	2 000	2 000	2 000	2 000	14 000
37215	EF	AUIN	0.10	100 160	100 000	50 000	100 000	100 000	850 000
38215	AU11	EF	0.13	199 550	200 000	50 000	200 000	200 000	2 000 000
40101	EF	AUIN	0.24	306 150	200 000	100 000	250 000	250 000	2 450 000
42156	EF	AUIN	0.37	81 670	60 000	20 000	40 000	100 000	650 000
42157	AU4	EF	0.24	39 240	40 000	10 000	40 000	40 000	500 000
44752	EF	AUIN	0.11	150 060	150 000	150 000	150 000	150 000	1 000 000
45210	AU8	IF	0.59	74 810	–	25 000	30 000	30 000	450 000
45273	AU12	IF	0.08	106 360	–	50 000	75 000	–	1 500 000
47213	IF	AUIN	0.72	21 090	–	20 000	6 000	6 000	120 000
47215	IF	AUIN	0.76	15 750	15 000	5 000	15 000	15 000	200 000
48001	AU14	IF	1.17	8 430	–	8 000	5 000	–	15 000
48153	IF	AUIN	1.02	15 620	5 000	5 000	10 000	10 000	60 000
52708	EF	AUIN	0.77	78 850	–	40 000	50 000	–	880 000
81400	AE5	IF	3.19	215	–	200	120	–	360
84206	IF	AEIN	2.21	645	–	600	600	–	1 800
84543	IF	AEIN	3.01	63	–	60	50	–	200
87210	AE4	IF	2.98	78	70	70	70	70	700
87214	IF	AEIN	1.98	670	–	600	400	–	4 000
87412	IF	AEIN	2.87	196	200	200	200	–	600
92143	MP	AU2	1.02	15 810	15 000	5 000	10 000	20 000	75 000
94153	MP	AE5	3.78	55	–	60	10	–	20
95123	MP	AU9	0.84	41 420	40 000	20 000	40 000	40 000	240 000
97214	MP	AU2	1.02	50 280	50 000	10 000	50 000	50 000	750 000
97841	MP	AE6	2.75	836	–	250	250	250	750

Notes

1. MOQ = manufacturing order quantity.
2. AU14 = automotive moulding machine 14, and so on.
3. AE5 = aerospace moulding machine 5, and so on.
4. EF = external finishing.
5. IF = internal finishing.
6. AUIN = automotive inspection.
7. AEIN = aerospace inspection.
8. MP = metal preparation.
9. All inventory where the next process is identified as ER has, in fact, either already been, or is awaiting to be despatched to an outworker.

Inventory

'Performance targets are an important part of the way we are judged as a company, as well as individuals. One area where we know we need to improve is working capital. For this reason', explained Sam Isaacs, 'we have been reviewing and analysing our inventory holdings particularly in terms of work-in-progress and finished goods. [The analyses given in this case have been confined to the automotive and aerospace markets. This is to keep the case analysis to a manageable size.] At the moment inventory levels are too high, especially given that we are a make-to-order business. As inventory is principally regarded as the responsibility of the operations function it is our task to identify and implement ways of reducing it. Exhibits 2 to 6 provide our initial review. The question is, however, what do we do from here?'

Exhibit 3   Review of inventory analysis

Exhibits 2, 4, 5 and 6 provide details of the inventory review completed in early June. A representative sample of part numbers was agreed for the inventory held in the following areas:

■ Blank preparation and blank stores   – Exhibit 4
■ Moulding, finishing and inspection areas – Exhibit 2
■ Finished goods inventory   – Exhibit 5

Exhibit 6 gives details relating to the data in Exhibit 5. As explained in the case narrative, Caltrex Engineering uses batch processes. Each part has been separated into a number of operations (the preparation of the material, blank preparation, moulding and so on) through which each part is progressed in line with a route sheet. Parts, although customized, are to manufacturing, standard products in that they have been made before and, therefore, are a known product in which investment has been made (for example, route sheets and moulds). Also, the blanks are made for one part and then the equipment is reset for the next part and so on. This format is similarly used in moulding, finishing and inspection.

Causal analysis
To undertake a causal analysis of the data given in Exhibits 2, 4, 5 and 6 you need to refer to the relevant sections in the accompanying text in Chapter 10.

Exhibit 4   Inventory and other data for a representative sample of parts in the blank preparation area and blank stores

Part #	Position within production process		cost per batch (£s)	Blank preparation			Moulding (# units)		
				# units			production planned in		last 12 months' sales
	present	next		inventory level at 31 May	planned production in June	MOQ	June	July	
70017	BS	AE8	0.81	155	–	600	–	–	450
71412	BS	AU7	0.65	15 720	–	15 000	15 000	–	60 000
72086	BS	AE8	0.92	275	–	1 500	–	–	3 400
72141	BS	AE22	1.24	110	–	100	40	–	80
72891	BS	AE12	1.42	1 065	1 500	500	1 000	1 500	10 000
73248	BS	AU9	0.72	8 140	–	4 000	8 000	–	16 000
74152	BS	AU4	0.89	4 020	–	2 000	4 000	–	8 000
74260	BS	AE6	0.76	915	–	800	700	–	700
75143	BS	AE4	1.08	430	–	500	100	–	200
75147	BS	AE8	0.81	75	–	500	–	–	425
76123	BS	AU1	0.54	10 090	10 000	10 000	8 000	8 000	130 000
77521	BS	AU5	0.82	8 110	20 000	20 000	–	12 000	50 000

Notes

1. BS = Blank stores.
2. AE8 = aerospace moulding machine 8, and so on.
3. AU7 = automotive moulding machine 7, and so on.
4. MOQ = manufacturing order quantity.
5. The present position within the production process (column 2) for all the above parts is blank stores. Parts having been formed go into the blank stores awaiting allocation to the next process or go directly into the relevant moulding area. Typically, high volume part numbers fall into the latter category.

Exhibit 5 *Finished goods inventory, planned production, MOQ and other data for a representative sample of parts*

Part #	cost per part (£s)	inventory level at 31 May	production planned in June	production planned in July	MOQ	planned call-offs June	planned call-offs July	last 12 months' sales	agreed inventory level
					# units				
03521	4.66	596	–	–	260	–	—	25 650	–
06702	2.75	584	3 000	3 000	1 000	2 500	2 300	26 425	–
07444	6.20	120	–	–	120	80	–	160	–
07615	3.08	1 535	–	–	1 200	600	600	7 200	–
07616	4.56	1 207	–	–	140	200	200	5 500	–
07618	2.96	1 100	–	–	2 000	–	50	650	–
07778	3.14	5 085	4 000	4 000	2 000	4 000	3 500	40 000	5 000
08445	2.81	210	200	100	100	250	250	7 500	–
10094	4.73	5 901	–	–	2 500	–	–	8 700	–
11136	2.32	8 895	–	–	2 750	2 200	1 850	18 400	–
12136	2.12	5 063	–	–	–	2 600	1 550	12 150	–
12727	3.13	8 037	1 500	–	1 500	3 250	2 675	24 010	–
14460	4.75	180	300	300	300	346	346	7 460	–
19782	4.14	4 400	2 500	2 500	2 500	–	4 650	20 000	4 000
24711	5.12	153	–	–	200	–	–	2 650	–
24713	3.96	750	–	1 500	1 500	–	1 000	5 150	–
25303	2.68	425	–	–	–	–	–	480	–
28420	5.05	160	–	–	300	–	–	240	–
28423	3.24	7 308	1 750	–	1 000	4 500	2 600	29 400	–
28743	3.06	341	380	–	–	200	200	1 120	–
34226	2.47	27 500	30 000	20 000	10 000	24 000	22 500	328 500	25 000
37891	2.32	1 152	–	–	–	420	370	2 990	–
43071	3.86	4 567	5 250	3 500	1 750	4 270	4 350	49 500	4 000
48522	3.33	332	–	–	430	120	180	1 560	–
53062	3.10	2 000	1 000	1 000	1 000	2 000	2 000	44 500	–
56669	3.14	2 150	2 000	2 000	2 000	–	6 000	28 400	–
57375	2.56	39 910	48 000	48 000	6 000	46 500	47 000	290 900	45 000
57376	3.08	4 146	–	1 100	550	–	3 000	20 070	–
57554	3.54	31	–	–	150	–	–	40	–
59528	2.36	63 914	–	–	20 000	22 000	22 000	226 400	–
60123	4.52	28	60	60	60	40	60	480	–
64265	2.42	11 471	9 000	12 000	3 000	10 000	10 000	65 500	10 000
66446	4.86	1 519	1 650	1 650	550	1 500	1 500	9 650	1 500
69123	4.15	3 816	3 600	2 400	1 200	3 800	2 800	37 550	3 000
71685	2.96	12	420	–	–	70	70	450	–
72142	4.01	967	–	–	550	–	–	4 070	–
73712	3.51	2 598	–	–	1 500	1 000	1 000	15 000	–
82595	4.05	6 521	6 000	6 750	750	6 500	6 500	72 000	6 000
87431	4.56	284	160	–	160	135	140	1 780	–
96537	3.75	750	1 050	1 050	1 050	1 100	1 350	8 560	–

Notes

1. MOQ is manufacturing order quantit. It is not included for bought-in products.
2. Supplier's minimum order quantity for bought-in products is £400.
3. See Note 6, Exhibit 2.

Exhibit 6   *Comments on finished goods inventory*

Part #	Comments
03521	Customer has cancelled call-offs in the last 3 months.
06702	Overproduction due to inaccurate scrap rate
07444	To meet customer's future orders.
07615	To meet customer's future orders.
07616	Customer has reduced scheduled call-offs in the last month.
07618	Overplanned as a result of manufacturing order quantity.
07778	Customer agreement to hold a minimum of the equivalent of 1 month of sales in stock at all times, together with reduced call-offs in the last 3 months.
08445	Overproduction due to inaccurate scrap rate.
10094	Customer has cancelled call-offs in the last 3 months.
11136	To meet customer's future orders.
12136	Supplier's minimum order quantity.
12727	To meet customer's future orders.
14460	Overplanned as a result of manufacturing order quantity.
19782	Customer agreement to hold a minimum of the equivalent of 1 month of sales in stock at all times, together with reduced call-offs in the last 3 months.
24711	Overproduction due to inaccurate scrap rate.
24713	Overplanned as a result of manufacturing order quantity.
25303	Supplier's minimum order quantity.
28420	Overplanned as a result of manufacturing order quantity.
28423	To meet customer's future orders.
28743	Supplier's minimum order quantity.
34226	Customer agreement to hold a minimum of the equivalent of 1 month of sales in stock at all times, together with minimum batch sizes.
37891	Supplier's minimum order quantity.
43071	Customer agreement to hold a minimum of the equivalent of 1 month of sales in stock at all times, together with minimum batch sizes.
48522	Overproduction due to inaccurate scrap rate.
53062	To meet customer's future orders.
56669	To meet customer's future orders.
57375	Customer agreement to hold a minimum of the equivalent of 1 month of sales in stock at all times, together with minimum batch sizes.
57376	To meet customer's future orders.
57554	Overproduction due to inaccurate scrap rate.
59528	To meet customer's future orders.
60123	Overproduction due to inaccurate scrap rate.
64265	Customer agreement to hold a minimum of the equivalent of 2 months of sales in stock at all times, together with minimum batch sizes.
66446	Customer agreement to hold a minimum of the equivalent of 2 months of sales in stock at all times, together with inaccurate scrap rates.
69123	Customer agreement to hold a minimum of the equivalent of 1 month of sales in stock at all times.
71685	Supplier's minimum order quantity.
72142	Customer has cancelled call-offs in the last 3 months.
73712	Customer has reduced scheduled call-offs in the last 6 months.
82595	Customer agreement to hold a minimum of the equivalent of 1 month of sales in stock at all times, together with minimum batch sizes.
87431	To meet customer's future orders.
96537	Overplanned as a result of manufacturing order quantity.

Fabritex

The room bore all the hallmarks of a long meeting. The Fabritex management team relaxed in their chairs. Empty coffee cups patterned the boardroom table. Not for the first time Charles Franklin, the company chairman, reflected on the quality of the business-based discussions and the noticeable financial improvements over the last 18 months.

'Well I think we're agreed. Next year we'll target Pearlwear as one of our major areas for sales growth.' Charles glanced around and got the nods of approval he was anticipating.

'Good. However, before we finish for today, let us review the issues around how we will grow our share of the Pearlwear business.'

Charles looked towards his sales and marketing director. 'Perhaps you can start us off, John.'

BACKGROUND

Fabritex is part of the Wardman Group which manufactures a range of textiles for a wide variety of fashion and industrial applications as well as having interests in engineering, furniture and finishings. Because of intense competition from the Far East, particularly on price, the UK textile industry had undergone major reorganization and much of the overcapacity in the sector had now been squeezed out.

Fabritex focuses on knitted fabrics for garment manufacturers, mainly for lingerie. These customers in turn sell either to major retailers or through independent outlets. Some of the garment manufacturers sell under their own brand name but many are making products to retailers' specifications to be sold under a retailer's own name.

Much of the development of new fabrics is done by manufacturers like Fabritex or even prompted by suggestions from raw material suppliers. Fabritex believes its strength lies in developing innovative fabrics that look good and perform well technically. Even when customers like a supplier's new fabric design this does not guarantee that supplier all their business, particularly over the longer term. It is common

This case study was written by Terry Hill (Templeton College, University of Oxford) and R Lily as the basis for class discussion and not as an example of good or bad management. © AMD Publishing.

for customers to show designs to their other suppliers with the intention of dual or triple sourcing, a commercial practice accepted within the industry.

The life of a particular fabric can vary widely from a few months to several years. It all depends on the popularity of the material with the final consumer. As part of the fashion industry the search for a new and different feel or look is a constant task, essential to a company's future growth and prosperity.

After a struggle in the early days to become profitable, Fabritex has increased profits to the point where they are above average for the Group. Sales at £45m have grown rapidly in the last two years and similar growth levels are forecast over the next few years. The management team believes that the basic manufacturing and engineering capability is in place which will underpin the continued sales growth. This view has the support of the Group but funds for investment are limited and Fabritex still has to demonstrate that it can outperform its competition rather than just hold its own.

MARKETING

Fabritex regards its market as a number of distinct segments that reflect differences in product, geography and type of customer. The customers are described as 'branded', selling under their own product name, or 'non-branded'. Customers are also grouped by garment type and divided into lingerie and outerwear (see Exhibit 1) and they can appear in several segments. The product distinction relates to the way the fabric is knitted, either warp or weft.

Many segments have a degree of seasonality associated with the type of garment in which the fabric is used. If a garment is well received, repeat orders for fabrics may come very quickly. Forward demand is therefore not easy to predict, particularly for new fabrics.

Responding to Charles Franklin's request John Watson (the sales and marketing director) pulled himself forward, shuffled through the pile of papers in front of him and began:

The segment in which we have chosen to grow is UK lingerie warp knit which currently generates £15.9m sales, about 35 per cent of our total sales revenue. Within this segment Pearlwear sales total £4.2m. As you are aware, Pearlwear is a premium company with an internationally recognized brand name manufacturing in Europe and the Far East. Pearlwear sales and its share of its markets are both growing. Where it places those additional sales and grows capacity is in part, as you would expect, related to the performance of its manufacturing plants. Initially we intend to grow our share with Pearlwear's UK factory, which we estimate to place purchase orders to the value of some £30m, of which we have only £4.2m, or 14 per cent. The opportunity to grow is, therefore, realistic.

The Pearlwear brand name is key in selling its products and that has implications for us. We have to remain competitive on price to avoid losing share but the name of the game is conformance quality. If we have any significant problems with the quality of our fabrics then Pearlwear will take its business elsewhere.

So far our two companies have worked well together over a number of years and we appear to have a good understanding of its requirements. Also, the management team at Pearlwear's UK plant is committed to developing sound customer supplier relations. And this is by no means a lip service statement. Pearlwear is keen to discuss problems and has, on a number of occasions, co-operated on changes that have affected the way both

Exhibit 1   *Sales forecast by segment*

Segment	Current year forecast (£m)	Next year forecast (£m)
UK lingerie warp knit		
Branded	12.3	15.9
Non-branded	3.6	3.6
Sub-total	15.9	19.5
UK lingerie weft knit		
Branded	5.3	15.6
Non-branded	0.9	0.9
Sub-total	16.2	16.5
Export lingerie warp knit		
Branded	5.4	6.3
Non-branded	0.0	0.0
Sub-total	5.4	6.3
Export lingerie weft knit		
Branded	0.9	1.2
Non-branded	1.2	1.2
Sub-total	2.1	2.4
UK outerwear		
Branded	0.9	0.9
Non-branded	3.3	3.3
Sub-total	4.2	4.2
Export outerwear		
Branded	0.6	1.2
Non-branded	1.5	1.5
Sub-total	2.1	2.7
Total	45.9	51.6

companies work. If we are proactive in those developments then we will undoubtedly be able to grow our share next year.

Pearlwear currently splits its business between three or four main suppliers. Some fabrics are allocated to only one company for the life of the fabric and some are ordered from two or more suppliers. Pearlwear seems to be happy with its current suppliers and overall share has not changed much even though demand from the UK plant has increased significantly over the last five years. We continue, however, to be very much the minority supplier taking about 14 per cent of Pearlwear's total business.

Where we are the sole supplier for a fabric, Pearlwear is absolutely dependent on us. The annual sales of these 'sole supplier' fabrics are £2.7m and should grow by about 10 per cent next year. Responding to short lead times on sales orders is important but even more crucial is meeting our promises on delivery. Nothing gets Pearlwear more upset than having to reorganize its production schedules due to our missing agreed delivery promises.

John paused for a sip of cold coffee and noticed the wry look from Mike Stewart, the operations director, after his last comment.

'We do recognize the delivery issue, John,' said Mike, 'but from an operations point of view the pattern of orders is very unpredictable. Some of these fabrics have regular orders. Demand for other fabrics keeps going over time but we never know when we will see the next order. This affects our response for example on raw material inventory. And short runs do reduce our capacity due to changeover losses.'

John Watson nodded and then continued:

When Pearlwear sources a fabric from two or more suppliers, the company that wins the lion's share is usually the one that can supply to the shortest promise date for an initial order. Of course, thereafter a supplier must hit its delivery promises consistently. Failure to deliver on time can affect our share of jointly sourced products. Mike's point about a mixture of regular and irregular orders applies to these fabrics as well, although probably to a lesser extent.

Price can also influence the volume split when a fabric is running regularly with joint suppliers. At the moment I estimate Pearlwear's total purchases of fabrics that are shared by two or more suppliers are £5.1m per annum and we have 30 per cent of this. The spend should grow by 10 per cent next year.

The fabrics that are only sourced from one of our competitors constitute the biggest part of Pearlwear's annual purchases of £21.9m. Some of these fabrics are reaching the end of their life cycle and I think purchases will decline next year, perhaps to £20.4m. If we are selective there may be opportunities on the higher volume fabrics to become a second supplier. The attraction to Pearlwear would be to gain more insurance on obtaining short delivery lead times. The usual reason we do not have a share is that we have not provided the design and performance characteristics of particular fabrics for which Pearlwear is looking. On occasions we believe we can but we have not been close enough to Pearlwear's designers to convince them that we have the technical know-how. Designers have their favourite suppliers, for whatever reason, so cultivating that relationship is important. So, the way forward is to carefully target some fabrics and get our technical people working closely with theirs.

Also, we may have to sweeten our move a bit on price to get them through the hassle of approving us. My initial assessment suggests that next year, if we really go for it, we could gain perhaps 7 per cent of the sales that currently go solely to one of our competitors. But it will mean a special team in the technical department.

Finally we need to consider new fabrics. Next year about £1.2m of Pearlwear's purchases will come from fabrics currently under development. The value of these fabrics can grow substantially in later years if they include some real winners. To get our slice of this business (we should be looking at half), the criteria are the same as those we have just considered. First, the fabrics must look good and perform well. Second, if the designer is sympathetic to Fabritex and works with us on the development clearly we have a better chance of supplying a production fabric. And on some, attractive prices can then help tip the balance.

John paused and looked round his colleagues. 'If we can achieve all those objectives we will take a quarter of the Pearlwear business in the UK lingerie warp knit segment. And that accounts for most of the growth required in our overall business forecast.'

'Thanks John, for a clear overview of the position on Pearlwear. Before our session next week I would like you to circulate a statement along those lines.' Charles Franklin then turned to his operations director, 'Also Mike, I would like you to tell us how we are performing against the operations issues raised. After that we can start to review the technical situation.'

OPERATIONS

The basic manufacturing task is knitting the fabric and then dyeing it. There are two knitting processes known as warp and weft. They use different machine types giving different fabric characteristics. The dyeing is done at another plant in the group located 12 miles away. Part of the dye plant is dedicated to Fabritex's requirements with the remaining capacity being used to process fabric from other customers from outside the Wardman Group.

A fabric is described by the specification that identifies the knitted fabric and the 'shade' that results from dyeing.

Knitting times for fabrics vary substantially. Some typical knitting times for Pearl-wear orders are shown in Exhibit 2. The knitting machines require skilled staff support to complete a set-up on a fabric change. Set-up or changeover times for warp knitting average four hours. (A set-up or changeover is where the required quantity for one fabric is completed, the machine is stopped and then reset to make the next fabric. During this set-up or changeover, no saleable output is produced.) The knitting machines are manned over three shifts covering 24 hours per day, five days per week. Overtime at weekends is commonly worked to supplement capacity.

Knitted fabric is called greige and is held in store until the required batch size for dyeing has been reached. No two knitting machines produce exactly the same fabric so dye batches unique to a knitting machine are usually accumulated before dyeing is commenced. The dyeing process determines the shade of a fabric. Setting up the process consists of loading the greige onto beams, which is done off-line, and loading the beams onto the machine which only takes about 20 minutes. Some colour sequences require the dyeing machine to be cleaned before use which takes about two additional hours. Typical dye times are seven hours for white and nine hours for coloured shades but about 10 per cent of dyed fabrics are unsatisfactory and have to be redyed. These times include an overall allowance for cleaning where necessary. The dye plant works a basic 24 hours per day for four days per week. Four dyeing units are used solely for Fabritex work.

Exhibit 2   *Sample of knitting times for Pearlwear fabrics*

Order	Specification	Quantity (metres)	Knitting time (hours)
43651	PN503	250	140.8
43600	PN522	500	289.9
43360	PN523	200	96.4
44754	PN704	1200	578.3
43671	PN713	450	236.8
43900	SA12	1100	354.8
44826	SA9	400	190.5
44849	SK24	900	371.1
44852	SK28	400	142.9
46096	SK33	2600	298.9
44347	SK51	74	41.1
44784	TD468	700	53.5

Notes

1. The term 'specification' identifies the knitted fabric before dyeing.
2. The knitting time includes an allowance for set-up.

The dyed fabric is shipped back to the knitting plant where it is inspected and finished before delivery to the customer. On average this takes about six days. For new or difficult fabrics the customer may require a sample of the fabric before approval is given for delivery.

Fabrics are normally made to order. On receipt of a customer enquiry a promise date is given based on knowledge of the fabric, raw material availability and current knitting loads. The planning system is based on actual times for completing past orders. When a customer places an order it is then scheduled on the system. Losses in the knitting and dyeing processes can be high and unpredictable, and the volume of the final fabric is unlikely to match exactly the order quantity.

Some key customers place orders for greige stock prior to orders for final fabrics. Marketing is also allowed to place orders for greige stock to cover special situations agreed by the management team. An example would be in anticipation of a large order where the required knitting capacity would mean an unacceptably long lead time to the customer. If marketing misread the situation Fabritex can end up with unwanted greige stock to be gradually disposed of at lower prices.

THE WAY FORWARD

Charles Franklin was determined to give his team a strong lead at what he saw as a crucial stage in Fabritex's development.

> I have a lot of confidence in the group of people sitting round this table and in the people out there working for us. We have done well in recent years in growing the business. Now is the time to be ambitious. Now is the time to build on our success and deliver a further big increase in sales revenue. We can show the Wardman Group that Fabritex is the place in which to invest for the future. Pearlwear is a major customer and represents a big opportunity. Our two companies have developed together over a number of years. We know the people in Pearlwear and the way they like to do business.
>
> Competition for the Pearlwear business is and will continue to be tough. But it is time we moved from being a minority supplier. Our target must be to secure half the Pearlwear business. We have to do this by improving our communications at all levels and by fast and reliable response to their orders. We currently have the manufacturing capacity to respond. This way we can drive the sales revenue from the current £4m to something close to £15m.

Following the meeting Mike Stewart set about collecting some information for his operations analysis which is given in Exhibits 3 to 6.

Exhibit 3 *Sample of Pearlwear orders showing required delivery times*

Order number	Specification	Shade	Quantity (metres)	Order value (£s)	Date order received		Customer required delivery	
					Week #	Day #	Week #	Day #
42322	SK28	Black 1	424	1823	10	3	15	2
43360	PN523	Beige	200	736	16	4	33	1
43600	PN522	White 0	500	2600	13	2	18	3
43651	PN503	Beige 4	250	920	2	2	7	4
43671	PN713	Beige 4	450	1665	21	2	29	4
43893	PN522	White 0	600	3120	19	3	25	1
43900	SA12	White 0	1100	5280	7	4	16	1
43904	SK28	Black 1	600	2844	4	3	15	3
43906	SK28	Champagne 73	400	1896	18	1	29	1
43924	SA9	White 0	330	1584	10	1	13	1
43985	PN704	White 0	700	2499	4	4	8	1
44207	PN522	White 0	1600	8320	25	4	33	4
44212	SA12	Black 1	300	1482	16	4	23	2
44213	SK24	White 0	800	3680	22	3	27	4
44214	SK24	Black 1	750	3555	22	2	31	2
44224	SA9	Black 1	300	1482	36	3	42	1
44347	SK51	Beige 4	74	204	16	4	21	3
44354	SK33	White 0	555	1487	15	3	28	1
44643	SK51	White 0	778	2085	15	4	22	1
44649	SK51	White 0	178	477	33	3	38	2
44650	SK51	White 0	709	1900	23	2	30	1
44662	SK33	White 0	709	1900	14	3	20	4
44663	SK33	White 0	140	375	28	3	32	1
44674	SK51	White 0	555	1487	33	1	37	3
44687	SK51	White 0	1993	5341	18	3	23	4
44754	PN704	White 0	1200	4284	13	2	23	1
44755	PN704	Black 1	100	368	18	2	28	1
44784	TD468	White 0	700	5054	22	3	24	4
44825	SA12	White 0	1000	4800	19	1	22	4
44826	SA9	Champagne 73	400	1976	23	1	34	1
44827	SA9	Black 1	500	2470	30	4	34	2
44832	SA12	Black 1	400	1976	34	3	38	1
44849	SK24	White 0	900	4140	14	4	20	2
44852	SK28	Champagne 73	400	1720	28	4	34	2
44935	SA12	Champagne 73	500	2470	31	5	35	3
44952	SK33	White 0	1993	5341	5	4	16	1
44976	SA12	Champagne 73	300	1482	32	5	40	1
45060	TD468	Black 1	150	1116	35	1	39	1
45074	SA9	Champagne 73	150	741	17	1	23	3
45075	SK24	Black 1	200	948	19	1	21	3
45175	SK24	White 0	400	1840	34	4	41	1
46096	SK33	White 0	2600	6968	8	4	19	1
2611	SK51	White 0	2400	6432	22	2	27	1
2612	SK51	White 0	2400	6432	13	1	19	2
2613	SK51	White 0	2400	6432	20	4	28	2
2614	SK51	White 0	2800	7504	29	4	38	4
2669	SK33	White 0	1400	3752	15	2	19	4
42302/1	SK24	Black 1	500	2370	13	2	18	4
43231/1	SK24	New Black	700	3318	28	3	34	4
43651/1	PN503	Beige 4	200	736	4	2	15	3
43901/2	SA12	Black 1	1050	5187	18	1	26	2

(Continued)

Exhibit 3   *Sample of Pearlwear orders showing required delivery times (cont'd)*

Order number	Specification	Shade	Quantity (metres)	Order value (£s)	Date order received		Customer required delivery	
					Week #	Day #	Week #	Day #
43902/1	SA12	Champagne 73	350	1729	23	3	32	2
43985/2	PN704	White 0	300	1071	20	1	29	2
44075/1	PN522	Black 1	500	2675	16	1	20	3
44784/1	TD468	White 0	700	5054	28	3	35	1
44825/1	SA12	White 0	1000	4800	12	4	17	3

Notes

1. Fabritex use week numbers 1 to 52 and day numbers 1 to 5 only.
2. The orders above are typical Pearlwear orders over a sample period.

Exhibit 4   *Regularity of Pearlwear orders*

Fabrics ordered on an irregular basis	Fabrics ordered on a regular basis
PN503	SK51
PN523	PN522
SA9	PN704
SK28	PN713
SK33	SA12
	SK24
	SK51
	TD468

Notes

1. The classification of Pearlwear fabrics was made by the Fabritex production planner.
2. The classification will change over time.

Exhibit 5   *Fabritex share of Pearlwear spend by fabric*

Specification	Estimated share of Pearlwear spend (per cent total)	Specification	Estimated share of Pearlwear spend (per cent total)
PN503	100	SA42	0
PN522	21	SA45	0
PN523	100	SK24	42
PN640	0	SK28	29
PN704	100	SK33	100
PN713	100	SK51	100
SA12	100	TD680	0
SA9	100	TD468	32

Notes

1. The table shows the sales and marketing director's estimates of Fabritex's share of the Pearlwear spend on a selection of fabrics.
2. 100 per cent of the total means Fabritex is the sole supplier.
3. 0 per cent of the total means Fabritex does not supply the fabric.

Exhibit 6   *Sample of Pearlwear orders showing promised and actual delivery times*

Order number	Quality	Shade	Fabritex promised delivery		Fabritex actual delivery	
			Week #	Day #	Week #.	Day #
42322	SK28	Black 1	18	1	20	1
43360	PN523	Beige	39	1	44	3
43600	PN522	White 0	22	3	26	1
43651	PN503	Beige 4	12	3	23	1
43671	PN713	Beige 4	39	2	43	4
43893	PN522	White 0	25	1	29	1
43900	SA12	White 0	18	4	24	2
43904	SK28	Black 1	18	1	20	3
43906	SK28	Champagne 73	29	1	32	2
43924	SA9	White 0	16	2	21	2
43985	PN704	White 0	9	3	21	3
44207	PN522	White 0	38	1	43	1
44212	SA12	Black 1	26	4	25	4
44213	SK24	White 0	32	3	33	4
44214	SK24	Black 1	35	3	35	1
44224	SA9	Black 1	44	2	42	5
44347	SK51	Beige 4	21	3	22	1
44354	SK33	White 0	29	3	33	4
44643	SK51	White 0	22	1	25	1
44649	SK51	White 0	39	1	42	2
44650	SK51	White 0	30	1	29	4
44662	SK33	White 0	22	1	23	4
44663	SK33	White 0	34	4	34	3
44674	SK51	White 0	38	4	41	4
44687	SK51	White 0	23	4	27	2
44754	PN704	White 0	23	1	22	1
44755	PN704	Black 1	28	1	27	1
44784	TD468	White 0	26	1	32	1
44825	SA12	White 0	25	3	28	1
44826	SA9	Champagne 73	34	1	41	3
44827	SA9	Black 1	38	3	37	1
44832	SA12	Black 1	42	2	40	5
44849	SK24	White 0	24	3	24	1
44852	SK28	Champagne 73	37	3	37	4
44935	SA12	Champagne 73	35	3	33	5
44952	SK33	White 0	17	2	22	1
44976	SA12	Champagne 73	42	4	40	3
45060	TD468	Black 1	38	4	38	4
45074	SA9	Champagne 73	23	3	26	2
45075	SK24	Black 1	22	1	28	3
45175	SK24	White 0	40	4	40	2
46096	SK33	White 0	20	2	26	4
2611	SK51	White 0	27	1	29	5
2612	SK51	White 0	19	2	23	2
2613	SK51	White 0	28	2	30	3
2614	SK51	White 0	38	4	40	5
2669	SK33	White 0	25	2	23	1
42302/1	SK24	Black 1	28	1	30	5

(Continued)

Exhibit 6   *Sample of Pearlwear orders showing promised and actual delivery times (cont'd)*

Order number	Quality	Shade	Fabritex promised delivery		Fabritex actual delivery	
			Week #	Day #	Week #	Day #
43231/1	SK24	New Black	34	1	38	2
43651/1	PN503	Beige 4	15	4	25	1
43901/2	SA12	Black 1	31	3	32	2
43902/1	SA12	Champagne 73	32	2	36	5
43985/2	PN704	White 0	31	1	34	5
44075/1	PN522	Black 1	25	2	31	3
44784/1	TD468	White 0	36	5	35	5
44825/1	SA12	White 0	22	3	23	2

Notes

1. Fabritex uses week numbers 1 to 52 and day numbers 1 to 5 only.
2. The orders above are typical Pearlwear orders over a sample period.

Georgian Frames

Georgian Frames is a small company engaged in making and installing new Georgian-style, premeasured windows to replace existing windows in the homes of its customers. Exhibit 1 details the activities required to complete the task of removing the old and installing a new window. Although occasionally more than one window

Exhibit 1   *Principal activities involved in replacing a window on site*

Activity	Time units (½ hour) to do the task, depending upon the number of men available			Minimum number of men required to do the job
	1 man	2 men	3 men	
Load vehicle at yard and prepare	2	1	1	1
To site	2	2	2	1
Unload and check the window size	1	½	½	1
Prepare site	2	1½	1	1
Remove old frame	2	1½	1	1
Offer new frame to the opening	–	1	1	2
Load old frame to vehicle	1	½	(note 7)	1
Finish installation	4	3	2	1
Load tools, and so on to vehicle	1	½	(note 7)	1
Return to yard	2	2	2	1
Load old frame and tools to vehicle	2	1	½	(note 7)

Notes

1. Where two windows and other items are loaded onto a vehicle with three men, the time taken will be the same as that for one window and other items with two men.
2. It is customary at this company for the vehicle driver to participate in the window installation activities.
3. The activity times given are the average for these tasks and take account of allowances for fatigue, rest and mid-morning and mid-afternoon breaks.
4. In the network diagram (Exhibit 2) the work throughout is carried out by two men. The men, on returning to the yard, do other work such as priming and sanding window frames.
5. The time to travel from one site to another would take ½ hour.
6. Activity 'remove old window frame' is not dependent upon 'prepare site'.
7. For three men, the activities 'load old window frame to vehicle' and 'load tools, and so on to vehicle' are combined into the one activity 'load old frame and tools to vehicle' which takes ½ of one time unit.

This case study was written by Terry Hill (Templeton College, University of Oxford). It is intended as the basis for class discussion and not as an example of good or bad management. © AMD Publishing.

will be installed at a site, at present about 75 per cent of all jobs involve a single-window installation. The critical path diagram representing this set of activities is shown in Exhibit 2.

The recent company sales growth has necessitated allocating more men to window installation on a full-time basis. However, there are increasingly days when it is necessary to install a window on two separate sites. While Georgian Frames wishes to maintain sales growth, it needs to keep capital investment to a minimum. Therefore, it does not wish to purchase a second vehicle (necessary to transport men, tools and windows to the customer's premises) unless it is essential. In addition, it also needs to keep labour costs to a minimum in order to stay competitive, while maintaining acceptable profit levels.

Exhibit 2   *Network diagram for the activities given in Exhibit 1 with a two-man team*

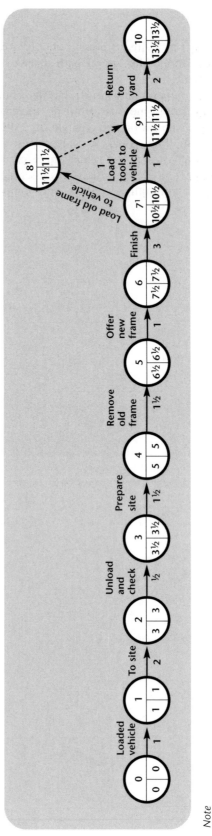

Note

1. Activities 7, 8 and 9 are shown to run in parallel. If it were decided to run these activities in sequence then the overall time taken would be the same.

Ghent Fireworks plc

In March, last year, Ghent Fireworks (GF) plc celebrated 100 years in the fireworks business. It had, in its time, experienced most of the growth problems of a typical manufacturing company, but was now an established name in the UK markets for its firework products.

Perhaps the most significant change in direction for the company occurred five or six years ago when, based upon its traditional business and reputation as a fireworks manufacturer, GF applied and gained registration on the UK Ministry of Defence's list of assessed contractors, having met the requirements as laid down in relevant Defence Standards. This successful application now opened up home and export markets for all types of pyrotechnic products. Typical of these would be smoke generators in a range of colours, hand-held, ground, grenade and trip-wire flares, small arms simulators (single and multi-shot), explosion, flame and smoke simulators, thunderflashes and rocket motors.

SALES

While sales for fireworks showed a steady growth, pyrotechnic sales had increased noticeably in the past three years, to the point where sales last year exceeded for the first time those of fireworks; current sales are anticipated to be higher still (see Exhibits 1 and 2).

Fireworks

By far the biggest proportion of firework sales (value and units) was to the general public, and the trend in recent years had been to sell them in boxes through whole-sale and retail outlets. GF sells boxes of fireworks in seven sizes with current retail prices up to £75.00. Other firework sales were for large orders from organizations of different types. These orders would typically comprise fireworks at the top end of the price range sold to the general public, or more normally from their wide range of

This case study was written by Terry Hill (Templeton College, University of Oxford). It is intended as the basis for class discussion and not as an illustration of good or bad management. © AMD Publishing.

Exhibit 1   Actual and forecast sales

Sales (£m)	Current year minus							Current year[1]
	7	6	5	4	3	2	1	
Fireworks	3.2	3.5	3.5	3.9	4.1	4.5	4.7	5.0
Pyrotechnics[2]	–	0.2	0.5	0.5	1.2	3.9	5.0	5.9
Total	3.2	3.7	4.0	4.4	5.3	8.4	9.7	10.9

Notes

1. Current year figures are forecasts.
2. Exports for pyrotechnic products were 70 per cent last year and are expected to increase to 75 per cent this year.

Exhibit 2   Types of firework, current catalogue

Firework category	# sizes in each category
Lights	10
Showers	16
Fountains	34
Rockets	20
Catherine wheels	7
Roman candles	18
Volcanoes	14
Shells	48
Mines	5

designs in the product categories of displays, set pieces and daylight fireworks. To fulfil these orders (which comprised some 10 per cent of the total value of firework sales) the top end of the price range and daylight fireworks were usually taken from existing finished goods stock and the specials (that is, displays and set pieces) which comprise four-fifths of these orders were made to a customer's specification. The range of fireworks sold currently is shown in Exhibit 2.

About 85–90 per cent of all GF's fireworks sales are sold in line with Bonfire Night on the 5 November each year. (Bonfire Night is celebrated in the UK to mark the failed attempt by a group of Catholics to blow up the Houses of Parliament in 1605. The incident is known as the Gunpowder Plot.) Orders are taken at the spring toy fairs at Brighton and Harrogate, or by direct order. Delivery of all these orders is made from August onwards and customers normally settle their invoices in either November or December each year.

Pyrotechnics

Sales for pyrotechnic contracts have increased significantly in the last three years and are forecast for this year at £5.9m (see Exhibit 1). The size of contracts awarded so far has varied from £40 000 to £2.5m. The latter contract was in fact awarded last month – the previous largest contract had been for £1.8m. Contracts currently in manufacture or recently finished had values ranging from £52 000 to £750 000. Each contract received is always for one product only, such is the nature of the business.

Exhibit 3   *Chance of GF receiving a pyrotechnic contract for a product they have made before*

# years after receiving the first contract	Chance of receiving an order with the same product specification[1] (per cent)
1	Nil
2	10
3	15
4	15
5 and over	20

Note

1. The low chances of receiving a repeat order are attributable to the fact that the range of products required by GF's customers is very wide, and although many of these products' specifications may not be changed, the tendency is for customers to order several years' requirements at a time. Combine this with the fact that GF may not be asked to tender or may not get the order, then the chances of receiving a contract for the same product are small.

Thus, if a customer wanted a number of products it would be required to place a contract to cover each product, even if two or more contracts were placed with the same supplier. The chances of GF receiving a contract for a product which it had made before are given in Exhibit 3.

Pyrotechnic sales are the responsibility of the managing director, Ray Livingstone, although the preparation of quotations and the control of the commercial side of the contracts is handled by the quotations and contracts department which reports to the commercial director as shown in Exhibit 4. Ray considers that this segment of GF's sales is the area for growth within the company:

Now that we are becoming established in this market, the opportunity to maintain current sales growth should be achievable. However, sales are not as predictable as on the fireworks side of our business for two important reasons. The first is that we are not certain which contracts, if any, we shall secure. This leads to the problem, therefore, of deciding how many and for which contracts to tender. Too few or too many orders won will bring its own set of operations problems – a case in point is the £2.5m contract we have just received. Furthermore, as we are not well established in pyrotechnics it would be ill-advised to turn down the opportunity to tender if asked. Many of our orders are for export contracts and dealing with different cultures has its own set of problems. The second reason is that not being well established also means that we are less certain about our customers and the nature of the repeat business from them, even though this would be for different products.

MANUFACTURING

GF moved to its present site on the outskirts of Dundee in the mid-1950s. The present site is an arrangement of about 30 small production units which have been added to over the years. The limitations on the amount of explosives which can be held in a

Exhibit 4   *Ghent Fireworks organisation chart*

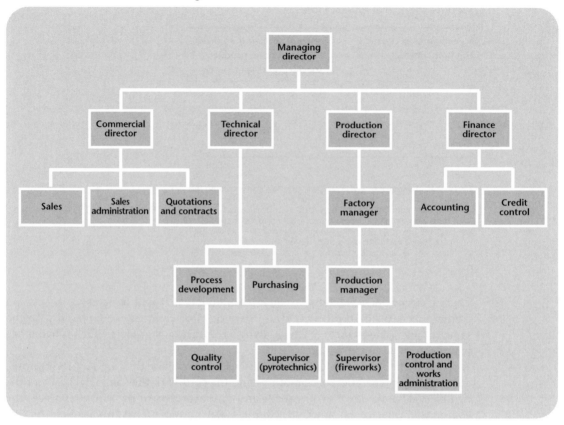

given area forces this organizational configuration onto GF and any other manufacturing company in this line of business.

GF has a total of 143 employees, of whom 104 are direct workers. Manufacturing usually works on a single shift basis from 7.30 am to 4.00 pm except in times of high throughput. At these times extra people have been employed on a part-time basis spanning a wide range of 2½–5 hour daytime shift combinations. Recently though, when a large contract has been going through manufacturing the company has worked two 12-hour shifts based on the full-time workforce and supplemented by part-timers and a few temporary full-timers who also worked the 12-hour shift pattern.

Fireworks

The manufacturing process for fireworks comprises four steps or stages as shown in Exhibit 5. Each of these main steps (except stage 3 which takes place after stage 2) is completed in a separate building because of the ruling on explosives described earlier.

All fireworks are packed into boxes or against a specific customer order. However, completion of this stage will always depend upon the appropriate mix of fireworks being available. Thus Box 17 comprises 17 different types of firework from within the categories giving in Exhibit 2, all of which have to be available before packing can commence.

Exhibit 5   *Manufacturing process for fireworks*

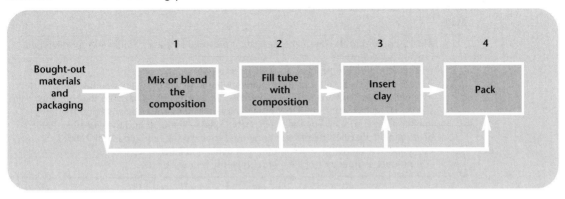

Whereas the mixing and filling activities are confined to small areas, packing takes place in a larger factory area which has been designated solely to firework packing. Fireworks after stage 3 in the process are now ready for packing. On completing stage 3 they are stacked into containers and transported to the packing area.

Although fireworks are made to a written specification, the filling operation is less than exact. Typically, a bundle of fireworks are strapped together by a rubber band and the composition is poured into them. By spreading the composition by hand and shaking, the firework tubes are filled before the clay is inserted.

Pyrotechnics

The manufacturing process to complete pyrotechnic products is similar from one to the next, as outlined in Exhibit 6. Working to the quality requirements of relevant Defence Standards (for either UK or export sales – in fact, being a Ministry of Defence registered company is almost a prerequisite to win export contracts for pyrotechnic products), the specification against which GF quoted goes first to process develop-

Exhibit 6   *Manufacturing process for pyrotechnic products*

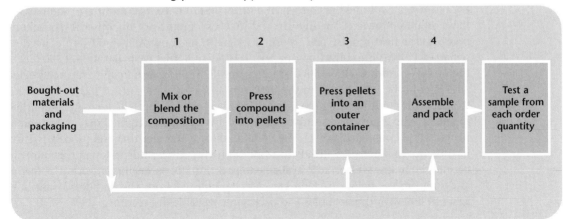

Exhibit 7   *Operations stages to produce a flare*

Stage	
1	Mix compound to the product specification provided by the customer and specified by process development.
2	Press compound into pellets – a simple press is used.
3	Assemble or press pellets into the required outer containers – again, a simple press is used.
4	Assemble ignitor and any other components (for example, a spike) onto the container. Paint, stencil, silk screen, heat shrink the required identification onto the container. The identification is specified by the appropriate Defence Standard and the customer. Process development specifies the process to be used to make the required identification.
5	Cap, tape flares together, pack in outer container and label.
6	Test product samples out of each order quantity processed.

ment. This function then specifies the appropriate way in which the product should be manufactured. Once these process specifications have been established they are handed over to production who can then schedule them into manufacturing once the required components and packaging are available. A more detailed summary of the processes through which a typical pyrotechnic product goes is given in Exhibit 7.

PRODUCTION PLANNING AND CONTROL

The production planning and control function is provided by the production control and works administration department (see Exhibit 4) which reports to the production manager. The procedures are outlined in Exhibit 8.

Fireworks

Following the peak sales in November each year, fireworks are manufactured initially in line with sales forecasts and then later in line with the firm sales orders received from spring onwards. Individual orders that do not relate to 5 November sales are met as and when they are required. To keep manufacturing steady, the aim is to produce each month one-twelfth of the forecast annual sales. The procedure used is to order materials, and other requirements in line with these sales forecasts and then make the same quantity of the high volume fireworks each month, and to make two months of some of the lower volume fireworks one month, and then two months of the other lower volume fireworks the next month, and so on. 'If we are to meet our August-onward deliveries', remarked Phil Mills, production director, 'it is essential that we make about £390 000 of fireworks each month. If we fail to do this we will find it very difficult to meet our deliveries later in the year. Based on the trade-offs and associated costs, it has been decided to adopt this method rather than any alternative.' Production schedules are established in line with inventory levels and anticipated deliveries of the required materials, components and packaging. However, the combination of the fact that the process is fairly flexible and the fireworks already in work-in-progress allows the packing programme to be adjusted in line with what is available to pack and the packaging in stock. The manufacturing process before packing can also be adjusted from the laid-down schedules again in line with the materials and packaging available in inventory.

| Exhibit 8 | *Production planning and control procedures* |

Fireworks

Production planning and control is based primarily on forecast sales in the first few months of each financial year (that is, 1 December onwards) and later (after the spring toy fairs and receipt of direct orders) on the basis of sales orders. Placing purchase orders with appropriate suppliers based on a monthly schedule, which is two months firm (that is, a committed schedule) and two months tentative.

Production schedules are laid down against these material, component and packaging deliveries with daily adjustments made according to what combinations of materials/components/packaging are in stock and in order to minimize manufacturing disruptions. To achieve this, the production control and works administration department works closely with the relevant production supervisor.

Pyrotechnics

The procedure involved in pyrotechnic contracts is as follows:

1. *Tender.* A tender is made by the quotations and contracts department, based upon an assessment of past contracts of a similar nature and a working knowledge of the operations involved to complete the work involved. However, there is no formal feedback of information from production to quotations and contracts of actual production achievement (for example, actual throughput times) nor is this information systematically collated by production for this purpose.

2. *Order received.* Where a tender is successful and an order is received, the specified delivery date of the tender is then triggered off on the basis of order receipt. Hence, a tender will specify that the delivery required is, say, four months from receipt of the order.

3. *Parts are ordered.* These usually take one month. However, if parts have a longer lead time then this is taken into account when setting the specified delivery time.

4. Process development is then completed on the basis of an advanced batch for some 50 sets of materials, components and packaging. These are completed in the process development department but do not normally involve production in these procedures. This department then produces a process specification to be followed by manufacturing.[1] However the specification does not normally include a synopsis for production of the problems, difficulties and 'things to watch for' as experienced by the process development department. It will include a proofing procedure which details the tests to be made and sample size to be taken from each manufacturing order quantity.

5. Production converts the process specification into a set of working instructions:

   (a) tasks involved;
   (b) safety precautions to be taken (for example footwear and protective clothing);
   (c) explosive limits to be adhered to.

6. Materials are then issued in line with the relevant Defence Standard and a record of which material was used and the supplier is kept with the order quantity of products. This is to allow all materials, and so on to be traced in case of problems later in the process or when the product is being used by the customer.

7. Each order quantity is then proofed (see Exhibit 9).

Note

1. As the process equipment and conditions of working are very different (for example, laboratory as against high volume manufacturing) the failure of process development to develop the suggested process specification in line with the conditions in which manufacturing will work, leads to many of the initial 'proofing' failures.

Pyrotechnics

A pyrotechnic contract has typically to be delivered within four months of GF receiving the order. Although delivery times do relate, to some extent, to the size of the contracts, the bigger the quantity involved, then the longer the delivery lead time, and vice versa. The procedure used to schedule this into production is given in Exhibit 8. The first step is for process development to determine the best way to manufacture the particular product. Using laboratory process facilities, process development will select from a limited number of different ways of making the product in order to meet the agreed specification. The increase in work in this department means that it takes on average one month to issue a process specification. The quality control department is responsible for testing the samples taken from the production order quantities which comprise a contract, and Exhibit 9 provides an analysis of the number of sample failures generally experienced.

The other activity that delays the start of manufacturing is the procurement of production quantities of materials, components and packaging. To meet the Ministry of Defence (MoD) standards, all suppliers must be on the MoD register. This restricts the number of suppliers from which companies such as GF may choose. It has taken up to six weeks to procure production quantities of some items (quantities sufficient for some 50 products can normally be obtained in a week by process development) but usually it takes up to three to four weeks from receipt of an order to production quantities being received.

When the first order quantity is completed, a sample is taken for 'proofing' as explained in Exhibit 9. However, manufacturing, under pressure to meet the delivery promise on a contract, invariably has no option but to continue to manufacture without waiting for the results of the proofing phase. If changes subsequently have to be made then the rework involved is completed by production as soon as possible.

INVENTORY

The results of an inventory check at the end of February, earlier this year (the first quarter of the current financial year) are shown in Exhibit 10. The inventory check showed a 10 per cent loss on the evaluation of fireworks (that is, the value of work-in-progress (WIP) for fireworks was 10 per cent less than expected, based upon the materials issued). This, however, was not considered unusual and is accounted for by the material losses in the manufacturing process, especially at the 'fill tube with composition' stage. However, this same check on WIP for pyrotechnics is computed at the end of each contract and normally there is little need to adjust the WIP value.

THE FUTURE

Ray Livingstone concluded:

The increase in pyrotechnic sales in recent years has been important on two counts. Firstly, it has given us an important boost in overall sales revenue. Secondly, it has provided us with an alternative product range in itself which also provides a balance in activities to being solely in fireworks, with the added advantages in cash flow. Fortunately, we have such a flexible workforce that we can move them from fireworks to

Exhibit 9   *Sample failures for pyrotechnic contracts and their source*

In order to complete a pyrotechnic contract, production manufactures a number of order quantities which typically equate to two shifts of work (this size of order quantity is considered sensible in terms of the explosive limits and the volume it represents going through the different processes). Each order quantity has to be 'proofed' (that is, inspected) by the quality control department (QCD). For example (and in line with the customer specification) these will comprise vibration testing, ignition burn length and damp test. The size of sample taken from an order quantity reduces over the production runs to meet the whole contract quantity and in line with the failure rates observed. To complete the test procedures on the first sample takes at least two days and sometimes five or more. Tests on later samples take less time.

If a sample fails the proofing then manufacturing will be stopped until the problem has been checked out. This may result in an internal manufacturing process change or a rejection of a particular component(s) and discussion with the supplier(s) involved.

Order quantity	Samples taken that fail proofing by QCD (per cent)
1st	25
2nd	10
3rd	Occasional
4th	Rare
5th onwards	None

Source of failure	Percentage of total failure
Production process	95
Component supply	5

pyrotechnics and vice versa without much disruption. Similarly, we can increase our capacity temporarily with part-time and full-time employees. In fact, winning the recent pyrotechnic contract for £2.5m has meant that we have now deicided that to meet all our sales commitments in fireworks and pyrotechnics we shall have to run a second shift as we did once before with a large contract. Our permanent employees will be divided into two groups so as to form the basis for each shift. We are now recruiting temporary staff to bring the shift members up to the required level. Achieving delivery on the contracts is not only important in itself but also has significant consequences in terms of cash flow.

Exhibit 10   *Inventory value by category and operations type (£000s) at 1 March, current year*

Product category	Raw materials/ components	Work-in-progress	Finished goods[1]	Total
Fireworks	210	175	1070	1455
Pyrotechnics	120	350	–	470
Total	330	525	1070	1925

Note

1. The opening finished good inventory for fireworks on 1 December last year was £0.37m (which is normal for this time of year) and nil for pyrotechnics. The other categories of inventory have remained steady throughout these 3 months.

Holmgren Engineering AB

Thanks for detailing your findings, Peter. As we've all had copies of your report for some time, I now suggest we open up the discussion on your proposals.

John Svensson, CEO of Holmgren Engineering AB (HE), was addressing the management team following Peter Wiklund's presentation on his proposed changes to the layout and process for the future manufacture of the Hetvatten range of products.

BACKGROUND

Holmgren Engineering AB (HE) was established almost 40 years ago. Initially it was a small heating engineering firm started by Benny Holmgren offering a range of related services. It grew and later expanded into the manufacture of its own products. It continued as a family business until it was taken over some 10 years ago by Karlsson Invest, a conglomerate with a range of businesses involved in building and construction-related activities. The last few years have seen a continued increase in sales although there has been a slight fall-off in profits (see Exhibit 1).

Based in Halmstad, HE was in the industrial conurbation centred on Gothenburg in the south west of Sweden (see Exhibit 2). Although initially an installer of equipment and provider of support services, HE was now only involved in the manufacture and selling of water storage systems. In fact, since it was taken over by Karlsson Invest it has moved even more into developing and manufacturing water storage products which included mains pressure heating systems.

Products

HE manufactures a range of products on its Halmstad site. The part of its range addressed by Peter Wiklund's report was sold under the Hetvatten Plus trademark. This comprises a family of products which vary by size of heating coil and storage capacity (see Exhibit 3).

This case study was written by Terry Hill (Templeton College, University of Oxford) and P. Åhlström (Stockholm School of Economics). It is intended as the basis for class discussion and not as an example of good or bad management. © AMD Publishing.

Exhibit 1   *Profit and loss account – current and past two years (SEK 000)*

	Current year –2	Current year –1	Current year
Sales revenue	49 200	54 840	61 776
Cost of sales	(40 200)	(43 872)	(52 272)
Gross profit	*9 000*	*10 968*	*9 504*
Distribution costs	(888)	(936)	(1 248)
Administration expenses	(3 024)	(3 360)	(3 696)
Trading profit	*5 088*	*6 672*	*4 560*
Interest payable	(84)	(1 236)	–
Amounts written off	–	(744)	(12)
Profit before tax	*5 004*	*4 692*	*4 548*
Tax	(708)	(1 320)	(1 080)
Profit after tax	*4 296*	*3 372*	*3 468*
Dividends	(1 452)	(1 140)	(708)
Retained profit transferred to reserves	*2 844*	*2 232*	*2 760*
Retained profit brought forward	+1 812	+4 644	+6 876
Retained profit carried forward	*4 656*	*6 876*	*9 636*

Notes

1. Inventory	Current year –2	Current year –1	Current year
Raw material and components	3 144	5 052	5 352
Work-in-progress	180	144	168
Finished goods	720	924	1 680
Total	4 044	6 120	7 200

2. Work-in-progress includes issued raw materials plus part-made products.
3. SEK = Swedish kronor.

These products are made in Halmstad and sell throughout Sweden and parts of Europe. Normally, the delivery lead time is three to four weeks, but shorter deliveries can usually be met if necessary.

MANUFACTURING

The Hetvatten Plus product range is basically made to a standard design and configuration. Larger houses and growing demand for hot water has led to an increase in the product range over the last decade. However, in manufacturing terms, the current range is not difficult to handle. The principal changes concern the external dimensions of the product and the different sizes of heating coil. But these require few, if any, alterations to the basic design.

The present layout and other related cost information are given in Exhibits 4 and 5. Currently, products are made in order quantities of five. As shown in Exhibit 4, an order quantity moves through the different processes with the operations completed on all five products before the total order quantity is moved to the next stage.

Exhibit 2   *Outline map of Northern Europe*

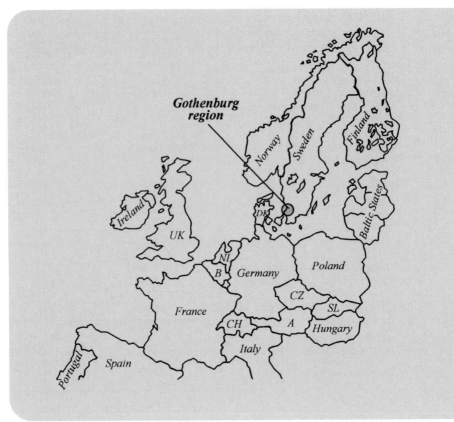

Notes

A	=	Austria
B	=	Belgium
CH	=	Switzerland
CZ	=	Czech Republic
DK	=	Denmark
NL	=	The Netherlands
SL	=	Slovak Republic

Exhibit 3   *Hetvatten Plus product range*

Model	Storage capacity (litres)	Dwelling types			Dimensions[1] height × width (cm)
		# bedrooms	# baths	# showers	
A	120	2 or 3	1	–	1500 × 500
B	140	2 or 3	1	1	1500 × 550
C	160	2–4	1 or 2	1 or 2	1500 × 600
D	180	3–4	1 or 2	1 or 2	1600 × 600
E	200	3–5	2	1–3	1700 × 600

Note

1. Refers to the physical dimensions of each model.

Exhibit 4   *Present factory layout*

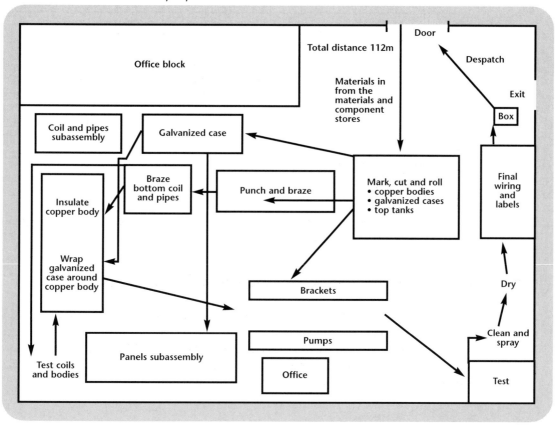

PRODUCTION SCHEDULING

The production programme is agreed weekly. Based on known orders and forecast sales it looks four weeks ahead with week 1 fixed and weeks 2 to 4 tentative.

Currently, parts are bulk ordered with weekly call-offs agreed at the beginning of each month. Most material and components are delivered on the first day of each week with sufficient parts for the production planned for that week and held in the material and components stores, which is located on the same site but in a different building from the one outlined in Exhibit 4.

Working on agreed weekly schedules (see Exhibit 6), materials are issued to the production area on a daily basis.

PRODUCTION ENGINEERING REPORT

The report presented by Production Engineering reviewed the current manufacturing procedures used to make the Hetvatten Plus Range. Its principal recommendation was to change the layout and the way of manufacturing these products. In essence, products would now be made in order quantities of one compared to the current order

Exhibit 5   *Costs (SEK) per unit*

Category		Models				
		A	**B**	**C**	**D**	**E**
Cost per unit	Material	4200	4800	6360	7068	7 908
	Labour	1260	1284	1320	1464	1 656
	Overheads	900	900	900	900	900
	Total	6360	6984	8580	9432	10 464

Notes

1. Costs are based on an average weekly production of 100 units.
2. SEK = Swedish kronor.

quantity of five. Also, products would be transferred by rollers with staff pushing them from one work station to the next.

OVERVIEW OF THE PROPOSED CHANGES AND BENEFITS TO BE GAINED

On John Svensson's invitation, Peter Wiklund gave an overview of the proposed changes and also detailed the benefits to be gained. Using an overhead projector, Peter explained the detail and rationale of the proposals and highlighted the benefits that would result. What follows is a summary of Peter's presentation and the key points of clarification requested by those at the meeting.

Exhibit 6   *Production figures for weeks 11–18 of the current year*

Models	Units produced in the following week #							
	11	**12**	**13**	**14**	**15**	**16**	**17**	**18**
A	10	15	10	10	10	10	10	15
B	15	15	10	10	10	15	10	15
C	40	40	40	30	40	40	40	40
D	30	30	25	20	35	30	30	30
E	5	5	10	10	5	5	10	5
Total	*100*	*105*	*95*	*80*	*100*	*100*	*100*	*105*

Notes

1. The above production figures are representative of the mix of models produced in the current year.
2. Issues to the shop floor are in order quantities of five.
3. The number of boilers is based on the planned capacity within a week and the mix of boilers scheduled to be manufactured.
4. Week 14 included a public holiday and, therefore, comprised only four working days.
5. All products are included in figures for the week in which they were completed. Therefore, no part-made boilers are included in the above figures.

Exhibit 7   *Evaluation of alternative approaches to manufacturing, used as a basis for selecting the changes to be introduced*

#	MTO versus MTS	Batch size	Sub-assembly stock yes (✓) or no (✗)	Dimension and score[1]						Total score
				Efficiency	Inventory	Speed of throughput	Space/ movement	Response/ variability	Quality	
1	MTS	5	✓	1	4	3	4	3	4	19
2	MTS	5	✗	3	3	4	3	3	2	18
3	MTS	1	✓	2	3	1	2	3	2	13
4	MTS	1	✗	4	2	2	1	3	1	13
5	MTO	5	✓	1	3	3	4	1	4	16
6	MTO	5	✗	3	2	4	3	1	2	15
7	MTO	1	✓	2	3	1	2	1	2	11
8	MTO	1	✗	4	1	2	1	1	1	10

Note

1. 1 = good; 4 = poor.

Exhibit 8   *Proposed factory layout*

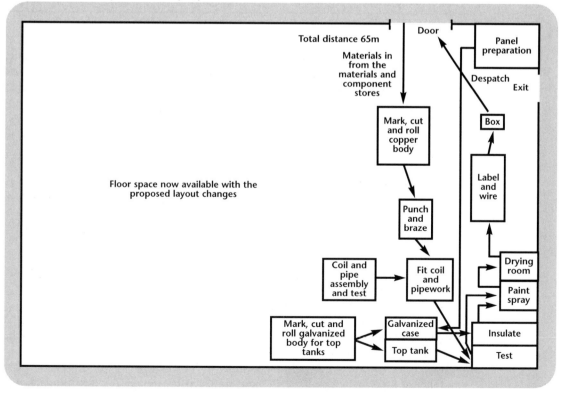

Exhibit 9   *Summary of proposed manufacturing changes for the Hetvatten Plus range of products*

The changes proposed and the principal benefits resulting from them have been summarized below:

Current manufacturing
- Currently manufacturing makes the Hetvatten Plus products by an order quantity of five products at a time.
- All five products go to operation 1 where the work is completed before all five products go to operation 2 and so on through the entire process.

Move to flow production
- Under the 'flow' production system, batches of five will be eliminated and work will be carried out on a batch of one.
- The physical structure of manufacturing will be altered to a U-shape production line (Exhibit 8).
- Single boilers will be moved on trolleys around the line.
- Subassembly components will be made off the main line and added to the part-made boiler on the line.
- A JIT process will be set up for raw material suppliers from stores to the line, and a JIT process will operate with component suppliers.

Human resource changes
- Currently operators concentrate their work on one area, but may be required to assist on different sections, or move to the subassembly area if the preceding stage is longer and holds up the flow of the batches.
- In the process flow system there will be less need for operators to move around. They will be assigned specific tasks and will keep to that operation through the day (this may consist of two or three steps). This should improve productivity as there will be less time lost through walking about. However, the new U-shaped flow system enables operators to maintain eye contact and allows each operator to have a better view of the whole process.

'As you know', explained Peter at the beginning of his review, 'a typical boiler comprises four principal subassemblies – copper body, top tank, galvanised casing and the electrical unit. As shown in the current layout (see Exhibit 4), these subassemblies are produced in separate systems and come together, as required, at the assembly stage. You can also see from the layout's details that the distance travelled totals 112 metres.

One of the initial tasks was to evaluate the current system and propose changes on whether to:

■ make-to-order (MTO) or make-to-stock (MTS)
■ make in order quantities (whether of five or a different quantity) or make individually (one-piece flow)
■ hold stocks of subassemblies or make them as part of the final product assembly stage.

To help in this evaluation we used Exhibit 7 which also gives the scores we agreed on each dimension for the eight options.'

'My recommendation, in the first instance, is to adopt option 7 [Exhibit 7] as holding subassembly stock will take some pressure off the system. Later, when the revised arrangement is running well we can eliminate this feature.' Details of the revised layout and other changes are given in Exhibits 8 and 9.

'However, to be able to change successfully to the new way of working will require a number of tasks to be completed. These are listed in the report I distributed earlier [see Exhibit 10]. Once the changes have been implemented we expect to gain the following advantages.' Peter then went through the list of advantages as given in Exhibits 11 and 12 and explained each in full.

'Given the need to improve our overall performance and the premium we are giving for reducing costs and taking out overheads then I feel that these changes are ones which will, in themselves, lead to noticeable inventory reductions, additional floor space needed to make new products in the future and shorter manufacturing lead times for the Hetvatten Plus product range. For these reasons I wish to implement these proposed changes as quickly as possible.'

Exhibit 10   *Tasks to be completed as part of the change to one-piece flow production*

Before the move to the one-piece flow production we need to undertake the following tasks:

1. Remove changeover times (particularly on punches).
2. Estimate the need for any two-man lifting requirements.
3. Develop a U-shaped manufacturing layout to minimize distances between operations.
4. Position tooling and materials close to the relevant operations.
5. Establish standard work methods.
6. Balance the line capacity.
7. Encourage teamworking, particularly through a new payment system, setting consistent performance targets and adopting a different management style.
8. Reduce or eliminate delays in spray painting.
9. Control dust from the rockwool insulation operation.
10. Possibly eliminate the final water test.

Exhibit 11   *Advantages of the one-piece flow process*

---

1. The advantages accruing from 'one-piece flow' are that it:
- reduces the floor area required, with the freed-up space being used for the manufacture of a new product
- increases quality
- facilitates teamworking
- reduces the walking distances involved
- increases flexibility
- reduces work-in-progress (WIP) inventory
- leads to higher control of throughputs
- increases focus for the continuous improvement teams
- improves operator's overall vision by means of the U-shaped layout

2. The advantages accruing from making-to-order as opposed to making-to-stock are:
- lower finished goods stock
- increased flexibility in production planning
- lower raw material stocks
- ability to cope with higher product variety
- materials can be delivered directly to the work stations

3. The advantages relating to the presence of subassembly stock within the process are that it:
- facilitates labour balancing
- affords the opportunity to make and feed parts to the point of use
- enables faster throughputs
- improves stock level control with the use of Kanban systems

---

Exhibit 12   *Specific advantages to be gained from the proposed changes in manufacturing*

The advantages accruing from the proposed changes in manufacturing include:

1. **Reduction in labour content** – less walking due to the smaller working area under the revised conditions.

2. **Elimination of set-up times** – the purchase of additional equipment (see Exhibit 13) means that set-ups will be eliminated.

3. **Reduced tooling costs** – the elimination of tool changes (see 2 above) means that some SEK 36 000 of tool damages per year would also be eliminated.

4. **Raw material inventory** – it has been agreed to change the call-off arrangements with suppliers. Materials (and particularly the high value items) are to be delivered more frequently. However, it is intended to hold raw material inventory steady even though sales revenue will increase in the next year by 44 per cent. Later it is intended that the supplier delivers some items (particularly the high value items) directly to the line on a daily basis.

5. **Work-in-progress inventory** – with the reduction of batch sizes from five to one, work-in-progress inventory will be reduced to SEK 36 000.

6. **Finished goods inventory** – the orientation of the company from a make-to-stock to a make-to-order approach will result in the finished goods inventory ceiling being reduced from a high of 1750 units (or equivalent of SEK 10 500 000) to a maximum of 300 units (or equivalent of SEK 1 800 000).

7. **Floor space** – the change in order quantities from five to one will result in a 50 per cent saving in floor space (see Exhibit 8).

8. **Distance travelled by a typical product** – resulting from the floor space gains, the product in future will travel 65 as opposed to 112 metres (see Exhibits 4 and 8).

Exhibit 13   *Additional equipment investment*

As part of the shop-floor changes the following additional equipment was purchased in order to reduce material movements, the time of operations and the number of set-ups involved.

Equipment description		#	Costs (SEK)	
			Per unit	**Total**
Folding machine		1	30 000	30 000
Roller		1	18 000	18 000
Punches	small	3	7 200	21 600
	large	1	9 600	9 600
Fly presses		2	9 600	19 200
Air test unit		1	18 000	18 000
Jenny		1	1 200	1 200
Lifting table		1	18 000	18 000
Create test area, introduce racking/storage bins and other layout changes		1	12 000	12 000
Total		12	–	147 600

McDonald's Corporation

INTRODUCTION

It is a cold Thursday afternoon in early December in Eastborough, a small town in southern England. Some of the hardy shoppers are busily making day-to-day purchases with others getting organized for Christmas. The main shopping area is pedestrianized, and at the end of the street, shining through the gloomy light, is a bright yellow M indicating the site of one of the town's two McDonald's restaurants.

Through the main entrance the interior is warm and well lit, with a hubbub of activity around the counter area. It is a medium-sized restaurant with seating for 193 people, divided between two floors. The restaurant is open seven days a week, from 7.00 am to midnight.

Asking a few customers why they use McDonald's produces few surprises. An energetic six-year-old nudges his younger sister and declares, 'We like the chicken nuggets.' Their mother explains: 'It's convenient at the end of our shopping, right in the town centre. It's not too expensive and the children like the food.'

It is not only the food that appeals to the younger generation. The two youngsters dash over to a tree laden with balloons and flags to make their selection. The restaurant encourages this idea of the 'McDonald's Experience', with a strong focus on what appeals to children. Children's parties for special occasions, such as birthdays, are regularly catered for and special events, like face-painting, are frequently organized. On the previous Mother's Day, daffodils were available for children to give to mother. On Father's Day, phone cards were distributed, so that children could ring the lucky parent.

But the age range using the Eastborough restaurant is wide. As an older couple explain: 'The service is quick and you know what to expect. The quality of the food on this visit will be as good as when we came in last week and the week before.'

The themes of knowing what to expect in terms of product quality and speed of service at a reasonable price, in clean and bright surroundings, are reiterated by other customers.

The original philosophy was laid down by Richard and Maurice McDonald shortly after the Second World War: 'Everything prepared in advance, everything uniform. All geared to heavy volume in a short amount of time.'

This case study was written by Terry Hill (Templeton College, University of Oxford) and R Lily. It is intended as the basis for class discussion and not as an example of good or bad management. © AMD Publishing.

The success of the McDonald's approach led to dramatic growth. Ray Kroc, the driving force in the expansion of the McDonald's chain, was first appointed as a franchisee by the McDonald brothers in 1954, in San Bernadino, California. Kroc bought all rights to the McDonald's concept for $2.7 million in 1961. By 1963 the 500th restaurant had opened in the USA and in 1967 the first restaurants were opened in Canada and Puerto Rico. In 1968, the Big Mac was introduced and the 1000th restaurant opened. By 1996 McDonald's had 21 000 restaurants in 101 countries. Sales exceeded $30bn.

In the UK, the first restaurant was opened in 1974 in South-east London. The number has now risen to some 750 outlets employing over 40 000 people with sales of £1bn.

STORE LAYOUT

The Eastborough store layout comprises a seating area, spread across two floors, and a working area (see Exhibit 1). In quiet periods, sections of seating are closed off for cleaning. The seating area is patrolled by dining area hosts/hostesses, whose primary role is to keep the area clean and tidy.

The main sections in the working area (see Exhibit 2) are the:

■ counter – this restaurant has 10 stations for tills
■ production area – here food is prepared and held in bins prior to serving to customers
■ grill area where the meat products are grilled
■ chicken station where chicken and fish are cooked.

SERVING CUSTOMER ORDERS

As the burger fast-food industry has become more competitive, McDonald's have steadily expanded the range of food and drinks provided from the original offering of burgers, drinks and fries. Above the counter, five brightly lit panels display the menu (see Exhibit 3). In addition to being sold as individual items, many of the products are packaged into special offers, listed as Extra Value Meals. For example, the Big Mac Meal consists of a Big Mac, a drink and a portion of fries. One panel exhorts customers to 'Make It Large – have large fries and a large soft drink with your Extra Value Meal'. In addition to the standard menu, special promotional items are added from time to time. Recent promotions include Ribs and a Double Cheeseburger.

Customers entering the restaurant typically divide into those who know exactly what they want, and join immediately the shortest queue, and those who first stand and study the menu panels for a short period. When the customer reaches the front of the queue and asks for his food, the counter person employs two selling techniques. The first is known as 'selling up'. For example:

'Hamburger and fries, please', requests the customer.
'Would you like large fries?' says the counter person.

'Selling up' involves augmenting the order, by either suggesting a larger portion or an additional item, such as a drink.

Exhibit 1   *Overall layout of Eastborough restaurant*

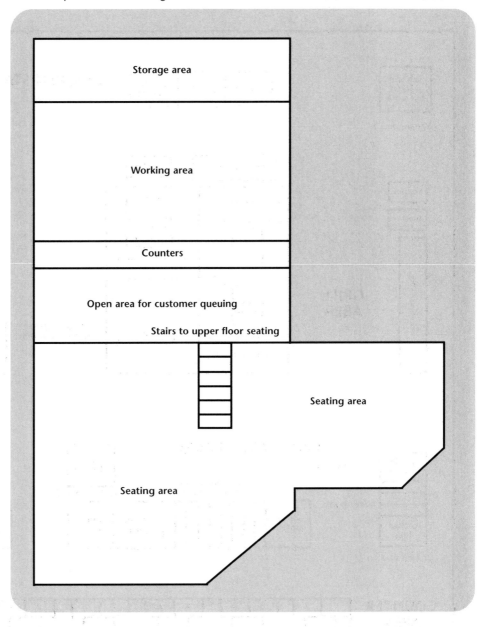

The other technique is called 'suggestive selling'. Here an order for a 'Big Mac and medium fries' would be greeted by suggesting to a customer the nearest Extra Value Meal alternative (for example a Big Mac Meal) which would cost a little more than the original order but give better overall value. The policy of suggestive selling leads to an increased sale as the alternative offering automatically includes additional items, such as drinks or fries.

Exhibit 2   *Eastborough restaurant working area*

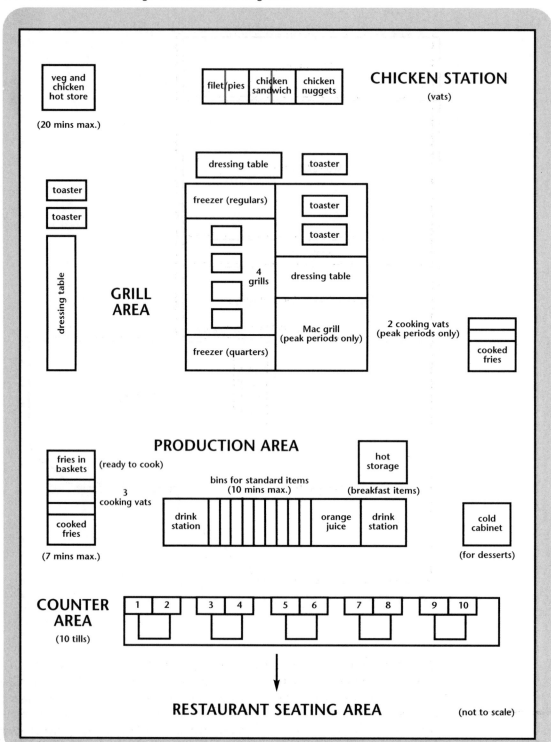

Exhibit 3   *The menu*

The menu in the Eastborough restaurant is displayed on five brightly lit panels set over the counter area with details of what is on offer – see below:

Menu items

Sandwiches
Hamburger   Vegetable Deluxe
Cheeseburger   Big Mac
Filet-O-Fish (100 per cent pure cod)   McChicken Sandwich
Chicken McNuggets (6 pieces)

Extra Value Meals
The Extra Value Meal includes a portion of fries, a drink and the main item. Medium or large refers to the fries and the drink.

# 1	Big Mac Meal	Medium or large
# 2	McChicken Sandwich Meal	Medium or large
# 3	¼ Pounder Meal with Cheese	Medium or large
# 4	Vegetable Deluxe Meal	Medium or large
# 5	Chicken McNuggets 6 pieces Meal	Medium or large
# 6	Filet-O-Fish Meal	Medium or large

Quarter pounders
■ Regular   ■ With cheese   ■ Deluxe

French fries
■ Regular   ■ Medium   ■ Large

Children's Happy Meals
Hamburger Meal
Cheeseburger Meal
Chicken McNuggets 4 pieces Meal

Beverages
Milk Shakes (four flavours)   Natural Mineral Water
Coca Cola   Semi-skimmed Milk
Diet Coke   Pure Orange Juice   ■ Regular or large
Sprite   Coffee   ■ Regular or large
Fanta Orange (still)   Tea
Super Size Soft Drinks   Hot Chocolate

Breakfast (served until 11.00 am)
Big Breakfast Meal   Sausage and Egg McMuffin Meal
Pancakes and Sausage Meal   Bacon and Egg McMuffin
Sausage Bacon and Egg McMuffin Meal   Scrambled Eggs and English Muffin
Big Breakfast   Hash Brown Potatoes
Pancakes and Sausage   English Muffin with Jam
Pancakes and Syrup

The counter person punches the order into the till. For the standard items listed below, the food would be available in the bins in the production area.

■ Big Mac   ■ Quarter pounder with cheese
■ Filet-O-Fish   ■ Chicken sandwich
■ Chicken nuggets   ■ Hamburger
■ Cheeseburger   ■ Vegetable Deluxe

The counter person then picks the food in a set sequence:

- cold drinks
- hot drinks
- fries
- boxed burgers/sandwiches
- wrapped burgers/sandwiches

The drinks machines have a selection of buttons, corresponding to the drink sizes on offer, to dispense the appropriate amount. Different-sized serving containers are used for portions of regular, medium and large fries.

The sequence for a typical order for a Big Mac, coffee and fries to eat in the restaurant, goes as follows:

- punch order into the till, as the customer details the items
- place tray on counter
- pour coffee and place on tray
- walk over to fries and fill container
- on way back to counter, take Big Mac from bin
- place items on tray
- take the money

If an item of food is not available in the production area, the counter person calls the order to the production person who calls the food order to the grill area. The item is then prepared as a priority. In slack periods, certain standard items with low demand are only cooked to order. In the Eastborough restaurant, Filet-O-Fish and Vegetable Deluxe fall into this category.

When an order is not immediately available, the counter person takes the money for the order (the till can only deal with one current order), asks the customer to stand aside and wait, and starts to deal with the next person in the line. At the server's discretion, the customer is requested to take a seat and the order is brought over by the staff. This might apply to an elderly customer or a parent struggling with several children.

If a customer requests a non-standard item, for example, a Big Mac with no cheese, the counter person identifies the non-standard item when punching the order into the till. This causes a 'grill slip' to be printed at a terminal in the grill area. When the item of food is prepared, the grill slip travels with it to the production area. The production person then calls the counter person to indicate that the order is available.

The restaurant aims not to exceed a maximum time for the customer waiting in line of two minutes and a maximum waiting time of one minute from the order being placed. Periodically, actual performance on waiting times is checked, using a stopwatch.

At the Eastborough restaurant, customers eating the food in the restaurant account for 64 per cent of sales. The balance is for takeaways.

PRODUCTION PLANNING

Production planning is guided by a computer package. The schedule manager, who can be either the restaurant manager or the first assistant manager, prepares daily a chart of projected sales by hour throughout the day. The previous three weeks' sales

Exhibit 4   *Examples of manning levels for the Eastborough restaurant*

		Supervision	Dining area	Counter area	Grill area	Total
1	Quiet period – for example, weekday afternoon	1	1	2	3	7
2	Medium activity – for example, Monday to Thursday lunchtime	1	2	4	5	12
3	Busy period – for example, Saturday lunchtime	3	8	13	24	48

and the sales for the same period last year are used as inputs to the schedule manager's prediction. From the sales forecast, the computer package generates proposed bin levels by product for the production area. The resulting chart is displayed on the wall. In practice, the production person, who controls the bin levels, uses the chart as a guide, but can often spot more precisely a surge or fall in demand. For example, there is often a time in the afternoon when many schoolchildren call in at the restaurant before catching their buses out of town.

The computer also helps in planning manning levels. From a weekly sales forecast, a package generates the required crewing levels for the different areas of the restaurant. The crewing levels are affected by both volume and product mix. The level of demand varies substantially. For the Eastborough restaurant, the periods of high demand are lunchtimes, Friday evenings after 5.00 pm, and all day on Saturdays and Sundays. Some typical manning levels are given in Exhibit 4.

The Eastborough restaurant employs a total of 100 staff, of whom only 12 are full-time. The age profile reflects the UK average, with 70 per cent of employees between 16 and 20 years old. Pitching the number of staff at the right level throughout the week is key to the smooth operation of the restaurant. If the staffing level proves to be out of line with actual demand, then the options are limited. If there are excess staff, the manager will ask if anyone wishes to go home. If demand is unexpectedly high, staff not scheduled to work are contacted, but there is no guarantee that they will be available and willing to come into work at short notice. In periods where staff loads fall short of actual demand everybody has to operate that much more 'slickly'. To facilitate this the manager ensures that all employees are allocated to the jobs in which they perform most efficiently, known as 'aces in their places'. All managers, including the restaurant manager, carry out routine food preparation if required by the level of customer demand.

PRODUCTION CONTROL

To handle the high volumes and meet the fast service required, there is a defined McDonald's approach to each aspect of preparing and serving the food and drinks on offer. At the start of the day the production person runs the bins in the production area up to the required levels by requesting sufficient products from the grill area and chicken station. In periods of high demand there is a person allocated to the job of 'the bin'. The task involves managing the flow of products, calling for production as needed, keeping the bin stock organized and fresh, thereby acting as the interface between the staff preparing food and the counter staff who serve the customers. During slow periods counter staff would normally call orders from the back as needed to maintain minimum inventory levels. To guarantee that customers are only served with hot and fresh products, food is held for no longer than 10 minutes after wrapping before either being sold or discarded.

The production person works closely with the food preparation areas and roles change slightly as different areas come under pressure. Normally, the production person will fetch the food, when ready, from the grill area. Food from the chicken station and quarter pounders from the grill area are normally boxed at the station and taken to the production person.

As explained earlier, food is held for a maximum of 10 minutes in bins in the production area. This is indicated by a purpose-designed clock hanging over the production area. The outer rim of the clock has a series of numbers in different colours. These are repeated, but offset on the inner rim. When the clock hand reaches a new number on the outer rim a corresponding plastic tag is placed in the bin. If food before that tag is still in the bin when the number is reached on the inner rim of the clock, then that food is removed and discarded.

Sue Kemp, who often runs the bin during busy times on her shift, described her job:

> Having worked here for some time, I have a good sense of when our peaks occur and how demand levels vary. But, there will still be times when I am caught out. I'll build up the bin before the peak starts and then try to run production as smoothly as possible through the busy times. You never known how many people will come in and this causes problems and at busy times can increase staff pressure to the point of causing some tension. There are charts telling us how much stock to hold at different volume levels, but I need to watch what is selling, gauge customer flows and take into account how experienced the production staff are to judge how much to have in the bin. I'd rather have too much than keep a customer waiting.

PREPARING PRODUCTS

The main products use several common ingredients, as illustrated in Exhibit 5. All food preparation is carried out according to carefully detailed rules. For example, fries must be left for a minimum of 45 minutes to defrost, before cooking. This is to minimize the amount of water reaching the fry vat. When cooking fries, a duty timer sounds after 30 seconds, indicating that the fry basket must be lifted from the shortening and shaken. (Shortening is the medium in which fries are cooked.) This separates the fries and prevents air mixing with the shortening. Fries must be cooked for three minutes, plus or minus five seconds. The maximum holding time for fries is seven minutes, after which the fries must be discarded. During busy periods an operator works full-time on cooking the fries. In slack periods, cooking the fries is covered by the counter staff.

In order to ensure that employees are familiar with these rules, they are documented for each product in the form of an observation check list (OCL). The OCL is also used in assessing an employee's level of proficiency.

Exhibit 5   *Main product ingredients*

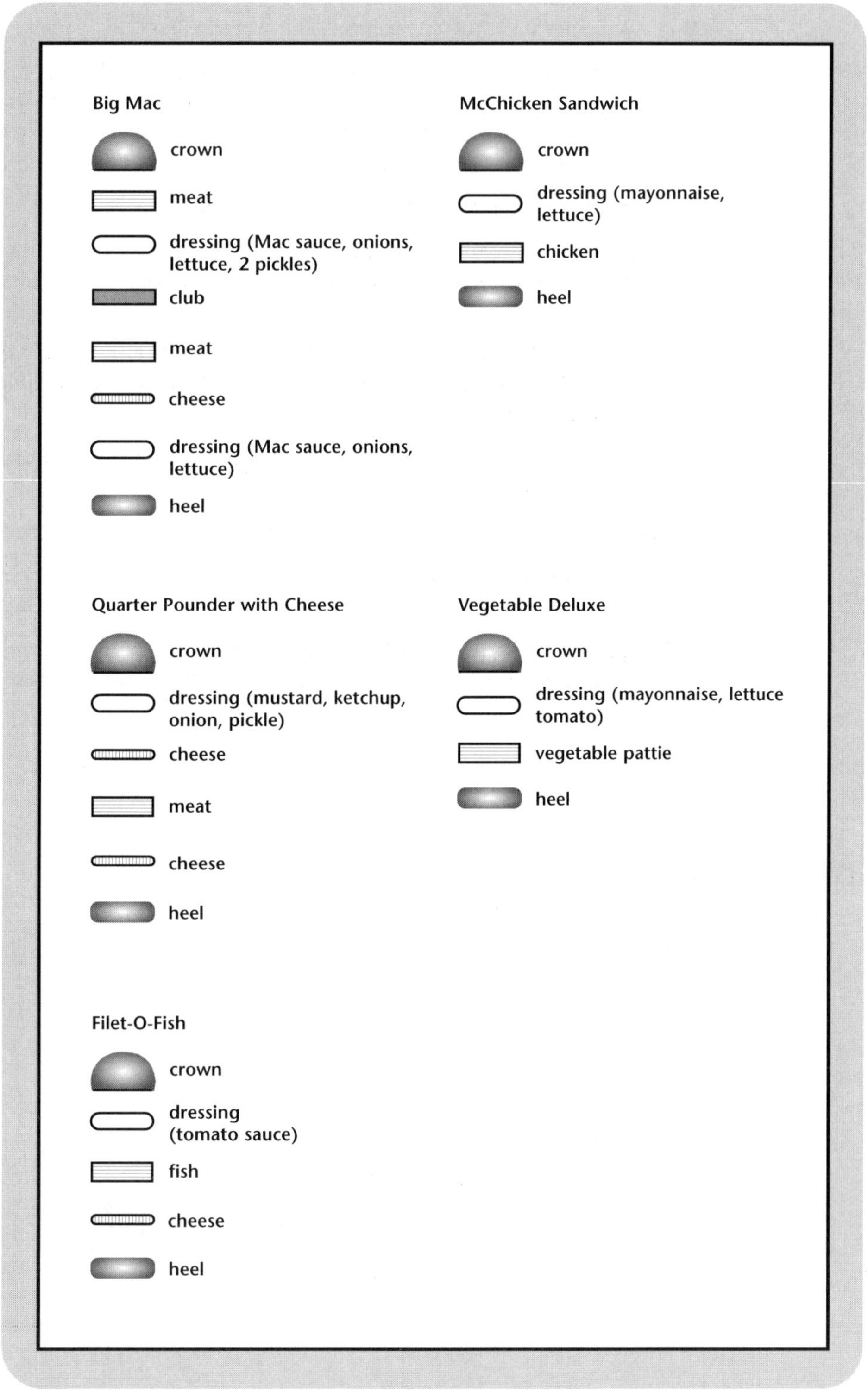

Big Mac

crown

meat

dressing (Mac sauce, onions, lettuce, 2 pickles)

club

meat

cheese

dressing (Mac sauce, onions, lettuce)

heel

McChicken Sandwich

crown

dressing (mayonnaise, lettuce)

chicken

heel

Quarter Pounder with Cheese

crown

dressing (mustard, ketchup, onion, pickle)

cheese

meat

cheese

heel

Vegetable Deluxe

crown

dressing (mayonnaise, lettuce tomato)

vegetable pattie

heel

Filet-O-Fish

crown

dressing (tomato sauce)

fish

cheese

heel

A typical sequence for preparing food goes as follows:

■ A call comes from the production person 'Four Big Macs, please'.

■ The bun for the Big Mac is in three sections, designated the 'heel', the 'club' and the 'crown'. The operator on the dressing table loads the four heels and clubs of the buns into the toaster. After 35 seconds a timer sounds on the toaster and the operator transfers the heels and clubs onto the dressing table.

■ The operator loads the crowns into the toaster.

■ At the same time, the grill operator, prompted by the timer alarm, lays eight pieces of meat onto the grill. The grill takes exactly 42 seconds to grill both sides of the meat.

■ During this time the operator at the dressing table puts the Mac sauce, onions, lettuce and cheese onto the heels and clubs. Sauces are delivered in preset amounts from a dispenser.

■ Two pickled gherkins, which, according to the relevant OCL, must not be touching, are placed on the club.

■ The grill operator puts a piece of meat onto each dressed heel and club.

■ The dressing table operator assembles the buns, adds the now toasted crowns, stacks the buns and gives them to the production person at the next station.

■ The product is then wrapped and placed in the rack, with the appropriate time card. The whole process, shown in Exhibit 6, takes about two minutes.

Exhibit 6   *Preparing the Big Mac*

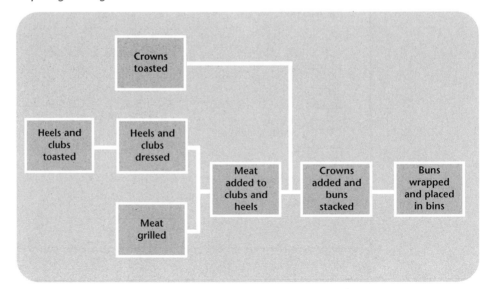

STAFF TRAINING

Good teamwork and familiarity with the set routines for dealing with customers, storing the food and preparing the meals, are essential to the successful operation of a McDonald's restaurant.

After joining McDonald's, staff are expected to reach a set level of expertise, designated 5-star, within five months, or 10 months if a part-timer. An employee's performance is assessed against a given task using the appropriate OCL. Each OCL details precisely, step by step, how a product should be prepared. To achieve 5-star status, an employee must have undertaken two satisfactory OCLs for each area of operation. The restaurant manager and each area leader carry out one OCL each day. Because of the high number of staff, this is a major activity for the restaurant manager.

It is customary to work alongside the employee being assessed for a period on the particular task and then mark up the OCL. Any 5-star employee is qualified to carry out an OCL assessment. A pass on an OCL requires a 90 per cent mark on each of the two sections on the check list. The first section covers food preparation and the second general issues, such as neatness and cleanliness of the uniform. All the OCLs are filed.

EXTERNAL AUDIT

Each quarter, an external audit is carried out, usually by the manager of another McDonald's restaurant. Fifteen employee files are selected and the restaurant is graded based on the OCL scores achieved. Annually, the restaurant is subjected to a more intensive audit, known as 'full field'. A group of supervisors from other restaurants complete OCLs on all operations, over a period of one dayshift and one nightshift. In this and other ways, the corporate tradition of managing all outlets under the motto QSC & V (Quality, Service, Cleanliness and Value) is reinforced.

FINANCIAL TARGETS

Restaurant managers have to agree each month with their area supervisors a financial target for the next month's revenue. Daily cash sheets are filed, showing takings. Progress is reviewed at mid-month with the area supervisor.

Northmore Finance Direct

'The next phase', explained Sam Boston, operations director at Northmore Finance Direct, 'is to determine how to broaden our product range in the "direct" market so as to enable us to build a business that can sustain adequate growth and provide a broader sales revenue platform in the future. The initial steps of testing and proving this product strategy are now successfully completed and arrangements are now in hand to develop the case for an investment of some £12m to be made during the next 12–18 months in order to deliver the systems and procedures that will need to be in place to handle these new products.'

BACKGROUND

Retail credit facilities had been developed in the 1950s to meet the growing demands of customers. The white and electrical goods sectors were some of the first where this facility was successfully introduced. In the early 1960s, Northmore Bank bought out a personal loan company (Axia Loans) with the aim of developing the opportunities to sell different forms of loan finance to existing and new customers.

Part of this growth was initiated by Northmore Bank writing to its customers to advise direct finance opportunities. The success that followed and the opportunity for future growth of personal loan products led to the decision five years ago to separate Northmore Finance Direct (NFD) from Northmore Bank with the former's task to concentrate on developing the personal loans market. At that time some 75 staff were transferred to an office block across from an existing Northmore site in Guildford together with existing IT systems. Within a few months agreement was reached to take an exact copy of the account management IT system, delete the data entries and use the program for the new loan business. This program was supplied and managed by Software Data Systems, a third-party supplier. Within three years, the growth and opportunities in the personal loans market were further signalled when NFD moved into the phase of TV advertising.

NORTHMORE FINANCE DIRECT – THE CONCEPT

The increasing use of the telephone as a medium for marketing and selling within a range of financial services has gathered pace since first introduced in the late 1980s. The NFD vision coupled a recognition of the opportunity and growing importance of this selling channel to:

■ using different media opportunities from doorstep drops to press and TV advertising as ways of stimulating awareness within the general public to the availability of personal loans

■ create a service that would meet the changing needs and expectations of customers in terms of its user friendly, quick response and flexible nature

■ build on the strength of a bank.

The decision to separate NFD clearly reinforced the intent by Northmore Bank to develop the personal finance loan market using direct channels. In those early days, the need to maintain and accelerate sales revenue growth was one of the newly-

Exhibit 1   *Trends within NFD for the last six years*

Aspect		Current year minus					Current year
		5	4	3	2	1	
New business volumes (£s) (per cent of total)	traditional	100	100	100	82	63	33
	direct	–	–	–	18[1]	37	67
	total	100	100	100	100	100	100
Customer accounts (per cent of total)	traditional	n/a	n/a	100	91	71	61
	direct	–	–	–	9	29	39
	total	n/a	n/a	100	100	100	100
Average monthly applications (indexed)	traditional	100	150	367	300	317	167
	direct	–	–	–	100	600	1150
	total	100	150	367	300	717	933
# staff (FTEs) indexed		100	134	439	536	1182	1512

Notes

1. The current year minus 2 figure for new business volumes for the direct channel is based on a part year only.
2. The figures for traditional business includes both 'original' and 'affinity'.
3. The figures for direct business include:

    ■ TV and press advertising   ■ newspaper inserts
    ■ mailshots to NFD customers   ■ doorstep drops

4. Two years ago 70 per cent of all applications were received by post and 30 per cent by telephone. So far this year, 7 per cent have come by post and 93 per cent by telephone.
5. n/a = not available.
6. FTEs = Full-time equivalents.
7. The total figures in the section 'Average monthly applications (indexed)' relate to the total applications and are not the sum of the individual figures for 'traditional' and 'direct'.

fledged company's principal tasks. The drive to grow sales was appropriately high on the corporate agenda and the results are provided in Exhibit 1.

Expanding its customer base was the key factor in achieving this. In the early days, the customer list of Axia Loans (the company bought out by Northmore Bank) was an essential input into the company's sales activities. As advertising grew so did the company's own customer base. But the need to expand also led to the company looking for affinity partners as a new source of potential customers. These arrangements enabled NFD to have access to a partner's customer list under an agreed commercial arrangement. (Affinity partnering arrangements centred on the purchase and use of another company's mailing list.) Currently, the number of listings totals 15. Exhibit 2 gives details of some of the contracts while Exhibit 3 gives details of the agreement with one partner with a very large customer listing.

- **Traditional** – comprises applications that result from mailings to the customer lists that were part of the Axia Loans purchase plus any repeat business from these customers. The rate of loan interest offered at the time of a mailing is at a fixed level.

- **Affinity** – comprises applications that result from mailings to the customer lists belonging to other corporations. Again, the rate of loan interest is at a fixed level.

- **Direct** – applications in this segment are a direct result of NFD's activities. They comprise 'repeat' business that involves non-TV-based advertising channels, as well as TV advertising. Additionally, interest rates are not fixed but vary in line with the principle of 'rate for risk'. In this way, the loan rate offered reflects an applicant's personal circumstances concerning the degree of risk involved in making a

Exhibit 2　　　*Details of past and current affinity partnerships*

Details of affinity partnerships regarding the size and status of the mailing lists involved			
Size of mailing list (000s)	**# partnerships**		
	Total	Terminated	Ongoing
10–50	4	–	4
50–100	2	2	–
100–200	5	2	3
200–500	6	1	5
500–1000	2	–	2
1000–2000	1	–	1
2000+	1	1	–
Total partnerships (#)	21	6	15
Total mailing list (000s)	8721	3970	4751

Note

Total numbers on the mailing list are the actual numbers involved.

Exhibit 3   *Details of the customer service procedure required and agreed with one affinity customer having a large mailing list*

TELEPHONE ANSWERING TARGETS

- Telephone answering

  95 per cent to be answered within three rings
  97 per cent to be answered in total

- Monitoring the quality of calls

  Northmore Bank Accreditation

  All telephone operators are to go through an intensive training programme and are expected to attain Northmore Bank's service quality standards. Every individual will be accredited against these standards to ensure that the service quality standards are maintained:

  – Three calls per week per person will be taped to ensure that each operator continues to achieve the accreditation standard.

  – If operators fail to meet this standard they will be given alternative duties until given further upgraded training. Subsequent to this all calls will be taped for constant monitoring until the minimum standards are either attained or the operator given alternative duties.

APPLICATION PROCESSING TARGETS

- **Written application form processing**

  100 per cent processed on the same day of receipt

- **Quality of application**

  Accuracy level – minimum 99 per cent
  1 in 10 postal and 3 applications per telephone operator per day are to be checked for accuracy

- **Agreement form/decline letter notification**

  100 per cent produced overnight for dispatch by first-class post the following day

- **Payment of the loan from receipt of the agreement form**

  100 per cent paid same day received, signed with cheques produced overnight for dispatch by first-class post the following day

- **Procedure for handling agreements that are not taken up**
  The

  All customers not returning an agreement within 5 working days will receive a telephone call/letter.

  initial contact will be followed up at 10 days and again at 15 days if the agreement form has still not been returned

- **Welcome calls**

  100 per cent of new accounts will receive a call to welcome the customer to Northmore Finance Direct between 4 and 6 working days of the dispatch of the cheque

DECISION TARGETS

- **Immediate decisions**

  60 per cent of decisions are to be automatic

- **Speed of decision on referred applications (hours of operation 0800–2100)**

  3 hours maximum. Initially will attempt to telephone customers with a decision, including requests for further information. Irrespective of telephone contact, confirmation of the decision will be printed overnight for dispatch by first-class post the following day

GENERAL CORRESPONDENCE TARGET

- **Response to written correspondence**

  100 per cent of post received will be sent a response the same day. This could be an acknowledgement with a full response to follow. The maximum time for full response to more complicated correspondence will be 5 working days

personal loan. Whereas traditional and affinity businesses are based on a fixed rate included as part of the advertisement, 'rate for risk' allows the rate to be varied as explained earlier and hence increases the catchment area and eventually the number of agreements made.

NORTHMORE FINANCE DIRECT – THE ORIGINS

In the early years, the traditional activity enabled NFD to 'get off the ground', while affinity arrangements helped to fuel the required volume growth. The decision to use TV advertising as a medium for accessing a broader applicant base coupled with the 'rate for risk' principle of assessing and agreeing applications changed the profile of NFD.

Having taken the strategic view that the core of its personal loan business needed to be centred on a direct, telephony-based product, where to locate operations to meet these new dimensions was a key step that could affect the quality of the support required. The strategy was to build a brand that would stand on its own. If successful, it was estimated that after about five years some 80 per cent of its business would be self-generated by customers. The first five years investment in advertising (the annual TV advertising budget alone is about £10m) and other brand-building activities needed to be made in order to get to a position where future investments would be lower and made primarily to reinforce brand recognition rather than stimulate new business. Thus, most applications in the future would not be made as a direct result of advertising, but due to existing customers initiating calls based on the strength of the brand and the association of NFD's name with personal loan opportunities. During the first five years, however, the advertisement-led demand resulted in customer calls characterized by high peaks with different timescales depending on the medium used. Some of these patterns, that are now used as part of the Call Centre Model (referred to later in the case), are included as Exhibit 4.

Whereas the initial NFD activity had been suitably accommodated near to Northmore Bank's existing facilities and thus the transfer of staff was not a factor affecting the setting up of the required operation, the increase in volumes in the last two to three years and the change in orientation and accelerated growth anticipated with TV advertising resulted in the need for more office space and the opportunity to consider where best to locate the operations activities to support direct business activities.

The alternatives narrowed down to Guildford and Leicester, and as a telephony-based facility is not location dependent, then the choice concerned issues other than geography. The final decision to develop NFD in Leicester was principally made in recognition of the dynamic nature of TV advertisements and the need for operations to be able to effectively support the short-term response patterns involved (see Exhibit 4). Locating in Leicester would thus avoid bringing existing contracted agreements, work patterns and cultures from the past into a facility where the demands on operations were markedly different. A fresh start seemed to make a lot of sense.

OPERATIONS

The corporate decision to create NFD as a stand-alone facility signalled the real development of the direct personal loan business. Direct marketing had been initiated with some press advertising and mail shots to NFD customers and by two years ago

Exhibit 4   *Examples of the impact of different types of media on operations*

Below are three examples of the response patterns which result from different types of media both in terms of the shape and timescales involved:

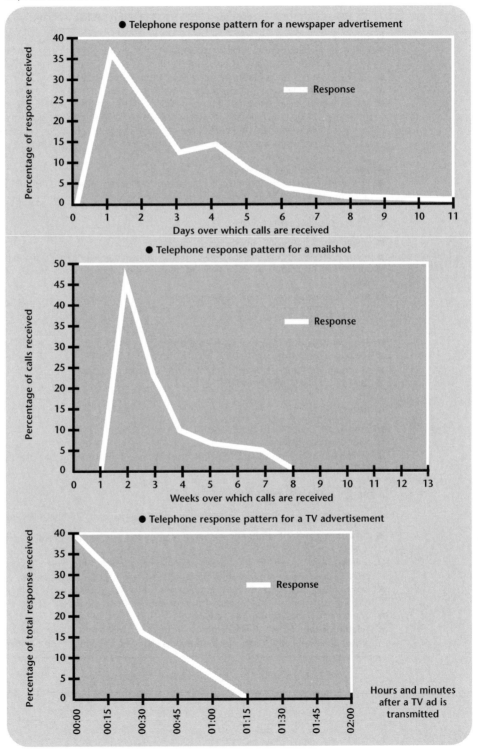

Exhibit 5   *Media options: direct and indirect characteristics*

DIRECT CHARACTERISTICS

1. TV advertising – direct response (DRTV) and brand response (BRTV)

- overall annual spend equates to some 35 000 spots
- DRTV – generates immediate response and call volumes
  - 'shelf life' about 1 hour
- BRTV – builds brand awareness at different times of the day
  - stimulates calls over a longer time period than DRTV
- the number of calls generated varies depending on the slot purchased. For example
  - '11.00 coffee time' – low response but considered to be quite cost-effective
  - between the two halves of major 'soap' – very high brand awareness and call responses, but too extreme to manage effectively the resulting call handling capacity requirement
- spot costs reflect viewing levels
- TV companies hold the right to allocate and/or reallocate slot times. Gazumping is not uncommon and up to 25 per cent of all slots can be reallocated at short notice

2. Press advertisements

- media spend totals 500 press advertisements
- many press advertisements are booked over a month in advance to aid planning
- 'distress' space (that is, short, usually 24 hours, notice placements) is offered occasionally at low prices
- trend to generate more calls at the weekend

3. Door drops

- comprises the distribution of 25 million leaflets
- very cost-effective
- uncertain lead times re delivery – part of the low-cost dimension
- run size usually 5 million leaflets

4. Inserts

- media spend equates to 1.4 million packs
- cost-effective medium
- mailed using Sort 3 (that is, third-class post) as part of the cost-effective delivery
- delivery lead times can vary up to 14 days

INDIRECT CHARACTERISTICS

Response patterns are also influenced (sometimes quite markedly) by the following:

- **Geography and TV channels** – different regions and TV channels produce varying response levels
- **Source** – Affinity partners have different consumer characteristics. Freemans, for example, produce a very high proportion of postal rather than telephone applications
- **Seasonality** – it is too early yet to understand the effects of seasonality. So far, Northmore Direct has only experienced one Christmas period and two Easter periods
- **The weather and competitor activity**
- **Telephone familiarity** – the acceptance of the direct channel to market appears generally to be growing in popularity. Consumer behaviour is changing dynamically on different days of the week

over 1 million letters were being sent monthly to prospective customers. However, in the early days the need to increase volumes and meet sales targets was the overriding corporate priority. New ideas and alternatives to existing approaches were part of the experimental environment that drove the company forward. As sales grew so did operational requirements. However, in these early times operations was absorbed in keeping pace with growth, coping with the changing patterns of demand and meeting the day-to-day tasks as they occurred. One outcome was that operations gave too little time to learning about the different demands resulting from the array of marketing plans and initiatives. In part, operations got caught up with the general ground swell in activity and did not keep pace with the essential developments called for by the learning curve associated with high growth. Relying on inherited IT systems that were bespoke and not well suited to personal loan products, operations found itself with too little insight into what it was being asked to do. Even the performance measures in place were insufficiently robust to provide operations with the input into corporate discussion about growth and what constituted necessary support from operations.

Although marketing and operations discussed major initiatives, the result was too often a compliant response from operations, more by default than design. Commitments were asked for and duly given. The outcome was far from satisfactory.

Two years ago, NFD appointed Sam Boston to the position of operations director. One of his first tasks was to evaluate the current position and decide on the best way of improving it.

> Getting the basics right [explained Sam] became a priority task. The business had an excellent 'can do' culture and a very strong and necessary entrepreneurial spirit. But, operations developments had not kept pace. Staff efforts to get around systems constraints were unstinting [he recalled] but, the solutions were largely paper based and 'band aid' in nature. Systems needed to become more robust, match the needs of the expanding business and more automated in order to free up staff time for doing what they do best – talking to customers.
>
> Operations management skills had also not kept pace. Performance measures, analyses and an understanding of the core processes needed to be in place as the basis for improving key operations activities.
>
> The other big step was a planning tool, a way of modelling the impact of different forms of advertising on capacity [see Exhibit 5]. Without this, we would still be in the times of feast and famine that were a hallmark of the early years. In fact, this development was an essential prelude to our successful move into TV advertising that is characterized by higher peaks of activity over shorter timescales. Also, the models help marketing and operations to have a shared understanding of the issues affecting both sides. They provide a common language to help ensure that we both work together to improve overall business performance.
>
> Since these early days we have now set realistic performance targets [see Exhibit 6 for some of the key ones] and use data to help us understand market developments and take an increasingly proactive role in developing products, customers and market support [see Exhibit 7]. Also, as we expand our business we know that we are moving away from the 'safer' customer profiles into those which carry more risk [see Exhibit 8]. We need to develop operations to meet these and similar characteristics if we are to maintain our past success into the future.

Exhibit 6 *Service levels – current standards*

Aspect of service		Standard
Answering calls	average speed	10 seconds
	# to be answered within 15 seconds	80 per cent
	maximum # calls to voicemail or abandoned	2 per cent
All post to be acknowledged within		24 hours
Data input accuracy		98 per cent
Referred applications turnaround		80 per cent in 4 hours

LEICESTER CALL CENTRE

The use of TV as an advertising medium for personal loans was new not only to NFD but also to the market in general. Given the pioneering nature of the project, the first phase was to test the market in three regions within the UK. Operationally, this was a major initiative especially given the decision to open every hour of every day throughout the year. To minimize the overall risks during this test phase, it was decided to subcontract the telephony tasks to an outside supplier. During the first months the third-party telephony unit undertook the prime tasks of handling calls and the other duties of the personal loan advisers. However, if the market test proved a success, the intention was always to bring this function in-house, so a dedicated team under separate management was set up. The Leicester site was designated and the facilities were refurbished and equipped, key appointments, such as the call centre manager, made and staff recruited and trained in line with a planned start-up.

With the success of the test phase, a full national 'rollout' was launched. To help the transition in operations, the third-party support and Leicester Call Centre ran in parallel for the first six months, gradually moving over this time from an 80/20 to a 20/80 responsibility for call handling. After that, the call centre was on its own.

The need to plan and collaborate key activities was a major factor in the functions of the business coming together. Arranging capacity in line with anticipated volumes in particular was recognized as a core activity. At the beginning this was particularly difficult with no historic market data to go on. Over the period that followed, improvements became the priority task in operations. As Pam Whitely (the call centre manager) explained:

> From the beginning it was apparent that operations needed to become involved in the discussions on markets. Anticipating the volume of calls and the capacity, which needed to be available to support and maintain required service levels, was an essential task. The operations and marketing functions have worked together to gain a comprehensive understanding of the dynamics which drive these issues and have jointly developed a number of predictive volumes and resources models. The media agency used to promote NFD also participates in this process on a quarterly basis in order to optimize the use of capacity and minimize costs in line with the amount of business written. How we

Exhibit 7   *Operations data monitoring market responses over time*

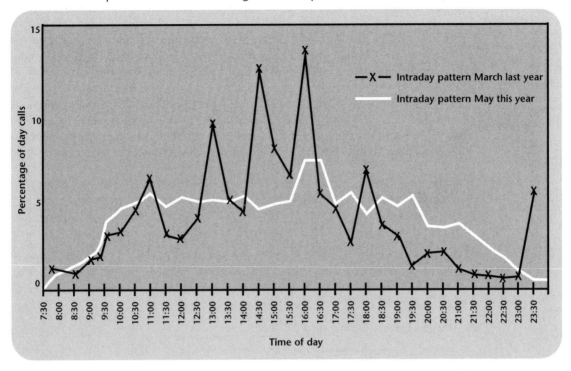

Exhibit 8   *Operations data monitoring the levels of potential fraudulent applications in Northmore Bank*

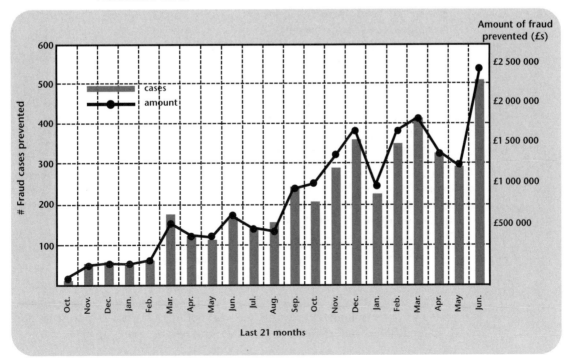

achieve this is directly affected as much by the level of capacity and capability in the call centre as by the marketing and advertising plans that stimulate initial demand.

She went on to explain that the broad statements of demand were translated first into capacity statements covering each month, then each week and finally planning call centre capacity on a half-hourly basis with service levels measured every 15 minutes. In the same way, marketing's predictions covering the number of calls are forecast half-hourly as is the number of calls delivered. 'It is essential that all involved become better at providing relevant inputs into this dynamic service equation. The better the inputs then the better the outputs. Creating then meeting demand makes for a better business,' concluded Pam. Other features within the centre are outlined below.

■ Marketing plans, as explained earlier, are translated into the number of calls first at a monthly level for aggregate planning purposes and then to a weekly and finally a daily basis. In capacity terms this needs to be translated into the number of personal loan advisers (PLAs) at the level of each half-hour of the day.

■ Telephony support is available every hour of every day in the year. The capacity allocations reflect the anticipated daily demands and these together with other key factors are monitored on a half-hourly basis each day. Exhibit 9 provides an example of the detail recorded in this control document.

■ The procedure followed by a PLA is as follows:

   – customer telephones in
   – PLA asks a series of set questions
   – the information given by a customer is fed into the system which advises the rate to be offered – the 'rate for risk' principle
   – printed confirmation of the offer is generated by the system and mailed to the prospective customer
   – customer signs the agreement
   – cheque is mailed on receipt of the signed agreement
   – the loan is then managed

For some 80 per cent of applications, a PLA is able to tell a customer immediately whether or not the loan is agreed and the interest rate to be applied. The 20 per cent that are referred go to the credit department at Guildford where each case is reviewed by underwriters on a first-in first-out basis. Referred customers can telephone later using a different number to find out if their loan has been approved.

■ To enable a PLA to advise a decision, the data files need to be available in terms of access. The current system is supplied, maintained and managed by an outside agency. Currently, the 'system is up' (that is, the data are available for a PLA to advise a decision) at the following times:

Mon to Fri	0700–2200
Sat	0700–2100
Sun	0700–1700

At other times, the system information is being downloaded which typically takes some two or three hours. When the system is not up, PLAs take handwritten notes of an application and then key this in when the system is next up.

Exhibit 9   Call centre – daily measurement

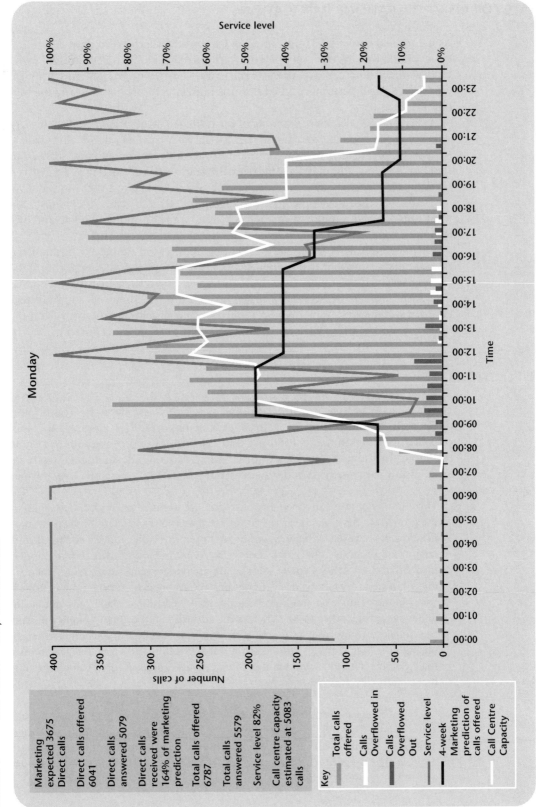

RATE FOR RISK – OPERATIONS IMPLICATIONS

As mentioned earlier, NFD introduced a loan product to be priced on a 'rate for risk' basis. In other words the rate offered to customers would be based on their own individual circumstances, rather than on the market norm where a standard, uniform rate was offered to all customers. In addition, lending decisions risked losing the business opportunity.

A clear and detailed understanding of the credit risk issues was critical to this strategy. This involved being able to analyse the risk for each customer accurately, to make the loan decision and set a price accordingly. In the early traditional days, such an understanding was less important as the standard rates were very high (25–35 per cent on occasions) and customer's expectations involved a delay before a decision was given.

Credit scorecard developments to address these issues became a core task. Also, as most calls are from unknown customers, it is vital to continue to update and improve these skills and to keep abreast of changes in the market circumstances.

Telemarketing skills are also critical in operations. Starting in new business acquisition, the success of NFD is heavily dependent on optimizing sales opportunities, from chasing accepted customers who have not drawn down their loan through to selling insurance products (which has a major influence on income). In addition, telemarketing techniques are fundamental to relationship development with customers in a direct business, starting with initial welcome calls to telephone contact early on.

REFLECTIONS

Looking back, NFD has grown significantly over the last few years. The initiative to direct mail customers to advise personal loan opportunities has fuelled a business currently growing annually at 50 per cent. The initial step of moving to the current Guildford site using existing staff and IT systems was an understandable step to take so as to minimize investment and other costs in the start-up phase of a new business.

> The vision of offering an 'open all hours' product seems to be fit for today's lifestyle and the growth we have seen bears witness to that fact [reflected Sam Boston]. To meet the needs of the next developments within NFD then investments discussed in the opening section are essential. The key business drivers underpinning this reflect the developments that need to be made to address inherited issues and future requirements. For a direct business, operations needs to become the engine which drives the customer relationship rather than operations' classically perceived role of being only responsible for undertaking back office tasks. Whereas the advertisement or brand name will stimulate the initial customer call, transacting the business, identifying customer needs, maximizing sales opportunities afforded by a call and fulfilling customer expectations needs to be clearly seen, understood and delivered by operations. Adding value is the name of the game!

With the TV-based products successfully launched, the business is now developing a deeper branded strategy, addressing opportunities to widen our product range and deepen relationships with our customers. The discussion embodies a clear recognition of the role that operations, marketing and other key functions need to play together to win in our chosen markets.

Operations Control and Scheduling: Short Cases

ASH ELECTRICS

Ash Electrics plc is a manufacturer of doorbells, door chimes, switches, industrial alarm bells and a range of small transformers. Producing some five million units per year (from a 38 cm diameter bell to a replacement bulb in a lighted switch) the company sells to electric wholesalers throughout the UK and abroad. One of its important selling features is to meet home orders on a same-day-as-receipt basis while the dispatch of export orders only waits for the next appropriate shipping arrangements.

The range of manufacturing activities includes coil winding, simple cropping and punching and other operations such as bending, forming and crimping simple components for later assembly. The principal activity, however, is the assembly, test and packing of products from the necessary bought-out and made in-house components, mouldings and parts. In outline, the operations process is shown in Exhibit 1. In order to reduce manufacturing costs and work-in-progress (WIP) inventory holdings, the company has standardized many components in each of the products from fixing screws through to clips, bobbins, coils, lamps and multi-language instruction leaflets. Besides the metal bars or domes which produce the sound, the principal material used is plastic. Plastic bases, front pieces and components are bought in from outside suppliers to meet demand forecasts for each final product.

The company works on 13 four-week periods and the period forecast sales, by product, is provided. In addition, the forecast end-of-period finished goods inventory holding is also known. It is expected that anticipated differences between actual and forecast sales will be reflected in the production programme so that the actual end-of-period finished goods inventory is as close as possible to the forecast level. These adjustments are made at the start of each period when firm production outputs are agreed.

The case studies in this section on operations control and scheduling – Ash Electrics, Hunting Swift, Platt Green Electronics, Richmond Plastics and Spencer Thompson – were written by Terry Hill (Templeton College, University of Oxford) for class discussion and not as illustrations of good or bad management. © AMD Publishing.

Exhibit 1　　*Outline of the operations process*

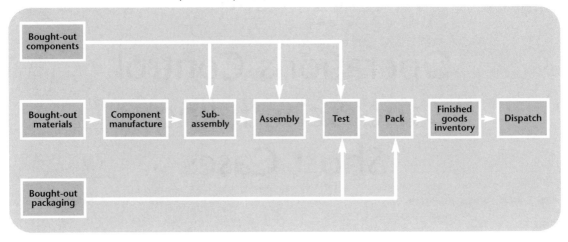

HUNTING SWIFT

Hunting Swift (HS) manufactures a range of pumps and turbines for the petrochemical industry. The current product range consists of 20 basic units offered in a total of 110 sizes (that is, some 5 sizes per unit) and, on average, each size can be manufactured in up to 10 different materials. All products are manufactured to the very precise standards of the American Petroleum Institute in order for HS to avail itself of world export markets and the rigorous international requirements of the industry.

Typically a unit consists of some 350 parts of which about 120 require some machining. The other 230 are bought-out components which go into the final assembly. The machining processes within the company comprise 21 work-centres such as centre lathes, turners, millers, drills and borers. The machining requirements of the different parts vary greatly from as little as a single operation of 3 minutes on one work centre to as high as a total of 13 hours on some 8–10 operations spread over 7 work-centres. About 65 per cent of machined parts are common to more than one type of end-product and in a typical year there are 1000 of these common parts, the cumulative demand for which exceeded 28 000 items (see Exhibit 2). Once all the materials are on site, the majority of the manufacturing process time is taken up in the machine shop.

HS submits tenders to the major oil companies and civil engineering contractors who design and build petrochemical plants. The order quantities are small with a maximum of four similar units on any one order. Total unit sales in recent years have risen to about 280 for all pumps. A similar quantity is anticipated for the coming year. The delivery time offered to customers for a typical unit is six months with some suppliers quoting a three months delivery on castings. At the other end of the delivery spectrum some small items are held in stock or are same-day delivery.

The products supplied by HS have a long life and consequently generate a significant demand for spares. For instance, in the last full year there were 300 orders for spares. These orders were for 1400 different parts with typically, several different parts on each order. When the order quantities for each part were totalled, they exceeded 12 000 items and accounted for about 50 per cent of the total sales revenue. The

Exhibit 2   *Typical demand patterns for common parts*

Demand for parts	# parts	# items
0–10	488	1 939
11–20	213	2 912
21–50	168	5 112
51–100	78	5 420
101–200	30	3 894
201–300	11	2 543
301–500	7	2 757
501–1000	5	3 653
Total	1000	28 230

typical delivery time for spare parts was also quoted as six months where many machining operations were required. Other parts (for example small components where the quantities required were high but they were either bought out or require little machining) were quoted two to three months for delivery.

PLATT GREEN ELECTRONICS

Platt Green Electronics (PGE) is a small company that manufactures and assembles a small range of oscilloscopes. There is only one basic product but this is sold in four versions: mains supply, direct current (DC) supply, battery pack (including charger) and mains pack. The oscilloscopes are also sold with or without a probe and connector. These latter items are also sold individually.

The operations process involves the following principal phases: purchasing materials and components, metal fabrication, printed circuit boards (PCB) manufacture, PCB test, subassembly, assembly, test pack and dispatch. The policy of the company is to use outworkers to complete parts of these processes with the others being performed inside the plant. The oscilloscope cases and drilled blanks to take the components are fabricated in the metal shop. From these, subassemblies are made which, together with other parts, are then assembled before test and packing. The component parts and subassemblies for each product are shown in Exhibit 3.

The present workforce comprises three full-time and two part-time staff, employed at the plant with 12 outworkers who can allocate up to 20 hours per week to PGE's

Exhibit 3   *The number of components and subassemblies by product type*

Product	# components		# subassemblies
	Made-in	Bought-out	
Mains	20	85	9
DC	32	105	10[1]
Battery pack	26	92	6
Mains pack	30	70	4
Total	108	352	29

Note

1. Eight of these subassemblies are also common to the mains version of this product.

Exhibit 4 *The operations process*

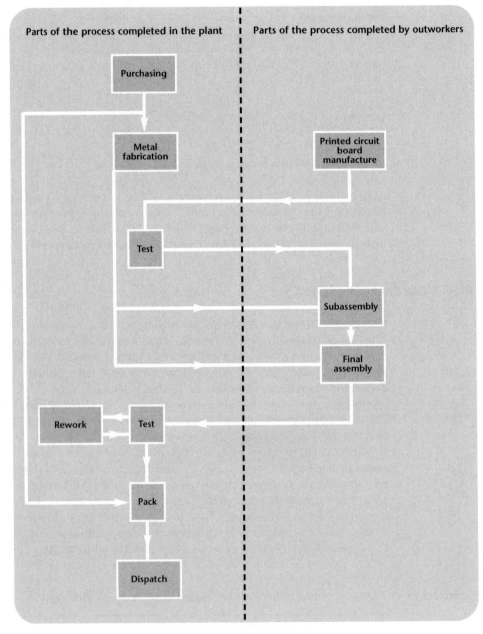

work – see Exhibit 4. Production levels average 20 oscilloscopes per week. Probes and connectors are bought in and require little additional work. The products are sold as standard items to meet a range of different industrial applications.

The weekly production levels, although averaging 20 units, can vary from week to week depending upon the number of oscilloscopes requiring rework after final assembly test. The amount of time it takes to correct the faults can vary from 0.5 to 6.0 hours. At the moment, the full-time staff are responsible for the rework activity.

Exhibit 5   *Number of machines by machine group*

Moulding machine group	# machines
1	29
2	14
3	10
4	4
Total	57

RICHMOND PLASTICS

Richmond Plastics produces a wide range of products that fall into three categories: items that it sells to several customers, items that are designed for one customer who calls off from a blanket order with the required notice, and items made on a subcontract basis.

The first two items are for products that typically have a number of bought-out components added to them and require specific labels and packaging before they can be assembled and packed. While some subcontract items also fall into this category, others comprise products that are bulk-packed into secondhand cartons and require no labels.

The principal manufacturing processes involved are injection moulding and assembly. A typical product has one or more parts that are moulded. These then go direct to assembly or into WIP stores prior to assembly. After assembly and packing the products go into the finished goods warehouse. The injection moulding machines are grouped into one of four sizes with each mould going onto one size of machine (see Exhibit 5).

As many of the products are bulky and the volumes can total up to 4000 shots per shift, it is important to keep WIP inventory to a minimum. (A multi-impression mould will produce in each shot the number of components on that mould.) The mould shop works on a 24-hour basis for five days per week with some weekend working on particular orders as necessary. The assembly department rarely works overtime except to meet the peak demands prior to Christmas – the normal working week is 37.5 hours. In addition, Richmond Plastics occasionally subcontracts work to one or two other moulding companies in times of high demand. When this happens, some of the products are returned to Richmond Plastics as WIP for inspection, assembly and packing while others (usually where quality is less critical) are assembled and packed at the subcontractor's premises and then delivered to Richmond Plastics' finished goods warehouse.

SPENCER THOMPSON

Spencer Thompson (ST) is a firm of professional accountants that provides both accounting, finance and management consultancy services to its clients. ST has offices throughout the UK with the largest in central London.

At the central London office, there is a word processing centre and proofreading department that prepares the majority of reports for clients, together with internal documents, statements, reporting procedures and information papers. There is a manager, supervisor, nine processing staff and three proofreaders employed to provide this facility. The documents received for preparation vary in length from a few pages up to 250 pages or more. The estimated sizes of documents that users of the centre projected when booking facilities ahead of time frequently differed greatly from the final version that the centre eventually received.

The average output of each person on the word processing phase of the service is 500 lines per day including initial processing and corrections. The demand placed upon the processing facility varies as does the lead time required to meet client and consultancy assignment deadlines.

The process to complete a report or other document consists of initial processing, editing if required, proofreading, making corrections and proofreading the corrections. The three proofreaders provide the editing and proofreading capability in the process. However, in some situations the person writing the report may wish to take the initial typed document, edit or revise the text and then put it back into the process. In some cases, the revisions may be extensive.

Each proofreader averages about 70 pages of work a day. This average covers a typical mix of work and includes the checking of corrections.

PAK
Television

Given the increase in other areas of our business, we really need to clarify how much work we have and can expect in our television production sector. Furthermore, [explained Geoff Marsh, founding partner of the company] there is a real opportunity to expand in other directions and we need to assess how much and how quickly we may need to expand.

BACKGROUND

PAK Television (PAKT) has been involved in producing successful television programmes for over 12 years. The company is now one of the UK's largest independent production companies producing a wide range of entertainment and factual programmes from its offices near Birmingham in central England.

The company is jointly managed by Geoff Marsh and Johannah White. Geoff was the founding partner but has recently been spending a large portion of his time on other aspects of related work as a way of helping to grow overall sales revenue. Johannah is responsible for the day-to-day operations of the company and has an Executive Producer's role on many of PAKT's television projects. 'Johannah', as Geoff explained, 'has extensive production experience and is a tough negotiator when it comes to budgets and contracts'. Throughout the past few years PAKT has developed an enviable reputation for producing high-quality, innovative productions, on time and within budget. In all it has produced over 200 hours of network television for all the major broadcasters.

OPERATIONS

The process of making a television programme, from generating the concept to delivering a video tape to the broadcaster, can take from anything between six months and

This case was written by Terry (Templeton College, University of Oxford) and AJ Hill (UMIST) and AJ Mayers (UMIST) as a basis for class discussion and not as an example of good or bad management. © AMD Publishing.

Exhibit 1   *The process from an idea being generated to the delivery of a completed product*

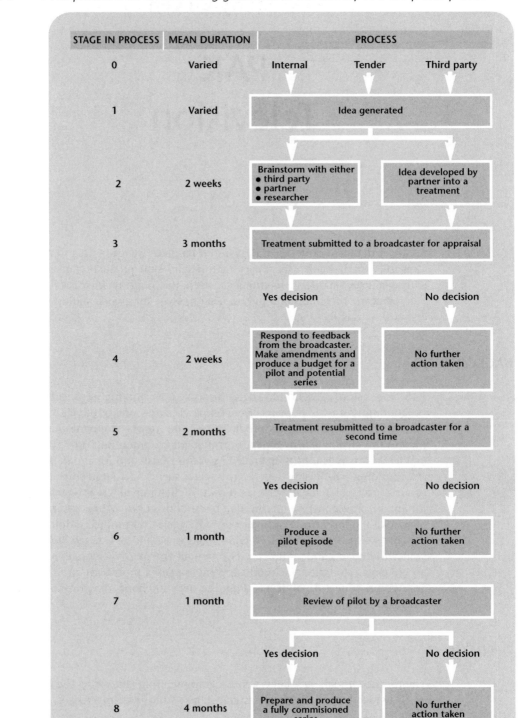

three years. Typically, however, it takes about 12 months and follows the general path described in Exhibit 1.

The first, and most difficult stage, is generating the concept or idea for a programme. 'This can take various forms', explained Johannah 'from a topic that you have found interesting and think other people would think the same, to a word or phrase scribbled on the back of an envelope that will spark a chain of thoughts when you come back to it. Whatever form it may take, ideas come from the following three sources:

1. **Internally** – the idea comes from an employee of the company, usually one of the partners.

2. **Tender** – broadcasters who want a specific type of programme to fill a space in their schedule and will propose an idea for development.

3. **Third party** – where an outside organization or person has an idea but needs the programme-making expertise and reputation of a company such as PAKT to develop and sell it.

Inspiration and the generation of ideas are hard things to quantify in terms of the time it takes to develop. However, on average we generate internally five ideas a month, receive six tenders a year direct from major broadcasters and are approached twice a month by third parties.'

At this point the ideas are usually verbal and need to be developed into something more tangible, this is Stage 2 of the process. The outcome at this stage is a document called a 'treatment'. This gives a brief outline of how the proposed programme would work, the audience to whom it is aimed and its proposed transmission in terms of the length of the programme, the day to be shown and the time of day it was to be scheduled. A treatment is either written by one of the partners working on the idea in isolation, or by a team of the relevant people working together (Stage 2, Exhibit 1). On average this stage takes two weeks to complete.

Once a treatment has been prepared it is then sent to a broadcaster for appraisal (Stage 3). A decision is reached and a broadcaster will respond with a 'no', in which case no further action is taken, or a 'yes' in which case the idea goes to Stage 4. The time it takes to get a response can vary widely, although a period of three months is around the mean.

Stage 4 involves responding to the feedback from broadcasters. This may require modifying the treatment in ways they feel would improve the show, the preparation of a detailed budget for the programme or series should it be commissioned and also the preparation of a budget for a pilot, normally a non-transmittable episode designed to give a broadcaster more of an idea as to what the programme would look like. In all, the stage takes an average of two weeks to complete. The revised treatment and relevant information is then resubmitted to the broadcaster for further review. On average the broadcaster takes two months to undertake this step.

Broadcasters then decide whether they wish to proceed with a project. If a 'no' decision is given, then no further action is taken. If the answer is 'yes' then a pilot episode will be produced.

Once the pilot programme has been completed (this normally takes PAKT about one month) the tape will be sent back to the broadcaster who will review it and then make the final decision whether or not to proceed with the full programme (Stage 7).

Exhibit 2 *Rejection rates as ideas progress through each stage*

Stage	Cumulative loss rates at each stage (per cent of total)	Cumulative net ideas going forward to the next stage (per cent of total)
0–1	0	100
1–2	0	100
2–3	0	100
3–4	57	43
4–5	57	43
5–6	79	21
6–7	79	21
7–8	93	7

It is uncertain how long this step will take. However, typically a decision would be reached after one further month. For those pilots which are given the final go-ahead it will take an average of four months to prepare and produce a fully commissioned series (Stage 8).

The number of ideas that successfully make it from the original concept to a commissioned programme is shown in Exhibit 2. These data show that many ideas are rejected at each stage and, on average, for every 100 ideas only seven result in a fully commissioned series.

Thus, of 100 treatments which are submitted to a broadcaster for approval, 57 will typically be given a 'no' decision and 43 will typically be a 'yes' decision. Subsequently when these 43 are resubmitted (Stage 5) a further 22 will receive a 'no' decision leaving only 21 of the original 100 ideas going into Stage 6. Finally, of the 21 pilot programmes, 14 receive a 'no' decision while the remaining 7 pilot programmes go on to Stage 8 where a fully commissioned series is produced by PAKT.

CAPACITY AND DEMAND

At present PAKT has three full-time staff, hiring additional personnel as and when they are needed. They consist of the two partners (Geoff Marsh and Johannah White) and James Bentley, the production manager. The weekly hours that each of these work on TV productions is typically 20, 60 and 50 respectively. Exhibit 3 shows the average number of hours that each employee would spend at each stage of the process detailed in Exhibit 1.

The current demand on their time is shown in Exhibit 4, which gives the number of current projects at each stage of the process along with how many hours of work have already been completed at the respective stages by each member of staff.

LOOKING FORWARD

'Following our continued success over the last few years', explained Geoff Marsh,

the time and opportunity has come to increase our range of services while growing the throughput and sales of existing products. Our full-time team is well established but we

Exhibit 3   The hours of work which have to be completed by the three full-time staff at each stage in the process

Stage of process	# hours of work at each stage		
	Geoff Marsh	Johannah White	James Bentley
1	2	2	0
2	1	25	4
3	0	0	0
4	5	20	2
5	0	0	0
6	15	150	160
7	0	0	0
8	380	480	540

Exhibit 4   The current projects in progress and the total work (hours) completed on all these projects at each stage in the process

Stage of process	# current projects	Total work completed on all current projects		
		Geoff Marsh	Johannah White	James Bentley
1	10	20	20	0
2	12	12	120	5
3	10	0	0	0
4	5	10	60	5
5	2	0	0	0
6	0	0	0	0
7	0	0	0	0
8	1	375	460	500

need to consider increasing this while keeping the mix of full- and part-time staff to reflect the variable patterns of demand we experience. As both Johannah and James will feature in our intended expansion then the first step in addressing this requirement is to establish our existing demand and capacity position in our largest segment, television programme production. Until we know where we are in this important segment it will not be possible to identify how much work we can take on elsewhere.

Ransom Electronic Products

'The problem is to increase the output from our manufacturing unit in Ransom Electronic Products (REP). It seems to me that what is required is the application of basic industrial engineering to the situation in order to get better bench layouts, work flow, materials handling and so on. And, furthermore,' continued Peter Bullen, chairman of Ransom Electronic Products, 'we need to act quickly.' Peter Bullen was addressing the board of directors of REP, a wholly owned subsidiary of Ransom plc. (Plc means public limited company and in the United States equates to being incorporated.) The other members of the board were Jim Latham, managing director, and Tony Richards, a non-executive director who was an executive with the principal company, Ransom plc. This particular agenda item had been raised at an earlier meeting in February and had been formally minuted for this meeting in July.

BACKGROUND

Ransom had started business in the field of electronics about 10 years before. Part of the original arrangements had been to subcontract the manufacture of 'special' items for customers to a small, local company. As the company's sales grew, Ransom put money into the local subcontractor, leading to a 49 per cent share of the business.

Five years ago the company bought out the remaining 51 per cent of the shares (held by the original owner), and since that time it had operated as an independent but wholly owned subsidiary. The following year this subsidiary was renamed Ransom Electronic Products and was relocated into the same premises as its parent company.

Jim Latham has been with REP since it was partly owned by Ransom plc. When it was bought out, the original owner stayed on for a few months and then eventually left. Jim Latham seemed the natural successor to run REP, and he took up the role as managing director in June of the same year.

This case was prepared by Terry Hill (Templeton College, University of Oxford). It is intended for class discussion and not as an illustration of good or bad management. © AMD Publishing.

Exhibit 1   Attendance hours in the three months ended 30 June of the current year, analysed by main activities

Employee	Recorded hours during the month			
	April	May	June	Total
Metalwork				
F. Hurst	160	128	176	464
M. Abbott	160	144	160	464
D. Inskip	174.5	150.25	167.25	492
M. Jenner	–	–	80	80
	494.5	422.25	583.25	1500
Assembly/Wire				
J. Latham	90	112	105	307
M. Tower	92	190.75	136	418.75
P. Dyer	90	94.5	90	274.5
M. Parkes	80	84	88	252
P. Hanlan	188	187	194	569
D. Gurner	184	159.25	225.5	568.75
F. Nott	–	139	14	153
D. Gray	–	–	155.5	155.5
	724	966.5	1008	2698.5
Test				
J. Lees	187.5	215.5	241	644
Total	1406	1604.25	1832.25	4842.5

Notes

1. J. Latham's hours reflect the estimated time he spent on productive work.
2. National holidays, annual holidays and sickness have been deducted from the recorded available hours as appropriate to give attendance hours.
3. Mary Pickard is not included in the above information (see Exhibit 2).

Source: Skill Lab International invoices, pay records and internal time sheets.

ORGANIZATION AND STAFFING

REP is a small production unit with some 13 staff members in addition to Jim Latham. Of these, 10 are full-time, while the other three (including one clerk/typist) work on a part-time basis. The actual attendance hours in the three months ended 30 June of this year and analysed by main activities are given as Exhibit 1, while Exhibit 2 gives an organization chart for the company.

Of the 10 full-time employees, seven work on a subcontract basis and are supplied by Skil Lab International plc, who specialize in providing tradesmen and other specialist labour. REP had adopted this policy primarily because it found, and is still finding, difficulty in recruiting skilled staff; second, it allows flexibility in labour capacity, especially in the present situation of employee protection legislation.

At present, and for some time now, REP receives all its orders from Ransom, and it is not seen, at this stage, that this pattern will change. In fact, the increase in Ransom sales has been significant over the last two years, and this is shown in the REP sales revenue figures for the past four years as given in Exhibit 3.

Exhibit 2   *Organization chart for Ransom Electronic Products*

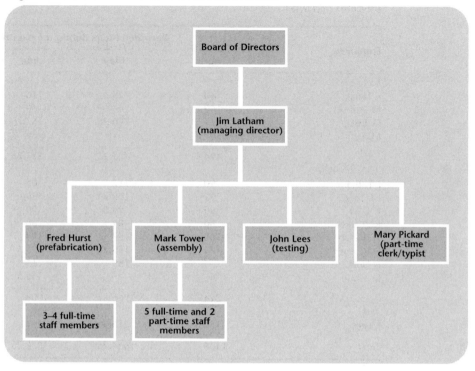

Note

1. Mary Pickard works the other part of her day for Ransom plc.

PRODUCT MIX

A recent analysis of the invoiced sales for the 12 months ended 30 June – the financial year ends on 31 December but, as a check on current trends, the 12-month period to 30 June has been analysed, see note 5 to Exhibit 3 – had been completed as a check on the split between 'standard' and 'special' products (see Exhibits 4 and 5). This revealed that over 95 per cent of the work was made up of these two types of product, with the remainder consisting of repairs, refurbishing and factored items. As Peter Bullen said, 'It's the same picture as for previous years, and I see little change in the future. We are in the "standards market" supplying over 60 per cent to Ransom from our standard catalogue.'

PERFORMANCE

Sales had grown steadily in the last four years (see Exhibit 3), but in the latter part of last year and during the first six months of this year demand had risen sharply.

When a sales order was received from Ransom, the first task was to estimate the labour and material content of the work involved. For standard items, past labour estimates were used, but for specials, estimates were agreed between the planning

Exhibit 3   *REP's balance sheet and profit/loss statement for the last five years (£000s)*

	Current year minus				Current year
	4	3	2	1	
Fixed assets	5.7	13.3	10.2	10.0	9.7
Current assets					
Inventory	10.2	14.5	13.6	19.7	30.1
Debtors	0.7	0.3	1.0	0.8	0.3
Cash	–	0.1	0.1	0.1	0.1
Amount due from holding company	16.7	6.8	8.0	11.9	44.8
Total	**33.3**	**35.0**	**32.9**	**42.5**	**85.0**
Capital and retained profits	4.7	3.6	6.6	10.7	24.3
Loan from holding company	12.0	13.2	13.2	13.2	13.2
Current liabilities					
Creditors	11.7	11.5	9.8	14.2	27.8
Bank	4.9	6.7	3.3	4.4	19.7
Total	**33.3**	**35.0**	**32.9**	**42.5**	**85.0**
Sales	64.3	68.2	66.6	90.3	163.8
Less cost of goods sold	25.7	39.8	44.4	50.4	79.7
Gross profit	**38.6**	**28.4**	**22.2**	**39.9**	**84.1**
Direct expenses					
Labour	17.9	16.1	20.9	33.4	72.7
Tools	1.7	0.9	0.9	0.6	1.6
Workshop	0.3	0.2	0.1	0.2	0.2
Depreciation	0.8	1.3	0.7	0.5	0.8
R&D	1.1	0.5	0.1	–	–
Delivery	0.2	0.1	0.1	–	–
Net profit	**16.6**	**9.3**	**(0.6)**	**5.2**	**9.0**

Notes

1. Fixed assets are net of depreciation.
2. All sales figures are net of commission.
3. All figures have been rounded.
4. The current year's figures are projected on the basis of the first six months of trading up to 30 June.
5. The financial year ends on 31 December. Information in this case refers to the 12-month period to 30 June as the most recent set of figures for a 12-month period.

function of Ransom and Jim Latham. The labour estimates for the work completed in the period April to June of this year, together with the March work-in-progress already completed on sales in these months and the June work-in-progress completed for items to be finished from July onward are given in Exhibit 6. It was considered that no work-in-progress from any months previous to March related to April, May and June sales.

WORKING ARRANGEMENTS

Although REP was legally a separate company within the Ransom group it was, in principle, a small production unit almost totally captive to supplying the needs of its parent company. On the one hand, this had the advantage of providing a full order book, without any sales effort, and keeping the sales and manufacturing functions

Exhibit 4   *Analysis of monthly invoiced sales on an actual and cumulative basis for the 12 months to 30 June of this year*

Month	Standard £s			Special £s			Repair (cum.) £s	Factor (cum.) £s	Total £s	
	Act.	Cum.	Total Cum. %	Act.	Cum.	Total Cum. %			Act.	Cum.
July	3 900	3 900	62	2 200	2 200	35	–	200	6 300	6 300
August	5 900	9 800	58	3 000	5 200	31	–	1 800	10 600	16 900
September	2 100	11 900	45	7 500	12 700	48	–	2 000	9 700	26 600
October	7 000	18 900	54	1 400	14 100	40	100	2 200	8 700	35 300
November	3 700	22 600	55	1 900	16 000	39	100	2 300	5 700	41 000
December	6 900	29 500	59	900	16 900	34	100	3 000	8 600	49 600
January	3 600	33 100	61	800	17 700	33	100	3 100	4 600	54 200
February	7 300	40 400	60	5 500	23 200	35	200	3 100	12 800	67 000
March	3 600	44 000	61	1 600	24 800	34	300	3 200	5 400	72 400
April	1 700	45 700	59	4 000	28 800	37	300	3 200	5 700	78 100
May	9 900	55 600	63	200	29 000	33	400	3 400	10 300	88 400
June	6 700	62 300	62	5 000	34 000	34	400	3 500	11 800	100 200
Total	62 300	62 300	62	34 000	34 000	34	400	3 500	100 200	100 200

Notes

1. All values have been rounded to the nearest £100.
2. The columns for 'Repair' and 'Actual' only show cumulative values. Therefore, the total actual will not add up to the analysed values because actual sales (except for July last year) are not given for 'Repair' and 'Factor' (factored items) sales.
3. Act. = actual, and cum. = cumulative.

Source: J Latham.

Exhibit 5   *Standard products ordered in the 12 months ended 30 June of this year*

During this 12-month period, 150 orders for standard products were received from Ransom plc. The total number of standard products requested in these 150 orders was 86, and the frequency with which each product was ordered is shown below

# Standard products	# Orders received for each standard product	Percentage of total orders received
56	1	65
19	2	22
8	3–5	10
2	6–10	2
1	10+	1
86	150	100

separate in terms of pressures and changes, while on the other hand, enjoying the link between sales and manufacturing experienced in a normal corporate situation.

The philosophy towards pricing also reflected this relationship in that the profit set for REP was one of making a small profit at the end of each year. It was intended that the profit for the group would be made at the sales point in the company and not shared between manufacturing and sales.

Exhibit 6   *Estimated productive work relating to the period 1 April to 30 June of this year*

The details below relate to the amount of work invoiced.

Taken from relevant invoice details in the period 1 April to 30 June the figures represent the amount of work by manufacturing category, invoiced during this period. In addition, details are given on the amount of work-in-progress carried over at 31 March and also the amount that was in the system at 30 June.

Period	Metalwork	Assembly/Wire	Test
March work-in-progress	437.50	323.00	–
April sales	149.50	250.75	12.50
May sales	401.75	867.33	52.50
June sales	164.50	558.25	231.41
June work in progress	421.50	226.25	–

Notes

1. All figures are in hours.
2. It was considered that no work-in-progress from months up to and including February related to the April–June sales figures above.
3. The June work-in-progress figures relate to work completed in the above period, but the 'value' for this work would not be seen in the form of invoiced sales until July onward, when the items, once completed, would be delivered, then invoiced in the usual way.

As explained earlier, there existed an important link between the project engineers of Ransom and REP. The procedure was that a salesman requested a quotation for a job. A project engineer would then discuss the requirements with the salesman and produce a drawing of the job, together with any other information relevant to manufacturing the system and equipment. Then the project engineer would discuss these requirements with Jim Latham in order to determine:

1. Labour estimates and, from these, labour costs for each stage in manufacturing (including test).
2. Material estimates.
3. Delivery dates.

On this basis, a quotation would be prepared for submission to the customer. Those quotations accepted by customers were passed internally from project engineering (Ransom) to purchasing (Ransom). A purchase order was prepared and sent through to Jim Latham in REP. Jim Latham would then add this purchase order to his file of outstanding orders. Each month, orders completed formed the basis of an invoice from REP to Ransom. Part-completed work would not be invoiced; however, where there was more than one item on the purchase order and one or more of these were completed, then these would be delivered and invoiced in the normal way.

Currently, there are still only two project engineers based at Ransom who have responsibility for the task described here. A problem experienced, however, was that the information link between sales (Ransom), project engineering (Ransom) and manufacturing (REP) was becoming increasingly less defined. This was due to a lack of time, more complicated specials quoted for, and the increase in marketing effort, resulting in more enquiries/quotations being required. In addition, the sales value of orders was increasing (one current quotation was five to six times larger than any currently received and processed. On the whole, this increase in sales value was due to the fact that the specials were more complex. The more complex the order, then the more intricate was the manufacturing process, particularly at the assembly/wire stage.

It appeared that due to the pressure on project engineers described here, there had been a significant increase in the interpreting, redesigning and development task of the REP staff when assembling and wiring a job. An additional factor experienced in the last six to nine months was that the customer and/or salesman were requesting modifications during the manufacturing stage. This added to the problem referred to earlier where manufacturing (REP) had to resolve these definitions, overcome problems in design and agree to changes and modifications in the original design, in order to ensure that the specification would be met. This 'defining' process was taken into account at the labour estimation stage, although it was difficult to fully appreciate what was needed until the requirements had been provided by information giving detailed design and specifications (see Exhibit 7).

At the moment, Jim Latham undertook a part 'working on the manufacturing side of the product' and part management role within REP. This suited him well as he considered that he was able to keep a finger on the pulse at both ends of the organization (see Exhibit 1).

FORWARD LOAD

Sales for the 12 months to June of this year had been just over £100 000. This had represented an increase on the previous year (Exhibit 3), but the future requirement was estimated as being much higher. In order to assess the extent of the increased demand in the future months, the present outstanding orders (net of any work already completed and so falling into the category of work-in-progress) were analysed to extract this information. Working from his outstanding order file and from the original labour estimate agreed with project engineering (Ransom), Jim Latham compiled the information given in Exhibit 8.

Exhibit 7   *Total labour hour comparison between quoted and actual for six recently completed 'large specials'*

Order #	Metalwork		Assembly/Wire		Test		Planning		Total	
	Quoted	Actual	Quoted	Actual	Quoted	Actual	Quoted	Actual	Quoted	Actual
A6791	8	80	32	56	8	8	8	8	56	152
A5522	3	45	50	170	5	40	5	8	63	263
A6690	2	4	20	24	–	4	3	5	25	37
A5495	10	120	160	150	80	150	20	20	270	440
A4940	10	5	6	6	–	0.5	3	2	19	13.5
A4527	1.5	4	5	24	–	4	–	2	6.5	34
Total	34.5	258	273	430	93	206.5	39	45	439.5	939.5

Notes

1. Actual hours were estimated by Jim Latham and the staff concerned.
2. The specials analysed were chosen on the basis of value (£s) and information availability.
3. The hours compared above are the total for the order – for the order number A6791, the quantity was 8, but all other specials were singles.
4. These specials were representative of more recent orders.

Source: Jim Latham and project engineering (Ransom).

Exhibit 8   *Estimated outstanding work (#hours) at 30 June*

Purchase order	Quantity	Item	Metalwork Each	Metalwork Total	Assembly/wire Each	Assembly/wire Total	Test Each	Test Total	Total estimated work
A6775	500	A025	–	–	0.50	250.00	0.17	83.00	333.00
A8033	8	Special	30.00	240.00	160.00	1280.00	40.00	320.00	1840.00
A8099	1	2 VPR systems	2.00	2.00	2.00	2.00	0.50	0.50	4.50
A8035	39	126 box	2.00	78.00	3.00	117.00	0.50	19.50	214.50
A8362	1	2/3 Con 240 V	–	–	1.00	1.00	0.25	0.25	1.25
A8621	1	MTD system	60.00	60.00	–	–	–	–	60.00
A8787	12	1540	4.00	48.00	5.00	60.00	0.50	6.00	114.00
A8788	3	Specials	3.00	9.00	–	–	–	–	9.00
A8856	1	Box/2 bridge SW	10.00	10.00	30.00	30.00	2.00	2.00	42.00
A8910	1	Special	–	–	6.00	6.00	1.00	1.00	7.00
A9016	6	Unit/DC	1.00	6.00	3.00	18.00	0.50	3.00	27.00
A9016	6	Unit/mains	1.00	6.00	2.00	12.00	0.50	3.00	21.00
A9025	8	N/D system	4.00	32.00	5.00	40.00	0.50	4.00	76.00
A9055	2000	Clips	0.08	160.00	–	–	–	–	160.00
A9001	20	127 box	2.00	40.00	–	–	–	–	40.00
A9123	12	A/6 control	5.00	60.00	40.00	480.00	1.00	12.00	552.00
A9123	50	130 control	5.00	250.00	4.00	200.00	0.50	25.00	475.00
A9123	10	Standard	2.00	20.00	1.00	10.00	0.25	2.50	32.50
A9123	6	150 standard	2.00	12.00	10.00	60.00	0.50	3.00	75.00
A9123	1	70A	–	–	3.00	3.00	0.25	0.25	3.25
A9163	1	Special	10.00	10.00	30.00	30.00	3.00	3.00	43.00
A9190	1	Special	5.00	5.00	15.00	15.00	2.00	2.00	22.00
A9198	1	Standard	–	–	2.00	2.00	0.50	0.50	2.50
A9217	2	SLO	–	–	2.00	4.00	0.50	1.00	5.00
A9218	25	Control	2.00	50.00	8.00	200.00	1.00	25.00	275.00
A9232	20	N/D	8.00	160.00	5.00	100.00	0.50	10.00	270.00
A9235	50	400 PCB	–	–	–	–	–	–	–
A9240	1	150 standard control	2.00	2.00	11.00	11.00	0.50	0.50	13.50
A9795	8	6-1A	5.00	40.00	3.00	24.00	0.25	2.00	66.00
A9263	2	Special	–	–	25.00	50.00	2.00	4.00	54.00
A9284	1	Special	8.00	8.00	–	–	–	–	8.00
A9303	3	8-123	5.00	15.00	3.00	9.00	0.25	0.75	24.75
A9330	10	306	2.00	20.00	6.00	60.00	0.50	5.00	85.00
A9355	1	Modification	–	–	2.00	2.00	0.50	0.50	2.50
A9361	6	6-20	5.00	30.00	30.00	180.00	1.00	6.00	216.00
A9280	10	Control	1.00	10.00	3.00	30.00	0.50	5.00	45.00
A9405	150	Plates	0.80	120.00	–	–	–	–	120.00
A9415	1	126D			2.00	2.00	0.25	0.25	2.25
A9418	2	Special	30.00	60.00	15.00	30.00	4.00	8.00	98.00
A9425	10	Control	2.00	20.00	3.00	30.00	0.50	5.00	55.00
A9426	1	Special	15.00	15.00	30.00	30.00	2.00	2.00	47.00
A9428	1	Modification	0.50	0.50	–	–	–	–	0.50
A9429	1	Special	–	–	4.00	4.00	1.00	1.00	5.00
A9432	1	123 control	3.00	3.00	8.00	8.00	1.00	1.00	12.00
A9443	1	10A1	5.00	5.00	3.00	3.00	0.50	0.50	8.50
A9443	2	Special	15.00	30.00	30.00	60.00	2.00	4.00	94.00
A9443	1	Box	4.00	4.00	6.00	6.00	1.00	1.00	11.00
		Total		1540.00		3459.00		573.00	5572.00

The details relate only to those orders required in July and August this year. For orders required from September onward, the relevant outstanding file plus some recently confirmed sales orders (the internal paperwork for which was still in the pipeline, provided by the project manager in charge of project engineering in Ransom) were analysed in terms of their sales invoice value; the details are given in Exhibit 9. Also, an estimate of the number of working days available in these months is given as Exhibit 10.

In addition, Exhibit 11 outlines the possible production capacity (£s) available by transferring responsibility for some manufacture to one of the existing Ransom locations in Market Drayton (Shropshire), some 120 miles away. The reason behind this proposal is that both the company and Skil Lab International are finding it very difficult to recruit skilled assembly and wiring staff who are able to cope with the requirements of the work on hand. This is increasingly the situation with regard to specials, and Jim Latham considers that the most recently quoted-for specials will add significantly to the skill levels demanded at this stage in the process. 'Even the staff provided by Skil lab,' commented Jim Latham, 'often require training in what, to some, is a different and higher-level range of work. The trouble is that we can then only hope that they are happy to stay with Skil Lab, and also with us.'

The sharp increase in demand had led to a growing concern, and that is why this point had been tabled for the July meeting.

Exhibit 9 *Order and delivery situation on known significant orders as of 1 July for the period September this year to March next year*

Month required	Total sales value (£s)
September	21 500
October	18 700
November	17 300
December	14 200
January	12 000
February	12 000
March	12 000

Exhibit 10 *An analysis of the estimated labour capacity available in the period September this year to March next year*

Aspect	This year				Next year		
	September	October	November	December	January	February	March
# working days	21	22	22	16	22	20	22
Basic hours including estimated overtime	1685	2456	2624	1984	2720	2496	2720
Known/estimated holidays or absenteeism	–	–	128	10	120	80	120
Net hours available	1685	2456	2496	1974	2600	2416	2600

Notes

1. Basic hours include test.

Source: Jim Latham.

Exhibit 11   *Estimated production that would be available from the Ransom location at Market Drayton*

Month	Outputs (£s)
September	600
October	–
November	1300
December	900
January	1300
February	1300
March	1300

Notes

1. All space requirements at Market Drayton are available.
2. Production could not start until September of this year.
3. Initially, this production facility would take part-completed work from REP and finish it (hence £600 value in September).
4. From October, the new production unit would start the work from the beginning and this (plus the training needs required) would result in little output in this month.
5. The difficulties of recruiting, training and retaining staff have been carefully considered and taken into account at arriving at what are considered to be realistic estimates.
6. No one at this new unit has had production experience before. Consequently, someone from REP and/or Ransom would visit the site on two days a week.

Redman Company

Redman Company was a wholly owned subsidiary of Bomat Industries. Although all its sales were internal within the group, it was judged under normal commercial rules of which one was profit performance.

Its task was to take requirements and, having discussed these in detail with the 'customer', it would prepare initial drawings to ensure that the product met requirements. On the basis of this it would agree a price and delivery schedule and then proceed to manufacture it. The principal steps involved from that stage onwards are described below and summarized in Exhibit 1.

In order to meet the requirements of its customers, Redman Company would, in essence, prepare drawings and cost estimates in line with a customer's stated requirements and then arrange for the whole manufacturing task to be completed and delivered to the customer's premises.

With regard to manufacturing, the company would buy-in standard parts from suppliers and also seek quotations for and organize the making of any special parts from chosen subcontractors. The company would be responsible for issuing materials to both its own manufacturing unit and subcontractors. While much of this material was in inventory, any other material could be purchased locally, with guaranteed short deliveries. When the component parts were received from its subcontractors, Redman would bring these together with the relevant subassemblies made in-house and complete the final assembly prior to delivery.

When placing orders for component parts with local subcontractors, the company had developed a policy of requiring estimates, the acceptance of which coincided with the placement of the order (activity 6 in Exhibit 1).

Internal pressure to reduce costs had led the company to review its current practice. As part of this revision it had listed the activities involved and determined how long each one currently took to complete. Furthermore, it had estimated that for each day the total assembly duration could be reduced there would be a saving on each order of £200 per day. These savings were, however, not to be made without some additional costs. Details of these, together with the activities where potential reduction in time was available, are given in Exhibit 2.

This case was written by Terry Hill (Templeton College, University of Oxford). It is intended as the basis for class discussion and not as an illustration of good or bad management. © AMD Publishing.

Exhibit 1   *Schedule of principal activities in the manufacturing task*

Activity	Place at which the activity would be completed	Normal duration (days)
1. Assemble component parts and subassemblies to make the final product	Redman	10
2. Prepare final drawings	Redman	5
3. Make subassemblies	Redman	15
4. Make and deliver component parts	Subcontractor	20
5. Obtain estimates for special parts from relevant subcontractors[1]	Redman	20
6. Accept quotation and place an order on the relevant subcontractor[2]	Redman	3
7. Issue appropriate standard components and/or materials:[2]		
Internally	Redman	2
To subcontractors	Redman	5
8. Deliver to customer	Redman	4

Notes
1. Includes the decision on whether or not to subcontract the work.
2. Both activities 6 and 7 can start as soon as activity 5 has been completed.

Exhibit 2   *Opportunities to reduce total lead times and associated costs*

Activity	(A)	(B)	(C)
1. Assemble component parts and subassemblies to make the final product	10	8	60
2. Prepare final drawings	5	5	–
3. Make subassemblies	15	11	80
4. Make and deliver component parts	20	11	160
5. Obtain estimates for special parts from relevant subcontractors	20	20	–
6. Accept quotation and place an order on the relevant subcontractor	3	3	–
7. Issue appropriate standard components and/or materials:			
Internally	2	2	–
To subcontractors	5	2	40
8. Deliver to customer	4	4	–

Column A – the normal number of days required to complete each activity as given in Exhibit 1.
Column B – the shortest possible time (days) needed to complete each activity.
Column C – the increased costs (£) incurred for each day's reduction achieved in completing an activity (that is, reducing the normal time taken as shown in column B towards the shortest possible duration, as shown in column C).

Southwest Airlines

Since its foundation in 1967, Southwest Airlines has gone from strength to strength. Slowly expanding from its base in Dallas, the company has built up its operation to the point where it now serves 34 airports, with 124 planes in operation. Now worth around $1.2bn, the company is continuing to expand.

When describing Southwest Airlines, it is difficult to avoid superlatives. The lowest costs, the lowest fares, the highest levels of asset usage, the best labour relations, the highest wages in the industry; Southwest has all these things and a lot more. And at first glance, the company seems to have achieved these goals by running counter to industry practice: there are no operations hubs, there is no emphasis on service extras (quite the contrary) and there has been no heavy investment in IT. Southwest seems to deliberately concentrate on markets that other airlines do not regard as important.

So why have they succeeded? It would be easy to portray Southwest Airlines as a maverick organization, and over the years a lot of attention has focused on its president, co-founder and inspirational leader, Herb Kelleher. But, while not denying Kelleher's influence in creating a strong and enduring company culture, it has to be said that there is more to this picture than the presence of a dynamic leader. Southwest Airlines is, and has been from the beginning, an organization founded on a few basic success principles. It is somewhat surprising to find that behind the dynamic, thrusting exterior and the lively company culture there is an organization that is innately careful, even cautious, and risk-averse. While embracing change, Southwest also avoids change for its own sake; there are no grand designs, no plans to grow outside their own niche market and, in an age when globalization seems to be the word on everyone's lips, absolutely no desire to go global. Change in Southwest Airlines is always focused on one or both of the company's two goals: cutting costs and increasing numbers of passengers.

Part of this careful approach can probably be traced to Southwest Airlines' origins. This is a company that almost never got off the ground at all, and for years since has fought a campaign of guerrilla warfare against its larger rivals.

This case study was written by Terry Hill (Templeton College, University of Oxford). It is intended as the basis for class discussion and not as an illustration of good or bad management. © AMD Publishing.

GUERRILLA WARFARE

For the first four years of its existence, Southwest Airlines was an airline in name only, fighting for its existence against rivals who wanted to kill it at birth. When Southwest first applied for certification in Texas in 1967 its competitors, especially Braniff and Texas International, opposed the application through the courts, on the grounds that the Texas market was already saturated and could not support another airline. The case dragged on for years and funds began to run low; Herb Kelleher, then working as Southwest Airlines' corporate lawyer, was eventually reduced to providing his services for free.

Finally, after winning their case in the US Supreme Court, Southwest Airlines was allowed to fly, and in 1971 their first aircraft finally left the ground. Kelleher and his colleagues had learned a valuable lesson. Rather than fight their larger, wealthier competitors head on, they would adopt a classic strategy of guerrilla war: be where the enemy is not.

Over the years, Southwest has systematically targeted airports and routes overlooked or badly served by other airlines. Steering clear of the large, overserved and congested 'hub' airports, Southwest's preferred ground has been the mid-sized airports of the Midwest and the Sun Belt, cities like Little Rock, Las Vegas, Phoenix and Sacramento. Targeting smaller airports in this way means Southwest can hit other airlines where they are vulnerable. Smaller airports tend to be poorly served by the other major airlines, and lack of competition means fares are high. They also tend to have less traffic and are less congested. As a result, Southwest can compete against its rivals by offering lower prices and faster service. For short-hop commuters (most of Southwest's flights are of less than an hour's duration), these are deciding factors when choosing a service. This strategy has worked. In 75–80 per cent of the airports where it operates, Southwest is the largest carrier in terms of numbers of passenger boardings.

One example shows how Southwest can not only enter a market but build it into a highly profitable one. When the airline first entered the Los Angeles–San Francisco area, rival airlines operating from the two major airports charged from $80 to $220 for a one-way ticket. Southwest established a route between the two metropolitan centres, not using the major airports but flying from the smaller, less crowded airports of Oakland and Burbank. Its one-way tickets were offered at a range from $29 to $59. The result? At the start of the year, Oakland–Burbank was the 200th busiest airline route in the USA in terms of numbers of passengers. By the end of the year, it had risen to twenty-first busiest. Elsewhere in the state, Southwest moved to a position of dominance in the airport of Sacramento, the state capital, and it now carries 20–40 per cent of all passengers in and out of Sacramento. In fact, throughout California, Southwest Airlines now carries over 15 per cent of all airline traffic within the state.

The traffic growth on routes served by Southwest illustrates another 'guerrilla war' aspect to Southwest Airlines. Marxists call it the mobilization of the masses; marketeers call it motivating people to take up the offer. Southwest Airlines does not just see itself as being in the airline business: it is in the transportation business. To that extent, it is not just competing with other airlines, but with other forms of transportation including trains, buses and private cars. By offering fares at competitive rates and a swift, efficient service, Southwest is encouraging travellers to switch from other forms of commuting. If the traffic figures are anything to go by, it is succeeding.

There is a third 'guerrilla war' aspect to Southwest Airlines' operations: the lack of a central base. Most airlines operate on a 'hub and spoke' principle, flying the bulk of their passengers between major hub airfields and then transferring them to feeder flights going on to smaller airfields closer to their destination. Theoretically, at least, this is the most efficient model of operation for an airline. However, hub operations require considerable concentration of resources; and if a hub operation goes wrong, there can be severe knock-on consequences. Hubs also represent a point where an airline can be particularly vulnerable to competition; losing market in a hub airport means the associated feeder traffic dries up as well.

Southwest, almost unique among major US airlines, uses a 'point to point' system. Its route diagram looks more like a spider web than the spokes of a wheel. Most of its flights are of short duration (the average is 55 minutes). Therefore, there is no defined centre of operations, no point where Southwest can be said to be particularly vulnerable. Anyone attempting to seriously challenge Southwest's dominance of the regional airline market would have to attack it on a number of points at once.

Such is the popularity of Southwest's service that cities all over the south-western USA frequently invite the company to begin operating services from their airports. Interestingly, few of these offers are taken up. Southwest is not an aggressive company in that it seeks to challenge its rivals at every opportunity. Instead, the company moves only when it can see a clear advantage. Entry into potential new markets is carefully considered. It has to be; Southwest's margins are wafer-thin, and it cannot afford to spend time on loss leaders building up a market. The company's policy is that a new route has to be profitable from day one.

But when Southwest does decide to go into a market, it goes in hard. New routes typically have a broad spread of flights, timed so that flights are never more than about an hour apart. Passengers are invited to turn up and go; with flights as regular as buses (for example, Southwest flies 78 times per day between Houston and Dallas), customers can travel at their convenience, not that of the airline. There are also no formalities of ticket reservation and collection; automatic ticket dispensers can process a credit card and dispense a ticket in under 20 seconds.

Within a short time after entry, Southwest Airlines comes to dominate the market, with affordable flights every few minutes acting like a magnet to pull passengers away from competing airlines. Many airlines would see this as suicidal, with large numbers of flights pushing up costs. Southwest looks at things differently; large numbers of flights allow fixed costs to be spread over a larger number of seats, while running costs are kept to the lowest level possible and are compensated for by the high volumes as Southwest becomes the airline of choice. This strategy also works, often dramatically. Five days after beginning flights from Little Rock, Southwest had scooped up 25 per cent of the market.

This strategy works not only as a means of breaking into new markets but as a means of deliberately attacking rivals. Coming down out of the hills, Southwest entered major airports like Phoenix and Chicago, attacking two competitors, America West and Midway, at their hubs. Unable to compete on price or service frequency, insufficiently flexible to switch their centres of operation, both rival airlines were driven into bankruptcy.

QUALITY WITHOUT FRILLS

Compared to many of its competitors, Southwest Airlines offers a distinctly no-frills service. There are no connections to other flights, and no baggage transfer. No meals are served. Seats cannot be reserved. The service resembles not so much an airline as a bus service with wings.

What the airline does offer is cheap, reliable, frequent service that gets passengers from A to B as fast as possible and with a minimum of fuss. There is a definition of quality which suggests that quality is determined by a product or service's fitness for the purpose for which it was designed. On that criterion, Southwest Airlines can be said to be offering a high-quality service.

One of the keys to the success of the service offering is the constant, continuous focus on the market. It has defined its niche with great success. Southwest's passengers are like commuters; they are going somewhere for a purpose, and they want to turn up and go without a lot of fuss or distractions. By not using travel agents to sell tickets, Southwest is able to cut out the agents' commissions and thus reduce its costs – and prices – still further. Because there are always plenty of planes flying and plenty of seats, no computerized reservation system is required; that is another cost saved, and another complication for the customer dispensed with. By operating a turn up and go policy, Southwest is able to offer what are on aggregate the cheapest fares of any airline in the USA. And, because it knows its market and knows that cheapness and reliability are what that market wants, Southwest has been continuously profitable since it first began operations. Not many airlines in the USA can say that.

Would this formula work in a different market? Possibly, but possibly not. Southwest knows its own market, and intends to stay there. Real strength, it is said, comes from knowing your own limitations and working within them. This is yet another area where Southwest Airlines would seem to have a lead over its rivals.

DOING MORE FOR LESS

Over and over again, the statistics show that Southwest wins by simply working harder than its rivals. Planes turn around faster, and operations has fewer staff. The average number of flights from each airport gate each day is 10½: the industry average is less than half that number. Southwest's planes spend an average of 11 hours a day in the air, compared with an industry average of eight.

Strategy is focused on keeping operations simple, efficient and inexpensive. Staffing levels are kept to the minimum to do the job. The same applies to infrastructure. IT, for example, is kept deliberately simple and functional. There is no elaborate computerized system needing support and maintenance. The ticket machines were designed by some Southwest Airlines staff members one evening in a bar in Denver, and the prototypes were subsequently built by them in their spare time, using off-the-shelf components.

The frequent take-offs and landings use more fuel and mean Southwest must pay more in landing fees, but still Southwest has the lowest cost per seat-mile of any major airline, less than half that of its major rival USAir. By working its assets harder – that is, by keeping its planes in the air for more hours per day – Southwest has been able to reduce its load factor (defined as the number of paying passengers as a proportion of total seats on each flight required to break even) to just 55 per cent; again, lower than the industry average. This, in turn, means that planes can fly with fewer passengers, meaning more flights can be offered, which increases the number of options available to customers... and so, on it goes.

Speed and flexibility are keys, operationally as well as tactically. Southwest Airlines ground staff can turn an aircraft around in 15 minutes; most airlines take up to an hour. Superbly trained, staff know their roles intimately, and the result, when a plane taxies up to the gate, is an efficient routine that might be envied by the pit crew of a Grand Prix racing team. The technical side is equally efficient. Southwest flies just one type of aircraft, the Boeing 737, and just three versions of that; spares and maintenance routines can thus be standardized, cutting down still further on costs. Southwest also operates new, fuel-efficient aircraft, rather than trying to make do with an ageing fleet as some of its competitors (unsuccessfully) have done.

LEADING BY EXAMPLE

There is no doubt that Herb Kelleher himself has been one of the critical factors in the success of Southwest Airlines. A brilliant lawyer, he is also a strategist and an inspiring leader of people. Colleagues comment on his personality, his mental brilliance, his sense of humour, his ability to gain the respect and trust of his employees. This is a man who can in the same day chair a board meeting and do an Elvis Presley imitation at a company party.

Kelleher believes in leading by example rather than by direction. If staff work overtime, he turns up in person to thank them. And once a quarter he spends a day in the front line: serving drinks with the cabin crew, working with the baggage handlers, selling tickets, getting to know both passengers and staff.

This is a tactic that can easily backfire; employees are notoriously adept at sniffing out when their bosses are 'slumming' in hope of ingratiating themselves with the staff. But Kelleher's genuine commitment is never doubted. Where his company is concerned, he wears his heart on his sleeve.

Evidence of this is easily come by. When the Gulf War drove fuel prices up, airline staff set up a payroll deduction programme to help offset the increased costs. The programme, set up without Kelleher's knowledge, quickly raised over $130 000. This was a tiny amount in terms of the overall fuel bill. In terms of the sacrifice made by staff, and as evidence of their commitment to the firm, this was an enormous gesture. Even the name of the programme – Fuel from the Heart – showed the strength of feeling.

Kelleher is a leader rather than a manager. Within the company, staff at all levels are given wide discretion in carrying out their duties; they know what is expected of them, and are free to work out how to give the best service possible. Kelleher's role is more fundamental; he is the central focus of the company's culture, the pillar around which that culture revolves.

A CULTURE OF COMMITMENT

Kelleher's commitment to the firm is one of the building blocks of the company's culture. The struggle for survival in the early days, and Kelleher's role in it, have passed into Southwest Airlines legend. Events like Fuel from the Heart have also become part of that legend.

History is important in Southwest Airlines. The walls of the corporate headquarters in Dallas are lined with memorabilia: old advertisements, photographs of employees and corporate events, even mannequins displaying examples of staff uniforms. The effect is something like a cross between someone's family photo album and a museum.

But this is not just reverence for the past; it is recognition that the past is something that can be built on.

Contradictions abound. Nearly all staff are union members; yet the company also has the highest rate of employee ownership of any major airline. As a result, Southwest also has one of the best records of any airline in terms of labour relations. The high levels of employee ownership – plus one of the highest pay levels in the industry – make for labour peace. Another superlative: Southwest also has the airline industry's lowest ratio of staff turnover. And when the airline does hire, it can take its pick from applicants; in one year, the company received over 60 000 applications for just 1400 jobs.

The lowest prices in the industry, the highest pay in the industry: can this be right? Clearly it can. Southwest Airlines gets by with fewer staff, half or less than the usual number of boarding agents and ground staff (and remember that ground staff turn planes around much faster than any other airline). But those staff work hard and are committed to their jobs, their customers and the company. One intriguing facet to the company's recruitment programme is the use of customers, frequent flyers, to join interview panels. By using customer input directly into the recruiting process, the company hopes to recruit staff whose personalities match customers' expectations.

Close personal contact with customers is another feature of the company's culture. In return, customers tend to be extraordinarily loyal. Frequent flyers get to know staff, not only cabin crew but also ground staff, and are often on first-name terms. Customers are encouraged to tell the company about their likes and dislikes, and they respond; about 5000 letters from customers are received every month, and all are read and answered.

THE QUIET REVOLUTIONARIES

The airline industry is notoriously fraught with perils. More than 100 airlines have gone bankrupt in the USA in the last decade, including some giants of the industry. Half the rest are desperately trying to stave off bankruptcy; few are consistently profitable.

Against this background, Southwest Airlines stands out. It does almost everything counter to industry logic; and its performance figures are equally contradictory to industry norms. Most compelling of all, the airline's managers have never got cocky. They continue to be fanatical about cutting costs; they continue to be devoted to their niche, and to their customers. They continue with a corporate culture that promotes heroes, and that involves customers and staff alike in constant innovation and improvement. They take nothing for granted.

Southwest Airlines has achieved something of a revolution in the airline industry in its region by not only taking passengers away from rivals but by growing markets and increasing passenger traffic overall. Quietly, working within their own self-defined limits, the company has become a major player in the airline industry. This is a company that embraces change: as Herb Kelleher has pointed out, the airline industry is full of change: how can it be passive when its major assets are moving at over 500 miles per hour? But above all, it is a company that knows itself, knows its customers, and is intent on doing whatever it takes to provide the best service possible.

The Ipswich Hospital NHS Trust

It all began after I attended a one-day course on 'Quality for Hospital Pharmacists' [explained the head of pharmacy at the Ipswich Hospital] This not only fired me up but also confirmed that the problems we faced and opportunities that we had were not, by any means, unique. But, more importantly, it provided a way forward. It offered an approach which was easy to explain and made sense in practice. Since that time all the staff have attended a similar programme, and continuous improvement teams have been formed. Initial work has started and progress in other areas is under way. We all believe this to be a sustainable initiative as it is core to the tasks and services we provide.

BACKGROUND

The Ipswich Hospital NHS Trust is a large hospital on the edge of the town with over 800 beds. In a typical 12-month period the hospital handles more than 100 000 in-patients and new out-patients, with follow up out-patients (existing out-patients seen a second, third and more times) totalling about a further 150 000 visits. There are currently nine medical directorates for which wards are allocated in line with in-patient demand (see Exhibit 1).

The Department of Pharmacy offers a range of core and non-core services to the rest of the hospital (see Exhibit 2). These are typically provided during weekdays between 8.30 am and 5.30 pm with an additional on-call, out-of-hours service. Increasingly some of the services are provided on the wards or in other areas within the hospital. This reflects the growing need to give specialist help at the point of provision, the growing range of drugs available with its attendant diversity and the subsequent need to recognize and control the side effects of and between different medications.

This case study was prepared by Terry Hill (Templeton College, University of Oxford) as the basis for class discussion and not as an illustration of good or bad management. © AMD Publishing.

Exhibit 1   *General hospital information*

Directorates		# wards and specialist units
General	Medicine	7
	Surgery	6
Elderly services		6
Maternity and gynaecology		6[1]
Trauma and orthopaedics		4
Paediatrics		2
Specialist surgery		1
Oncology and haematology		1
Anaesthetics		1[1]

Note

1. Includes a specialist unit.

THE CONTINUOUS IMPROVEMENT INITIATIVE

On his return from the one-day programme on 'Quality for Hospital Pharmacists', the head of pharmacy discussed the potential use of these ideas and approaches with the senior pharmacists in the department. The decision to undertake this initiative was agreed in principle and arrangements for all staff (pharmacists, technicians, assistants and clerical) to attend a similar day's training on quality were concluded. The costs for this training were met by all the major drug companies. To accommodate the need for releasing staff, three one-day courses were arranged with about one-third of the staff (see Exhibit 3) attending at a time.

'The initiative itself, its department-wide scope, and the fact that everyone went through the same one-day programme were a real help in getting everyone on board,' explained the head of pharmacy. 'In addition, there was one unforeseen advantage. This came from the need for everyone to co-operate in order to cope with the normal workload in the pharmacy department on the days when the programmes were held, as only two-thirds of the staff were here. This, in many ways, increased the level of co-operation so essential for the success of this type of initiative.'

The 'away days' as the one-day programmes were called, covered many aspects including mission statements, role of continuous improvement initiatives, useful techniques to use (for example, brainstorming), procedures to follow and how to go forward. On completing the away days the Continuous Improvement Programme (CIP) was officially launched with a steering group and four sectional improvement teams (SITs) to organize the programme, identify priorities and set up additional teams to address selected key areas where required (see Exhibit 4). To provide additional momentum, the pharmacist with specific responsibility for quality assurance was given the role as the CIP co-ordinator. The steering group comprised one member from each SIT, the head of pharmacy and the CIP co-ordinator.

The CIP co-ordinator was a member of each SIT in order to provide co-ordination across the whole activity. Membership of the SITs is given in Exhibit 3.

Exhibit 2   *Department of pharmacy information*

---

1. Core services – the following services are provided for all directorates:

	Activities	
Supply	■ in-patient ■ out-patient ■ discharge prescription	dispensing
	■ distribution ■ portering	
Procurement	■ purchasing ■ invoice reconciliation ■ clerical ■ financial data provision	
Clinical	■ drug information ■ prescription monitoring ■ patient counselling ■ stock 'top up' ■ ward stock control ■ therapeutic drug level ■ monitoring	
Manufacturing	■ licensable manufacturing ■ pre-packaged drugs ■ resuscitation box ■ provision ■ quality control ■ extemporaneous dispensing	

2. Non-core services – the following services are provided to some but not all the directorates:

■ ward round participation
■ directorate liaison role
■ self-medication scheme
■ centralized intravenous additive scheme (CIVAS)
■ cytotoxic drug reconstitution
■ education and training to nursing and other healthcare staff

---

The SITs' role was to undertake projects themselves, to identify potential areas for improvement and suggest a team to undertake the task. This would be chosen from all the staff within the department to reflect existing workloads, the CIP itself and the knowledge of and involvement in the issues under review.

Many of the improvements were simple in nature, easy to implement and yet provided a clear sign to all of what could be achieved. An example from each of the SITs is provided below to illustrate the type of problems reviewed and the improvements undertaken:

■ **Clinical services** – the provision of ward visits by pharmacists had developed over several years. This involved prescription monitoring, drug information provision, patient counselling as well as the drug supply function. However, on checking it was clear that the service provided to the wards varied according to the pharmacist

Exhibit 3   *Pharmacy department staff and section improvement team members*

1. Pharmacy department staff

Grade	# FTEs
Pharmacists	13.5
Technicians	16.0
Assistants	5.0
Clerical	3.5

2. Section improvement team (SIT) members

Clinical Services		Dispensing	
Pharmacy manager	1	Pharmacists	2
Pharmacists	2	Technicians	2
Technicians	1	CIP co-ordinator	1
CIP co-ordinator	1		

Manufacturing		Stores and Distribution	
Pharmacists	2	Pharmacy resource	
Technicians	3	Manager	1
CIP co-ordinator	1	Technicians	3
		CIP co-ordinator	1

Note

FTEs = full time (staff) equivalents.

involved. The team, therefore, drafted and agreed standards for these clinical pharmacy activities in order to raise standards and to allow performance to be audited.

■ **Dispensing** – the basic procedure within the dispensary is to dispense drugs for both in-patients and out-patients. The initial dispensing is typically undertaken by dispensing technicians with the final check completed by a pharmacist.

   As pharmacists working in the dispensary were involved in several tasks (for example giving advice to medical staff, ward staff and out-patients) the benches on which dispensed prescriptions were held awaiting a final check, very often became congested. The team suggested plastic trays to separate prescriptions and thereby simplifying checking. These trays were also colour coded to indicate the level of urgency involved and hence enable priorities to be set.

Exhibit 4   *Steering group and the four section improvement teams*

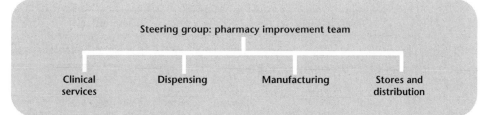

■ **Manufacturing** – staff rotate in the manufacturing department on a three-month basis. Some staff may only be seconded to this department once a year. In order to help refresh and/or update staff on the basic rules of 'good manufacturing practice' a document was compiled containing basic information and highlighting any procedures that have been recently revised.

■ **Stores and distribution** – out-of-date stock was analysed in terms of value and cause. As a result, stock levels of individual items were adjusted, a regular review of expensive items was installed and a weekly monitoring of any stock with a short shelf life was initiated.

REVIEWING PROBLEMS

As well as the one-day programmes on quality arranged for all staff, supporting documents were distributed and discussion sessions were held on what to do and the next steps to take. 'In the early days' explained the CIP co-ordinator, 'it was more necessary to give a lead on translating the ideas into a way of working and helping groups to begin identifying and resolving improvement ideas. Part of the approach was to categorize problems into one of three types (see Exhibit 5).

'To help start the programme the section teams chose Internal 1 type problems as they were easy to implement. The four examples given earlier were typical of these. However', explained the CIP co-ordinator, 'we have broadened the scope of the problem types to include more complex but, hopefully, more rewarding improvement opportunities. Two of these on which initial information has been gathered are to improve the effectiveness of the portering service, the procedures to handle the return of non-stock drugs to the pharmacy department and also the procedures used to recycle and redistribute them.

The porters' problem

A group was set up to look at the effective use of the porters' time. The team comprised one person from each of the four SITs, the two departmental porters and the CIP co-ordinator. Requests for items to be dispensed for in-patients are made in one of three ways:

■ stock items for wards where orders arrive in a black box via one of the porters
■ non-stock items for individual patients
■ medication requests for patients who have been discharged and will go back to their own home.

Exhibit 5   *Categories of problems*

Problem type		Description
Internal	1	Concerning only one section in the pharmacy department
	2	Concerning two or more sections in the pharmacy department
External		Involves one or more departments outside the pharmacy department

The latter two types of request come directly from a ward, via a ward pharmacist or in a ward's red bag via one of the porters.

Drugs and other items that wards require are distributed as follows. Requirements for these items are either requested by a ward or listed by pharmacists on their ward rounds:

- **Bulk fluid items** (for example, one litre bags of dextrose and sodium chloride) are taken by two technical assistants who go round from ward to ward in line with stated needs.

- **Black boxes** are used to transport stock items to wards and departments. These orders are given out in bulk form (that is not broken down into quantities for individual patients). These boxes are also used by a ward as a means of returning unused drugs to the pharmacy department.

- **Red bags** are used to transport non-stock orders and dispensed medication to and from wards. Several deliveries of red bags are made in a single day from the dispensary.

Requests for urgently needed drugs were often telephoned through and nursing staff would then bring down the relevant prescription and collect the drugs. Most prescriptions, however, were collected by the pharmacy department porters using the red bag system and distributed either later that day or on the next day. As a general rule, 15 per cent of all requests for 'urgent drugs' were required immediately, 80 per cent for delivery that day and 5 per cent, the following day.

Exhibit 6   *Tasks undertaken and service provided by the Department of Pharmacy porters*

General information

The Department of Pharmacy employs two porters whose prime task is to collect the empty boxes and bags used to distribute drugs around the hospital and to then deliver these back to the wards, theatres and special units when the required drugs have been dispensed.

Controlled drugs (for example, pethidine and morphine) and other drugs are handled in the same way except that controlled drugs have to be signed for on receipt by one of the nursing staff on the relevant ward.

The two porters share the wards. The split reflects the distances involved and size of the wards in terms of average number of patients and range of illnesses (for example, intensive care units *vis-à-vis* an orthopaedic ward).

All wards have one red bag and one black box which are marked with the name of the ward.

The daily routine

1. Collection of boxes and bags is completed between 08.00 and 09.30 each day. The pharmacy staff then dispense the requirements for the wards.
2. At around 10.45 one set of boxes is delivered, with the remaining wards being delivered from 11.30.
3. Any controlled drug requests are delivered in the morning rounds with additional requirements being met in the afternoon.
4. Between 13.45 and 14.30 the porters again collect the bags from the wards and the procedure in the morning is replicated with the afternoon deliveries (which are typically fewer) taking place between 16.00 hours and the end of the working day at 17.00.
5. In between the collecting and delivering parts of their task, the two porters undertake general work around the department and also make journeys to deliver the one-off requests for drugs and other medicines when available.

Exhibit 7   Fishbone analysis completed on 'why the porters' time is not used effectively'

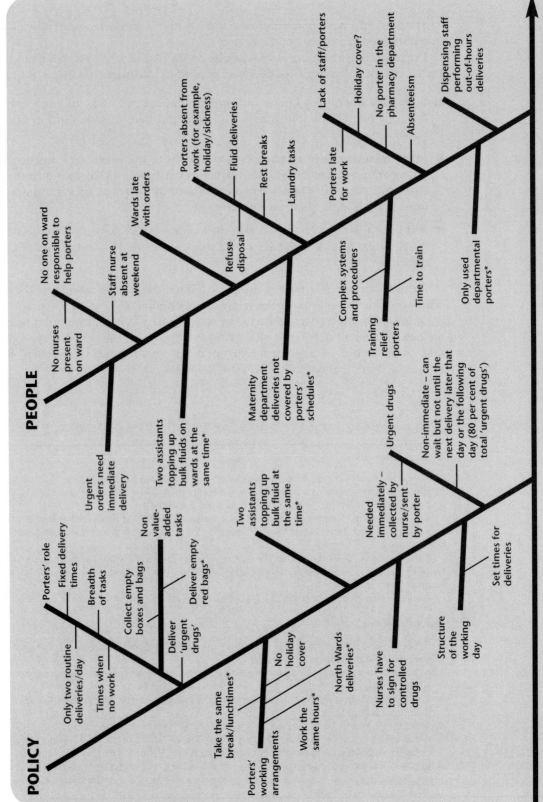

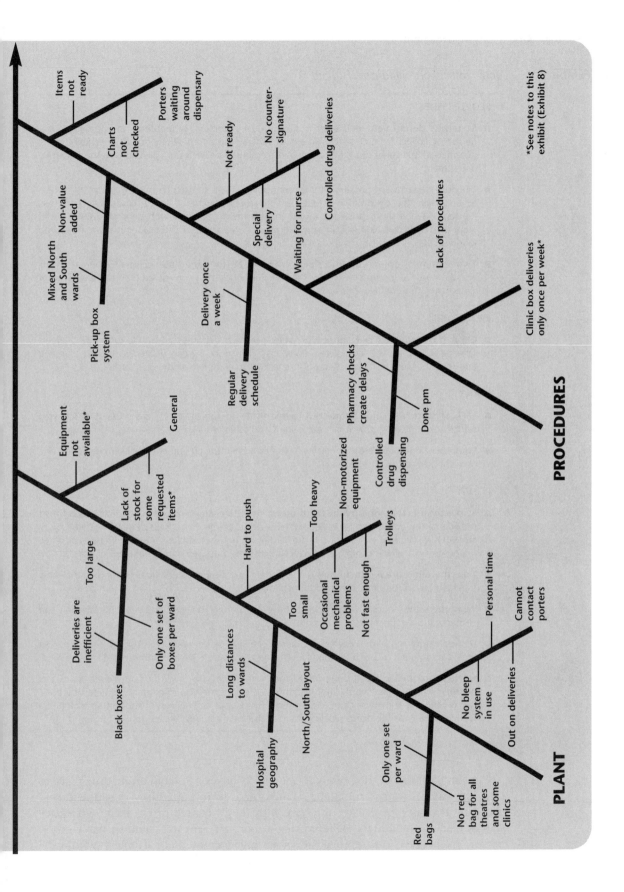

PLANT

Deliveries are inefficient

Black boxes
— Too large

Only one set of boxes per ward

Lack of stock for some requested items*

Equipment not available*

General

Hospital geography
— Long distances to wards
— North/South layout

Hard to push

Trolleys
— Too small
— Too heavy
— Occasional mechanical problems
— Non-motorized equipment
— Not fast enough

Red bags
— No red bag for all theatres and some clinics

Only one set per ward

No bleep system in use
— Personal time
— Cannot contact porters
— Out on deliveries

Pick-up box system
— Mixed North and South wards
— Non-value added

Charts not checked
— Items not ready

Porters waiting around dispensary

Regular delivery schedule
— Delivery once a week

Special delivery
— Not ready
— No counter-signature
— Waiting for nurse

Controlled drug deliveries

Pharmacy checks create delays

Controlled drug dispensing
— Done pm

Lack of procedures

Clinic box deliveries only once per week*

PROCEDURES

*See notes to this exhibit (Exhibit 8)

Exhibit 8   *Notes to fishbone diagram (Exhibit 7)*

---

1. PEOPLE ISSUES

■ **Maternity department deliveries not covered by porters' schedules** – the porters do not deliver or collect from this department as part of their normal schedule. Consequently, the pharmacy department does not schedule the timing of deliveries or collections to the maternity department.

■ **Only use department porters** – the current policy is only to use pharmacy department porters to undertake the distribution and collection service described in the case study narrative. Previously, when short, porters from other departments or those with general hospital duties were used but, due to a lack of knowledge and experience of the tasks this alternative is no longer used.

■ **Two assistants topping up bulk fluids on wards at the same time** – currently, two assistants visit the wards to top up or replenish the bulk fluid stocks. It is considered that only one assistant is necessary to undertake this task.

2. PROCEDURES

■ **Clinic box delivered only once per week** – certain deliveries are made just once a week, whereas all others are completed every day. The once-a-week deliveries present planning difficulties because of the existing tight schedules to complete all the daily tasks.

3. PLANT

■ **Lack of stock for some requested items** relates to the pharmacy department not having sufficient inventory so that it can meet ward and other requests on an 'on-demand' basis.

■ **Equipment not available** – on review it was found that the equipment (for example boxes) was only checked at the time of use.

4. POLICY

■ **Two assistants topping up bulk fluids on wards at the same time** – the pharmacy department provides a 'top-up' service for bulk fluid items (for example 1 litre bags of dextrose and sodium chloride) which does not require technical know-how to complete. Also, this task was noted under section 1 of this exhibit, entitled 'People Issues', but presenting a different dimension.

■ **Take the same break/lunchtimes** – the porters' work schedule includes starting at the same time and taking the same break and lunchtimes.

■ **Work the same hours** – as mentioned above, the porters' work schedules include starting and finishing at the same time.

■ **Deliver empty red bags** – porters occasionally have to deliver empty red bags to a ward so that the ward can put its waste into a bag for collection by a porter. There is only one red bag per ward.

■ **North Ward deliveries** – deliveries to the North Ward are made first. However, as clinical pharmacists visit these words later in the day, many of the dispensed items required by these wards were not known or completed in time for the porters' delivery. This then necessitated a second delivery as the drugs would fall under the 'non-immediate' category of 'urgent drugs'.

The principal role of the porters was to collect boxes/bags containing drug requests from the various wards and clinics, return these to the pharmacy department and distribute the boxes/bags later that day with the dispensed drugs inside. Pharmacy staff (including the porters) believed that a more efficient use could be made of the porters' working day 'to improve the service given to internal customers (within the department) and external customers (within the hospital)'. Over a period of several months data were collected on the work undertaken and service provided by the porters, details of which are given in Exhibit 6. In addition, a fishbone analysis was prepared showing where porters' time was not efficiently used, a copy of which is provided as Exhibit 7, with accompanying notes provided as Exhibit 8.

As explained earlier, in addition to the collection and delivery service provided by the portering staff, wards, theatres and other units need drugs and other medicines on a more urgent basis and, therefore, cannot wait for the next scheduled delivery by the porters. In these instances, nursing staff telephone the department with the request and later collect the items personally or they were delivered by other pharmacy staff as needs be. This happened throughout the day and as Exhibit 9 shows the average number of calls that led to a delivery/collection by other than the two porters. The figures given here are based on a representative four-week period.

Certain drugs in general use (for example, paracetamol, aspirin and some anti-biotics) were kept on each ward. The dispensing of these was handled and controlled by the nursing staff and requests to 'top up' levels were made on a regular basis.

'Although most requests are adequately dealt with by the current arrangements,' explained the lead person of the improvement team on this review, 'the nature of medi-cine and hospital service is that there are many requests and the demand from wards and other units is, understandably, ongoing through the day. [The data given in Exhibit 9 show the extent of the calls.] What we also discovered when analysing this "other" demand was that as many as 60 per cent of the requirements are not needed immedi-ately but cannot wait until the next porters' round. However, if we could increase the number of porters' deliveries then the intermittent demand would reduce noticeably.'

The lead person of this SIT then explained that although there is much pressure on the dispensing side of the department's work, fitting in an additional delivery schedule would not add to the total dispensing workload. 'In fact, the very opposite as "formal" demands would replace the "informal" nature of these requirements and at the same time take away some of the urgency associated with these requests', she reflected.

The problem of non-stock drugs

As explained earlier, frequently-used drugs are normally held by a ward as part of its own stock. Drugs with low and irregular demand are classed as non-stock drugs (that is, not part of the ward stock) and are issued as and when required. The non-stock drugs are generally referred to as 'yellow labels' which refers to their distinctive pack-aging. The procedure for handling yellow label items is now explained. During the daily ward visits, a pharmacist monitors each patient's drugs chart and requests the supply of any drug not routinely stocked by a ward. The number of tablets to be provided is determined on a sliding scale that reflects the nature of the ward. An initial provision is made and as the 'run out' time approaches all the non-stock items for a patient are topped up by a further 8 or 15 days according to each situation. When non-stock drugs are no longer required (for whatever reason), the bottles containing the residue stock are returned to the pharmacy department.

Because of the high cost of drugs directorates throughout the hospital were actively looking for ways to reduce costs. Recently, for example, the Elderly Services Direc-torate had approached the Department of Pharmacy to discuss how they may be able to reduce this element of cost.

Until 18 months ago, non-stock drugs returned to the pharmacy department would, where possible and where appropriate, be checked, recycled and reissued and

Exhibit 9   *Number of calls by nursing staff for urgently needed drugs and other medicines that were collected by nursing staff or delivered by Department of Pharmacy staff when a porter was not available*

Time of day	# calls by nursing staff
0830–0930	3.1
0930–1030	6.9
1030–1130	10.0
1130–1230	10.2
1230–1330	29.5
1330–1430	22.0
1430–1530	16.4
1530–1630	6.6
1630–1730	32.4
1730 onwards	26.8

the directorate in question credited with the full savings. Loosely-packed tablets (that is, those not individually blister packed but dispensed in a bottle) would, for reasons of patient safety, invariably be incinerated, whereas those in blister packs would invariable be recycled and reissued. However since that time, growing workloads and staff reductions had meant that all non-stock drugs (whether loosely packed or in a blister pack) returned were now incinerated.

To find out the size of the yellow label returns in terms of drug costs and the time involved for a pharmacy technician to check and restock the returns, an analysis of all non-stock returns was made over a four-week period. This also involved reintroducing the practice of checking and where possible, recycling the drugs in question. Details of this study are given in Exhibit 10, and these data provide a representative sample of the returns made. Based on the yellow labels returned from five of the wards in the Elderly Services Directorate and whether or not they could be recycled, the annual value of all non-stock tablets returned for the whole hospital was estimated at about £45 000.

To reduce the cost of yellow label returns the team recognized the need to address both causes and symptoms. The reasons were identified by the elderly care standards group working with the pharmacy continuous improvement team selected to address this problem. They identified the following reasons why yellow labels were returned:

■ patient discharged
■ drugs discontinued
■ patient's death
■ duplicate supply on the ward
■ patients transferred to another ward, but the drugs were not sent with them.

In order to identify the causes, the nursing staff recorded the reason why any yellow label tablets were returned. The results are shown in Exhibit 11.

The analysis completed also examined the issues behind each of these reasons, the results of which are given in Exhibit 12.

Exhibit 10   *An analysis of a representative sample of all the yellow label returns from five elderly care wards during a typical four-week period*

The follow details are for a representative sample of all yellow label returns received from five elderly care wards during a typical four-week period – a total of 20 days.

1. The time involved by pharmacy technician staff includes a 15 per cent uplift to cover starting and finishing the procedure and normal rest allowance.
2. The total value of the drugs recycled in this period was 68 per cent of all the drugs returned. The other 32 per cent were considered not suitable for reuse and were incinerated for reasons of safety.
3. On several days in this four week period there were no returns recorded. The sample below was chosen to reflect typical recycled yellow label values and the time needed to recycle these items by a pharmacy technician.

Day # in the the four-week period	Yellow labels			Pharmacy technician time to recycle the item (minutes)
	Total # returned	Recycled items only		
		#	Total value (£s)	
1	13	11	66.49	12
	7	7	25.03	14
	9	5	21.04	18
	10	10	15.16	12
5	20	8	44.04	13
	7	5	9.52	10
	18	14	50.64	15
8	7	4	7.97	6
	14	13	24.74	18
	4	1	0.49	4
	15	14	33.40	35
	2	2	6.19	12
10	12	6	48.65	9
11	7	1	0.63	15
	2	0	–	2
	6	5	18.18	14
	5	3	7.64	5
	8	7	43.79	7
16	26	9	17.19	40
	8	2	2.17	6
	9	3	1.37	16
	6	1	0.10	8
20	38	26	125.25	55
	22	13	47.25	50
	17	10	12.40	15
	31	28	187.56	65

The CIP review

'Although it is not many months ago since this programme started, the results are very encouraging. Staff involvement is high and we have attempted to keep a "sensible" level of activity to maintain interest and yet create a manageable load. The porters and yellow label analyses', explained the head of pharmacy, 'are an important departure as it is spreading the initiative across the department and the hospital at the same time. This not only presents an opportunity for larger savings but also helps to further integrate the pharmacy department's activities into the hospital as a whole and link us more firmly with our external customers and their needs. Here's hoping', he concluded, 'that the latest two initiatives will yield sizeable and realizable results. That would be a big boost for us all.'

Exhibit 11   *Reasons why yellow labels were returned*

Reasons		Per cent of total
Discontinued use of drug		39
Patient	discharged	41
	died	9
	transferred	6
Duplicate supply		1
Other		4
Total		100

Exhibit 12   *Reasons why yellow labels are returned*

Discussion around the reasons why yellow labels are returned provided the following information:

1. **Drugs discontinued** – this was always the result of a doctor's decision to change a patient's drugs for medical reasons.

2. **Patient discharged** – when patients were discharged, the non-stock drugs that they were taking would always be returned to the pharmacy department. The hospital specialist responsible for a patient would then prescribe the same or some of the same items to take home. The reasons for this procedure was to ensure control and to avoid patients taking medicines which may have been appropriate during their hospital stay, but not in the post-hospital phase of their treatment. It was considered that because of the risks the associated need to control drug prescription could not and should not be changed.

3. **Patient transferred** – this is where a patient was transferred from one ward/unit to another inside the hospital.

4. **Duplicate supply** – drugs already held on the ward, but their availability had not been identified.

5. **The sliding scale** – the normal procedure was to issue a further 8 or 15 days' supply of a non-stock drug 2 days before the current supply would be used up. The choice of 8 or 15 days was based on a 1- and 2-week timescale.

The Turn of an Unfriendly Card

First State Bank of California thought it could relocate its centre for producing credit cards and update its technology at the same time, improving efficiency and saving costs. Instead, they ended up with cost overruns, long delays and an even longer list of angry customers. What went wrong?

It started off as a relatively simple cost-cutting measure. First State Bank's (FSB) credit card production centre is where cards are encoded and embossed (see Exhibit 1) and then dispatched in line with agreed schedules. The centre was to be relocated from its existing premises in the Los Angeles suburb of Burbank to a less expensive location in Pasadena. At the same time, executives in charge of credit card services decided to introduce new and more efficient card processing technology. It all seemed quite sensible; combine the move with the new technology and get all the pain over with in one go. But things did not quite work out that way.

First, and unforeseen, a problem of potential credit card fraud arose just as the move was about to start. Measures were at once taken to deal with this. The high profile nature of credit card fraud and the large and growing size of associated losses meant that additional controls were introduced and tight monitoring of every step in the service delivery system was the order of the day. These actions were essential and

Exhibit 1 *The tasks of embossing and encoding*

Cards in corporate colours and printed with corporate logos and information such as 'valid from', 'expires end' and, on the reverse side, authorized signatory statements are received by the production centre from suppliers in this form. The centre then embosses and encodes the cards in line with its customers' requirements. The embossed data (the raised printing on a card) cover the account number, relevant start and end dates and the user's name. Inserting data such as the customer's name, account number and other coded details onto the magnetic strip is known as encoding.

This case was written by Terry Hill (Templeton College, University of Oxford) It is intended as the basis for class discussion and not as an example of good or bad management. © AMD Publishing.

fast detection was paramount. But the increased security lengthened the time it took, resulted in increased backlogs and caused delays in issuing cards to customers. Customer complaints streamed in.

Staff and managers at the centre were still trying to pick up the pieces when the move began. Delays caused by the move were compounded by further delays when the new technology developed unexpected glitches.

Senior executives at FSB noted the problem and tried to find out what was going on. Unfortunately, the management information system (MIS) had dried up. The project team to manage the move included two FSB managers, but the head of the team, an outside consultant on a short-term contract, had simply not established formal MIS reporting procedures. Regular project meetings were the key link between the project team and senior management, but, because in the early stages all seemed to be going well, senior managers had stopped attending these. By the time the situation reached critical point, the gap between solution and problem was too wide to bridge by a single span – effective control had been gradually eroded.

Once the project team leader's contract expired and he left the project, FSB managers were able to identify the issues and problems fully, take action and reassert control.

Eventually, the backlog cleared and the centre was able to operate as forecast. In the meantime, 18 months of stress had resulted in unhappy staff and even more unhappy customers. The full cost of FSB's cost-cutting measure is only just beginning to emerge.

MOVING FORWARD

'Venerable' and 'trustworthy' are words sometimes considered synonymous with FSB. It is indeed one of California's oldest banks, founded during the gold rush days of the nineteenth century; reputedly, its first deposit was a sack of gold dust from diggings in the hills above Sacramento. But FSB has moved with the times. Early this century it set its sights on becoming the leading commercial bank in California and although it has never quite overtaken its rivals, it now has 1100 branches and is the fourth largest deposit-taker in the state.

Some years ago, the company began the process of moving its headquarters from San Francisco to Los Angeles, to be, as bank President Gerry Wilcox put it, 'closer to the centre of the action'. The move was phased over three years, with the transferral of credit card services to a location in Burbank. The process went smoothly – indeed, more smoothly than anticipated. The move complete FSB was ready, in the words of its President 'to begin competing in the twenty-first century'.

The move was a success, and FSB began closing the gap on its larger rivals. One area where FSB was particularly successful was in the marketing of credit cards. Although the United States already has an enormous number of credit card issuers, FSB started to carve a place for itself by offering lower interest rates and service charges, targeting some previously untouched affinity group markets, and introducing a wide range of personalized cards. Aggressive direct sales campaigns encouraged people to switch from their present card to an FSB Visa or Mastercard, and these too had some success.

However, even though the move had gone more smoothly than anticipated, the costs of the move had been greater than forecast. The top brass at FSB began looking at cutting costs. Among other measures, Wilcox ordered a review of FSB's property portfolio. High up on the list of expensive properties came the credit card production centre's location in Burbank. FSB's vice-president in charge of operations, Juan Antonio Perez, instigated a search for new premises and came up with a suitable site in Pasadena, still in the Los Angeles area and within a reasonable distance of group headquarters. The owners of the Pasadena site were willing to do a straight swap, their building for the Burbank location plus a favourable price adjustment. Within a few months the paperwork was signed and the move scheduled.

SECURITY AND EFFICIENCY

As it happened, the decision to move came at a time when credit card services (CCS) was undergoing a number of changes. Several new products were coming on-stream, including two that marketing classed as crucial to its product strategy. Also, and again as a cost-cutting measure, CCS was planning staff reductions in response to FSB's corporate directive. Operating units were required to make reductions, and the production centre was no exception, having been set a target for reductions from 56 to 37 staff over 18 months.

New, highly automated credit card production technology had also become available, that required only one person to handle all stages of producing a new card. As a consequence the production centre managers were confident that they could cut staff costs and increase productivity at the same time. The centre produced around 10 million cards annually and was currently running at full capacity given its existing technology. According to the targets set by the marketing plan 14 million cards a year would be needed in the near future.

Until 18 months ago, all the centre's customers were internal (that is, within FSB and it subsidiaries). To increase sales revenue, marketing proposed to sell the card preparation capability to other companies outside FSB. Since then, this segment has grown rapidly and been an increasingly important factor in overall sales revenue growth. In many ways the new, non-FSB customers were similar to the centre's traditional customers wanting fast delivery, the ability to meet the specification of each card and service system security. Although price was a factor, it was more so with non-FSB customers. But even here, it was not a key criterion for gaining and retaining contracts. As Juan Perez put it. 'We're in the credit card age where you can't really survive in modern day America without one. No credit card in this country and you're like a fish out of water. What we aim to offer our customers is security and efficiency. We have to get cards to our customers safely and as quickly as possible'.

Juan Perez admits that card services managers were initially unhappy when told of the proposal to relocate the production centre. Card services executives were called in for a meeting with himself and Gerry Wilcox shortly after the Pasadena site had been chosen. At that time the senior card services manager had expressed reservations about the effect the move would have on the new product launch and on the downsizing and new technology initiatives. However, they were assured that the move would be phased, there would be a full month to test the new premises before the move would begin and full training in the new technology would be provided. The department would 'barely feel the bump' was the way it was explained. In fact, by introducing the new technology at the same time as the move, the department would be able to get all its transition problems over in one go.

The business case for the move seemed unanswerable. The new building would cost $2.3m to fit out, and the hardware and software installation for the new card-processing technology would require another $4.2m. Further costs, particularly for IT investment, were estimated at $100 000 and severance payments to redundant staff would cost around $250 000. The total investment required would be just under $7m.

Against this, FSB could expect to save in rental, maintenance and staff costs around $9m in the first three years and not including the benefits of the agreed price adjustments on the buildings. Furthermore, the new premises (which provided better facilities, particularly in terms of security and cabling) and the new technology offered opportunities to develop further income streams, by providing additional services to both internal and external customers. The proposition was presented to card services as 'an answer to their prayers'; they could bring in the new technology, cut staff, develop new products and new customers all at once. All they had to do was move premises.

An agreement was reached over the timing of the move; the first phase would start in July of the following year, and the move would be made over four months on a product-by-product basis. Card services began discussions with the human resources department over laying-off redundant staff, and Perez gave the bank's property services arm the go-ahead to close the deal on exchanging premises.

BAD DAY IN BURBANK

A month before the proposed move, card services manager, Frank Dexter, wrote in a memo to Gerry Wilcox:

> We have detected a very large increase in reports of lost cards. There was a slight rise in March and then a more pronounced one in April. Last month we received reports of 345 lost cards, the highest ever recorded. Looking at the dollar value of purchases made on these cards at the time they are reported stolen, I think we must conclude that we are dealing with a serious case of fraud.
>
> Subject to your approval, I am contacting the postal service authorities and also the police. I will delay this if it is deemed necessary to give public relations time to prepare a statement.

Gerry Wilcox immediately telephoned Frank and gave permission for the authorities to be contacted. He also set up a special audit team to conduct an investigation inside card services.

In the end, the source of the fraud was never detected. The special audit team, the post office and the police all drew blanks. To be sure, however, the special audit team recommended that double-checking procedures should commence at once throughout the card-issuing process, particularly in the production centre at Burbank. This recommendation was approved just a week before the first phase of the move to Pasadena was due to begin.

The impact on the production centre was immediate. Double-checking meant that two people had to check information at certain key stages of card production. For security purposes (that is, to avoid collusion), they could not always be the same two people at each stage. Carefully designed workflows were interrupted and productivity dropped like a stone. Within three months, delivery time for cards had increased from three to four days to three to four weeks.

Customer complaints mounted. So did complaints from staff. Already concerned about the move, unsure about the new technology and knowing that some of their colleagues were due to be laid off, employees at the production centre found their work patterns severely disrupted. Some felt that the increased security measures reflected on their own honesty. Morale declined, and the centre's operations manager reported an increase in sick days taken by staff.

'I am convinced', Frank Dexter says now, 'that we could have managed the problem caused by the additional security checks. We could even have managed them in conjunction with the move and the introduction of new technology. The problem is, we never knew what was going to happen in time to take preventive action. We were always two steps behind.'

THE MAN FROM INEX

To oversee the move to Pasadena and the introduction of the new systems, FSB had established a three-person management team. Two of the team were FSB managers, Carrie Burnett from card services and Alex Orloff from operations. The team leader, Tom Maxwell, was an outside consultant from the consultancy firm Inex. He had been contracted for a year to plan and oversee the move and its implementation. Inex was an experienced consultancy company that had played an important role in the relocation of FSB's head office from San Francisco to Los Angeles. However, Tom Maxwell had never worked with FSB before.

Progress reports were logged onto the FSB management information system, but there was also a project group set up to oversee these developments. This consisted of the three team members, Frank Dexter, and four other senior managers (three from card services and one from IT). This project group had been meeting with the management team on a monthly basis since the management team was first established. Dexter chaired the meetings initially, but Maxwell did most of the talking. He had, as Carrie Burnett later recalled, 'a unique management style, at least in my experience. He was very confident and gave the impression that everything was well under control. He was well-spoken and his manner was always reassuring. He reminded me a bit of a doctor dealing with a patient.'

Nine months after the recommendation was approved the detailed plans for the move were in place. Project meetings were rapidly becoming a formality. The project did not seem particularly difficult to start with and was going smoothly; Maxwell was confident that everything would take place according to plan. Like Burnett, the senior managers took his assurances at face value and stopped showing up for meetings, preferring to pull reports off the MIS. Dexter himself was becoming increasingly preoccupied with the fraud issue and was content to leave the move in the hands of Maxwell and his team.

MORE DELAYS

The technology supplier for FSB's credit card production centre was – and still is – Amcard International, one of the leading suppliers of this kind of technology. Many of the leading banks used Amcard, and there was a long relationship between the company and FSB. Tom Maxwell, explained Frank Dexter, was not exactly told to use

Amcard as the supplier, 'but he was guided in that direction. After all, we already knew about the new technology, and its capabilities. It fitted our plans.'

With existing technology, the different steps in card production were performed at different work stations, each with a particular piece of equipment and a member of staff required to operate it. Amcard's new AM-9, however, combined all these steps into one process carried out by a single machine – and operated by a single member of staff. Fewer machines were required, less floor space was need and fewer staff were necessary.

Amcard was contracted to supply 12 of the new AM-9s, and the software required to operate them. The original contract was to have been signed nine months before the move. This would have allowed a period in which the software would be tested. The plan also included time for staff to be trained on the new processes. In this way the new technology could be phased in – as each team was trained appropriate card production orders would be switched to the new site and existing equipment closed down.

Six months before the planned move, however, the contract had still not been signed. Amcard, anxious that the deal might be about to fall through, contacted Tom Maxwell and was assured that all was well. Early in January he met with Amcard's local managers and signed the contract. Although Amcard agreed to reduce its lead times slightly, the planned delivery was now October, some three months after the relocation would start.

'The first I heard of this', says Frank Dexter, 'was in early July.' It was just after the fraud issue had been reported to the police and Dexter, preoccupied, passed an offhand comment to Burnett during a meeting on a separate issue that he was looking forward to seeing the new machines. Burnett 'looked stunned. She didn't say anything, nothing at all.'

'Of course I didn't say anything', says Burnett. 'What could I say? Tom had reported the delay at the project board meeting, but Frank wasn't there. He'd also logged the report onto the MIS. I assumed Frank had made a mistake.' But in fact, Tom Maxwell had never directly reported the delay to Dexter or any other senior manager. Confident of his own abilities, he had assumed he could manage the delay and still bring the project in on time.

HOW DOES THIS WORK, AGAIN?

By mid-July, part of the plan was rolling out – and part of it was not. Amcard, as per contract, began conducting two-day training sessions on site in Burbank, with a demonstration machine that had been set up for the purpose. Tom Maxwell gave the okay for the training sessions to go ahead, despite the backlog of work that was already building up thanks to the security checks – and despite the fact that the staff would not now be using the new machines for real for another three months.

There were also complaints that the training was not detailed enough. Whereas formerly each staff member was only responsible for a part of the production process, now they were required to manage the whole thing. It was not only the technology that was unfamiliar, it was the job itself.

Predictably, by the time staff were settled into their new office in Pasadena, they had forgotten most of what they learned. The old machines had to be moved over from Burbank and crammed in as best was possible in floor space that had been designed to accommodate the AM-9s; then they had to be taken out and the Am-9s installed in a rush. There was no time for any more training; the backlog of card orders had now reached critical proportions, and staff were told they would have to learn 'on the job'. Amcard provided a technical representative on site for the first week, and a telephone helpline after that; but even with this assistance, production was slow for the first month.

PAPER CHASE

One final misunderstanding compounded the situation. The AM-9s, in addition to processing the cards themselves, also processed the paper templates. Marketing had advised that five different templates were needed, and the project team had proceeded on this assumption. They had then turned to the technical specification and looked at the paper required for the templates. Amcard's recommendation was to use paper of 110–120 grams weight. But paper was expensive, and costs were overrunning. Burnett and Orloff agreed with Maxwell's suggestion that they save money by using a lighter weight of paper. They settled on 90 grams – not so much lighter, it was thought, to make a difference – and ordered one million sheets (about one months' supply) to be ready for the rollout of the new machines. Then marketing dropped a bombshell. The templates arrived in late September, about two weeks before the delivery of the new machines. Instead of the promised five, there were 17. Staff had just two weeks to learn these and how to use them before putting them into production.

Within the first week of operation with the AM-9s in October, the scale of the error over paper weight became clear. The paper was too light to feed properly through the machines. The form feeds tended to scoop up two or three sheets at a time, which would then slip and jam inside the machines. On the first day of operation, machine downtime averaged 40 per cent. With help from the Amcard technical rep, staff managed to reset the form feeds, but the paper continued to slip and jam. As well as lost time there was high wastage.

By the first of November, the project team gave in. The remainder of the million sheets were scrapped and the costs written off. A further million sheets of 120 gram paper were ordered, with a request for emergency delivery. Another $80,000 had been lost.

LATE, LATE, LATE

By mid-November, even with proper paper and the machines working as designed, production had dropped to 25 000 cards per day, exactly half that required. Back in Burbank office, the complaints hotline was receiving over 100 calls a day, from branches and from customers, concerning delays to cards. According to the company's complaints procedure, each complaint had to be written out and then faxed to the relevant department. Carrie Burnett recalls seeing the faxes 'like a blizzard' in the Pasadena office, coming in faster than they could be dealt with. Responding to the complaints took much time and contributed to more delays.

However, life started to become easier. The Inex contract with Tom Maxwell expired at the end of November and was not renewed. Carrie Burnett took over as manager of the production centre, and was given full access to whatever resources she needed to get the situation under control. Alex Orloff stayed on as her deputy, and was able to persuade IT to assign them technical staff on a full-time basis until the problems could be sorted out. By working overtime, staff have now managed to clear most of the order backlog; waiting times are down to about 10 days, and production has reached 90 per cent of optimum. Frank Dexter believes the centre will be back on track in another three months, and ready then to carry on with plans for expansion.

But what price has had to be paid? The forecast cost savings from the move have been largely eroded. The potential is there for productivity gains and new product introductions; that part of the plan, at least, was merely put back in time. But the real cost, in disgruntled customers, remains to be counted. In the end, just how badly FSB will be affected will have to be measured by the number of customers who defect to other card issuers – or the number who, confronted with one of FSB's slick marketing presentations, hold up their hands and say, 'Thanks, but no thanks!'

Tile Products plc

Tile Products plc is a small company which makes fire-retardant ceiling tiles. The tiles are plaster mouldings made to any size or pattern, but the standard size is 2 feet square and the company offers a range of 10 patterns. Any customer requiring either a tailor-made size or pattern, would be charged the setting-up costs which entail the production of a one-off mould from which the tiles would then be produced.

After the initial work by the founder of the company, Ben Graham, upon whose ideas the tile is based, sales had begun to increase over the past three to six months. Sales for the first 12 months of business and the first six months of this second year are given in Exhibit 1. Ben Graham is currently solely responsible for sales besides having overall control over production and the financial aspects of the business.

Exhibit 1   *Tile sales in the first 18 months of business*

	Year 1	Year 2					
		Jan	Feb	Mar	Apr	May	Jun
Standard tiles							
Classic	2 050	–	1400	–	–	–	–
Georgian	2 850	–	–	600	650	–	400
Victorian	3 800	1000	–	–	250	1000	500
Modern	2 400	–	–	800	–	400	100
Simplicity	2 850	–	–	900	–	300	300
Scandinavian	1 600	–	500	–	–	–	900
American	–	–	–	–	–	400	600
Scottish	–	–	–	–	500	700	300
Floral	2 800	700	–	–	–	–	600
Heraldic	750	–	100	–	300	200	300
Customer's own design	1 000	–	–	–	200	400	–
Total	20 100	1700	2000	2300	1900	3400	4000

Notes

1. All figures are in number of tiles produced.
2. Some designs (for example Heraldic) tend to be ordered as part of a ceiling pattern rather than as the main design.
3. Once moulds are available then tile process production time is the same for each design. There are some minor set-up times involved, but these are of little significance.
4. American and Scottish designs were not introduced until April of year 2.
5. Taking into account public and other holidays, employees work for 46 weeks of each year.

Source: company records.

This case was written by Terry Hill (University of Oxford). It is intended as the basis for class discussion and not as an illustration of good or bad management. © AMD Publishing.

Exhibit 2   *Existing shopfloor layout*

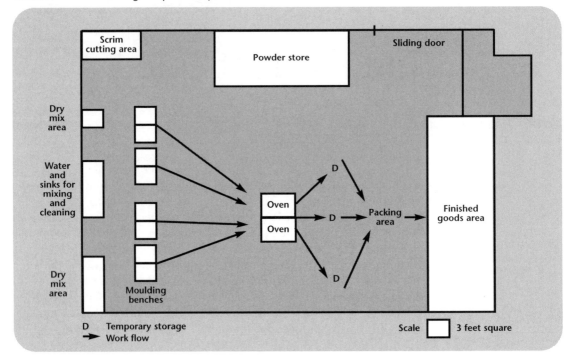

PRODUCTION

Arthur Marshall, the production supervisor, is responsible for the day-to-day control of production. He has been with the business from the early days. As output requirements increased, the company had employed two additional moulders – Ian Yates and Maurice Coles – who were now both fully trained. For at least half his time Arthur Marshall does the production jobs of either moulding or packing besides helping, as do Ian and Maurice, to unload materials and load up dispatches.

The working week is from Monday to Friday, 8.00 am to 4.30 pm with half an hour for lunch. If overtime is worked it is usually in the evening, but occasional Saturday working is arranged depending upon order volumes and delivery requirements.

The layout of the factory is shown in Exhibit 2 and the method of working is described in Exhibit 3. Although some tiles are made-to-stock, production tends to follow sales orders because of the lack of information on sales patterns and volumes. It is anticipated, however, that once sales have reached a higher level, then production will be against sales forecasts for each pattern type.

Exhibit 3   *Current methods of working*

Moulding

A moulder mixes the dry materials in the appropriate area, moves to the water sink and completes the mixing stage. He returns to the moulding bench and pours the mixture into the mould. He then goes to the scrim cutting area, cuts scrim (a synthetic gauze to help bond the tile) to the appropriate size and returns to the moulding bench. He places the scrim into the mould and then puts down the

(Continued)

Exhibit 3   *Current methods of working (cont'd)*

lid of the mould. The required pattern is in the mould base and the scrim, therefore, is placed in what will be the back of the tile. At the end of the initial drying cycle, the tile is lifted from the mould, carried to the oven and hung by lugs which form an integral part of the back of the mould. The moulder returns to the mould, cleans off any excess plaster and then repeats the process. The normal practice is to cut two or three pieces of scrim at a time and place them near at hand. This saves a journey to the scrim cutting area.

Typically a moulder works three moulds and very occasionally four. A person working all the time on moulding makes, on average, 60 tiles in an eight-hour day. In addition, the moulders and Arthur Marshall unload and load vehicles besides packing tiles once they have been baked in the ovens.

Drying
The drying process is in two stages. The initial drying or setting takes place in the mould as described above. This takes 15 minutes from pouring the plaster mixture into the mould to the time for lifting. The second drying stage takes place in the ovens. There are currently two fixed-position ovens each of which has a capacity to hold 90 tiles. When the oven has a full load (although occasionally this part of the process is started with a part-load due to delivery requirements) the heat is brought up to the required temperature of 75 °C and the tile is baked for eight hours.

Packing
When the tile has been oven-dried, it is allowed to cool for a minimum time of 30 minutes. Then the ovens are unloaded and the tiles are stacked on edge between the ovens and packing area (see Exhibit 2). When the tiles have accumulated or delivery requirements are pressing, each tile is packed individually and then four tiles are packed into an outer carton. The packed tiles are then stored in the finished goods area, by pattern, and up to three outer cartons high (the cumulative weight restricts storage height).

Dispatch
Sales orders are met from stock (unless it is a special tile and then these are made only to order) and the finished goods are stored in such a way as to facilitate stock rotation and so ensure that the older tiles are dispatched first.

Technical note
The materials used in making fire-retardant ceiling tiles are relatively fast setting which precludes the opportunity to make larger mixes than is the present practice. Consequently, each moulder may only mix sufficient for one moulding cycle which ensures that the required technical specification is achieved.

COMPANY PERFORMANCE

Following a loss in the first year, the position has improved by the end of the first half of year 2 (see Exhibit 4). Sales for the second half of year 2 are running at a level slightly higher than in the first six months and the company has submitted tenders for some very large orders. Ben Graham's immediate concern is production capacity: a good moulder would produce, under current methods of working, a maximum of 60 tiles per day.

Ever since the start of the business Ben Graham's attention had been directed towards the product. It had been necessary to refine the fire-retardant qualities of the tiles and improve the other aspects of tile quality while trying to reduce the costs of raw materials. Considerable steps have been achieved in this direction and arrangements are now in progress to get the appropriate certification for the fire-retardant properties of this newly designed tile. Once this has been achieved, Graham's aim is to reduce the price per tile in line with the material savings available with the new design. This would enable the company to increase sales by achieving greater market penetration with the lower price tile.

Exhibit 4 Information on the first 16 months of business

	Year 1	Year 2
Sales (£)		
Standard designs	56 000	43 900
Customers' designs	3 600	2 490
	59 600	46 390
Direct costs (£)		
Materials	13 800	9 700
Moulding labour	15 550	8 700
Packaging	3 800	2 660
Packing labour	1 200	700
Dispatch	2 000	1 400
	36 350	23 160
Manufacturing profit	21 250	23 230
Indirect costs		
Salaries	15 100	7 950
Mould and other manufacturing costs	3 500	2 100
Other overhead costs	7 100	4 000
	25 700	14 050
Net profit (loss)	(4 450)	9 180

Notes
1. 'Customers' designs' sales include the costs of moulds. These were for year 1 £600 and for the first six months of year 2, £470.
2. Salaries include the owner and 50 per cent of the supervisor.
3. Year 2 figures are for the first six months only.
4. The average selling price of a tile in year 1 was £3.00. In year 2, the selling price had averaged £3.28 and there had been some increase in direct and other costs.
5. Because of the relatively short life of a mould, these costs are treated as revenue expenditure.

Source: company records.

STUDY OF OPERATIONS METHODS

With the increase in sales of existing tiles and the anticipated uplift in orders following a decrease in price as described above, Ben Graham had requested a study of operations methods in order to establish the facilities and labour required for these higher volumes. The results of this preliminary investigation are given in Exhibit 5.

Exhibit 5 Study of existing methods

Moulding	Standard minutes[1,2]
Load mould (including mix ingredients)	1.30
Cut scrim[3]	0.27
Inital setting of tile in the mould	15.00
Unload tile to oven and hang	1.50
Packing	
Pack four tiles, then to an outer carton and stack	4.70

Notes
1. Standard times include an appropriate allowance for rest.
2. All times include the travel elements involved.
3. Cut scrim time is based on cutting 3 pieces of scrim per journey. The standard time of 0.27 is the average time per piece.

Too Short
the Day

Giles Chamberlain, the production manager of the Playhouse Theatre, set out for work on Monday morning. Over the weekend he had drawn up a priority list of the important longer-term tasks he needed to accomplish and now took the opportunity of reviewing them. Among the important items was the need to find new suppliers for several high-cost materials and those materials used in relatively large quantities in order to reduce the ever-increasing production costs. However, to help achieve this he needed to develop and agree new procedures with the administrator about planning the production of shows. This would not only help to reduce overtime working and the casual labour bill but would also mean that materials could be ordered in advance and so enable lower prices to be secured rather than the present position where sourcing was usually based on fast delivery. In addition, he had been requested some months ago to draw up plans and expenditure estimates with the stage manager (see Exhibit 1) regarding proposals to provide new facilities on stage to offer more scope to designers and less work to provide the necessary requirements of a typical production. Finally, he had to discuss the increased use of modular stage designs with the head of carpentry in order to reduce the timber costs and construction time to produce a show.

By the time he reached the theatre he was pleased about the approaching day and anticipated taking steps towards the resolution of these tasks, some of which he had intended getting down to over the last six to nine months. As he entered the building, the stage manager, Ian Salter, called him and explained that he needed more casual labour than planned due to the agreed changes made last Friday to the forthcoming play *The Sons of Light*. They discussed the proposed increases and agreed on the course of action to take. He asked Ian to advise him on the outcome and to let his secretary, Mary Wright, know the costs involved. In the conversation, Ian had also reminded Giles of several items which needed either purchasing or progressing from suppliers.

On entering his office, Giles found on his desk some invoices and also the time sheets for the casual labour employed last week. In order not to keep the pay procedure waiting, Giles checked the wage claims, made one or two notes and authorized for payment those without queries. He then checked the invoices and telephoned the head of electrics (Jim Beagle), the head of carpentry (Fred Bates), the head of sound

This case was prepared by Terry Hill (Templeton College, University of Oxford) as the basis for class discussion and not as an illustration of good or bad management. © AMD Publishing.

Exhibit 1 *Organization chart for the production manager's responsibilities at the Playhouse Theatre*

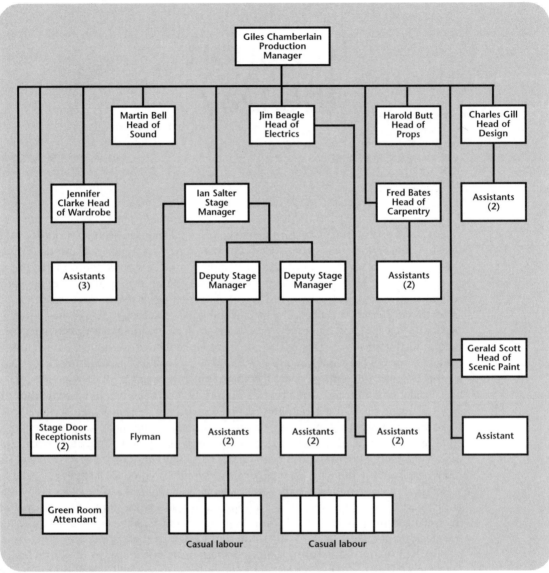

Note

In addition, Mary Wright, one of the staff in the administrative section, is detailed to provide secretarial support to the production manager.

(Martin Bell) and head of wardrobe (Jennifer Clarke) to confirm the items and quantities had been received. Neither Jim Beagle nor Jennifer Clarke answered so he made a mental note to ask them later in the day. He then made several telephone calls to outside suppliers in line with his earlier discussion with Ian Salter and asked for information to be put into the post.

Giles then telephoned Mary Wright to ask her to come up to his office. While he waited, he telephoned the local fire officer to check a point of detail that had come up in conversation with the assistant director (see Exhibit 2) late last week. Following the discussion he checked his file containing details of the local fire regulations and marked the appropriate section. Just then, Mary entered. He discussed some points of administrative detail and handed over the signed invoices and authorized casual labour time sheets. Mary handed over the morning mail and explained one or two points.

After a coffee break, Giles then went down to the stage area to check on the progress being made on the alterations for the current production *The Bottom Drawer*. He walked over to Ian Salter to ask how the work was progressing. 'The problem is fitting the rostrum onto the stage', explained Ian. 'Fred (the head of carpentry) is working on an idea I have in order both to ensure fit and to keep it stable once in position.' Giles discussed the idea with both Ian and Fred and together they came up with another possibility. Giles looked on as first one idea then the other was tried. Further discussion took place until a satisfactory solution was reached. Before leaving the stage area, Giles then checked the casual labour time sheet queries with Ian, particularly about the level of overtime that had been worked, asked Ian to get overtime authorized in future, reinforcing the necessity to keep all costs within production budgets.

Giles then set off to see the head of wardrobe, Jennifer Clarke, to discuss the final cost of the current production and tomorrow's proposed trip to London with the head of design, Charles Gill, to buy new costumes for a future production of *Anyone for Denis?* The discussion addressed costs, costume resale policies and the budget limits for the new costumes. Before he left, Giles also checked out the invoice query he had had that morning. By the time this discussion was over and Giles had walked back to his office, it was lunchtime. He made a few notes on points that had been made in the morning and then went off to lunch.

When he returned, there was a note from the theatre director's secretary advising him that his meeting with the director would have to be put back to 3.30 pm. He then made a telephone call to a supplier of special effects to order a smoke gun for a future production. As he was discussing the request, Mary Wright entered with letters for him to check and sign together with the second delivery of mail. Having cleared the letters, Mary made one or two points contained in these and then left. Giles checked through both lots of mail in detail, made some notes and prepared his replies. He then telephoned Mary and asked her to come to his office at about 3.00 pm.

As he got up, a telephone call came through from a company enquiring about a shower unit which it had loaned to the theatre for a production which finished earlier in the year. Giles then left the office and immediately bumped into Gerald Scott, head of scenic paint. Gerald discussed the need for some particular paints he required and asked if the request could be dealt with urgently. Giles agreed to this and continued into the stage area. He checked with Ian Salter that the earlier problem was now resolved. Ian also took the opportunity to enquire if he could use the theatre's large van to pick up some props for the next production, to which Giles agreed. On seeing Jim Beagle he crossed over and asked him about some queries on invoices concerning the purchase of electrical equipment and consumables. Giles then continued on to the carpentry shop to discuss with Fred Bates the next production in terms of deadlines for props and scenery. Fred also took the opportunity of handing over purchase requisitions for tools and timber, explaining that some of the items were urgent. On returning to his office, the administrator telephoned him about a touring theatre due the month after next. He asked Giles to note in his diary the date of a meeting he had

Exhibit 2   *Playhouse Theatre organization chart*

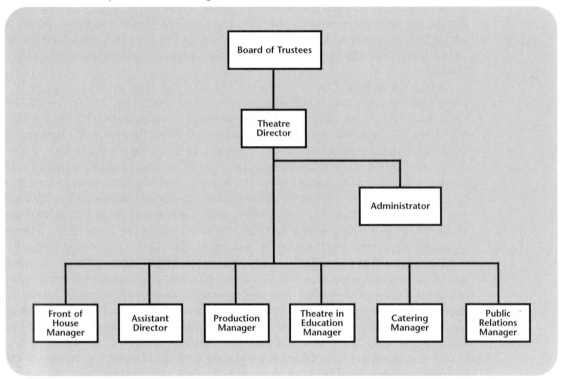

arranged to discuss the detailed requirements with the touring theatre's agent. Just then Mary Wright entered and from then until his scheduled meeting at 3.30 pm he dictated letters, handed over filing and recorded dates in both diaries. Mary also asked him to call in to see the assistant director about an employee later that afternoon.

Meetings with the theatre director took place at least twice weekly. They involved discussions on a number of issues such as, like today's, an up-to-date progress report on the current production, rehearsals for the next two productions and the forward planning for both in-house and touring shows. Like most meetings, this one lasted about 45 minutes and Giles, on leaving it, had a list of points to check out and to confirm the detailed arrangements made. This information was normally required within 24 or 48 hours, at the latest, and formed part of the next meeting's agenda.

When he left the director's office he called in to see the assistant director and checked through the terms of employment details for a new member of staff due to start next week. He also mentioned the fire regulation query and agreed to let the assistant director have sight of the relevant section. He then went to see Harold Butt, head of props, to ask about the shower unit query. Harold explained that it had been broken after the production had ended, and consequently, was thrown away some weeks ago. Giles asked some questions on detail and then returned to his office, telephoned Martin Bell and Jim Beagle and asked them to come to see him. He then called the company about the shower unit, explained the problem, asked the price involved and agreed for them to send an invoice for the replacement cost. When Martin and Jim arrived, he discussed details of the special effects required for the next two productions, checked the up-to-date position and the lead times involved for those parts which were not yet ready. He noted the points and completion dates discussed in order to report back to the theatre director. He then telephoned Charles Gill, head of design, to ask him to come up to the office. Between Jim and Martin leaving and Charles arriving, Giles telephoned a paint supplier regarding the artistic paints request and also made an appointment to talk to an artist's agent about the requirements for a one-man show booked into the theatre in three weeks' time. By then Charles had arrived. Giles asked for a progress report on the design implications for three future productions: *The Irresistible Rise of Arturo UI*, *The Miser* and *Atarah's Band*. As a result of this discussion, Giles agreed to schedule further discussions with all those involved in these productions as time was now pressing in order to ensure that all aspects of these shows could be scheduled on time. He again made appropriate notes in order to report the details back to the director.

Giles then went back to the stage area as he had arranged to supervise a trial fit-up for the next production. He discussed aspects with the heads of the departments involved, noted the agreements and asked them to assess the deadlines to meet the necessary changes. By the time this was finished, the scheduled stage conversion back to that evening's performance had begun. Just as he was about to leave the stage area, Giles was beckoned by the front of house manager who wanted to discuss the provision of cover for two people (one on holiday and one who was ill) for tomorrow's matinee and evening performance. Giles agreed to arrange the cover, and went back to his office. He then made a series of notes following the afternoon's discussions and, when he glanced at his watch it was 6.40 pm. Time to go home.

Busy? he asked himself. Too busy he thought. He had, on reflection, covered all the necessary aspects of his job, and put a lot of necessary effort and pressure behind the important tasks to ensure that present and future shows would be successful productions. But he had spent no time at all on the longer-term tasks he had set himself that morning. 'I seem to be doing well', he thought, 'and both my superiors and subordinates seem to appreciate the job I do and the role I fulfil. But, what is my job? Earlier today, it all seemed so clear, but now I am not so sure.'

ASSIGNMENT QUESTIONS

1. What do you think of Giles Chamberlain's day?
2. Comment on the situation described in the case study and be prepared to propose any changes which you think would be beneficial.

Weavers Homoeopathic Products

The use of alternative medicines has continued to increase over the last few decades and sales for our products have reflected this growth, explained John Mason, chief executive officer of Weavers Homoeopathic Products (WHP). In particular, sales of our creams and ointments have grown year on year and the initial contract with a leading UK retail pharmacy chain has recently been renewed. Furthermore, this new contract not only includes two additional products but also shows a marked increase in volumes for existing ones.

BACKGROUND

WHP has been a manufacturer of homoeopathic products since the early 1920s. These comprise creams, ointments and tablets for a wide range of ailments and conditions. The company is part of Breugen, a French-based conglomerate principally involved in foods and pharmaceuticals. The group has a number of manufacturing sites in the UK and the rest of Europe but WHP is the only one that makes and sells homeopathic products. The manufacturing unit is located on the outskirts of Winchester in the west of England.

PRODUCTS

Homoeopathic products use natural ingredients (for example calendula flowers) that, in liquid form, are added to the tablet, ointment or cream to arrive at the end-product. WHP makes a range of products. Although sales of tablets and ointments show some growth, there has been a marked increase in the sales of creams over the last few years.

This case study was written by Terry Hill (Templeton College, University of Oxford) It is intended for class discussion and not an example of good or bad management. © AMD Publishing (UK).

Exhibit 1   *Current sales information*

1. Product split

Product type	Per cent of sales (£s)
Creams and ointments	70
Tablets	30
Total	100

2. Customer types

Customer type	Per cent of total sales	# customers
Multiple retailers	48	2
Small independent retailers	29	310
Wholesalers	22	22
Other	1	*

* The number of customers in this group totals several hundred. The customers vary over time but always comprise low volume orders.

Exhibit 2   *Detail of last year's sales (units)*

Tablets	Annual sales (# bottles or blisters)
Painkillers	158 100
Indigestion	126 400
Arthritis	82 000
Sleeping	61 800
Anxiety	55 300
Diarrhoea	38 100
Anti-nausea	21 400
Migraine	15 600
Relaxation	9 200
Appetite suppressant	4 600
Bronchitis	2 400

Creams and ointments	Annual sales (# tubes)
Skin moisturiser 101	374 600
Sun cream	350 700
Antiseptic cream	163 100
Dry skin cream	129 200
Pain relieving cream	112 800
Hair pomade	105 500
Insect repellant cream	95 400
Acne cream	90 100
Nappy rash ointment	88 700
Healing ointment	61 000
Strain ointment	32 100
Chilblain ointment	25 700
Burn ointment	19 300
Haemorrhoid ointment	4 600

Note

The difference between a cream and an ointment is that the latter is oil based and the former is not. As a non-oil-based product, a cream can be absorbed by the skin.

As shown in Exhibit 1, sales are made to four types of outlets. Sales to the multiple retailers have grown significantly since their introduction and now account for almost half the total. 'This trend is likely to continue,' explained Bob Dale (VP marketing), 'given the new contracts signed last week. Our two best selling creams have, as we hoped, taken off and schedules from the big two retailers have been increased significantly. Whereas last year we sold a total of about 1.7 million tubes of all our creams and ointments (see Exhibit 2) the projections for next year show an increase of more than 35 per cent. Given the two recent contracts with multiple retailers we are confident of meeting, if not exceeding, these projections.'

'Most products are sold from stock,' confirmed Bob Dale. 'The exceptions are the special orders placed by doctors and pharmacists for any product whether it is a tablet, ointment or cream. These are handled on a one-off basis in the dispensary. But most sales are for standard products that are made against forecasts or known call-offs. Having products in stock to meet delivery requirements is important for all customers but particularly so for the multiple retailers who measure our delivery reliability performance on a weekly basis. Meeting schedules, therefore, is a prerequisite for growing sales particularly in this segment.'

SALES ORDERS

Orders are received by telephone, on-line (in the case of the two multiple retailers), post, fax and from sales representatives. The relevant paperwork is then created in the sales office. For small and medium volume orders the invoices are sent to the dispensary where the orders are then picked and packed. Inventory for some low volume demand products is kept in this area. The inventory for the other low volume demand products is kept in the finished goods warehouse. Any specials (low volume demand products not kept in stock) are made up in the dispensary and then handled as other low volume orders. Depending on parcel weight, orders are sent by mail or by private carriers. Larger volume orders go to the finished goods warehouse where they are picked and packed before being delivered by the same private carrier service referred to earlier.

MANUFACTURING

The manufacturing process for each product starts with the production of the 'mother tincture'. The natural ingredients are crushed to a pulp (or fine powder if appropriate) and dissolved in alcohol. The 'mother tincture' is the undiluted version of a product and is used in the manufacture of tablets, creams and ointments. The tinctures are typically produced on a seasonal basis in line with the availability of the actual ingredients. All active ingredients are held in the potency room (see Exhibit 3).

Products for which there is regular demand are kept in stock. Other products are only made on receipt of an order as explained in the next sections. Currently, manufacturing quantities produced are for a minimum of 1 working day with high demand products made for two or occasionally three working days. This is to avoid the set-ups incurred on product changes.

Doctors, pharmacists and retail outlets specializing in homeopathic medicines frequently place orders for products that are of low demand. These are not kept in

Exhibit 3   *Shop floor and dispatch layout*

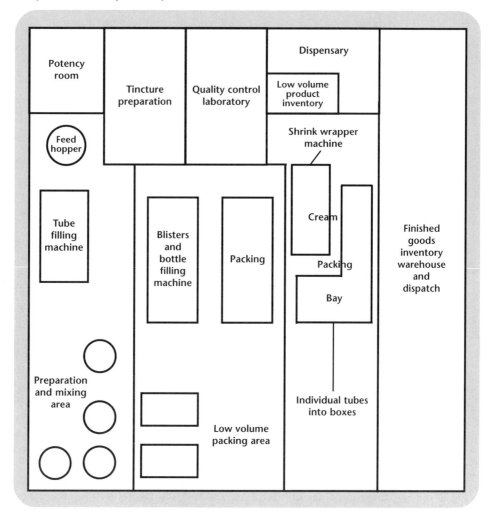

stock and so are manufactured only on receipt of an order. All those orders for small quantities (one or two tubes of a cream, for instance) are manufactured in the dispensary. Here, on receipt of an invoice, a member of the dispensary staff checks the product formula, collects the ingredients and prepares and packs the product.

Tablets

Standard base tablets are purchased as a raw material and the actual ingredient is added on the packing line. The tablets are then loaded into a feed drum which passes them through the active ingredient dispenser. At this point the tablets are then either routed through to blister pack or bottle machines depending upon the packing requirements. The tableting machine has been designed to switch from blister to bottle pack, but can only feed one pack form at a time. Details of set-up times and throughput speeds are given in Exhibit 4.

Exhibit 4　　*Tablet and cream manufacture*

Product	Operation	Set-up time (minutes)	Throughput speed (No./minute)
Tablets	Blister pack	60	60
	Bottle fill	30	70
Creams and ointments	Tube fill	50	36
	Tube pack	–	72

Notes

1. Both blister and bottle packs of tablets are hand-packed in the same area (see Exhibit 3).
2. To reduce changeover times, manufacturing order quantities are designed to be either one or two working days in length.

Creams and ointments

Creams and ointments go through the same manufacturing procedures. The first step is to make a standard cream or ointment base to which the active ingredient is added. This is then transferred to the feed hopper which, in turn, is linked to the tube-filling machine. Once filled, the tubes are sent on pallets to the cream-packing bay where six tubes are placed into a box before they are shrink wrapped. All tubes are 27 cm in size. Two operators run the tube-filling machine. One operator is responsible for filling and refilling the hopper with product and keeping the filling machine supplied with empty tubes. The second operator takes the filled tubes, stacks them into a tray and then carries each tray to an area where it is collected and taken to the cream packing bay. The hopper takes sufficient cream/ointment to fill 1000 tubes, and there are 374 empty and 300 filled tubes respectively in a tray. Whenever the hopper is empty or a tray is full/empty, the designated operator stops the filling process to complete the necessary task of getting more empty tubes or taking filled tubes to the designated area. Whereas filling the hopper takes five minutes, removing/collecting a tray of tubes only takes half a minute in each instance.

Both operators can undertake either job on the cream-filling line and typically work half a day on each task. The key is to keep the filling machine fully loaded with empty tubes. This requires the full attention of the operator at the front of the machine. At the other end, the task is lighter and only occupies the person about 50 per cent of the time when the machine is running. Filled tubes are discharged onto a small working area where they are collected, several at a time, and placed in a tray.

Working patterns

The 'normal working' day comprises 7 hours with one 15-minute period during both the morning and afternoon when all operators take a break. Lunchtime is one hour but does not form part of the working day. The two, shorter, 15-minute breaks, on the other hand, do form part of the rest and relaxation associated with a normal working day. (There is a need for rest to form part of the day. Typically, the 'rest allowance' would be about 15 per cent of a working day. This allowance is often taken, in part, as scheduled breaks (similar to the 15-minute breaks described here) or shorter breaks taken at individually chosen times. Lunchtime is normally unpaid and does not, therefore, form part of a working day.) During these breaks all equipment is stopped but there are no further delays when the machines are restarted.

THE FUTURE

'The new contracts and increased schedules for our cream products have confirmed our view that the projected forecast sales growth will be met,' concluded John Mason. 'Holding finished goods inventory (see Exhibit 5) is essential in the support of our customers and to meet their lead time and on-time delivery expectations. With future sales showing considerable growth, we are now in the process of checking whether we can make these projected volumes. An increase of 35 per cent looks to be a major task.'

Exhibit 5   *Finished goods inventory levels for the cream and ointment products*

Product	Current inventory (# of tubes)
Skin moisturiser 101	48 386
Dry skin cream	46 056
Healing ointment	34 185
Hair pomade	23 284
Antiseptic cream	16 490
Insect repellant	16 012
Nappy rash ointment	14 506
Sun cream	12 889
Haemorrhoid ointment	10 210
Chilblain ointment	9 024
Acne cream	8 155
Burn ointment	6 810
Pain relieving cream	5 216
Strain ointment	649

What They Teach You at Disney U

'Just remember: two Ds, two Ss and three emotions.' Thirty-six pencils record this information in notebooks, ensuring that their owners will know, if asked, the names of the Seven Dwarfs: Doc and Dopey, Sleepy and Sneezy, Happy, Grumpy and Bashful.

The mnemonic for Snow White's friends is an essential element of the curriculum at Disney University at Walt Disney World Resort, whose principal function is to indoctrinate more than 16 000 new employees each year to the unique ways of the Walt Disney Company. The plain office building that serves as a schoolhouse, located on the northern edge of Walt Disney World Resort near Orlando, Florida, swarms with seasonal workers hired for the summer rush. The instructor, identified by his name tag only as Jim, has the blond coiffure, youthful athleticism and breezy confidence of a college fraternity president. The coat of his grey suit hangs as casually from his shoulders as an open beach shirt, and a shock of yellow hair juts straight out over his forehead like a sun visor.

This is an orientation class, but it is not called orientation – nor are the new workers known as employees. They are cast members, and the class is known as traditions. Throughout the day the cast members will learn other Disney terms. Ninety per cent of the labour force, hourly employees from street sweepers to store clerks to ride operators, wear costumes, not uniforms. They are not on duty but on-stage. During breaks they are off-stage. Visitors are guests; cast members are hosts and hostesses.

'Working at Disney', Jim had said at the start of the class, 'is like going to a foreign country. You have to learn a new language and a new culture.' At a time when employees' attitudes, productivity and quality of work are problems throughout corporate America, Disney seems immune to the maladies of the age. America's leading corporations – from General Electric to General Motors – have dispatched executives to Disney University to discover how Disney inspires its staff to meet the company's exacting standards.

No visitor has to spend much time in the park before he begins to wonder whether Disney feeds some magic potion to its employees, perhaps learned from a certain former sorcerer's apprentice. So confident is Disney that cast members will charm guests that it has devised ways to force contact. One example: many of the wares in the park's ubiquitous gift shops bear no price tags, requiring shoppers to ask the cost.

© Used by permission from Disney Enterprises Inc.

If all this frenzied friendliness makes Walt Disney World Resort sometimes seem a bit like Stepford South, its success is beyond dispute. Sixty per cent of Walt Disney World Resort's visitors are repeaters. Together, Walt Disney World Resort, Disneyland Paris Resort, Paris, Tokyo Disneyland Resort, Japan and their California cousin, Disneyland Resort, accounted for $5.5bn of the company's almost $23bn in 1998 revenues. The company's ability to retain workers is rare in the service sector, which nationally suffers from a 40 per cent annual turnover; Disney's is lower by one-third. For office and administrative workers, Disney's attrition rate drops to a mere 6 per cent.

None of this happens by accident. Disney's hiring policies are designed to find workers who will fit the company mould. Disney takes people who are normally gregarious and trains them to be more so. Looks do not matter; attitude and personality do. The casting department puts more weight on interviews than résumés; Disney wants people who look questioners in the eye.

Today the pressure on casting is greater than ever, for this summer alone they were looking to hire 2000. Disney cannot be as selective as it once was; the labour pool in Central Florida has shrunk as a result of the boom Walt Disney World Resort started. At one time Disney had ten job seekers for every hourly position; now the ratio is three to one. (For managerial positions the reverse is true. This year Disney will fill 300 jobs for which it will receive 70 000 résumés.) More and more representatives of Florida's large semi-retired population are showing up on Walt Disney World Resort work lines. Disney recruits hourly workers on 130 college campuses and advertises in major markets for positions in hotels and restaurants.

All new employees must attend traditions classes before starting work, even those hired for a week at spring break. There, in a classroom decorated with posters and pictures depicting great moments in the company's history (for example Mickey Mouse's first cartoon, *Snow White and the Seven Dwarfs*, *Fantasia*, the opening of Disneyland Park) they are inoculated with the Disney corporate culture. Everything in the room has a purpose: the shape of the table (round to instil a sense of teamwork), the method of introductions (each person gives not only his own name but that of the person to his right again to instil a sense of teamwork), the taking of a test on Disneyland Park that involves remembering the names of as many Disney characters as possible in an allotted time period (and each table consults on answers, again to instil a sense of teamwork). In case someone has somehow missed the point, Jim makes it again: if one employee makes a mistake, a guest goes home unhappy. 'We never say, "it's not my job",' he warns. "If someone asks us a question, we know the answer. If we see a piece of trash on the ground, we pick it up.'

Like all instructors, Jim is not assigned to the university permanently. Nor is he an executive. He is an hourly employee – intended to be a role model – who conducts the class one day a week for one year. Disney puts a time limit on teaching to ensure that its instructors will be fresh and enthusiastic. Some are still in their first year with the company.

More teamwork, 'Disney is a first-name company', Jim tells the class. That is tradition number one. If the policy promotes informality, it is also meant to reduce individuality. So are the company's strict grooming standards. 'Why do we have them?' Jim asks rhetorically. 'To make everyone blend in, to promote the whole show, not individuals.' Men cannot have moustaches, beards, long sideburns or hair touching the ears or collar. Women may wear one small ring on each hand and earrings no larger than a penny (a recent liberalization from previously mandated posts); they cannot have long or brightly painted fingernails, large hair decorations or long necklaces. Thanks to Walt Disney World Resorts, Orlando must be one of the world's principal markets for plain black shoes. Acceptable styles are displayed in a glass case near the area where cast members pick up their costumes; twice a month a shoemobile makes the 25-mile drive from town.

The morning session ends with a 3-minute videotape called 'Making Magic'. It shows employees volunteering to take pictures of guests, so that the whole family can be in the picture, as well as doing other good deeds. At the end, Michael Eisner and President Frank Wells are joined by Mickey and Donald (Disney's first-name policy extends to omitting even their surnames) while the tune of 'When you wish upon a star' swells in the background.

Disney manages to Disneyfy its employees despite an hourly pay scale that begins at $6.25, which company officials describe as competitive for service workers in the Orlando area. There are raises after six months, a year and annually thereafter, but all hourly positions carry a salary cap regardless of longevity. The carrot is that Disney promotes liberally from within.

Disney's low-entry-level-pay but fast-advancement system enables the company to retain employees who have the ability to move up without offering rewards to those who do not. Based on performance, hourly workers are promoted and can join the management ranks as salaried workers. On the other hand, image-conscious Disney prefers not to fire anyone, since it views every human being on the planet as a potential customer and does not want to offend a single one. Instead, it tries to find new positions for problem employees, something that is easy enough to do at a park with 1100 job descriptions and steady turnover.

Underlying all this is an unflagging company-wide obsession with excellence. Disney workers paint every trash can to blend with nearby scenery; they steam-clean every piece of pavement and wash every window in the Magic Kingdom and Epcot every day. Disney designers stayed in low-budget hotels around the park and then pencilled in extra soundproofing and double sinks for the Caribbean Beach resort in order to beat the competition. Disney gardeners have trimmed the oaks on Main Street, USA, in the Magic Kingdom to the identical shape every day since the park opened; they have clipped the shrubbery in heavily travelled areas into shapes of penguins, elephants, swans and camels. The gardeners travel enough miles on lawn mowers each year to circle the earth 14 times. Atop the Italian Pavilion in Epcot is a four-foot angel; though it is too high for visitors to discern, Disney coats it with the most expensive gold paint available; 14-carat gold leaf.

In all this there ought to be lessons for the rest of corporate America. It sounds so simple; take the long-term view, insist on quality, recognize that courtesy pays, offer low-level employees incentives for advancement rather than money, hire by giving more weight to personality than credentials and expand by filling the public's needs rather than your own.

Wilson Pharmaceuticals plc

Wilson Pharmaceuticals had been manufacturing and selling its mouth ulcer treatment (Ulcercare) for the last 15 years. At the time of its introduction there had been few products in this area of healthcare. The product consisted of a small glass bottle, with a cork and printed label. The bottle was filled with a pink fluid (the chemical formulation for which had been derived by Wilson's own research laboratories) leaving enough room to fit a cotton bud in the neck of the bottle without inducing spillage. Twelve double-ended cotton buds were included in the pack, providing sufficient for 24 individual applications

The treatment was made by dipping one end of a cotton bud into the fluid and then applying it directly to the infected area within the mouth. The package was made from rolled card tube. This tube was in three parts – a single inner and two close-fitting outer tubes, each closed with a card disc which formed the top and bottom of the pack (see Exhibit 1). Inside the inner tube was a small card cup into which the glass bottle fitted. This cup was surrounded by corrugated paper sheet which held it firmly in the inner tube. The cotton buds fitted between the glass bottle and the corrugated paper, thus providing additional protection for the bottle. The top and bottom of the outer tube were closed by a label, and the disc of the top tube was covered by a circular label.

Over the past 18 months, sales for Ulcercare had been declining steadily. Enquiries revealed that two large competitors had introduced their own products in this range, which were lower in price than Ulcercare. The current profit margin enjoyed by Wilson's product, although above average, was not sufficiently high to withstand a price reduction in line with the competitors' products.

As part of their review of the situation, the executives involved turned to the question of product costs, details of which are included as Exhibit 2.

This case was prepared by Terry Hill (Templeton College, University of Oxford) and KHA Negal. It is intended as the basis for class discussion and not as an illustration of good or bad management. © AMD Publishing.

Exhibit 1   *The current production design*

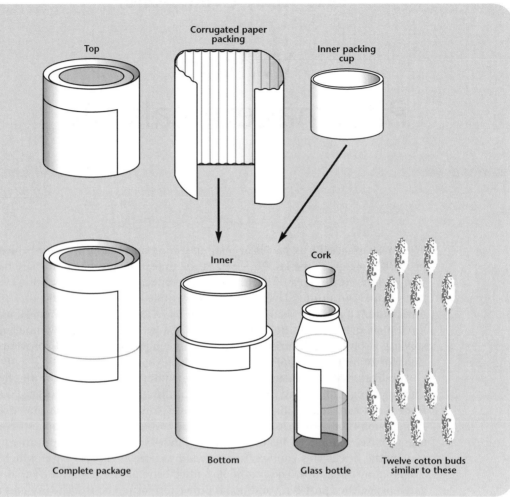

Exhibit 2   *The cost of breakdown for Ulcercare*

Cost/100 items	Materials (£)
Ulcer fluid	2.55
Bottle	1.85
Cork	0.95
Bottle label	0.25
Card cup	0.80
Corrugated paper	0.20
12 double-ended cotton buds (total)	1.76
Inner tube	1.05
Top tube	1.33
Bottom tube	1.33
Tube label	0.65
Disc label	0.25
Assembly and packing labour	3.86
Total materials and labour	16.83

Yuppie Products

The Yuppie Products Company produces a line of furnishings for hotels and restaurants. Among the items manufactured is the Yuppie Executive water pitcher whose product structure is shown in Exhibit 1. Components A and B are manufactured by the firm's plastic moulding shop and components C, D, E and F are purchased from a supplier. The Yuppie Executive water pitcher is completed by the final assembly department located at the firm's plant in Geneva. (A flow diagram indicating the different manufacturing stages in the Geneva plant is shown in Exhibit 2.)

The firm's products are supplied to customers from stock held in the company's distribution centres which are located in Amsterdam and Rome. A distribution requirements planning (DRP) system is used to plan and schedule the replenishment of inventory at the distribution centres and the scheduling of production operations at the Geneva plant. (See Exhibit 3 for sample information used by the DRP system). This information is updated daily by the company's computer system.

Exhibit 1   *Product structure*

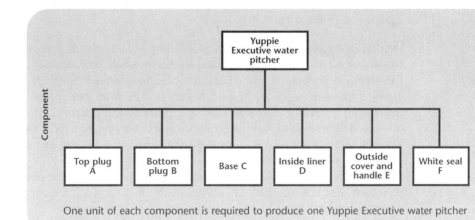

One unit of each component is required to produce one Yuppie Executive water pitcher

This case was prepared by Professor William Lee Berry as a basis for class discussion rather than to illustrate either effective or ineffective handling of an administrative situation. Copyright by IMEDE, Lausanne, Switzerland. IMD International, resulting from the merger between IMEDE, Lausanne, and IMI, Geneva, acquires and retains all rights. Reproduced by permission.

Exhibit 2   *Manufacturing system*

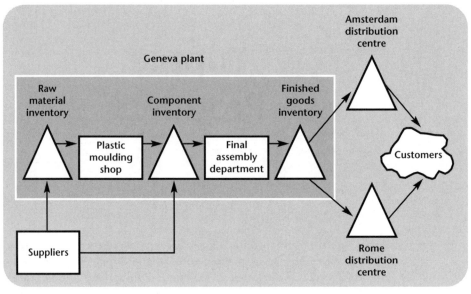

THE DRP SYSTEM

The firm's distribution requirements planning system includes four main elements:

1. Time-phased order point (TPOP) records for each end-product stocked at a distribution centre (Exhibit 3, Part A).
2. Time-phased master production scheduling records for each end-product produced by the Geneva plant (Exhibit 3, Part B).
3. Time-phased material planning records for each component part manufactured or purchased by the Geneva plant (Exhibit 3, Part C).
4. Shop-floor control reports used to schedule production in the various plant departments (Exhibit 3, Part D).

A standard format is used for all of the time-phased planning records. The first row contains a weekly forecast of demand for the product item. The second row contains the delivery schedule for any orders that have been relayed for shipment to the distribution centres or for production in the plant. The third row provides a projection of the closing inventory each week, and the fourth row indicates planned orders that are scheduled for release so that inventory shortages are not incurred. The schedule for the planned orders takes into account the order quantity, lead time and safety stock information for each item as shown below the item record.

The DRP system co-ordinates the planning of operations in the distribution centres, the plant and the suppliers (as illustrated by Exhibit 4). For example, the planned order row information in the distribution centre TPOP records is summarized and displayed as the gross requirements row in the master production scheduling records (see arrow A in Exhibit 3). Likewise, the master production schedule (MPS) row information in the master production scheduling records is used to calculate the gross requirements in the material requirements planning records for the component items, using bill of material information (see arrow B in Exhibit 3, Part B to Part C).

Exhibit 3   *Distribution requirements planning worksheet*

Part A: Distribution centre planning records

Yuppie Executive water pitcher
Amsterdam distribution centre

		Week							
		1	2	3	4	5	6	7	8
Forecast[1]		10	10	10	10	10	10	10	10
Scheduled receipts[1]		20	0	0	0	0	0	0	0
Projected available	10	20	10	20	10	20	10	20	10
Planned shipments[1]		20		20		20			
Firm planned shipments									

Order quantity = 20 units
Transportation lead time = 2 weeks
Safety stock = 5 units

Yuppie Executive water pitcher
Rome distribution centre

		Week							
		1	2	3	4	5	6	7	8
Forecast[1]		20	20	20	20	20	20	20	20
Scheduled receipts[1]		0	0	0	0	0	0	0	0
Projected available[2]	45	25	5	25	5	25	5	25	5
Planned shipments[1]			40		40		40		
Firm planned shipments									

Order quantity = 40 units
Transportation lead time = 1 week
Safety stock = 5 units

Part B: Master production scheduling (MPS) records

Yuppie Executive water pitcher
Geneva central warehouse

		Week							
		1	2	3	4	5	6	7	8
Gross requirements[1]		20	40	20	40	20	40	0	0
Scheduled receipts[1]		0	0	0	0	0	0	0	0
Projected available[2]	40	20	40	20	40	20	40	20	40
MPS[1]		60		60		60	0	0	0

MPS order quantity = 60 units
Production lead time = 1 week
Safety stock = 10 units

A

B

Exhibit 3   *Part C: Materials requirement planning records*

Item A – top plug

		Week							
		1	2	3	4	5	6	7	8
Gross requirements[1]		60	0	60	0	60	0	0	0
Scheduled receipts[1]		60	0	0	0	0	0	0	0
Projected available[2]	65	65	65	5	5	5	5	5	5
Planned orders[1]		0	0	0	60	0	0	0	0

Order quantity = 60 units
Production lead time = 1 week
Safety stock = 5 units

Item B – bottom plug

		Week							
		1	2	3	4	5	6	7	8
Gross requirements[1]		60	0	60	0	60	0	0	0
Scheduled receipts[1]		0	0	90	0	0	0	0	0
Projected available[2]	35	−25	−25	5	5	35	35	35	35
Planned orders[1]		0	90	0	0	0	0	0	0

Order quantity = 90 units
Production lead time = 3 weeks
Safety stock = 5 units

Item C – base

		Week							
		1	2	3	4	5	6	7	8
Gross requirements[1]		60	0	60	0	60	0	0	0
Scheduled receipts[1]		0	0	120	0	0	0	0	0
Projected available[2]	15	−45	−45	15	15	75	75	75	75
Planned orders[1]		0	120	0	0	0	0	0	0

Order quantity = 120 units
Purchasing lead time = 3 weeks
Safety stock = 10 units

Part D: Shop-floor control reports

Plastic moulding department scheduling report				
Shop order number	Component item	Order quantity	Order due date[1]	Machine time (in days)[3]
10-XXY	A	60	week 1	3
10-XZV	Z	20	week 1	1
10-XXX	G	45	week 2	2
10-XYZ	B	90	week 3	4

1. As of the beginning of the week.
2. As of the end of the week.
3. The plant works five single-shift days per week.

Exhibit 4 *Distribution requirements planning information system*

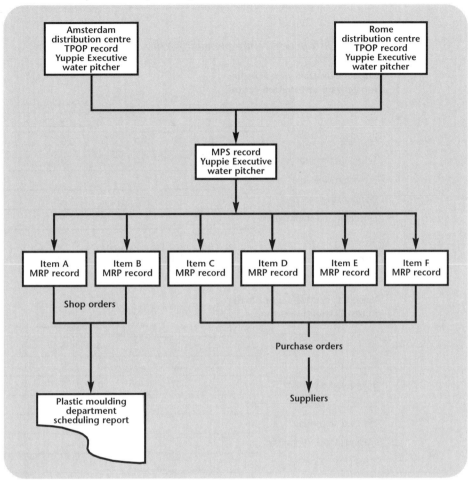

Finally, information in the material requirements planning records is used to establish priorities for the scheduling of production in the plant. Orders are scheduled in sequence according to their due date. The due dates for open shop orders contained in the scheduled receipts row of the material requirements planning records are shown on the scheduling reports for individual departments in the plant. For example, the due date of week 1 for the order of 60 units for item A is shown both in the material requirements planning record for this item, and on the scheduling report for the plastic moulding department in Exhibit 5, Part D. Currently, two open shop orders for Yuppie Executive water pitcher components are waiting to be processed in the plastic moulding department – items A and B. All of the orders shown on the plastic moulding department scheduling report are made complete in one operation, and are subsequently ready for the final assembly department.

The material requirements planning record for item C, the base, is shown in Exhibit 5, Part C; this item is produced by a plastic moulding company in Taiwan. Because of lengthy overseas shipment times, the purchasing lead time for this item is a firm three weeks and the current open order of 120 units will not be received until the beginning of week 5.

Exhibit 5   *Distribution requirements planning worksheet*

Part A: Distribution centre planning records

Yuppie Executive water pitcher
Amsterdam distribution centre

		Week							
		1	2	3	4	5	6	7	8
Forecast[1]		10	10	10	10	10	10	10	10
Scheduled receipts[1]		20	0	0	0	0	0	0	0
Projected available[2]	10								
Planned shipments[1]									
Firm planned shipments[1]									

Order quantity = 20 units
Transportation lead time = 2 weeks
Safety stock = 5 units

Yuppie Executive water pitcher
Rome distribution centre

		Week							
		1	2	3	4	5	6	7	8
Forecast[1]		20	20	20	20	20	20	20	20
Scheduled receipts[1]		0	0	0	0	0	0	0	0
Projected available[2]	~~45~~								
Planned shipments[1]	35								
Firm planned shipments									

Order quantity = 40 units
Transportation lead time = 1 week
Safety stock = 5 units

Part B: Master production scheduling (MPS) records

Yuppie Executive water pitcher
Geneva central warehouse

		Week							
		1	2	3	4	5	6	7	8
Gross requirements[1]									
Scheduled receipts[1]									
Projected available[2]	40								
MPS[1]									

MPS order quantity = 60 units
Production lead time = 1 week
Safety stock = 10 units

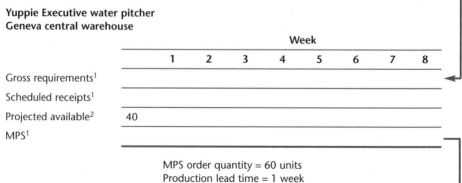

Exhibit 5   *Part C: Materials requirement planning records*

Item A – top plug

					Week			
	1	2	3	4	5	6	7	8
Gross requirements[1]								
Scheduled receipts[1]	60							
Projected available[2]	65							
Planned orders[1]								

Order quantity = 60 units
Production lead time = 1 week
Safety stock = 5 units

Item B – bottom plug

					Week			
	1	2	3	4	5	6	7	8
Gross requirements[1]								
Scheduled receipts[1]			90					
Projected available[2]	35							
Planned orders[1]								

Order quantity = 90 units
Production lead time = 3 weeks
Safety stock = 5 units

Item C – base

					Week			
	1	2	3	4	5	6	7	8
Gross requirements[1]								
Scheduled receipts[1]			120					
Projected available[2]	15							
Planned orders[1]								

Order quantity = 120 units
Purchasing lead time = 3 weeks
Safety stock = 10 units

Part D: Shop-floor control reports

Plastic moulding department scheduling report				
Shop order number	Component item	Order quantity	Order due date[1]	Machine time (in days)[3]
10-XXY	A	60	week 1	3
10-XZV	Z	20	week 1	1
10-XXX	G	45	week 2	2
10-XYZ	B	90	week 3	4

1. As of the beginning of the week.
2. As of the end of the week.
3. The plant works five single-shift days per week.

Index